Springer Series on Environmental Management

Robert S. DeSanto, Series Editor

Environmental Effects of Off-Road Vehicles

Impacts and Management in Arid Regions

Edited by
Robert H. Webb
Howard G. Wilshire

With 149 Figures

Springer-Verlag
New York   Heidelberg   Berlin

Robert H. Webb
Department of Geosciences
University of Arizona
Tucson, Arizona 85721 U.S.A.

2/1986
geog.

Howard G. Wilshire
U.S. Geological Survey
345 Middlefield Road
Menlo Park, California 94025 U.S.A.

On the cover—Desert motorcycle race—the annual Barstow to Las Vegas race, last run in 1974. Permit applications have subsequently been denied because of excessive damage to natural and cutural resources. Amendments to the California Desert Plan proposed by the Bureau of Land Management for 1982 call for reinstituting this event. Published with permission of the National Geographic Society.

Library of Congress Cataloging in Publication Data
Main entry under title:
Environmental effects of off-road vehicle use.
  (Springer series on environmental management)
  Bibliography: p.
  Includes index.
  1. All terrain vehicles—Environmental aspects. 2. Arid regions ecology. I. Webb, Robert H. II. Wilshire, Howard Gordon, 1926-   . III. Series.
  QH545.A43E58 1983   574.5′222   82-10479

Typeset by Ms Associates, Champaign, Illinois
Printed and bound by Halliday Lithograph, West Hanover, Massachusetts
Printed in the United States of America

9 8 7 6 5 4 3 2 1

ISBN 0-387-90737-8   Springer-Verlag New York Heidelberg Berlin
ISBN 3-540-90737-8   Springer-Verlag Berlin Heidelberg New York

Series Preface

This series is dedicated to serving the growing community of scholars and practitioners concerned with the principles and applications of environmental management. Each volume is a thorough treatment of a specific topic of importance for proper management practices. A fundamental objective of these books is to help the reader discern and implement man's stewardship of our environment and the world's renewable resources. For we must strive to understand the relationship between man and nature, act to bring harmony to it, and nurture an environment that is both stable and productive.

These objectives have often eluded us because the pursuit of other individual and societal goals has diverted us from a course of living in balance with the environment. At times, therefore, the environmental manager may have to exert restrictive control, which is usually best applied to man, not nature. Attempts to alter or harness nature have often failed or backfired, as exemplified by the results of imprudent use of herbicides, fertilizers, water, and other agents.

Each book in this series will shed light on the fundamental and applied aspects of environmental management. It is hoped that each will help solve a practical and serious environmental problem.

Robert S. DeSanto
East Lyme, Connecticut

Preface

This book was conceived as a result of a public meeting on the environmental effects of human uses of resources in the California Desert Conservation Area. Clearly, one of the most controversial subjects discussed at this meeting was the use of recreational off-road vehicles (ORVs) and their effects on the natural desert terrain of California. Such environmental problems, and the controversies they arouse, are found all over the world—in Australia, Canada, Spain, and Italy to name a few countries. Nonrecreational vehicles also cause adverse environmental effects in arid areas. Chief among these are military vehicles and vehicles used in exploration for minerals. Serious problems resulting from such uses have been reported from the western United States, the Near-East deserts, North Africa, Peru, Australia, Russia, and China.

Our purpose in publishing this book is to provide authoritative information on the physical and biological impacts of vehicles on the desert ecosystems. We then use this information to formulate general management guidelines for recreational ORV use in deserts. The chapters of this book are divided into five main categories: (1) the physical effects, (2) the biological effects, (3) the rehabilitation potential, (4) case histories of specific problem areas, and (5) management concepts and practices.

Under physical effects, the types of soils commonly found in arid lands and their rates of formation are described (Chapter 2). These desert soils are vulnerable to modification by vehicles, and the nature of such modifications is described in Chapters 2 through 4. The effects of these modifications on accelerating water and wind erosion are presented in Chapters 5 and 6.

Under biological effects, the vegetative communities of deserts are described, emphasis being placed on deserts of the western United States. The effects of ORVs on those communities are discussed in Chapters 7, 8, and 10. The effects of vehicle noise on desert vertebrates and the general impacts of vehicles on dune fauna and flora are examined in Chapters 9 and 10, respectively.

Under rehabilitation, reclamation techniques for physical systems of the desert are covered in Chapters 11 and 12, and for vegetative communities in Chapters 16 and 17. The degree and rate of natural recovery of soils and vegetation in disturbed arid lands are described in Chapters 13 through 15.

Under case histories, specific ORV problem areas in Australia and the United States are described in Chapters 18 through 20. These diverse studies illustrate the great range of adverse environmental effects caused by ORVs. Some of these effects could be anticipated; others were a surprise, thus emphasizing the need for thorough planning and careful plan implementation.

The environmental effects of ORVs as described in these 20 chapters are potentially so severe, and the incompatibility of mechanical recreation with passive recreation so universal, that special planning and regulatory considerations must be applied if ORVs are to be accommodated. Management concepts and practices, including regulations, funding, and education, are covered in Chapters 21 through 23.

As a consequence of the rapid escalation of recreational ORV use in the western United States in the late 1960s and 1970s, most studies specifically related to this activity have been made in the United States, and most of these concern the California deserts. Moreover, the concepts and practices dealt with in this book are also those developed in the United States since more ORVs are used there than elsewhere in the world. However, the physical and biological effects of ORV use in arid areas are the same everywhere. Thus, the conclusions and recommendations in this book are generally applicable to arid lands throughout the world.

Contributors to the book were asked to use language that was readily understood by interested laypersons, land managers, recreation planners, and policy makers. The comprehensive reference lists of important technical reports should be useful to all readers, particularly in indicating potential lines of investigation. The book is intended for use as background material for undergraduate and graduate courses in environmental and recreational planning, not merely as it applies to ORVs in the desert, but also as it applies to any modification of the physical and biological resources of those lands.

A great many people have given graciously of their time and knowledge in helping make this book a reality. We are especially indebted to David

Sheridan and Robert Stebbins for editorial and scientific help early in the book's history, to Catherine Campbell, Ronnie Frankel, and Lindsay Ardwin for editorial help in later stages, and to Ruby Christenson, Barbara Gessner, Irene Jimenez, Julie Kirchner, Tia Marshall, and Mary Milan for typing assistance.

None of the opinions expressed by any of the contributors necessarily reflects official viewpoints or policies of any government agency or other institution.

Robert H. Webb
Howard G. Wilshire

Contents

Contributors

John Adams, Bureau of Land Management, 1695 Spruce Street, Riverside, California 92507, U.S.A.

Michael C. Bondello, Science Department, Allan Hancock College, 800 S. College Drive, Santa Maria, California 93454, U.S.A.

Robert S. Boyd, Biological Sciences Department, California State Polytechnic University, Pomona, California 91768, U.S.A.

Bayard H. Brattstrom, Department of Biology, California State University, Fullerton, California 92634, U.S.A.

Gilbert D. Brum, Biological Sciences Department, California State Polytechnic University, Pomona, California 91768, U.S.A.

R. Bruce Bury, Fish and Wildlife Service, Fort Collins Field Station, 1300 Blue Spruce Drive, Fort Collins, Colorado 80524, U.S.A.

Susan M. Carter, Biological Sciences Department, California State Polytechnic University, Pomona, California 91768, U.S.A.

Harold E. Dregne, International Center for Arid and Semi-Arid Land Studies, Texas Tech University, Lubbock, Texas 79409, U.S.A.

Christopher D. Elvidge, Department of Applied Earth Sciences, Stanford University, Stanford, California 94305, U.S.A.

David Gilbertson, Department of Geosciences, University of Arizona, Tucson, Arizona 85721, U.S.A.

Dale A. Gillette, CIRES, University of Colorado, Boulder, Colorado 80309, U.S.A.

Walter L. Graves, Farm Advisor, Bldg. 4, 5555 Overland Avenue, San Diego, California 92123, U.S.A.

Bernard Hallett, Quaternary Research Center AR60, University of Washington, Seattle, Washington 98195, U.S.A.

Burchard H. Heede, USDA Forest Service, Rocky Mountain Forest and Range Experiment Station, Tempe, Arizona 85281, U.S.A.

Mary Ann Henry, 609 Saratoga, China Lake, California 93555, U.S.A.

Bern S. Hinckley, Department of Geology, University of Wyoming, Laramie, Wyoming 82070, U.S.A.

Richard M. Iverson, Department of Applied Earth Sciences, Stanford University, Stanford, California 94305, U.S.A.

Burgess L. Kay, Department of Agronomy and Range Science, University of California, Davis, California 95616, U.S.A.

William J. Kockelman, Planner, Palo Alto, California 94303, U.S.A.

Earl W. Lathrop, Department of Biology, Loma Linda University, Loma Linda, California 92354, U.S.A.

Roger A. Luckenbach, College Eight, University of California, Santa Cruz, California 95064, U.S.A.

John K. Nakata, U.S. Geological Survey, 345 Middlefield Road, Menlo Park, California 94025, U.S.A.

William Popendorf, School of Public Health, University of California, Berkeley, California 94720, U.S.A.

Peter G. Rowlands, Bureau of Land Management, 1695 Spruce Street, Riverside, California 92507, U.S.A.

Robert H. Webb, Department of Geosciences, University of Arizona, Tucson, Arizona 85721, U.S.A.

Hans-Rudolph Wenk, Department of Geology and Geophysics, University of California, Berkeley, California 94720, U.S.A.

Howard G. Wilshire, U.S. Geological Survey, 345 Middlefield Road, Menlo Park, California 94025, U.S.A.

1
Introduction[1]

William J. Kockelman

The Wonders and Fragility of Arid Areas

Some people perceive arid areas as "God-forsaken wasteland." Bury and Lucken-bach (Chapter 10) point out that some people are unaware of the rich life found in arid areas. Peter Aleshire (1979, p. 143) reports for *The Desert Sun* in Palm Springs that:

> The public is just beginning to realize the value of this arid region. The sun-seared mountains offer geologic histories stretching back 600 million years. The harsh environment has wrung fascinating biological adaptations from a rich variety of plants and animals which live there. And ancient Indian cultures have left their artifacts scattered through-out the region. It is a land which harbors the oldest living things: the lowly creosote bush, which some botanists claim can live to be 10,000 years old. The marks of wind and rain on the land are clear, but scien-tists have also found square miles of ground covered with pebbles which have not been moved for thousands of years. It is one of the most easily scarred landscapes in the world, and perhaps the slowest to heal.

Far from being a wasteland, arid areas have many plants and animals; for example, over 90 species of shrubs, perennial herbs, and annuals, and almost 100 different species of reptiles, amphibians, birds, and mammals may live in the Upper Johnson Valley ORV open area in California's Mojave Desert according to a report by the U.S. Bureau of Land Management (1976, pp. 46-50).

---

[1]The views and conclusions contained in this chapter are based on the author's studies or experiences and do not necessarily represent the official viewpoint or policy of any govern-mental agency.

In addition to the low rainfall and high evaporation rates, extreme temperatures are a characteristic of arid areas. For example, daily seasonal temperatures vary from 14°F (10°C) at Deep Springs Valley, California, in January to nearly 117°F (47°C) at Death Valley in July; nevertheless, arid areas have magnificent flowers. The mere fact that plants grow in such a hostile environment is amazing. Plants make unusual adaptations—dual root systems, deep "tap" roots, stem-storage of water until needed, and the shedding of leaves to reduce evaporation. White (1975, pp. 27, 28) notes that:

> There are . . . animals so well adapted to the desert environment that they seldom need to take in water by drinking, nor lose it by excreting. Others store water in extra stomachs, or additional lengths of intestines, or can subsist on the water in their tissues for an extraordinary time. All desert animals can browse on . . . plants that appear totally dry and which bristle with ferocious defenses.

Some arid-area animals possess structural adaptations. For example, the desert tortoise stores water under its shell; some arthropods allow water to condense on their bodies and then take in the water droplets directly. Some of the adaptations that plants and wildlife take to avoid drought and to conserve water are noted by Lathrop and Rowlands (Chapter 7).

The living forms in arid areas contain genetic information on how to survive in harsh environments. Stebbins (1974, pp. 298, 301) likens the isolated ecological systems to a series of archipelagos, each possessing its own distinctive characteristics and biota, and notes that, "Perhaps some of the desert grasses harbor genes potentially useful in breeding disease-resistance or other desirable traits into our cereals." Arid areas are also places of extraordinary beauty. Stebbins (1978) described the Imperial Sand Hills of California after the Chocolate Mountains had shed their runoff water:

> The water brings forth a surge of life . . . . The ponding area is a biologist's paradise. The stark, buff-colored dunes and stands of yellow-green paloverde are reflected in the glassy waters. There are giant creosote bushes reaching heights of 12 feet. The waters soon teem with fairy shrimps and spadefoot tadpoles . . . . one may witness the charming sight of long-billed curlews and other water birds moving about among the dunes as they work the edges of the ponds. I have travelled many parts of the world, but have found no place more fascinating.

Sometimes the wonders and contradictions of America can be seen more clearly through the eyes and minds of foreigners such as Jon Manchip White (1975). In his *The Great American Desert,* he sees and tells of the interweaving of the desert, mountains, settlements, trails, peoples, and their culture of the southwest. He concludes his second chapter (p. 33) by saying:

> Such, then, is the desert: a great brown patch on the skin of the American continent. It is belied by its name. The desert is not flat. It is pinched and folded into mountains and mesas, buttes and canyons. The desert is not drab. Its tawny hide, lit up by the quintessential daylight,

is spattered with violet and purple and burnt orange. The desert is not featureless. It sports a thousand distinct and individual growths. The desert is not silent. It continually sings, murmurs, skirls, or whispers.

In prehistoric times, some arid areas were lush savannahs with broad lakes. Today, they contain a wealth of fossils. Paleontologists have unearthed prehistoric camels, saber-toothed cats, three-toed horses, and other species from the fossil beds. Sheridan (1979, p. 19) writes as follows about the rich archeological resources of arid areas:

> Artifacts of human occupancy can be traced back about 12,000 years. There are hints that man may have been present 50,000 to 80,000 years ago. The desert contains the largest concentration of prehistoric art anywhere in the world, including petroglyphs (carvings on rock), pottery, and intaglios, the rarest form of prehistoric art. People living in the desert thousands of years ago created vast designs (intaglios) by scraping aside a layer of dark pebbles at the surface and exposing lighter material beneath. Some of these intaglios are geometric designs or mazes—up to 2 miles in diameter; others are human and animal figures, the longest of which is 489 feet.

Like the artistic designs made then, the scars made today can also be expected to last a thousand years. Plants and animals depend upon the thin layer of topsoil. When the surface is disturbed, the underlying soil or sand can blow or wash away leaving a barren area where the making of new soil capable of supporting plants and animals can take hundreds or even thousands of years. In addition, Heede (Chapter 12), notes that the abuse of one part of a desert will have grave consequences on the other parts.

The term "desertification" is a relatively new term, not precisely defined, but generally describing the gradual reduction in the productivity of land because of excessive human use. Most of the world's arid areas are vulnerable. The United Nations has begun to give careful attention to the process of desertification, which is occurring at an increasing rate in the world's arid areas. These areas provide harsh and difficult environments to those who use them and when they fail to take their delicate ecosystems into account, desertification can result. The UN conference on desertification convened in 1977 and prepared a world map of desertification. Figure 1-1 shows large parts of the United States with a high degree of desertification hazard and shows the western part of the arid lands having a high human pressure. Figure 1-2 shows the status of desertification in the United States.

Sheridan (1981, p. 121), notes that about 225 million acres (91 million hectares) of land in the United States are undergoing severe desertification—an area roughly the size of the 13 original states; he concludes that desertification in the arid United States is "flagrant." Some of the effects of desertification go aloft for all the world to see. Six dust plumes covering 690 square miles (1,700 km^2) of the western Mojave Desert were photographed by the National Aeronautics and Space Administration satellite on January 1, 1973. The cause of the dust

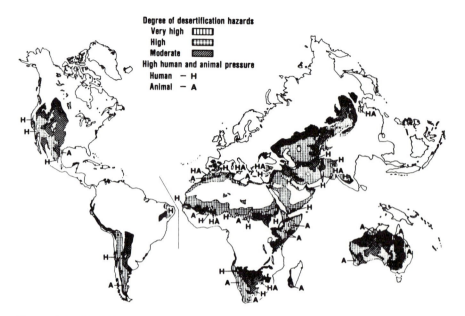

Figure 1-1. World map of desertification (from Food and Agriculture Organization of the United Nations and the United Nations Educational, Scientific and Cultural Organization, Figure 1, © FAO/UNESCO, 1979). Reproduced by permission.

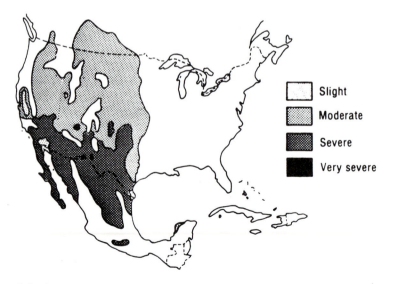

Figure 1-2. Status of desertification in North America (from Dregne, © Clark University, 1977). Reproduced by permission.

was identified as man's destabilization of the natural surface through various human activities, including ORV (off-road vehicle) use (Bowden et al., 1974). A former director of the U.S. Bureau of Land Management (BLM) (Silcock, 1973) emphasized in testimony before a U.S. House of Representatives subcommittee that ORVs can cause damage to the whole gamut of lands administered by BLM and can affect soils, water, air, plants, animals, and all living things.

The causes of desertification are usually considered to be overgrazing, cutting of trees and bushes for fuel, and other uses beyond the carrying capacity of the land. However it is clear that lands used for ORVs are also showing symptoms of desertification. For example, the American Association for the Advancement of Science Committee on Arid Lands (1974, p. 500) reported that the recreational pressure being exerted on the desert resources of southern California is "almost completely uncontrolled" and that the area has suffered greater destruction than any other arid area. The committee concluded that the present unregulated ORV use of arid areas is "a serious threat to the preservation of the environment in a desirable and stable condition . . . ."

In an environmental impact statement, the U.S. Bureau of Outdoor Recreation (1974) noted that practically no area of the public land is free from potential damage by ORVs and in some areas, where improperly or indiscrimately used, ORVs can cause great harm to man and his natural environment; and that even when properly operated, the impact may be great and, in many instances, irreversible. The U.S. Congress [1976, Sec. 601.(a)] in its Federal Land Policy and Management Act requiring the Secretary of the Interior to prepare a plan for the management, use, development, and protection of federal public lands within the California Desert Conservation Area found that:

> The California desert environment is a total ecosystem that is extremely fragile, easily scarred, and slowly healed.
> Its resources are seriously threatened by pressures of increased use particularly recreational use.
> Its resources can and should be provided for in a multiple use and sustained yield management plan to conserve resources for future generations and to provide, where appropriate, for ORV use.

Chipping and McCoy (1982, p. 12) conclude their study of Pismo Beach and Monterey Bay sand dunes:

> A rapid rate of environmental degradation of sand dunes has been documented in two separate environments. Should the trend continue at its present rate, it is possible that in a few years there will be no pristine coastal dune environment remaining in California, and that associated ecosystems will be damaged beyond hope of recovery.
>
> Damage to wildlife, especially plants, may be irreversible, as many species in the sand dune ecosystem are rare or endangered. The impact of vehicles on dune stability at Pismo Beach will probably result in increased sand advancement rates into farmland and lakes, and at Monterey Bay the sand will advance into farmland, freeways, and housing developments.

A California Department of Parks and Recreation (1975, p. 15) report describes the emotional conflict between ORV users and nonusers and concludes "It is clear that some of the differences between ORV users and those who protest their intrusion and the damage they cause will be irreconcilable."

The Problem Is Recognized

Three primary aspects of ORV use may be easily recognized—pleasure for ORV users, conflict with other users, and effect on resources. ORV use in the arid areas has existed since the turn of the century, but was not identified until recently as a recreation use having conflicts and effects. For example, the comprehensive report on *Land and Water for Recreation* prepared by Clawson (1963) for Resources for the Future does not refer to ORV use; the recreation activities projected through the year 2000 by the U.S. Bureau of Outdoor Recreation (1971) do not include ORV use; and the U.S. Department of Interior (Bureau of Outdoor Recreation, 1973) first nationwide outdoor recreation plan barely mentions motorized recreation.

In the early 1960s there were fewer than half a million registered motorcycles, but in 1972 there were about 5 million, in 1976 over 8 million, and today, over 12 million. The Motorcycle Industry Council (1980, p. 7) estimates that 4.7 million motorcycles were used by 11.7 million people in 1978 for off-highway recreational purposes. These figures do not include snowmobiles, dune buggies, and four-wheel ORVs. During the last 10 years, the demand for public-use areas has greatly increased. The problems of ORV use have been recognized by both user and conservation groups, state and federal agencies, professional societies, many scientists, the U.S. Council on Environmental Quality, state courts, Congress, and two former presidents.

In 1972, the problems were so apparent that the president issued Executive Order 11644 to control the use of ORVs on federal public lands. Federal agencies charged with public-land management were directed to adopt policies to protect public resources, promote safety among all users, and minimize conflicts among various kinds of uses. In 1977, another president issued Executive Order 11989 to provide for immediate closure of areas or trails to ORVs causing considerable adverse effects (Fig. 1-3).

In 1972, and every year since 1974, the U.S. Council on Environmental Quality has reported on ORV problems. In its fifth annual report, the Council (1974, p. 209) observed that ". . . the problem is still growing at an unprecedented rate, and virtually no effective new controls have as yet been accomplished." In its tenth annual report, the Council (1979, p. 421) noted that ORVs have continuing serious adverse impacts on public lands and that serious conflicts continue to exist between ORV users and desert homesteaders, hikers, scientists, and environmentalists.

The Geological Society of America (1977) Committee on Environment and Public Policy has considered the impacts and management of ORVs. After identifying the environmental impacts, the committee concluded (p. 6) that the harsh impacts of ORVs on the natural systems "have destroyed evolutionary gains of such antiquity that recovery will be exceedingly slow . . . that many delicate interdependencies between organisms and their habitats, having been obliterated by ORVs, can never be restored." Rasor (1977, p. v) notes in his report on state approaches to trailbike recreation facilities and management that:

> The American Motorcyclist Association (AMA) has long recognized that there are areas where trailbike use should be prohibited, and even areas where any type of recreational use should not be allowed. Such areas would include ecologically sensitive areas, areas of geologic or archeological significance, locations where such use could be detrimental to endangered wildlife habitats or nesting areas and locations that are established primarily for another recreational purpose.

EXECUTIVE ORDER 11644

Use of Off-Road Vehicles on the Public Lands

An estimated 5 million off-road recreational vehicles—motorcycles, minibikes, trail bikes, snowmobiles, dune-buggies, all-terrain vehicles, and others—are in use in the United States today, and their popularity continues to increase rapidly. The widespread use of such vehicles on the public lands—often for legitimate purposes but also in frequent conflict with wise land and resource management practices, environmental values, and other types of recreational activity—has demonstrated the need for a unified Federal policy toward the use of such vehicles on the public lands.

NOW, THEREFORE, by virtue of the authority vested in me as President of the United States by the Constitution of the United States and in furtherance of the purpose and policy of the National Environmental Policy Act of 1969 (42 U.S.C. 4321), it is hereby ordered as follows:

SECTION 1. *Purpose.* It is the purpose of this order to establish policies and provide for procedures that will ensure that the use of off-road vehicles on public lands will be controlled and directed so as to protect the resources of those lands, to promote the safety of all users of those lands, and to minimize conflicts among the various uses of those lands.

SEC 2. *Definitions.* As used in this order, the term:

(1) "public lands" means (A) all lands under the custody and control of the Secretary of the Interior and the Secretary of Agriculture, except Indian lands, (B) lands under the custody and control of the Tennessee Valley Authority that are situated in western Kentucky and Tennessee and are designated as "Land Between the Lakes," and (C) lands under the custody and control of the Secretary of Defense;

(2) "respective agency head" means the Secretary of the Interior, the Secretary of Defense, the Secretary of Agriculture, and the Board of Directors of the Tennessee Valley Authority, with respect to public lands under the custody and control of each;

(3) "off-road vehicle" means any motorized vehicle designed for or capable of cross-country travel on or immediately over land, water, sand, snow, ice, marsh, swampland, or other natural terrain; except that such term excludes (A)

any registered motorboat, (B) any military, fire, emergency, or law enforcement vehicle when used for emergency purposes, and (C) any vehicle whose use is expressly authorized by the respective agency head under a permit, lease, license, or contract; and

(4) "official use" means use by an employee, agent, or designated representative of the Federal Government or one of its contractors in the course of his employment, agency, or representation.

SEC 3. *Zones of Use.* (a) Each respective agency head shall develop and issue regulations and administrative instructions, within six months of the date of this order, to provide for administrative designation of the specific areas and trails on public lands on which the use of off-road vehicles may be permitted, and areas in which the use of off-road vehicles may not be permitted, and set a date by which such designation of all public lands shall be completed. Those regulations shall direct that the designation of such areas and trails will be based upon the protection of the resources of the public lands, promotion of the safety of all users of those lands, and minimization of conflicts among the various uses of those lands. The regulations shall further require that the designation of such areas and trails shall be in accordance with the following—

(1) Areas and trails shall be located to minimize damage to soil, watershed, vegetation, or other resources of the public lands.

(2) Areas and trails shall be located to minimize harassment of wildlife or significant disruption of wildlife habitats.

(3) Areas and trails shall be located to minimize conflicts between off-road vehicle use and other existing or proposed recreational uses of the same or neighboring public lands, and to ensure the compatibility of such uses with existing conditions in populated areas, taking into account noise and other factors.

(4) Areas and trails shall not be located in officially designated Wilderness Areas or Primitive Areas. Areas and trails shall be located in areas of the National Park system, Natural Areas, or National Wildlife Refuges and Game Ranges only if the respective agency head determines that off-road vehicle use in such locations will not adversely affect their natural, aesthetic, or scenic values.

(b) The respective agency head shall ensure adequate opportunity for public participation in the promulgation of such regulations and in the designation of areas and trails under this section.

Figure 1-3. Executive Orders 11644 and 11989, Use of Off-Road Vehicles on the Public Lands.

(c) The limitations on off-road vehicle use imposed under this section shall not apply to official use.

SEC. 4. *Operating Conditions.* Each respective agency head shall develop and publish, within one year of the date of this order, regulations prescribing operating conditions for off-road vehicles on the public lands. These regulations shall be directed at protecting resource values, preserving public health, safety, and welfare, and minimizing use conflicts.

SEC 5. *Public Information.* The respective agency head shall ensure that areas and trails where off-road vehicle use is permitted are well marked and shall provide for the publication and distribution of information, including maps, describing such areas and trails and explaining the conditions on vehicle use. He shall seek cooperation of relevant State agencies in the dissemination of this information.

SEC. 6. *Enforcement.* The respective agency head shall, where authorized by law, prescribe appropriate penalties for violation of regulations adopted pursuant to this order, and shall establish procedures for the enforcement of those regulations. To the extent permitted by law, he may enter into agreements with State or local governmental agencies for cooperative enforcement of laws and regulations relating to off-road vehicle use.

SEC. 7. *Consultation.* Before issuing the regulations or administrative instructions required by this order or designating areas or trails as required by this order and those regulations and administrative instructions, the Secretary of the Interior shall, as appropriate, consult with the Atomic Energy Commission.

SEC. 8. *Monitoring of Effects and Review.* (a) The respective agency head shall monitor the effects of the use of off-road vehicles on lands under their jurisdictions. On the basis of the information gathered, they shall from time to time amend or rescind designations of areas or other actions taken pursuant to this order as necessary to further the policy of this order.

(b) The Council on Environmental Quality shall maintain a continuing review of the implementation of this order.

RICHARD NIXON

THE WHITE HOUSE,
February 8, 1972

EXECUTIVE ORDER 11989

Off-Road Vehicles on Public Lands

By virtue of the authority vested in me by the Constitution and statutes of the United States of America, and as President of the United States of America, in order to clarify agency authority to define zones of use by off-road vehicles on public lands, in furtherance of the National Environmental Policy Act of 1969, as amended (42 U.S.C. 4321 *et seq.*), Executive Order No. 11644 of February 8, 1972, is hereby amended as follows:

SECTION 1. Clause (B) of Section 2(3) of Executive Order No. 11644, setting forth an exclusion from the definition of off-road vehicles, is amended to read "(B) any fire, military, emergency or law enforcement vehicle when used for emergency purposes, and any combat or combat support vehicle when used for national defense purposes, and".

SEC. 2. Add the following new Section to Executive Order No. 11644:

"SEC. 9. *Special Protection of the Public Lands.* (a) Notwithstanding the provisions of Section 3 of this Order, the respective agency head shall, whenever he determines that the use of off-road vehicles will cause or is causing considerable adverse effects on the soil, vegetation, wildlife, wildlife habitat or cultural or historic resources of particular areas or trails of the public lands, immediately close such areas or trails to the type of off-road vehicle causing such effects, until such time as he determines that such adverse effects have been eliminated and that measures have been implemented to prevent future recurrence.

"(b) Each respective agency head is authorized to adopt the policy that portions of the public lands within his jurisdiction shall be closed to use by off-road vehicles except those areas or trails which are suitable and specifically designated as open to such use pursuant to Section 3 of this Order."

JIMMY CARTER

THE WHITE HOUSE,
May 24, 1977

Figure 1-3. (continued)

The National Association of Conservation Districts (1980) adopted a general resolution with respect to ORVs at its 34th annual convention in Houston, Texas. The resolution supports "responsible state actions addressing the problems of environmental damage, vandalism, theft, and irresponsible advertising . . ." (Fig. 1-4).

The problem has been recognized by more than half the states, which in turn have adopted registration and licensing laws. A few states and some counties have regulatory controls. The Santa Clara County Board of Supervisors (1980), in adopting an ordinance (Kockelman, Chapter 23, Fig. 23-3) regulating ORVs, found that ORV activities have:

a strong potential for adversely impacting both the site of the activity and the surrounding neighborhood;

already adversely impacted many areas of the country;

resulted in the destruction of natural soil stabilizer, in soil displacement, in stripping of vegetation, and in mechanical erosion;

Serious damage to vegetation on critical areas, to dirt roads and trails, and to stream-banks and water courses from the careless operation of off-road vehicles is causing increasingly costly problems on both private and public lands. Accelerated soil erosion, increased flooding, and damage to structures and improvements are a burden on private landowners, as is the problem of potential liability created when ORV operators trespass on private lands. Also related to the increased use of ORVs has been an alarming increase in theft and vandalism, particularly to isolated properties.

At the same time, NACD recognizes that ORVs are useful tools for the farmer, rancher, logger and others who live and work in remote locations. They are a legitimate form of recreation for urban people which, if properly and responsibly carried out, can cause minimum damage to the environment and private property owners.

NACD urges the manufacturers of all forms of off-road vehicles to take the lead in an intensive national campaign to promote environmentally sound use of the vehicles and respect for the land and improvements of private owners. This is particularly needed in line with television advertising, which too often depicts ORVs being used in highly damaging ways.

NACD urges state associations to support the development of state legislation such as the model act contained in NACD's 1980 publication entitled Private Lands and Public Recreation. This will help ease some of the problems of access, trespass and liability that exists in many states today. In addition, we support responsible state actions addressing the problems of environmental damage, vandalism, theft and irresponsible advertising caused by certain elements within the ORV user's community.

Adopted by the National Association of Conservation Districts (1980).

Figure 1-4. General resolution on off-road vehicles adopted by the National Association of Conservation Districts (1980).

greatly reduced soil moisture, increased temperature in the soil, and increased runoff of rain water; and

increased the erosion potential and decreased the land's ability to retard erosion.

Recently, Presiding Justice Gardner (1980, p. 6) in upholding San Bernardino County Ordinance No. 1590, which provides that no person may drive a motor vehicle over land belonging to another without that person's written permission, concluded that "The fragility of the desert ecology supports the local ordinance."

What Must Be Done?

The fragility of arid-area ecosystems is commonly cited as a basis for specific protective actions or policies. Generally, this perception is founded only on casual observations rather than on quantitative study. Casual observations of ORV effects on desert landscapes indicate that denudation is rapid, water and wind erosion of soil are accelerated, and the effects are long lasting, as shown by the persistence of roads and trails that have been unused for decades. From these causal observations, it may be deduced that some effect is being registered in wildlife communities by modification and destruction of their habitat.

A definition of the potential threat of ORVs to arid areas depends upon quantitative assessment of these impacts. However, an understanding of the variability and functioning of national desert systems is first required. Such understanding can be approached first by comparing damaged systems with adjacent similar undamaged terrain, and second by making controlled experiments in previously undamaged areas. Ideally, both of these approaches will lead to predictive models that are essential for good management.

Four steps are necessary to solve most problems. First, identify the problem or goal; second, consider or suggest plans to solve the problem or reach the goal; third, select the most appropriate plan; and fourth, implement the selected plan. In this book, the editors and authors have taken the first two steps. Twenty chapters cover most of the biological and physical problems caused by ORVs in arid areas. These chapters carefully document the ORV impacts and clearly identify the need for scientific information and its use by planners, managers, and decision makers. The last three chapters set forth management concepts, practices, regulations, and education for meeting ORV-user needs, protecting resources, and avoiding conflicts. All that remains is to select the most appropriate plan and to act upon it.

References

Aleshire, P. 1979. High-stakes conflict over the California desert: Dune buggies versus flowering cactus. Calif. J. 10(4):143–145.

American Association for the Advancement of Science, Committee on Arid Lands. 1974. Off-road vehicle use. Science 184(4135):500, 501.

Bowden, L. W., R. Huning, C. F. Hutchinson, and C. W. Johnson. 1974. Satellite photograph presents first comprehensive view of local wind. The Santa Ana. Science 184:1077–1078.

California Department of Parks and Recreation. 1975. The Off-Road Vehicle. A Study Report. The Resources Agency, Sacramento, California, 62 pp.

Chipping, D. H., and R. McCoy. 1982. Coastal sand dune complexities: Pismo Beach and Monterey Bay. Calif. Geol. 35(1):7–12.

Clawson, M. 1963. Land and Water for Recreation. Published for Resources for the Future. Rand McNally, Chicago, 144 pp.

Dregne, H. E. 1977. Desertification of arid lands. Econ. Geogr. 53(4):322–331.

Food and Agricultural Organization of the United Nations and the United Nations Educational, Scientific and Cultural Organization. 1977. Proc. Conf. on Desertification. Nairobi, Kenya, August 29–September 9, 1977.

Gardner, R. C. 1980. *Sports Committee District 37 A.M.A., Inc., v. County of San Bernardino.* Court of Appeal, Fourth District, Second Division, State of California. 4 Civil 21617, Superior Court No. 169018, 7 pp.

Geological Society of America. 1977. Impacts and Management of Off-road

Vehicles. Report of the Committee on Environment and Public Policy. Geological Society of America, Boulder, Colorado, 8 pp.

Motorcycle Industry Council, Inc. 1980. The Recreational Trailbike Planner. Newport Beach, California, Vol. I, No. 9.

National Association of Conservation Districts. 1980. General Resolution No. 59 Off-Road Vehicles. 34th annual convention, Houston, Texas. February 10–14, 1980.

National Association of Conservation Districts. Undated. Private Lands and Public Recreation. (Brochure.) League City, Texas.

Rasor, R. 1977. Five State Approaches to Trailbike Recreation Facilities and Their Management. American Motorcycle Association, Westerville, Ohio, 64 pp.

Santa Clara County Board of Supervisors. 1980. Ordinance No. NS-1019.1 To Prohibit Operation of Off-Road Motor Vehicles on Private Property Without a Permit. (Adopted May 13, 1980.) San Jose, California, 2 pp.

Sheridan, D. 1979. Off-Road Vehicles on Public Land. Council on Environmental Quality. U.S. Government Printing Office, Washington, D.C., 84 pp.

Sheridan, D. 1981. Desertification of the United States. Council on Environmental Quality, U.S. Government Printing Office, Washington, D.C., 142 pp.

Silcock, B. 1973. Testimony before the Public Lands Subcommittee of the Interior and Insular Affairs Committee of the House of Representatives, February 9, 1973.

Stebbins, R. C. 1974. Off-Road Vehicles and the Fragile Desert. Am. Biol. Teacher 36(4, 5):203–208; 294–304.

Stebbins, R. C. 1978. Letter to David Sheridan, U.S. Council on Environmental Quality, Washington, D.C., January 12, 1978.

U.S. Bureau of Land Management. 1976. Environmental Analysis Record for Competitive Off-Road Vehicle Events Designated Vehicle Use Area 30–Upper Johnson Valley. Riverside, California, District Office, High Desert Resource Area, 50 pp.

U.S. Bureau of Outdoor Recreation. 1971. Selected Outdoor Recreation Statistics. U.S. Government Printing Office, Washington, D.C., 145 pp.

U.S. Bureau of Outdoor Recreation. 1973. Outdoor Recreation–A Legacy for America. 2416-00066, U.S. Government Printing Office, Washington, D.C., 89 pp.

U.S. Bureau of Outdoor Recreation. 1974. Final Environmental Statement, Department Implementation of the Executive Order 11644 Pertaining to Use of Off-Road Vehicles on the Public Lands. January 10, 1974, p. 9.

U.S. Congress. 1976. Federal Land Policy and Management Act of 1976, as Amended. 94 Public Law 579, 90 Stat. 2747, 43 U.S. Code 1701 et seq.

U.S. Council on Environmental Quality. 1971. Third Annual Report, p. 139; 1974, Fifth Annual Report, pp. 207–210; 1975, Sixth Annual Report, pp. 243–245; 1976, Seventh Annual Report, pp. 93–94; 1977, Eighth Annual Report, pp. 81–83; 1978, Ninth Annual Report, pp. 303–305; 1979, Tenth Annual Report, pp. 421–422; 1980, Eleventh Annual Report, pp. 348–357. U.S. Government Printing Office, Washington, D.C.

White, J. M. 1975. The Great American Desert. George Allen & Unwin LTD., London, 320 pp.

PART I

Physical Effects of Off-Road Vehicle Use

2

Soil and Soil Formation in Arid Regions[1]

Harold E. Dregne

Introduction

Soil is the biochemically weathered mantle on the Earth's surface that sustains life, functions as a vast reservoir for the collection and storage of water, and absorbs and neutralizes agricultural, domestic, and industrial wastes. As the sustenance for ecosystems, soils can be viewed as the most important part of the natural environment; yet of all parts of the environment, soils are probably the most abused. With declines in the productivity in arid regions continuing as a result of land misuse, the need for rational management of soils is paramount. Off-road vehicle (ORV) use is one of the serious management problems in the arid regions, and management of ORV use to minimize the disturbance to soils requires knowledge of what kinds of soils occur in arid lands and how they form.

The climatic region with which this book is concerned comprises the zones shown on the map of Figure 2-1 as "hyperarid" and "arid." The semiarid zone is excluded unless specific reference is made to it. Figure 2-1 was adapted from the 1977 UNESCO map showing the world distribution of arid and subhumid climates (UNESCO, 1979). Boundaries on this map differ somewhat from the widely used 1952 UNESCO map drawn by Meigs (1952). The climatic basis for the 1977 map is the ratio of annual precipitation to annual potential evapotranspiration (Table 2-1). The terms "deserts" and "arid regions," as used here, are synonyms that refer to the hyperarid and arid climatic zones of Figure 2-1. The

---

[1] The views and conclusions contained this this chapter are based on the author's studies or experiences and do not necessarily represent the official viewpoint or policy of any U.S. government agency.

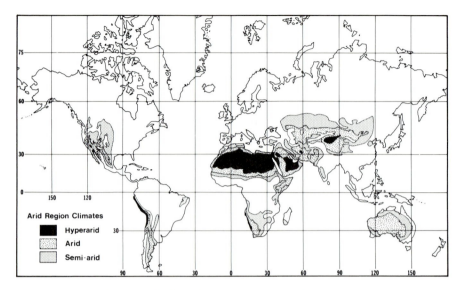

Figure 2-1. World distribution of arid climates.

region includes what are known as the Chihuahuan and Sonoran Deserts of the United States and Mexico, the Great Intermountain Basin between the Rockies and the Sierra Nevada and Cascade Mountain ranges, the Central and Imperial Valleys of California, and a number of local "deserts" contained within other vegetation or physiographic units.

Soils of Arid Regions

Soils of arid regions reflect the current environment in which they occur and the climates to which they have been exposed, over what sometimes amounts to a million or more years. Prehistoric climates are sure to have included wet and dry periods that undoubtedly influenced present-day soils. Evidence of this is most obvious in Australia where landscapes are old and soils reflect past humid cli-

Table 2-1. Classification of Arid Region Climates[a]

Aridity class	Precipitation/potential evapotranspiration
Hyperarid zone	<0.03
Arid zone	0.03–0.20
Semiarid zone	0.20–0.50

[a]Data from UNESCO (1979).

mates as well as recent arid conditions. As the result of short-term and long-term climatic effects, arid regions soils are as variable as those in the humid regions.

For the world's deserts as a whole, gravelly soils are by far the most extensive in areal distribution. They usually are deep, are coarse-textured throughout the profile, have only a weak B horizon or no B horizon at all, and are covered with a desert pavement of gravels and stones. Desert pavements are also called, appropriately enough, desert armor and are the surface materials that distinguish the gobi of China and the reg of North Africa. Stony pavements protect the underlying soil from the impact of raindrops and the erosive force of wind. They also provide a bearing surface for vehicular traffic as long as the stones and gravels remain in place.

Sandy soils and sand dunes are next most extensive but are especially widespread in the hyperarid climatic zones. Barren moving dunes covering tens and hundreds of square kilometers in immense sand seas (called *ergs* in the western Sahara) are sometimes more than 100 m high. They occur principally in the Sahara, the Empty Quarter of the Arabian Peninsula, and the Takla Makan Desert of China. Large dune fields also occur in the somewhat less arid deserts of northern China, Soviet Central Asia, and elsewhere. Whereas moving sand dunes show little or no indication of the horizon formation that distinguishes soils, vegetated sandy surface materials will usually have an easily observable A horizon.

Clay soils are not extensive on a world scale but do occupy large areas in the arid regions of Australia and the Sudan. Their very low permeability severely inhibits soil formation and horizon differentiation. Clay soils are most common in and near playas.

Temperature, precipitation pattern, and topographic position are the main determinants of the kind of soil found in arid and semiarid regions. Soils of the smooth to gently sloping uplands tend to be most strongly influenced by—and most representative of—the regional climate and have, in the past, been called zonal soils. Where slopes are steep, soils tend to be shallow due to erosion, whereas in depressions soils are usually fine textured and deep as the result of sediment deposition.

Classification

Soils of the hyperarid and arid climatic zones belong almost exclusively to three orders of the United States comprehensive soil classification system (Soil Survey Staff, 1975). These are the Aridisol, Entisol, and Vertisol orders. Aridisols may not show considerable development; Entisols and Vertisols show little development and are, therefore, pedologically young. Absolute age of soils does not determine whether they are young or old. Vertisols are young even though a playa may be 50,000 years old. Deposition of new clayey sediments keeps Vertisols "young" by slowing the development of horizons. Conversely, an "old" argillic Aridisol can form on the surface of a plain which has little erosion and

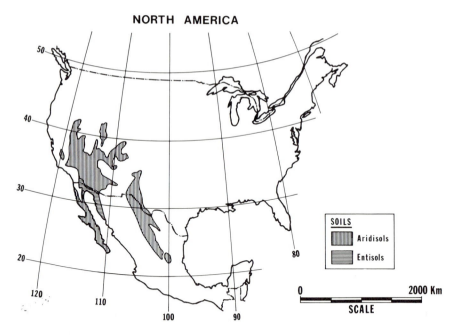

Figure 2-2. Arid region soils of North America.

deposition in a period of 10,000 years. Figure 2-2 is a map of the soils of the hyperarid, arid, and semiarid zones of North America (Dregne, 1976).

Aridisols come in two kinds, one with an argillic (clay-enriched) B horizon (Table 2-2) and the other without an argillic horizon (Table 2-3). Some of them are calcareous to the surface but most are not. The presence of the argillic (Bt) horizons in the Aridisol of Table 2-2 indicates that the soil has experienced a considerable degree of development and is several thousand years old. The ca horizons in the Aridisol of Table 2-3 are highly calcareous, the top one (Clca) being an indurated carbonate horizon (calcrete). Both of these Aridisols have a desert pavement of stones and gravels on the surface.

Entisols and Vertisols have either a weakly developed B horizon or none at all. In the dry lands, two kinds of Entisols are dominant: sandy soils and gravelly soils on uplands. A third kind, recent alluvium, is found along stream channels. Vertisols are deep clays that crack badly upon drying. They may be derived from marine deposits, be formed in place from rocks such as basalt, or originate from sediments deposited in depressions.

Profile characteristics of the two major kinds of Entisols in the arid regions are illustrated in Tables 2-4 and 2-5. The Entisol of Table 2-4 is representative of the gravelly soils that are found on alluvial fans and piedmonts in the Southwest. It is covered by a desert pavement, is alkaline from the surface downward, and is calcareous below 8 cm. The organic matter content is low. The other common Entisol is a sand dune soil (Table 2-5) that is low in everything except sand. This particular sample came from a stabilized dune about 10 m high that

Table 2-2. Profile Characteristics of a Well-Developed Aridisol (Typic Haplargid)

Depth (cm)	Horizon	Particle size			Textural class[a]	pH	C.E.C.[b]	Organic matter (%)
		Sand (%)	Silt (%)	Clay (%)				
0–8	A	82	12	6	LS	7.6	4.3	0.3
8–23	B21t	75	13	12	SL	7.6	8.2	0.4
23–48	B22t	75	13	12	SL	7.6	8.9	0.4
48–81	B3	83	11	6	LS	7.6	4.2	0.2
81–102	Cca	81	13	6	GLS	8.3	4.4	0.1

[a]LS, loamy sand; SL, sandy loam; GLS, gravely loamy sand.
[b]C.E.C. = cation exchange capacity, me/100 g.

Table 2-3. Profile Characteristics of a Weakly Developed Aridisol (Typic Calciorthid)

Depth (cm)	Horizon	Particle size			Textural class[a]	pH	C.E.C.[b]	Organic matter (%)
		Sand (%)	Silt (%)	Clay (%)				
0–5	A2	71	19	10	SL	7+	10.4	0.4
5–13	B	73	15	12	SL	7+	12.3	0.6
13–18	C1ca	64	18	18	SL	7+	14.4	0.3
18–48	C2ca	73	16	11	SL	7+	11.8	0.4
48–69	C3ca	81	12	7	LS	7+	6.4	0.2
69–94	C4ca	79	14	7	LS	7+	7.3	0.2
94–132	C5ca	77	13	10	SL	7+	7.3	—

[a]SL, sandy loam; LS, loamy sand.
[b]C.E.C. = cation exchange capacity, me/100 g.

Table 2-4. Profile Characteristics of a Gravelly Arid Region Entisol (Typic Torriorthent) on an Alluvial Fan

Depth (cm)	Horizon	Particle size			Textural class[a]	pH	C.E.C.[b]	Organic matter (%)
		Sand (%)	Silt (%)	Clay (%)				
0–8	A	69	26	5	GSL	7+	9.4	0.3
8–33	C1ca	76	15	8	VGSL	7+	7.8	0.4
33–56	C2ca	73	17	10	GSL	7+	8.8	0.5
56–74	C3ca	78	14	8	GLS	7+	7.6	0.6
74–112	C4ca	91	5	4	VGS	7+	4.7	0.1

[a]GSL, gravelly sandy loam; VGSL, very gravelly sandy loam; GLS, gravelly loamy sand; VGS, very gravelly sand.
[b]C.E.C. = cation exchange capacity, me/100 g.

Table 2-5. Profile Characteristics of a Sandy Arid Region Entisol (Typic Ustipsamment)

Depth (cm)	Horizon	Particle size			Textural class[a]	pH	C.E.C.[b]	Organic matter (%)
		Sand (%)	Silt (%)	Clay (%)				
0–8	A	96	2	2	S	7.5	1.7	0.4
8–30	C1	98	1	1	S	7.3	1.0	0.1
30–65+	C2	97	2	1	S	7.3	0.9	0.03

[a]S, sand.
[b]C.E.C. = cation exchange capacity, me/100 g.

had a sparse cover of shrubs and grasses. If the dune had been mobile, it would not have had an A horizon because the mixing of the surface sand as the dune moved under the force of the wind would have obliterated any signs of horizon formation.

Characteristics of a typical Vertisol are shown in Table 2-6. Vertisols of playas are generally saline in the hyperarid climatic zone but are likely to be nonsaline in the arid zone.

Distribution

The gross character of the soil pattern in the arid regions, as related to landscapes, tends to be a function of slope. At the low points in the landscape where land surfaces are level, as in closed basins and floodplains of streams, cracking clay Vertisols (Torrents) and variably textured alluvial Entisols (Fluvents), respectively, are found. On the slopes leading out from the basins and streams, coarse-textured Entisols (Orthents) of variable depth are the principal soils. Higher on the landscape, gently sloping plains, if present, may have sand dunes (Psamments), gravelly calcareous Aridisols (Orthids), or coarse- to medium-textured argillic Aridisols (Argids). Farther up, on the steeper slopes of alluvial fans and desert mountains, the Entisols (Orthents) found there may be gravelly and deep or rocky and shallow.

In North America, calcium carbonate is present within the upper 2 m of soil nearly everywhere. Frequently, gypsum also is present in large amounts, particularly in the Pecos River watershed of New Mexico and Texas and in the Tularosa Basin of New Mexico, where gypsum crystals constitute the sands of the White Sands National Monument. Gypsum and calcium carbonate occur together in soils, with calcium carbonate the dominant salt in most cases. Gypsiferous soils usually belong in the Aridisol order and the Calciorthid or Gypsiorthid great group. There are few instances of indurated gypsum horizons occurring in North American soils although they are widespread in the USSR, North Africa, Iraq, and Australia (Cooke and Warren, 1973). Indurated siliceous horizons are also not common in the arid regions of North America.

Although giant sand dunes are frequently associated with deserts in people's minds, they are rare in North America. The only large systems of sand dunes are the Algodones Dunes in California, the White Sands of New Mexico, and El Grande Desierto in the Mexican state of Sonora.

Soil Formation

Soil formation is a function of the character of the surface materials from which the soils are derived, the slope of the land, climatic and vegetative conditions, and the length of time over which development has occurred. Soil formation is the transformation of rock into soil, where rock refers to consolidated or unconsolidated bedrock and to alluvial and aeolian deposits. The degree of soil for-

Table 2-6. Profile Characteristics of a Playa Vertisol (Typic Torrert)

Depth (cm)	Horizon	Particle size			Textural class[a]	pH	C.E.C.[b]	Organic matter (%)
		Sand (%)	Silt (%)	Clay (%)				
0–5	A	6	30	64	C	8.2	33.1	1.0
5–23	AC	6	28	66	C	8.4	32.2	0.8
23–48	C1	6	32	62	C	8.4	31.1	0.4
48–115	C2	6	29	65	C	8.4	30.4	0.4

[a] C, clay.
[b] C.E.C. = cation exchange capacity, me/100 g.

mation is measured by the amount and kind of horizon differentiation that has occurred. Well-developed soils have several clearly defined genetic horizons, including a B horizon, whereas poorly developed soils have few obvious genetic horizons.

The conditions favoring rapid soil formation are a humid and warm climate, heavy vegetative cover, a gently undulating well-drained upland position on the landscape, and medium-textured and poorly consolidated surface materials. Formation will be slow in an arid climate where biological activity is subdued, slopes are steep or flat enough to accumulate runoff water, and the surface materials are consolidated or very gravelly. In an arid environment, whether hot or cold, chemical weathering is very slow since it is dependent upon water. Physical weathering certainly is a factor in hot arid climates due to the large temperature changes from day to night but chemical weathering is the major driving force in soil formation. The relation of rainfall to the intensity of soil formation, according to Jenny (1941), appears on a graph as a S curve, with low intensity in the arid regions and high intensity in the humid regions. This relation suggests that in the hyperarid zones the rate of soil formation is very slow, just as biological activity is very slow.

Soil formation is a process of weathering and translocation. Chemical weathering produces secondary clays, oxidizes and reduces minerals, and brings about hydration, hydrolysis, and solution of minerals and salts. Weathering and the translocation of organic matter, clay, carbonates, sequioxides, and soluble salts from the surface soil and their accumulation at greater depth or their complete removal from the soil system leads to horizon differentiation. Both chemical weathering and translocation of substances are very slow in hyperarid zones and slow in arid zones.

Due in part to the low degree of soil development associated with aridity, the pattern of soils in the arid and hyperarid climatic zones tends to be similar throughout the world. Another consequence of the rainfall-soil development relation is that many of the gravelly or stony upland soils in hot and dry regions such as the southwestern United States are not much different from the surface materials from which they have been developed. This lack of soil development is most obvious on gravelly slopes of the desert mountains in Arizona and California and on sand dunes. An A horizon, the presence of which is the first indicator that geologic surface materials are being transformed into soils, is frequently either absent, difficult to detect, or only a few centimeters thick in those soils. The exception is seen on old, deep, level to gently sloping, medium-textured materials, which may have well-defined argillic B horizons. Calcic (carbonate) subsurface horizons are much more common than argillic B horizons. The physical environment in deserts is harsh, vegetation is sparse, and life in general is precarious. Soil formation is slow and easily disrupted. Recuperative powers after disruption are weak because biological activity, which is the main force influencing the rate of soil formation, is low except when occasional rains induce a growth of ephemeral vegetation. It is this lack of resiliency to disruption that leads people to refer to desert soils as fragile.

Recovery after disruption by human activity is faster in the wetter climatic zones, but any change that leads to moderate to severe sheet and gully erosion or to dune formation is likely to have effects that will last for decades or centuries. Once a dune or a gully has appeared or the soil stripped from a slope in the arid regions, a change will have occurred that is, to all intents and purposes, permanent, with no chance of a return to the original soil conditions.

Development is also slow in soils of closed depressions, principally due to the high clay content, low permeability, high salinity, and continual deposition of new sediments. Montmorillonitic expanding clays dominate the clay mineral complex in depressions, whether the soils are in the hyperarid or arid climatic zones. Soils in depressions usually have no B horizons, display deep cracks when dry, and are classified as Vertisols.

Rate of Soil Formation and Age of Desert Soils

Quantitative data on the time it takes to form a soil are virtually nonexistent. One of the many reasons for the lack of data is the difficulty of determining whether a particular soil has reached a stage of development that is in equilibrium with the environment. Another is the fact that the rate of soil formation varies greatly with the climate, the slope of the land, and the type of parent material present (Joffe, 1949). A sand deposit in a humid climate and in a well-drained position on the landscape weathers and forms a mature soil relatively rapidly, perhaps in as little time as 1000 to 1500 years (Jenny, 1941). In an arid climate having a little less than 250 mm annual precipitation and in medium-textured unconsolidated material on a gentle slope, about 2200 years were required to form a well-defined calcic C horizon (Gile and Hawley, 1968). A calcrete subsurface horizon may require several tens of thousands of years to develop (Gile et al., 1966). More to the point, perhaps, Hunt (1972) mentions alluvium deposited 2000 years ago in the Denver area, where annual precipitation is about 350 mm, which still has only very weakly developed profiles.

Although rates of formation of mature soils amount to thousands of years, soil formation begins shortly after parent material has been exposed to a new environment. With the possible exception of one abiotic soil reported for Antarctica (Horowitz et al., 1972), there are no known lifeless soils on the Earth's surface, even in the center of the Sahara. Biological activity is a powerful force that contributes to the physical and chemical weathering that transforms rock material into soil.

To a pedologist, soil age is a function of the time the soil material has been exposed on the land surface without experiencing deposition or erosion at a rate exceeding that of soil formation. Within the same climatic zone and in similar parent material, there may be young (immature) soils on river floodplains and on steep slopes at the same time there are old (mature) soils on level surfaces. The time over which soil-forming processes have been operating may be chronologically the same but with different results. Land surfaces in arid Australia, for example, have not been altered by catastrophic events such as glaciation for over a million years, yet there are immature and mature soils almost side by side.

One of the few detailed and comprehensive studies undertaken on the influence of time on soil formation in the arid regions is that by Gile and Hawley (1968) in New Mexico. The parent material was noncalcareous alluvium dating from Mid-Pleistocene to the present, annual precipitation was about 200 mm, and the vegetation zone was desert grassland. Table 2-7 shows the age of the geomorphic surface and the kind of soil occurring on that surface.

The first two manifestations of soil formation are a slight accumulation of organic matter and the appearance of a weakly vesicular layer at the surface. Air trapped beneath the thin surfical crust that forms when raindrops strike the surface of the ground is responsible for the vesicular layer characteristic of most arid region soils (Springer, 1958; also see Chapter 11). In subsequent centuries, carbonate accumulation occurs due to release of calcium from the parent material or wind-laid deposition of calcium salts on the surface, followed by downward translocation and deposition. If there were no accumulation of carbonates in the subsoil an argillic B horizon would slowly begin to form.

Transformation of the rock particles into soil did not, in the test area, produce a recognizable calcic or argillic subsurface genetic horizon within about

Table 2-7. Influence of Age of Geomorphic Surface on Soil Characteristics[a]

Age of surface (years)	Soil name	Soil characteristics
100(?)	Entisol (torripsamment)	Thin gray A horizon; vesicular in places; slight accumulation of organic carbon
100(?) to 1000	Entisol (torrifluvent)	Slight evidence of carbonate accumulation; thin strata absent
1100 to 2100	Entisol (torrifluvent)	Weak distinct horizon of carbonate accumulation in gravelly materials
2200 to 4600	Aridisol (calciorthid)	Weak calcic horizon of carbonate accumulation in low-gravel matertials; prismatic and subangular blocky structure
Late Pleistocene	Aridisol (haplargid) (paleorthid)	Haplargid: Oriented clay coatings in Bt horizon; calcic horizon Paleorthid: Indurated calcic horizon; single laminar layer
Mid-Pleistocene	Aridisol (paleorthid)	Indurated calcic horizon; multiple laminar layers

[a]Data from Gile and Hawley (1968).

2000 years; only Entisols were developed. However, most of the original bedding in the alluvium had disappeared as a consequence of root and animal disturbance and carbonate accumulation. It required something more than 2000 years to form a Calciorthid, which is an Aridisol with a calcic subsurface horizon. Geomorphic surfaces of Late Pleistocene age (more than about 10,000 years old) were developed enough to have an argillic horizon (Haplargid) or indurated carbonate horizons (Paleorthid). The Mid-Pleistocene Paleorthid was more indurated than the earlier one.

Interpretation of the time required to produce an argillic horizon in an arid environment, which Table 2-7 indicates at more than 4600 years and probably more than 10,000 years, is complicated by the fact that Pleistocene climates were both wet and dry. It is quite possible that the Haplargid actually was formed during a wetter period of the Pleistocene. This raises doubts about the relevance to modern environments of horizon formation in soils older than about 5000 years.

A somewhat similar analysis of the influence of soil age on development was made in the subtropical continental climate of the Punjab River plain of Pakistan (Ahmad et al., 1977). Annual precipitation, however, was about 500 mm. In that area, where soil development should be faster, between 10,000 and 20,000 years were required to develop an argillic horizon.

All of the meager evidence indicates that soil formation in the hyperarid and arid zones requires thousands of years to do more than increase the surface organic matter content, develop a vesicular or platy surface structure, and darken the color of the surface soil, even in the absence of significant erosion or deposition. That being the case, it is futile to speak of recovery from disturbance of soils in those regions in any time frame related to human occupancy.

The Effect of ORVs on Desert Soils

Direct soil damage due to ORVs is principally of two kinds: (1) disruption of the surface soil (Chapter 3) and (2) compaction of surface soil and subsoil (Chapter 4). Disruption of the surface soil, especially, leads to numerous problems. If the surface soil is disturbed by the impact of vehicles or the knocking over of shrubs, susceptibility to wind and water erosion is increased (Chapters 5 and 6), decomposition of what little organic matter may be present is accelerated, soil aggregate stability is further weakened, inorganic surface crusts form which encourage greater runoff (Chapters 3 and 4), germination and emergence of seedlings is inhibited (Chapter 7), less water enters the soil, and the environment becomes more harsh for the plants and animals that live in and on the soil. Vegetation protects the soil from erosion, and once that protection is lost soil degradation can be very rapid (Figs. 2-3 and 2-4). The effect is longer lasting than elsewhere on the gravelly upland soils in the driest part of the arid regions, where there is little or no vegetative cover and soil recovery is very slow (Chapter 14). The permanent effect is least on barren sand dunes and on the clay flats of playas.

Figure 2-3. Gully erosion in urban park, Niger.

Figure 2-4. Severely eroded sandy soil, Texas.

Figure 2-5. Caravan of four-wheeled vehicles in California desert.

Vehicle tracks across desert pavement, on the other hand, may remain easily visible for decades or centuries (Figs. 2-5 and 2-6; see Chapter 11).

Conclusions and Management Recommendations

Aridisols and Entisols of various kinds are the most extensive soils in hyperarid and arid climate zones. Vertisols can be found throughout the arid regions in any climatic zone. Extensive fields of barren sand dunes are largely confined to the hyperarid zones.

Arid region soils vary greatly in their susceptibility to ORV damage. Susceptibility to permanent damage is greatest on sloping land in the hyperarid and arid climatic zones. Susceptibility is high on steep slopes, on gravelly and sandy surfaces of gentle slopes, and on stabilized (vegetated) sand dunes in the drier climates. Susceptibility is low on barren sand dunes and the clay flats of playas.

Two groups of soils require minimal regulation of ORV traffic: barren, fixed sand dunes and clay flats (Chapters 4 and 5). There are esthetic problems associated with tracks across the surfaces and there may be a small amount of localized air pollution due to wind erosion, but significant troublesome changes in the land surface are unlikely to occur. Changes in the biota which are sustained by these soils cannot be ignored, however (see Chapters 8, 9, 10, and 19).

The remainder of the soils in hyperarid and arid zones are in a very different category. They are sensitive to vehicular damage having both short-term and

Figure 2-6. Start line for the Barstow to Las Vegas cross country motorcycle race. This wave, one of two, has 1,500 motorcycles lined up across a one-mile long start line. The enormous damages caused by the 1974 race resulted in denial of permit applications for subsequent races.

long-term effects. Once the soil surface in the climatic zones having less than 200 to 250 mm of rain is disturbed, recovery is extremely slow (see Chapters 13 and 14). Aside from the esthetic injury, there will be accelerated water and wind erosion leading to increased air pollution and sediment production (Chapters 5, 6, and 20). There is no possibility of setting a realistic permissive level of vehicular use; any use will be destructive. If there is to be recreational vehicular use, it should be on an acceptable sacrifice area. It should be remembered, however, that there can be no acceptable sacrifice area unless the much greater runoff and sediment produced can be tolerated downslope of the sacrifice area.

References

Ahmad, M., J. Ryan, and R. C. Paeth. 1977. Soil development as a function of time in the Punjab River plains of Pakistan. Soil Sci. Soc. of Am. J. 41: 1162–1166.
Cooke, R. U., and A. Warren. 1973. Geomorphology in Deserts. B. T. Batsford, Ltd., London, 398 pp.

Dregne, H. E. 1976. Soils of Arid Regions. Elsevier Scientific Publishing Company, Amsterdam, 237 pp.

Gile, L. H., and J. W. Hawley. 1968. Age and comparative development of desert soils at the Gardner Spring radiocarbon site, New Mexico. Soil Sci. Soc. Am. Proc. 32:709–716.

Gile, L. H., F. F. Peterson, and R. B. Grossman. 1966. Morphological and genetic sequences of carbonate accumulation in desert soils. Soil Sci. 101: 347–360.

Horowitz, N. H., R. E. Cameron, and J. S. Hubbard. 1972. Microbiology of the dry valleys of Antarctica. Science 176:242–245.

Hunt, C. B. 1972. Geology of Soils. W. H. Freeman and Company, San Francisco, 344 pp.

Jenny, H. 1941. Factors of Soil Formation. McGraw-Hill Book Co., Inc., New York, 281 pp.

Joffe, J. S. 1949. Pedology. Pedology Publications, New Brunswick, New Jersey, 622 pp.

Meigs, P. 1952. World distribution of arid and semi-arid homoclimates. In: UNESCO, Reviews of Research on Arid Zone Hydrology: Arid Zone Research, 1:203–210.

Soil Survey Staff. 1975. Soil Taxonomy. Agricultural Handbook No. 436. U.S. Dept. Agriculture, U.S. Government Printing Office, Washington, D.C., 754 pp.

Springer, M. E. 1958. Desert pavement and vesicular layer of some soils of the Lahontan Basin, Nevada. Soil Sci. Soc. Am. Proc. 22:63–66.

UNESCO. 1979. Map of the World Distribution of Arid Regions. MAB Technical Notes 7, UNESCO, Paris, 54 pp. Scale, 1:25,000,000.

3
The Impact of Vehicles on Desert Soil Stabilizers[1]

Howard G. Wilshire

Introduction

Because of climatic conditions, deserts have an apparently sparse plant cover. Shrub communities of deserts in the western United States change progressively in composition, density, and size of individuals with increasing height above valley floors, reflecting progressive changes in temperature and abundance, depth, and composition of water (Hunt and Durrell, 1966). The soil between shrubs may appear bare, but it is commonly occupied by microfloral crusts and at least seasonally supports annual plants, whose root systems continue to have a stabilizing effect even if the plant has died. In fact, the sparsity of shrubs creates soil-moisture conditions favorable to microflora (Friedmann and Galun, 1974). Extensive areas of soil not protected by vegetation are covered by rock pavements, commonly of great antiquity. Even here a floral niche is found by diaphanous algae. Even bare soil is protected by silt-clay (mechanical) or salt crusts.

One of the functions of these organic and inorganic features of the desert surface is soil stabilization. In natural desert systems, a dynamic equilibrium is maintained among these features and the underlying soils that minimizes the rate of geomorphic change. The balances appear to be delicate, however, and a role of stabilization played by any of these components may change to one of enhancement of erosion when its distribution is modified (De Ploey et al., 1976). The sensitivity of these surface stabilizing components to disruption or destruc-

---

[1]The views and conclusions contained in this chapter are based on the author's studies or experiences and do not necessarily reflect the official viewpoint or policy of any U.S. government agency.

tion by vehicles is well known (Webb and Wilshire, 1978), but much less is known about the systemic effects of these changes and the rates of recovery (Chapter 14).

Macrofloral Elements

Although desert shrubs and trees are commonly sparse, they tend to have extensive near-surface root systems which help stabilize the soil beyond the limits of the plant crowns (Chew and Chew, 1965; Cloudsley-Thompson and Chadwick, 1964). The root systems of desert annuals produced in the dry season are very small and poorly developed, and those produced in wetter seasons are small compared to those of shrub seedlings (Went, 1979). In the North American deserts, roots of winter annuals usually penetrate to depths of only about 5 to 15 cm. Nevertheless, these roots have a well-developed rhizosphere which is a major force in binding soil particles (Went and Stark, 1968). The plant foliage protects underlying soil because it intercepts rainfall and reduces the energy transferred to the soil. Because they increase surface roughness, macrofloral elements reduce surface runoff and wind velocities, thereby retarding erosion of the soil; coppice dunes or mounds of fine-grained material under desert shrubs are common. Below certain limiting densities, however, plants may induce turbulence in surface runoff which, on sufficiently steep slopes, may increase soil erosion (De Ploey et al., 1976); similar effects can be anticipated for wind erosion.

The destructive effects of modern recreational off-road vehicles (ORVs) on desert macroflora is well established (Keefe and Berry, 1973; Wilshire et al., 1978; Chapter 8). Off-road vehicles destroy smaller plants at very low levels of use, and even the larger, more resilient, deep-rooted plants such as creosote bush *(Larrea tridentata)* succumb to repeated vehicular impacts. Annual plants in the process of germination are so sensitive that a single vehicle pass can destroy them, and even mature plants are uprooted and crushed at very low levels of ORV use. Small shrubs, especially brittle ones such as saltbush (the genus *Atriplex*), are sensitive to ORV disturbance and generally are not large enough to discourage vehicle operators from driving over them. Shrubs such as creosote bush are commonly large enough to discourage direct impacts, but in areas of heavy use they are progressively worn down and finally destroyed (Fig. 3-1). Thus, in areas of creosote bush scrub communities in the California deserts, there is a progressive reduction in the protective cover of vegetative communities as the more sensitive species are eliminated by ORV use (Keefe and Berry, 1973; Chapter 8).

Large shrubs, particularly thorny ones, and trees usually are not directly struck by vehicles, although Joshua trees *(Yucca brevifolia)* as much as 3 m tall and junipers *(Juniperous osteosperma)* as much as 3.5 m tall occasionally have been destroyed by direct impacts (Fig. 3-2). These plants, however, as well as smaller ones are being destroyed slowly over much wider areas by erosion and sedimentation caused by vehicular denudation of adjacent land. Junipers as much as 5 m tall, oak trees more than 7 m tall, and Joshua trees as much as 3 m

Figure 3-1. Stoddard Valley, Mojave Desert. Root mounds of creosote shrubs. The spacing of shrubs in less disturbed adjacent terrain suggests that even the root mounds of many shrubs have been obliterated by intensive vehicular use.

Figure 3-2. West of Reno, Nevada, Great Basin Desert. 3 m juniper flattened by 4-wheel vehicle. Note damaged trees on opposite side of trail as well.

tall have been destroyed by root undercutting caused by wind erosion and
accelerated runoff from ORV-stripped land (Wilshire et al., 1978).

Sediment from ORV-stripped slopes commonly buries plants, especially at
the base of steep slopes, where sediment buildup may temporarily exceed the
capacity of sediment-removal processes (Fig. 3-3) or adjacent to disturbed dunes
and sand sheets (Fig. 3-4). Measurement of fencepost exposures at the edge of
an ORV-destabilized dune in the Kettleman Hills, California shows a high flux of
sand movement (Table 3-1). Denudation of watersheds has caused flooding and

Figure 3-3. Jawbone Canyon, Mojave Desert. View down deeply eroded 4-wheel
vehicle trail showing large debris fan that has buried vegetation on flood plain.
Note person on debris fan for scale.

Figure 3-4. Piute Butte, Mojave Desert. Vegetation in process of burial by sand blown from dune buggy trails visible in upper right of photograph.

sedimentation of sensitive floodplain habitats in a number of heavily used ORV areas. Examples are the semiarid Ballinger Canyon and Hungry Valley (Fig. 3-5) in the Transverse Ranges, California, and Dove Spring Canyon and Jawbone Canyon in the northwestern Mojave Desert. Sedimentation is sufficient to completely bury vegetation between shrubs over substantial areas, thereby creating wind fetches and high-runoff surfaces where they did not previously exist.

Recovery of vegetation from ORV damage has been quantitatively monitored at several arid land sites. Lathrop (Chapter 13) showed that about 35% of the vegetative cover in vehicle trails and about 18% in a heavily used road left by military maneuvers had returned in approximately 38 years. Rowlands et al. (1980) studied the effects of controlled ORV use of three areas in the Mojave Desert on summer and winter annual vegetation. They found incomplete recovery of density and proportions of species of both summer and winter annuals in vehicle tracks after 3 years despite unusually high rainfall in two of the years. They concluded that:

> Recovery from compaction is long term. We believe that several centuries may be too conservative for recovery time.

At the Panoche Hills, California site (Snyder et al., 1976), a vegetative cover consisting largely of filarie *(Erodium circutarium)* with minor amounts of annual grasses had improved from about 20% to 39% in 4 years after closure to motorcycle use; motorcycle use had been permitted for 2 years. In the same period

Table 3-1. Kettleman Hills, California: Exposure of Fence Posts at the Edge of a Sand Dune Destabilized by Off-Road Vehicles, Illustrating Sand Flux with Time

Post	Date[a]				
	3/19/77	8/19/77	3/6/78	5/8/78	10/17/80
1					123
2					124
3		137	132		130
4	127	125	123	123	120
5	105	105	105	103	103
6	99	98	97	99	97
7	81	87	85	82	76
8	61	64	68	62	33
9	62	64	64	56	−14
10	97	95	102	94	20
11	101	107	114	88	36
12	103	106	115	111	40
13	103	103	Removed	−	−
14	71	68	Removed	−	−
15	82	74	63	49	−20+
16	63	57	51	−50+	−20+
17	74	61	69	76	39
18	83	88	83	104	62
19	112	116	98	112	68
20	119	112	117	105	55
21	124	104	116	109	65
22	99	75	85	99	65
23	73	78	80	103	79
24	76	96	87	113	105
25	127	130	110	133	128
26	121	135	107	123	101
27	114	129	110	113	107
28	137	155	139	152	136
29	93	92	87	96	
30	93	101	87	95	
31	63	66	48	65	
32	41	41	In edge of diversion gully		
33	18	19			
34	Buried	−7			

[a]Each number represents the length of post in centimeters above the sand at the time of measurement, negative numbers indicating complete burial.

vegetative cover in the unused area increased from 66% to 75%, representing improvement from the effects of grazing, which was also prohibited. The conclusion of Snyder et al. (1976) that the 5% per year rate of improvement would

Figure 3-5. Hungry Valley, Transverse Range, California. Burial of vegetation on flood plain by debris washed from motorcycle trails.

probably not continue because of compaction and erosion in the trails is borne out by continued accelerated erosion of the area (Wilshire, 1981). Vollmer et al. (1976) measured significant reduction in density of spring annuals in a track traversed 21 times by a truck, but no significant difference in tracks made by a single pass of the truck. This study was limited to the first growing season after the traverses. Results of quantitative studies of vegetation recovery from other types of disturbances (Chapters 13, 14) indicate that recovery rates in the desert are likely to be very slow. In areas such as Ballinger Canyon, Hungry Valley, and western Mojave Desert localities weeds such as Russian thistle *(Salsola iberica)* and adaptible native annuals such as buckwheat *(Eriogonum* sp) are major components of the vegetation reoccupying closed areas. In above-average rainfall years, heavily used areas may show substantial growth of annuals in the disturbed parts. However, the reduced moisture-retaining capacity of the disturbed soils apparently results in early dieoff, and the surface is quickly returned to a state highly vulnerable to erosion (Fig. 3-6). Areas where gully erosion has started are even slower to recover (Chapter 12).

Figure 3-6. Red Rock Canyon, Mojave Desert. Eroded 2- and 4-wheel vehicle trails more than 3 years after closure.

Microfloral Elements

Lichen, fungal, and algal crusts are widespread in arid lands (Cooke and Warren, 1973; Kovda et al., 1979; Skujins, 1975; Hunt and Durrell, 1966; Cameron, 1969; Cameron and Blank, 1966; Went and Stark, 1968; Taylor, 1979; Friedmann and Galun, 1974; Dregne, 1976) and are locally the principal contributors to surface stability (Fig. 3-7). Taylor (1979) recognizes three main types of fungi in deserts: a slow-growing darkly pigmented type; a fast-growing type that exploits transient favorable conditions much as flowering annuals; and an intermediate type that is brightly pigmented and grows at a moderate rate. In Death Valley, California, the composition and density of the microflora change systematically from flowering plants, to algae, to fungi, to bacteria as the saltpan is approached (Hunt and Durrell, 1966). Seasonal variations in species composition and abundance reflect seasonal variations in the organic and nutrient content of the soils (Taylor, 1979). Microflora stabilize soil by binding it with thallial filaments and metabolic products (Bond and Harris, 1964; Cameron and Blank, 1966; Skujin, 1975; Watson and Stojanovic, 1965; Went and Stark, 1968), by armoring the surface (Cameron and Blank, 1966; Bolyshev, 1964, quoted by Cooke and Warren, 1973; Dregne, 1976; Shields et al., 1957), and by increasing surface roughness.

Algal crusts are common in sandy and clayey soils of the desert. In sandy soils, algae typically form moderately dense mats of filaments about a centi-

Figure 3-7. Bloomington, Utah. Surface stabilized mainly by darkly pigmented lichen. A single traverse by a vehicle is sufficient to destroy the crust.

meter below the surface. Well-formed mats barely a centimeter thick can support an overhang of 10 cm and more. Algal mats also occur at the surface of clayey and sandy soils in many desert areas (Friedmann and Gulan, 1974), and diaphanous algae occur commonly under translucent rocks that protrude from the surface (Cameron and Blank, 1966). Alkaline, fine-grained soils may favor algal growth on the surface (Dregne, 1968). In little-disturbed areas, extensive lichen crusts are found on bajada surfaces between minor runoff channels, whereas algal mats occupy the channels themselves except for deposits left by the most recent runoff (Fig. 3-8). Encroachment of lichen into edges of active channels is indicated by erosion of the organic crusts. In more disturbed areas and in some areas where the surface is naturally active (as in sand sheets and playas), algal crusts of varying strength are more widespread than lichen crusts. Possibly there is a cyclic invasion of algae into areas of active physical surface processes; algal buildup might be followed by conversion to lichen; erosion, and invasion again by algae. Lichen crusts commonly have surface relief (2 to 5 cm) sufficient to constitute an important microsurface roughness factor (Fig. 3-8). This effect reduces surface wind and runoff velocity and inhibits channelization of runoff.

Lichen and algal crusts are strong enough to protect underlying soil from raindrop impact; but they also increase runoff (Shields et al., 1957; Cooke and Warren, 1973; Dregne, 1976; Chapter 4). In places crusts have been removed in an effort to increase water availability (Miller and Gifford, 1975). However, in a water-deficient environment it is likely that biological systems evolve to maxi-

Figure 3-8. Southeast of Baker, California, Mojave Desert. Intershrub areas are stabilized by a lichen crust with surface relief of 2 cm. The light colored shallow wash has a well-developed algal crust.

mize usage of available water. If so, artificial modification of runoff characteristics may well affect some part of the natural system adversely, whether or not that has been observed; for example, microfloral crusts may act to retard the loss of soil moisture. Moreover, well-developed microfloral crusts are effective deterrents to wind erosion and particle entrainment during runoff; their removal to enhance rainfall infiltration exposes the soil to accelerated wind and water erosion (Chapters 5, 6).

The vulnerability of microfloral crusts to disturbance by vehicles is readily evident (Fig. 3-7). Although the strength of crusts is sufficient to protect the underlying soil from wind and water erosion, it is no match for the stresses generated under vehicle tires. A single pass of a vehicle which is operated in a manner that induces large shear stresses (Chapter 4) destroys even the best developed crusts on sandy soils. When the mode of operation of the vehicle is such that mainly compressive stresses are induced, one pass commonly does not destroy the crust. The number of such passes required to destroy the crusts is not known but is likely to be small. One pass of a vehicle inducing mainly compression across well-developed lichen crusts crushes the lichen and makes it much finer textured but apparently does not kill it. In general, however, all of the soil-stabilizing functions of the microfloral crusts are quickly eliminated in areas of ORV use.

Very little is known about the recovery of microfloral crusts that have been disturbed by vehicles. Observations in deserts of the southwestern United States indicate rapid recovery of a coherent lichen crust in areas of slight disturbance, perhaps within months or a few years, in some localities, but in other nearby areas recovery is incomplete even after 4 decades. Rapid recovery is seen, for example, in several generations of motorcycle tracks (Fig. 3-7) in which the relatively young tracks are completely barren of lichen, and the relatively older ones have been reoccupied by new-growth lichen. Such "recovered" crusts do not have the surface relief of undisturbed crusts, and even tracks formed by a single pass of a vehicle commonly remain as indentations that channel runoff. More heavily disturbed areas probably take longer to recover. Motorcycle Enduro courses in an area of well-developed algal crusts in the northwestern Mojave Desert showed no recovery in at least 2 years. In severely disturbed areas in the southcentral Mojave Desert used for military maneuvers, lichens and algae have reoccupied some areas disturbed about 40 years ago, but lichens have apparently not reoccupied areas disturbed 16 years ago. In the harsher climate of the Skidoo townsite in Death Valley National Monument (Chapter 14), lichen crusts have not reoccupied heavily disturbed areas 63 years after abandonment. Nothing is known about recovery of species composition or about biological functions of microfloral crusts disturbed by ORVs.

Inorganic Elements

Three types of inorganic crusts are common in arid lands: desert pavement, silt-clay (mechanical) crusts, and chemical crusts. If developed beyond certain limiting levels, all protect the underlying soil by retarding wind and water erosion.

Desert pavements form by winnowing of the fine fraction by wind or water, by upward movement of large fragments as a result of cyclic freezing and thawing or wetting and drying, or a combination of these processes (Cooke and Warren, 1973; Chapter 11). Other contributing factors include breakdown of large rocks at the surface by freezing and thawing, salt wedging, and biological processes (Cooke, 1970). Mature desert pavements not only protect the underlying soil from erosion but also reduce runoff, increase infiltration, and retard evaporation (Epstein et al., 1966; Hillel and Tadmore, 1962; Kovda et al., 1979; Yair and Klein, 1973; Yair and Lavee, 1974). Less dense stone covers may increase runoff, especially those with smaller stone sizes (Yair and Lavee, 1976) and accelerate the development of silt-clay crusts between the stones. Yair and Klein (1973) observed an inverse relation between slope angle and slope erosion which they interpreted as a result of greater stone cover on steeper slopes. On the other hand, De Ploey et al. (1976) have shown that dispersed stone cover (and plant cover) may increase erosion rates by enhancing turbulent flow. On sufficiently steep slopes, such currents can aggressively erode soil between the stones. It is apparent that disruption of stone pavements is likely to increase erosion rates by exposing uncrusted soil. Decreasing the density of the stone cover, moreover, can change the role of the cover from protective to erosion enhancing.

Figure 3-9. (a) Rice Air Field, Mojave Desert. Granule-small pebble lag developed on surface that was stripped about 40 years ago. (b) Undisturbed surface adjacent to 9a. Stabilizing elements consist of larger pebbles than seen in 9a and much more abundant organic litter and remnants of annual plants than are present in the disturbed area.

The rate of recovery of desert pavement is quite variable depending on the processes producing the pavement as well as the lithology of the soil on which it forms. Mature pavements have formed in as few as 24 hours under severe wind conditions (Wilshire et al., 1981). Sharon (1962) conducted an experiment to determine the rate of formation of desert pavement on a surface stripped of 90% of its cover. An immature crust had reformed on 60 to 80% of the surface in 5 years. The rates of pavement formation by wind and water erosion appear to decrease with time (Sharon, 1962), as do the erosion rates of other disturbed surfaces (Megahan, 1974). Sharon (1962) estimated that the fine-grained material winnowed out during restoration of the immature pavement was equivalent to a layer 15 to 20 mm thick. Formation of the mature pavement described by Wilshire et al. (1980) was accompanied by surface lowering of 7 to 8 cm. Symmons and Hemming (1968) estimated that a pavement in the southern Sahara was equivalent to the stone distributed through a soil thickness of 4.3 cm. Thus, substantial erosion is associated with restoration of desert pavements. Coarse particles have been observed to move upward 1 to 2 cm in 4 to 22 cycles of wetting and drying (Cooke and Warren, 1973; Springer, 1958). Desert pavement has recovered slightly in Wahmonie ghost town in the Mojave Desert, 51 years since it was abandoned (Webb and Wilshire, 1980), in single tank tracks formed about 40 years ago in the Vidal area, Mojave Desert, California, and in stripped zones of the Rice Air Field (Fig. 3-9), constructed about 40 years ago in the eastern Mojave Desert. Zones stripped for strafing runs about 40 years ago (Fig. 3-10) in the Mohave Mountains, Arizona have not yet recovered. These areas

Figure 3-10. Mojave Mountains, Arizona, Sonoran Desert. Edge of strafing run that was stripped by bulldozer about 40 years ago, showing lack of recovery of rock pavement.

represent a wide variety of terrain types in widely separated parts of the Mojave and Sonoran Deserts.

Silt-clay (mechanical) crusts have been extensively described and interpreted (Cooke and Warren, 1973; Dregne, 1976; Kodova et al., 1979; Chapter 4). In arid lands, they consist of a skin less than 1 mm thick sealing a thicker hardened zone as much as 5 cm thick (Epstein and Grant, 1967; Evans and Buol, 1968; Farres, 1978; McIntyre, 1958a, b). Experiments have shown that the process of sealing occurs during rainfall by breakdown of soil aggregates, redistribution of the fine particles, and compaction by raindrop impact (Epstein and Grant, 1967; Farres, 1978; McIntyre, 1958a, b; Tackett and Pearson, 1965; Chapter 4). A rapid increase in modulus of rupture during the first 9 minutes of simulated rainfall indicated extensive sealing, especially in less clayey soils (Epstein and Grant, 1967). Upon drying, a fairly impermeable crust forms on many types of soils (Kemper and Miller, 1975). That processes other than raindrop compaction contribute to the mechanical crusts is evident from their occurrence on thin mudflows that have congealed on steep to vertical surfaces (Fig. 3-11); cementation may be a major contributing factor (Gifford and Thran, 1975; Uehara and Jones, 1975).

Eckert et al. (1979) studied the effects of ORVs on mechanical crusts and showed that moderate ORV use on crusted soils reduced infiltration and increased sediment yield from erosion. After the crust reformed, the infiltration

Figure 3-11. North of the Yucca Valley, California, Mojave Desert. Mechanical crust developed on vertical surfaces of a road cut.

rate was less than that of the freshly disturbed soil, and sediment yield remained higher than that from undisturbed surfaces. Off-road vehicles also encouraged the formation of mechanical crusts in place of the organic crusts they damage (Chapters 4 and 5). Stripping of organic crusts and organic litter by ORVs exposes soil and allows inorganic crusting. This crusting reduces infiltration rates and increases runoff and sediment yield on most desert soils (Chapter 5).

Recovery rates of mechanical crusts are not known. It is apparent that recrusting of disturbed surfaces occurs rapidly, in a matter of months or at most no longer than the first rain. However, recovery of the original functions of the crust has not been studied over a period sufficient to determine whether and when fully functional crusts are restored.

Chemically precipitated crusts occur widely but not abundantly in arid lands (Dregne, 1968; Watson, 1979), mostly in proximity to dry lakes. Chlorides dominate toward the center of the playa, and then sulfates, followed by carbonates away from the center (Dregne, 1968; Hunt, 1966). Little information is available on the effects of ORVs on salt crusts or their rates of recovery. Wilshire and Nakata (1976) noted severe rutting and compaction of the surface of a dry-lake bed by motorcycles. Subsequent salt crystallization was localized by track indentations. Hunt (1966) noted preservation of 70-year-old wagon tracks on salt crusts in Death Valley. The effects, if any, of disturbance of these crusts on wind erosion rates is unknown.

Conclusions

It is evident that all of the principal natural soil-protective elements in the desert are highly vulnerable to vehicle use. A single vehicle pass can destroy many types of annual and some perennial plants, desert pavement, and microfloral and mechanical crusts, although hundreds of passes may be required to destroy tough, deep-rooted shrubs such as creosote bush. Rates of indirect destruction through erosion, sedimentation, and modification of surface-runoff patterns are probably much slower, on the order of years to decades.

Less is known about rates of recovery of the soil stabilizers, but in general, the processes of natural restoration operate slowly or at very infrequent intervals. Thus, disturbance of the soil stabilizers leaves the soil susceptible to accelerated erosion for prolonged periods. In the event of substantial soil loss, loss of relic soil, or loss of relic vegetation, recovery may never take place or may take place only on a time scale that is not relevant to human uses. Such losses are irreversible. Another effect not discussed here is the loss of biological functions associated with deterioration of organic stabilizers (Dregne, 1976; Farnsworth et al., 1978; Rychert et al., 1978; Sheridan, 1981; Skujins, 1975; U.S. Department of the Interior, 1980; Westman, 1977).

Because of the vulnerability of the desert to ORVs, selection of areas in which usage is to be permitted should involve consideration of the stability and resiliency of the soil. Criteria for evaluating motorcycle trails have been pro-

Table 3-2. Guide for Rating Soil Limitations for Off-Road Vehicle Trails, Data from U.S. Department of Agriculture (1979)

Property	Limits			Restrictive feature
	Slight	Moderate	Severe	
1. USDA texture	—	—	Ice	Permafrost
2. Fraction >3 in. (wt pct) (surface layer)	10	10–25	25	Large stones
3. Depth to high water table (ft)	2	1–2	0–1	Wetness, ponding
4. Erosion Factor (k) X percent slope	2	2–4	4	Erodes easily
5. USDA texture (surface layer)[a]	—	—	SC, SIC, C	Too clayey
6. USDA texture (surface layer)	—	LCOS, VFS	COS, S, FS	Too sandy
7. Unified (surface layer)	—	—	OL, OH, PT	Excess humus
8. Slope (Pct)	0–25	25–40	40	Slope
9. Coarse Fragments (wt pct) (surface layer)[b]	40	40–65	65	Small stones
10. USDA texture (surface layer)	—	SIL, SI VFSL, L	—	Dusty
11. Flooding occas.	None, rare	Frequent	—	Floods
12. Other[c]	—	—	—	Fragile

Note: Off-road motorcycle trails are those used primarily for recreational use with trail-type motorcycles. Little or no trail preparation is done and the surface will not be vegetated or surfaced. Considerable soil compaction on the trail is expected. Soils are rated on the properties that influence erodibility, trafficability, dustiness, and safety to the operator. Soil properties considered are stoniness, slope, wetness, texture of the surface layer, and flooding. Slope affects the soil erodibility and safety to the operator. Large stones thrown from wheels may endanger riders that follow. Wetness and flooding affects frequency of use. Surface texture affects erodibility, trafficability, and probability of dust. If the soil is observed to be easily damaged by use or disturbance, rate "Severe-fragile." (U.S. Department of Agriculture, 1979)

[a] Soils in UST, TOR, ARID, BOK, XER suborders, great groups, or subgroups rate one class better.

[b] 100—I passing No. 10 sieve.

[c] If the soil is easily damaged by use or disturbance, rate "Severe fragile."

posed by the U.S. Soil Conservation Service (Table 3-2), and standards exist for four-wheel vehicle routes (Megahan, 1976). The application of standard engineering practices in the construction of trail systems and containment of increased runoff and sediment can help achieve the goals of (United States) Presidential Orders 11644 and 11989 by reducing the adverse environmental effects of off-road vehicles.

References

Bond, R. D., and R. Harris, Jr. 1964. The influence of the microflora on physical properties of soils: I. Effects associated with filamentous algal and fungi. Austral. J. Soil Res. 2:111–123.

Cameron, R. E. 1969. Abundance of Microflora in Soils of Desert Regions. Tech. Rept. 32-1378, National Aeronautics and Space Administration-Jet Propulsion Laboratory, Pasadena, California, 16 pp.

Cameron, R. E., and G. B. Blank. 1966. Desert algae: soil crusts and diaphanous substrata as algal habitats. Tech. Rept. No. 32-971, National Aeronautics and Space Administration-Jet Propulsion Laboratory, Pasadena, California, 41 pp.

Chew, R. M., and A. E. Chew. 1965. The primary productivity of a desert scrub *(Larrea tridentata)* community. Ecol. Monogr. 35:355–375.

Cloudsley-Thompson, J. L., and M. J. Chadwick. 1964. Life in Deserts. London, G. T. Foulis and Co., Ltd., 218 pp.

Cooke, R. U. 1970. Stone pavements in deserts. Ann. Assoc. Am. Geogr. 60: 560–577.

Cooke, R. U., and A. Warren. 1973. Geomorphology in Deserts. University of California Press, Berkeley, California, 374 pp.

DePloey, J., J. Savat, and J. Meoyersons. 1976. The differential impact of some soil loss factors on flow, runoff creep and rainwash. Earth Surf. Proc. 1: 151–161.

Dregne, H. E. 1968. Surface materials of desert environments. In: W. G. McGinnies, B. J. Goldman, and P. Paylore (Eds.), Deserts of the World. The University of Arizona Press, Tucson, Arizona, pp. 290–377.

Dregne, H. E. 1976. Soils of Arid Regions. Elsevier Scientific Publishing Co., Amsterdam, 237 pp.

Eckert, R. E., M. K. Wood, W. H. Blackburn, and F. F. Peterson. 1979. Impacts of off-road vehicles on infiltration and sediment production of two desert soils. J. Range Management 32:394–397.

Epstein, E., and W. J. Grant. 1967. Soil losses and crust formation as related to some soil physical properties: Proc. Soil Sci. Soc. Am. 31:547–550.

Epstein, E., W. J. Grant, and R. A. Struchtmeyer. 1966. Effects of stones on runoff, erosion, and soil moisture. Proc. Soil Sci. Soc. Am. 30:638–640.

Evans, D. D., and S. W. Buol. 1968. Micromorphological study of soil crusts. Proc. Soil Sci. Am. 32:19–22.

Farnsworth, R. B., E. M. Romney, and A. Wallace. 1978. Nitrogen fixation by microfloral-higher plant associations in arid to semiarid environments. In: N. E. West and J. Skujins (Eds.), Nitrogen in Desert Ecosystems. Dowden, Hutchinson & Ross, Inc., Stroudsburg, Penna., pp. 17–19.

Farres, P. 1978. The role of time and aggregate size in crusting process. Earth Surf. Proc. 3:243–254.

Friedmann, E. I., and M. Galun. 1974. Desert algae, lichens, and fungi. In: G. W. Brown, Jr. (Ed.), Desert Biology, Vol. 2. Academic Press, New York, pp. 165–212.

Gifford, R. O., and D. F. Thran. 1975. Bonding strength of silica cementations. In: J. W. Carey and D. D. Evans (Eds.), Soil Crusts. Tech. Bull. 214, Agricultural Experiment Station, University of Arizona, Tucson, Arizona, pp. 28–30.

Hillel, D., and N. Tadmore. 1962. Water regime and vegetation in the central Negev highlands of Israel. Ecology 43:33–41.

Hunt, C. B. 1960. The Death Valley Salt Pan, Study of Evaporites. U.S. Geological Survey Professional Paper 400-B, pp. B456–B458.

Hunt, C. B. 1966. Hydrologic Basin, Death Valley, California: Geochemistry of the Saltpan. U.S. Geological Survey Professional Paper 494-B, pp. B40–B103.

Hunt, C. B., and L. W. Durrell. 1966. Plant Ecology of Death Valley, California: Distribution of Fungi and Algae. U.S. Geological Survey Professional Paper 509, pp. 55–66.

Keefe, J., and K. Berry. 1973. Effects of off-road vehicles on desert shrubs at Dove Springs Canyon. In: K. G. Berry (Ed.), Preliminary Studies on the Effects of Off-Road Vehicles on the Northwestern Mojave Desert: A Collection of Papers. Privately published, Ridgecrest, California, pp. 45–57.

Kemper, W. D., and D. E. Miller. 1975. Management of crusting soils: Some practical possibilities. In: J. W. Carry and D. D. Evans (Eds.), Soil Crusts. Tech. Bull. 214, Agricultural Experiment Station, University of Arizona, Tucson, Arizona, pp. 1–6.

Kovda, V. A., E. M. Samoilova, J. L. Charley, and J. J. Skujins. 1979. Soil processes in arid lands. In: D. W. Goodall, R. A. Perry, and K. M. W. Howes (Eds.), Arid-Land Ecosystems: Structure, Functioning and Management. Cambridge University Press, Cambridge, pp. 439–470.

McIntyre, D. S. 1958a. Soil splash and the formation of surface crusts by raindrop impact. Soil Sci. 85:261–266.

McIntyre, D. S. 1958b. Permeability measurements of soil crusts formed by raindrop impact. Soil Sci. 85:185–189.

Megahan, W. F. 1974. Erosion Over Time on Severely Disturbed Granitic Soils; A Model. Forest Service Research Paper INT-156, U.S. Department of Agriculture, Intermountain Forest and Range Experiment Station, U.S. Government Printing Office, Washington, D.C., 14 pp.

Megahan, W. F. 1976. Tables of geometry for low-standard roads for watershed management considerations, slope staking, and end areas: Forest Service General Tech. Rept. INT-32, U.S. Department of Agriculture, U.S. Government Printing Office, Washington, D.C., 104 pp.

Miller, D. E., and R. O. Gifford. 1975. Modification of soil crusts from plant growth. In: J. W. Cary and D. D. Evans (Eds.), Soil Crusts. Tech. Bull. 214, Agricultural Experiment Station, University of Arizona, Tucson, Arizona, pp. 7–16.

Rowlands, P. G., J. A. Adams, H. B. Johnson, and A. S. Endo. 1980. Experiments on the effects of soil compaction on establishment, cover, and pattern of winter and summer annuals in the Mojave Desert. Unpublished draft appendix for the California Desert Conservation Area Management Plan and EIS, U.S. Bureau of Land Management, pp. 170–222.

Rychert, R., J. Skujins, D. Sorenson, and D. Porcella. 1978. Nitrogen fixation by lichens and free-living microorganisms in deserts. In: N. E. West and J. Skujins (Eds.), Nitrogen in Desert Ecosystems. Dowden, Hutchinson & Ross, Inc., Stroudsburg, Penn., pp. 20–30.

Sharon, D. 1962. On the nature of hamadas in Israel. Z. Geomorphol. 6:129–147.

Sheridan, D. 1981. Desertification of the United States. Council on Environmental Quality, Washington, D.C., 141 pp.

Shields, L. M., C. Mitchell, and F. Drouet. 1957. Alga- and lichen-stabilized surface crusts as soil nitrogen sources. Am. J. Botany 44:489–498.

Skujins, J. 1975. Soil Microbiological and Biochemical Investigations. III. Tunisian Presaharan Project, Annual Report, 1974: United States/International Biological Program, Desert Biome. Utah State University Press, Logan, Utah.

Snyder, C. T., D. G. Frickel, R. F. Hadley, and R. F. Miller. 1976. Effects of Off-Road Vehicle Use on the Hydrology and Landscape of Arid Environments in Central and Southern California. Water Resources Investigations 76-99, U.S. Geological Survey, 45 pp.

Springer, M. E. 1958. Desert pavement and vesicular layer of some soils of the desert of the Lahontan Basin, Nevada. Soil Sci. Soc. Am. Proc. 22:63–75.

Symmons, P. M., and C. F. Hemming. 1968. A note on wind-stable stone-mantles in the southern Sahara. Geogr. J. 134:60–64.

Tackett, J. L., and R. W. Pearson. 1965. Some characteristics of soil crusts formed by simulated rainfall. Soil Sci. 99:407–413.

Taylor, E. C. 1979. Seasonal distribution and abundance of fungi in two desert grassland communities. J. Arid Environ. 2:295–312.

Uehara, G., and R. C. Jones. 1975. Bonding mechanisms for soil crusts: Part I. Particle surfaces and cementing agents. In: J. W. Cary and D. D. Evans (Eds.), Soil Crusts. Tech. Bull. 214, Agricultural Experiment Station, University of Arizona, Tucson, Arizona, pp. 17–28.

U.S. Department of Agriculture, Soil Conservation Service. 1979. National Soils Handbook, Part II, Guide for Rating Soil Limitations for Off-Road Vehicle Trails, Section 403.6(b).

U.S. Department of the Interior. 1980. Desertification in the United States: Status and Issues. Working review draft. U.S. Department of the Interior, Washington, D.C., 486 pp.

Vollmer, A. T., B. G. Maza, P. A. Medica, F. B. Turner, and S. A. Bamberg. 1976. The impact of off-road vehicles on a desert ecosystem. Environ. Management 1:115–129.

Watson, A. 1979. Gypsum crusts in deserts. J. Arid Environ. 2:3–20.

Watson, J. H., and B. J. Stojanovic. 1965. Synthesis and bonding of soil aggregates as affected by microflora and its metabolic products. Soil Sci. 100: 57–62.

Webb, R. H., and H. G. Wilshire. 1978. An annotated bibliography of the effects of off-road vehicles on the environment. U.S. Geological Survey Open File Report 78-149, 28 pp.

Webb, R. H., and H. G. Wilshire. 1980. Recovery of soils and vegetation in a Mojave Desert ghost town, Nevada, U.S.A. J. Arid Environ. 3:291–303.

Went, F. W. 1979. Germination and seedling behavior of desert plants. In: D. W. Goodall, R. A. Perry, and K. M. W. Howes (Eds.), Arid-Land Ecosystems: Structure, Functioning and Management. Cambridge University Press, Cambridge, Massachusetts, pp. 477–489.

Went, F. W., and N. Stark. 1968. The biological and mechanical role of soil fungi: Proc. Nat. Acad. Sci. (U.S.A.) 60:497–505.

Westman, W. E. 1977. How much are nature's services worth? Science 197:960–964.

Wilshire, H. G. 1981. Sensitivity of organic and inorganic desert soil stabilizers to vehicular impact. In: J. Latting (Ed.), The California Desert: An Introduction to Natural Resources and Man's Impact. California Native Plant Society Special Publication No. 5, In press.

Wilshire, H. G., and J. K. Nakata. 1976. Off-road vehicle effects on California's Mojave Desert. Calif. Geol. 29:123–132.

Wilshire, H. G., J. K. Nakata, and B. Hallett. 1980. Field observations of the December, 1977 windstorm, San Joaquin Valley, California. In: T. L. Péwé (Ed.), Desert Dust: Origin, Characteristics, and Effects on Man. Geological Society of America Special Paper 186, pp. 233–251.

Wilshire, H. G., S. Shipley, and J. K. Nakata. 1978. Impacts of off-road vehicles on vegetation. Transactions of the 43rd North American Wildlife and Natural Resources Conference, 1978, Washington, D.C., Wildlife Management Institute, pp. 131–139.

Yair, A., and M. Klein. 1973. The influence of surface properties on flow and erosion processes on debris covered sloped in an arid area. Catena 1:1–18.

Yair, A., and H. Lavee. 1974. Areal contribution to runoff on scree slopes in an extreme arid environment—a simulated rainstorm experiment. Z. Geomorphol. Suppl. 21:106–111.

Yair, A., and H. Lavee. 1976. Runoff generative process and runoff yield from arid talus and mantled slopes. Earth Surf. Proc. 1:235–247.

4

Compaction of Desert Soils by Off-Road Vehicles[1]

Robert H. Webb

Introduction

> Whenever you put a foot down on forest or range land, you are—to a
> degree—compacting the soil. The hooves of cattle, the wheels of
> vehicles, the weight of a dragged log; these can compact the soil too.
> Soil compaction is a common and universal process. (Lull, 1959)

The use of off-road vehicles (ORVs) is widespread and a recognized management problem in the deserts of the southwestern United States and elsewhere
(Sheridan, 1980). One of the most important and long-lasting effects of ORV
use is the compaction of soil caused by the force of rolling wheels. Compaction
can be defined as the application of forces to a soil mass which results in an increase in density and strength. Soil compaction is known to be a contributing
factor to accelerated soil erosion (Snyder et al., 1976; see Chapter 5) and a cause
of decreased plant growth (see Chapters 7 and 13) in deserts. Hence, a quantitative prediction of soil compaction is of fundamental importance in the formu-
lation of management plans designed to minimize adverse impacts of ORVs on
soils.

Compaction and its effects on soil properties are well known in agricultural
(see Barnes et al., 1971) and engineering practice (Lambe and Whitman, 1979),
but information on compaction in rangelands is generally incomplete. Many
authors have reported compaction resulting from vehicle use, livestock grazing,

---

[1] The views and conclusions contained in this chapter are based on the author's studies or
experiences and do not necessarily represent the official viewpoint or policy of any U.S.
government agency.

human trampling, logging operations, and even raindrop impacts (Lull, 1959), but few have attempted to quantify changes in soil properties as functions of the intensity of use. A review of the literature on ORV impacts reveals that a theoretical framework is needed to explain and predict the many effects noted but unexplained in past studies. For example, Webb et al. (1978) noted that different soil types varied widely in susceptibility to compaction effects in central California and that only one soil, a clay loam, resisted compaction. Wilshire and Nakata (1976) noted that some dry playa clays in the Mojave Desert were compacted minimally by motorcycle traffic, while coarser soils on alluvial fans were significantly compacted, but offered no explanation for the difference. Weaver and Dale (1978) measured soil density increases with increasing use by horses, hikers, and motorcycles in Montana but did not relate the changes other than qualitatively to the type of impact or the number of passes. The increase in soil density after ORV use is commonly greatest just below the surface instead of at the surface (Arndt, 1966; Snyder et al., 1976) and has been measured to depths greater than 1 m (Snyder et al., 1976). Most studies have ignored the influence that slight compaction can have on soil properties while concentrating on severe soil compaction.

Most aspects of soil compaction—compactibility differences among soil types, variation of density change with depth, the rate of change of soil densities with increasing intensity of use, and the resulting change in infiltration properties—have been studied in detail and can be understood and partially predicted using the principles of soil mechanics and soil physics. Because compaction affects all soils in a similar manner, compaction of desert soils can be deduced from general theory and observed effects on soils of more humid regions in addition to being directly measured. The question that is to be addressed in this chapter is not whether compaction results from ORV use, but how much and what the consequences of the compaction are.

An Example of ORV Compaction of Soils:
Experimental Results for Controlled Motorcycle Traffic

In order to directly study motorcycle-induced compaction, four trails representing 1, 10, 100, and 200 motorcycle passes were created in March 1979 near Fremont Peak, western Mojave Desert, California (Webb, 1982). The soil present, a loamy sand, was chosen for study because it was representative of a large area of the Mojave Desert and had a low gravel content, which lessened problems with soil property measurements. The motorcycle used, a 175-cc dirt bike with a 73-kg rider, was ridden on straight trails at a constant velocity. The moisture content at which the soil was compacted (6.2%) appeared to be typical of the moisture status of this soil between spring rains; the soil was slightly drier (4.1%) from 0 to 30 mm depth.

The motorcycle trails were very noticeable immediately after the impact (Fig. 4-1). The one-pass trail had definite knob imprints with a slight surface indentation; no berm was present beside the one-pass trail. The other trails were

(a)

(b)

Figure 4-1. Photographs of the Fremont Park study area giving a comparison of the undisturbed terrain with motorcycle trails. Photographs (d) and (e) were taken approximately 2 months after the impact, whereas (a), (b), and (c) were taken immediately after the impact. (a) Undisturbed view. (b) View of one-pass trail. Three tracks are shown crossing the *Atriplex torreyi* in the foreground.

(c)

Figure 4-1. (c) 10-pass trail.

(d)

Figure 4-1. (d) 100-pass trail.

(e)

Figure 4-1. (e) 200-pass trail.

about 0.30 m wide or approximately three times the width of the motorcycle tire. While annual vegetation remained in the one-pass trail, most of the annuals had been destroyed after 10 passes. Definite berms were present beside the 100- and 200-pass trails, and the center of these trails was approximately 10 to 30 mm below the adjacent undisturbed soil.

Significant compaction was measured at the soil surface and at depth in the soil profile in all four trails. The penetration resistance of the soil, as measured with a 30° cone penetrometer (Carter, 1967), increased in all trails. Penetration resistance is an integrated measure of soil texture, clay mineralogy, density, and moisture content (Baver et al., 1972) and is considered an index of the effective soil strength. Penetration resistance varied linearly with depth in the undisturbed soil while penetration resistance curves for the center of vehicle (Fig. 4-2) indicate that the greatest change (inferred to be the maximum density increase) occurred between 30 and 60 mm depth. Penetration-resistance increases were measurable to a depth of 0.12 m in the one-pass trail and to a depth of 0.21 to 0.25 m in the 10-, 100-, and 200-pass trails. Measurement variability increased with depth, especially below 0.25 m because the soil contained significantly more gravel below this depth.

The bulk density in the 0 to 60 mm depth range increased as a logarithmic function of the number of passes according to the least-squares-fit equation

$$\rho_d = 1.60 + 0.034 \, ln \, (n), \quad r^2 = 0.79 \tag{4-1}$$

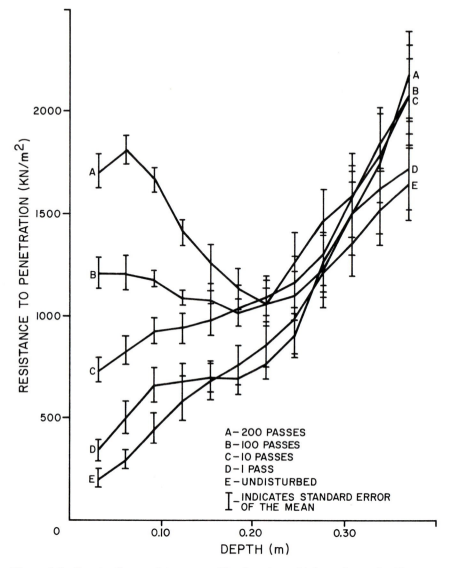

Figure 4-2. Penetration resistance profiles for the vehicle trails at the Fremont Peak study site. The standard error was calculated as the standard deviation divided by the square root of the number of passes.

where ρ_d is the dry bulk density (in metric tons per cubic meter, or t m^{-3}), n is the number of passes (not corrected for actual trail width), and r^2 is the coefficient of determination (Fig. 4-3). According to this relation, the rate of density increases in the 0 to 60 mm depth range will decrease in proportion to the inverse of the number of passes, and thus the greatest density increases and related property changes per pass will occur during the first few passes.

Consistent differences were measured in the response to rainfall of the un-

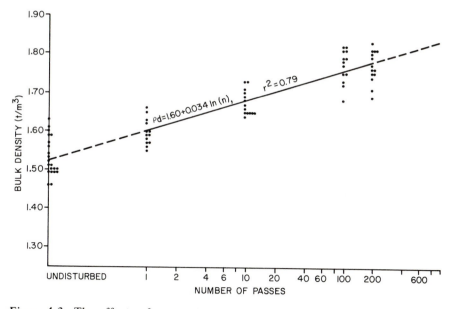

Figure 4-3. The effects of repeated motorcycle passes on the bulk density in the upper 0 to 6 cm of loamy sand at the Fremont Peak study site.

disturbed soil and the 100- and 200-pass trails. The undisturbed soil could withstand an artificial rainfall intensity of 46 mm hr^{-1} for the 100- and 200-pass trails, respectively (Webb, 1982). The time required before ponding occurred varied greatly but in general decreased with increasing rainfall intensity. Figure 4-4 shows the decrease of terminal infiltration rates, as measured with double-ring infiltrometers (Bertrand, 1965; Webb, 1982), with increasing numbers of vehicle passes. This variation can be expressed as

$$I_t = 81 - 9.7 \, ln \, (n), \quad r^2 = 0.68 \tag{4-2}$$

where I_t is the terminal infiltration rate (mm hr^{-1}). Equation (4-2) demonstrates that soil compaction has a dramatic effect on infiltration rates and that the effect is dependent on the number of vehicle passes. The relatively low r^2 obtained in the least-squares fitting reflects the high spatial variability inherent in I_t, especially in undisturbed soils (Fig. 4-4).

This example illustrates the problems inherent in direct measurement of soil compaction for land-use management purposes. Although the data contained in Figures 4-2, 4-3, and 4-4 are useful for planning purposes, they represent one soil type compacted at one moisture content by a specific type of ORV. Additional vehicle trails would have to be created while the soil was at different moisture contents to completely evaluate this soil's response to ORV impacts. The need for additional controlled studies may be reduced by using information from other sources, including engineering and agricultural studies, to illustrate and possibly predict the probable behavior of this and other soils under vehicle tires.

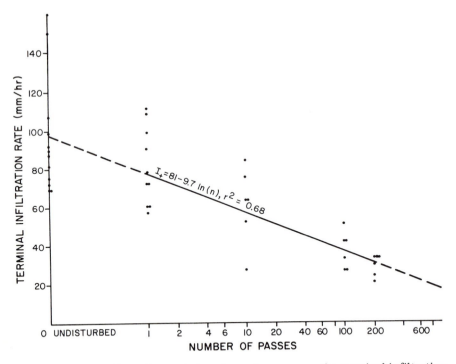

Figure 4-4. The effect of repeated motorcycle passes on the terminal infiltration rate of the Fremont Peak loamy sand.

The Compaction Process

The goal of the land-use manager concerned with ORV compaction should be the prediction of compaction prior to ORV use so that adverse impacts can be minimized, and prediction methods for compaction must consider the forces generated when an ORV tire comes into contact with the soil. Any surface loading of soil results in normal and shear stresses that can compress and deform soils to increase the soil density; brief discussions of these stresses are given by Lambe and Whitman (1979), Harris (1971), Karafiath and Nowatzki (1978), and Reece (1977), and readers are urged to use these sources for more detailed information.

The density of the soil increases as the magnitude of the normal and shear stresses increases above the strength of the soil to resist deformation. Compaction is often characterized in terms of changes in bulk density, pore spaces, bulk volume (the inverse of bulk density), or the void ratio (the ratio of void volume to solid volume). The conceptual model of Reece (1977) and the similar one of Bailey and Vanden Berg (1968) suggest that the shear and normal stresses are both important in soil compaction, but their relative importance changes as the soil density increases or the pore space, bulk volume, and void ratio decrease.

Before any model can be applied, however, the stress distribution under the vehicle tires must be either measured or simulated.

Stress Distributions Under Vehicle Tires

Use of any model for predicting compaction requires knowledge of the magnitude and distribution of the applied stresses in the soil. Pressure distributions beneath vehicle tires have been measured by numerous investigators (see Cohron, 1971), but measurement of pressure distributions requires disturbances of *in situ* soil in addition to complicated techniques. The stress distribution created by knobby or treated tires is very complex because high shear stresses are induced locally at the contact between the knobs and the soil surface as a result of the sharp edges (Karafiath and Nowatzki, 1978). The effect of these stresses dissipates with depth and becomes indistinguishable from the general normal and shear stresses generated by the weight of the entire wheel; therefore, average ground pressure can be used to model stresses under the entire wheel as a continuous surface loading. Surface pressure is seldom uniform under a pneumatic tire but either concentrates along the sides because of sidewall stiffness (Karafiath and Nowatzki, 1978) or is maximum at the center of the tire. Studies by Soehne (1958) and Reeves and Cooper (1960) suggest that the most realistic model of stresses under a tire involves a loading with the surface pressure distributed so that the maximum pressure occurs in the center.

Several investigators have suggested the use of elasticity theory to predict the distribution of stresses with depth under vehicle tires (Lull, 1959; Soehne, 1958). The distribution of stresses beneath the center of the rear tire of a 175-cc motorcycle was calculated using theory of elasticity and various contact geometries and distribution of surface pressure. Numerous assumptions are required for this model (Lambe and Whitman, 1979), but alternative models (plasticity theory; Karafiath and Nowatzki, 1978) require large numbers of data on soil properties. The elastic solutions used here were the uniform circular and rectangular (Poulos and Davis, 1974); uniform elliptical loading (Deresiewicz, 1960); the Hertzian problem of nonuniform circular loading (Hamilton and Goodman, 1966; Timoshenko and Goodier, 1970); and Newmark graphical solutions for the actual contact area of the tire knobs (uniform and nonuniform loadings, Poulos and Davis, 1974). In all cases, the surface pressure averaged 78 kN m^{-2} over the contact area of the tire. The calculated stresses were not substantially different, so the stresses were averaged from all six solutions to obtain the stress distribution shown in Figure 4-5. It is particular interest that all solutions provide a similar stress distribution despite the differences in the contact geometry. Although this discussion has been limited to a vehicle at rest or moving at a constant velocity, similar stresses will result with loading from an accelerating or braking vehicle (see Hamilton and Goodman, 1966).

One of the main criticisms of application of elasticity theory to compaction problems is the lack of compensation for soil property change as the soil com-

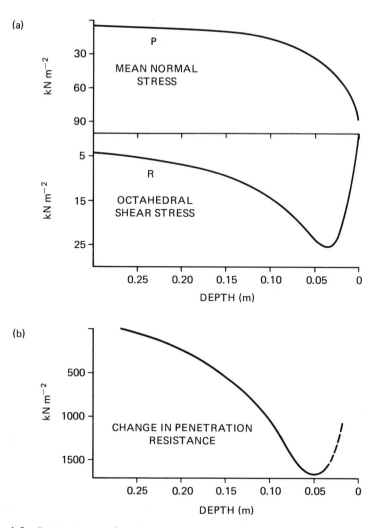

Figure 4-5. Comparison of calculated stresses with the change in penetration resistance. (a) Calculated octahedral normal and sheer stresses under the rear tire of a 175-cc motorcycle using six solutions from elasticity theory for different contact geometries. (b) The difference between the mean penetration resistance measured in the undisturbed soil and the 200-pass trail.

pacts. Stress calculations for initial vehicle passes can be corrected for changing soil properties using Froehlich concentration factors (Soehne, 1958). Cohron (1971) reported that stress distributions calculated using this technique gave results similar to measured stress distributions. However, in the case of motorcycle compaction near Fremont Peak, the soil after 200 passes showed little additional nonelastic deformation with each successive pass; hence, the variation of penetration resistance with depth probably reflects the distribution of applied stresses.

The Variation in Compaction with Depth

The magnitude and variation of density increase with depth is of great importance when the recovery time of a compacted soil is to be considered, because soil loosening processes operate most quickly at the ground surface (Chapter 13). Compaction variation with depth is a function of the distribution of stresses with depth, but the relative contribution of normal and shear stresses in causing density increases with depth is the subject of some debate. Hovland and Mitchell (1972) studied the effects of a sphere rolled on sand to aid in the understanding of the causes of compaction under vehicle tires. Measurement of a cross section of the sphere's path (Fig. 4-6) showed a zone of increased density directly beneath the sphere and zones of loosening, resulting from shear displacements, along the sides of the sphere's path; maximum compaction occurred at the surface beneath the center of the sphere. The authors concluded that the compression beneath the sphere was correlated with the normal-stress distribution predicted with an elastic solution for a circular, uniformly loaded area.

Other authors have reported that the initial compaction of a soil was directly related to the normal stress. Soehne (1958) found porosity changes in several different soils to be proportional to the logarithm of the applied pressure. Because the normal stress decreases with depth below an applied load (Fig. 4-4) and the amount of density increase is proportional to the applied stress, these results suggest that the maximum density increase must occur at the surface.

However, many other investigators have measured a zone of maximum compaction below the surface. Raghaven et al. (1977) measured a maximum density increase in a zone 0.12 to 0.26 m below tracks created by tractor tires in clay soils. Chancellor et al. (1962) studied deformations under a rigid, 0.15-m diameter piston driven into a sandy loam and reported that the maximum density increase occurred at a depth of 50 mm below the piston face. Reicosky et al. (1981), studying a loam, measured maximum compaction at a depth of 50 to 60 mm beneath a 50 mm by 50 mm metal plate in a simulation of compac-

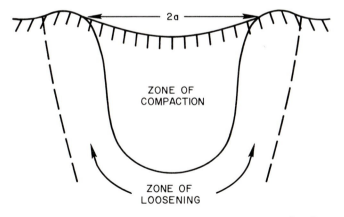

Figure 4-6. Schematic cross section of the path of a sphere of radius a rolling in uncompacted sand (redrawn from Hovland and Mitchell, 1972).

tion under tires. Therefore, volume changes are not proportional only to the mean normal stress but must be considered as complex functions of both the shear and normal stresses.

Models of soil compaction combined with predicted stress distributions can be used to better understand the variation in density increase (as inferred from penetration-resistance measurements) with number of motorcycle passes and depth as shown in Figure 4-2. The initial motorcycle pass caused compaction directly beneath the tire to a depth of about 12 cm with possible loosening below that depth to approximately 25 cm. Subsequent passes compressed the soil to a greater depth, and the magnitude of the compression, as indicated by the change in penetration resistance, resembles the calculated distribution of stresses under the motorcycle tire (Fig. 4-4). The density increase caused by the motorcycle loading is no longer significant below about 0.25 m; at this level the mean normal stress is about 6% of the surface pressure and of the same order of magnitude as the hydrostatic stress generated by the weight of the soil. The slightly less compacted soil near the surface could have been caused by lower moisture in the surface soil than the subsurface soil; by high local shear stresses induced by the knobby tires, which compacted the surface to the "critical void ratio" (Lambe and Whitman, 1979), whereupon the surface soil could no longer increase in density while the subsurface soil could in response to additional vehicle passes; or by compaction in response to the maximum shear stress in addition to compression caused by the normal stress.

The exact mechanism causing the variation of compaction with depth is not well understood and should be the subject of future research, but the available evidence suggests that the third mechanism (maximum shear stress) is probably most important. The variation of density increase with number of passes and depth under other vehicular loadings should be similar, with the depth and magnitude of the maximum compaction being determined from tire geometry, pressure distribution at the soil surface, the soil texture, and moisture content at the time of compaction.

Time Dependence of Compaction

The speed at which an ORV traverses soil is an important consideration for compaction. Bodman and Rubin (1948) measured the time dependence of volume change with both applied normal and shear stresses. In general, their results indicate that for a given applied stress the bulk volume decreases as an exponential-decay function, and that the influence of compression occurs more quickly than does shearing. Dexter and Tanner (1974) also found the exponential-decay relationship and reported that coarse-textured soils respond faster to applied stresses than do fine-textured soils. This time dependence is due to the reorientation of particles and increases if drainage occurs in response to loading (Lambe and Whitman, 1979). These studies indicate that faster moving ORVs will cause less compaction than slower moving ORVs. However, Vomocil et al. (1958)

found that although decreasing vehicle speed increased the amount of compaction, the effect was small when compared with the influence of moisture content. Also, greater surface disruption can be expected under vehicles moving at higher speeds.

Empirical Models of Compaction in Sandy Soils

Ideally, a land manager concerned with ORV effects on a specific soil would be able to use soil mechanics to predict the amount of soil compaction without actually disrupting large amounts of undisturbed soil. Unfortunately, tire-soil interactions are very complicated mechanically and empirical relations between applied pressure and density increases are more useful for the prediction of soil compaction. Fortunately, substantial information is available on how soil properties change with vehicle passages so approximation models can be formulated without a rigorous experimental verification. It should be noted that no approximations should be made without some experimental data, such as the undisturbed density and Proctor compaction curves (see next section).

Compaction is typically expressed as some measure of soil density increasing as a function of the applied pressure. Terzaghi and Peck (1948) developed an equation for the compression of subsurface clays under an overburden load, the form of which is applicable to compaction under vehicle tires. They expressed the change in void ratio e as a function of the change in overburden pressure as a result of surface loading, P, as

$$e = e_1 - C \ln \left[(P_1 + \Delta P)/P_1 \right] \tag{4-3}$$

where e_1 and P_1 are initial void ratio and overburden pressure, respectively, and C is the compression index (Terzaghi and Peck, 1948). Hovanesian and Buchele (1959) presented the following empirical equation for density change with applied stress

$$\rho = \rho_1 + B \ln \left[(P/P_1 + K)/(1 + K) \right] \tag{4-4}$$

where ρ is the bulk density, ρ_1 is the initial bulk density, B is a parameter analogous with the Terzaghi-Peck compression index C, and K is a parameter usually set to zero. Soehne (1958) measured density increases as a logarithmic function of applied pressure for one loading, and Raghaven et al. (1976) expanded Soehne's equation to include multiple vehicle passes and initial moisture content with the assumption that the applied pressure equalled the number of tractor passes times the pressure per pass. They reported an empirical equation specific to their sand soils as

$$\rho_d = 1.44 + 0.0855 \ln (nP) + 0.312 \ln (w) \tag{4-5}$$

where ρ_d is the dry bulk density, n is number of passes, P is pressure per pass, and w is a moisture content greater than the optimum for compaction (no value for r^2 was reported). Use of this equation requires the assumption that the con-

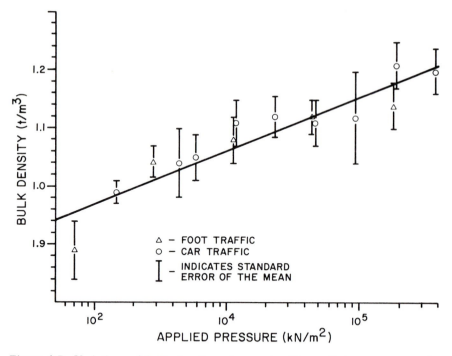

Figure 4-7. Variation of bulk density of a sand with applied pressure, or the pressure per pass times the number of passes (adapted from Liddle and Greig-Smith, 1975).

tribution of stress from each tire passing over a point is additive with respect of its influence on soil density change. Such an equation appears to be valid up to a high density where shearing and loading history become important (Bailey, 1971) but does not apply to the loading of a high-density soil.

Equation (4-5) as written applies to compaction under tractor tires and can be generalized to include other types of applied loads. The results in Figure 4-3 show a strong correlation between bulk density and the number of motorcycle passes for the Mojave Desert loamy sand. The bulk density increase at 6.2% moisture content and 0.60 mm depth can be expressed in the form of Equation (4-4) as

$$\rho_d = 1.39 + 0.034 \ln (nP), \quad r^2 = 0.79 \tag{4-6}$$

where ρ is the sum of ground pressure from front and rear tires.

Liddle and Greig-Smith (1975) studied compaction in sand under foot and automobile traffic at unspecified moisture contents and included ground pressures for each as a part of their data. Their results, recalculated and plotted in Figure 4-7, indicate that the bulk density can be related to the applied pressure per pass times the number of passes independently of the type of impact (foot or car). The resulting equation is

$$\rho_d = 0.69 + 0.04 \ln (nP), \quad r^2 = 0.86 \tag{4-7}$$

where P is applied pressure from any source. Despite the fundamental differences between the stresses below hiking boots and tires, it appears that both types of loading affect soil density in the same functional manner.

Williams and MacLean (1950) studied the efficiency of different machinery used for compacting soil during construction projects and also found similar empirical relationships (recalculated and shown in Table 4-1). These results suggest that such equations as (4-7) fit experimental compaction data better if the compacting machine is a sheepsfoot roller, especially as the clay and silt contents of the soil increase. In all soil types, the rate of density increase per pass is greatest using the sheepsfoot rolers, although Williams and MacLean (1950) found that these rollers could not compact sand. Compaction under knobby vehicle tires should be very similar to compaction under sheepsfoot rollers because both create high local shear stresses under sharp-edged knobs.

All of these equations represent empirical approximations of the compaction process and should be used when only an estimate of the mean density increase is desired. Use of these equations requires that all factors influencing compaction, including vehicle speed, acceleration/braking, initial soil moisture content, and spatial variability of soil properties, be lumped into the B term of Equation (4-4); hence, B can be considered a random variable distributed with a mean and variance in most practical problems. Therefore, usage of these equations provides only a range of densities which could result from a given number of vehicle passes, and if the density is assumed to be distributed normally, confidence intervals for the predicted density range can be calculated.

Table 4-1. Comparison of Empirical Equations for Density Increases Under Different Compacting Equipment[a]

Soil type	Texture[b]	Equation[c]	r^{2d}	w^e (%)
Gravel-sand	54-36-3-7	$\rho = 1.45 + 0.11\ ln\ (nP)^f$	0.96	7.5
Clay		$\rho = 0.95 + 0.13\ ln\ (nP)^g$	0.88	5.5
Sand	10-80-6-4	$\rho = 1.53 + 0.08\ ln\ (nP)^f$	0.92	9.0
Loam	0-22-45-23	$\rho = 1.20 + 0.08\ ln\ (nP)^f$	0.79	15.0
		$\rho = 0.90 + 0.12\ ln\ (nP)^g$	0.96	12.0
Clay loam	0-21-45-34	$\rho = 1.19 + 0.07\ ln\ (nP)^f$	0.83	16.5
		$\rho = 0.81 + 0.12\ ln\ (nP)^g$	0.96	14.0
Clay	0-5-31-64	$\rho = 0.86 + 0.09\ ln\ (nP)^f$	0.71	20.5
		$\rho = 0.68 + 0.12\ ln\ (nP)^g$	0.83	15.5

[a]Calculated from Williams and MacLean (1950).
[b]% gravel — % sand — % silt — % clay.
[c]Where ρ is dry density (m tons/m³) and nP is the number of passes multiplied by the pressure per pass.
[d]r^2, coefficient of determination.
[e]w, moisture content during compaction.
[f]7.3 and 2.5 m ton rollers.
[g]Club- and taper-foot rollers.

Effect of Moisture Content and Soil Texture on Compaction

Considerable information is available concerning compaction of different soils at different moisture contents. This variation in "compactibility" is usually expressed in Proctor compaction curves (Webb, 1982). Figure 4-8 shows that in general soils (excluding pure clays or sands) exhibit three stages of compaction resistance with increasing moisture content: (1) the soil becomes more resistant to compaction as the moisture content increases from dry to a low value; (2) as the moisture content increases further, the soil becomes less resistant to compaction until an intermediate ("optimum") moisture content is reached for maximum compaction; and (3) the resistance to compaction increases as the moisture content increases above the optimum.

Soil texture is the major factor determining the magnitude of density increases under applied loads. Bodman and Constantin (1965) considered soil as packed spherical particles and predicted that the minimum volume of a mixture of "coarse," "medium," and "fine" spherical particles would occur when the mixture was 72, 20, and 8% by volume of coarse, medium, and fine particles, respectively. Mixtures of equal-size particles such as sands or clays will not compact as much as mixtures of different sizes of particles according to this argument. They found empirically that the maximum bulk density for soil mixtures occurred when the sand component was 80% and the texture was equivalent to

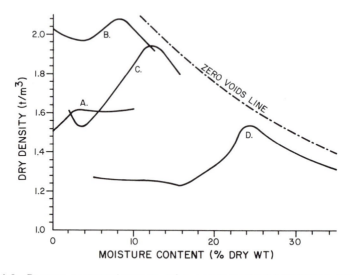

Figure 4-8. Proctor compaction curves for various soils. (a) Well-sorted fine sand under a kneading compactor (Bodman and Constantin, 1965). (b) Loamy sand under 25 hammer blows on three layers (this study). (c) Loam under 20 blows on three layers (Weaver and Jamison, 1951). (d) Clay under 20 blows on three layers (Weaver and Jamison, 1951).

a loamy sand. Soil mixtures with more sand or more clay did not compact as much, as shown in Figure 4-8. However, Williams and MacLean (1950) found that mixtures of soil and gravel, as is commonly found in deserts with lag gravel surfaces, can be compacted to higher densities than loamy sands (Table 4-1). Kezdi (1979) explains that soils which are most compactible have a wide distribution in particle sizes with the compactibility being determined primarily by the ratio of small to large particle diameters and the percentage of large particles present. Hence, any poorly sorted soil is highly susceptible to compaction.

The soils of arid regions typically have textures of sandy loam, loamy sand, and sand at the surface with some degree of soil development (Chapter 2). Frequently the soil has abundant gravel in the profile, leading to very poorly sorted conditions, and usually has a gravel, cobble, or stone cover. These soils are present on fans and bajadas, which occupy a great proportion of desert land area, while more resistant clay-rich soils are prevalent only near playas, which occupy only 1% of the desert land area (Cooke and Warren, 1973; see Chapter 6). Depending on the stage of soil development and the age of the soil, a clay-enriched B horizon may be present either near the surface or at a small (<200 mm) depth. The typical desert soil can be considered dry most of the year, with wetting occurring infrequently to shallow depths, although the soil may remain somewhat wetted during winter and spring months. Hence, most desert soils have textures which can be considered highly susceptible to compaction from ORVs, although the typical dryness of the desert soil affords some protection. Most desert soils are armored with a lag gravel or pavement which appears to resist compaction; in reality, this pavement which is often underlain by a vesicular horizon, is easily disrupted (Chapter 11) and the subsurface soil compacted.

Effects of Soil Compaction on Infiltration Rates

Numerous investigators have reported increased runoff and severe erosion problems in soil compacted by vehicles. Although ORVs alter surface conditions in a number of ways conducive to accelerated water erosion (Iverson, 1980; Chapter 5), the most important property change leading to increased erosion is the decreased infiltration rate in vehicle trails caused by compaction. Reductions in infiltration rates are commonly linked to decreases in total soil porosity (Eckert et al., 1979; Hillel, 1980) and the magnitude of the decrease has been shown to depend upon the soil moisture content, soil texture, and compacting load (Akram and Kemper, 1979). Rubin (1949), Archer and Smith (1972), and Reicosky et al. (1981) showed systematic decreases in total porosity and changes in the size distribution of pores with increasing compacting land. Knowledge of the changes in the volume distribution of pores and the saturated conductivity are important if infiltration rates into compacted soil are to be predicted or estimated.

Experimental Verification of Porosity Changes in Compacted Soil

The compacted loamy sand in the motorcycle trails near Fremont Peak had a different distribution of effective pore sizes than did the undisturbed soil (Webb, 1982); the pore volumes are shown in Table 4-2 expressed as volume per 100 g of soil (after Rubin, 1949). The macropores (radii >4.5 μm), the most important for moisture transport, were the only ones to be significantly affected by the compaction, and the decrease in the volume of macropores closely reflected the decrease in total porosity. Also, the data for intermediate (1.5 to 4.5 μm) and micro- (<1.5 μm) pores suggested that there was no net increase in the volume of small pores, although increases in the intermediate and micropores have been reported in compacted soil (Hillel, 1980; Reicosky et al., 1981; Rubin, 1949). Webb (1982) also reported that the greatest changes in pore volume occurred in pores with radii greater than 150 μm.

Models of Infiltration in Unsaturated Soils

Infiltration is controlled by the energy potential in and conductivity properties of the soil mass (Hillel, 1980). The energy potential, the driving force behind infiltration, consists of a gravitational potential, a pressure potential caused by capillary attraction forces, and other potentials created by temperature and chemical gradients. These potentials are usually expressed in the units of length as head (ψ). The pressure head can be positive or negative if the moisture potential is greater or less than atmospheric pressure. The soil is saturated when the pressure head ψ is greater than zero and generally unsaturated when ψ is less than zero (suction head). Some soils, particularly fine-textured or compacted ones, remain saturated for small values of ψ until ψ_a, the air-entry value, is reached (Hillel, 1980). ψ increases negatively as the soil moisture content θ decreases and the relationship between ψ and θ is determined by the pore-volume distribution.

The conductivity of soil moisture is a function of both the porosity and the interconnection of soil pores. The conductivity K decreases as the moisture content decreases, or as ψ increases negatively. The conductivity at saturation, K_s, can be considered qualitatively as a function of the cube of the total soil porosity (Scheidegger, 1974), although it is also a function of the size of soil pores and the tortuosity of the moisture-flow path. Rubin and Steinhardt (1963) demonstrated analytically that ponding occurred when the rainfall intensity exceeded K_s and continued longer than the time period required for the surface soil to become saturated, called the "time to ponding."

Infiltration into different soils has been predicted from theoretical and empirical models of flow through porous media (see Baver et al., 1972). The Richards equation

$$C(\psi)\frac{\partial \psi}{\partial t} = \frac{\partial}{\partial_z}\left[K(\psi)\left(\frac{\partial \psi}{\partial z} + 1\right)\right]$$

(4-8)

Table 4-2. Comparison of the Distribution of Pore Sizes in the Motorcycle-Compacted and Undisturbed Soil at the Fremont Peak Study Area

Number of motorcycle passes	Bulk density (t m^{-3})	Total pore volume (cm^3 100 g^{-1})	Volume of pores >4.5 μm (cm^3 100 g^{-1})	Volume of pores 1.5–4.5 μm (cm^3 100 g^{-1})	Volume of pores <1.5 μm (cm^3 100 g^{-1})
0 to 3 cm depth					
Undisturbed	1.52	29.1	23.0	1.4	4.7
1 pass	1.58	26.3	19.7	1.6	5.0
10 passes	1.66	23.1	17.3	1.4	4.5
100 passes	1.73	20.7	15.2	1.3	4.2
200 passes	1.72	21.1	16.0	1.2	3.9
3 to 6 cm depth					
Undisturbed	1.59	25.6	19.2	1.1	5.4
1 pass	1.62	24.9	18.6	1.3	4.9
10 passes	1.66	23.3	17.3	1.2	4.7
100 passes	1.75	20.1	13.9	1.0	5.2
200 passes	1.80	18.6	12.8	1.1	4.7

where ψ is soil water pressure head (or suction head in unsaturated soils), $C(\psi)$ is specific moisture capacity ($\partial\theta/\partial\psi$), θ is the volumetric moisture content, $K(\psi)$ is the unsaturated hydraulic conductivity, z is vertical distance, and t is time, is the basis for most theoretical models of infiltration. The most commonly used semiempirical model is the Green and Ampt equation (Mein and Larson, 1973)

$$f = K_s \left[1 + (\theta_s - \theta_i) S/F \right] \tag{4-9}$$

where F is the cumulative infiltration during the rainfall event, f is the infiltration rate (dF/dt), K_s is the saturated hydraulic conductivity, θ_s and θ_i are the saturated and initial moisture contents, respectively, and S is the pressure head at the wetting front. Both models of infiltration require knowledge of soil moisture-retention and conductivity properties, and these properties are dependent on the porosity and distribution of pore sizes in the soil.

The Richards equation, Equation (4-8), requires as input data the moisture-retention or $\theta-\psi$ curve, and the unsaturated conductivity or $K-\psi$ curve. This equation is more accurate than Equation (4-9) but it is not useful because it requires the $\theta-\psi$ and $K-\psi$ curves, both of which vary substantially spatially and with depth and are difficult to measure. The Green and Ampt equation, Equation (4-9), requires knowledge of K_s, θ_s, and S for solution. K_s can be expected to decrease dramatically as the total porosity decreases. θ_s is very nearly equal to the total soil porosity (not necessarily equal, because of entrapped air) and decreases as the soil density increases. S, the pressure head at the wetting front, has been calculated as the area under the $K-\psi$ curve (Mein and Farrell, 1974; Mein and Larson, 1973), the form of which could also change as a result of pore-size distribution changes.

These equations suggest that decreases in the total porosity and changes in the distribution of pore sizes are expected to reduce infiltration rates and affect the nature of water movement in soils.

Models of Unsaturated Moisture Flow in Compacted Soils

Numerous investigators have attempted to predict moisture flow in soils from pore-volume distributions by modeling flow through a porous medium as flow through a bundle of capillary tubes of varying diameters. These models have had limited success in application to real soils, and although some equations predict the unsaturated conductivity, or $K-\psi$, curves better than others (Mualem, 1976), none of the available models is effective in predicting K_s. Moreover, Scheidegger (1974) notes that in general a unique relationship between porosity and K_s cannot exist because K_s also depends on the distribution and interconnection of pores. Therefore, any prediction of infiltration into compacted soils requires some measurement of compacted soil conductivity properties.

The prediction of infiltration into ORV trails requires knowledge of how

K_s varies with the number of vehicle passes. For motorcycle trails near Fremont Peak, K_s probably decreased in a manner similar to the decrease in terminal infiltration rate I_t as shown in Figure 4-4. These values of I_t are estimated to be 3 to 10% higher than K_s using equations for infiltration from a shallow ponded water source (Baver et al., 1972, p. 374). Reduction of the mean values for I_t by 10% yields mean values of K as $K_u = 1.4$, $K_1 = 1.2$, $K_{10} = 0.92$, $K_{100} = 0.43$ mm min^{-1}. These K values have important implications for describing qualitatively the response of the soil to rainfall because the intensity required before ponding occurs must exceed the saturated conductivity of the soils (Mein and Larson, 1973; Rubin and Steinhardt, 1963). Assuming that these values of K are the true mean values of K_s, the rainfall intensity required to initiate ponding in the 200-pass trail, R_{200}, will be less than the intensity required for the ponding in the undisturbed soil, R_u. Furthermore, it follows that $R_{200} < R_{100} < R_{10} < R_1 < R_u$. This indicates that on the average ponding with possible runoff will occur under lower rainfall intensities in the motorcycle-compacted soil than in the undisturbed soil.

The Green and Ampt equation, Equation (4-9), was used to model infiltration into the undisturbed soil and vehicle trails. The soil was assumed to be uniformly compacted with K_s, θ_s, θ_i, and S constant with depth for simplicity, although the Green-Ampt equation can be applied to layered soils (Childs and Bybordi, 1969). S was calculated as the area under the relative $K-\psi$ curve obtained by the method of Jackson (1972), and θ_s was assumed equal to the mean total porosity (Table 4-3). Three initial conditions were used to illustrate the infiltration properties of the undisturbed and compacted soils: (1) initially dry soil under a rainfall intensity of 1.4 mm min^{-1}; (2) soil at field capacity ($\theta_i = 0.14$; Webb, 1982) under an intensity of 1.4 mm min^{-1}; and (3) initially dry soil under an intensity of 2.8 mm min^{-1}.

Figure 4-9 shows the calculated infiltration rate versus time relation for the undisturbed soil and vehicle trails at initial condition (1). Because the rainfall intensity equals K_u, the infiltration rate f_u for the undisturbed soil is constant with time and no ponding occurs. However, R exceeds K_s for the vehicle trails so f decreases asymptotically toward the respective K_ss and ponded or excess

Table 4-3. Summary of Input Parameters to the Solutions of the Green-Ampt Equation for Infiltration in Compacted Motorcycle Trails

Number of passes	K_s (mm min^{-1})	θ_s	θ_o	S (mm)
Undisturbed	1.4	0.437	0.0–0.14	13.5
1 pass	1.2	0.410	0.0–0.14	21.0
10 passes	0.92	0.380	0.0–0.14	26.4
100 passes	0.55	0.350	0.0–0.14	34.6
200 passes	0.43	0.341	0.0–0.14	34.5

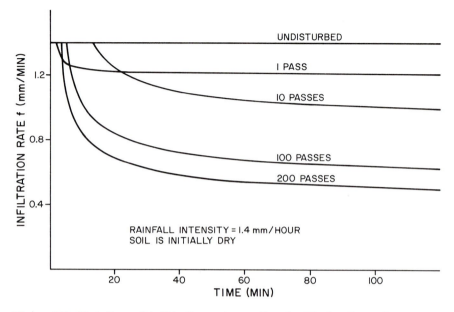

Figure 4-9. Variation of infiltration rate predicted with the Green-Ampt equation with time for the undisturbed soil and vehicle trails.

water available for runoff appears at the soil surface. The time to ponding for the vehicle trails varies between 2 and 14 min for this intensity; in general, the time to ponding would probably be less than 30 min for this soil (Webb, 1982). The difference between f_u and all other f curves is the rate at which excess becomes available for runoff at any given time. The amount of excess water at 30, 60, and 90 min generally increased with increasing motorcycle passes (Table 4-4). Note that a greater amount of water was available for runoff when the soil was wet; this indicates that the potential for runoff from soils is greater when the soil contains residual moisture. The depth to the wetting front was usually greater at any time in the undisturbed soil than in the compacted soils, which indicates that moisture penetrates deeper into the undisturbed soil. Greater depth of moisture penetration in undisturbed soils than in those compacted by ORVs has been observed elsewhere in the Mojave Desert (Iverson and Hinckley, pers. comm., 1980).

This example shows the utility of the Green-Ampt equation, (4-9), in predicting infiltration into ORV-compacted soil. The equation requires only three parameters (K_s, θ_s, and S) in addition to two initial conditions (θ_i and R), and these parameters can be easily varied spatially or with depth. Calculation of these infiltration rates would complement a hydraulic analysis of overland flow in ORV trails (Iverson, 1980) needed for the estimation of erosion rates (see Chapter 5).

Table 4-4. Excess Water (Available for Runoff) and Depth to Wetting Front Data Obtained with the Green-Ampt Equation Solved for Three Initial Conditions

Number of passes	Time = 30 min		Time = 60 min		Time = 90 min	
	Excess water (mm)	Depth (mm)	Excess water (mm)	Depth (mm)	Excess water (mm)	Depth (mm)
R = 1.4 mm min^{-1}, $\theta_i = 0.00$						
Undisturbed	0	9.6	0	19.2	0	28.8
1	0.4	9.1	1.0	18.0	1.6	26.8
10	0.1	10.6	1.1	19.2	2.2	27.3
100	1.1	8.8	3.1	14.9	5.4	20.5
200	1.5	7.7	4.0	12.8	6.6	17.4
R = 1.4 mm min^{-1}, $\theta_i = 0.14$						
Undisturbed	0	14.2	0	28.5	0	42.7
1	0.5	13.4	1.1	26.8	1.7	40.2
10	1.9	15.9	5.0	29.7	7.8	41.2
100	3.1	13.1	7.2	22.5	11.3	31.4
200	3.6	11.2	8.3	19.6	12.5	26.0
R = 2.8 mm min^{-1}, $\theta_i = 0.14$						
Undisturbed	2.9	12.7	6.8	23.0	10.5	32.5
1	4.6	9.3	9.4	18.1	13.9	26.4
10	3.9	11.6	9.1	20.1	14.4	28.1
100	5.0	9.0	11.3	15.1	17.7	20.7
200	5.9	8.0	12.6	13.1	18.9	17.4

Raindrop Impact Effects

Soil compaction under vehicle tires decreases the saturated conductivity and increases the potential for runoff from a given area, yet the rainfall intensity required to initiate runoff is commonly considerably less than the measured conductivities. An important phenomenon which should be considered when modeling infiltration or managing soils is the decrease in conductivity at the soil surface resulting from surface crusting and/or raindrop compaction on bare or disturbed soils (Chapter 3).

Some surface crusts result from the breakdown of soil aggregates under raindrop impacts after the aggregates absorb sufficient moisture to weaken structurally (Farres, 1978). The disaggregated particles form a relatively smooth crust at the soil surface which varies 0.1 to 5 mm in thickness and "washes" several centimeters below the surface to create a zone of decreased porosity (Farres, 1978; McIntyre, 1958a). After the rainfall, platy particles can settle in the pores at the surface, further reducing conductivities (Hillel, 1960; McIntyre, 1958b), and compounds such as silica and lime are deposited as the soil dries, increasing the crust's strength (Uehara and Jones, 1974). Investigators studying soil crusting have found the underlying soil conductivity to be greater than the crust conductivity by a factor of 5 (fine sandy loam; Tackett and Pearson, 1965), 100 to 100,000 (remolded sandy loam; Hillel, 1964), and 2000 (fine sandy loam; McIntyre, 1958a). Lowdermilk (1930) found that runoff from crusted, bare soil was 3, 9, and 16.5 times the runoff from uncrested, litter-covered soil for a fine sandy loam, a sandy clay loam, and a clay loam, respectively. Eckert et al. (1979) report that the infiltration rate in an ORV trail was reduced from 2.1 to 1.1 cm hr^{-1} as a result of surface crusting in a Mojave Desert sandy loam. The problem of surface crusting is commonly most severe in soils of arid regions with aggregates which are not stable when saturated (Hillel, 1960).

Raindrop compaction occurs concurrently with surface crusting and may influence surface conductivities even in the absence of unstable aggregates. Lunt (1937) and McIntyre (1958b) suggested that raindrop compaction of the surface soil caused significant infiltration decreases in sandy soils. Many investigators have reported increased density and penetration resistance as characteristics of soil surfaces after rainfall events (Hillel, 1960; Lunt, 1937; Tackett and Pearson, 1965) and these changes decrease the soil conductivity as a result of porosity changes. The effects of raindrop compaction would be most severe in loamy sands, because these are the soils most susceptible to density increases under loading (Bodman and Constantin, 1965). Epstein and Grant (1967) measured density increases of 1.15 to 1.65 t m^{-3} and 0.83 to 1.14 t m^{-3} at 0 to 5 mm depth in two silt loams as a result of raindrop compaction and the deposition of particles in pores by percolating water.

These two processes act in concert to cause infiltration rate decreases in soils with both undisturbed and disturbed surfaces. Future research on infiltration into compacted soils in ORV areas should be concerned with the formation of rainfall crusts in vehicle trails and their relation to infiltration and overland flow properties. Eckert et al. (1979) report that crusting had an important effect both on infiltration and sediment yields, but their results were for very small (0.14-m^2) plots. Iverson (1980) and Hinckley and others (Chapter 5) suggest that erosion in arid regions may be caused by long recurrence interval storms; hence the occurrence of surface crusts may lower the infiltration rate sufficiently that severe erosion may occur from less-intense storms of shorter recurrence interval. Surface crusting in ORV trails is an important process which must be considered if runoff and erosion are to be predicted quantitatively.

Summary and Management Considerations

Soil compaction tests and existing theory are used to explain and partially predict the effects of ORV use on soil properties. While most existing information on compaction comes from tests on soils in more humid regions, this information can be generalized to all types of ORVs and desert soils with varying moisture contents. Use of ORVs on soil causes compaction; the only question is the amount and significance of the resultant density increase.

Any surface loading creates stresses in the soil which affect soil properties to a finite depth. Field measurements in the Mojave Desert indicate and elasticity theory suggests that the greatest increases in density during ORV compaction occur at a shallow depth instead of at the soil surface, and this depth appears to be roughly related to the geometry of the tire contact with the soil. The density of the soil near the surface increases as a logarithmic function of the number of vehicle passes, which indicates that the greatest changes in soil properties occur within the first few passes. The density change resulting from ORV compaction can be approximated as an empirically derived logarithmic function of the number of passes times the applied pressure per pass.

Soil infiltration rates also decrease as logarithmic functions of the number of ORV passes because of total porosity decreases and changes in the distribution of soil pores. Theoretical analysis of field measurements indicates that the rainfall intensity required to initiate runoff is less in compacted than in undisturbed soils and decreases with increasing numbers of vehicle passes. A review of the literature indicates that disruption of the soil surface by vehicle traffic leads to raindrop crusting, which also dramatically decreases infiltration rates. This suggests that the combination of decreased porosities caused by compaction and crusting caused by raindrop impacts and other processes can cause greatly increased runoff and concurrent increased erosion potential in ORV trails.

Additional information on compaction indicates that the soils most susceptible to density increases are loamy sands or very coarse, gravelly soils with a wide range of particle sizes. In addition, these soils are susceptible to density increases at all moisture contents although the rate of density increases with the number of ORV passes may be greater when the soil is wet than dry. Most naturally occurring soils will compact under ORV traffic but the soil types which probably will be least affected will be sands and clays where the bulk of the soil particles are about the same size. It should be noted that clays will compact significantly when wet. ORV use should be limited to areas where soils are not susceptible to compaction (e.g., sand dunes and dry lakes in deserts) during times of the year when the soil is dry.

References

Akram, M., and W. D. Kemper. 1979. Infiltration of soils as affected by the pressure and water content at the time of compaction. Soil Sci. Soc. Am. J. 43: 1080–1086.

Archer, J. R., and P. D. Smith. 1972. The relation between bulk density, available water capacity, and air capacity of soils. J. Soil Sci. 23(4):475–480.

Arndt, W. 1966. IV. The effect of traffic compaction on a number of soil properties. J. Agric. Eng. Res. 11:182–187.

Bailey, A. C. 1971. Compaction and shear in compacted soils. Trans. Am. Soc. Agric. Eng. 14(2):201–205.

Bailey, A. C., and G. E. Vanden Berg. 1968. Yielding by compaction and shear in unsaturated soils. Trans. Am. Soc. Agric. Eng. 11(3):307–311, 317.

Barnes, K. K., W. M. Carleton, H. M. Taylor, R. I. Throckmorton, and G. E. Vanden Berg. 1971. Compaction of Agricultural Soils. American Society of Agricultural Engineering Monograph, St. Joseph, Michigan, 471 pp.

Baver, L. D., W. H. Gardner, and W. R. Gardner. 1972. Soil physics. 5th ed. John Wiley and Sons, New York, 498 pp.

Bertrand, A. R. 1965. Rate of water intake in the field. In: C. A. Black (Ed.), Methods of Soils Analysis. Part 1. American Society of Agronomy Monograph 9, Madison, Wisconsin, pp. 400–412.

Bodman, G. B., and J. Rubin. 1948. Soil puddling. Soil Sci. Soc. Am. Proc. 13: 27–36.

Bodman, G. B., and G. K. Constantin. 1965. Influence of particle-size distribution in soil compaction. Hilgardia 36(15):567–591.

Carter, L. M. 1967. Portable recording penetrometer measures soil strength profiles. Agric. Eng. 48:348–349.

Chancellor, W. J., R. H. Schmidt, and W. H. Soehne. 1962. Laboratory measurement of soil compaction and plastic flow. Trans. Am. Soc. Agric. Eng. 5: 235–239.

Childs, E. C., and M. Bybordi. 1969. The vertical movement of water in stratified porous material. 1. Infiltration. Water Resources Res. 5(2):446–459.

Cohron, G. T. 1971. Forces causing soil compaction. In: K. K. Barnes, W. M. Carleton, H. M. Taylor, R. K. Throckmorton, and G. E. Vanden Berg (Eds.), Compaction of Agricultural Soils. American Society of Agricultural Engineering Monograph, St. Joseph, Michigan, pp. 106–122.

Cooke, R. U., and A. Warren. 1973. Geomorphology in Deserts. B. T. Batsford, Ltd., London, 398 pp.

Deresiewicz, H. 1960. The half-space under pressure distributed over an elliptical portion of its plane boundary. Trans. Am. Soc. Mech. Eng., J. Appl. Mech. 82E:111–119.

Dexter, A. R., and D. W. Tanner. 1974. Time dependence of compressibility for remoulded and undisturbed soils. J. Soil Sci. 25(2):153–164.

Eckert, R. E., Jr., M. K. Wood, W. H. Blackburn, and F. F. Peterson. 1979. Impacts of off-road vehicles on infiltration and sediment production of two desert soils. J. Range Management 32(5):394–397.

Epstein, E., and W. J. Grant. 1967. Soil losses and crust formation as related to some soil physical properties. Soil Sci. Soc. Am. Proc. 31:547–550.

Farres, P. 1978. The role of time and aggregate size in the crusting process. Earth Surf. Proc. 3:243–254.

Hamilton, G. M., and L. E. Goodman. 1966. The stress field created by a circular sliding contact. Trans. Am. Soc. Mech. Eng., J. Appl. Mech. 88E:371–376.

Harris, W. L. 1971. The soil compaction process. In: K. K. Barnes, W. M. Carleton, H. M. Taylor, R. K. Throckmorton, and G. E. Vanden Berg (Eds.), Compaction of Agricultural Soils. American Society of Agricultural Engineering Monograph, St. Joseph, Michigan, pp. 9–44.

Hillel, D. 1960. Crust formation in loessial soils. Seventh International Congress of Soil Science, Madison, Wisconsin 1:330–338.

Hillel, D. 1964. Infiltration and rainfall-runoff as affected by surface crusts. Trans. Eighth Intl. Congress Soil Sci., Bucharest, Vol. 2, pp. 53–60.

Hillel, D. 1980. Fundamentals of Soil Physics. Academic Press, New York, 413 pp.

Hovanesian, J. D., and W. F. Buchele. 1959. Development of a recording transducer for studying effects of soil parameters on compaction. Trans. Am. Soc. Agric. Eng. 2:78–81.

Hovland, H. J., and J. K. Mitchell. 1972. Model studies of the failure mechanism associated with a sphere rolling down a soil slope. J. Terramech. 9(1):37–50.

Iverson, R. M. 1980. Processes of accelerated pluvial erosion on desert hillslopes modified by vehicular traffic. Earth Surf. Proc. 5:369–388.

Jackson, R. D. 1972. On the calculation of hydraulic conductivity. Soil Sci. Soc. Am. Proc. 36:380–382.

Karafiath, L. L., and E. A. Nowatzki. 1978. Soil Mechanics for Off-Road Vehicle Engineering. Trans Tech Publishers, Clausthal, Germany, 515 pp.

Kezdi, A. 1979. Soil Physics: Selected Topics. Developments in Geotechnical Engineering Series No. 25. Elsevier Scientific Publishing Company, Amsterdam, 160 pp.

Lambe, T. W., and R. V. Whitman. 1979. Soil Mechanics, SI Version. John Wiley and Sons, New York, 553 pp.

Liddle, M. J., and P. Greig-Smith. 1975. A survey of tracks and paths in a sand dune ecosystem. I. Soils. J. Appl. Ecol. 12(3):893–908.

Lowdermilk, W. C. 1930. Influence of forest litter on runoff, percolation, and erosion. J. Forestry 28:474–491.

Lull, H. W. 1959. Soil Compaction on Forest and Range Lands. U.S. Forest Service Misc. Publ. 768. 33 pp.

Lunt, H. A. 1937. The effect of forest litter removal upon the structure of mineral soil. J. Forestry 35:33–36.

McIntyre, D. S. 1958a. Permeability measurements of soil crusts formed by raindrop impact. Soil Sci. 85:185–189.

McIntyre, D. S. 1958b. Soil splash and the formation of surface crusts by raindrop impact. Soil Sci. 85:261–266.

Mein, R. G., and D. A. Farrell. 1974. Determination of wetting front suction in the Green-Ampt equation. Soil Sci. Soc. Am. Proc. 38:872–876.

Mein, R. G., and C. L. Larson. 1973. Modeling infiltration during a steady rain. Water Resources Res. 9(2):384–394.

Mualem, Y. 1976. A new model for predicting the hydraulic conductivity of unsaturated porous media. Water Resources Res. 12(3):513–522.

Poulos, H. G., and E. H. Davis. 1974. Elastic solutions for soil and rock mechanics. John Wiley and Sons, New York, 411 pp.

Raghaven, G. S. V., E. McKyes, I. Amir, M. Chasse, and R. S. Broughton. 1976. Prediction of soil compaction due to off-road vehicle traffic. Trans. Am. Soc. Agric. Eng. 19(4):610–613.

Raghaven, G. S. V., E. McKyes, E. Stemshorn, A. Gray, and B. Beaulieu. 1977. Vehicle compaction patterns in clay soil. Trans. Am. Soc. Agric. Eng. 20(2): 218–220.

Reaves, C. A., and A. W. Cooper. 1960. Stress distribution under tractor loads. Agric. Eng. 40:20–21.

Reece, A. R. 1977. Soil mechanics of agricultural soils. Soil Sci. 123(5):332–337.

Reicosky, D. C., W. B. Voorhees, and J. K. Radke. 1981. Unsaturated water flow through a simulated wheel tract. Soil Sci. Soc. Am. J. 45(1):3–8.

Romkens, M. J. M. 1979. Soil crusting—when crusts form and quantifying their effects. In: Infiltration Research Planning Workshop. Part 1. State of the Art Reports. U.S. Department of Agriculture, Agricultural Research, Science and Education Administration, Peoria, Illinois, pp. 36–39.

Rubin, J. 1949. The influence of externally applied stresses upon the structure of confined soil material. Unpublished Ph.D. thesis, University of California, Berkeley, California.

Rubin, J., and R. Steinhardt. 1963. Soil water relations during rain infiltration: I. Theory. Soil Sci. Soc. Am. Proc. 27:246–251.

Scheidegger, A. E. 1974. The Physics of Flow Through Porous Media. 3rd ed. University of Toronto Press, Toronto, 353 pp.

Sheridan, D. 1980. Off-Road Vehicles on Public Lands. Council on Environmental Quality, Washington, D.C., 84 pp.

Snyder, C. T., D. G. Frickel, R. F. Hadley, and R. F. Miller. 1976. Effects of Off-Road Vehicle Use on the Hydrology and Landscape of Central and Southern California. U.S. Geological Survey Water Resources Investigation 76-99, 30 pp.

Soehne, W. 1958. Fundamentals of pressure distribution under tractor tires. Agric. Eng. 39:276–281, 290.

Tackett, J. L., and R. W. Pearson. 1965. Some characteristics of soil crusts formed by simulated rainfall. Soil Sci. 99(6):407–413.

Terzaghi, K., and R. B. Peck. 1948. Soil Mechanics in Engineering Practice. John Wiley and Sons, Inc., New York, 566 pp.

Timoshenko, S. P., and J. N. Goodier. 1970. Theory of Elasticity. 3rd ed. McGraw-Hill Book Company, New York, 567 pp.

Uehara, G., and R. C. Jones. 1974. Bonding mechanisms for soil crusts. In: J. W. Cary and D. D. Evans (Eds.), Soil Crusts. Tech. Bull. 214, Agricultural Experiment Station, University of Arizona, Tucson, Arizona, pp. 17–28.

Vanden Berg, G. E. 1966. Triaxial measurements of shear strain and compaction in unsaturated soil. Trans. Am. Soc. Agric. Eng. 9(4):460–463, 467.

Vomocil, J. A., E. R. Fountaine, and R. J. Reginato. 1958. The influence of speed and drawbar load on the compacting effect of wheeled tractors. Soil Sci. Soc. Am. Proc. 22:178–180.

Warkentin, B. P. 1971. Effects of compaction on content and transmission of water in soils. In: D. D. Barnes et al. (Eds.), Compaction of Agricultural Soils. American Society of Agricultural Engineering Monograph, St. Joseph, Michigan, pp. 126–153.

Weaver, H. A., and V. C. Jamison. 1951. Effects of moisture on tractor tire compaction of soil. Soil Sci. 71:15–23.

Weaver, T., and D. Dale. 1978. Trampling effects of hikers, motorcycles, and horses in meadows and forests. J. Appl. Ecol. 15:451–457.

Webb, R. H. 1982. Off-road motorcycle effects on a desert soil. Environ. Conserv. (in press.)

Webb, R. H., H. C. Ragland, W. H. Godwin, and D. Jenkins. 1978. Environmental effects of soil property changes with off-road vehicle use. Environ. Management 2(3):219–233.

Williams, F. H. P., and D. J. MacLean. 1950. The compaction of soil: a study of the performance of plant. Road Research Technical Paper No. 17, Department of Scientific and Industrial Research, Road Research Laboratory, London, 46 pp.

Wilshire, H. G., and J. K. Nakata. 1976. Off-road vehicle effects on California's Mojave Desert. Calif. Geol. 29(6):123–132.

5

Accelerated Water Erosion in ORV-Use Areas[1]

Bern S. Hinckley, Richard M. Iverson, and Bernard Hallet

Introduction

Virtually every element of the Earth's landscape is to some extent the product of erosion. Denudation and sedimentation are inevitable geologic phenomena that man may regard as either benevolent or pernicious depending on the place and time. Erosion of upstream fertile lands, for example, leads to enrichment of the prolific Nile and Mesopotamian floodplains, nuturing the first agriculturalists (Moss and Walker, 1978). From another point of view, modern agricultural researchers commonly estimate that only 0.1 to 0.8 mm year^{-1} of soil removal can be sustained indefinitely without loss of productivity on croplands (U.S. Department of Agriculture, 1975). Yet erosion of thin topsoils, rapid sedimentation of streams and lakes, and gullying of landscapes are in some areas esthetic and economic problems of massive proportions. Figure 5-1, for example, illustrates a Mojave Desert hill slope where erosion has become a serious problem following slope modifications by vehicles. The problem, however, is not erosion per se, but rather erosion rates, and the adjective "accelerated" is commonly applied to erosion rates considered to be significantly greater than "natural."

By far the most important erosive agent is water, moving either as overland flow (commonly augmented by impacting raindrops) or in channels and streams. In some areas hillslope erosion also occurs by landsliding and soil creep and, particularly in arid areas, wind may be an important erosive agent (Chapter 6).

---

[1] The views and conclusions contained in this study are based on the authors' studies or experiences and do not necessarily represent the official viewpoint or policy of any U.S. government agency.

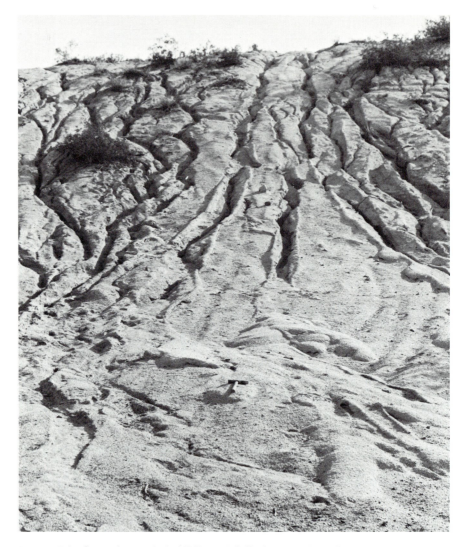

Figure 5-1. Severely eroded ORV-used hill slope at Red Rock Canyon in the northwestern Mojave Desert, California. No gullies were present prior to ORV use. Small sediment levees on the edges of some gullies and smooth depositional lobes of sediment in the foreground suggest that some of the eroded material moved downslope in thick slurries. Hammer in foreground provides scale.

Finally, as evidenced by the "rooster tail" of sediment behind a spinning tire, there are the direct erosional effects of man's activities. In this chapter we address the magnitude and processes of accelerated water erosion on arid hill slopes modified by off-road vehicle (ORV) traffic. We discuss the relative sensitivity of desert surfaces to this erosion and the management implications thereof.

Erosion Measurement and Natural Erosion Rates

The growing use of ORVs, particularly on arid lands, has spurred considerable effort to document and analyze their conspicuous effect on erosion rates. Various workers (e.g., Stull et al., 1979; Wilshire, 1979) have reported ORV-induced erosion rates 5 and 50 times greater than natural rates. To consider usefully the available data on ORV use and erosion rates in general, however, it is first necessary to examine the several ways in which erosion is measured.

The most common methods of measuring water erosion rates have been either to monitor sediment flux past a stream-gaging station or to periodically survey the sediments collecting in reservoirs. In either case, downstream point data are extrapolated over upstream areas to assign average erosion rates. The fact that such rates almost invariably increase as drainage basin size decreases reflects the complex interplay of erosion and deposition through which sediment moves down a drainage system (Langbein and Schumm, 1958; Piest and Miller, 1975). The smaller the basin studied, the closer the calculated erosion rate should be to the actual lowering of the ground surface. For drainage basins smaller than about 1.8 km^2 calculated values range from zero for extremely arid areas to a high of 31.3 mm $year^{-1}$ for a basin in the loess hills of Iowa (Schumm, 1963), and reports from the arid and semiarid southwestern United States vary from 0.01 to 1.0 mm $year^{-1}$ (U.S. Department of Agriculture, 1964).

A second difficulty with extrapolating erosion measurements is the failure to distinguish contributing areas; for steep slopes and floodplains, shales and granites, vegetated and barren sections are often evaluated with no regard for disparate erosional susceptibilities. Because some areas of a drainage basin contribute little or no sediment, erosion rates for those areas from which most of the sediment is actually derived will be higher than the basinwide averages. Therefore, the most accurate erosion-rate data are likely to come from small basins where erosion-related properties of the landscape are nearly constant. Data from stock reservoirs in the Cheyenne River Basin, Wyoming (250 to 360 mm $year^{-1}$ precipitation), for example, distinguish erosion rates of 0.1 mm $year^{-1}$ on an "incoherent," very sandy formation, 0.2 mm $year^{-1}$ on a very sandy loam, 0.5 mm $year^{-1}$ on a sandy loam, and 0.9 mm $year^{-1}$ on clay loams and silty clay loams (Hadley and Schumm, 1961).

A more difficult and areally limited method of determining erosion rates involves direct measurement of sediment removal at a single point. While the problems of basin size and contributing areas are thus solved, such data tend to be highly variable due to dependence on extremely local climatic, topographic, soil, vegetation, and land-use factors. LaMarche (1968) used root exposures of long-lived bristlecone pines to monitor surface lowering in very coarse material of a White Mountains, California (320 mm $year^{-1}$ precipitation) basin. He calculated erosion rates of 1.1 mm $year^{-1}$ from the steep banks of incising channels, 0.2 mm $year^{-1}$ on long, steep (30°) midslopes, and 0.3 mm $year^{-1}$ from steep crestal slopes. Using a similar technique on stony, sandy silts in the Piceance Basin, Colorado (330 mm $year^{-1}$ precipitation), Carrara and Carroll (1979) calculated average hillslope lowering rates of 0.35 mm $year^{-1}$ for the period 100 to 400 years B.P. and 1.8 mm year^{-1} for the last 100 years, when cattle grazing became common in the area. Badlands slopes underlain by silts and clays in South Dakota, in contrast, showed up to 46 mm year^{-1} of erosion as measured with steel stakes (Hadley and Schumm, 1961). On a more typical arid soil of silts, sands, and gravel near Santa Fe (300 mm year^{-1} precipitation) Leopold et al. (1966) monitored several hundred erosion stakes to derive an average erosion rate of 4.6 mm year^{-1} for an estimated 65% of a 9.6-km^2 drainage basin that was undergoing net erosion. While soil creep and minor landsliding were found to be very significant locally (7.6 mm year^{-1}) the authors did not believe these processes contributed more than a minor amount to the predominantly water-derived erosion rates basin-wide.

In conclusion, knowledge of a net "erosion rate" can be far removed from an understanding of the actual sediment movement within a basin. On one hand, reservoir and stream-load data may indicate high erosion rates due to sediment removal from channels rather than from hillsides. Conversely, severe interfluve and slope erosion may cause buildup of debris aprons and floodplains with very little monitored sediment leaving the basin. Thus, to analyze the significance of ORV modification of natural erosion rates, comparison to similarly measured data or compensation for dissimilar measurement technique is critical.

Erosion Rates in ORV-Use Areas

Studies of the effects of off-road vehicles on erosion rates have been made using a variety of techniques. Snyder et al. (1976) monitored reservoirs in the Panoche Hills, California (190 mm year^{-1} precipitation) and found that an ORV-used, 0.05-km^2 drainage basin produced eight times the runoff of an adjacent unused basin. Basinwide erosion rates averaged 1.0 mm year^{-1} in the used area, whereas no measurable sediment was produced from the unused area. Analogous to the point erosion measurement methods described above are surface transects made across ORV trails. Estimation of original surface levels allows calculation of the net erosion at any point along such a transect, and repeated surveys provide erosion rate data by simple comparison. Workers in Dove Springs Canyon, California (140 mm year^{-1} precipitation) have documented up to 150 mm year^{-1} of erosion (Snyder et al., 1976), and in Ballinger Canyon, California (250 mm year^{-1} precipitation) 220 mm year^{-1} using this method (Stull et al., 1979). Results of other ORV transect studies from a variety of environments can be found in Wilshire and Nakata (1977) and Webb et al. (1978).

While the simple fact that ORV use leads to accelerated erosion in many areas is very important, it is also important from both scientific and management points of view to understand the various factors and processes controlling such erosion. The measurement techniques discussed so far are of a generally descriptive nature and typically suffer from three limitations: (1) they represent the effects of fairly short time periods (usually less than 10 years) and thus likely do not include the effects of intense storms with long return periods; (2)

the rainfall volume and intensity required to generate the observed result is usually unknown; and (3) the actual processes of erosion are rarely observed. A solution to these problems that preserves the advantages of point erosion data is the use of simulated rainfall to study erosion on carefully monitored and bounded plots.

The following discussion draws heavily upon data acquired by the authors as a result of over 50 such plot experiments concentrated in three ORV-use areas in the western Mojave Desert, California. In these experiments simulated rainfall was applied to 1.0 m^2 plots for 20 min at an average intensity of 66 mm hr^{-1}. Rainfall properties simulated those of a storm with a return period of about 100 years in this area (Iverson, 1980). Details of experiment sites, procedures, and apparatus are described in Hinckley (1980) and Iverson (1980); principal measurements included those of slope inclination, surface and subsurface soil texture and strength, rainfall input, runoff and sediment yield, runoff velocity and flow channelization, and grain-size distribution of the eroded material. Results indicated significantly greater erosion (typically a 10 to 20-fold increase) on ORV-used plots compared to adjacent unused plots. The processes involved in such erosion will be addressed in two groups: (1) changes in the frequency and volume of runoff, and (2) changes in soil erodibility and runoff erosivity.

ORV Effects on Runoff Volume and Frequency

Since a prime requisite for water erosion is the production of runoff, its magnitude and frequency of occurrence are of critical importance. In arid areas, runoff generally occurs as a result of rainfall intensities exceeding infiltration rates (as opposed to saturating the soil column as happens in humid areas with high groundwater tables). Thus, ORV effects on runoff production are dependent on vehicular modification of soil infiltration capacities. Measurements by several researchers show that soil compaction and disruption and consequent reduction of infiltration capacity almost inevitably result from ORV activity (Chapter 4). Statistical analyses of our own data conclusively demonstrate a significant decrease in average infiltration rate and a consequent increase in volume and duration of runoff following ORV use (Hinckley, 1980).

Many moderate or low-intensity desert storms, which produce no rainfall excess on undisturbed surfaces, may easily exceed the lowered infiltration capacities of ORV-used areas. For example, our field investigations during natural rains of relatively low intensity, 4.0 mm hr^{-1} and 10.0 mm hr^{-1} in Dove Springs Canyon, California and Stoddard Valley, California, respectively, showed that local ponding and runoff occurred on heavily used soils whereas adjacent unused areas showed no signs of impending runoff. Observations of unused experimental plots where no runoff was generated under heavy simulated rainfall suggest that intensities in the 40 to 60 mm hr^{-1} range are necessary to produce runoff on undisturbed hillslopes. Comparison to hourly precipitation data for selected Mojave Desert locations (National Oceanic and Atmospheric

Administration, 1973-1978) indicates that over this 6-year period, runoff would have occurred five times or more on used surfaces near Mojave, Boron, Dagget, Baker, and Needles, whereas only one event at one location, Needles, was of sufficient intensity to produce runoff on a natural surface similar to those of our experiments. Available data do not permit analysis of instantaneous rainfall intensities so the above evaluation may not be precise in delineating the actual number of runoff events, but it is clear that runoff will be much more frequent on used areas than on unused. The effect of reduced infiltration will also be great where both vehicle-used and -unused surfaces produce runoff, for runoff will both start earlier and proceed at a greater rate on the vehicle-used surface.

ORV Effects on the Erosion Process

In addition to producing greater and more frequent runoff, effects of ORV traffic cause modifications that leave desert surfaces more susceptible to water erosion. These may be classified as (1) modifications to soil surface stabilizers that enable runoff to more easily acquire sediment, and (2) modifications to the configuration of the ground surface that enable runoff to more effectively transport sediment.

Surface Stabilizers and Soil Erodibility

Erosion of natural desert hillslopes is commonly limited by the rate at which particles can be detached from the ground surface. Soil stabilizers (i.e., surface crusts, erosion lags of coarse particles, desert pavements, and vegetation) inhibit detachment of soil particles by rainfall and runoff (Chapter 3). Although the effects of stabilizers are less evident in arid than in humid regions (Moss and Walker, 1978), our work demonstrates their significance in affecting desert hill slope erosion (Iverson et al., 1981).

Stabilizers protect soil particles from the direct force of raindrop impact, which is an extremely important agent for initiating sediment movement on hill slopes. While raindrop strikes alone appear to be minimally effective in moving particles downslope (Morgan, 1978), raindrops impacting on or near shallow overland flows play a key role in enabling such flows to entrain particles (Moss et al., 1979; Young and Wiersma, 1973). Grains too large or too firmly affixed to be entrained by the flow are often set into motion by energetic raindrops striking near the grains, and after this initial entrainment the flow is commonly competent to transport these particles downslope (Iverson, 1980). The protective effect of surface stabilizers can thus place an important constraint on natural hill slope erosion rates.

Surface stabilizers are disrupted by the direct mechanical action of off-road vehicles so that infiltration rates are decreased (Chapter 4) and the number of exposed and detached soil particles is greatly increased. Erosion is then limited only by the capacity of overland flow to transport sediment. This capacity is closely related to the rate at which the flow expends energy, known as the flow power and simply defined as

$$P = \rho s q \sin \theta$$

where P is the temporally and spatially averaged flow power per unit surface area of the hillslope, ρ is the density of the fluid (water plus suspended sediment), g is gravitational acceleration, q is mean runoff discharge per unit width of hillslope, and θ is approximated by the angle of slope inclination. From this simple equation it is evident that average overland flow power is dependent on only two parameters that vary: runoff discharge per unit width of hillslope and the steepness of the hillslope, because ρ and g normally may be taken as constant. Furthermore, available data suggest that overland flow sediment transport capacity increased more than linearly with increasing flow power, being proportional to flow power raised to an exponent of about 1.5 (Iverson, 1980; Kilinc and Richardson, 1973). This means, for example, that a doubling of runoff volume due to ORV-induced infiltration reduction will more than double the erosive capacity of the flow.

Surface Configuration and Runoff Erosivity

Off-road vehicle traffic also increases overland flow sediment transport capacity by causing surface changes that alter runoff hydraulics. On natural desert hill slopes, runoff is usually diverted by microtopograhic obstructions and follows rather indirect flow paths as it moves downslope; and intermittent ponding with consequent energy dissipation and sediment deposition at short (less than 1-m) slope-length intervals is common (Fig. 5-2a). Off-road vehicle use modifies hillslopes by creating relatively smooth trails (usually oriented directly upslope) and smoothing obstructions perpendicular to the trails. Substantial tread ruts are commonly incised up and down the slopes. Runoff on surfaces used by ORVs thus follows straighter flow paths, is more readily channelized, and less often decelerates and ponds than does runoff on natural hillslopes (Fig. 5-2b). The resultant effect of these changes is a considerable reduction in hydraulic resistance to overland flow. [Iverson (1980) gives a quantitative discussion of this phenomenon.] Frictional dissipation of flow energy is thus decreased following ORV use of desert hill slopes, and greater runoff energy is available to perform the work of sediment transport.

Channelization of runoff in vehicle tracks or trails has especially important implications for accelerated erosion. Many investigators (e.g., Kirkby and Kirkby, 1974) have noted that measurable erosion on natural desert hill slopes is often confined to areas of channelized flow, and our own field observations suggest that erosion on vehicle-used slopes is greatly facilitated by the channelizing effect of vehicle tracks. Such an effect can be anticipated from the observed proportionality of overland flow sediment transport capacity to runoff power raised to an exponent larger than one. If, for example, runoff occurring over the entire slope width is localized onto half that width, runoff power will vanish

(a)

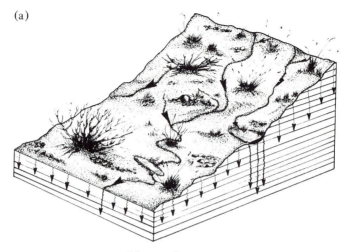

Unused

(b)

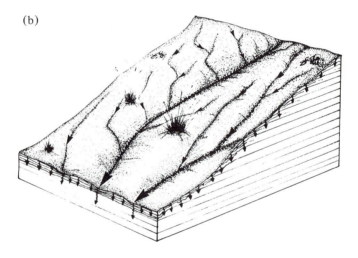

Used

Figure 5-2. Schematic diagrams illustrating changes in surface water behavior resulting from off-road vehicle use in arid environments. (a) A typical unused surface characterized by high infiltration capacities, considerable microtopographic roughness (leading to indirect runoff paths and intermittent ponding), and abundant surface stabilizers. (b) A typical vehicle-used surface characterized by disrupted, compacted soil (leading to lowered infiltration capacities), considerable microtopographic smoothness and tread ruts oriented up and down the slope (leading to direct runoff paths and increased sediment transport capacity), and few surface stabilizers. The net effect of these changes is almost inevitably accelerated erosion.

over the sector lacking flow, but will double over the sector receiving localized flow. Doubling runoff power will more than double sediment transport capacity, so total transport capacity averaged over the entire slope will increase. This effect can be magnified many times when runoff is channeled into a narrow vehicle track, leading to vastly increased erosion rates following ORV hill slope modification.

Effect of Slope Length

An additional effect of altered runoff hydraulics is that, following ORV use, runoff more rapidly builds up to maximum, steady-state discharges, which allows sediment to be scoured from longer portions of hill slopes. This effect is deduced from the observed reductions in hydraulic resistance to flow and soil infiltration capacity on ORV-used hill slopes through application of a kinematic wave overland flow model (Iverson, 1980). Theoretically, net erosion can occur along an entire slope length only when sediment transport capacity continuously increases downslope; this occurs only after runoff discharge reaches a steady state and increases continuously downslope. Substantial reduction by ORVs of the time required for runoff to attain maximum discharges may be of particular importance to accelerated erosion on long desert hill slopes. Buildup of flow to steady-state levels near the base of long, hydraulically rough slopes requires considerable time that often exceeds the duration of excess rainfall during desert storms. Net erosion may thus not occur there under natural conditions. Reduction of infiltration and surface roughness imparted by ORV use markedly increases the probability and magnitude of net erosion on these long slopes.

Debris Flows

Where severe surface disruption by ORVs is accompanied by a sharp subsurface soil permeability contrast, hill slope erosion may occur by way of debris flows. Such flows are particularly common on steep slopes having soils that are shallow, granular, and underlain by a layer than prevents free drainage of infiltrating rainwater (e.g., bedrock or a zone of ORV-compacted material). Under these conditions soils may readily saturate to an extent that leaves them unable to withstand shearing stresses in the downslope direction. A slurry or sludgelike mass of soil and water then flows downhill, leaving behind a conspicuous scar or channel from which material has been scoured and depositing a smooth lobe of material on the valley floor. We have generated small debris flows on steep (24°) ORV hillclimbs in Dove Springs Canyon by applying simulated rainfall at an intensity of 60 mm/hr for 18 min. Field evidence for larger debris flows on particularly steep ORV-used hill slopes with granular soil is abundant (cf. Wilshire, 1979), suggesting that this may be an important component of accelerated erosion in such areas.

Erosion Prediction

Because of the obvious importance of soil erosion, a great deal of work has been done in examining predictive relationships, especially for agricultural areas. The most widely used system of water erosion prediction at the present is the Universal Soil Loss Equation (USLE) (U.S. Department of Agriculture, 1975; Wischmeier, 1959):

$$E = (R)(K)(LS)(C)(P)$$

where E is soil loss, R is the rainfall erosivity factor, K is the soil erodibility factor, S is the slope factor, L is the slope-length factor, C is the cropping factor, and P is the management factor. Although not all researchers attempting erosion prediction have adopted the USLE, most agree on at least the general factors to be considered. The following discussion will center on the USLE as but one example of a variety of similar relationships.

The first component (R) expresses the importance of rainfall characteristics in affecting erosion rates. Multiplication of rainfall total kinetic energy (a function of rainfall volume and raindrop impact velocity) and rainfall intensity forms an energy-intensity (EI) parameter reflecting rainfall erosivity. Dragoun (1962) working in Nebraska, Johnson and Hanson (1976) in Idaho, and our own studies in the Mojave Desert confirm the predictive superiority of such an EI parameter over simpler expressions of total rainfall or rainfall intensity. Although one may derive an expression relating EI and erosion, actual prediction of soil loss over some period of time in the desert will be seriously hindered by the variability of precipitation. Jaeger (1957) reports annual precipitation variation from 0.3 to 250 mm for a single Mojave Desert station and Cooke and Warren (1973) cite a variation of 0 to 390 mm year^{-1} from the Atacama Desert of Chile. Considering this and the fact that many desert storms will produce no runoff under natural circumstances, accurate prediction of water erosion rates in arid areas for periods of less than several tens of years is very unlikely.

Slope length and slope factors (LS) express the effects of topography on erosion. Various workers have developed empirical and theoretical models using linear, power, and polynomial relationships to express the general tendency for soil erosion to increase with slope gradient (see, for example, reviews by Bryan, 1979; Smith and Wischmeier, 1957). Our own data indicate significant linear correlation ($r^2 = 0.64$) between slope and sediment yield on unused plots but weaker correlation on used plots ($r^2 = 0.48$). Thus, proposal of a single slope-erosion relationship to cover used as well as unused surfaces might be suspect. Our plot data do not address slope-length considerations explicitly, although consideration of surface characteristics suggests that following ORV modification erosion may occur over the full length of longer hill slopes.

The soil erodibility factor (K) in the USLE is a complex, empirically derived function of soil texture, composition, structure, and permeability. Evaluation of the average soil for our desert plot experiment (18% silt and clay, 63% sand, and 19% gravel) places it in or below the lowest U.S. Department of Agriculture designated erodibility class (U.S. Department of Agriculture, 1975) under natural conditions and only slightly higher (due to decreased permeability) under vehicle-used conditions. Since we have observed greatly increased erosion following ORV use, however, we must assume (1) the reason for erosion increases lies elsewhere than in permeability/infiltration changes and/or (2) the USLE assessment of the importance of soil infiltration capacity is inadequate in this case. The validity of the first point is supported by the significant changes in runoff hydraulics and particle detachment resulting from ORV modification of surface characteristics, and the second point clearly applies to at least the range of storms where modification of infiltration rates determines whether runoff will be generated. In either case, it is clear that standard application of USLE procedures does not adequately express the erosion increases resulting from ORV activity. As with the effects of slope, evidence suggests that the entire, interrelated erosional "system" behaves somewhat differently on ORV-used hill slopes than on natural equivalents.

A cropping or vegetative factor (C) is a common component in erosion prediction. Its significance in the desert, however, is less clear than in more humid environments. Cooke and Warren (1973) cite vegetation cover of 21% in some Arizona desert areas (our measurements of perennial crown coverage from study sites in the western Mojave vary from 2 to 10%) and conclude that the erosion controlling effects of vegetation are relatively small. The effect of ORV activity on vegetation reduction is explored in detail by Lathrop (Chapter 8), but the effects of reduced vegetation on erosion rates in desert areas are not thoroughly understood.

The parallels between agricultural and desert lands are sufficient to allow qualitative application of a USLE-type approach, but actual quantitative prediction of desert erosion is seriously hindered by several factors: (1) desert precipitation variability may preclude prediction of any but long-term erosion rates; (2) whereas erosion will almost certainly increase with increasing slope, the exact form of the relationship may be dependent on ORV use; (3) ORV modification of soil properties requires that a USLE-style approach consider used and unused soils as essentially two different types, thus hampering prediction of post-ORV erosion rates based on initial conditions. With large quantities of data and the addition of a "management" factor (P) to account for artificial disturbances, some of these difficulties might be alleviated, but at the present such a massive, empirical solution is not possible and a method for distinguishing the relative sensitivity of desert surfaces to ORV-induced erosion increases is needed.

One development of such a method is provided by the following prediction equations which were derived from regression analyses of data resulting from our rainfall simulation erosion plot studies in the western Mojave. The sediment yields predicted are only for the storm simulated. Thus, sediment yield predictions assigned to various areas are more useful in ranking the relative sensitivity of sites than in predicting actual soil loss. Because simulated rainfall was generally sufficient to produce runoff and erosion on both used and unused areas, however, these should be conservative estimates of relative sensitivity under storms less intense than those simulated. ORV effects on soils and slope variables are implicit in the analysis of each factor because only the increases in sediment yield following ORV use are predicted. The multiple linear regression equation:

$$S = 1.24(EI) + 57.9(\theta) + 34.6(D) - 1299$$

where S is the increase in sediment yield (gm), EI is the rainfall energy intensity (J mm/min^{-1}), θ is the slope angle (degrees), and D is the percentage of fine (less than 0.125-mm) particles on the undisturbed surface, has a correlation coefficient of 0.85. Alternatively, the equation:

$$S = 1.37(EI) - 197(C) + 476$$

where C is the infiltration rate (cm/hr) of the undisturbed plot, has a correlation coefficient of .91.

Analysis of these equations over the natural ranges of the various parameters indicates that the most important parameter by far is EI (total rainfall kinetic energy $\times$ average 20-min intensity). Even over the small, controlled range of EI for our simulated storms, this factor accounts for as much variation in predicted sediment yield as does the full naturally occurring range of any other parameter. Undisturbed infiltration rate and slope are of approximately equal importance in accounting for the variation of predicted sediment yield increases in these equations, identifying areas with low infiltration rates or steep slopes as most susceptible to ORV-induced erosion increases. Finally, the stabilizing influence of coarse surface particles is seen in the positive relationship between abundant surface fine particles and increased erosion.

Summary

It has been demonstrated repeatedly that off-road vehicle activity on arid landscapes nearly always results in greatly increased erosion. While some areas may react more severely than others, evidence strongly suggests that erosion will be significantly increased in virtually every case. Increased water erosion results principally from two ORV modifications of natural hill slopes: (1) ORVs compact and disrupt the soil, infiltration capacity is reduced, and both the frequency and intensity of runoff are increased; (2) ORV activity destroys or disperses surface stabilizers and creates relatively smooth trails (usually up and down slope), leading to greater concentration and erosive effectiveness of runoff. Quantification of the amount of ORV-induced erosion increase is difficult due to the variety of erosion measurement techniques, each producing slightly different results, that have been applied to both natural and disturbed areas, and to a dearth of knowledge of natural erosion rates in the desert. Prediction of surface sensitivity to erosion increase is possible, however, in relative terms. A large body of general erosion studies as well as the results of desert-specific experiments indicate areas of low-intensity, short-duration storms, of low slope and/or high infiltration capacity, and of abundant coarse surface material will be least sensitive.

It should be remembered that our analyses have addressed water erosion only. Where this type of erosion is minimized, others (e.g., wind erosion or direct mechanical erosion) may not be, and various deleterious effects on flora and fauna may still be significant.

Management Recommendations

Both physically and chemically, soils form the base of the desert ecosystem. Desert soil formation is generally so slow that on a human time scale the resource is essentially nonrenewable (Chapter 2). Thus, the importance of soil in land-use management decisions surpasses simple consideration of the esthetics of rutted landscapes. Unfortunately, the rates and processes of soil erosion by water in the desert and the long-term effects of ORV landscape modification are not precisely understood. Certain effects, however, are so dramatic that the management implications are clear even within the present state of knowledge. It seems certain that to prevent substantial loss of soil and consequent overall environmental deterioration every effort should be made to prevent extension of existing ORV use to any as yet unimpacted desert areas. Where it is decided that ORV use will occur, that use should be confined to small drainage basins where the off-site effect of the increased runoff and sediment can be in some measure controlled. The importance of avoiding steep slopes to limit erosion increases is well supported and the necessary data for planning are readily available. Likewise, it is apparent that use patterns that create trails and ruts running directly upslope greatly reduce the surface's resistance to erosion.

The positive relationship between high-intensity and long-duration rainstorms and sensitivity to ORV-induced erosion is also solid; however, detailed data for area classification are sorely lacking. That the Needles area appeared the most likely to produce runoff is significant, for it suggests that the eastern Mojave may receive more severe storms than the west. This general pattern is documented by Huning (1978), who notes that the bulk of eastern Mojave precipitation falls as high-intensity summer thunderstorms as opposed to less intense winter rains in the west. The effect of the eastern thunderstorms is "less infiltration and greater runoff" (Huning, 1978, p. 83). Such generalization may not be very useful from a planning perspective, but considerable refinement of this pattern may be possible through acquisition of unpublished local weather records. Especially important in erosion analysis is correlation of measured rainfall intensities to runoff occurrence. Such observations are likely much more common in original weather logs and journals than in published summary data.

Additional data acquisition is also necessary to classify soil sensitivities. Soil mapping in the Mojave Desert south of Barstow (U.S. Department of Agriculture, 1970) demonstrates the representativeness of the soils of our rainfall simulation experiments, and studies by Eckert et al. (1979) support out assignment of low relative sensitivity to soils with abundant surface gravel. Much work remains, however, in desert-wide inventories of soil infiltration capacity, surface characteristics, and soil textures.

Clearly, the desert is extremely sensitive to accelerated erosion due to ORV use. We are just beginning to understand the rates and processes of that erosion and many aspects of the problem remain to be thoroughly explored. Coupled with unanswered questions about long-term recreational demands are serious doubts about the desert's ability to sustain ORV use. The decision to defer recreational demands can be made many times, the decision to proceed with ORV use only once.

References

Bryan, R. B. 1979. The influence of slope angle on soil entrainment by sheet-wash and rainsplash. Earth Surf. Proc. 4:43–58.

Carrarra, P. E., and T. R. Carroll. 1979. The determination of erosion rates from exposed tree roots in the Piceance Basin, Colorado. Earth Surf. Proc. 4: 307–318.

Cooke, R. U., and A. Warren. 1973. Geomorphology in Deserts. University of California Press, Berkeley, California, 374 pp.

Dragoun, F. J. 1962. Rainfall energy as related to sediment yield. J. Geophys. Res. 67:1495–1501.

Eckert, R. E., Jr., M. K. Wood, W. H. Blackburn, and F. F. Peterson. 1979. Impacts of off-road vehicles on infiltration and sediment production of two desert soils. J. Range Management 32:394–397.

Hadley, R. F., and S. A. Schumm. 1961. Hydrology of the Upper Cheyenne River Basin. U.S. Geological Survey Water-Supply Paper 1531, 198 pp.

Hinckley, B. S. 1980. Factors affecting off-road vehicle erosion acceleration in the Mojave Desert, California. Unpublished M.S. thesis, Department of Applied Earth Sciences, Stanford University, Stanford, California, 78 pp.

Huning, J. R. 1978. A characterization of the climate of the California desert. Bureau of Land Management, Riverside, California, CA-060-C17-2812, 220 pp.

Iverson, R. M. 1980. Processes of accelerated pluvial erosion on desert hillslopes modified by vehicular traffic. Earth Surf. Proc. 5:369–388.

Iverson, R. M., B. S. Hinckley, R. H. Webb, and B. Hallet. 1981. Physical effects of vehicular disturbances on arid landscapes. Science 212:915–917.

Jaeger, E. C. 1957. The North American Deserts. Stanford University Press, Stanford, California, 308 pp.

Johnson, C. W., and C. L. Hanson. 1976. Sediment sources and yields from Sagebrush Rangeland Watershed. In: Proceedings of the Third Federal Inter-Agency Sedimentation Conference. Water Resources Council, Sedimentation Committee (PB-245-100), pp. 1-71 to 1-80.

Kilinc, M., and E. V. Richardson. 1973. Mechanics of soil erosion from overland flow generated by simulated rainfall. Hydrology Papers, No. 63, Colorado State University, Fort Collins, Colorado, 54 pp.

Kirkby, A. V. T., and M. J. Kirkby. 1974. Surface wash at the semi-arid break in slope. Z. Geomorphol. Suppl. 21:1521–2176.

LaMarche, V. C. 1968. Rates of slope degradation as determined from botanical evidence, White Mountains, California. U.S. Geological Survey Professional Paper 352-I, 36 pp.

Langbein, W. B., and S. A. Schumm. 1958. Yield of sediment in relation to mean annual precipitation. Am. Geophys. Union Trans. 39:1076–1084.

Leopold, L. B., W. W. Emett, and R. M. Myrick. 1966. Channel and hillslope processes in a semi-arid areas, New Mexico. U.S. Geological Survey Professional Paper 352-G, 60 pp.

Morgan, R. R. C. 1978. Field studies of rainsplash erosion. Earth Surf. Proc. 3: 295–299.

Moss, A. J., and P. H. Walker. 1978. Particle transport by continental water flows in relation to erosion, deposition, soils, and human activities. Sediment. Geol. 20:81–139.

Moss, A. J., P. E. Walker, and J. Hutka. 1979. Raindrop-stimulated transportation in shallow water flows: an experimental study. Sediment. Geol. 22: 165–184.

National Oceanic and Atmospheric Administration. 1973–1978. Hourly precipitation data for California. Environmental Data and Information Service, National Oceanic and Atmospheric Administration, U.S. Department of Commerce, Washington, D.C.

Piest, R. F., and Miller, C. R. 1975. Sediment sources and sediment yields. In: V. A. Vanoni (Ed.), Sedimentation Engineering. American Society of Civil Engineers, New York, pp. 437–487.

Schumm, S. A. 1963. The disparity between present rates of denudation and orogeny. U.S. Geological Survey Professional Paper 454-H, 13 pp.

Smith, D. D., and W. H. Wischmeier. 1957. Factors affecting sheet and rill erosion. Trans. Am. Geophys. Union 38(6):889–896.

Snyder, C. T., D. G. Frickel, R. F. Hadley, and R. F. Miller. 1976. Effects of off-road vehicle use on the hydrology and landscape of arid environments in central and southern California. U.S. Geological Survey Water Resources Investigations 76-99, 27 pp.

Stull, R., S. Shipley, E. Hovanitz, S. Thompson, and K. Hovanitz. 1979. Effects of offroad vehicles in Ballinger Canyon, California. Geology 7:19–21.

U.S. Department of Agriculture. 1964. Summary of Reservoir Sediment Deposition Surveys Made in the United States Through 1960. Miscellaneous Publication No. 964, 61 pp.

U.S. Department of Agriculture. 1970. Report and General Soil Map of the Southwestern Desert Area of San Bernardino County, California. Soil Conservation Service and Mojave Desert Soil Conservation District, U.S. Department of Agriculture, 87 pp.

U.S. Department of Agriculture. 1975. Guides for Erosion and Sediment Control in California. Soil Conservation Service, U.S. Department of Agriculture, Davis, California, 105 pp.

Webb, R. H., H. C. Ragland, W. H. Godwin, and D. Jenkins. 1978. Environmental effects of soil property changes with off-road vehicle use. Environ. Management 2(3):219–233.

Wilshire, H. G., and J. K. Nakata. 1977. Erosion off the road. Geotimes 22(7): 27.

Wilshire, H. G. 1979. Study of 9 sites used by off-road vehicles that illustrate land modifications. U.S. Geological Survey Open-File Report 77-601, 26 pp.

Wischmeier, W. J. 1959. A rainfall erosion index for a universal soil loss equation. Soil Sci. Soc. Am. Proc. 23:246–249.

Young, R. A., and J. L. Wiersma. 1973. The role of rainfall impact in soil detachment and transport. Water Resources Res. 9:1629–1636.

6

Accelerated Wind Erosion and Prediction of Rates[1]

Dale A. Gillette and John Adams

Introduction

When vulnerability of the soil to wind erosion is coupled with high surface winds, large-scale damage to agriculture, transportation, and human habitation can result (for example McCauley et al., 1980; Wilshire et al., 1980). The effects of off-road vehicles (ORVs) on areas of arid or semiarid soils may continue long after the ORV event if some physical property of the soil is altered so that natural resistence to damage by wind and rainfall is decreased. Soils disturbed by ORVs may be subject to wind erosion where they were resistent before disturbance (Gillette et al., 1980). Documentation of wind erosion events which occurred after the disturbance of arid and semiarid land is reported by Nakata et al. (1976) and by Wilshire (1980).

Theoretical Considerations

The rate at which a soil erodes for a given wind speed depends on the physical properties of the soil. It is convenient to consider the erosion of soil as a function of wind speed in terms of threshold velocity u_t (the minimum velocity at which erosion takes place) and the rate of erosion once the threshold velocity is exceeded. Bagnold (1941) showed for desert sands and Chepil and Woodruff

[1] The views and conclusions contained in this chapter are based on the authors' studies or experiences and do not necessarily represent the official viewpoint or policy of any U.S. government agency.

(1963) showed for farm fields that the total movement of soil expressed in terms of flux q through an area perpendicular to the wind and to the soil and having unit width but infinite height is proportional to the cube of the friction velocity. The friction velocity, u_*, may be defined as a parameter in the equation for neutral wind profiles near the ground,

$$u_2 - u_1 = u_*/k \ln (z_2/z_1) \tag{6-1}$$

where u_2 and u_1 are near wind speeds at the heights z_2 and z_1 in the constant flux layer and k is von Karman's constant. The friction velocity is related linearly to wind speed close to the ground in periods of high wind so that the rate of erosion is also roughly proportional to the third power of the wind speed above threshold velocity. Gillette (1977) measured dust production from farm fields in west Texas and found for the sandy soils of this area that total soil horizontal flux, q was roughly expressed as

$$q = 4 \times 10^{-7} u_*(u_* - u_{*_t}) \tag{6-2}$$

where q is expressed in g cm-sec^{-1}, u_* is the friction velocity in cm sec^{-1}, and $u_{*_t} = 25$ cm sec^{-1}, the mean threshold velocity for the loose, sandy soils tested.

The production of fine particles smaller than 0.02 mm can be expressed as a flux, F_a, through a surface of unit area parallel to the ground (Fig. 6-1). The increase with wind speed for this flux was also proportional to u_*^3 for sandy soils but was found to increase at an even greater rate for a soil having a loamy-sand texture. Thus fine particle production may increase with wind speed at a greater rate than soil movement as a whole, indicating that a breakage of soil aggregates into finer particles occurs with increasing wind speed (Gillette and Walker, 1977). Figure 6-1 shows different ratios for fine particle production compared to total soil movement for differing soil textures.

Chepil and Woodruff (1959) have shown that erodibility of soil increases with the weight fraction of soil occurring in aggregates smaller than 0.84 mm. Chepil (1956) showed soil moisture is effective in reducing wind erosion only if it exceeds the -15 bar soil moisture, and soil movement is roughly inversely proportional to the ridge roughness, expressed as a mean depth of furrows, and vegetative residue, expressed as a density of organic material on the soil surface (Chepil and Woodruff, 1959).

Experimental Results

Gillette et al. (1980) measured threshold velocities for desert soils in disturbed and undisturbed states along with many descriptors of the physical condition of the soil. Soil was disturbed by driving a three-quarter ton pickup truck once over the soil. The tires were of knobby tread design and the truck was accelerated, the result being that the surface material was loosened, mixed, and displaced. The soil property having the highest correlation with the threshold velocities that were measured is the mode of the dry-aggregate size distribution, or the size of the aggregate found most frequently.

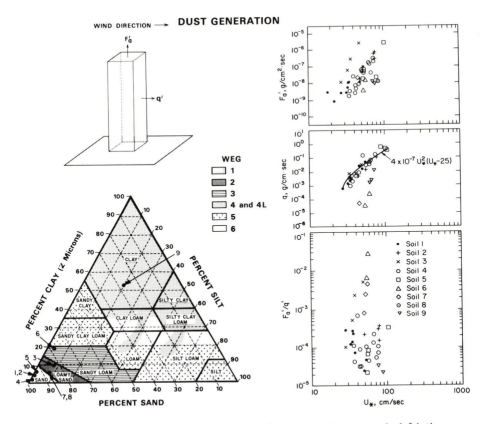

Figure 6-1. Textures of sample soils; total soil movement versus wind friction velocity; vertical flux of particles smaller than 0.02 mm versus wind friction velocity; ratio of vertical flux of particles smaller than 0.02 mm to total soil movement per unit area per time versus wind friction velocity. Wind erosion groups are denoted WEG (Lyles, 1976; figure after Gillette, 1977).

For all tests in which a threshold velocity was reached (i.e., all tests except undisturbed soil of clay content $>20\%$)

$$u_{*_t} = 64 + 0.0055\,d_M \quad r^2 = 0.41,\ \text{d.f.} = 63 \qquad (6\text{-}3)$$

where u_{*_t} is the threshold friction velocity, r is the correlation coefficient, d.f. is the degrees of freedom, and d_M is the mode of the solids dry-aggregate size distribution in microns.

The threshold friction velocity u_{*_t} can be expressed for undisturbed soils as

$$u_{*_t} > 200 \text{ cm sec}^{-1} \text{ for } c > 20\%$$

$$u_{*_t} = 390 - 3.3s \quad r^2 = 0.52,\ \text{d.f.} = 25,\ \text{for } c < 20\% \qquad (6\text{-}4)$$

where c is the percentage of clay-size particles and s is the percentage of sand-size particles in the soil.

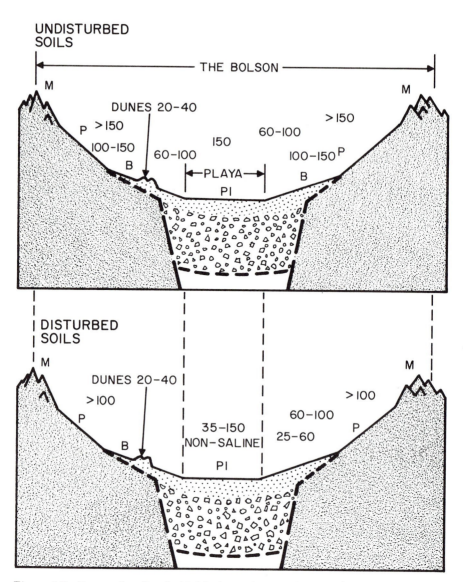

Figure 6-2. Ranges for threshold friction velocities (cm sec^{-1}) superimposed on a generalized cross section of basin and range structure (after Reeves, 1977) to show limits of the bolson and intermontane basin. M, mountains; P, pediment; B, bajada; Pl, playa. Vertical scale greatly exaggerated. Threshold velocity data from Gillette et al. (1980).

For soils which have been disturbed, u_{*_t} can be expressed as

$$20 < u_{*_t} < 60 \text{ cm sec}^{-1}, s > 90\%$$

$$u_{*_t} = 14.5 + 0.0071 d_M + 1.59 c_c \quad s < 90\% \quad r^2 = 0.59, \text{d.f.} = 12 \quad (6\text{-}5)$$

where c_c is the colloidal clay content taken as the percentage of soil particles smaller than 0.5 μm.

The relationships for u_{*_t} of undisturbed soils (Equations 6-4) demonstrates that the threshold velocities of undisturbed soils depend on soil texture, with fine-textured soils having high threshold velocities and sandy soils having lower threshold velocities. The relationships for disturbed soils (Equation 6-5) show that the threshold velocities for finer pulverized soils are lower, while coarser pulverized soils having higher fine-clay content have larger threshold velocities. The above measurements may be related to arid region geomorphology as shown in Figure 6-2. Playas and pediments are least affected by ORV disturbances while alluvial, bajada, and desert flats are most affected by ORV disturbance in lowering the threshold velocities. The threshold friction velocity of active dunes are hardly affected by ORV disturbance.

With respect to Clements' et al. (1957) comparison of areas of desert surface types (Table 6-1), it follows that the soils of the southwestern United States are highly susceptible to wind erosion following ORV disturbance as a whole, while other deserts are less susceptible to ORV-induced accelerated wind erosion. By subtracting areas of desert mountains, volcanic cones and fields, and bedrock fields from the areas for desert surface types in Table 6-1, the percentage of non-rock surfaces were found for the southwestern United States, Sahara, Libyan, and Arabian Deserts. The percentage of these areas of fans, bajadas, and flats, of dunes, and of playas was found and is shown in Table 6-2. As is shown, the dominant surface type in the southwestern United States deserts is flats, fans, and bajadas while sand dunes predominate in the other deserts.

Table 6-1. Comparison of Desert Surface Types in Some of the World's Deserts[a]

Surface type	Southwestern U.S.	Sahara Desert	Libyan Desert	Arabian Desert
Playas	1.1	1	1	1
Bedrock fields (incl. hammadas)	0.7	10	6	1
Desert flats	20.5	10	18	16
Regions bordering through-flowing rivers	1.2	1	3	1
Fans and bajadas	31.4	1	1	4
Dunes	0.6	28	22	26
Dry washes	3.6	1	1	1
Badlands and subdued badlands	2.6	2	8	1
Volcanic cones and fields	0.2	3	1	2
Desert mountains	38.1	43	39	47
Total	100.0	100.0	100.0	100.0

[a]From Clement et al. (1957).

Table 6-2. Percentage of Total Desert Surface Areas Considered as Wind-Erodible Soil (from Table 6-1)

	Southwestern U.S.	Sahara Desert	Libyan Desert	Arabian Desert
Fans, flats, bajadas	84	25	35	40
Dunes	1	64	41	52
Playas	2	2	2	2

Expected Conditions of Soils Which Are Vulnerable to ORV Disturbance

Since the largest damage to arid soils is expected to occur in alluvial fans, bajadas, and desert flats, the problem of wind erosion damage can be outlined as follows:

1. The texture of the soil is likely to be sandy.
2. The total soil movement is a function of the wind velocity. As seen in the work of Gillette (1977), this function should be proportional to u_*^3 which was found for all sand-textured soils tested.
3. Dust production is also a direct function of wind speed, with F_A proportional to u_*^3 (Gillette, 1977).
4. Sandy soils require a relatively small distance for wind erosion to come to an equilibrium horizontal mass flux q. This distance called the fetch, is dependent on the looseness of the sandy soil and the dimension of the disturbance of the parallel to the wind direction.
5. The effect of ridge roughness and vegetative residue in reducing wind erosion are expected to be minimal in deserts.
6. During most of the year soil moisture is less than that at -15 bars, which indicates that soil moisture will have little effect on reducing wind erosion (Chepil, 1956).
7. The size and distribution of vegetation are very important to wind erosion estimates since vegetation acts to absorb some of the wind stress which induces movement of soil particles. On desert flats, fans, and bajadas, this vegetation is quite variable and probably is very important in determining wind erosion intensity. ORV pit areas, where ORV events are staged and vehicles are parked, are typically almost denuded.
8. In summary, the characteristics which a soil vulnerable to wind erosion after ORV disturbances would possess are a sandy texture, very low moisture content, flat aspect, and surface almost devoid of vegetative residue. The major variables controlling the amount of soil movement would seem to be the coverage and height of vegetation and length of the ORV disturbance parallel to the wind direction.

Calculation of Wind Erosion Rates

A brief outline of the method used to calculate wind erosion of soils was given by Gillette (1977). The method requires computation of "wind tunnel erodibility" x used as a correction factor for Equation (6-2) and a correction of the friction velocity u_* for soil moisture content. An equation for x is given by Chepil and Woodruff (1959) as

$$x = 1500\, I/(RV)^{1.26} \tag{6-6}$$

where R is ridge roughness (average depth of furrows in cm), V is density of vegetative residue in kg ha^{-1}, and I is an erodibility index based on the percentage of soil mass in aggregates greater than 0.84 mm (given in Table 6-3). The momentum flux u_*^2 was corrected for the erosion-inhibiting effects of moisture content according to the relation of Chepil (1956)

$$u_*^2 = (u_*')^2 - \frac{6}{\rho}\left(\frac{w}{w'}\right)^2 \tag{6-7}$$

where u_*' is the uncorrected friction velocity (cm sec^{-1}), ρ is the density of air (g cm^{-3}), w is the amount of water held by the soil, and w' is the amount of water by the same soil at -15 bars pressure.

The horizontal mass flux (in g cm-sec^{-1}) can be calculated with the equation

$$q = 0.16LX/5030\,(u_*/78)^3, \quad \text{for } LX/5030 \leqslant 1$$
$$q = 0.16\,(u_*/78)^3, \quad \text{for } LX/5030 > 1 \tag{6-10}$$

where L is the length of exposed soil parallel to the wind (m) and u_* is the corrected friction velocity (cm sec^{-1}). This formula was derived from the author's data and from Chepil's work on the effect of field length on erosion (Chepil, 1957). Alternatively, the amount of wind erosion could be predicted using data shown in Figure 6-1 since many of the conditions for ORV disturbed desert soils are similar to the soils for which Figure 6-1 was constructed.

Expected Yearly Wind Erosion

Wind erosion predictions for individual events are very difficult because of changing wind speed and direction. A more useful quantity to land-use planners would be the amount of wind erosion predicted on an annual basis. For a given soil we may calculate the annual expected wind erosion, E, by

$$E = \int_{u_{*_t}}^{\infty} q(u_*)f(u_*)du_* \tag{6-11}$$

where $q(u_*)$ is wind erosion as a function of wind friction velocity, $f(u_*)$ is the probability density function of u_*, and u_{*_t} is the threshold friction velocity of the soil.

Table 6-3. Soil Erodibility Index I Based on Percentage of Soil Fractions Greater than 0.84 mm in Diameter as Determined by Dry Sieving[a]

Percentage of soil fractions greater than 0.84 mm:

Tens	Units									
	9	8	7	6	5	4	3	2	1	0
9										0.02
8	0.02	0.03	0.03	0.04	0.05	0.06	0.07	0.08	0.09	0.10
7	0.12	0.14	0.16	0.20	0.25	0.30	0.35	0.40	9.45	0.5
6	0.55	0.60	0.65	0.70	0.75	0.80	0.85	0.90	0.95	1.0
5	1.1	1.2	1.3	1.4	1.6	1.8	2.0	2.2	2.5	2.8
4	3.1	3.4	3.7	4.0	4.3	4.9	4.9	5.2	5.6	6.0
3	6.5	7.0	7.5	8.0	8.5	9.0	9.5	10.5	11.0	12.0
2	13	14	15	16	17	18	19	20	21	23
1	25	27	30	33	36	39	43	17	51	55
0	70	80	100	120	150	175	280	450	1000	—

[a]From Chepil and Woodruff, 1959.

For desert fans, flats, and bajadas, the major change to soils by ORV disturbance is the lowering of the threshold velocity. For the sake of an illustration, a soil is chosen which has no vegetation and whose distance of disturbance parallel to the wind is sufficient to give equilibrium erosion. Then, approximately

$$E = K \int_{u_t}^{\infty} u^3 \, f(u) du \qquad (6\text{-}12)$$

where K is a constant and u is the wind speed. The form for $f(u)$ was found by plotting wind data for various locations in the Mojave Desert. Figure 6-3 shows two cumulative probability distribution plots, one apparently normally distributed (from China Lake, California) and one apparently log-normally distributed (from Desert Center, California).

The equation for E was evaluated with arbitrary value for K using the wind data for Desert Center, California. The results shown in Figure 6-4 show that if a threshold wind speed is lowered below 65 km hr^{-1} that a dramatic increase of wind erosion would be expected until the surface regained equilibrium conditions either by wetting and drying cycles or by deflation of soil to a stable layer. Since the threshold velocities for desert flats, fans, and bajadas are in general more than 65 km hr^{-1}, the wind erosion from these landforms would be expected to increase dramatically following disturbance. Playa soils would have much smaller increases in wind erosion due to higher values than 55 km hr^{-1} for threshold velocities of disturbed playa soils. Dune soils are highly erodible for both disturbed and undisturbed states (unless the dunes are stabilized by vegetation) and therefore do not have greatly increased erosion rates following disturbance.

Length of Time the Desert Surface is Vulnerable to Wind Erosion

The length of time that the surface will be vulnerable to wind erosion depends on the time needed to accomplish the following:

1. Erode the loose soil away so that the new surface is protected by aggregated subsurface soil or so that sufficient numbers of nonerodible elements such as cobbles are exposed at the soil surface (see Chapter 5).
2. Reform a surface crust from the loose material (see Chapter 3). This can happen if clay or water-soluble salts are present in the loose material in sufficient quantity and sufficient moisture to wet the loose material is added.

Thus, the length of time required for surface restoration is highly dependent upon the composition of the soil, wind events following the disturbance of the soil, and frequency of rainfall. The permanent loss of material from a desert soil to large-scale transport is of fine-clay material and low-density organic material. Since these two components of the soil have been associated with agricultural productivity, one would assume a loss of the potential plant-nuturing capacity of the soil due to wind erosion.

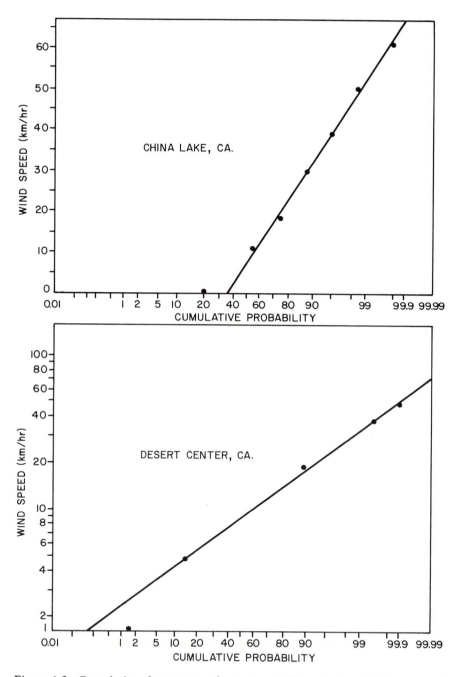

Figure 6-3. Cumulative frequency of winds at China Lake, California, and Desert Center, California. Note that the distribution for China Lake is roughly normal and the distribution for Desert Center is roughly log normal.

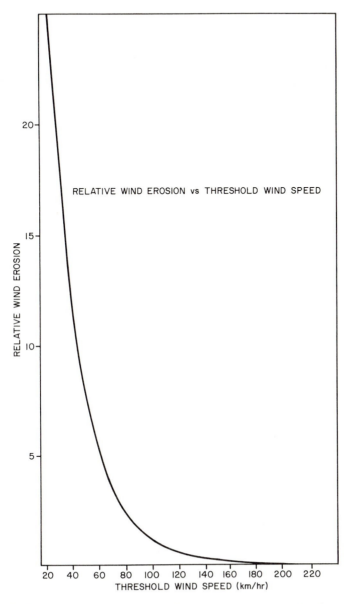

Figure 6-4. Relative wind erosion vs. threshold velocity for the Desert Center wind data. This is a plot of E vs. threshold wind speed, u_t (see text).

Conclusions and Management Recommendations

Because of the major lowering of the threshold velocity for desert flats, fans, and bajadas into the range of moderately frequent winds, ORV disturbances act to increase dramatically wind erosion on these desert land forms. In the American southwest these desert landforms are predominant, in contrast with other deserts, such as the Sahara, where dunes cover larger areas. Wind erosion increases on sand dunes and on playas are less dramatic due to the relatively high threshold velocities for disturbed playa soils and low threshold velocities for undisturbed dune soils.

Thus a management recommendation to reduce wind erosion effects would be to discourage ORV use on alluvial fans, bajadas, and desert flats in favor of dune areas and playas. Since the soils of individual playas may become distintegrated if a great amount of physical grinding by the wheels of ORVs is applied, whereas dune soils will be much less affected, dune areas of the desert would be preferred to playas when the management objective is to reduce the amount of wind erosion caused by ORV use. Failure to make reduction of wind erosion a management goal will lead to larger areas of the desert being subjected to such erosion. However, in many areas of ORV activity, wind erosion will be limited by short erosion fetches or coarse surface materials. Greater amounts of wind erosion will occur from disturbed areas with relatively large dimensions, such as pit areas, campsites, or roads or larger trails parallel to the direction of strong winds.

References

Bagnold, R. A. 1941. The Physics of Blown Sand and Desert Dunes. Methuen, London, 265 pp.

Chepil, W. S. 1956. Influence of moisture on erodibility of soil by wind. Soil Sci. Soc. Am. Proc. 20:288–292.

Chepil, W. S. 1957. Width of field strips to control wind erosion. Tech. Bull. 92, Kansas State College of Agriculture and Applied Science, Manhattan, Kansas, 16 pp.

Chepil, W. S., and N. P. Woodruff. 1959. Estimations of Wind Erodibility of Farm Fields. Production Research, Report No. 25, U.S. Department of Agriculture, 21 pp.

Chepil, W. S., and N. P. Woodruff. 1963. The physics of wind erosion and its control. In: A. G. Norman (Ed.), Advances in Agronomy, Vol. 15. Academic Press, New York, 301 pp.

Clements, T., T. H. Merriam, R. O. Stone, J. L. Eimann, and H. L. Reade. 1957. A Study of Desert Surface Conditions. Tech. Report EP-53, Quartermaster Research and Development Command, U.S. Army Natick Laboratories, Natick, Massachusetts, 111 pp.

Cooke, R. U., and A. Warren. 1973. Geomorphology in Deserts. University of California Press, Berkeley and Los Angeles, California, 374 pp.

Doehring, D. O. 1980. Geomorphology in arid regions. Binghampton Symposia in Geomorphology. International Ser. No. 8. Allen Unwin., Winchester, Maine, 276 pp.

Gillette, D. A. 1977. Fine particulate emissions due to wind erosion. Trans. Am. Soc. Agric. Engr. 20:890–897.

Gillette, D. A., and T. R. Walker. 1977. Characteristics of airborne particles produced by wind erosion of sandy soil. High plains of west Texas. Soil Sci. 123: 97–110.

Gillette, D. A., J. Adams, A. Endo, D. Smith, and R. Kihl. 1980. Threshold velocities for input of soil particles into the air by desert soils. J. Geophys. Res. 85:5621–5630.

Lyles, L. 1976. Wind erosion: Processes and effect on soil productivity. Paper 76-2016 presented at the Annual Meeting of the American Society of Agricultural Engineers, June 27, 1976, Lincoln, Nebraska.

McCauley, J. F., C. S. Breed, M. Grolier, and D. Mackinnon. 1980. The U.S. duststorm of February, 1977. In: T. L. Péwé (Ed.), Desert Dust: Origin, Characteristics, and Effect on Man. Geological Society of America Special Paper 186, 123–147.

Nakata, J. K., H. Wilshire, and G. Barnes. 1976. Origin of Majove Desert dust plumes photographed from space. Geology 4:644–648.

Reeves, C. C., Jr. 1977. Intermontane basins of the arid western United States. In: D. O. Doehring (Ed.), Geomorphology in Arid Regions. Proceedings of the Eighth Annual Geomorphology Symposium, State University of New York, Binghamton, New York, pp. 7–25.

Wilshire, H. G. 1980. Human causes of accelerated wind erosion in California's deserts. In: D. R. Coates and J. D. Vitek (Eds.), Thresholds in Geomorphology. George Allen and Unwin Ltd., London, pp. 415–533.

Wilshire, H. G., J. K. Nakata, and B. Hallet. 1980. Field observations of the December, 1977 Windstorm, San Joaquin Valley, California. In: T. L. Péwé (Ed.), Desert Dust: Origin, Characteristics, and Effect on Man. Geological Society of American Special Paper 186, 233–251.

PART II

Biological Effects of Off-Road Vehicle Use

7
Plant Ecology in Deserts: An Overview[1]

Earl W. Lathrop and Peter G. Rowlands

Introduction

> The love of nature is after all an acquired taste. One begins by admiring the Hudson-River landscape and ends by loving the desolation of the Sahara. (Van Dyke, 1901)

The vulnerability of desert vegetation to off-road vehicle (ORV) impacts, and in particular, the probable longevity of these impacts, is well established for the southwestern deserts of North America. Because of the many similarities of the world's deserts to those of the United States, consideration of the vegetation of the world's deserts is also important to management of ORVs. The objective of this chapter is to give the reader an overview of some of the more important aspects of the vegetation ecology and dynamics of the world's deserts. The emphasis is on the deserts of the southwestern United States since the authors are most familar with this region in both a scientific and practical sense. However, we have no reason to believe that generalizations and concepts gleaned largely from studies of the vegetation of North American deserts will not be applicable to the arid and semiarid regions of other continents, especially when the vegetation types can be considered "matched" (Pielou, 1979) or homologous. In areas with similar climates, similar life forms tend to dominate in the natural vegetation even though such areas may be floristically distinct (Mueller-Dombois and Ellenberg, 1974). The physical communalities among the deserts

---

[1] The views and conclusions contained in this chapter are based on the authors' studies and experiences and do not necessarily represent the official viewpoint or policy of any U.S. government agency.

of the world, including those associated with soils, geomorphology, and climate as described elsewhere in this volume, together with the vegetational, in the sense of life form, and structural/functional development would lead one to believe that the responses of desert vegetation to perturbations, for example, those created by motorized vehicles, will follow similar patterns.

The chapter is divided into three parts. The first part deals with the physical and vegetational settings of the world's deserts, and the second deals with productivity and vegetation dynamics. The decision to concentrate on productivity (especially changes in productivity in time and space) is based on the assumption that productivity as a variable is the best indicator of plant response to changes in the environment, and that a basic understanding of the dynamics of plant productivity in deserts is essential to assess the impacts on vegetation due to both natural and anthropogenic factors. According to Whittaker (1975, p. 197A), productivity may be the single most significant attribute of natural communities. It is appropriate to consider its magnitude and variability in different desert communities since all biological activity (including human) within the world's deserts is dependent upon the production of green plants. Moreover, all vegetational changes in plant assemblages, whether subtle or drastic, relative or absolute, are a manifestation of changes in the net production of individual plant species relative to others. Such changes occur within varying time scales, including those associated with long-term geologic change, succession (as defined in Miles, 1979), revegetation, and recolonization, and short-term fluctuations within plant assemblages where no directional changes in vegetation are evident within a defined region of time. Vegetational changes are discussed in a section on vegetation dynamics; ORV effects are described as an example of antropogenic factors. Some ideas on the nature of desert successional phenomena are described. Finally, some concluding remarks are made concerning the possible effects and management problems created by ORVs in arid regions.

Other valuable reviews of desert vegetation and vegetation dynamics are presented in Johnson (1968), McCleary (1968), Walter (1973), Whittaker (1975), McGinnies et al. (1968) and Chapters 8, 13, 14, 15, 16, and 17, to which the reader is referred for additional information.

Physical Setting

Distribution and Climate

One-fifth of the Earth's surface is made up of desert which supports less than 4% of the world's population. Each of the continental landmasses, including the interior of Australia, contains arid or semiarid regions. The largest of these areas occurs in the Eurasian-Palearctic region which includes the Sahara and deserts of Asia Minor, India, Tibet, China, and Mongolia; a huge region which stretches from the west coast of Africa to central China. Coastal deserts occur in Peru and Chile; a 100-km-wide band of land adjacent to the Pacific Ocean which receives little or no rainfall, and parts of southern Africa. The major deserts of North

America are the Mojave, Sonoran, and Great Basin of the southwestern United States and Chihuahuan Deserts of Mexico. They are for the most part desertic but in general receive much more precipitation than the majority of the world's deserts (Fig. 7-1 and 7-2).

Although often associated in the popular mind with great heat and accumulation of sand, deserts are more properly defined as regions of aridity (Axelrod, 1964). "True" deserts result from a deficiency in the amount of precipitation received relative to water loss by evaporation (Logan, 1968; Major, 1977). Arid climates are products primarily of Subtropical High Pressure Belts that lie between the Westerlies on the poleward side and by the Trade Winds (Easterlies) on the equatorial side. In these belts air masses are descending and dry so that rainfall is minimal, relative humidity is low, and insolation is intense owing to the sparsity of clouds (Daubenmire, 1978). Topography can also be a causal factor for a region of aridity. Mountains may act as barriers, cutting off moisture-laden clouds that otherwise might sweep across and deposit rain in the deserts. Such areas are rain-shadow deserts (Logan, 1968). A cold ocean current can have the same effect by robbing rain from clouds. The Atacama Desert off the coast of Peru, the Namib of South Africa, and the coastal portion of western Baja California are examples of what Logan (1968) has termed cool coastal deserts: those deserts are cool coastal phases of the subtropical deserts caused by the Subtropical High Pressure Belts.

Some deserts result from a merging of two or more of the above types; the Mojave Desert, for example, receives little winter precipitation because of its rain-shadow position in the lee of the Sierras and Transverse Ranges and little summer precipitation because of the dominance of the Subtropical High (Axelrod, 1964). Classification of the climates of deserts, based on causes of their aridity, is shown in Table 7-1 (Logan, 1968).

The most obvious common characteristic of all the desert regions is aridity, which is generally defined by geographers as an annual rainfall of 250 to 380 mm or less (Leopold, 1961; McGinnies et al., 1968). Some rain falls on all desert lands, though it might not fall every year. Some spots in Baja California go rainless for 4 or 5 years in a row, and the hamlet of Dakhla in the Sahara went 11 years without a trace of rain, though its average is 130 mm per year. Such an average is often the product of rare, unpredictable downpours (Leopold, 1961). In the deserts of low and middle latitudes, there are nevertheless well-defined winter and summer seasons attended by relative wetness and dryness, coolness and heat. In areas with the Mediterranean type of climate—dry summers and moist, mild winters, such as southern California and North Africa—the rains come in winter. In the typical continental climate of central Mexico, the precipitation comes in the form of summer thundershowers (Leopold, 1961).

Thermally, the deserts of the world may be divided into:

1. Warm-winter deserts, such as the Sahara and Sonoran
2. Cool-winter deserts, represented by the Great Basin and Gobi Deserts
3. Cool-coastal deserts, as the Namib and western Baja California (after Logan, 1964).

Figure 7-1. The major deserts of North and South America.

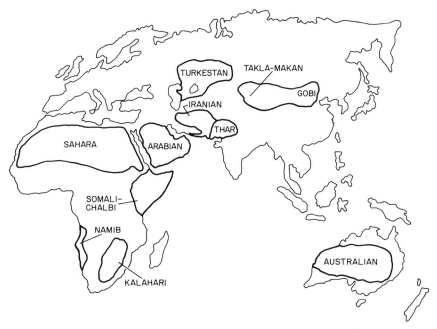

Figure 7-2. The major deserts of Eurasia and Australia.

Table 7-1. Climatic Classification of the World's Deserts[a]

Desert	Climatic type			
	Subtropical	Cool coastal	Rain shadow	Continental interior
Mojave	X (summer)		X (winter)	X (in part)
Sonoran	X		X (in part)	
Great Basin			X (in part)	X (in part)
Chihuahuan	X			
Kalahari	X			
Namib		X		
Sahara	X			
Somali-Chalbi	X			
Arabian	X			
Iranian				X
Thar	X			
Turkestan				X
Takla-Makan				X
Gobi				X
Australian	X			
Monte-Patagonia			X	
Atacama-Peruvian		X		

[a] After Logan (1968).

The warm-winter deserts are characterized by extreme summer heat and a great diurnal range; but their insolation, while high in summer, is greatly reduced in winter. Winter minima are extremely variable from place to place, being determined by the local landform configuration: while the lowlands (i.e., closed basins) are often far below freezing, the hill slopes may be frost free. Although temperatures in the cold-winter deserts commonly drop far below freezing during the winter, their summers are warm to hot. Both diurnal and seasonal ranges are very great, as is the range in insolational input.

The cool coastal deserts are paradoxical in that while they are virtually rainless, they are drenched in sea fog much of the time. Their temperatures are extremely mild—only a few degrees warmer than the neighboring seas—and daily and seasonal ranges are exceedingly low.

Vegetation

Because of the problems of defining "desert" and information deficiencies, "there is little common ground for comparing the vegetation of one desert with another with any degree of precision" (McGinnies et al., 1968). However, McGinnies goes on to state that certain characteristics are held in common, to a degree, by the vegetation of all deserts of the world. McCleary (1968, p. 142), in comparing desert floras with those of deciduous forests and chaparral, states that

> whereas the latter two types of vegetation result from a somewhat limited set of conditions, deserts are determined by such diverse factors as continental position, rain shadow effects, proximity to cool ocean currents, high pressure air systems, etc., so that the various floras are apt to be rather distinctive.

Some deserts, however, can be compared, such as the Sonoran and the Sahara. Likewise the Great Basin and the Gobi have many things in common, such as floras, life forms, and physiognomy of vegetation (McCleary, 1968). Differences are also pointed out by McCleary (1968, p. 142):

> Both the Australian and the Thar Deserts are partially due to high pressure systems; nevertheless, their vegetative components are not at all alike. Both the Namib and Atacama regions are arid chiefly because of cold ocean currents that parallels their shores, but the Namib has predominantly leaf succulents while the Atacama has an abundance of stem succulents. The Australian deserts have no close counterparts anywhere in the world.

Vegetation of the world deserts, while not directly comparable for reasons mentioned previously, is perhaps best characterized by brief floristic and physiognomic descriptions available from the literature. Floristic classifications are based on species list and are often presented as vegetation types or "associations of dominant species" of the region. Physiognomic classifications seek to classify vegetation based upon its outward appearance, or life-form composition.

In addition, morphological, anatomical/structural, and physiological/metabolic criteria could be used to classify vegetation.

Mojave. In the Mojave Desert, creosote bush scrub (Munz and Keck, 1949, 1950; Thorne, 1976; Thorne et al., 1981; Vasek and Barbour, 1977; Vasek and Thorne, 1977) with *Larrea tridentata* (creosote bush) and *Ambrosia dumosa* (burro bush) occupies 70% of the area. This vegetation occurs on well-drained sandy flats, bajadas, and upland slopes from below sea level in Death Valley to as high as 1500 m. After winter rains, the creosote bush scrub and dune areas may support a rich annual vegetation, producing the great flower shows for which the Mojave Desert is well known. There are relatively few species of summer annuals, some of the most prevalent being *Pectis papposa* (chinchweed), *Bouteloua barbata* and *B. aristidorides* (gramma grasses), *Mollugo cerviana* (Indian chickweed), *Euphorbia setiloba* (spurge), and *Boerhaavia erecta* (five-winged ringstem). Other important perennial species include *Encelia farinosa* (brittle bush), *Hymenoclea salsola* (cheese bush), *Atriplex* spp. (saltbush), *Acamptopappus sphaerocephalus* (goldenhead), *Stipa speciosa* (needle grass), *Hilaria rigida* (galleta grass), *Oryzopsis hymenoides* (rice grass), *Opuntia* spp. (prickly pears, chollas), as well as other species of cacti, *Lycium* spp. (box thorn), and many others. Often an overstory of *Yucca brevifolia* (Joshua tree), or below 100 m more often *Yucca schidigera* (Mojave yucca), develops within this very complicated vegetation type.

Two other important communities of this desert region are the cheesebush scrub (Hunt, 1966; Johnson, 1976) and succulent scrub (Thorne et al., 1981). The former vegetation type occurs in drainage channels of Mojave Desert washes, with component species including *Hymenoclea salsola, Chrysothamnus paniculatus* (black-banded rabbit brush), *Brickellia incana* (wooly brickella), *B. oblingifolia, Baccharis* spp. (broom), *Ambrosia eriocentra, Cassia armata* (desert cassia), the ubiquitous *Larrea,* and occasionally *Acacia greggii* (cat's-claw acacia) and *Chilopsis linearis* (desert willow). The mixed desert scrub vegetation type is generally found above 300 m on rocky or heavy, well-drained soils of the upper bajadas of desert mountains. Component species include species of *Opuntia, Agave* (century plant), *Nolina* (Bigelow's nolina), *Echinocereus* (mound cactus), *Mammilaria* (fishhook cactus), and *Coryphantha,* and *Echinocactus* and *Ferocactus* (barrel cacti). *Larrea* and other shrubby perennials such as *Encilia farinosa* and *Ambrosia dumosa* are associated with cacti in this community.

Blackbush scrub (Thorne et al., 1981; Vasek and Barbour, 1977; Vasek and Thorne, 1977; Knapp, 1965) dominated by *Coleogyne ramosissima* (blackbush), is essentially a Great Basin type but is common in Mojave Desert mountain ranges. Basins and broad low areas with alkaline soils often support a variety of saltbush scrub communities (Vasek and Barbour, 1977; Thorne, 1976; Johnson, 1976) dominated by species of *Atriplex.* Associated species include *Grayia spinosa* (hop sage), *Ceratoides lanata* (winter fat), *Artemisia spinescens* (bud sagebrush), *Menodora spinescens* (spiny menodora), *Kochia americana* (red sage), *K. californica, Suaeda torreyana* (seep weed), *Allenrolfea occidentalis* (iodine bush), and *Haplopappus acradenius* (alkali goldenbush).

The vegetation types of the Mojave Desert are dominated by scrub, in particular *Larrea, Atriplex, Coleogyne,* etc. Thus the overall physiognomy of this
desert is woody and succulent scrub, of low to moderate diversity, succulent
woodland *(Yucca brevifolia, Y. schidigera),* and occasional "islands" of evergreen
woodland (juniper-pinyon woodland of Thorne et al., 1981) in the eastern Mojave mountains.

Sonoran. Unlike many deserts, which have a physiognomic dominance of a
single life form, i.e., shrubs, the Sonoran Desert is an "arboreal desert" with
many trees and large cacti (Axelrod, 1979). Species which give the Sonoran this
characteristic include *Bursera* spp. (elephant trees), *Carnegia gigantea* (sahuaro),
Cercidium microphyllum (little-leaved palo verde), *C. floridum* (border palo
verde), *Chilopsis linearis* (desert willow), *Dalea spinosa* (smoke tree), *Parkinsonia
aculeata* spp. (retama), *Pitheocolobium sonorae,* and *Prosopis juliflora* (mesquite). Shrub species which complement the trees are, among others, *Acacia
constricta, A. greggii, Condalia globosa* (crucillo), *Encelia farinosa, Ambrosia
dumosa, A. deltoides, Fourquieria splendens* (ocotillo), *Larrea, Lycium parishii,*
and *Simmondsia chinesis* (jojoba) (Daubenmire, 1978). Vegetation of the foot-
hills and upper portions of bajadas of the Sonoran Desert are both floristically
and morphologically diverse (Daubenmire, 1978). Drier plains and lower bajadas,
however, often exhibit a dominance of *Larrea, Ambrosia,* and *Lycium.* Lower,
undrained basins favor the dominance of *Atriplex polycarpa* or other halophytes
such as *Allenrolfea occidentalis, Sarcobatus vermiculatus* (greasewood), and
Suaeda torreyana (Daubenmire, 1978).

Great Basin. The Great Basin Desert experiences quite severe conditions of winter cold and great annual ranges of temperature (Logan, 1968). This desert is a
"cold-desert shrubland" dominated by low shrubs mixed with cool-season
grasses (Stoddart et al., 1975). The dominant community, which is widespread
and common at higher elevations, is sagebrush scrub (Jaeger and Smith, 1966;
Knapp, 1965, Thorne, 1976). *Artemisia tridentata* (Great Basin sagebrush) pre-
fers deep soils or well-drained slopes, whereas *A. nova* tends to occur on heavy
soils and rocky substrates under relatively warmer and drier climatic conditions
(Thorne et al., 1981). Other component species of sagebrush scrub are
Coleogyne, Ceratoides, Purshia spp. (bitter brush), and *Tetradymia* spp. (cotton
thorn) (Thorne, 1976). There is occasionally an overstory of scattered pinyons,
junipers, or joshua trees. Two other Great Basin vegetation types associated with
sagebrush are hop sage scrub (Johnson, 1976), dominated by *Grayia spinosa,*
and blackbrush scrub (Thorne, 1976; Vasek and Barbour, 1977) dominated by
Coleogyne ramosissma. The former vegetation type generally occurs around
1200 m in elevation in sandy-loamy soils which are moderately rocky. Blackbrush scrub is widespread on rocky upper bajadas from about 1000 m to 2000 m
(Rowlands, 1980).

A community of more or less spinescent, microphyllous shrubs of uniform
physiognomy that occurs in the broad desert valleys of the Great Basin Desert,
often on alkaline soils, is shadscale scrub. Component species include *Atriplex*

confertifolia (shadescale), *A. canescens, Ceratoides, Artemisia spinescens, Grayia, Menodora spinescens, Gutierrezia* spp. (matchweed), and *Coleogyne* (Thorne, 1976). The most important grass associates to the shrubs of the Great Basin Desert are *Agropyron spicatum* (wheat grass) and *Sitanion* spp. (squirrel-tail), with other important grasses including *Oryzopsis hymenoides, Hilaria jamesii, Stipa comata, Agropyron smithii, Elymus cinereus* (rye), and *Poa* spp. (bluestems) (Stoddart et al., 1975).

Chihuahuan. There is a considerable floristic and vegetational difference between the Chihuahuan and other desert regions of North America (McCleary, 1968). It is a region of small cacti, more like the Mojave than the Sonoran, and is also characterized by an extremely high number of liliaceous and amaryllidaceous species of the genera *Yucca* and *Agave* (McCleary, 1968). The western margin of the Chihuahuan Desert is drawn at the eastern margin of the vast zone of short gramma grassland occupied in substantial part by species of *Bouteloua*. These grasslands gradually give way eastward to shrub desert community types (Johnston, 1974). The southern boundary, which occurs in northeastern Zacatecas and western San Luis Potosi of Mexico, is a high plateau which at present is floristically a mixture of grassland elements with a few desert elements including the northern chaparral. The eastern boundaries are largely marked by a gradation to chaparral-like woodland formations on limestone or dolomite (Johnston, 1974).

Johnston (1974) lists a number of community types for the Chihuahuan Desert. The unifying and widespread "vegetational matrix" is the microphyllous desert scrub dominated by *Larrea* and *Fluorensia cernua* (tarbrush). *Flourensia* is considered to be a Chihuahuan Desert indicator (McCleary, 1968). Next in coverage is a shrub-desert community type called by H. S. Gentry as "chaparrillo," occurring on calcareous rocks. Component species include *Acacia* spp., *Parthenium incanum, P. argentatum* (guayule), and often *Viguiera multiflora* (virguiera) and *Larrea*. The remainder of the more important community types occupy vast areas of moderately to highly elevated mountain slopes and tops. These include: (1) chaparral with *Quercus* (oak), *Fraxinus* (ash), *Garrya* (silk tassel), *Rhus* (sumac), *Ceanothus* (wild lilac), etc; (2) "matorral rosetofolia" dominated by *Agave lecheguilla;* and (3) "izotal" scrub dominated by large rosetted species such as *Yucca filifera, Y. carnerosana,* and *Dasylirion wheeleri* (Johnston, 1974).

Physiological Plant Ecology

Deserts are characterized by a large excess of potential evaporation over rainfall; thus desert organisms are under strong natural selection to conserve the limited supply of water. Adaptations of desert organisms, plant or animal, to this water shortage take two forms: avoidance of drought and conservation of water (McNaughton and Wolf, 1979). All successful desert organisms usually combine the two forms in order to cope with the environment.

Annuals are able to avoid water stress as dormant seeds and restrict growth to periods of adequate moisture (Richardson, 1977). Daubenmire (1978) reported the seeds of desert annuals do not all germinate at one time after rains, thus assuring survival of the population.

The nonsucculent shrubs typically have extensive root systems that are either deep and depend on infrequent subsurface moisture or are shallow and depend on more frequent light rains (Daubenmire, 1978). Both succulent and the non-succulent shrubs are water conservers. However, many xerophytic shrubs use considerable water and are not structurally adapted for low transpiration when water supplies are ample (McKell et al., 1971). When stomata of desert shrubs are open and water supply is adequate, transpiration rates are high. However, the thick layer of cutin, on most sclerophyllous leaves, often causes low cuticular transpiration when the stomata are closed (McKell et al., 1971).

Stomata on leaves of desert shrubs usually close during midday, and as water supply becomes critical transpiration is reduced to a very low rate (Daubenmire, 1978). Further, stems often remain green for many years to avoid complete loss of photosynthesis with leaf fall. Many desert shrubs and trees have deciduous leaves which are replaced only after adequate rains (Daubenmire, 1978). Many desert plants are succulents, although they are not found in most of the desert region (Daubenmire, 1978). These plants can store large quantities of water to use during periods of drought.

Another frame of reference concerning adaptation of plants in response to the desert environment is in relation to classification of desert plants by photosynthesis types. Three fundamentally different types of photosynthesis are distinguished by the metabolism and structural traits of plant species (McNaughton and Wolf, 1979). They are either C_3 species, which uptake CO_2 during the day and use ribulose diphosphate as the primary CO_2 acceptor; CAMs (Crassulacean Acid Metabolism) (most succulent species), which uptake CO_2 at night and store it in the form of malic acid; or C_4, which use phosphoenolpyruvate as the initial CO_2 acceptor. The latter species are generally summer active and include annuals such as *Pectis papposa,* both annual and perennial grasses (*Bouteloua* spp., *Hilaria* spp.), and shrubs, most notably many members of the genus *Atriplex.* The C_3 type of photosynthesis is the most widely distributed type, common to all algae and most vascular plants.

The ecological significance of these types, as they relate to desert plants, partly concerns water-use efficiency (McNaughton and Wolf, 1979). CAM species minimize water loss by opening their stomata only during the cool night hours instead of the daytime, when high temperatures would promote rapid evaporation if the stomata were open. These succulent species stockpile CO_2 for later use; during the day they carry on photosynthesis with the stomata closed (Richardson, 1977). The C_4 plants have a water-use efficiency intermediate between those of C_3 and CAM plants (McNaughton and Wolf, 1979). This is an adaptation to semiarid habitats intermediate between those of zerophytic CAM and mesophytic C_3 plants. The C_3 plants have a greater net photosynthetic rate than the CAM plants although they experience greater water loss compared to the CAM plants (McNaughton and Wolf, 1979). High photosynthetic capacity has been attributed to C_4 plants, greater than for C_3 plants and CAM plants, in this order (Szarek, 1979).

It has been proposed that C_4 plants have selective advantage because of their exceptionally high rates of photosynthesis at high light intensities and warm temperature (McNaughton and Wolf, 1973). However, Szarek (1979), in his report on primary productivity of the four North American deserts, stated that all four of the communities studied were dominated by C_3-type plants. McNaughton and Wolf (1973) stated that many desert annuals are C_3 plants and that some may have photosynthetic rates as high as C_4 plants at similar light-saturation properties, although their temperature optima were lower. The plants grow rapidly following winter rains and thus complete their life cycles when temperatures are relatively cool.

Productivity of Vegetation in Arid and Semiarid Lands

Although Grime (1979) considers true deserts to be "unproductive" in terms of yearly increases in the standing crop of vegetation, probably "areas of low productivity" is a better descriptive term. Even so, in areas which can collectively be defined as desertic in the sense that potential evapotranspiration exceeds precipitation (Logan, 1968; Major, 1977), there is a broad range of mean potential yearly productivity which depends upon the physiographic and climatic nature of the region in question. Within a single desert, for example the Sonoran Desert, the potential productivity of the various vegetation types follows principally a temperature/precipitation gradient which is influenced and modified by topographic relief (Whittaker and Niering, 1975; Whittaker, 1975). Secondary factors influencing potential primary productivity may include salinity [especially when salinities of the ground water exceed 6%; little or no higher plant life grows in such areas (Hunt, 1966)] and edaphic conditions other than salinity, including soil compaction (Rowlands et al., 1980), nutrient availability, and high concentrations of toxic chemicals (both natural and man produced). Substrate stability is also important; unstabilized sand dunes are often very low in productivity. In general, the potential primary productivity of a plant community is inversely proportional to the relative degree of environmental stress.

Environmental stresses are common in desert ecosystems and restrict the production potential to levels below that of most other ecosystems (Szarek, 1979; Grime, 1979). These environmental stresses relate mainly to the large ratio of potential evapotranspiration to precipitation characteristics of the desert environment. Another characteristic of many desert environments is persistent wind, which also tends to increase the rate of evapotranspiration. Walter (1973, p. 113) reports that:

> Phytomass production is subject to certain variations in one and the same region. It is higher in a year with good rainfall, lower in a bad year. These variations, however, are not proportional to the absolute

amount of rain and are somewhat damped by the fact that the species composition of the vegetation cannot change very rapidly: only the plants already existing alter their rates of development.

Productivity of desert annuals tend to vary considerably from season to season and from year to year, depending on the nature of the rainfall. Wiggins (1964, p. 2) aptly summarizes this phenomenon:

> The term "average annual rainfall" has little significance for desert regions, for the "average" includes wet and dry periods alike without taking into account the fluctuations that occur from year to year. Leibig's Law of the Minimum operates with a vengence under desert conditions, where the differences between adequate and inadequate rainfall are delicately balanced.

Daubenmire (1978), in reference to annuals of the North American deserts, reports that annuals which germinate at the start of autumn or winter rains have a longer period of development and grow larger than annuals which respond to summer rains.

Productivity of desert plants is closely associated with the plants' ecophysiological adaptation, particularly concerning water economy (Walter, 1973). Xerophytes which grow wherever their roots can reach water are termed phreatophytes; these plants are able to maintain a certain degree of photosynthesis and hence produce organic matter. Ephemerals are able to exploit the excess water which the perennials are unable to utilize in a year of good rain; they simply do not develop to any great extent during years of drought. Szarek (1979), in studies of primary productivity in the four North American deserts, found that photosynthetic and water use efficiencies vary among the four North American deserts, due to differences in climate and microenvironment of the site selected for intensive study.

The Magnitude of Primary Productivity in Arid Lands

According to both Whittaker (1975) and Daubenmire (1978) the potential net primary productivity of the world's deserts varies from 0 to 2500 kg (dry wt) ha^{-1} $year^{-1}$ with a mean of around 400 kg ha^{-1} $year^{-1}$ and a world wide total of 1.7×10^9 metric tons $year^{-1}$, about 0.01% of the Earth's net primary production from all sources. In comparison, productivity in the open ocean varies between 20 and 4000 kg ha^{-1} $year^{-1}$, and in the tundra of arctic and alpine areas it is 100 to 4000 kg ha^{-1} $year^{-1}$. The net primary production in mature stable temperate forests varies from 6000 to 28,000 kg ha^{-1} $year^{-1}$ and that of the tropical rain forest from 1000 to 35,000 kg ha^{-1} $year^{-1}$. Plant biomass per unit area of deserts worldwide averages 7000 kg ha^{-1} as opposed to 300,000 to 350,000 kg ha^{-1} in temperate forests and around 450,000 kg ha^{-1} in tropical rain forests. Under extreme desertic conditions biomass may be as low or lower than 200 kg ha^{-1} (Whittaker, 1975). Considering that they occupy about 22% of the land surface, the phytomass in deserts is a rather small, 0.8% of the land total (Walter, 1973; Whittaker, 1975).

Production of Perennial Plants

Yearly above-ground productivity of perennial plants in desertic regions has been estimated as anywhere between less than 100 to over 2000 kg dry weight per hectare per year (Table 7-2). The highest production occurs in desert grassland or steppe types. Such areas are properly defined as semidesert or semiarid and generally mean annual precipitation exceeds 250 mm year^{-1} but is usually less than 600 mm year^{-1}. According to information given in Walter (1973) above-ground production of arid southwestern African grassland increases linearly at about 1000 kg ha^{-1} year^{-1} for every 100-mm increase in mean annual precipitation and approaches 5500 kg ha^{-1} year^{-1} in some areas. This is an extremely high value and areas with such high productivity and mean annual precipitation (about 6000 mm year^{-1}) are really subhumid. Whittaker's upper limit of 2500 kg ha^{-1} year^{-1} is probably a realistic value for the maximum yearly production in desert and semidesert regions.

Next highest in overall productivity are semidesert thorn scrub types with collumnar cacti or other succulent species (Whittaker, 1975; Whittaker and Niering, 1975), with an annual above-ground productivity approaching 1300 kg ha^{-1} year^{-1}. The lowest productivity is found in desert scrub, where mean annual productivity may be as low as 100 kg ha^{-1} year^{-1} (Walter, 1973) to around 1000 kg ha^{-1} year^{-1} (Whittaker and Niering, 1975). Some special habitats such as unstable sand dunes or salt pans may have 0 to 100 kg ha^{-1} year^{-1} net plant productivity.

Below-ground productivity of desert plants often outstrips above-ground productivity. Working in a shadescale scrub vegetation in western Utah on the Desert Experiment Range (1600-m elevation), Holmgren and Brewster (1972) found that the total phytomass above ground was 2400 kg ha^{-1} as compared to 15,300 below ground (12,350 kg in roots alone). Above-ground productivity was 280 kg ha^{-1} year^{-1} for perennial plants compared to 2300 kg ha^{-1} year^{-1} below ground. The total production above and below ground compared quite well with similar values published by Rodin and Basilovich (1968, cited in Holmgren and Brewster, 1972) for Eurasian deserts, which were 1220 kg ha^{-1} year^{-1} for dwarf semishrub desert, 2500 kg ha^{-1} year^{-1} for subtropical desert, and 4200 kg ha^{-1} year^{-1} for steppe; and with the results of Pearson (1965) who measured 2400 kg ha^{-1} year^{-1} in the cold-desert steppe of eastern Idaho. Below-ground productivity was about 9 to 10 times that of above-ground productivity as reported by Holmgren and Brewster (1972) and Rodin and Basilovich (1968) but only about two times greater in the studies by Pearson (1965). Total above- and below-ground plant biomass in desert communities analyzed by Whittaker and Niering (1975) varied between 6000 and 21,000 kg ha^{-1} year^{-1} (Table 7-3); however, below-ground productivity in their study was based only on plausible root/shoot ratios for different growth forms and is probably an underestimate. Holmgren and Brewster (1972), on the other hand, directly measured underground biomass.

West (1972), working in Curlew Valley, Utah found that the 3-year average of above- and below-ground plant biomass was 6410 kg ha^{-1} and 16,070 kg

Table 7-2. Above-Ground Net Primary Productivity of Some Selected Desert and Semidesert Regions of the World and in Particular the Southwestern United States

Vegetation type	Location	Production (dry wt, kg ha^{-1} year^{-1})	Reference
Semidesert grasslands	South Africa	1000–6000[a]	Walter (1973)
Aristida grasslands	South Africa	1600	Walter (1973)
Bouteloua desert grasslands	Tucson, Arizona	1385	Whittaker and Niering (1975)
Larrea-Flourensia-Prosopis	Southern Arizona	1310	Chew and Chew (1965)
Spinose-suffrutescent desert scrub	Tucson, Arizona	1286	Whittaker and Niering (1975)
Cold-desert steppe	Eastern Idaho	1230	Pearson (1965)
"Moist southern desert"	Kazakstan, USSR	1200	Laurenko et al. (1955)
Cercidium-Franseria desert scrub	Tucson, Arizona	1052	Whittaker and Niering (1975)
Cold-desert steppe	Upper Snake River, Idaho	920	Blaisdell (1958)
Creosote bush scrub	Tucson, Arizona	918	Whittaker and Niering (1975)
Steppe	Northern Mongolia	400–500	Walter (1973)
Larrea-Lycium	Rock Valley, Nevada (1965–1968)	408	Wallace and Romney (1972)
Steppe	Central Asia	150–440	Rodin and Basilevich (1968)
Shadescale scrub	Southwest Utah	280	Holmgren and Brewster (1977)
Larrea-Lycium	Rock Valley, Nevada (1971–1974)	278	Turner (1975)
Desert scrub	Gobi Desert	100–200	Walter (1973)

[a] 1000 kg production per hectare per year for every 100 mm increases in mean annual precipitation.

Table 7-3. Summary of Biomass and Production Estimates for Four Desert Plant Communities from the Santa Catalina Mountains, Arizona, along an Elevational Transect[a]

	Bouteloua curtipendula desert grassland	Spinose-suffrutescent desert scrub	Cercidium microphyllum/ Franseria deltoidea desert scrub	Larrea tridentata desert scrub
Biomass (dry kg ha^{-1})				
Trees[b]	640	12,080	3,780	4,290[b]
Shrubs[c]	1,510	850	1,140	2.5
Herbs	.483	112	4	Tr
Moss and lichens	–	–	Tr	–
Selaginella	Tr	53	–	–
Total above ground	2,633	13,095	4,924	4,923
Total above and below[d]	6,000	21,000	6,000	6,000
Net productivity (kg ha^{-1} year^{-1})				
Trees	163	833	512	917
Shrubs	624	333	536	0.6
Herbs	598	120	44	0.03
Total above ground	1,385	1,286	1,052	918
Total above and below[d]	2,800	2,100	1,700	1,400
Biomass accumulation[e] ratio (B/P)	1.9	10.2	4.7	4.7

[a] Data from Whittaker and Niering (1975).
[b] Includes small trees and arborescent shrubs as well as canopy shrubs in Larrea tridentata desert shrub.
[c] Shrubs include subordinate true shrub and all semishrubs.
[d] No root data available; below-ground estimates based on plausible root/shoot ratios for different growth forms.
[e] Total biomass/net annual production.

ha^{-1} for *Ceratoides lanata* and 12,660 kg ha^{-1} and 13,130 kg ha^{-1} for *Atriplex confertifolia*, respectively. The average productivity over this period was 700 and 840 kg ha^{-1}. Total biomass of the *Ceratoides* dominated community was 18,480 kg ha^{-1}, 74% as roots; and 17,300 kg ha^{-1} for the *Atriplex*-dominated community, 87% as roots.

The biomass accumulation rate (B/P), which is the ratio of biomass to net productivity, can be used to characterize productivity in vegetation (Whittaker and Niering, 1975; Whittaker, 1975). Biomass represents productivity which has accumulated in the community, and as the biomass to net productivity ratio increases the relative percentage of gross productivity used for plant community respiration increases. As succession proceeds, an increasing proportion of the community biomass tends to be above ground and the biomass accumulation ratio generally increases as succession proceeds toward "climax" (Whittaker, 1975).

The B/P ratio in *Bouteloua* desert grassland is only 1.9, indicating a fairly rapid turnover of plant material. B/P is 4.7 in both *Cercidium-Ambrosia* and *Larrea tridentata* desert scrub and 10.2 in spinose-suffrutescent desert scrub (Table 7-3). The latter value is comparable to that which can be associated with the shadescale vegetation studied by Holmgren and Brewster (1972) where the ratio of B/P was 8.6. Turner and MacBrayer (1974) report the standing above-ground biomass in Rock Valley, Nevada, as 2300 kg ha^{-1} whereas below-ground biomass was 4540 kg ha^{-1}; hence, the B/P ratio was approximately 5.6, a value comparable to that of the Sonoran creosote bush scrub measured by Whittaker and Niering (1975).

As far as their B/P ratios are concerned, desert scrub communities with an overstory seem to resemble more "mature" communities with a relatively higher rate of respiration and slower turnover, whereas desert grasslands resemble more "juvenile" communities in that B/P ratios are comparatively low and turnover is high. These are the most readily exploited by grazing animals, domestic or otherwise. Desert scrub communities lacking an overstory are intermediate and in general the magnitude of the B/P ratio reflects the life form complexity of the vegetation, i.e., the greater the number of stories (herbs, subshrubs, woody shrubs, small trees and collumnar cacti, etc.) the higher the B/P ratio.

In general, the B/P ratio would increase with time in an area undergoing secondary succession and would be on the whole lower in areas recently disturbed (because these areas will in most cases be populated by pioneer annuals and short-lived perennials with little biomass tied up in roots and secondary tissues). But a low value for B/P within a stand relative to some other comparable adjacent area would not necessarily indicate that the latter was disturbed or in an earlier successional stage. For example, if mesquite should move into a desert grassland as a consequence of moderate disturbance by grazing, the B/P ratio subsequent to this influx would be higher after the disturbance in the "disclimax" than it was before.

Effects of Environmental Factors on Primary Production

Precipitation, and in some cases, temperature as it effects evapotranspiration, are the principal environmental factors affecting productivity in deserts. Wallace and Romney (1972) found that shrub weights in a *Larrea-Lycium* community comprised about 75% of the total primary productivity measured over a 3-year period and the magnitude of this percentage seemed to vary inversely with total precipitation. Annuals appeared to be more sensitive to low amounts of rainfall and to changes in seasonal distribution of rainfall than did shrubs. Net primary productivity totals were closely correlated with differences in fall and winter rainfall (Table 7-4).

Blaisdell (1958) correlated climatic data with herbage production in Idaho sagebrush-steppe vegetation in the region of the upper Snake River, Idaho. Precipitation in the area averaged about 250 mm year^{-1} and was evenly distributed but with a slight concentration in May and June. Temperatures rose to about 37°C during the summer but dropped to as low as −39°C during the winter. The original vegetation was an open stand of *Artemisia tridentata* intermixed with a vigorous stand of perennial grasses and forbs. Grazing over a period of many years increased the importance of *Artemisia* to that of the predominant species. Yearly production varied from 550 to almost 1200 kg ha^{-1} year^{-1} (Figs. 7-3 and 7-4). Blaisdell discovered that correlations were highest between herbage production and July-March rainfall and that there was a negative correla-

Table 7-4. Relationship Between Precipitation for Each Year and Productivity Measurements from Rock Valley[a]

Year and month	Rainfall (mm)	Production average (kg ha^{-1} year^{-1})			Ratio of shrubs to herbs
		Herbaceous	Shrubs	Total	
1965 to 1999					
Jul.–Oct.	14.6				
Nov.–Feb.	137.0				
Mar.–Jun.	12.5	185	488	673	2.63
1966 to 1967					
Jul.–Oct.	12.0				
Nov.–Feb.	44.7				
Mar.–Jun.	43.4	45	305	350	6.78
1967 to 1968					
Jul.–Oct.	68.9				
Nov.–Feb.	70.4				
Mar.–Jun.	16.0	248	431	679	1.73

[a]From Wallace and Romney (1972).

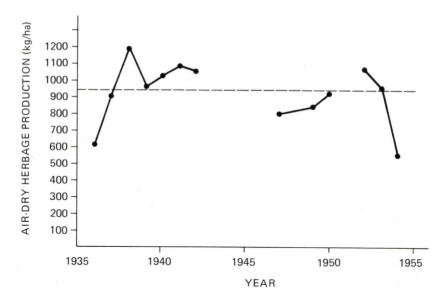

Figure 7-3. Total annual herbage production of perennial grasses, forbs, and shrubs at the U.S. Sheep Experiment Station, 10 km north of Dubois, Idaho (cold desert shrub—steppe vegetation) between 1936 and 1954 (data from Blaisdell, 1958).

tion between production and April-June rainfall (i.e., during the growing season). In general, precipitation during certain seasons was rather closely related to herbage weight of vegetation as a whole or groups of species but in only a few instances was it related to production of individual species. The poorest correlations were generally with the least abundant species and low production was often associated with high spring temperatures. He concluded that when adverse environmental factors (frost, insects, rodents, disease, etc.) affect certain species, other species are often able to utilize the moisture made available, increase their yield, and thus compensate for the loss of yield from the affected species. Therefore, various factors can disrupt performance of individual species without seriously disrupting overall community-environmental relations; hence oscillations in total production are dampened. There also seems to be some evidence (McNaughton, 1977; Mellinger and McNaughton, 1975) that oscillations in net productivity of a community in response to environmental perturbations will be lower in amplitude in stands of vegetation with a higher species diversity than stands of similar types with lower species diversity.

Production of Annual Plants

Cain and Castro (1959) show annual plant species as constituting 15 to 58% of the local flora in 12 of the world's deserts and 42 and 47% in Death Valley and the Salton Sink of California, respectively. In most forests, annuals generally

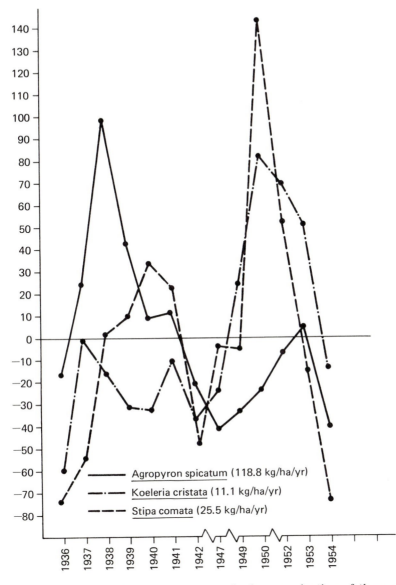

Figure 7-4. Percentage change from average herbage production of three native grasses on the upper Snake River plains of Idaho (from Blaisdell, 1958).

make up less than 10% of the flora. Johnson et al. (1978) observed that annual species made up 60% of the flora of Johnson Valley and 82 to 88% of the flora of Lucerne Valley in the Mojave Desert. They stated that this distiribution pattern indicated that the annual habit had special evolutionary significance as a component of the vegetation of hot arid regions, an idea more fully developed by Grime (1979). Desert annual plants are drought evaders which complete their entire lifespan during relatively short periods of time (during the winter, and in some areas during the summer) when abundant supplies of moisture are available. When active, they have heavy rates of carbon assimilation; most of this is allocated to seed production (Mooney et al., 1976).

In southwestern North America, two different groups of annuals have evolved: a few species of summer annuals that germinate during hot weather after summer convectional storms and which predominantly exhibit the C_4 photosynthetic pathway; and winter annuals which abound during the cool moist winter and early spring. Winter annual species number in the hundreds and are predominantly C_3 plants (Johnson, 1975, 1976; Johnson et al., 1978; Mulroy and Rundel, 1977).

According to Beatley (1976) winter annuals are widely fluctuating components of the Mojave Desert and transitional communities and are a distinctive feature of warm-desert vegetation. The requirements of the winter annual life cycle—which begins with germination following rainfall in the autumn, followed by slow vegetative growth of the seedlings (consisting of an unelongated stem and leaves in rosettes or tufts) and overwintering in the low temperatures of winter when the seedling low-temperature requirements are fulfilled, and completion of the life cycle with flowering, fruiting, and death the following spring— all precisely fit the climatic regimes of the Mojave and other deserts in the southwestern United States. The processes of speciation have resulted in many species in many families exhibiting the winter annual habit, all derived from the floras of adjacent regions (Beatley, 1976).

The majority of winter annual seedlings probably do not survive to maturity. Survival is high through the winter months. Most losses occur in early spring at the time of rapid growth of all the vegetation components and the associated rapid depletion of moisture in the soils (Beatley, 1967). Over the years, the phenology of desert annuals as it relates to environmental factors has captured the interests of many (Beatley, 1967, 1969, 1974, 1976; Went, 1948, 1949; Went and Westergaard, 1949; Johnson et al., 1978) and there is still disagreement as to the precise nature of these phenological relationships.

The spatial distribution and production of annual plants in the California Desert is very closely associated with the proximity to shrubs or even old shrub mounds where the original plant has died and disappeared (Muller, 1953; Norton, 1974; Went, 1942). However, the pattern is not always consistent from one place to another even when areas being compared are very similar in their physical characteristics (Johnson et al., 1978). As a generalization, however, the intershrub species are far less productive than the canopies of desert shrubs for desert winter annuals. This is no doubt in part a reflection of increased nutrient availability produced by accumulation of litter under these shrubs and possibly concentration of runoff around the base of the shrubmound due to water repellency of the soil beneath the shrubs (especially *Larrea*) proper (S. Adams et al., 1970). Other possible explanations are that the density of soil is considerably lower in shrub mounds, shrubs have a larger interception storage that holds water which otherwise might run off, and shrubs greatly reduce evapotranspiration from the soil and annuals beneath the shrub. The presence of a long-lasting water repellent layer, increased nutrient availability, lower soil strength and density, or a combination of these factors would also explain why annual plants still form halos around abandoned shrub mounds.

The production of winter annuals may outstrip that of perennials in favorable years (Norton, 1974). The extent of production of winter annuals is highly dependent upon the frequency, amount, and time between precipitation events (Beatley, 1969, 1974; Johnson et al., 1978). According to Norton (1974), annual production in the Mojave Desert was 3.2 kg ha^{-1} in 1972, a dry year, and 430 kg ha^{-1} in 1973, a wet year. Beatley (1969) measured production of winter annuals on the Nevada Test Site in three desert plant communities from 1964 through 1966 (Table 7-5); productivity values ranged from 0 to 616 kg ha^{-1} on sites with undisturbed soils and seasonally were two to five times higher on burned sites than on unburned ones in the same area. Maximum production during this period occurred on a burned site and was 753 kg ha^{-1}, with *Bromus rubens,* an introduced grass, contributing most of this biomass. If contributions from this species were disallowed, overall biomass was greatest in the 38 Mojave Desert communities, least in Great Basin Desert, and intermediate in the transitional communities.

Seasonal vegetative productivity and reproductive success of desert annual species was highly variable from plant to plant, from site to site, and from season to season. Measurements of total productivity with the objective of defining either the mean or extreme productivities in any given kind of desert vegetation are difficult in all the vegetation components because of spatial and temporal variations which require recognition, measurement, and definition (Beatley, 1969). Working in a *Larrea-Lycium* community in southern Nevada, Wallace and Romney (1972) reported production of winter annual plants as 130 to 260 kg ha^{-1} in 1966, 30 to 70 kg ha^{-1} in 1967, and 200 to 280 kg ha^{-1} in 1968. Net above-ground production of annual plants in 1973 exceeded that of perennial species (573 kg ha^{-1}) by almost 100 kg ha^{-1}, and production of annuals in Rock Valley in 1974 dropped to 17.4 kg ha^{-1} (Turner, 1975). Production of winter annual plant species in Nevada was therefore quite variable and highly dependent upon both the amounts and the pattern of winter precipitation (Beatley, 1969; Wallace and Romney, 1973).

Even higher levels of production for desert annuals were observed in data collected from the western and central Mojave Desert of California by Johnson and Rice (unpublished) of the U.S. Bureau of Land Management (Table 7-6). Production varied from around 450 to 900 kg ha^{-1} in the western Mojave Desert near Ridgecrest and from around 590 to over 1000 kg ha^{-1} in Johnson Valley. Only at two sites, however, did the production of native plants exceed that of introduced annuals (mostly *Erodium cicutarium* and *Schismus* sp.). In the Sonoran Desert of south-central Arizona, Patten (1975), Halvorsen and Patten (1975), and Patten and Smith (1974) measured production of winter annual species as about 950 kg ha^{-1} in 1973 and less than 100 kg ha^{-1} in 1974.

Table 7-5. Minimum (m), Mean ($\bar{x}$), and Maximum (M) Values of Dry Biomass of Winter Annual Plants in Three Mojave Desert Plant Communities on the Nevada Test Site, 1964 to 1966[a]

Vegetation type	No. of sites	Dry biomass (kg ha^{-1})								
		1964			1965			1966		
		m	$\bar{x}$	M	m	$\bar{x}$	M	m	$\bar{x}$	M
Mojave Desert										
Larrea (undisturbed)	38	1	60	442	0	19	75	40	160	616
Transitional desert										
Coleogyne-Grayia-Lycium[b]	20	1	61	329	1	35	518	27	180	753
Great Basin Desert										
Atriplex and Artemesia	10	1	62	138	0	41	185	1	25	92

[a]Data from Beatley (1969).
[b]Means on three burned sites within this type averaged 228, 365, and 540 kg ha^{-1} in 1964 to 1966. Much of this plant biomass was due to *Bromus rubens*, an introduced grass.

Table 7-6. Estimated Standing Crop of Desert Annuals (kg ha^{-1}) from Several Locations in Two Mojave Desert Regions[a]

	Precipitation = 42 mm[b] Western Mojave Desert				Precipitation = 47 mm[c] Central Mojave Desert	
	T31S, R36E Sec 34	T31S, R41E Sec 6	T28S, R41E Sec 10	Southwest of Ludlow	Central Johnson Valley	North-central Johnson Valley
Natives	64	2	160	685	435	133
Nonnatives	428	443	742	0	151	1002
Total	492	446	902	685	586	1135

[a]Data collected by H. B. Johnson and Carl Rice, March 1977 (Johnson and Rice, unpublished).
[b]Measured from Oct. 1976 to Feb. 1977 at Randsburg, California.
[c]Measured from Oct. 1976 to Feb. 1977 at Daggett, California.

Production by summer annuals is generally much less than winter annuals in those areas where cool season precipitation is dominant or equal to warm season in importance. One of the reasons must be that summer convectional storms in the southwestern United States tend to be localized, spotty, and often quite unpredictable. Thames (1975) reported productivity values for August through October of 1974 of 154 kg ha^{-1} between the trees and shrubs and 44, 60, and 36 kg ha^{-1} under *Cercidium microphyllum, Larrea tridentata,* and *Olneya tesota,* respectively, near Tucson, Arizona. Production of summer annuals does not seem to be influenced by the presence of shrubs to the same extent as winter annuals, a fact recognized by Johnson et al. (1978), who speculate that the contrasting distribution of winter and summer annuals may produce materials that can inhibit the growth of winter annuals later on. Rowlands et al. (1980) reported that intershrub biomass estimates of summer annuals in Stoddard Valley, south of Barstow, California (mostly *Bouteloua barbara, Euphorbia setiloba,* and *Pectis papposa*) amounted to 190 kg ha^{-1} in 1977 and 225 kg ha^{-1} in 1978. These values are about the same order of magnitude as those reported in Thames (1965).

Vegetation Dynamics in Arid Lands

Although community processes are often very slow in arid and semiarid lands, desert and semidesert vegetation is dynamic. Changes in space are brought about in response to complex environmental gradients (Whittaker, 1975, Whittaker and Niering, 1965, 1975). In some cases, floristic units can be identified which correspond to peculiar environmental conditions, for example calciphyte communities (Raven and Axelrod, 1976). In most cases, vegetation changes along continua (both in space and time) as was shown by Whittaker and Niering (1965) for a Sonoran Desert mountain range. Competition does not usually produce sharp boundaries between species populations and evolution of species in relation to one another does not produce well-defined communities with similar distributions. Centers and boundaries of species populations are scattered along the environmental gradient (Whittaker, 1975).

Changes Over Geologic Time

Temporal changes in desert vegetation can be both long- and short-term phenomena, and either may be cyclic. Long-term changes may be brought about by climatic shifts following changes in the Earth's crust (Axelrod, 1979).

The effects on vegetation involve tremendous changes in species distribution in response to climatic shifts and in some cases evolution and adaptive radiation of new plant species. According to Axelrod (1979), regional deserts such as the Sonoran and Mojave are relatively young, their constituent species adapting to ever increasing dryness, surviving and proliferating in localized dry sites and refugiae. Prior to the Early Holocene, most of the present-day desert scrub vegetation had not yet developed and woodland vegetation persisted up to this time in the Mojave and Sonoran Deserts, 600 to 1000 m below its present lower elevational limit (Van Devender, 1977; Van Devender and Spaulding, 1979; Wells, 1976; Wells and Berger, 1967). Thus, an enormous change in the general aspect of the vegetation of southwestern North America took place as a direct result of the ending of the Wisconsin glacial period.

Changes Caused by Climatic Cycling and Normal Fluctuations

Changes in vegetation of a lesser but nonetheless significant magnitude are also brought about by short-term climatic cycling. Hastings and Turner (1965) document the gradual if irregular decline in winter precipitation in southern Arizona over a period of about 100 years (summer rainfall did not noticeably change) together with a 1.5 to 2.0°C increase in mean annual temperature. As a result, there has been a tendency for the vegetational zones of the desert to re-treat upward in elevation and for large influxes of brush into desert grassland. This situation may have been exacerbated by overgrazing. These sorts of climatic changes are probably not long enough in duration to produce major evolutionary effects on populations of perennial plant species. However, a problem arises in determining which vegetational changes represent random local fluctuations and which if any indicate general conditions from which long-term variations in climate can be inferred (Hastings and Turner, 1965).

Random, local fluctuations in climate produced by normal variability in climatic events produce continual changes in the population densities, cover, and productivity of both annual and perennial plant species but different plant species seldom respond to these changes in similar manners.

> Year to year comparisons of maps of plant cover on permanent quad-rants show continual changes; one perennial species is replaced by another; areas occupied by vegetation become barren, and barren areas become occupied; annuals and seedlings of perennials appear and dis-appear. Two parts of the same community may be undergoing similar changes at the time, or what seem to be directly opposite changes may be occurring. (Blaisdell, 1958, p. 27)

Hastings and Turner (1965) suggested that over a period of years, desert vegeta-tion either will reflect the unpredictabilities and inequitabilities of precipitation by exhibiting a mosaic of stable, decadent, and thriving stands within the same region, or desert vegetation must in some ways be adapted to wide variation in rainfall or it could not exist where it does now. Even if extended over a period of many years and reinforced by temporal variability, except for their first years of existence, long-lived perennial plant species which may produce seed for well over a century are probably little affected by climatic extremes due to spatial inequalities (Hastings and Turner, 1965).

Research by Miller (1976) showed that stable age distributions are impossible for long-lived species. Correlations between either basal area or density of peren-nial species and precipitation were low in studies by West et al. (1979) in southern Idaho, indicating that pulses of regeneration are not strongly related to precipitation and that most plants in this cold-desert sagebrush community were highly plastic with regard to size. West et al. (1979) found no stable age-size relationship, and that stands of individuals which are approximately the same size are created which give the appearance of being even aged, but are in fact uneven aged. The authors concluded that community stability is achieved more through having the competitive vacuum filled by established plant plasticity in age-size relationships rather than through changes in age-class distributions. Regeneration of semidesert plant communities by "pulses" or "episodic phenomena with irregular incidences of large numbers of individuals entering the population due to favorable conditions" was not found to be important in the cold-desert scrub-steppe studied by West et al. (1979), but they suggested that pulses of plant regeneration may be more pronounced in the hot-desert environments since soil moisture recharge from snow in the cold-winter semidesert is probably more dependable than that derived from the often heavy, but sporadic pulses of precipitation in the warm deserts to the south. This remains to be seen, however; if most desert plant communities turn out to be plastic in their age-size distribution, the implications for plant demographic, successional, or revegetation studies are obvious: in order to obtain a valid age-class distribution, each individual perennial plant in the desert community in question would have to be aged independently since no reliable monotonically increasing curvilinear or linear relationships of increasing size to age could be derived.

Changes Caused by Human Disturbances

> It is impossible in these times to develop a "natural" ecology, one that
> ignores the import of man. Ecology should inspire a wiser management
> of nature; the feedback should work. (Margalef, 1968)

The ways in which man can bring about changes in the vegetation of arid and semiarid lands are legion. However, the major forces of change are probably agricultural development, livestock grazing, mining and energy development, urban expansion, groundwater removal, modification of the landscape by road construction, and the off-road vehicle (ORV). The discussion below is limited to the effects of off-road vehicles.

Research by Vollmer et al. (1976) showed clear differences between numbers of annuals in ruts of tracks produced by a motor vehicle and in other undisturbed parts of a *Larrea-Lycium* community in Nevada. Their results were probably due to the effects of soil compaction on the germination, growth, and establishment of the annual species present.

Most of the experimental studies of soil compaction and its effects on plant growth have been done in agricultural systems. If other conditions are not limiting, increases in soil strength due to compaction will reduce the rate of both emergence and root elongation (Taylor et al., 1966) and the proportion of seedlings emerging or proportion of roots which penetrate the impeding, high-strength layer (Carter and Tavernetti, 1968; Carter et al., 1965; Taylor, 1971;

Taylor et al., 1966, 1967). The limitations on root development in high-strength soils result in an increased demand for water to meet the requirements of evapotranspiration; if additional water is not supplied plants lapse into water stress and the plants wilt and die. Grimes et al. (1975) showed that soils whose resistances were greater than 1790 kNm^{-2} restricted growth of both cotton and corn seedlings growing in a sandy loam soil. Taylor (1971) believes that monocots may be more successful in germinating and penetrating high-strength soils and soil crusts, because monocots exert a thrust concentrated as a point load at the tip of the coleoptile, whereas dicots must push or pull large cotyledons through the soil. Wells (1961) found that *Stipa speciosa,* a rhizomatous bunch grass, was one of the early invaders on the abandoned but highly compacted streets and avenues of a Nevada ghost town. Another perennial bunch grass, *Oryzopsis hymenoides,* is also important as an early invader in disturbed desert sites (see Chapter 14). Although plant growth is inversely correlated with bulk density (a measurement of soil compaction) it is limited critically by soil strength (Taylor and Gardner, 1963).

J. A. Adams et al. (1981) and Rowlands et al. (1980) studied the responses of desert annuals to differential compaction of the soil due to multiple passes of a four-wheel-drive truck and a motorcycle from August 1977 through June 1979 in Stoddard Valley, California. They found that the strength of drying compacted soil increased at a much greater rate than the strength of drying uncompacted soil, and that more highly compacted soil showed an extremely large increase in penetrometer resistance when compared to the adjacent control after drying (J. A. Adams et al., 1981). Significant reductions in the cover of annuals occurred more than a year after tracks had been created by as few as one truck pass on wet soil, five motorcycle passes on wet soil, or 20 truck passes on dry soil.

Plant response to compaction varied greatly with species (annual grasses were generally less affected by soil compaction than annual dicots) or with rainfall characteristics during a growing season. The unusually heavy spring rains in 1978 and 1979 tended to ameliorate somewhat the reductions in plant density which might otherwise occur during years of normal spring rainfall (Rowlands et al., 1980). Figure 7-5 illustrates the relationship between the cover of winter annual plants, soil penetration resistance, and the number of passes by a four-wheel-drive vehicle. The penetration resistance at 12 cm depth in wet soil caused by three vehicle passes is around the same order of magnitude as that causing negative responses in agricultural crops. Note that the initial response of *Schismus barbatus,* an introduced annual grass, to compaction is an increase in cover up to three passes, followed by an overall decrease in cover with successive passes (the rather abrupt decline in cover at five passes may be an artifact caused by unusual site characteristics). The total cover of annual species was reduced almost 50% by one pass of the vehicle and declined only very little thereafter. The biomass of summer annuals as measured in September 1978 also showed an overall decline with number of passes. The summer annual grass, *Bouteloua barbata,* behaved similarly to *Schismus,* increasing in biomass up to three passes and then

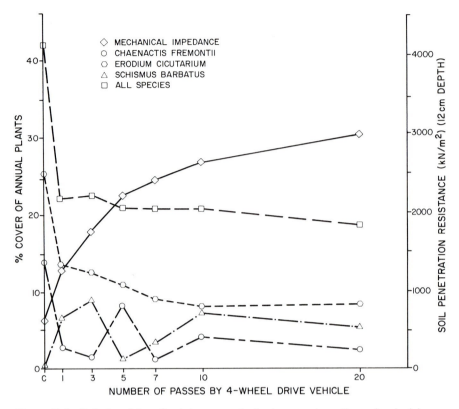

Figure 7-5. Relationship of winter annual plant cover to soil mechanical impedence and the number of passes of a four-wheel-drive vehicle over desert soil at field capacity (from Rowlands et al., 1980).

Table 7-7. Biomass of Summer Annuals Harvested in Stoddard Valley, September 1978, from a Control Plot and the Tracks Created by Multiple Passes of a Four-Wheel-Drive Vehicle[a]

No. of passes treatments	Width of track (m)	Biomass (g m^{-2})	
		Bouteloua barbata	*Pectic papposa*
Control	—	79.0	88.4
1	0.23	173.3	10.4
3	0.30	153.4	12.0
5	0.30	78.1	13.7
7	0.40	37.2	4.2
10	0.40	96.7	6.8
20	0.45	42.2	7.6

[a]From Rowlands et al. (1980).

declining (Table 7-7). *Pectis papposa,* a dicot, showed an abrupt decline after only one pass. Similar results were obtained from a motorcycle disturbance, but a greater number of passes along the same path were required as compared to the four-wheel-drive vehicle (Rowlands et al., 1980). Both J. A. Adams et al. (1982) and Rowlands et al. (1980) concluded that the greater increase of soil strength in drying compacted soil as compared to uncompacted soil is responsible for the observed reduction in annual desert plant growth even on areas with a relatively small amount of compaction.

Plant Succession in Arid Lands

The subject of plant succession in arid lands appears never to have been well studied. For example, McGinnies et al. (1968) do not devote a single portion of their book *Deserts of the World* to the general subject of plant succession. Research done in North American deserts by Muller (1940), Shreve (1942), Pianka (1974), and Beatley (1976) has tended to minimize the importance of succession in the vegetation dynamics of this region. On the other hand, studies by Wells (1961), Vasek et al. (1975), Vasek (1980b), and Webb and Wilshire (1980) have interpreted successional patterns in deserts as being different from those in more mesic ecosystems in that subsequent to disturbance, short-lived pioneer perennial species, for example the grasses *Stipa speciosa* and *Oryzopsis hymenoides* and the subshrubs *Hymenoclea salsola* and *Gutierrezia,* increase in the community and the role of pioneer annuals is diminished. Most of these plants are often already present in the undisturbed community in "naturally" disturbed sites such as washes. When the competition from the "climax shrubs" has been removed they quickly fill the void, only to be forced out again in time (according to Vasek et al., 1975, perhaps millenia) as the long-lived dominant shrubs regain their ascendency. However, data collected by Lathrop (1978) and Sulenski (1972) show that such a stage is clearly neither necessary nor sufficient for the natural revegetation of disturbed arid lands. If these "pioneer shrubs" are not present in the general region to form a pool of invaders the long-lived shrubs simply replace themselves either by seedlings or by resprouting (Vollmer et al., 1976) as asserted by Muller (1940), Shreve (1942), and Beatley (1976) in a sort of "autosuccession."

In describing plant succession in central southern Nevada, Beatley (1976, p. 72) states:

> The region abounds in large and smaller areas where the original vegeta-
> tion cover has been wholly or partially removed and the soils have been
> grossly modified. In the Mojave and transition desert areas, recovery of
> vegetation is an exceedingly slow process, to be considered in terms of
> centuries of time. At the higher elevations and higher rainfalls of the
> Great Basin Desert, recovery is a matter of at least several decades. Here
> increases in rainfall and decreases in temperature are reflected by in-
> creased organic matter accumulations, and the whole complex of vari-

ables contributes to increased rates of the soil-forming processes at the higher elevations. Removal of the tree and shrub vegetation and physical disturbance of the soils present a greatly modified environment in which seedlings must become established. However, even here, although the species representation may differ markedly from that of the original community, it is usually species of the original community that become reestablished and survive in the modified environment.

Characteristic of the whole region is the continuing occupancy of disturbed sites by species of the original vegetation of the area, with population expansions in some species and disappearance or reduced populations in other species. But essentially nowhere is there the intercalation of floristically discrete assemblages—several stages between pioneer and climax communities—which occurs in orderly and predictable sequence in humid regions plant succession.

It is quite clear that whether or not one accepts succession as an important aspect of desert vegetation dynamics depends on exactly how one defines succession. However, one thing is sure; plant "succession" or "revegetation after disturbance," or whatever the phenomenon is termed, is certainly not comparable to that described by Odum (1971) which occurs in mesic systems. After a review of research on succession in deserts, Rowlands et al. (1980) concluded that:

1. Many authors fail to distinguish between a true succession, as defined by Pickett (1976), Whittaker (1975), or Odum (1971), and simple reestablishment. Often there is a failure to substantiate what Shreve (1942) has called a reaction upon the environment of specific plant species within the successional scheme. In some cases, there may be differences in interpretation depending upon what measurements (i.e., cover, density, biomass) or synthetic indices (e.g., importance values) are used and manipulated in analyzing the data.

2. One should be careful to distinguish between true succession and the effects of spatial zonation due to environmental gradients, and vegetation cycling due to recurrent changes in the environment.

3. Since the effect of plants on soil profile development in deserts is minimal, particularly with regard to organic horizons, succession, as defined and studied in mesic ecosystems, may have little relevance in desert areas with respect to soil-plant interactions.

4. Since water is a limiting factor in true desert and is always very scarce, the biological factors which would be otherwise operating to form soils (e.g., soil microflora) do so at a very slow rate (Chapter 2). The dominant species within the desert flora are rigorously adapted to such environmental stresses as drought, high levels of salinity and alkalinity, and low soil nutrient content. In mesic ecosystems, denudation results in drastic changes in both soil water balance and nutrient balance, creating, after disturbance, a situation to which the climax vegetation is poorly adapted. In deserts, the "climax" vegetation, or more properly the species constituents of the local stable

zonal vegetation, are adapted to an already very arid and otherwise stressful environment which denudation disrupts proportionally less. As a result, reestablishment of the original vegetation by reseeding, or in some cases vegetative reproduction as with certain shrubs, rhizomatous grasses, and succulents commences, upon alleviation of the disturbance with the onset of favorable climatic conditions.

With respect to succession occurring after abatement of a chronic disturbance, favorable climatic conditions may involve the kind of "catastrophic climatic events" described by Holmgren and Hutchings (1977) whose comments on vegetational change after suspension of grazing might well apply to disturbances in general. Elimination of disturbances which have produced compositional changes in vegetation may not alone terminate or reverse changes induced by such disturbances. It may only be under the most favorable of conditions that seedlings of the former species can become established in competition with those species which have developed under the conditions of disturbance.

5. Because longer lived perennials have a slow rate of growth, a "stage" of vegetational development with "pioneer" perennials may predominate over the young representatives of the former vegetation; however this "stage" is clearly not a necessary component of the recovery process, and may be absent in many cases. The latter with time will eventually regain their ascendancy. The former may be present to a greater or lesser degree depending upon local conditions since many are plants which are normally found in washes and other naturally disturbed situations (most have seeds which are wind disseminated). They thrive in disturbed situations probably because of release from competition with the long-lived dominant perennial species shortly after denudation.

6. Because of the extremely long periods of time necessary to develop certain scrub communities, that is, creosote bush scrub with clone formation (Vasek, 1980a), the factor of evolutionary changes in plant species within the sequence of vegetational change cannot be ignored.

7. A climax community as defined by Odum (1971) cannot be distinguished in deserts; however, successional patterns in unproductive environments, as envisioned by Grime (1979), are observable.

8. Vegetational change, both cyclic and successional, does take place in arid and semiarid ecosystems. Occasionally, a true succession may be identified such as on dry lake margins (Vasek and Lund, 1980). In general, most vegetational changes are successional or fall somewhere between the interpretations of Shreve (1942), Muller (1940), and Beatley (1976) and those of Wells (1961), Webb and Wilshire (1980), and Vasek (1980b). Such sequences of vegetational development in arid areas might be termed parasuccession.

9. As in other ecosystems of the world, the time required for complete recovery after denudation of arid and semiarid vegetation is on the order of centuries or even millenia.

10. Until long-term studies are made in a variety of sites, discussions of plant succession on deserts will have to be labeled largely theoretical.

Overall Effects and Management of Off-Road Vehicles in Arid and Semiarid Vegetation Types

Experiments have shown that one pass of a four-wheel-drive truck on wet soil creates soil compaction sufficient to significantly reduce the cover and density of several species of annual plant species in the Mojave Desert. Some species such as *Schismus barbatus* and *Bouteloua barbata* at first respond positively to the compaction created by up to three passes of a truck on wet soil. Even these species declined as mechanical impedence of the wet soil exceeded 1800 kN m^{-2}, a value which also appears to be a threshold value for agricultural crops. Soil strength values above 2500 kN m^{-2} probably exceed the tolerance level of most plant species, native, introduced, cultivated, or otherwise.

In general, the response of annual plants to soil compaction is a function of: (1) the type of soil compacted, (2) the intensity of compaction, (3) the time of compaction relative to changes in soil moisture levels, (4) the amount and pattern of precipitation falling after compaction has occurred, (5) the chemical and physical properties of the soil at different sites, (6) the species of plant, (7) substrate heterogeneity, and (8) the way response is measured by the investigator. There is no reason to assume that newly germinated seedlings of perennial species should not behave similarly to annual plants in their response to compacted soils.

Severe water erosion in areas with shallow soil underlain by material impervious to roots, as on many hillclimb areas, may greatly reduce potential for growth of perennial plants. Water erosion on deeper soils or those whose parent material can be penetrated by roots will not be as detrimental to plant growth. Accelerated water or wind erosion may disperse nutrient elements which have been accumulating underneath shrubs and thus reduce the number of sites which are favorable to plant growth. Accelerated wind erosion may also decrease soil productivity by removing surface soil, which often has higher concentrations of nutrient elements essential to plant growth.

Surface shearing, which uproots and disrupts root systems, and crushing of foliage, root systems, and seedlings are the direct impacts of ORVs on vegetation. These impacts can cause changes in patterns and composition of vegetation as reflected in changes in plant density, cover, and species diversity within a site. Changes may be more or less intense depending upon the intensity and rate of use by ORVs, regional and local climates, topography, and soil type, among other factors. Densities of perennial plants in heavily used desert areas have been reported to have declined by 38 to 100% as compared with adjacent relatively unused areas (Chapter 8). Likewise, plant cover may decline 35 to 85% and species diversity 24 to 82%, depending upon the intensity of use (Hall, 1980).

After reviewing the literature dealing with the direct effects of ORVs on vegetation, Hall (1980) concluded that from the research gathered and analyzed, generalizations as to the effects of ORV use on arid and semiarid vegetation can be predicted: (1) ORV use will reduce perennial plant cover and above-ground biomass and the degree of loss is dependent on the intensity of use. (2) A reduction in perennial plant density often occurs in ORV use areas, especially in areas of "moderate" to "heavy" use. The terms "moderate" and "heavy" have not been quantitatively defined but are relative terms and may vary somewhat from site to site. (3) In areas of ORV use (primarily open or competitive areas), the smaller shrubs are often the first to be damaged and eliminated. (4) Annual species are affected in similar ways to the perennials. However, slight disturbances may cause no measureable differences with regard to either annual or perennial plants or show some positive response by increasing cover or diversity. (5) Some perennial plants can recover from ORV impacts if the plant crown has not been completely killed, and if sufficient time is given between impacts some species will resprout (Lathrop, 1978; Vollmer et al., 1976). The best estimates on resprouting perennial plant recovery appear to be around 10 to 20 years, but soil recovery maybe much longer, requiring centuries (Chapters 13, 14) or even millenia.

The management of ORVs really cannot be attempted within the context of sustained yield or "carrying capacity" as is often done with livestock grazing. Unlike ORV use, livestock grazing produces tangible benefits in the form of food production and proper management can maximize such production while minimizing environmental impacts. The strategies used may include some form of complex seasonal or rotational system, strict control of stocking rates, or a combination of these strategies designed to ensure that serious injury does not occur to the growth processes of the constituent rangeland plant species, all of which are to some extent exposed to herbivorous activity, domestic or native. Such management strategies cannot be applied to ORV recreation. Moreover, attempts to regulate numbers of ORVs within an area as one would adjust stocking rates would be difficult if not impossible (see Chapter 4). ORV recreation tends to require large areas of land which are not easily enclosed by fences or other devices, making enforcement of limits on user numbers a formidable task. ORV recreation is therefore a highly consumptive use of rangelands which is not conducive to sustained-yield management.

However, minimizing impact to vegetation is possible under the proper conditions. Use intensity should be kept as low as possible and strictly managed. Concentrated use, whether in race courses or "fellowship" areas (campgrounds, etc.) should be avoided, particularly on steep slopes. Areas already damaged and denuded of vegetation should be managed specifically for ORV use, rather than expanding activity into undisturbed areas. Revegetation of such areas is impossible as long as the area is being used (Chapters 15, 16, and 17). Restoration requires reconditioning and total recovery of the disturbed area such that predisturbance conditions, including species composition, are precisely replicated. On a practical level, restoration of disturbed land occurs only through the process of natural revegetation and recovery, which may take centuries to millenia due to the great environmental stresses in arid environments. The desert is not "tough" as some off-road enthusiasts have so glibly put it, and restoration as a management objective is for all practical purposes unattainable as long as ORV activity occurs, even on an irregular basis.

Because there are no known examples in the plant world of a growth strategy which enables plant species to withstand both the rigors of a stressful environment *and* the viscissitudes of continued disturbance (Grime, 1979) and because revegetation (whether natural or man induced) is such a slow process, the idea of rest and managed rehabilitation of heavily used ORV areas is rarely worthy of consideration even if unlimited funds are available. It is important in this regard to remember that irrespective of "claims" to the contrary, *no study or attempt at artificial rehabilitation and revegetation of desert disturbance has been an unqualified or even a qualified success* (Chapters 15, 16, and 17). Rest and reuse should only be considered in areas impacted by highly dispersed ORV events; however, it must be ensured that such areas are closed after the event and monitored until recovery is deemed to be complete. Other management strategies could involve limiting use to areas where vegetation is naturally scarce, such as playa (dry lake) surfaces or active sand dunes. Unfortunately, these areas often contain other sensitive resources, such as rare or endangered wildlife (Chapters 9 and 10), so not all of these places will be available for use.

Acknowledgments

This study was supported by the U.S. Bureau of Land Management, Desert Plan Program, Riverside, California. Special appreciation goes to Hyrum B. Johnson and other members of the Desert Plan Program for the guidance and help they gave. Thanks goes to Robert F. Thorne for help in determination of plant specimens during the field work phase of these studies and for his critical review of pertinent portions of the manuscript.

References

Adams, J. A., E. S. Endo, L. H. Stolvy, P. G. Rowlands, and H. B. Johnson. 1982. Controlled experiments on soil compaction produced by off-road vehicles in the Mojave Desert, California. J. Appl. Ecol., 19:167–175.

Adams, S., B. R. Strain, and M. S. Adams. 1970. Water-repellent soils and annual plant cover in a desert scrub community of southeast California. Ecology 51: 590–700.

Axelrod, D. I. 1964. History of Western Deserts. Lecture notes, NSF Institute in Desert Biology, Arizona State University, Tempe, 2 pp.

Axelrod, D. I. 1979. Age and Origin of Sonoran Desert Vegetation. Occasional Papers of the California Academy of Sciences, No. 132, 74 pp.

Beatley, J. C. 1967. Survival of winter annuals in the northern Mojave Desert. Ecology 48:745–750.

Beatley, J. C. 1969. Biomass of desert winter annual plant populations in southern Nevada. Oikos 20:261–273.

Beatley, J. 1974. Phenological events and their environmental triggers in Mojave Desert ecosystems. Ecology 55:856–863.

Beatley, J. C. 1976. Vascular plants of the Nevada Test Site and central southern Nevada ecologic and geographic distributions. National Technical Information Service, TID-2688 DAS, Springfield, Virginia, 316 pp.

Blaisdell, J. P. 1958. Seasonal Development and Yield of Native Plants on the Upper Snake River Plains and Their Relation to Certain Climatic Factors. U.S. Dept. of Agriculture Tech. Bull. 1190, 68 pp.

Cain, S. A., and G. M. de O. Castro. 1959. Manual of Vegetation Analysis. Harper, New York, 325 pp.

Carter, L. M., and J. R. Tavernetti. 1968. Influence of precision tillage and soil composition on cotton yields. Trans. Am. Soc. Agric. Eng. 11:65–67, 73.

Chew, R. M., and A. E. Chew. 1965. The primary productivity of a desert-shrub *(Larrea tridentata)* community. Ecol. Mongr. 35:355–375.

Daubenmire, R. 1978. Plant Geography. Academic Press, New York, 388 pp.

Grime, J. P. 1979. Plant Strategies and Vegetation Processes. John Wiley and Sons, Chichester, U.K., 222 pp.

Grimes, D. W., R. J. Miller, and P. L. Wiley. 1975. Cotton and corn root development in two field soils of different strength characteristics. Agron. J. 67: 519–523.

Hall, J. A. 1980. Direct impacts of off-road vehicles on vegetation. In: P. G. Rowlands (Ed.), The Effects of Disturbance on Desert Soils, Vegetation and Community Processes with Emphasis on Off-Road-Vehicles; A Critical Review. U.S. Dept. Interior, Bureau of Land Management, Desert Plan Staff Special Publication, Riverside, California, pp. 63–74.

Halvorsen, W. L., and D. T. Patten. 1975. Productivity and flowering of winter emphemerals in relation to Sonoran desert shrubs. Am. Midl. Naturalist 93: 311–319.

Hastings, J. R., and R. M. Turner. 1965. The Changing Mile. University of Arizona Press, Tucson, Arizona, 317 pp.

Holmgren, R. C., and S. F. Brewster, Jr. 1977. Distribution of organic matter reserve in a desert shrub community. U.S. Dept. Agriculture Forest Service Research Paper INT-130, 15 pp.

Holmgren, B. C., and S. S. Hutchings. 1972. Salt desert shrub response to grazing use. In: C. M. McKell, J. P. Blaisdell, and J. R. Goodin (Eds.), Wildland Shrubs—Their Biology and Utilization. Proc. Int. Symp., Utah State Univ., Logan, Utah, pp. 153–165.

Hunt, C. B. 1966. Plant Ecology of Death Valley, California. U.S. Geological Survey Professional Paper 509, U.S. Government Printing Office, Washington, D.C., 68 pp.

Jaeger, E. C., and A. C. Smith. 1966. Introduction to the Natural History of Southern California. University of California Press, Berkeley, California, 104 pp.

Johnson, A. W. 1968. The evolution of desert vegetation in western North America. In: G. W. Brown (Ed.), Desert Biology, Special Topics on the Physical and Biological Aspects of Arid Regions, Vol. 1. Academic Press, New York, pp. 101–140.

Johnson, H. B. 1975. Gas exchange strategies in desert plants. In: D. M. Gates and R. B. Schmerl (Eds.), Perspectives of Biophysical Ecology. Springer-Verlag, New York, pp. 105–120.

Johnson, H. B. 1976. Vegetation and plant communities of southern California deserts—a functional view. In: J. Latting (Ed.), Plant Communities of Southern California. California Native Plant Society Special Publication 2, pp. 125–162.

Johnson, H. B., F. C. Vasek, and T. Yonkers. 1978. Residual effects of summer irrigation on Mojave Desert annuals. Bull. So. Calif. Acad. Sci. 77:95–108.

Johnston, M. C. 1974. Brief resume of botanical, including vegetational, features of the Chihuahuan Desert region with special emphasis on their uniqueness. In: R. Wauer and A. H. Riskind (Eds.), Transactions of the Symposium on Biological Resources of the Chihuahuan Desert Region U.S. and Mexico. U.S. Dept. Interior National Park Service Trans. and Proc. Ser. No. 3, pp. 335–359.

Knapp, R. 1965. Die Vegetation von Nord-und Mittleamerika und der Hawaii Inseln. G. Fisher Verlag, Stuttgard, 373 pp.

Laurenko, E. M., V. N. Andreez, and V. L. Loenteef. 1955. Profile of productivity of natural above-ground vegetation of the USSR from the tundra to the deserts. Bot. Ahur. 40:415–419.

Lathrop, E. W. 1978. Plant Response Parameters to Recreational Vehicles in the California Desert Conservation Area. Final Report, Contract No. CA-060-CT7-2824, Desert Plan Program, U.S. Bureau of Land Management, Riverside, California, 240 pp.

Leopold, A. S. 1961. The Desert. Life Nature Library, Time Incorporated, New York, 192 pp.

Logan, R. F. 1964. Desert Climates: Causes, Types, Effects. Lecture notes, Axelrod (1964) citing Logan, NSF Institute in Desert Biology, Arizona State University, Tempe, Arizona, 2 pp.

Logan, R. F. 1968. Causes, climates, and distribution of deserts. In: G. W. Brown (Ed.), Desert Biology, Special Topics on the Physical and Biological Aspects of Arid Regions, Vol. 1. Academic Press, New York, pp. 21–50.

Major, J. 1977. California climate in relation to vegetation. In: M. G. Barbour and J. Major (Eds.), Terrestrial Vegetation of California. John Wiley and Sons, New York, pp. 11–74.

Margalef, R. 1968. Perspectives in Ecological Theory. University of Chicago Press, Chicago, Illinois, 111 pp.

Martin, S. C., and D. R. Cable. 1974. Managing Semidesert Grassland Shrub Ranges: Vegetation Responses to Precipitation, Grazing, Soil Texture, and Mesquite Control. U.S. Dept. Agriculture Forest Service Tech. Bull. 1480, 45 pp.

McCleary, J. A. 1968. The biology of desert plants. In: G. W. Brown (Ed.), Desert Biology, Special Topics on the Physical and Biological Aspects of Arid Regions, Vol. 1. Academic Press, New York, pp. 141–194.

McKell, C. M., J. P. Blaisdel, and J. R. Goodin. 1971. Wildland Shrubs—Their Biology and Utilization. U.S. Dept. Agriculture Forest Service General Technical Report INT-1, 494 pp.

McGinnies, W. G., B. J. Goldman, and P. Paylore. 1968. Deserts of the World: An Appraisal of Research into Their Physical and Biological Environments. University of Arizona Press, Tucson, Arizona, 788 pp.

McNaughton, S. J. 1977. Diversity and stability of ecological communities; A comment on the role of empiricism in ecology. Am. Naturalist 111:515–525.

McNaughton, S. J. 1979. Grazing as an optimization process. Am. Naturalist 113:691–703.

McNaughton, S. J., and L. L. Wolf. 1979. General Ecology. Holt, Rinehart and Winston, New York, 702 pp.

Mellinger, M. V., and S. J. McNaughton. 1975. Structure and function of successional vascular plant communities in central New York. Ecol. Mongr. 45: 161–182.

Miles, J. 1979. Vegetation Dynamics. Methuen, New York, New York, 80 pp.

Miller, R. R. 1976. Models, metaphysics and long-lived species. Bull. Ecol. Soc. Am. 57:2–6.

Mooney, H. A., J. Ehleringer, and J. A. Berry. 1976. High photosynthetic capacity of a winter annual in Death Valley. Science 194:321–323.

Mueller-Dombois, D., and H. Ellenburg. 1974. Aims and Methods of Vegetation Ecology. John Wiley and Sons, New York, 547 pp.

Muller, C. H. 1940. Plant succession in the *Larrea-Flourensia* climax. Ecology 21:206–212.

Muller, C. H. 1953. The association of desert annuals with shrubs. Am. J. Bot. 40:53–60.

Mulroy, T. W., and P. W. Rundel. 1977. Annual plants: Adaptations to desert environments. Bioscience 27:109–114.

Munz, P. A., and D. D. Keck. 1949. California plant communities. El Aliso 2: 87–105.

Munz, P. A., and D. D. Keck. 1950. California plant communities. El Aliso 2: 199–202.

Munz, P. A., and D. D. Keck. 1959. A California Flora. University of California Press, Berkeley, 1681 pp.

Norton, B. E. 1974. United States/International Biome Program studies in the desert biome. Bull. Ecol. Soc. 55:6–10.

Odum, E. P. 1971. Fundamentals of Ecology. W. B. Saunders Co., Philadelphia, Pennsylvania, 574 pp.

Patten, D. T. 1975. Phenology and function of Sonoran Desert annuals in relation to environmental changes. US/IBP Desert Biome Research Memorandum 75-10, Utah State University, Logan, Utah, 12 pp.

Patten, D. T., and E. M. Smith. 1974. Phenology and function of Sonoran Desert annuals in relation to environmental changes. US/IBP Desert Biome Research Memorandum 74-12, Utah State University, Logan, Utah, 12 pp.

Pearson, L. C. 1965. Primary production in grazed and ungrazed desert communities in eastern Idaho. Ecology 46:278–285.

Pianka, E. R. 1974. Evolutionary Ecology. Harper and Row, New York, 365 pp.

Pickett, S. T. A. 1976. Succession, an evolutionary interpretation. Am. Naturalist 110:107–119.

Pielou, E. C. Biogeography. John Wiley and Sons, New York, 351 pp.

Raven, P. H., and D. I. Axelrod. 1976. Origin and relationships of the California Flora. University of California Publications in Botany 72, Berkeley, California, 134 pp.

Richardson, J. L. 1977. Dimensions of Ecology. The Williams & Wilkins Co., Baltimore, Maryland, 412 pp.

Rodin, L. E., and J. I. Basilovich. 1968. World distribution of plant biomass. In:

F. E. Eckardt (Ed.), Functioning of Terrestrial Ecosystems at the Primary Production Level. Proc. Copenhagen Symp. UNESCO, Paris, pp. 45-52.

Rowlands, P. G. 1980. Recovery, succession, and vegetation in the Mojave Desert. In: P. G. Rowlands (Ed.), The Effects of Disturbance on Desert Soils, Vegetation and Community Processes with Emphasis on Off-Road Vehicles. U.S. Dept. Interior Bureau of Land Management Desert Plan Staff Special Publication, Riverside, California, pp. 75-120.

Rowlands, P. G., J. A. Adams, H. B. Johnson, and A. S. Endo. 1980. Experiments on the effects of soil compaction on establishment, cover and pattern of winter annuals in the Mojave Desert. In: P. G. Rowlands (Ed.), The Effects of Disturbance on Desert Soils, Vegetation and Community Processes with Emphasis on Off-Road Vehicles. U.S. Dept. Interior Bureau of Land Management, Desert Plan Staff Special Publication, Riverside, California, pp. 135-164.

Shreve, F. 1942. The desert vegetation of North America. Bot. Rev. 8:195-246.

Smith, H. T. U. 1968. Geologic and geomorphic aspects of desert. In: G. W. Brown (Ed.), Desert Biology, Special Topics of the Physical and Biological Aspects of Arid Regions, Vol. 1. Academic Press, New York, pp. 51-100.

Stoddart, L. A., A. D. Smith, and T. W. Box. 1975. Range Management. McGraw Hill Book Co., Inc., New York, 532 pp.

Sulenski, R. J. 1972. The Natural Revegetation of Mine Sites in the Las Vegas Valley and the Feasibility of Allowing the Free Use Collection of Cacti and Other Desert Plants. Bureau of Land Management Report 7383-3042-53-00 (N-053), U.S. Bureau of Land Management, Las Vegas, Nevada, 41 pp.

Szarek, S. K. 1979. Primary production in four North American deserts. J. Arid Environ. 2:187-209.

Taylor, H. M. 1971. Effects of soil strength on seedling emergence, root growth, and crop yield. In: D. D. Barnes et al. (Eds.), Compaction of Agricultural Soil. American Society of Agricultural Engineers Monograph, pp. 292-305.

Taylor, H. M., and H. R. Gardner. 1963. Penetration of cotton seedling taproots as influenced by bulk density, moisture content, and strength of soil. Soil Sci. 96:153-156.

Taylor, H. M., G. M. Roberson, and J. J. Parker, Jr. 1966. Soil strength root penetration relations for medium to coarse-textured soil materials. Soil Sci. 102:18-22.

Taylor, H. M., G. M. Roberson, and J. J. Parker, Jr. 1967. Cotton seedling taproot elongation as effected by soil strength changes induced by slurring and water extraction. Soil Sci. Soc. Am. Proc. 31:700-704.

Thorne, R. F. 1976. California plant communities. In: J. Latting (Ed.), Plant Communities of Southern California. California Native Plant Society Special Publication 2, pp. 1-31.

Thorne, R. F., B. A. Prigge, and J. H. Henrickson. 1981. A flora of the higher ranges and the Kelso Dunes of the eastern Mojave Desert in California. Aliso 10:71-186.

Turner, F. B. 1975. Rock Valley Validation Site Report. US/IBP Research Memorandum 75-2, Utah State University, Logan, Utah, pp. 24-30.

Turner, F. B., and J. F. MacBrayer. 1974. Rock Valley Validation Site Report. US/IBP Research Memorandum RM 74-2, Utah State University, Logan, Utah, 64 pp.

Van Devender, T. R. 1977. Holocene woodlands in the southwestern deserts. Science 198:189–192.

Van Devender, R. R., and W. G. Spaulding. 1979. Development of vegetation and climate in the southwestern United States. Science 204:701–710.

Van Dyke, J. D. 1901. The Desert, Further Studies in Natural Appearances. Charles Scribner's Sons, New York, 233 pp.

Vasek, F. C. 1980a. Creosote bush: long-lived clones in the Mojave Desert. Am. J. Bot. 67:246–255.

Vasek, F. C. 1980b. Early successional stages in Mojave Desert scrub vegetation. Israeli J. Bot. 28:133–148.

Vasek, F. C., and M. G. Barbour. 1977. Mojave Desert scrub vegetation. In: M. Barbour and J. Major (Eds.), Terrestrial Vegetation of California. John Wiley and Sons, New York, pp. 835–867.

Vasek, F. C., and L. Lund. 1980. Soil characteristics associated with primary plant succession on a Mojave Desert dry lake. Ecology 69:1013–1018.

Vasek, F. C., and R. F. Thorne. 1977. Transmontane coniferous vegetation. In: M. Barbour and J. Major (Eds.), Terrestrial Vegetation of California. John Wiley and Sons, New York, pp. 797–832.

Vasek, F. C., H. B. Johnson, and D. H. Eslinger. 1975. Effects of pipeline construction on creosote bush scrub vegetation of the Mojave Desert. Madrono 23:1–64.

Vollmer, A. T., B. G. Maza, P. A. Medica, F. B. Turner, and S. A. Bamberg. 1976. The impact of off-road vehicles on a desert ecosystem. Environ. Management 1(2):115–129.

Wallace, A., and E. M. Romney. 1972. Radioecology and ecophysiology of desert plants at the Nevada Test Site. United States Atomic Energy Commission Office of Information Services, Washington, D.C., 439 pp.

Walter, H. 1973. Vegetation of the Earth. Springer-Verlag, New York, 235 pp.

Webb, R. H., and H. G. Wilshire. 1980. Recovery of soils and vegetation in a Mojave Desert ghost town. J. Arid Environ. 3:291–303.

Wells, P. V. 1961. Succession in desert vegetation on the streets of a Nevada ghost town. Science 134:670–671.

Wells, P. V. 1976. Macrofossil analysis of woodrat (Neotoma) middens as a key to the Quaternary vegetational history of arid America. Quat. Res. 6:223–248.

Wells, P. V., and R. Berger. 1967. Late Pleistocene history of coniferous woodland in the Mojave Desert. Science 155(3770):1640–1647.

Went, F. W. 1942. The dependence of certain annual plants on shrubs in southern California deserts. Bull. Torrey Bot. Club 69:100–114.

Went, F. 1948. Ecology of desert plants. I. Observation on germination in the Joshua Tree National Monument, California. Ecology 30:1–13.

Went, F. 1949. Ecology of desert plants. II. The effect of rain and temperature on germination and growth. Ecology 30:1–13.

Went, F., and M. Westergaard. 1949. The ecology of desert plants. III. Development of plants in the Death Valley National Monument, California. Ecology 30:20–38.

West, N. E. 1972. Biomass and nutrient dynamics of some major cold desert shrubs. US/IBP Research Memorandum RM 72-15, Utah State University, Logan, Utah, 24 pp.

West, N. E., K. H. Rea, and R. O. Harniss. 1979. Plant demographic studies in sagebrush-grass communities of southeastern Idaho. Ecology 60:376–388.

Whittaker, R. H. 1975. Communities and ecosystems, 2nd ed. Macmillan Publishing Co., Inc., New York, 385 pp.

Whittaker, R. H., and W. A. Niering. 1965. Vegetation of the Santa Catalina Mountains, Arizona (II) A gradient analysis of the south slope. Ecology 6: 429–452.

Whittaker, R. H., and W. A. Niering. 1975. Vegetation of the Santa Catalina Mountains, Arizona. V. Biomass production and diversity along the environmental gradient. Ecology 56:771–789.

Wiggins, I. L. 1964. Some observations on the effects of drought on desert vegetation. Lecture notes, Axelrod (1964) citing Wiggins. NSF Institute in Desert Biology, Arizona State University, Tempe, 2 pp.

8

The Effect of Vehicle Use on Desert Vegetation[1]

Earl W. Lathrop

Introduction

In recent years the delicate desert ecosystem has been challenged by increased use of off-road vehicles (ORVs) (Sheridan, 1979). Families bring dune buggies, motorcycles, and four-wheel-drive vehicles into the desert by the thousands on weekends (Luckenbach, 1975) and this motorized use of the desert has greatly affected the vegetation (Vollmer et al., 1976; Wilshire et al., 1978a, b). The main recreational uses include: (1) motorcycle races, (2) hill climbing, (3) sand dune travel, and (4) trail riding. Associated with these activities are "pit areas" where racers, hill climbers, ORV drivers, and spectators park their vehicles. After several gatherings the pit area is usually bare of vegetation and the soil is greatly compacted (Fox, 1973; Davidson and Fox, 1974; Wilshire and Nakata, 1976, 1977).

The purpose of this project was to study the impacts of vehicles on vegetation in nine locations representative of off-road vehicle use in the California deserts (Fig. 8-1). The impacts studied consisted primarily of hill-climbing areas (Figs. 8-2 and 8-3), motorcycle tracks at raceway sites (Figs. 8-4 and 8-5) and associated pit areas (Figs. 8-3 and 8-6).

---

[1] The views and conclusions contained in this chapter are based on the author's studies or experiences and do not necessarily represent the official viewpoint or policy of any U.S. government agency.

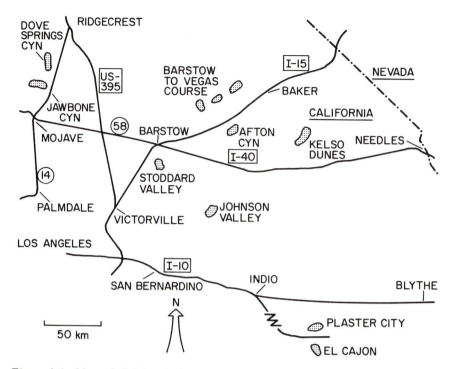

Figure 8-1. Map of California desert showing location of the study areas. Major highways and other landmarks are indicated.

Figure 8-2. Hillside showing motorcycle trails in Jawbone Canyon, T30S, R6E, Sec. 22 (May 1978).

Figure 8-3. Denuded canyon floor and hillside trails in Dove Springs Canyon, T29S, R37E, Sec. 8 (November 1978).

Figure 8-4. Race course site in a cheesebush scrub wash of the 1974 Barstow to Las Vegas race. The original tracks have been crossed and enlarged in some parts by more recent use. Photograph taken January 1978 at T12N, R5E, Sec. 28.

Figure 8-5. Pit area at the starting site of the Barstow to Las Vegas race, T10N, R4E, Sec. 6. Photograph (January 1978) shows accumulation of annuals *(Pectis papposa* and *Bouteloua barbata)* in track swales created primarily by recreational vehicles associated with the motorcycle race.

Figure 8-6. Large pit area near Plaster City, T16S, R11E, Sec. 5 (November 1977) showing vehicles lined up awaiting the events of a motorcycle race. The environmental impact on the vegetation is clearly visible in the photograph.

Methods

The study, undertaken August 1977 through July 1978, utilized aerial photographic and ground transect data as the primary methods for analysis of vegetation response. Study areas were located on aerial photographs for both disturbed (test) and undisturbed (control) sites. The ideal control was a comparable photograph before disturbance (1952, 1953). Dates for the test photographs were usually early to late 1970s. Transparent plot and transect grids were calibrated for each photograph for the purpose of measuring density and cover of perennial vegetation in test and control plots (Lathrop, 1978). Because the ORV activity in the study areas took place after the earlier photographs, such measurements were helpful in determining change in density and cover of the vegetation over time. While the changes noted were assumed to be primarily due to ORV activity, it is possible that "natural" effects could have contributed some of the change. Density is expressed as the number of individual perennial plants per hectare (ha). Cover measurements represent the percentage of the ground which is covered by the crown canopy of the perennial herbs and shrubs. Ground measurements, like the aerial photograph analyses, were used to calculate density and cover using standard formulas (Whittaker, 1975; Brower and Zar, 1977). While absolute values of aerial photograph measurements of vegetation were not directly comparable to similar ground measurements due to topography and resolution of the photographs, relative values were comparable; photographic analysis gave trends in the results similar to those of the on-site ground measurements. Vegetation at the study sites is composed primarily of perennial shrubs belonging to the creosote bush scrub, alkaline scrub, and desert dune sand plant communities as described by Thorne (1976) and to the cheesebush scrub community described by Johnson (1976).

Results

The effect of motorcycles and four-wheel-drive vehicles on vegetation is primarily due to direct destruction of plants and disruption and compaction of soil (Davidson and Fox, 1974). In addition to crushing of the foliage, root system and germinating seeds are damaged during compaction of the soil; the plants are also damaged by the superstructure of vehicles, so that the actual plant damage may occur over an area much larger than the track width (Wilshire et al., 1978b). Thus data presented in this section compare plant density and cover of the disturbed areas to equivalent undisturbed (control) areas to assess the effects of vehicles on vegetation.

Kelso Dunes

The Kelso Dunes, some of which stand between 182 and 213 m above the adjacent desert floor, have primarily a cover of perennial grasses (i.e., *Hilaria rigida*), perennial herbs (i.e., *Rumex hymenosepalus*), and shrubs. The scant shrub cover

on the foredunes consists mainly of creosote bush *(Larrea tridentata)* and burrobush *(Ambrosia dumosa)*. The plant community of the desert floor is of creosote bush scrub. Prior to closure of the Kelso Dunes to recreational use in 1973,
the scenic dunes, located 48 km southeast of Baker, had long attracted dune
buggy enthusiasts. Aerial photographic comparisons before (April 5, 1953) and
after (June 9, 1974) use by off-road vehicles in the dunes indicate a reduction in
shrub density of about one-half along both the foredunes and the desert floor at
the base of the dunes (Table 8-1). Ground transects taken by Kuhn (1974)
compared shrub density and cover in disturbed and undisturbed plots at the

Table 8-1. Aerial Photographic Comparison of Perennial Plant Density Before (Control) and After (Test) Use by Off-Road Vehicles in Test Areas of the California Desert

Area/site	N^a	Density (individuals per hectare)		Percentage change
		Before	After	
Kelso Dunes		1953	1974	
Desert floor	3,524	81		51
	1,721		40	
Fore dunes	1,139	40		50
	649		20	
Johnson Valley		1952	1977	
Pit areas	5,121	97		46
	2,709		52	
Plaster City		1953	1972	
Pit area	5,121	158		39
Race course	2,709		97	
Dove Springs		1952	1973	
Hillsides	12,242	340		46
	6,562		182	
Pit areas	6,972	329		60
	3,432		132	
Barstow to Vegas race		Nov. 26, 1974	Dec. 5, 1974	
Race course	3,596	2,478		46
	1,765		1,332	
El Cajon		Nov. 26, 1972	Dec. 5, 1974	
Race course	2,208	1,022		34
	1,450		672	

$^a N$, number of plants sampled.

dunes; his results show a reduction of density of 24 and 85% in the foredunes and desert floor, respectively. Vehicle use reduced the cover by 85 and 76% in foredunes and desert floor, respectively.

Johnson Valley

Johnson Valley has nearly a uniform cover of the creosote bush scrub community, except in an occasional wash where cheesebush scrub *(Hymenoclea salsola)* dominates. This region has had heavy use in the past by a variety of recreational vehicle activities, including hillclimbs by four-wheel-drive vehicles and motorcycle races. Shrub density, compared on photographs dated November 26, 1952 and May 28, 1977, was reduced 46% (Table 8-1) in the dominant creosote bush scrub community as a result of vehicle use.

Plaster City

Vegetation of the Plaster City study sites, located in the Yuha Desert area, consists mainly of creosote bush scrub and ocotillo *(Fouquieria splendens)* on the extensive pavemented terraces and on the gently sloping sandy alluvial fans. Alkaline scrub *(Atriplex hymenelytra)* dominates in the basins and dry sandy washes along with occasional smoke trees *(Dalea spinosa)* and cat's-claw acacia *(Acacia greggii)*. Analyses of three large off-road vehicle use areas (Figs. 8-3 and 8-6) with flat to rolling topography were done using before (May 1953) and after (November 26, 1972) aerial photographs. Mean density, calculated from counts of perennials on both sets of photographs showed a reduction of 39% for the three areas sampled (Table 8-1).

Stoddard Valley

The dominant vegetation on upper slopes of Stoddard Valley is creosote bush scrub, while saltbushes *(Atriplex canescens* and *A. confertifolia)* are the dominant perennials of the low areas. This popular recreational area has been used for a variety of competitive events, including dune buggy races and hill climbing. Ground transect measurements were used to compare vegetation density and cover in disturbed and undisturbed areas. Results indicate significant reduction of both mean density (91%) and cover (96%) due to off-road vehicle activity in this area (Figs. 8-7 and 8-8).

Afton Canyon

Ground transect comparisons of an undisturbed hillside of creosote bush scrub with a similar hillside with dense trails showed a respective reduction in density from 1425 to 315 per hectare and a corresponding reduction in cover from 5.5 to 1.3%. The nearby pit area, also of creosote bush scrub, had a density of 49 individuals per hectare compared to the control of 1912, with a similar drop in percentage cover (Figs. 8-7 and 8-8).

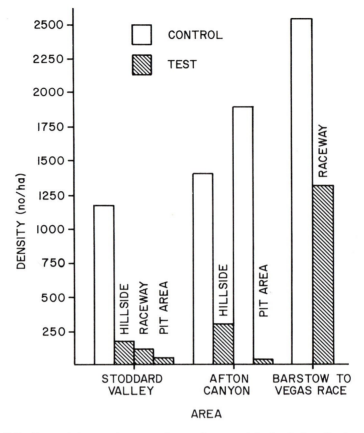

Figure 8-7. Ground transect comparison of perennial plant density in control and test areas of off-road vehicle sites. Number of individuals sampled (N) averages 117 at each site.

Jawbone Canyon

Vegetation cover at the study sites in Jawbone Canyon was primarily of cheese-bush scrub on the lower slopes and hills, and alkaline scrub *(Atriplex ploycarpa* and *Lepidospartum squamatum)* in the flatter areas. Associated perennial species in the cheesebush scrub here were: bladder sage *(Salazaria mexicana),* brittle bush *(Encelia virginensis), Ambrosia dumosa,* California buckwheat *(Eriogonum fasiculatum),* and Mormon tea *(Ephedra nevadensis).* Three steep hillsides in Jawbone Canyon, each with numerous trails in the vegetation cover caused by motorcycle hill climbing (Fig. 8-2), were measured for density and cover by ground transects, along with the attendant pit area. Mean density of the three disturbed hillsides was 48% less than the vegetation density of the adjacent undisturbed hillsides; density of the pit area was reduced by 82% compared to

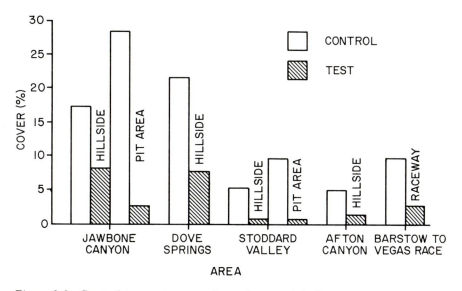

Figure 8-8. Ground transect comparison of perennial plant cover in control and test areas of off-road vehicle sites. N averages 146 each site.

its control. Likewise, there was a substantial (54% on hillsides and 91% in the pit area) decrease in vegetation cover at the same sites (Fig. 8-8).

Dove Springs

Vegetation of Dove Springs is essentially the same as that described for the nearby Jawbone Canyon. Aerial photographic comparisons in Dove Springs Canyon, before and after (1952 and 1973, respectively) ORV use indicates an average reduction in plant density of 46% on disturbed hillsides (Fig. 8-3). There was also a corresponding 60% reduction in plant density in the associated pit areas (Table 8-1).

Results of a ground transect comparison of a partially denuded hillside, used for hill climbing by ORVs, showed a reduction in vegetation cover of 64%, compared to the undisturbed control hillside (Fig. 8-8). When the extensive barren areas of the hillside site were included in the calculations, cover was reduced by 88% (see Fig. 8-10). Keefe and Berry (1973) also found completely barren areas within some of their transects when measuring vegetation cover in Dove Springs Canyon. The plant species diversity, using the formula of MacArthur (Whittaker, 1972), was found to be significantly different ($P = 0.01$) between the undisturbed and disturbed plots they measured.

Duck (1978), who also studied the Dove Springs site, states that ORV use caused decreases in vegetative density, cover, and diversity. He indicated that the main cause of the damage was direct destruction of shrubs by vehicles, and recovery of vegetation will be slow because of soil losses from steep slopes.

Barstow to Las Vegas Motorcycle Race

Vegetation along the Barstow to Las Vegas race route is highly variable from site to site. However, the main plant communities at the sites studied are creosote bush scrub on the alluvial fans, cheesebush scrub in the washes, alkaline scrub in the basins and playas, and perennial grasses *(Hilaria rigida, Stipa speciosa,* and *Oryzopsis hymenoides)* on small, low, dune areas. This race, held November 30,

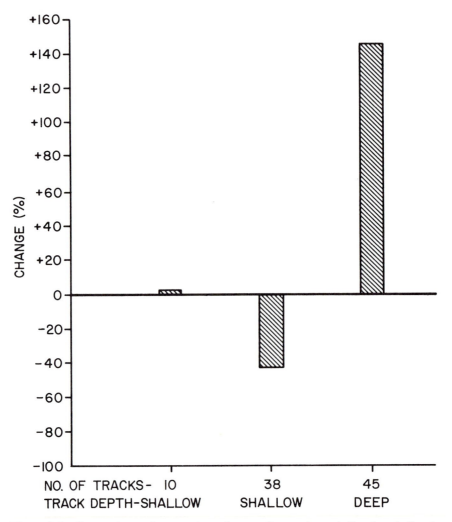

Figure 8-9. Comparison of percentage change of annual vegetation in relation to track density and depth within ground test sites at the starting area of the Barstow to Las Vegas motorcycle race. Percentage change values were determined from measurements of cover. $N = 500$ point samples at each site.

1974, was the last of eight annual events. Over 3000 riders participated, divided into two heats of 1500 motorcycles each (Horsley, 1979; U.S. Bureau of Land Management, 1975). The course had been changed somewhat from previous races (Luckenbach, 1975). The starting pit area and four sample sites along the first part of the racecourse were measured for plant density and cover by use of aerial photographs and ground transects.

To test for the influence of motorcycle tracking on annual plants, point-frame samples of foliage cover were taken in December 1977, in and out of tracks (Fig. 8-9). Deep, dense tracks showed a positive response to annuals (mainly *Pectis papposa* and *Bouteloua barbata*). Rowlands et al. (1980) explain possible reasons for this increase of annuals in track swales. They indicate there is a tendency for monocotyledons, grasses in particular *(Schimus barbtus* and *Bouteloua barbata)*, to tolerate light soil compaction better than some other plants and thus become more successful in these swales. Alternatively, the bar-and-swale surface texture seen in Figure 8-9 may have developed in material eroded from the disturbed areas. If so, the swales would not be compacted, and the positive response to annuals could result from concentration of water in the swales.

Photographic analysis of perennial vegetation at two raceway sites, approximately 24 km beyond the starting area of the race, utilized low-level aerial photographs of before (November 26, 1974) and after (December 5, 1974). Results indicate that the mean density was reduced by approximately one-half as a result of the 1-day race (Table 8-1). Ground measurements taken in the same vicinity as the aerial photographic sites indicated a similar decrease in density comparing control and raceway sites (Fig. 8-7). There was also a corresponding reduction in cover at the ground sites due to the race (Fig. 8-8).

El Cajon Motorcycle Club Race

The vegetation at this site is the same as described for Plaster City, which it is near. This race was held December 3, 1972, in the Yuha Desert in Western Imperial County, California, with 215 motorcycles participating in the four-lap race totaling 133 km. Three sets of aerial photographs were analyzed for this event: April 18, 1953; November 26, 1972; and December 12, 1972. This permitted an evaluation of vegetation change over a 19-year period prior to the race and again immediately before and after the race. In one area of the race route which had had some off-road vehicle activity prior to the race, the change in perennial plant density between the years 1953 and 1972, but before the race, was calculated. The resultant negative change in density was only 2.5%. The identical site was similarly measured, but on photographs taken immediately before and after the December 3, 1972 race. For this short period of time, there was a negative change in density of 23%. The mean drop in density for three other randomly selected race-route sites was 34% (Table 8-1).

Conclusions

Data from both aerial photographic analyses and ground transects are summarized in Figure 8-10. The mean percentage of vegetation density and cover, expressed as a percentage of the control vegetation, is shown for each of the nine study areas. The data indicate a highly negative response by perennial vegetation to most types and degrees of recreational vehicle use intensities as studied in the sample sites. The degree of negative impact on plants varies with conditions and intensity of use. Concentrated current or recent vehicle use in localized areas (heavily used weekend areas) tends to create the greatest reduction in vegetation cover, averaging 59% in the sites studied. One time or infrequent motorcycle races, with dissipated activity (not all following the same tracks) and with several years time allowance for vegetation recovery, reduced vegetation cover by an overall average of 42% in the sites studied. For comparison, the concentrated but distant-past use (Patton's training camps in the Mojave Desert) with 36 years for recovery shows an average reduction of vegetation in between the two previous response types of 50% (see Chapter 13).

Management Recommendations

In light of the results of this study and of others which have measured the impact of off-road vehicles on the California desert (see Webb and Wilshire, 1978), it is imperative that this type of recreation be carefully regulated to minimize damage to desert ecosystems. Although all of the sites measured were in Cali-

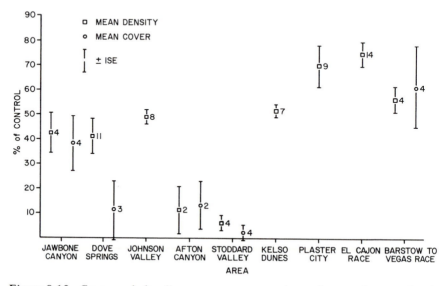

Figure 8-10. Cover and density means as a percentage of control vegetation in the ORV study areas. The number of study sites for each area is indicated beside each mean.

fornia deserts, it is reasonable to expect similar reductions in plant communities in other arid areas given the same type and intensity of use. Measurements of percentage composition at test sites indicate that off-road vehicle activities drastically reduce vegetation density and cover. Thus, it is important to avoid destruction of plants and to stay within the boundaries of areas open to ORV use. The environmental cost to vegetation within these open areas is heavy. Thus, this loss should be limited to these areas and not expanded into fresh territory. A rest-rotation system, where a particular open area is closed to permit vegetation "recovery," would not be feasible according to the data presented here. The data also indicate that perennial vegetation and ORV use are not compatible, and we apparently can only have one without the other.

Acknowledgments

This study was supported by the U.S. Bureau of Land Management, Desert Plan Program, Riverside, California. Special appreciation goes to Hyrum B. Johnson and other members of the Desert Plan Program for the guidance and help they gave. Thanks goes to Robert F. Thorne for help in determination of plant specimens during the field work phase of these studies and for his critical review of pertinent portions of the manuscript.

References

Brower, J. E., and J. H. Zar. 1977. Field and Laboratory Methods for General Ecology. Wm. C. Brown Co., Dubuque, Iowa, 194 pp.

Davidson, E., and M. Fox. 1975. Effects of off-road motorcycle activity on Mojave Desert vegetation and soil. Madrono 22:381–412.

Duck, T. 1978. The effects of off-road vehicles on vegetation in Dove Springs Canyon. Unpublished Report, Department of Biology, University of Redlands, Redlands, California, 12 pp.

Fox, M. 1973. Compaction of soil by off-road vehicles at three sites in the Mojave Desert. In: K. H. Berry (Ed.), Preliminary Studies of the Effects of Off-Road Vehicles on the Northwestern Mojave Desert: A Collection of Papers. Privately publ., Ridgecrest, California, pp. 1–13.

Horsley, C. E. 1979. Plant response to the Barstow to Las Vegas motorcycle race of November, 1974. Unpublished M.A. thesis, Loma Linda University, Loma Linda, California, 87 pp.

Johnson, H. B. 1976. Vegetation and plant communities of southern California Deserts—a functional view. In: J. Latting (Ed.), Plant Communities of Southern California. California Native Plant Society Special Publication 2, Riverside, California, pp. 125–162.

Keefe, J., and K. H. Berry. 1973. Effects of off-road vehicles on desert shrubs at Dove Springs Canyon. In: K. H. Berry (Ed.), Preliminary Studies on the Effects of Off-Road Vehicles on the Northwestern Mojave Desert: A Collection of Papers. Privately publ., Ridgecrest, California, pp. 45–57.

Kuhn, M. W. 1974. Environmental effects of off-road vehicles on the Kelso

Dunes. Paper presented at the annual meeting of the California Council for Geological Education, Bakersfield, California, May 5, 1974.

Lathrop, E. W. 1978. Plant response parameters to recreational vehicles in the California Desert Conservation Area. Final report, Contract CA-060-CT7-2824, Desert Plan Program, U.S. Bureau of Land Management, Riverside, California. Looseleaf, 240 pp.

Luckenbach, R. A. 1975. What the ORVs are doing to the desert. Fremontia 2:3–11.

Rowlands, P. G., J. Adams, H. B. Johnson, and A. Endo. 1980. Experiments on the effects of soil compaction on establishment, cover and pattern of winter and summer annuals in the Mojave Desert. In: P. G. Rowlands (Ed.), The Effects of Disturbance on Desert Soils, Vegetation, and Community Processes with Emphasis on Off-Road Vehicles; A Critical Review. U.S. Dept. of Interior, Bureau of Land Management, Desert Plan Staff Special Publication, pp. 135–164.

Sheridan, D. 1979. Off-Road Vehicles on Public Land. Council on Environmental Quality. U.S. Government Printing Office, Washington, D.C., 84 pp.

Thorne, R. F. 1976. The vascular plant communities of California. In: J. Latting (Ed.), Plant Communities of Southern California. California Native Plant Society Special Publication 2, Riverside, California, pp. 1–31.

U.S. Bureau of Land Management. 1975. Evaluation Report, 1974 Barstow-Las Vegas motorcycle race. U.S. Department of the Interior, Bureau of Land Management, Riverside, California, 130 pp.

Vollmer, A. T., B. G. Maza, P. A. Medica, F. B. Turner, and Sa. A. Bamberg. 1976. The impact of off-road vehicles on a desert ecosystem. Environ. Management 1(2):115–129.

Webb, R. H., and H. G. Wilshire. 1978. A Bibliography on the Effects of Off-Road Vehicles on the Environment. U.S. Geological Survey Open-File Report 78-149, 38 pp.

Whittaker, R. H. 1972. Evolution and measurement of species diversity. Taxon 21:213–251.

Whittaker, R. H. 1975. Communities and Ecosystems. MacMillian Publishing Co., Inc., New York, pp. 1–385.

Wilshire, H. G., and J. K. Nakata. 1976. Off-road vehicle effects on California's Mojave Desert. Calif. Geol. 29:123–132.

Wilshire, H. G., and J. K. Nakata. 1977. Erosion of off-road vehicle sites in southern California. In: K. Berry (Ed.), Proceedings of the Symposium on the Physical, Biological, and Recreational Impacts of Off-Road Vehicles on the California Desert. Southern California Academy of Sciences Special Publication (unpublished).

Wilshire, H. G., J. K. Nakata, S. Shipley, and K. Prestegaard. 1978a. Impacts of vehicles on natural terrain at seven sites in the San Francisco Bay Area. Environ. Geol. 2:295–319.

Wilshire, H. G., S. Shipley, and J. K. Nakata. 1978b. Impacts of off-road vehicles on vegetation. Transactions of the 43rd North American Wildlife and Natural Resources Conference, 1978, Wildlife Management Institute, Washington, D.C., pp. 131–139.

9

Effects of Off-Road Vehicle Noise on Desert Vertebrates[1]

Bayard H. Brattstrom and Michael C. Bondello

Introduction

With the increase in the human population in Southern California and the concomitant increase in the use of open spaces for recreation, it has become clear that the activities of off-road vehicles (ORVs) are causing considerable damage to the California deserts. Associated with this use is the spread of high-intensity sounds into formerly quiet desert regions, which suggest that these sounds might have severe impacts on the wildlife in the desert. Some initial studies done before and after motorcycle races indicated increases in the aggressive behavior of kangaroo rats (*Dipodomys* sp.) after a race passing through an area and the observation that many of the *Dipodomys* had bloody ears following the race. Following this, Bondello (1976) showed that excessive off-road motorcycle sounds (115 dBA) could damage the acoustical sensitivity of desert iguanas *(Dipsosaurus dorsalis)*.

The purpose of this study was first to measure natural and mechanized sound sources in the California desert with a special emphasis on sounds produced by ORVs. The second part of this study was to explore the effects of ORV noise on the behavior and hearing physiology of three species of desert vertebrates. We chose two sand dune dwelling forms, the Mohave fringe-toed sand lizard *(Uma scoparia)* and the desert kangaroo rat *(Dipodomys deserti),* and a desert dwelling amphibian, Couch's spadefoot toad *(Scaphiopus couchi).* All three species occur near areas with high ORV noise.

---

[1] The views and conclusions contained in this chapter are based on the authors' studies or experiences and do not necessarily reflect the official viewpoint or policy of any U.S. government agency.

The Nature of Sounds

Sound can occur in a continuous manner (as along a freeway or inside a steel mill). High intensity sounds have deleterious effects on human hearing if sustained for certain lengths of time. Table 9-1 presents some typical sound levels and some typical hearing impairments. As a result of known sound-level effects, the Office of Occupational Health and Safety (OSHA) has established decibel/ time exposure limits for certain occupations (e.g., 90 dBA for a maximum of 8 hr, 100 dBA for a maximum of 2 hr, etc.). It is well established that many musicians, snowmobile users, jackhammer workers, etc., suffer a considerable loss of hearing.

Table 9-1. Effects of Common Sound Pressure Levels

Example	Sound pressure in decibels (dBA)	Effect with prolonged exposure
Jet takeoff (close range)	150	Eardrum rupture
Aircraft carrier deck	140	
Armored personnel carrier	130	
Thunderclap, live rock music, discotheque, jet takeoff at 61 m, siren (close range)	120	Human pain threshold
Steel mill, riveting, automobile horn at 1 m	110	
Jet takeoff at 305 m, subway, outboard motor, power lawn mower, motorcycle at 8 m, farm tractor, printing plant, jackhammer, blender, garbage truck	100	Serious hearing damage (8 hr)
Busy urban street, diesel truck	90	Hearing damage (8 hr)
Garbage disposal, clothes washer, average factory, freight train at 15 m, noisy office or party, diswasher	80	
Freeway traffic at 15 m, vacuum	70	Annoying
Conversation in restaurant	60	Intrusive
Quiet suburb (daytime), conversation in living room	50	Quiet
Library	40	
Quiet rural area (nighttime)	30	
Whisper, rustling leaves	20	Very quiet
Breathing	10	
	0	Threshold of audibility

Sound can also occur at intermittent or unpredictable times. These "startle noises" have been shown to have many effects on humans including annoyance, disruption of activity, increase in heart rate, vasoconstriction, increase in blood pressure, stomach spasms, headaches, fetal convulsions, and ulcers.

Sounds are described in many ways. One measure of sound is the pitch or frequency (number of wavelengths per unit time, usually presented in kilohertz, kHz) and reflects the range of sounds as seen in the notes emanating from a piano. Another measure of sound is the intensity or loudness measured on the logarithmic decibel scale. Decibels are measured either on a A-weighted (dBA) or linear (dBL) scale; these scales differ in that lower and higher frequencies of the A network are penalized in order to approximate human acoustical sensitivities while linear measurements correspond to unweighted amplitudes of frequencies. In this study, dBLs were measured to determine unweighted sound pressure levels (SPLs) for relation to nonhuman animals and dBAs were measured for comparison with data in previous reports and potential applications to human acoustical research. Other measures of sound (especially music) relate to tone, modality, and quality and are not considered in this report.

Sound Pressure Levels in the California Desert

Materials and Methods

Between April 1977 and June 1978, sound pressure levels were measured at a number of different locations of varying elevation in the Colorado and Mojave Deserts of California. Ambient SPLs were measured for natural and mechanized sound sources. Natural sources included abiotic sounds of wind, rain, and water, and the biotic sounds of birds, rattlesnakes, anurans, and insects. Mechanized sound sources measured included aircraft, highways, rail vehicles, off-road motorcycles, other ORVs, transmission lines, power plants, and stationary facilities and impulse sounds.

A Bruel and Kjaer Precision Sound Level Meter Type 22-3 with Type 1613 Octave Band Filter Set (B & K 2203/1613) equipped with a condenser microphone and nose cone was used to monitor the environmental SPLs in decibels on the A-weighted (dBA) and linear, "fast" (dBL), scales with the microphone positioned perpendicular to the sound path. When possible, SPLs were monitored over the octave frequency spectrum from 0.0315 to 31.5 kHz. Single-incident events (aircraft overflights, vehicle passby, bird calls, etc.) were monitored for overall SPL. A tape recorder set at a recording speed of 19.0 mm sec^{-1} with microphone and plastic parabolic reflector recorded these incidents, and sonagraph analysis of these recordings was performed with a spectrograph. Distances of sound sources were determined from 15 to 180 m using a Ranging 620 Stereoscopic Rangefinder. A 25-m roll tape was used for distances less than 15 m. For distances greater than 180 m, ranges and elevations of known topographical landmarks were used to estimate distances.

A typical measurement of an incident involving determining the SPL and range of the sound source. If the incident was of sufficient duration, the SPL over the octave frequency spectrum would be determined. The time, duration, climatic data, and description of the incident was then recorded.

The effects of range, humidity, and natural barriers on attenuation of sounds were also determined. A battery-powered integrated circuit frequency generator amplified a signal through to a loudspeaker which produced an 80-dB square wave tone. This signal was projected over unimpeded desert surfaces, through plants and over sand dunes at various relative humidities. SPLs of six frequencies (1, 2, 4, 8, 10, and 12 kHz) were monitored with the B & K 2203/1613 octave filter set at distances from 0.5 to 6.0 m.

Results

Sound Pressure Levels of Natural Sound Sources. Naturally occurring sounds monitored in the California Desert during 1977 to 1978 ranged from 14.0 to 66.0 dBA and from 30.0 to 70.5 dBL. Lowest SPLs (14.0 dBA and 30.0 dBL) were measured during early morning hours under still conditions (wind 0 to 5 km hr^{-1}) and minimal local biotic activity (distant insects and birds). Highest SPLs (66.0 dBA and 70.5 dBL) were also measured during early morning hours under more severe abiotic conditions of either higher wind speeds (15 to 25 km hr^{-1}) or rushing streams. Thus, abiotic factors produced the lowest and highest SPLs that occurred under natural conditions (Fig. 9-1).

Among the total number of measurements taken within the natural SPL range of 14.0 to 66.0 dBA, 44% were between 20.5 and 25.0 dBA, 54.6% were less than 25.5 dBA, 82.6% were less than 35.5 dBA, and 90.5% were less than 45.5 dBA (Fig. 9-1a). Within the natural SPL range of 30.0 to 70.5 dBL, 55.5% of all measurements were below 45.5 dBL, 78.1% were below 50.5 dBL, and 93.1% were below 60.5 dBL (Fig. 9-1b). Thus, for all monitored natural SPLs, over 75% were below 40.5 dBA and 50.5 dBL and over 90% were below 45.5 dBA and 60.5 dBL.

Mean linear and A-weighted SPLs were monitored every 2 hr over a 24-hr period from 0600, April 16 to 0600, April 17, 1977 at Soda Springs (Fig. 9-2). Morning SPL minima (22.0 to 22.5 dBA and 30.0 to 31.0 dBL at 0600 hr) were measured during the absence of local biotic activity. Mean SPLs increased with the initiation of cricket chirps and bird calls. The noontime peak (24.3 to 27.5 dBA and 41.5 to 47.0 dBL) was measured during elevated wind speed (3 to 16 km hr^{-1}) and decreased to lower SPLs with still conditions. The advent of dusk initiated frog chorusing which increased SPLs to a midnight maximum (32.0 to 34.0 dBA and 45.0 to 48.5 dBL). Cessation of frog chorusing resulted in the early morning decrease to the dawn minimum (22.5 to 23.0 dBA and 30.5 to 33.5 dBL). As dawn broke at 0445, all animal sounds were temporarily halted, and resumed a few minutes later with the initiation of bird calls.

A variety of naturally occurring sound sources were monitored in the range of 14.0 to 66.0 dBA and 30.0 to 70.5 dBL. These sources and their SPL range

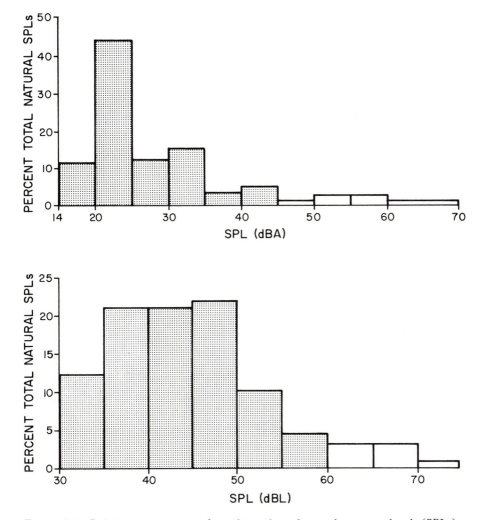

Figure 9-1. Relative percentage of total monitored sound pressure levels (SPLs) for natural desert areas in dBA (a) and dBL (b). Shaded area = over 90% of total monitored SPLs.

included still desert (14.0 to 27.0 dBA, 30.0 to 53.5 dBL), bird wingbeats (30.0 to 33.0 dBA), humming bees (29.0 to 34.0 dBA, 35.0 to 38.0 dBL), walking dog (35.0 to 36.0 dBA), windy desert (16.5 to 38.0 dBA, 39.0 to 70.5 dBL), trilling toads (36.0 to 39.0 dBA, 58.0 to 60.0 dBL), walking man (33.0 to 40.0 dBA), rainstorm (42.0 to 45.0 dBA, 50.0 to 56.0 dBL), calling locust (50.0 to 56.0 dBA), bird calls (26.0 to 60.0 dBA, 48.0 to 60.0 dBL), rattlesnakes (24.0 to 62.0 dBA, 30.0 to 62.0 dBL), and rushing streams (50.0 to 66.0 dBA, 56.0 to 68.0 dBL).

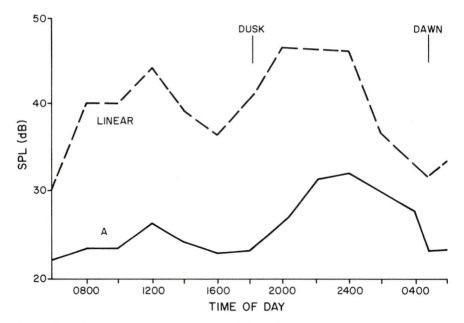

Figure 9-2. Peak sound pressure levels of Soda Springs Station monitored every 2 hr for 24 hr (0600, April 16 to April 17, 1977). Upper line, linear scale; lower line, A-weighted scale.

Various animal sounds monitored in the desert have SPLs between 26.0 and 56.0 dBA. Within this range, 76.9% of all measurements were less than 40.5 dBA, 84.6% were less than 45.5 dBA, and 92.3% were less than 50.5 dBA (Fig. 9-3a). Within the animal SPL range of 30.0 to 62.0 dBL, 73.7% of all measurements were less than 55.5 dBL and 91.1% were below 60.5 dBL (Fig. 9-3b). Thus, over 90% of all monitored animal sounds were less than 50.5 dBA and 60.5 dBL.

Attenuation of Animal Sounds. Animal sounds were seen to attenuate with distance as a function of the major frequency of the signal. The "rattle" signals of three species of rattlesnake were analyzed by sonagraph to determine their major frequencies. Major intensities of the three rattlesnakes' signals were located in the higher frequencies: 5 kHz for the Western Rattlesnake *Crotalus atrox,* 6.3 kHz for the Pacific Rattlesnake *C. viridis,* and 8 kHz for the Sidewinder *C. cerastes.* SPLs of all rattelsnakes measured abruptly attenuated with distance (Fig. 9-4).

The Cactus Wren, *Campylorhynchus brunneicapillus,* had a lower frequency call near 2 kHz (Fig. 9-4), in contrast to the high-frequency signal of rattlesnakes. At similar signal intensities (60 dBL) the Cactus Wren signal attenuated 12 dBL in 30 m, while the rattlesnakes' signal attenuated 30 dBL in 6 m. Thus, with similar conditions and signal intensities, the lower frequency signal persisted much farther through the environment than higher frequency signals.

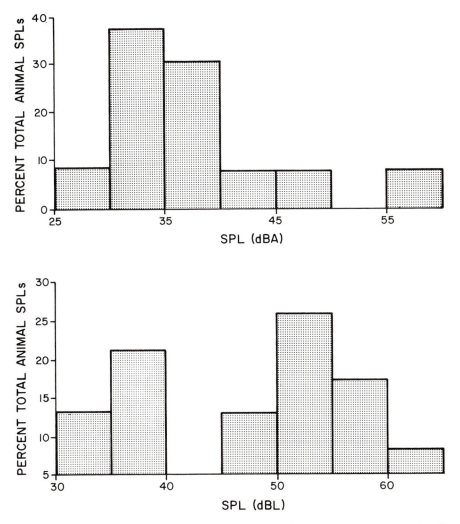

Figure 9-3. Relative percentages of total monitored animal sound pressure levels (SPLs) in dBA (a) and dBL (b).

Duration of Animal Sounds. Durations of animal calls varied. A Red-Tail Hawk monitored at 1525 hours, April 16, 1977 at Soda Springs had a call duration of 62 msec delivered three times within 1.5 sec at 709-msec intervals. This sequence was repeated periodically for over 1 min. A Cactus Wren monitored 0940, March 18, 1978 at Borrego Springs had a call duration of 125 msec delivered 15 times for 2.0 sec at 39-msec intervals. This sequence was repeated periodically for over 10 min until the bird flew off as a result of human intrusion. A Western Rattle-snake disturbed by 10 separate human intrusions responded with 10 continuous "rattles" with a mean duration of 21.7 sec over a range of 12.3 to 41.1 sec. When continuously disturbed by nearby tapping sounds the response was a con-

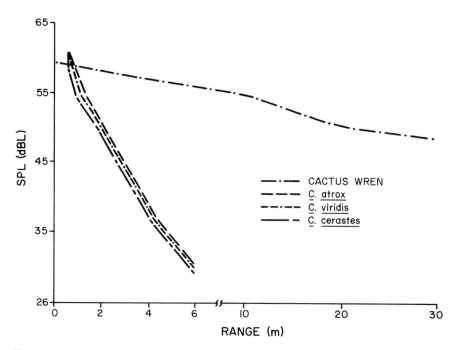

Figure 9-4. Comparison of the relative attenuation with distance of signals produced by a cactus wren and three species of rattlesnake (*Crotalus* spp.).

tinuous "rattle" with a duration of over 10 min, at which time the tapping was halted. Durations exceeding 1 hr of uninterrupted frog *(Hyla regilla)* chorusing at Soda Springs and toad *(Bufo punctatus)* trilling at Corn Springs are not uncommon during the spring. Thus, durations of animal sounds that were measured in the California Desert range from the very short (62 msec) to the very long (1 hr plus).

Peak SPLs of Off-Road Vehicles. Peak SPLs of ORVs were monitored at the Imperial Sand Dunes near a trail 1 km west of Glamis, California between 1300 and 1400 hr and 0.5 km south of Glamis near a staging area between 1400 and 1500 hr on March 19, 1978. SPLs of 61 ORVs were monitored at ranges of 3 to 70 m. Peak SPLs ranged from 78.0 to 110.0 dBL (Fig. 9-5).

Peak SPLs monitored between 1300 and 1400 hr ranged from 78.0 to 90.0 dBL for dune buggies with a mean of 83.5 dBL ($n = 7$), and from 85.0 to 92.0 dBL for motorcycles with a mean of 83.3 dBL ($n = 9$); one jeep had a peak SPL of 84.0 dBL. Peak SPLs monitored between 1400 and 1500 ranged from 82.0 to 100.0 dBL for dune buggies with a mean of 91.3 dBL ($n = 16$), from 80.0 to 92.0 dBL for pickup trucks with a mean of 85.9 ($n = 7$), and from 76.0 to 110.0 dBL for motorcycles with a mean of 91.3 dBL ($n = 15$). Two jeeps had peak SPLs of 92.0 dBL. Thus, mean SPLs increased with increased proximity to the pit area south of Glamis. The peak SPLs of 250-cc motorcycles driven 90 km

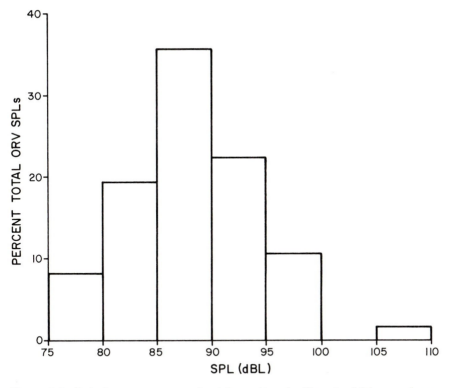

Figure 9-5. Relative percentages of total monitored off-road vehicle sound pressure levels (SPLs).

hr^{-1} at 30 m were 90.0 dBL for three motorcycles, 89.0 dBL for two, and 86.0 dBL for one. Thus, under similar conditions, an increase in the number of ORVs of the same type increased the peak SPL.

Of a total of 57 ORV SPLs monitored near Glamis, 64% were less than 90.5 dBL, 86.8% were less than 95.5 dBL, and 97.3% were below 100.5 dBL (Fig. 9-5).

Frequency Composition of Off-Road Motorcycle Sounds. The sounds of a 125-cc off-road motorcycle (89.0 dBA) monitored at 10 m had major energies concentrated between 2.5 and 4.5 kHz with minor energies between 0.5 and 6.5 kHz. Sounds of 30 massed 125-cc motorcycles (110.0 dBA) monitored at 10 m had major and minor energies concentrated near the same frequencies. The sounds of 30 massed 250-cc motorcycles (115.0 dBA), however, had major energies concentrated between 0.4 and 5.5 kHz with minor energies from 0.25 to 7.0 kHz.

Thus, an increase in the number of 125-cc motorcycles increased the SPL from 89.0 dBA to 110.0 dBA, but the major energies remained concentrated within the same frequencies. An increase in the engine size of massed motorcycles, however, changed the SPL from 110.0 dBA to 115.0 dBA and also extended the major energies to higher and lower frequencies.

Attenuation of Off-Road Vehicle Sounds. ORV sounds attenuated as a function of range, engine acceleration, and muffler type. Engine size was not a major factor in the attenuation of ORV sounds. Peak SPLs of an off-road truck driven 70 km hr^{-1} were 92.0 dBL at 10 m, 85.0 dBL at 25 m, 84.0 dBL at 40 m, and 80.0 dBL at 60 m. Thus, an increase in range decreased the peak SPL of the truck. A pair of dune buggies at Soda Springs idled at 50 m with peak SPLs below 80.0 dBL; when engines were accelerated, peak SPLs increased to 105.0 dBL. Thus, an increase in engine acceleration increased the peak SPL of dune buggies. Three Volkswagen dune buggies with straight tailpipes individually monitored at 30 m had peak SPLs between 82.0 and 86.0 dBL. Two other Volkswagen dune buggies equipped with glasspack mufflers monitored at the same distance had peak SPLs below 80.0 dBL. A Volkswagen dune buggy with a megaphone tailpipe had the highest peak SPLs (90.0 dBL at 30 m). Thus, the more Volkswagen dune buggy engines were muffled, the greater was their sound attenuation.

Durations of Off-Road Vehicle Sounds. Durations of ORV sounds varied with the mode of operation of the vehicle. When the ORVs moved rapidly over a trail the durations were similar to those of highway vehicles. ORV operators, however, often halted their vehicles, either to study the irregular terrain, view distant objects, search for companions, or examine their vehicles. At these times, engines were often left running with associated accelerations of engine speeds and increased SPLs. Durations of these episodes ranged from a few seconds to over 5 min at any one spot.

The ambient SPL of the Imperial Sand Dunes between 1300 and 1500 hr on March 19, 1978 was not less than 50 dBL. These minima were measured in the absence of nearby ORVs but distant (greater than 1 km) activities were audible.

Discussion

SPLs that occur in the California Desert (Fig. 9-6) are lowest for still deserts (14.0 dBA) and highest for bomb explosions (190.0+ dBA). Peak SPLs are lowest for naturally occurring sounds (27.0 to 66.0 dBA) and highest for mechanized sounds (70.0 to 190.0+ dBA). These data indicate the natural acoustical environment of desert areas to be one of relatively low ambient SPLs not normally exceeding 66.0 dBA (70.5 dBL) in the absence of mechanized disturbances (or thunder and earthquakes, which were not measured). Over 90% of the measured natural SPLs do not exceed 45.5 dBA (60.5 dBL). The sounds of animals normally increase the ambient SPLs of natural environments; however, no desert animal we studied created sounds that exceeded 56.0 dBA (62.0 dBL) and over 90% of animal sounds measured were below 50.5 dBA (60.5 dBL). Thus, SPLs of natural desert environments are unusually low, with minimum values during early morning hours.

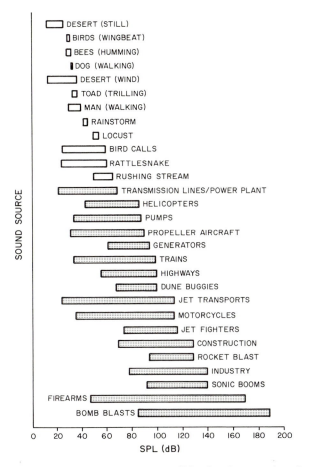

Figure 9-6. Relative sound pressure levels (SPLs) of natural and mechanized sound sources of the California Desert.

Mechanized sounds increase the SPLs of natural desert areas in all measured instances. These SPL increases ranged from 3.0 dBA (7.0 dBL) for transmission lines to over 160.0 dBA for bomb explosions. The types of mechanized sound and their relative occurrence in the desert are described in Bondello and Brattstrom (1978) and are briefly summarized below.

The occurrence of mechanized sounds in the desert depends somewhat on the specific location of an area. All visited areas receive sounds of aircraft overflights. Road and rail sounds obviously occur in areas proximate to traffic corridors. ORVs range through many areas, with heaviest concentrations near designated ORV sites. Stationary machinery sounds are restricted to the immediate vicinity of the sources and adjacent perimeters. Impulse sounds of firearms and evidence of their occurrence (discarded cartridge cases) also occur in many locations, with sonic booms, bombing, and mining explosions restricted to specified areas (military air routes, gunnery ranges, and mining quarries). Thus, the most pervasive of these sounds, those most frequently detected in remote desert areas, are sounds of aircraft overflights and ORVs. Due to wide-ranging mobilities of aircraft and ORVs, formerly inaccessible areas of the desert are now regularly overflown by aircraft and frequently traversed by ORVs. The result is a concomitant increase in the ambient SPLs of formerly remote natural areas. The most frequently occurring aircraft overflights, however, are distinguished by lower SPL increases than are those associated with the most frequently occurring ORV incidents.

The sounds of ORVs are more restricted to their immediate surroundings than those of jet aircraft. However, the versatility and large numbers of ORVs result in their penetration into nearly all areas of the desert with concomitant increases in the ambient SPLs of these regions. The peak SPLs associated with the most frequent desert ORV activity are usually much higher (78.0 to 110.0 dBA) than those of the most frequent aircraft overflights (44.0 to 66.0 dBL). The most frequently encountered ORVs are off-road motorcycles. Other ORVs also range far into the desert, but motorcycle incidents are the most frequent occurrences. Within 100 m, the peak SPLs of individual off-road motorcycles (76.0 to 110.0 dBL) exceed those of all naturally occurring sounds and when multiple motorcycle events occur, SPLs may rise higher (115.0+ dBA). Hare and Hound races, Enduros, and various individual motorcycle activities are presently authorized near Johnson Valley, Stoddard Valley, Plaster City, Cadiz Lake, Rand Mountain/Spangler Hills, and other areas of the California Desert; additionally, motorcyclists are permitted to explore many other regions. The result is a spreading of high-SPL motorcycle sounds, detectable for several kilometers throughout many desert regions.

The durations of high-SPL motorcycle incidents most frequently resemble those of highway traffic. However, where large concentrations of off-road motorcycles occur (pit areas, races, open areas), the durations of elevated SPLs may extend to several hours.

Off-road motorcycles, therefore, generate the most frequent pervasive, high-intensity sounds of all mechanized sound sources that occur in the California Desert. This phenomenon results from the large numbers of off-road motorcycles, their ability to penetrate all types of desert terrain, and their initially generated high SPLs.

The Effects of Dune Buggy Sounds on Hearing in the Mojave Fringe-Toed Lizard, *Uma scoparia*

Introduction

Animals exposed to high-intensity sounds suffer both anatomical and physiological damage, including both auditory and nonauditory damage. Most noise research, however, has been conducted on animals from nondesert habitats and only recently have the effects of ORV sounds been investigated in deserts.

High-intensity sounds of massed off-road motorcycles were shown to severely damage the acoustical sensitivity of the Desert Iguana, *Dipsosaurus dorsalis* (Bondello, 1976). Exposures of 115 dBA for durations of 1 and 10 hr both resulted in decreased cochlear responses to acoustic stimuli (Bondello, 1976). The *Dipsosaurus* study demonstrated that high-intensity ORV sounds can damage the peripheral auditory system of desert lizards. "Hearing," as measured by the changes in the electrical activity of the central nervous system in response to acoustical stimuli, was not monitored in the *Dipsosaurus.*

Transient changes in the electrical activity of the central nervous system in response to sound have long been observed in the electroencephalogram (EEG) of human and other vertebrates. The background EEG is often of greater amplitude than those transient changes elicited by acoustic stimuli. The observation of these smaller transient changes in EEG has been greatly facilitated by computer averaging techniques, which electronically summate the EEG signals. Through this technique the presumably random, larger background electrical activity factors itself out through successive additions, while the smaller time-locked acoustical responses grow into recognition patterns (Goldstein, 1973). These average evoked responses (AER) are used as criteria in the clinical evaluation of hearing for human and other subjects (Davis, 1976). The measurement of AERs of nonhuman subjects traditionally involves the placement of intracranial electrodes, in contrast to the extracranial placements normally made on human subjects (Keidel, 1976).

The purpose of this study was to determine the hearing thresholds of the Mojave fringe-toed lizard, *Uma scoparia,* using the AER technique and to determine the effect of ORV noise on the hearing thresholds. The AERs were recorded during the summer season to insure a proper intensity of response. Following the recording of a control AER, an individual lizard was subject to 8 min and 30 sec of dune buggy sounds of 95 dBA. Following the sound exposure, the AER of the lizard was again recorded and compared with the control response. In this way, the effect of the dune buggy sound on the individual lizard's hearing threshold was determined. These dune buggy sounds represent lower intensities and shorter durations than the maximum reported field values and have been used to make the study more relevant to exposures more likely to be experienced by lizards in the field.

Materials and Methods

Twenty *Uma scoparia* were captured by noosing, 5 km south of Rice, Riverside County, California on July 9, 1978. Lizards were placed into an acoustically insulated plastic container with internal dimensions of 66 cm × 30 cm × 30 cm; the boxes could reduce a 100-dBA external noise by 35 dBA. Subjects were immediately transported to California State University, Fullerton, California where the lizards were randomly separated into two separate acoustically insulated plastic containers with internal dimensions as above. Ten lizards were stored in each box on a substrate of sand taken from their home dunes. A 12-hr light, 12-hr dark cycle was maintained in each box with a 10-W bulb, and temperatures within the boxes ranged from 22°C in darkness to 39°C in light. Temperature decreased with distance from the light bulb, which established a thermal gradient in each container. Periodic checks of lizard cloacal temperatures showed that the lizards maintained their temperatures near the preferred 35.7°C reported by Brattstrom (1965). Lizards were maintained on a daily diet of *Tenebrio* larvae and water, and compartments were cleaned daily. Eight animals were used, seven for testing and one for mapping the electrical responses of the brain. Lizards were anesthetized with sodium pentobarbital injected intraperitoneally at a dosage of 30 to 40 mg ka^{-1} body weight. The subjects were ready for surgery within 25 min of injection. Anesthetized lizards were secured, dorsum up, in a sterotaxic device, placed inside a grounded copper Faraday cage, located within an acoustically insulated room. Details of electrode implantation and recording are presented in Bondello et al. (1979).

Lizards were maintained at a body temperature of 38°C ± 1°C during each test run by covering them with a warm water jacket. Head temperatures varied from cloacal temperatures by less than 1.8°C as determined by thermister placement.

Preliminary experiments were conducted from July 12 to August 10, 1978, with the actual measurement of AER for the seven test lizards occurring on August 11, 1978. A lizard was surgically implanted and, soon after, the first series of stimuli was presented. After this test, the lizard was disconnected from the sterotaxic apparatus and removed, with the electrode still implanted, to a quiet room for a period of 30 to 90 min. The lizard was then reinserted into the apparatus and the electrode reconnected. A second run was then made to determine any effect due to the process of disconnection and removal from the apparatus. After the second run, the lizard was again disconnected and removed to an insulated chamber. Here the lizard was exposed to a total of 500 sec of taped dune buggy sounds (95 dBA, 100 dBL). The subject was then reconnected to the apparatus and immediately tested for the third time. Thus, 21 runs were made (three runs per lizard), 14 before noise exposure and 7 directly afterwards. After the third run, lizards were removed, sacrificed, and prepared for histological examination.

High-intensity sounds of a 1971 Volkswagen "Baja Bug" were recorded onto a 30-sec loop tape, using a battery-powered tape recorder with condenser microphone. A simultaneous recording was made using a different recorder for later sonagraph analysis. The duration of the dune buggy sound was 25 sec for every 30-sec loop of the tape; the noise exposure was interrupted and not continuous. Twenty revolutions of the tape were played which resulted in a total sound exposure of 500 sec. A sound spectrograph was used to analyze the relative intensity distribution of the sounds over the frequency spectrum. A Bruel and Kjaer Precision Sound Level Meter Type 2203 with 1613 Octave Band Filter Set was used to monitor the overall intensity of the dune buggy sounds.

The dune buggy sounds were played to the lizards from the loop tape which was amplified through to a 20-cm coaxial loudspeaker. Signal intensity was increased until 95 dBA (100 dBL) was reached 8 cm in front of the speaker. This intensity is lower than the maximum (105 dBL) value actually recorded from dune buggies in the field (Bondello and Brattstrom, 1978).

Results

The intensities of the 1971 Volkswagen "Baja Bug" recorded and used in this study exceeded 95 dBA (100 dBL) at 5 m. Sonograph analysis revealed major energies concentrated below 1.0 kHz with minor energies extending to 2500 Hz and residual energies up to 8.0 kHz.

The typical response to a 0.1-msec pulse of 0.1 V (76 dBL) is given for the first control run of lizard 20. The response is characterized by alternating negative (upward) and positive (downward) deflections. The first negative (1N) peak occurs at 1.5 msec after the termination of the stimulus. This 1N peak is followed by the first positive (1P) peak at 2.5 msec, the second negative (2N) peak at 3.5 msec, and the second positive (2P) peak at 5.5 msec after the stimulus. The waveform then steadily rose to regain the normal baseline EEG pattern until the next stimulus was presented.

The amplitude of the control 1N peak varied with the stimulus intensity. Control 1N peak amplitudes ranged from 0.9 to 3.1 μV ($X = 1.67$) for stimulus intensities of 0.1 V (76 dBL), 1.1 to 5.3 μV ($X = 2.63$) at 0.2 V (80 dBL), 1.8 to 9.8 μV ($X = 5.59$) at 1.0 V (83 dBL), and 1.8 to 10.5 μV ($X = 5.70$) at 2.0 V (85 dBL). Increased stimulus intensities, then, tended to increase the amplitude of the 1N in the control runs up to intensities of 2.0 V (85 dBL; Fig. 9-7).

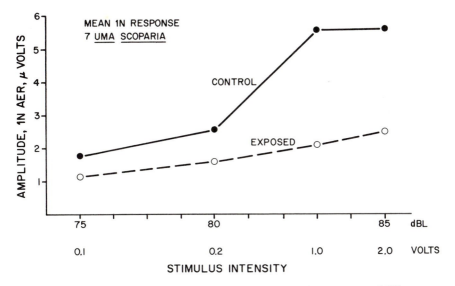

Figure 9-7. Comparison of the mean amplitude of the first negative (1N) average evoked response (AER) in microvolts for the control and exposed runs of seven *Uma scoparia* at four stimulus intensities of 0.1V, 0.2V, 1.0V, and 2.0V. Five hundred responses were averaged for each subject at each intensity.

Preliminary tests performed on the lizard used to electrophysiologically "map" the AER revealed that the amplitude of the 1N peak did not vary as a linear function of intensity. The magnitude of the 1N AER of the "map" lizard rose to a maximum at 1.0 V (83 dBL) and steadily fell to lower values with increased stimulus intensities of 2.0 V (85 dBL), 4.0 V (86 dBL), and 6.0 V (87 dBL). This nonlinear function after the maximum 1N peak is consistent with the findings of Werner (1972) and probably indicates that the increased acoustical input overloads the ability of the sensitive lizard ear to respond.

The latencies of the 1N peak following stimulation also varied with stimulus intensity. The 1N peaks of the first control run were 1.5 to 1.9 msec ($X = 1.55$) at stimulus intensities of 0.1 V (76 dBL), 1.0 to 1.5 msec ($X = 1.38$) at 0.2 V (80 dBL), 1.0 to 1.8 msec ($X = 1.21$) at 1.0 V (83 dBL), and 1.0 to 1.5 msec ($X = 1.07$) at 2.0 V (85 dBL). Thus, as the stimulus intensity was increased, the latency of the 1N response decreased (Fig. 9-8). These findings are consistent with AERs obtained from human subjects.

The experimental procedures of electrode disconnection and reconnection did not reduce the amplitude or shift the latency of the 1N response of any experimental subject. Comparison of the first and second control runs indicate that the careful manipulation of electrodes and animals did not contribute to any alteration of the characteristic amplitude and latency of the 1N response of *Uma scoparia.*

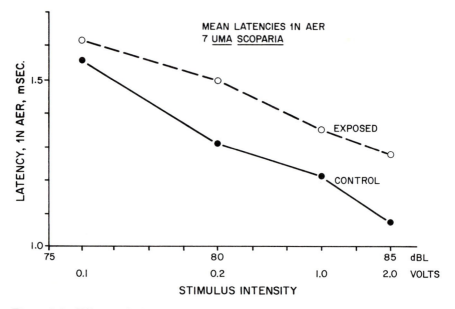

Figure 9-8. Effects of click intensity on the mean latency in milliseconds of the first negative (1N) average evoked response (AER) for the control and exposed runs of seven *Uma scoparia* at four intensities (same as in Fig. 9-7). Five hundred responses averaged for each subject at each intensity.

AERs of *Uma scoparia* significantly varied after exposure to dune buggy sounds. Comparison of first control runs with exposed (after sound treatment) runs showed the amplitude of the mean 1N responses to decrease (Fig. 9-7) and latencies to increase (Fig. 9-8) after exposure to dune buggy sounds. Decreased amplitudes and increased latencies of neural responses to standard auditory stimuli are diagnostic symptoms of hearing loss as described by Aran (1971). The decreased amplitudes and increased latencies caused by the dune buggy sounds are, therefore, interpreted as representing actual hearing losses in the exposed lizards. The seven *Uma scoparia,* therefore, suffered actual hearing loss after being exposed to 500 sec of 95-dBA (100-dBL) dune buggy sounds.

Discussion and Conclusion

These data indicate that dune buggy sounds of comparatively moderate intensity and short duration contain sufficient acoustical energies below 3 kHz to induce hearing loss in *Uma scoparia,* as evidenced by decreased amplitudes (Fig. 9-7) and increased latencies (Fig. 9-8) of the first negative responses of their AER. Sounds of equivalent or larger acoustical dosage may, therefore, be expected to inflict similar detectable hearing losses on *Uma scorparia.* We did not measure recovery times on these lizards, but the studies of Bondello (1976) on the desert iguana would suggest full recovery in 4 weeks. In the field, however, these lizards would probably be exposed to dune buggy sounds weekly.

The most frequently occurring, high-intensity sounds monitored in the California Desert over an 18-month survey were generated by ORVs, and individual ORVs have been monitored with SPLs as high as 110 dBL. The most frequently encountered ORVs in the California deserts are motorcycles; however, most motorcycles are unable to penetrate the interiors of the wide soft sand dune systems characteristic of the Imperial Sand Dunes, Devil's Playground, and the Rice Sand Hills. Sand dune systems, then, represent a greater challenge to ORV enthusiasts due to their relatively more difficult terrain. The result is that four-wheeled vehicle activity (jeeps, sand rails, dune buggies) tends to be most intensely concentrated on the sand dunes. Dune buggies are able to penetrate deep into the interior of sand dune systems due to their superior maneuverability and traction on the sandy substrate. Many areas within the dune periphery are, therefore, exposed to repeated episodes of high-intensity sounds. Dune buggies most often maximize engine speeds in order to maneuver over or through soft sand areas. Accelerated engine speeds produce similar elevations of SPLs; thus, high-intensity sounds are often characteristic of dune buggy activities.

Dune buggy sounds with major energies concentrated below 3 kHz have been monitored with intensities of 105 dBL at ranges of 50 m. Stationary dune buggies have been monitored with engines "revved" at high speed with subsequently high SPLs for durations exceeding 5 min (Bondello and Brattstrom, 1978). Wide-ranging dune buggies were observed deep within the dune interior, repeatedly crossing the same terrain. Dune buggies, then, may be characterized by high engine speeds (high SPLs), which often range widely over the dune systems, with repeated passages over selected terrain. Considering these intensely concentrated dune buggy activities on sand dunes (especially at ORV use areas such as Glamis, California), it becomes quite apparent that the cumulative acoustical dosages delivered at any one spot on the dunes system during an active spring or summer weekend morning are at least as great as those delivered to the lizards in this study. Thus, these high-intensity sounds are regularly occurring phenomena in the California desert regions during the spring and summer months.

The major energies of dune buggy sounds coincide with the frequencies of maximum acoustical sensitivity for *Uma scoparia*, 1.0 to 1.6 kHz, as determined by Werner (1972). *Uma notata notata*, the Colorado fringe-toed lizard, has a similar maximum acoustical sensitivity range, 1.0 to 2.0 kHz, and responds to intense acoustical stimulation (Wever and Peterson, 1963) in a pattern not unlike those described by *Uma scoparia* in this report. Thus, these data suggest that dune buggy sounds are inherently damaging to the hearing sensitivity of fringe-road lizards.

When disturbed in the field, *Uma scoparia* seldom escaped into deep burrows. Of the 20 *Uma scoparia* captured for this study, not one sought the refuge of nearby rodent burrows. Many hid among surface vegetation or burrowed only a few millimeters below the sand surface, often at the mouth of a rodent burrow. When *Uma scoparia* were pursued, their quick turn into the mouth of a burrow and rapid shallow burial near the entrance gave the impression of escape into the deep rodent burrow. Repeatedly, however, the lizards were found just beneath the surface near the entrance of the burrow. Similar escape strategies have been described for several species of *Uma*. Pough (1970) described shallow burial (less than 2 cm deep) or retreat beneath bushes as the escape responses of *Uma notata* to predators. He also described the tendency for *Uma* to preferentially locate themselves at sand depths of no more than 4 cm from the surface. Commins and Savitsky (1973) observed *Uma exsul* to "sand swim" when approached, hide beneath tumble weeds, or lie motionless and cryptically colored on sand surfaces. Carpenter (1967) noted a tendency for *Uma exsul* to lie in shallow burrow entrances.

Uma will seek the refuge of rodent burrows when soil and climatic conditions are favorable. In damp, compacted soil which receives summer rainfall, conditions are favorable for the maintenance of rodent burrow systems and *Uma scoparia* retreat to them rather than bury themselves in sand (Pough, 1970). Carpenter (1967) noted a similar tendency for *Uma exsul* and *Uma paraphygas* preferentially to retreat to rodent burrows rather than sand swim. *Uma* constructed its own burrows in moist sand under laboratory conditions (Pough, 1970).

When soil and climatic conditions are less favorable (less cohesive, dry wind-blown sand), fewer rodent burrows are maintained; hence fewer burrows are available as retreats. Because of the territorial behavior of *Uma*, crowding into burrows would probably not occur (Pough, 1970). Thus, more *Uma* will be forced to seek refuge outside of burrows during seasons of low burrow availability.

A shallowly buried lizard is more likely to receive a higher intensity sound exposure from a nearby dune buggy than would a deeply burrowed lizard. Our laboratory observations indicate that 4 cm of fine compacted sand from Rice, California, does not noticeably lower the SPL of a 95 dBA sound. Thus, due to restricted species distribution and shallow and surface escape tendencies, fringe-toed lizards are particularly prone to receive damaging, short-duration exposures of recurring dune buggy sounds. These exposures may be most intense during the most active ORV months of the spring and summer seasons.

Intense ORV activities of the spring and summer months, however, coincide with the reproductive season of all three species of *Uma* which occur in California. *Uma inornata* are reproductively active from March to September (Mayhew, 1965b), *Uma notata* from April to September (Mayhew, 1966a), and *Uma scoparia* from April to July (Mayhew, 1966b). All California species of *Uma* apparently reached their peak of reproductive activities in May (Mayhew, 1965, 1966a, b). Thus, during the most critical phase of their life cycle, the breeding season, their habitat is subjected to the most intense degree of ORV impact.

When the favorable environmental conditions of proper winter rains and abundant annual plant production do not occur, *Uma*'s preferred annually migrating insect prey may be scarce on the dunes. *Uma* are then forced to switch to a less easily obtained insect prey which frequent perennial plants. Their lowered energy intake may delay and subsequently decrease the reproductive success of *Uma* for the entire season. If drought conditions persist for several seasons, population sizes of *Uma* may be reduced (Mayhew, 1966b). Thus, the potential impacts of ORVs on *Uma* are especially high during conditions of drought, wherein populations are reduced in size and fewer rodent burrows are available as retreats. At these times of extreme dryness, and low annual plant production, the dune habitat of fringe-toed lizards is most sensitive to ORV impact.

The importance of hearing to *Uma* is probably related to prey acquisition and predator avoidance. Environmental sounds of potential importance: rustling of dry leaves by insects, insect sounds, digging and sniffing of dogs, crawling snakes on loose gravel, striking rattlesnakes, and swooping owls all produce low-intensity sounds which have strong components within the range of 1000 to 4000 Hz. These potentially important sounds coincide with the maximum acoustical sensitivities (0.9 to 3.5 kHz) of lizards of the families Iguanidae, Gekkonidae, Anguidae, and Teiidae (Campbell, 1969).

Good hearing ability is especially important for animals that inhabit quiet natural environments such as the desert where ambient sound pressure levels are often as low as 30 dBL (Bondello and Brattstrom, 1978). The attenuation of sounds due to increased temperature and decreased humidity (Harris, 1967) makes the desert an especially quiet environment. The regions within the perimeter of long, continuous sand dunes such as the Algodones Dunes, the largest in California and habitat of *Uma notata* (Norris, 1958), are especially quiet due to the establishment of shadow zones of suppressed noise. In these regions, the sand dunes act as a barrier preventing the intrusion of high-intensity ground-generated noise similar to acoustical barriers constructed near freeways (Federal Highway Administration, 1976). Due to the rapid attenuation of higher frequency sounds, reception of natural sounds above 1 kHz implies nearness and often danger to prey animals (Hardy, 1956). Thus, the importance and selective advantage of possessing and maintaining a healthy hearing apparatus capable of detecting subtle sounds within the 0.9 to 3.5 kHz range for *Uma scoparia* and other desert animals is again strongly implied.

The extreme vulnerability of the hearing apparatus of *Uma scoparia* to short durations of high-intensity sound is not demonstrated in humans. Human noise exposure limits set by OSHA prescribe a recommended cumulative exposure to 95 dBA noise not to exceed 4 hr. *Uma scoparia* suffered hearing loss with a cumulative exposure of 500 sec to 95 dBA sounds. Thus, the larger, more sophisticated, better protected human ear is capable of withstanding high-intensity sound exposures which easily damage the smaller, more simplistic lizard ear. OSHA and the Environmental Protection Agency (EPA) recommended noise guidelines established for the protection of human hearing, then, are not necessarily applicable to the protection of wildlife hearing. An acceptable vehicle noise limit in urban areas may, in a relatively short period of time, be capable of severely damaging the hearing of exposed wildlife populations.

Awareness of these pronounced differences between human and desert lizard auditory systems, the relative vulnerability to acoustical trauma of lizards, the importance of the detection of subtle low-intensity sounds in the daily lives of desert wildlife, the significance of the 0.9 to 3.5 kHz sensitivity range, the relative quiet of remote natural areas, are all fundamental to the specific understanding of the effects of dune buggy sounds on *Uma scoparia,* and more generally, to the effects of high-intensity mechanized sounds on wildlife.

The Effect of Motorcycle Sounds on the Emergence of Couch's Spadefoot Toad, *Scaphiopus couchi*

Introduction

Couch's spadefoot toad *(Scaphiopus couchi)* is a highly adapted semifossorial anuran that inhabits arid regions of the southwestern United States. The toad has a black, sickle-shaped "spade" on each hind foot that enables it to burrow to depths in excess of 50 cm beneath the desert surface. Within the burrow, *S. couchi* is able to avoid the environmental extremes of the harsh desert surface for periods which may exceed 1 year (Mayhew, 1965a).

Populations of *S. couchi* energe from their burrows with the first summer thunderstorms (June–July) and aggregate at temporary pools of water where mating occurs. Foraging may occur at some distance from these pools (McClanahan, 1967). Their eggs may hatch within 48 hours and larvae mature within 10 days. Within 3 months, their weight may increase by 110% and length by 1100%. Metamorphosis is rapid and often completed before the temporary pools dry up (Mayhew, 1965a).

After the seasonal summer thunderstorms have passed (September–October), individuals dig into their burrows and remain buried until the next summer's storms (McClanahan, 1967). They do not emerge during winter rains, although similar pools may form (Mayhew, 1965a). While buried in their burrows, *S. couchi* encounter physiological problems of food storage and water conservation (McClanahan, 1967).

The auditory system of *S. couchi* is quite different from that represented by other families of anurans. Most anurans have three distinct types of auditory nerve fibers with varying degrees of response which enable them to perceive sounds of lower, medium, and higher frequencies. *Scaphiopus couchi*, however, has only two distinct types of auditory nerve fibers, one that responds to lower frequencies and one that responds to higher frequencies.

The lower frequency sensitive fibers have a range of sensitivity from 0.1 to 0.7 kHz with their best response at 0.48 kHz (54 dBL). These fibers probably derive from the amphibian papilla of *S. couchi*'s inner ear and exhibit tone-on-tone inhibition. The higher frequency sensitive fibers have a range of sensitivity from 0.9 to 1.5 kHz with best response at 1.4 kHz (64 dBL). These fibers probably derive from the basilar papilla of the inner ear and do not exhibit tone-on-tone inhibition. The response properties of the higher frequency sensitive group corresponds to the major spectral energies and temporal patterns of *S. couchi*'s mating (1.3 to 2.1 kHz) and release (1.0 kHz) calls. The response properties of the lower frequency sensitive group, however, do not correspond to spectral patterns of known biological significance. Thus, detection of predators and other environmental low-frequency sounds has been suggested as the function of the fibers of the amphibian papilla (Capranica and Moffat, 1975).

The timing of the emergence of *S. couchi* during summer thunderstorms is of critical importance to the reproductive success of the population. Yet, the exact mechanism that initiates their emergence is not known. Prior to the rainy season on warm nights, *S. couchi* have been seen with only their eyes and snouts protruding from the surface (Bragg, 1965). Ruibal et al. (1969) eliminated rain as a necessary cue for emergence in that it was difficult to explain how a 1-mm rain could affect the soil environment at a depth of 30 cm. The exact environmental stimulus that is responsible for initiating the emergence of the spadefoot is thus not known.

The purpose of this investigation was to determine whether acoustical signals provided an environmental cue which could initiate the emergence of spadefoots. Specifically, we asked if, in the late fall, in the absence of water, mechanized sounds (such as that from ORVs) with low-frequency energies could trigger the emergence of a captive group of burrowed *S. couchi*. The results of these tests and spectral analysis of the introduced mechanized sounds are presented, and the ecological implications of *S. couchi* responses are discussed.

Materials and Methods

Twenty *S. couchi* were obtained from the Arizona-Sonora Desert Museum in late summer 1978 and allowed to acclimate in a 57-liter terrarium filled with 10 cm of sand collected near Rice, California and kept at an ambient air temperature of 22°C. The terrarium was placed on foam rubber pads 5 cm thick to insulate it from ground vibrations. A 20-cm coaxial loudspeaker, suspended 20 cm above the sand surface over the center of the terrarium, was connected to an amplifier which amplified a recording of mechanized sounds from a 30-sec loop tape, played back on a cassette recorder. The mechanized recording consisted of sounds recorded from 30 massed 250-cc motorcycles.

Seven experiments were performed with *S. couchi* individuals between October 10 and November 20, 1978. Experiments were conducted during early evening hours (1830 to 2130) and controls always preceded test runs. A bowl of fresh water was provided the spadefoots each week, but not until several days after each experimental session. Equal numbers of control and test runs were conducted at durations 10, 20, and 30 min; thus, a total of seven runs at 10 min, six runs at 20 min, and four runs at 30 min was conducted.

Test runs consisted of amplifying the motorcycle recording to an intensity of 95 dBA (100 dBL), and the number of spadefoots on the surface was then visually observed and recorded at 5-min intervals. If more than two toads were on the surface prior to the experimental session, the experiment was terminated. Controls were conducted under similar conditions except no sounds were introduced. Observations were initially made under red light; however, subsequent tests were performed under white light, and in one instance, no light, with no apparent change in *S. couchi* behavior.

Results

The number of individuals on the surface of the sand did not increase during control runs, but did increase during the test runs. The range of numbers for *S. couchi* on the surface was 0 to 2 ($X = 0.8$) for controls, and the number of toads on the surface during test runs was 1 to 7 ($X = 3.3$) after 10 min, 4 to 11 ($X = 5.7$) after 20 min, and 6 to 12 ($X = 7.5$) after 30 min exposure to motorcycle sounds. Thus, motorcycle sound exposure resulted in the emergence of toads and the longer the duration, the more toads emerged (Fig. 9-9).

Scaphiopus couchi exhibited quiescent behavior during control runs. Toads on the surface rested in crouched positions with ventral surfaces held near, and often in contact with, the sand surface. Their eyes were loosely closed or half opened; however, at times they opened widely as the toads peered out of the terrarium. Buccal pumping was slow and even at about one pump per second. Burrowed individuals, visible through the glass walls, remained motionless with eyes tightly shut and limbs held closely to their bodies. Buccal pumping was very slow and not easily detected.

Scaphiopus couchi behavior changed when motorcycle sounds were introduced. Toads at the surface blinked and widely opened their eyes, slightly

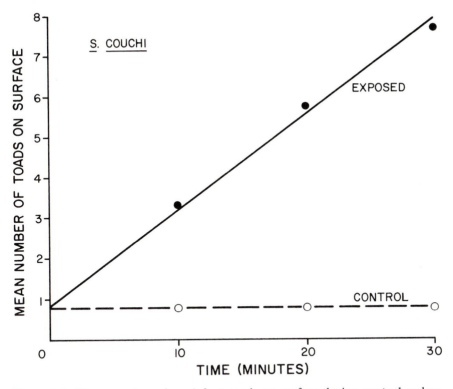

Figure 9-9. Mean number of spadefoot toads on surface during control and exposed experimental runs.

tensed, and raised their posture so that snouts were elevated about $30°$ from the substrate. Buccal pumping increased to about twice per second as toads became more active. After several minutes, some toads slowly moved around the terrarium as others hopped quickly across the enclosure. Most, however, moved near the sides of the terrarium and remained there. Toads visible in shallow burrows shook slightly, gulped several times, and slowly unfolded limbs from their bodies while their eyes remained tightly closed. Then, they would slowly, but persistently, nudge their snouts into the soil above their heads and force their bodies upward. In a few minutes, they managed to dig through several centimeters of soil and break through several millimeters of compacted sand crust to arrive at the surface. The toads often paused prior to emerging, with only their snouts and eyes protruding. At this time, their eyes slowly blinked open, while buccal pumping increased to once per second. Then, they either remained partially buried or totally emerged, with a cake of damp and dry sand coating their dorsal surface. The skin color of newly emerged toads was quite dark. Once on the surface they either remained near their burrows or slowly moved along the perimeter of the enclosure.

After the sounds were terminated, most of the toads remained at the surface. A few *S. couchi* that had not totally emerged dug back into their burrows, but the majority of the toads simply rested in stationary positions and peered out of the terrarium or moved slowly along the perimeter. Many toads were still on the surface several hours after sound exposure.

Analysis of the motorcycle sounds revealed that major energies were concentrated between 0.4 and 4.4 kHz, with minor energies between 0.25 and 7.0 kHz. The mechanized sounds, therefore, possessed major energies well within the range of the auditory nerve fibers of both the amphibian and basilar papillae of *S. couchi* (Capranica and Moffat, 1975).

Discussion and Summary

Recorded motorcycle sounds of intermediate intensity have been shown to elicit the emergence of captive burrowed *S. couchi*. The same toads under similar environmental conditions failed to emerge in the absence of recorded sounds. Thus, mechanized sounds can trigger the emergence of captive spadefoot toads. Further, increased durations of exposure stimulated more toads to emerge (Fig. 9-9). The late season (October–November), presence or absence of light, and absence of water from their enclosure did not deter the emergence of the toads in repeated experiments. These data indicate that acoustical signals alone can act as an environmental cue in eliciting the emergence of spadefoot toads. Similar results have been reported for *S. couchi* and *S. hammondi* by Dimmitt (1975) and Dimmitt and Ruibal (1980), wherein the sound of rainfall was suggested as the primary emergence cue. McClanahan (1967) also reported that captive *S. couchi* remained alert to sound while burrowed in leucite containers and sounds from a hand drill initiated a digging response.

It is true that in this experiment the spadefoot toads were placed in a relatively shallow terrarium with a hard bottom. It may well be that sound waves from the recording traveled through the soil, bounced off the bottom of the terrarium and traveled past the toads a second time. The vibrations set up in the sand may not resemble those encountered in the field where attenuation of the sound occurs with increasing soil depth, yet the studies of Dimmitt (1975), Dimmitt and Ruibal (1980), and McClanahan (1967) suggest that deeply burrowed spadefoot toads are apparently able to monitor and respond to surface environmental sounds.

The ecological importance of their emergence response to acoustical stimuli may be understood by recalling the seasonal patterns of *S. couchi* behavior. *Scaphiopus couchi* emerge only after the summer thunderstorms have begun and temporary pools have formed. Although similar pools may form during winter rains, the toads do not emerge (Mayhew, 1965a). These observations indicated that rain, and subsequent temporary pools of water, do not provide the necessary environmental cues to bring the toads to the surface. This observation is consistent with the conclusions of Ruibal et al. (1969) in which it could not be explained how 1 mm of surface rain could affect *S. couchi* individuals at a depth of 30 cm or more. Summer thunderstorms must, therefore, provide environmental cues other than rain which may account for the emergence of *S. couchi*.

Summer thunderstorms are brief, intense, violent episodes of rainfall that differ in many respects from the low-intensity rainstorms of the winter. The most obvious difference is the greatly increased electrical activity produced by thunderstorms. Lighting strokes produce thunderclaps with intensities up to 120 dBA (Miller, 1975) and with sound components whose low-frequency signals (0.030 to 0.130 kHz) can be monitored thousands of miles from the thunderstorm (Holzer, 1955). The resultant violent acoustical shockwaves certainly contain sufficient energies in the appropriate frequency ranges to alert even the most deeply burrowed S. couchi.

The emergence of S. couchi in response to motorcycle sounds represents a potentially deleterious impact on the toad populations. These toads were induced to emerge during the wrong season, in the absence of water, and in the presence or absence of light. They were not reinforced with food or water, yet they repeatedly emerged in subsequent sound exposures over several weeks. Thus, the spadefoots appear to be "locked in" to this response, without regard to critical environmental factors of water, food, or temperature.

The misinterpretation of acoustical cues by anurans has long been known. Florida treefrogs normally emerge from seclusion in response to the increased humidities which occur prior to thunderstorms. Thunder can induce several frogs to emit "rain calls" simultaneously. However, airplane noises can elicit the same response from *Hyla cinerea* (Bogert, 1960). Dimmitt (1975) and Dimmitt and Ruibal (1980) reported the emergence of spadefoot toads in response to sounds generated by an off-balance electric motor in the absence of reinforcing environmental conditions. Thus, misinterpretation of acoustical information by anurans is not an uncommon occurrence.

Recently emerged toads are severely stressed in that they are dehydrated and their fat reserves are depleted (McClanahan, 1967). The act of burrowing upward depletes energy reserves even more and dislodges keratinized layers of skin. Water and food must be available if the toads are to survive. If temperatures are not high enough, presence of appropriate insect prey and fat deposition may be affected and reproductive success would certainly be curtailed in that egg hatching and larval development would be slowed by the lower temperatures. Thus, if S. couchi were induced to emerge at any time other than the natural season of their emergence, they would most certainly suffer deleterious effects.

ORV activities generate sounds with intensity and frequency characteristics sufficient to reach burrowed S. couchi. ORV sounds monitored at the periphery of the Imperial Sand Dunes near Glamis, California, ranged from 76 to 110 dBL over a 1-hr period in March 1978. The ORVs were scattered over the dunes at various distances; however, most of the activities were concentrated on the periphery of the dunes. Individual or massed ORVs often generated high-intensity sounds for periods in excess of 5 min at any one spot (Bondello and Brattstrom, 1978). Both motorcycles and dune buggies generate sounds with major energies concentrated in the lower frequencies. Thus, ORVs certainly generate sounds of sufficient intensity and frequency to be received and misinterpreted by nearby burrowed spadefoot toads.

The potential impact of ORV sounds on spadefoot toad populations near ORV use areas is tremendous. The Glamis-Imperial Sand Dunes site represents one of these delicate areas. Mayhew (1965a) reported isolated populations of *S. couchi* located on the periphery of the Algodones Dunes 9.7 km northwest of Glamis, 3.2 km SE of Glamis, and 11.3 km SE of Glamis. The toads were apparently clustered along the eastern edge because the dunes act as a large dam in blocking runoff of rainfall from the Chocolate, Cargo Muchacho, and Picacho Mountains as the water flows toward the Salton Sea. The eastern periphery of the Algodones Dunes, which contains these relict populations of *S. couchi,* therefore, comprise a particularly sensitive area to ORVs or any other equivalently loud mechanized activity (e.g., gunnery, mining). Unfortunately, the Algodones Dunes near Glamis are widely known as "The Dune Buggy Capital of the World." ORV activities are prohibited only from the northern dune areas. Thus, the southern dunes are open to very intense ORV activity, particularly between March and June. The Glamis *S. couchi* population areas have, therefore, been subject to high-intensity sound exposures in recent years.

Recent field surveys of *S. couchi* in California by Dimmitt (1975) found intact populations of spadefoots throughout the regions northwest and northeast of Glamis in areas that are relatively free of ORV impact. However, *S. couchi* populations reported by Mayhew (1965a) 3.2 to 11.3 km southeast of Glamis clustered along the Algodones Dunes were not seen; this area has received intense ORV impact over the last 10 years. The current status of *S. couchi* within this ORV area is still unknown. The reliance of *S. couchi* on acoustical (Bondello and Brattstrom, 1979) and vibratory (Dimmitt, 1975) stimuli to elicit their emergence from subterranean burrows and their absence from formerly established localities, now intensely used ORV areas, certainly implies that ORVs have a disruptive influence on these populations.

The Effects of Dune Buggy Sounds
on Behavioral Thresholds of Desert Kangaroo Rats,
Dipodomys deserti

Introduction

Desert kangaroo rats, *Dipodomys deserti,* are typical residents of sand dune systems of the California Desert. Among the 13 species of *Dipodomys* within California (Ingles, 1965), *D. deserti* is considered the most specialized form (Nader, 1978). Adaptations of *Dipodomys* to arid environments include a variety of anatomical and physiological specializations. Among these specializations are adaptations for ricochetal locomotion, water metabolism and conservation, tolerance to high body temperatures, diestrous reproductive cycles, and subcortical control of hind limbs to facilitate rapid leaping motions.

The ear apparatus of *Dipodomys* represents an equally specialized adaptation to quiet arid regions (Webster, 1962). The middle ear cavities of Merriam kangaroo rats, *D. merriami,* are reported by Webster (1961) to be greatly enlarged, with a total volume greater than that of their braincase. This greater volume lowers the air pressure within the middle ear, which reduces the effect of dampening on sounds that strike the tympanic membrane (Webster, 1963). The middle ear ossicles are delicately suspended within the middle ear cavity and freely move, unencumbered by supportive ligaments common to most other mammals (Webster, 1961). The malleus is greatly lengthened and extends down over the large tympanic membrane, acting as a lever arm that transforms the relatively weak vibrations that strike the tympanic into stronger movements as the vibrations move down the ossicular membrane chain of the middle ear. Due to the large size of the tympanic membrane and the small size of the footplate of the stapes, weak pressure on the large tympanic membrane is transformed into strong pressure on the oval window. This "transformer ratio" is extremely high in *D. merriami* (97.2:1) and is relatively low in man (around 18.3:1). The specializations of the middle ear apparatus of *Dipodomys,* enlarged auditory bullae, freely moving middle ear ossicles, and high transformer ratios all act to greatly amplify sounds (near 97 times) and relay these vibrations into the inner ear (Webster, 1961).

The inner ear of *Dipodomys* is also specialized to respond to low-intensity vibrations. The cochlear duct has $4\frac{1}{4}$ turns, while $2\frac{1}{2}$ turns are common in mammals. Within the cochlear duct, the tectorial membrane is suspended over enlarged cells of Hensen, with only the "hairs" of the hair cells delicately embedded in the membrane. Thus, the inner ear is adapted for increased sensitivity to the reception of faint sound vibrations (Webster, 1961).

The central auditory system of *D. merriami* shows modifications of the nervous pathways to the brain (Webster et al., 1968) which are well correlated to the peripheral ear modifications. Nuclei of the central auditory system of kangaroo rats are prominant, with special enlargement of medial superior olivary nuclei and dorsal nuclei of the lateral lemniscus also apparent. The dorsal cochlear nuclei are organized into three cell-type layers, which comprise the majority of the acoustica. Two types of spindle-shaped cells of the lateral and medial superior olivary nuclei are present as are unique groups of large multipolar cells that lie between the dorsal nuclei of the lateral lemniscus and base of the inferior colliculus. The adaptations of the central auditory system of *Dipodomys,* therefore, serve to sufficiently strengthen and shorten their auditory pathways in order to rapidly relay acoustical information to the brain.

Cochlear microphonic studies on *D. merriami* showed the greatest sensitivities of their ears to occur between 1.0 and 3.0 kHz, with peak sensitivities at 1.2, 1.4, 1.8 to 2.2, and 2.6 kHz (Webster, 1962). Good sensitivity to low-frequency sounds was also seen by Moushegian and Rupert (1970) wherein 89% of nerve fibers studied in the ventral cochlear nucleus of *Dipodomys* had their best frequency responses below 4.0 kHz.

The importance to *Dipodomys* of detecting low-frequency, low-intensity environmental sounds has been shown by Webster (1962) and Webster and Webster (1971). Sounds produced by *D. merriami,* sidewinders *(Crotalus cerastes),* and screech owls *(Otus asio)*, although quite faint, were strongest within the range of 1.0–3.0 kHz. The reception of the sounds of these predators approaching, the snake's crawl and strike, the owl's wing beat, provides *Dipodomys* with ample warning to successfully evade capture, while hearing-impaired rats are captured. Thus, because of the quiet desert environment, *Dipodomys* have specialized ear and brain modifications which enable them to receive and rapidly process low-intensity sounds of critical environmental importance.

The purpose of this study was to attempt four separate observational experiments on *D. deserti* in order to isolate a specific behavioral response to acoustical stimuli and employ this response as a means of determining the hearing thresholds of *D. deserti*. These four experiments were to:

1. Observe and describe typical behaviors of solitary *D. deserti* in hopes of detecting a behavior which could be shaped as a response to auditory stimuli
2. Observe the typical behaviors of individuals exposed to live *C. cerastes* in order to describe their reactions during predator-prey encounters
3. Determine the behavioral hearing sensitivity of *D. deserti* by eliciting naturally occurring behavioral responses to auditory stimuli
4. Determine the behavioral hearing thresholds of *D. deserti* by the same methodology as previously, after their exposure to brief episodes of 95-dBA dune buggy sounds

Thus, we attempted to determine, through behavioral means, the effects of dune buggy sounds on the hearing of desert kangaroo rats. In an early phase of the experiment, it became apparent that naturally occurring behavior, a sand kick, was elicited from *D. deserti* whenever an intruder (i.e., the experimenter) was detected. This response was also deployed during subsequent encounters with *C. cerastes*. We endeavored to shape the experimental conditions to fit this response into a situation in which we could evaluate the hearing sensitivity of *D. deserti*.

Materials and Methods

Fourteen *Dipodomys deserti* were captured with Sherman live traps 5 km south of Rice, Riverside County, California, on August 8, 1978. The individuals were placed into large glass Mason jars supplied with cotton and bird seed, and packed into a specially constructed acoustically insulated wooden box that was lined on all sides with 7.5-cm-thick foam rubber pads. The animals were immediately transported to California State University in Fullerton, California, where they were transferred into individual plastic containers with internal dimensions of 13 × 15 × 27 cm covered by a 6.4-mm wire-mesh screen which held a substrate of fine sand collected from the dunes near Rice. The individual containers were stored on shelves of a specially assembled "igloo" of 15-cm thick styrofoam blocks. The *D. deserti* were therefore acoustically insulated on all sides, top and bottom, in this "igloo" which could reduce a 90-dBA external sound by 35 dBA.

The *D. deserti* were maintained in total darkness within the "igloo" except for a daily exposure to light around dusk, when the "igloo" was opened to feed the rats their daily ration of bird seed and occasionally fresh lettuce. Cotton and a small jar of water were also provided each rat. The soil was periodically strained to remove droppings and seed husks and occasionally replaced. The temperatures fluctuated daily in each container of the "igloo" from about 22°C during morning hours to 27°C during evening hours. This daily temperature increase was correlated with an increased state of activity for the rats, as monitored by a motion detector connected to a specially fabricated event counter. The rats maintained these behavioral activity cycles throughout their captivity.

Observations of *D. deserti* behavior were conducted over a 4-month period from August to December 1978 for one to several nights a week between 1900 and 2400 hr. Individuals were observed within a 420-liter aquarium that had been acoustically insulated with 7.6-cm-thick pads of foam rubber attached to top, sides, and floor of the enclosure, was filled with 10 cm of fine sand from the dunes near Rice, and was illuminated with a dim red light. The ambient temperature of the enclosure seldom varied from 22°C. Depending on the activities within the building, these sound levels in the enclosure fluctuated from a minimum of 22 dBA (52 dBL), corresponding to the same levels recorded at the Rice Valley sand dunes at 2200 hr, up to a maximum of 34 dBA (61 dBL). Most sound levels were near 33 dBA ± 1 dB. Solitary *D. deserti* were observed over a 2-month period and their stereotypic behaviors described. A behavioral classification scheme was then developed for later use in tabulating the frequencies and sequences of occurrence of these behaviors.

Over the same 4-month time period, kangaroo rats were placed into the enclosure which contained a live sidewinder *(Crotalus creastes)* in order to observe their typical behaviors during these encounteres. A total of 87 individual encounters between 14 *D. deserti* and 2 *C. cerastes* (38 and 45 cm snout-to-vent length) were observed. Individual behaviors of each animal were described for these encounters and tape recordings of sounds emitted during these interactions were recorded for later sonagraph analysis on a tape recorder. Again, behavioral classification schemes were developed for later use in tabulating frequencies and sequences of occurrences of specific behaviors for the rats during simulated encounters using a freeze-dried western diamond-back rattlesnake, *Crotalus atrox*. Behavior of the *C. cerastes* was tabulated during actual encounters with rats.

Two *D. deserti* were later observed to determine frequencies and sequences of specific behaviors that occurred when the rats were alone in the enclosure and when the rats were in the presence of the freeze-dried, coiled *C. atrox*. A total of 250 movements were observed for each rat alone and with the snake. Thus, a total of 500 movements were observed and tabulated for each condition and from these the frequencies (expressed as percentages of total movements) and sequences of occurrence of these behaviors were determined.

During encounters with either live or freeze-dried *Crotalus, D. deserti* were observed to deliver well-placed kicks of sand at the snake. These sand kicks were not delivered until the snake was detected. This sand-kicking behavior was, therefore, selected for use as a behavioral criterion which signaled detection of an intruder. Because *D. deserti* have a variety of special sensory capabilities (visual, acoustical, olfactory, tactile) which could detect the presence of a snake, the following experiments attempted to evaluate the relative effectiveness of each alerting sensory system, and eventually to isolate the responses of *D. deserti* to acoustical stimuli only, as a means of measuring responses of the behavorial hearing thresholds.

The enclosure was partitioned into two areas by an aluminum wire screen (mesh size, 1.5×2.0 mm) set at an angle of $45°$ to the substrate. The area into which the rats were introduced was illuminated by a dim red light located above the screen and directed toward the rats, and this area was about twice the size of the area behind the screen, which was kept in darkness. Beneath the screen ran a block of foam rubber, which completely separated the substrate into two sections. The arrangement of the screen and red light acted as a visual barrier, obliterating the view of objects placed behind the screen, and the foam rubber block acted as a barrier to any substrate vibrations or compression forces which may have emanted from objects placed behind the screen.

The effectiveness of these barriers was tested by first placing a freeze-dried snake in front of the screen, and then introducing a rat into the enclosure. The rat responded immediately by advancing cautiously toward the snake and turning to deliver sand kicks at it. The rat was then removed and the freeze-dried snake moved behind the screen. The rat was reintroduced and aside from a few exploratory movements near the screen, showed no indication of having detected the image of the snake coiled just in back of the screen. Thus, the screen apparently served as a good visual, as well as tactile barrier due to the foam rubber block.

The rat was again removed from the enclosure and a live *C. cerastes* was placed behind the screen. When introduced back into the far side of the enclosure, the rat cautiously advanced toward the screen, quickly detected the snake, and responded with a series of sand kicks at the screen. It was clear that this series of responses could not have been elicited by either visual or tactile stimuli. Removal of both the rat and the snake and replacement of the rat into the enclosure revealed that the rat no longer delivered sand kicks at the screen but repeatedly sniffed the screen for several minutes. This suggested that the rat responded to the reception of specific auditory or olfactory stimuli from the snake, and was not simply responding to the screen with sand kicks.

The rat was again removed to test these hypothesis. A snake-scented rag, rubbed over the body of the *C. cerastes,* was placed behind the screen. When reintroduced, the rat again repeatedly sniffed the screen, then suddenly became alerted, turned and kicked sand at the screen. A similar test using only a sterile, unscented cotton rag failed to elicit the sand kicking response. Thus, olfactory stimuli were presumably detected by the rat only at extremely close ranges.

A loudspeaker was placed behind the screen and, upon reintroduction of the rat, was found to elicit no sand kicking responses. When low-intensity static or hum was played through the speaker, the rat responded with repeated exploratory movements and sniffing at the screen, but no sand kicks. However, when the sounds of a *C. cerastes* crawling on sand were placed through the speaker, the rat responded with repeated sand kicks at the screen. Sand kicks were repeatedly elicited by acoustical simuli only, and apparently, the rat did not habituate to the sound, in that it always responded with sand kicks to their presentation. It was the specific auditory cue of *C. cerastes* crawling on sand that was used to measure the behavioral hearing threshold of *D. deserti*. Only those rats that responded 100% of the time with sand kicks to the sound of *C. creastes* crawling on sand were used in the behavioral hearing tests.

Due to the fluctuation of ambient sound levels within the enclosure by 1 or 2 dB, a more accurate method of assessing the stimulus intensity used in the behavioral hearing tests was devised. A millivoltmeter was connected in line between the tape recorder and the speaker, which allowed the precise speaker voltage which elicited the sand kicking responses of rats to be measured. When a response was first elicited, the speaker voltage was recorded, and after removal of the rat, the number of decibels above ambient of the sound produced by this speaker voltage was determined.

A typical behavioral hearing test began soon after a rat was introduced into the enclosure. When its explorations brought it to within 50 cm of the speaker, the tape recorder was quietly started and volume slowly turned up, from the minimum setting, at increments of 0.5 mV. When the first sand kick was observed, the recorder was stopped, voltage noted, and volume turned down again. The entire procedure was then repeated until several consistent readings were obtained. The two desert kangaroo rats used were quite consistent in these responses and did not deliver sand kicks until the stimuli were presented. Control experimental sessions to determine the behavioral hearing thresholds of the two rats were conducted for 3 weeks prior to November 20, 1978. The responses of the rats remained quite consistent from week to week; thus, the lowest voltages which elicited their sand kicking responses were considered to be their threshold of behavioral hearing. These voltages and their equivalent SPLs were recorded for later comparison with threshold levels obtained after the rats were exposed to dune buggy sounds.

Dune buggy sounds were played to the *D. deserti* from a loop tape through an amplifier which amplified the signal through to the loudspeaker. Signal intensity was increased until 95 dBA (10 dBL) was reached at the position of the rat. This intensity is lower than the maximum (105 dBL) value actually recorded from dune buggies in the field (Bondello and Brattstrom, 1978). The rats were housed in a small aluminum screen cage (6.4-mm mesh) placed 8 cm in front of the speaker during the sound exposures. Their behaviors were observed during the duration of the sound exposure, after which time their ears were examined with an otoscope to check for any physical signs of external or middle ear damage. The rats were immediately given a behavioral hearing test after their sound exposures and were then rechecked at weekly periods until December 11, 1978, at which time their behavioral hearing thresholds had returned to normal.

Results

Behavioral Hearing Tests on Desert Kangaroo Rats. The two *D. deserti* that positively responded to the presence of a live *C. cerastes* and freeze-dried *C. atrox* with sand kicks 100% of the time were tested to determine their behavioral hearing thresholds. Results of these tests indicate that *D. deserti* initially responded with sand kicks to recordings of *C. cerastes* crawls emitted at speaker voltages of 2.7 and 2.9 mV. These voltages correspond to SPLs of 35 dBA (63 dBL) and represent a difference of less than 1 dBA (1 dBL) above ambient. Rats did not respond with sand kicks to snake crawl sounds below these values; thus, they were considered to be the baseline behavioral hearing thresholds for each rat. Subsequent repeated tests conducted several weeks apart confirmed that these were indeed the behavioral hearing thresholds for each rat. These sound pressure levels were not audible to the experimenter without the aid of a stethoscope which was used to detect whether the speaker was indeed operating.

Behaviors of Kangaroo Rats Exposed to Dune Buggy Sounds. A 1971 Volkswagen "Baja Bug" produced sounds in excess of 95 dBA (100 dBL) at 5 m. Sonagraph analysis revealed energies of these sounds to extend from 0.085 to 8.0 kHz. Major energies were concentrated below 2.1 kHz, with maximum values at 0.3 kHz. Substantial energies were also apparent below 1.5 kHz.

Dipodomys deserti exposed to dune buggy sounds ran in circles, defecated, pushed at the opening of their cages, chewed on the wooden struts of their cages, started at each new sequence of recorded sounds, frantically groomed themselves and performed repeated slides, and finally shivered on hindlimbs below the speaker, with head lowered. After the sounds were terminated, the rats assumed a cautious stance with heads raised to about 20° above the substrate. No external or middle ear damages were found in either exposed rat.

Effects of Dune Buggy Sounds on Desert Kangaroo Rat Hearing Thresholds. The same stimulus and intensity required to elicit a positive sand kicking response in both *D. deserti* during control sessions failed to elicit a positive response in rats 10 min after their exposure to dune buggy sounds. Stimulus intensities had to be increased for both rats in order to elicit the sand kicking responses. These increases of intensity, measured in speaker voltages and decibels above ambient, for each rat respectively, were 5.5 mV and 8.0 mV. These increases correspond to increases above the ambient sound levels of 5.0 dBA (8.0 dBL) and 7.0 dBA (10.0 dBL), respectively. Even with the normal ±1-dB fluctuation, the increased SPLs still represent at least a doubling of intensity for the first rat, and a quadrupling of sound intensity for the second rat in order to elicit the same sand kicking response of the control sessions after being exposed to the dune buggy sounds. Both rats, therefore, suffered a temporary threshold shift in their behavioral hearing sensitivity.

Both rats gradually recovered their original behavioral hearing sensitivity, measured by speaker voltage intensity required to elicit a sand kicking response,

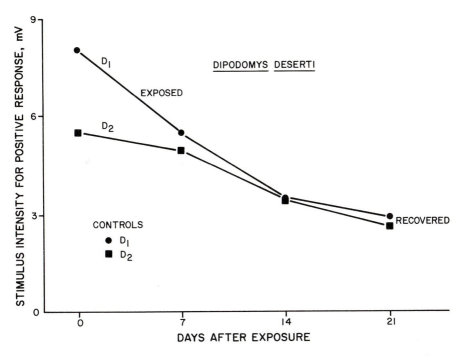

Figure 9-10. Graph depicting the temporary threshold shift and gradual recovery of behavioral hearing in two desert kangaroo rats *(D. deserti)* after exposure to 500 sec of noncontinuous dune buggy sounds of 95 dBA (100 dBL).

over a period of 3-weeks following their exposure to dune buggy sounds (Fig. 9-10). Neither rat, however, had fully recovered from the 500 sec of dune buggy sounds until the 21st day following exposure. During this 3-week period their hearing, while undergoing improvement, continued to be impaired when compared to their former hearing acuities during control sessions.

Discussion and Summary

The immediate effects of dune buggy sounds on the behavioral hearing of both *D. deserti* tested was to lower their hearing sensitivities and thereby raise their hearing thresholds by 4 dBL in one subject and 9 dBL in the other (Fig. 9-10). This means that the actual power intensity of the stimulus had to be increased by two times in the first subject and eight times for the second over what it had previously been in order to elicit the same response in these individuals. Expressed another way, these required increases in stimulus intensities represent decreases in the effective audible detection distance between the rats and the sound source previously observed in control sessions (40+ cm for each individual). Ten minutes after sound exposure, this warning distance dropped to less than 2 cm. Recovery from sound exposure thus gradually restored the effective warning distance, previously seen in controls. Seven days after exposure warning distances increased to at most 12 cm, after 14 days to a maximum of 21 cm, and the original warning distance (40 cm) was not achieved until 21 days after the sound exposures.

The normal striking distance of *Crotalus* generally has been reported as being between one-third and one-half of the total body length of the specific reptile, though some have been known to exceed this distance (Klauber, 1956). The *C. cerastes* used in this experiment was 48 cm in total length (45 cm in snout-vent length) and would therefore be expected to have a normal striking range of between 16 and 24 cm. Thus, for nearly 21 days following the sound exposure, under darkened conditions, both rats could conceivably have been approached, monitored, and successfully struck by this sidewinder, without having received detectable acoustical warnings.

Dune buggy sounds of 95 dBA (10 dBL) delivered in a noncontinuous duration of 500 sec, therefore, seriously impaired the behavioral hearing of *D. deserti* and deprived these animals of one of their primary dark-adapted predator detection senses. Thus, the dune buggy sounds immediately lowered the fitness of both *D. deserti* by removing their primary ability to detect the approach of predators in the dark for up to 21 days after their exposures.

Characteristics of the dune buggy sounds which contributed to the destruction of hearing and predator detection in *D. deserti* included their high sound intensities and the frequency components of their major sound energies. Sonagraph analysis indicated that major energies of the high intensity sounds were carried beyond 6.0 kHz with highest concentrations below 2.0 kHz. Thus, major sound energies occurred at the region of the most acute hearing sensitivity (1.2 to 1.4 kHz) of kangaroo rats as determined by Webster (1962).

The ears of *D. merriami* were overloaded near this region (1.5 kHz) by sound intensities of 20 dB re 1 dyne cm^{-2} by Vernon et al. (1971). This intensity corresponds to the 100-dB re 20 Pa exposure delivered in this study. Kangaroo rat ears may, therefore, be assumed to be quite vulnerable to sounds with high concentrations of energy in the region 1.0 to 3.0 kHz.

Dipodomys ears possess a variety of anatomical adaptations which promote the amplification of low-frequency sounds, presumably because this is the region in which critical environmental sounds (i.e., mammalian, avian, and reptilian predators) are most apparent. These adaptations include their enlarged auditory bullae, high tympanic membrane to stapes footplate transformer ratios, and unimpaired middle ear ossicles (Webster, 1961). All of these structures function to reduce the dampening of low-frequency sounds with the result that *Dipodomys* are more sensitive to lower frequency sound than most animals tested (Vernon et al., 1971). *Dipodomys*, therefore, have little means of preventing the full amplification into their ears of high-intensity, low-frequency sounds produced by dune buggies.

Field surveys (Bondello and Brattstrom, 1978) found that dune buggies produced sound intensities that were over twice as high (105 dBL), at ranges of 50 m, as those sounds used in this experiment. Other high-intensity dune buggy sounds, with similar acoustical characteristics, were monitored for continuous durations that exceeded 5 min. Thus, field sound exposures regularly exceeded the cumulative dosage required to elicit hearing loss in *D. deserti,* as reported in this study.

The intense concentration of dune buggies on sand dunes and their repeated penetrations into interior dunes, therefore, repeatedly spreads potentially destructive sounds throughout the restricted habitat of *D. deserti.* Much of this intense dune buggy activity occurs during late spring and early summer, which coincides with the breeding season of *D. deserti* of late January to mid-July (Nader, 1978). During the reproductive season, mothers of infant rats are known to retrieve their offspring by responding to repeated scratch-whines emitted by young (Eisenberg and Isaac, 1963). The effects of ORV penetrations on the reproductive success of local populations of *D. deserti* are not known; however, it is apparent that during the most critical phase of their life cycle, the habitat of *D. deserti* receives the heaviest impacts from dune buggies.

The intense ORV activities which presently occur on and near the sand dunes of the California Desert, then, clearly constitute a potential threat to the well-being of *D. deserti* and other dune inhabitants. Our study suggests that the magnitudes and frequencies of occurrence of ORV sounds in the California Desert present a clear and present danger to the wellbeing of the natural wildlife of arid regions.

Local populations of *D. deserti* are unlikely simply to move away from dunes where ORV activities occur. Because of their narrow habitat requirements they are restricted to the dune habitat and cannot move away from them into less impacted, differently composed regions (i.e., hardpan) which may border the dunes. They are not likely to move successfully into adjacent dune systems either. Conspecifics already occupy these areas and defend their territories with as much tenacity as all other *D. deserti.* Local populations of *D. deserti,* therefore, do not enjoy the option of successfully emigrating away from ORV-impacted dunes.

These kangaroo rats are too specialized to tolerate the disturbance to their habitat which would result from ORV activities, much as California kangaroo rats *(D. californica)* apparently could not tolerate the disturbance of habitats near the Geysers geothermal field (Hurley, 1977). The same specialized niche requirements which contribute to the success of *D. deserti* on undisturbed, quiet, productive sand dunes make this species totally intolerant of disturbances caused by ORVs. The intolerance of *D. deserti* cannot be too highly stressed. *Dipodomys deserti* construct too fragile burrows, defend territories too rigidly, and rely too heavily on unimpaired hearing for survival to tolerate even the most cursory of ORV penetrations into their dunes. None of the narrow niche requirements of *D. deserti* is subject to compromise without seriously jeopardizing the existence of local populations of these animals.

Summary and Management Recommendations

The foregoing studies indicate that ORV activities in the California Desert represent disruptive and often destructive influences on the native wildlife of this region. They show that the noise of dune buggies and motorcycles: (a) definitely caused hearing losses in animals with little or no recovery; (b) interfered with their ability to detect predators; and (c) caused behavior in an unnatural manner that put the animal in a situation which could result in death. Further, these studies indicate that ORV sound levels of lower intensity and shorter duration than those monitored in the desert can disrupt and destroy essential features of desert wildlife. Detrimental effects of ORV sounds result from the acute sensitivity of desert vertebrates to the reception of specific environmental sounds.

Several factors contribute to processes of natural selection which have made desert vertebrates so sensitive to the reception of specific counds. The intense heat and dryness which characterizes this region during the most active spring and summer months greatly reduces the effective conduction of sound in this experiment (Harris, 1967). Natural constraints of heat and dryness function to attenuate rapidly sounds of higher frequency while lower frequencies are carried for greater distances (Harris, 1967). The result has been that the reception of higher frequency sounds by prey animals implies nearness and often danger (Hardy, 1956). The ability to receive lower frequency sounds (below 3.0 kHz), therefore, benefits animals by extending the range at which important environmental stimuli (predator approach) are audible (Webster and Webster, 1971). Because critical environmental sounds are often of relatively low intensity (snake crawls and owl swoops) sensitive hearing acuity is essential to the survival of many desert vertebrates. The result of these natural selective forces has been the evolution of many types of desert vertebrates (spadefoot toads, lizards, kangaroo rats) with the ability to hear low-intensity, low-frequency sounds.

Bondello and Brattstrom (1978) and this chapter have shown that mechanized sounds have much higher intensities than naturally occurring desert sounds. The high forces required to operate heavy equipment and drive ORVs through sand and over rocks generate high-intensity sounds concentrated in the lower frequencies. These high-intensity, low-frequency sounds carry the farthest in desert air and are known to penetrate to distances exceeding 4 km (Rennison and Wallace, 1976). Mechanized sounds are, therefore, able to penetrate deep into desert habitats, beyond the specific location of sound sources. The superior maneuverability of ORVs has enabled their penetrations into vast regions of formerly quiet desert habitats and this occurs on a regular basis. ORVs, therefore, amplify their acoustical impact on the desert ecosystem by carrying high-intensity sound sources deep into the home ranges of hearing-sensitive animals.

ORVs are not the loudest mechanized sound source in the California Desert; however, they occur more frequently than any comparable high-intensity sound source. It is the penetrating, far-ranging nature of ORV use and concentrated use of specific fragile habitats that comprise the greatest acoustical threat to desert wildlife. The problem is not just the abilities of specific sounds to carry into desert regions, but the abilities of specific sound *sources* to penetrate deep into these reaches.

Sand dune inhabitants are particularly vulnerable to ORV sounds. Accounting for this vulnerability requires a brief review of the unique acoustical characteristics of sand dunes. Dune systems are characterized by intense heat and dryness which serve to rapidly attenuate sound conduction. These habitats also have high sloping barrier dunes on their peripheries, which crop to bowl-shaped depressions within interiors of dune systems. These high dunes act as acoustical barriers (Federal Highway Administration, 1976) which block the entrance of loud sounds into the interior dunes. Interior dunes, therefore, represent a "shadow zone" wherein sound levels are quite low (Bondello and Brattstrom, 1978) and it is here that many hearing-sensitive animals exist. Interior dunes are also regions that are heavily impacted by frequent, loud incursions of dune buggies. Sound exposures similar to these promptly devasted the hearing acuities of dune residents *(Uma* and *Dipodomys)* investigated in this report. Vertebrates of the dunes are simply incapable of absorbing the impact of even the most moderate of ORV sound exposures.

The best available scientific data, therefore, indicate that acoustical impacts of ORVs on the California Desert pose a clear and present danger to the well-being of desert vertebrates. Each class of vertebrate tested revealed that disturbing or destructive effects resulted from ORV sound exposures *less than* those which actually and regularly occur in the desert. Animals from quiet protected sand dunes *(Uma* and *Dipodomys)* were the more vulnerable and suffered immediate loss of hearing when exposed to these sounds. Recovery of *D. deserti* was gradual and took several weeks, during which time the demonstrated auditory abilities of prey animals to detect predator approach dropped below levels requisite for survival. Experimental evidence indicates that equivalent (or higher) cumulative doses of ORV sounds will, likewise, damage the hearing abilities of similar animals (Bondello et al., 1979).

The desert sand dunes represent a critical habitat to the animals that live only in these systems (e.g., *Uma scoparia* and *D. deserti*). The vital requirements of space, nutrients, shelter, breeding sites, dunes for buffering sounds, sand for grooming, burrow construction, food catching, cover, and concealment are provided only on these sand dune systems. Desert sand dunes are, thus, in every respect, critical habitats of these indigenous species of wildlife.

Based on the best available scientific data we, therefore, recommend that the following measures by taken to protect the unique habitats and wildlife of deserts.

1. Desert sand dune systems should be designated as "critical habitats."
2. Sand dune dwelling species should be afforded protected status to ensure their survival on undisturbed dune habitats.
3. ORV and other disturbing activities should be totally restricted from undisturbed desert sand dune systems and from their peripheries.

4. Recreational ORVs should be restricted from the wide-ranging use of public lands to minimize the spread of high-intensity sounds.
5. Public lands designated for ORV use should be regulated to ensure total confinement of ORV impacts to relatively small areas.
6. ORV designated areas should be located away from all undisturbed desert habitats, critical habitats, and all ranges of threatened, endangered, or otherwise protected desert species.

Acknowledgments

We wish to thank Anthony C. Huntley and Harry B. Cohen for assistance in the *Uma* study. This study was carried out under a contract with the Bureau of Land Management (CA-060-CT7-2737). We wish to thank Anthony Huntley, Mark Posson, Diane Tucker, and Nancy Jean Mann for their assistance, Mark Zolle for doing the illustrations, and many others who gave us ideas and encouragement.

References

Aran, J. M. 1971. The electrocochleogram. Arch. Klin. Exp. Ohr-Nas-u. Keklk.-Heilk. 198:128–141.

Bogert, C. M. 1960. The influence of sound on the behavior of amphibians and reptiles. In: W. E. Lanyon and W. N. Tavolga (Eds.), Animal Sound and Communication. American Institute of Biological Sciences Publication 7, Washington, D.C., pp. 137–320.

Bondello, M. C. 1976. The effects of high-intensity motorcycle sounds on the acoustical sensitivity of the Desert Iguana, *Dipsosaurus dorsalis*. M.S. thesis, California State University, Fullerton, California, 38 pp.

Bondello, M. C., and B. H. Brattstrom. 1978. Ambient sound pressure levels in the California desert. Report, Contract No. CA-060-CT7-2737, U.S. Bureau of Land Management, Riverside, California, 135 pp.

Bondello, M. C., A. C. Huntley, H. B. Cohen, and B. H. Brattstrom. 1979. The effects of dune buggy sounds on the telechephalic auditory evoked response in the Mojave Fringe-toed Lizards, *Uma scoparia*. Report, Contract No. CA-060-CT7-2737, U.S. Bureau of Land Management, Riverside, California, 31 pp.

Bragg, A. N. 1965. Gnomes of the Night. University of Pennsylvania Press, Philadelphia, Pennsylvania, 127 pp.

Brattstrom, B. H. 1965. Body temperatures of reptiles. Am. Midl. Naturalist 73: 376–422.

Campbell, H. W. 1969. The effects of temperature on the auditory sensitivity of lizards. Physiol. Zool. 42:183–210.

Capranica, R. R., and A. J. M. Moffat. 1975. Selectivity of the peripheral auditory system of spadefoot toads *(Scaphiopus couchi)* for sounds of biological significance. J. Comp. Physiol. 1:123–249.

Carpenter, C. C. 1967. Display patterns of the Mexican Iguanid lizards of the genus *Uma*. Herpetologica 23:285–293.

Commins, M. L., and A. H. Savitsky. 1973. Field observations on a population of the sand lizard, *Uma exsul.* J. Herpetol. 7:51–53.

Davis, H. 1976. Electrical response audiometry, with special reference to the vertex potentials. In: M. O. Keidel and W. O. Neff (Eds.), Handbook of Sensory Physiology: Auditory System, Vol. 3. Clinical and Special Topics. Springer-Verlag, New York, pp. 85–103.

Dimmitt, M. A. 1975. Terrestrial ecology of spadefoot toads *(Scaphious):* Emergence cues, nutrition, and burrowing habits. Ph.D. dissertation, University of California, Riverside, California, 80 pp.

Dimmitt, M. A., and R. Ruibal. 1980. Environmental correlates of emergency in spadefoot toads *(Scaphiopus).* J. Herpetol. 14:21–29.

Eisenberg, J. F., and D. E. Isaac. 1963. The reproduction of heteromyid rodents in captivity. J. Mammal. 44:61–67.

Federal Highway Administration. 1976. Highway noise, the noise barrier design handbook. FHWA-RD-76-58. U.S. Dept. Transportation, Washington, D.C., 102 pp.

Goldstein, R. 1973. Electroencephalic audiometry. In: J. Jerger (Ed.), Modern Developments in Audiology (2nd ed.). Academic Press, New York, 446 pp.

Hardy, H. C. 1956. Some observations on man's noise environment. Intl. Congr. Acoustics Proc. 2:37–43.

Harris, C. M. 1967. Absorption of sound in air versus humidity and temperature. National Aeronautics and Space Administration Contract Report 647, 236 pp.

Holzer, R. E. 1955. Studies of the Universal Aspect of Atmospheric Electricity. Final Report, Contract AF 19 (122)-254, University of California. In: Meterological Research Reviews 3(20), July, 1957.

Hurley, J. F. 1977. Effects of geothermal development upon small mammal communities at the Geysers Geothermal Field. M.S. thesis, University of California, Berkeley, California, 119 pp.

Ingles, L. G. 1965. Mammals of the Pacific States. Stanford University Press, Stanford, California, 506 pp.

Keidel, W. D. 1976. The physiological background of the electric response audiometry. In: W. D. Keidel and W. D. Neff (Eds.), Handbook of Sensory Physiology: Auditory System, Vol. 3. Clinical and Special Topics. Springer-Verlag, New York, 811 pp.

Klauber, L. M. 1956. Rattlesnakes: Their Habits, Life Histories, and Influence on Mankind, Vol. 1. University of California Press, Berkeley, California, 506 pp.

Mayhew, W. W. 1965a. Adaptations of the amphibian, *Scaphiopus couchi,* to desert conditions. Am. Midl. Naturalist 74:95–109.

Mayhew, W. W. 1965b. Reproduction in the sand-dwelling lizard, *Uma inornata.* Herpetologica 21:39–55.

Mayhew, W. W. 1966a. Reproduction in the arenicolous lizard, *Uma notata.* Ecology 47:9–18.

Mayhew, W. W. 1966b. Reproduction in the psammophilous lizard, *Uma scoparia.* Copeia 1966:114–122.

McClanahan, L. 1967. Adaptations of the spadefoot toad, *Scaphiopus couchi,* to desert environments. Comp. Biochem. Physiol. 20:73–99.

Miller, G. T. 1975. Living in the Environment. Wadsworth Publishing Co., Belmont, California, 470 pp.

Moushegian, G., and A. L. Rupert. 1970. Response diversity of neurosis in ventral cochlear nucleus of kangaroo rat to low-frequency tones. J. Neurophysiol. 33:351–364.

Nader, I. A. 1978. Kangaroo Rats: Intraspecific variation in *Dipodomys spectabilis* Merriam and *Dipodomys deserti* Stephens. Illinois Biol. Mongr. 49:1–116.

Norris, K. S. 1958. The evolution and systematics of the Iguanid Genus *Uma* and its relation to the evolution of other North American desert reptiles. Bull. Am. Mus. Nat. Hist. 114:247–326.

Pough, F. H. 1970. The burrowing ecology of the sand lizard, *Uma notata*. Copeia 1970:145–157.

Rennison, D. C., and A. K. Wallace. 1976. The extent of acoustic influence of off-road vehicles in wilderness areas. Paper presented at Natl. Symp. for Off-road Vehicles in Australia, Australian Natl. Univ., 19 pp.

Ruibal, R., L. Tevis, and V. Roig. 1969. The terrestrial ecology of the spadefoot toad, *Scaphiopus hamondii*. Copeia 1969:571–584.

Stebbins, R. C. 1966. A Field Guide to Western Reptiles and Amphibians. Houghton-Mifflin Co., Boston, 279 pp.

Vernon, J., P. Herman, and E. Peterson. 1971. Cochlear potentials in the kangaroo rat, *Dipodomys merriami*. Physiol. Zool. 444:112–118.

Webster, D. B. 1961. The ear apparatus of the kangaroo rat, *Dipodomys*. Am. J. Anat. 108:123–147.

Webster, D. B. 1962. A function of the enlarged middle-ear cavities of the kangaroo rat, *Dipodomys*. Physiol. Zool. 35:240–255.

Webster, D. B. 1963. Ears of *Dipodomys*. Nat. Hist. 74:27–33.

Webster, D. B., and M. Webster. 1971. Adaptive value of hearing and vision in kangaroo rat predator avoidance. Brain Behav. Ecol. 4:310–322.

Webster, D. B., R. F. Ackermann, and G. C. Longa. 1968. Central auditory system of the kangaroo rat, *Dipodomys merriami*. J. Comp. Neurol. 133:477–494.

Werner, W. L. 1972. Temperature effects on inner ear sensitivity in six species of iguanid lizards. J. Herpetol. 6:147–177.

Wever, E. G., and E. A. Peterson. 1963. Auditory sensitivity in three iguanid lizards. J. Aud. Res. 3:205–212.

10

Vehicular Recreation in Arid Land Dunes: Biotic Responses and Management Alternatives[1]

R. Bruce Bury and Roger A. Luckenbach

Introduction

Sand dunes are a biologically unique fraction of arid land ecosystems. In the southwestern United States they make up only about 0.6% of the surface area (Clements et al., 1957). Throughout this region they have a disjunct distribution and are highly variable, occurring at different elevations and climatic regimes. Desert dunes vary from hummocks less than 1 m high in washes or around dry lake beds to continuous masses covering 500 km² with peaks up to 200 m above the surrounding land. Most North American dunes are geologically recent, formed by wind-blown deposits from dry lake beds dating from the Pleistocene (10,000+ years B.P.) or earlier. Among the larger inland systems are those at the Great Sand Dunes National Monument (Colorado), White Sands National Monument (New Mexico), Big Dune (Nevada), and the Algodones (= Imperial Sand Hills), Eureka, Dumont, Kelso, Garnet, and Panamint Valley Dunes (California). Several of these are tourist attractions because dunes are intrinsically scenic and provide wilderness solitude.

Some people envision dunes as barren wastelands. They equate all dunes with the drifting sands of the Sahara Desert and are unaware of the rich life found on dunes during the blooming season for plants and during times of peak activity for the animals, many of which are fossorial, crepuscular, or nocturnal in habits. It is erroneous to think that dunes are devoid of life. Rather, they are "habitat islands" for a number of plants and animals that are especially adapted to sandy

---

[1] The views and conclusions contained in this chapter are based on the authors' studies or experiences and do not necessarily represent the official viewpoint or policy of any U.S. government agency.

soils. Biota of dunes possess unique dispersal or locomotory features, drought resistance, and ability to withstand high temperatures. Environmental constraints often are severe, but native biota survive under these peculiar conditions.

Several investigations have examined the impact of off-road vehicles (ORVs) on arid land biotic communities (for reviews see Bury, 1980; Bury et al., 1977; Berry, 1980; Sheridan, 1979; Stebbins, 1974; Vollmer et al., 1976; Webb and Wilshire, 1978; Chapters 11 and 13), but we know relatively little given the magnitude of the problem. Research projects have seldom been concerned with inhabitants of sandy or dune areas.

Sand dunes have in the past been remote, impassable to most wheeled vehicles, and inhospitable to people. However, the advent of ORVs has made dunes into centers of recreational driving. Development of the dune buggy opened sandy areas to ready access by thousands of visitors. Dune buggies are relatively light vehicles with open tubular frames, rear-mounted engines, and large, wide tires that are sometimes equipped with paddles for better traction in loose sand. A related machine used on dunes is a three-wheeled motorcycle with wide tires that is popular with young people. Other vehicles (four-wheel-drive trucks, motorcycles, tour buses) are also occasionally used on sand dunes. Operators of these machines enjoy driving on dunes because of the soft substrate, lack of cacti and boulders, and "challenges" of the dune slopes.

Usage of dunes for motorized recreation is substantial. For example, three of the five major dune systems in the California Desert are open to ORV use; one dune system was legally closed to use in 1976 in order to enhance its other values, particularly to protect two endangered plants (DeDecker, 1979). The large number of motorized vehicles being operated on limited dune areas is a management challenge. We here address the question of how native plants and animals respond to vehicular operation on dunes and, from a biological perspective, explore ways for improved management and protection of desert dune systems.

Dune Plants and Animals

Dune vegetation usually is sparse on ridges but may be dense on the flanks. For example, on the east side of the Algodones Dunes there is a microphyll woodland with tall trees (some more than 3 m high), including blue palo verde *(Cercidium floridum)*, screwbean *(Prosopis glandulosa)*, and ironwood *(Olneya tesota)*. Other plants also reach large size here. For example, creosote bush *(Larrea tridentata)* grows to 3 m in height, whereas 1.5 m is the maximum size in other areas. Such growth is dependent on water, which occurs as a relatively high water table for extended periods. The water mostly originates as runoff from nearby mountains that flows into the east flank and is retained by the high water-holding capacity of the sand.

In deep sands, perennials have deep roots and an ability to survive sand movements. These plants often form hummocks—hillocks of sand held in place by roots and stems—that are important stabilizers of blowing sand. On the Eureka Dunes (Inyo County, California), the endangered dune grass *Swallenia alexan-*

drae forms hummocks (Henry, 1979). In the Algodones system, mounds are formed by desert buckwheat *(Eriogonum deserticola)* and croton *(Croton wigginsii),* both threatened species (U.S. Bureau of Land Management, 1977), and by Mormon tea *(Ephedra trifurca).*

Other endangered or threatened plant species also occur in dunes. Eureka locoweed *(Astragalus lentiginosus* var. *micans)* and Eureka evening primrose *(Oenothera avita* spp. *eurekensis)* occur in the Eureka Dunes, and giant Spanish needle *(Palafoxia arida* var. *gigantea),* desert sunflower *(Helianthus niveus* spp. *tephrodes)* and sandfood *(Ammobroma sonorae)* frequent that Algodones system. *Ammobroma* (a parasite) is seldom encountered until moisture and food reserves nurture emergence of the single floret head (about 0.10 to 0.15 m in diameter) on the surface; otherwise the plant is subterranean (Armstrong, 1980).

Dunes are inhabited by a number of specially adapted animals. The White Sands area is home to a whitish phase of the plains pocket mouse *(Perognathus flavescens),* a form once described as a full species *(P. gypsi)* or subspecies *(P. apache gypsi;* see Benson, 1933; Hall and Kelson, 1959); *Perognathus apache* is now synonymous with *P. flavescens* (Findley et al., 1975). Although not restricted to dunes, several desert rodents are most abundant in areas of sandy deposits (Brown, 1973, 1975), e.g., the desert kangaroo rat *(Dipodomys deserti),* the pale kangaroo mouse *(Microdipodops pallidus),* and the desert pocketmouse *(Perognathus penicillatus).*

Several unique reptiles also colonize sand dunes. The fringe-toed lizards (genus *Uma*) are restricted to areas of eolian sands. *Uma* are adapted to existence in sand substrates through modifications for locomotion in soft sands (fringes on toes), cryptic coloration, special nasal "plumbing" for breathing while buried, ear flaps, and a countersunk lower jaw (Stebbins, 1944). Occupation of specific sand dune systems has lead to reproductive isolation and subsequent speciation in this genus (Norris, 1958). Three distinctive lizards occur on the White Sands dunes (Dixon, 1967): the White Sands prairie lizard *(Sceloporus undulatus cowlesi),* the bleached earless lizard *(Holbrookia maculata ruthveni),* and a light color phase of the little striped whiptail *(Cnemidophorus inornatus).* Although not limited to dunes, sidewinders *(Crotalus cerastes)* and shovel-nosed snakes *(Chionactis)* are most numerous in sandy regions. Sand dunes and eolian sands present a unique, severe environment that only a few specially adapted animals and plants have been able to colonize.

The Algodones Dunes: A Case Study

The greatest concentration of ORV recreation in the southwestern United States occurs at the Algodones Dunes, Imperial County, in southeast California (Fig. 10-1). The dunes are linear (about 65 km long) and vary from 6 to 10 km wide; some hills are as high as 100 m (Norris and Norris, 1961).

Access to this dune system is limited. Interstate 8 traverses the southern portion parallel to the United States-Mexico border and Highway 78 cuts across the

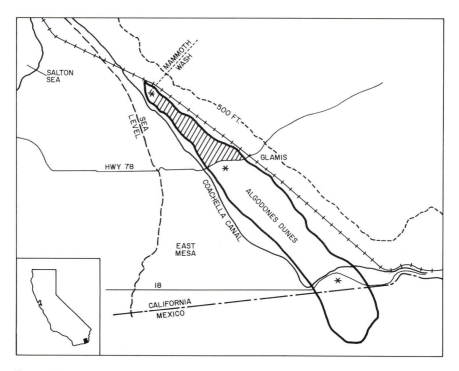

Figure 10-1. Location and features of the Algodones Dunes. Stars (∗) indicate areas now presently used for off-road vehicle recreation. Hatched lines indicate the location of the natural area.

north central area. The Coachella Canal with its maintenance roads are west of the dunes proper, whereas to the east a rail line and adjacent road (Ogilby-Niland route) parallel the dunes. ORV usage is centered near these paved or solid surfaces (Fig. 10-1). Paved turnouts and camping facilities are located south of Highway 78 at Osborn Park in the center of the dunes and along Gecko Road on the western flank.

At the present time, about 82% of the Algodones Dunes system is open to ORV use. The only closed portion is a natural area north of Highway 78. This closure was precipitated by concern from citizens and scientists desiring to provide protection for the dunes.

Intensive vehicular recreation has occurred since the late 1960s and has steadily increased. In 1978, there were over 500,000 visitor-use-days, principally related to ORV activities (R. Schneider, personal communication, 1980). Thousands of vehicles may be present on certain weekends.

Biotic Responses to ORV Use

The Algodones Dunes have a rich and varied biota. There are many sand-adapted plants, including five that are being considered for listing as threatened species (Westec Services Inc., 1977; U.S. Bureau of Land Management, 1977; Armstrong, 1980). The arthropod fauna is diverse but poorly known (Hardy and Andrews, 1976). Vertebrate life consists of at least 1 species of amphibian, 14 reptiles, 13 rodents, 3 large-sized mammals, and 50 birds, of which 15 species breed in the dune system (Hill, 1965; Franzreb, 1978; Luckenbach and Bury, in prep.).

In the spring of 1977 and 1979, we examined the ecological impacts of ORV use on the biota of the Algodones Dunes. We assessed the impact of vehicular usage on both perennial and annual vegetation, on populations of invertebrates, and on the reptiles and mammals that inhabit the dunes. Six sets of paired plots (areas with heavy ORV usage and those which were unused) were compared. Details of this study are provided elsewhere (Luckenbach and Bury, in prep.). A partial summary is given in Table 10-1.

Areas with heavy ORV use had little or no vegetation: two-thirds of these plots had virtually no herbaceous cover or any identifiable shrubby vegetation. On control plots there were 2.5 times the number of plant species, 10 times the density, 10 times the cover, and 4 times the volume of shrubby perennials as compared with ORV-impacted plots.

The ORVs run over and through vegetation (Fig. 10-2A) and in intensively used recreation sites there is virtually a total loss of all plant cover (Fig. 10-2B). There is a dramatic difference in the vegetation remaining in the closed natural area and in the adjacent ORV-used lands along Highway 78 (Fig. 10-3). It is obvious that ORVs have had a major detrimental impact on dune plant communities.

Impacts of ORVs on vertebrate life are also negative. Control plots had 1.8 times the number of species, 3.6 times the number of individuals, and 5.8 times more biomass of reptiles than did ORV areas. Unused sites also had 1.3 times more species, 2.2 times more individuals, and 2.2 times the amount of biomass of rodents than did ORV plots. Two sand-adapted species, the fringe-toed lizard *(Uma notata)* and the desert kangaroo rat *(Dipodomys deserti)*, were both severely reduced in areas frequently used for ORV recreation (see Chapter 9 for more information on ORV effects on these species).

The differences in animal life between areas used and unused by ORVs also is illustrated by a comparison of four pairs of sand-sweep transects (each 1 m × 1 km) established at right angles to Highway 78. These were swept each night and tracks recorded in the morning. Animal activity was appreciably less in areas where ORV use occurred (Fig. 10-4). Again, the evidence clearly indicates that ORV recreation decreases the abundance of vertebrates in desert dune systems. Similar impacts on invertebrate populations can be expected.

A Dilema of Management Alternatives

The three areas of greatest ORV impact are: (1) at the northernmost end of the dunes near Mammoth Wash, (2) in the north central portion of the dunes just south of Highway 78 for about 4 km along and east of Gecko Road, and (3) on both sides of Interstate 8 at the southern end of the dune system (Fig. 10-1). Some dune buggies travel alone or in convoys between Highways 78 and Inter-

Table 10-1. Comparison of the Biota on Control Versus ORV-Impacted Plots on the Algodones Dunes, Imperial County, California[a]

Biota	Control plots ($N = 6$)				
	No. individuals	No. species	Cover (m³)	Volume (m³)	Biomass (g)
Herbaceous plants (10-m² plots)	254 ± 264	3.5 ± 1.6			
Perennial plants (1000-m² plots)	139 ± 134	5.3 ± 1.5	94 ± 67	553 ± 688	
Lizards (2-ha plots)	39 ± 24	3.2 ± 2.4			488 ± 323
Rodents (1-ha plots)	17 ± 12	2 ± 1.3			1483 ± 787

[a]From Luckenbach and Bury in prep. Numbers are X ± S.D.

(a)

Figure 10-2. (a) Vegetated dune slope partially disrupted due to ORV activities.

Biota	Impacted plots ($N = 6$)				
	No. individuals	No. species	Cover (m³)	Volume (m³)	Biomass (g)
Herbaceous plants (10-m² plots)	15.5 ± 28	1.5 ± 1.7			
Perennial plants (1000-m² plots)	14 ± 29	2.2 ± 1.8	10 ± 21	14 ± 345	
Lizards (2-ha plots)	11 ± 12	2 ± 0.6			83 ± 69
Rodents (1-ha plots)	7.6 ± 10	1.3 ± 0.8			685 ± 799

(b)

Figure 10-2. (b) Area of the dunes (Osborn Park south of Highway 78) where all vegetation has been eliminated due to intensive ORV usage.

Figure 10-3. View of Highway 78 showing differences in habitat in the closed natural area (above road) and in the open ORV area (below the road).

state 8, principally along the center of the dunes. Some vehicles also illegally use the Coachella Canal service road for access to the central portions of the dunes. Illegal use of the northern Natural Reserve Area occurs from both the north and south, and along the flanks.

The U.S. Bureau of Land Management (BLM) regards the Algodones Dunes as an Area of Critical Environmental Concern (U.S. Bureau of Land Management, 1980). Three plan alternatives are listed for the Algodones Dunes (Fig. 10-5, A–C): Use, Protection, and Balanced (representing an assumed compromise position) Alternatives. These are only briefly discussed here.

The Use Alternative basically maintains the present unregulated status but assumes increased recreation, especially by extension of the Gecko Road and

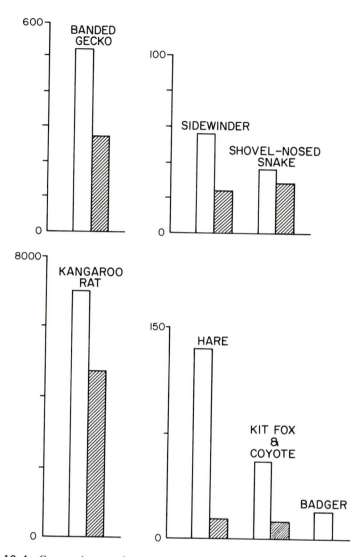

Figure 10-4. Comparisons of animal activity recorded on four 1 m X 1 km transects (sand sweeps). Total counts of tracks are shown. The control areas are open bars; ORV areas, closed bars.

construction of additional camping and recreational facilities along the length of the central portion of the dunes. According to this alternative, use by motorized vehicles would be allowed on existing roads, trails, and ways, and off road in all portions of the dunes except for the Natural Area. This plan is essentially one that permits intensive recreational use and development without regard for other natural resource values.

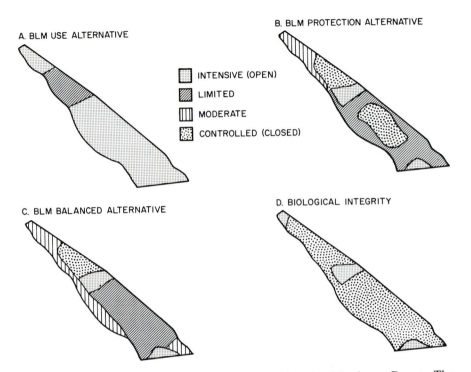

Figure 10-5. Four possible management plans for the Algodones Dunes. The three U.S. Bureau of Land Management alternatives quarter the dunes, whereas a biological option offers protection for the majority of the dunes through a north and south core area plus connecting corridors (not shown is the southern terminus of the dunes in Mexico) (redrawn from U.S. Bureau of Land Management, 1980).

The Protection Alternative would permit "intensive use" immediately south of Highway 78 and Interstate 8, and "limited use" at the extreme northern tip and along the central flanks of the dunes. The central ridge of the dunes and the area immediately north of Highway 78 would be classed as "controlled," wherein motorized vehicle travel would be prohibited *if* the area were to be designated as wilderness by Congress, If not so designated, ORV use could be allowed. Surprisingly, this alternative cannot protect most of the dune system from vehicular damage. The flanks of the central portion of the dunes would be in a "limited multiple-use" classification, meaning vehicles would be allowed on roads, trails, and ways; such use is impossible to control since travel routes are obscure in dune areas. Enforcement is difficult and ORVs could enter the protected areas.

The Balanced Alternative apparently is a compromise because it allows "intensive multiple-use" in the areas immediately south of Highway 78 and Interstate 8, confers a controlled classification on the area north of Highway 78 north to Mammoth Wash, and keeps the central portion of the dunes under a limited use classification. In reality, this is no different than the present usage pattern because the average dune buggy operator usually does not travel farther than 3 km from his campsite near a road. Thus, the central portion remains largely unvisited and unused for intensive dune buggy recreation.

A major problem of the proposed management schemes is that they functionally quarter the dune complex and present biological barriers to plant and animal dispersal and gene flow. All three alternatives fail to consider this problem of managing the dunes. Further, large-scale planning classifications apparently assume that the system is homogeneous. However, plant distributional studies (Westec Services Inc., 1977) have demonstrated that plant communities on the dunes are not uniformly distributed. Our field studies also indicate that the plants (the dune food base) and the associated food chain of arthropods and small vertebrates occur in a patchy distribution. Planning processes should acknowledge this mosaic, complex pattern of biota inhabiting dune systems.

Further, even limited ORV use causes some loss of plants and animals. For example, *Uma* bury themselves on the surface of the sand and passing ORVs can easily crush individuals. Also, *Dipodomys* prefer to den in depressions in the dunes where finer soil particles accumulate. Depressions are often driven through by operators of ORVs because of the challenges of driving up the slopes. Noise generated by vehicles can cause deafness or disrupt behavioral responses (Chapter 9). Thus even a limited amount of ORV activity could have drastic demographic consequences to certain sensitive species.

Present evidence clearly indicates that ORV activities are detrimental to resident plants and animals of the Algodones Dunes, and that many sensitive and threatened species are being negatively impacted by ORVs. None of the proposed management alternatives would adequately protect these features of the dune system. Thus we think another avenue should be explored as a way to manage this and other arid land dune systems.

A Biological Option

If natural resource management has a commitment to protection and enhancement of habitats and associated wildlife as well as to recreational opportunities, then decisions to ensure continued diversity and abundance of all life forms will always be difficult. In the Algodones Dunes, ORVs are decreasing the native biota, and areas with intensive ORV recreation are already depauperate in most resident plants and wildlife. It is clear to us that ORV recreation and biological resources are mutually exclusive, and that they should be separated from one another through distinct management units.

We propose that remaining populations of plants and animals be fully protected. In the Algodones Dunes, this requires setting aside core areas plus connecting corridors (Fig. 10-5D). The corridor areas are the homes of many unique species and also permit exchange between the core areas; this gene flow is critical to the long-term survival of species. The biological option dictates closure to ORV activities of most of the dunes except for three specific areas already denuded. Rather than have more diffuse and poorly defined areas for ORV activities, we suggest that there be specific recreation sites for intensive usage and that these biological "sacrifice" areas be limited in size. Closure of the majority of arid land dunes is the only choice if plant and animal communities are to persist.

At the same time, ORV recreation could continue in a modified form and perhaps even be more enjoyable to people who partake of this sport. In the Algodones Dunes, the three major ORV areas would remain open (Fig. 10-1 and 10-5D). These are now accessible and the preferred areas for ORV activities. Limited improvements (more paved turnouts, campsites) adjacent to heavy use areas would improve access and overnight accommodations while concentrating ORV usage. The open areas constitute about 125 km^2 of land, a sizeable area for any recreational pursuit and an area that is suitable for a variety of ORV activity (i.e., short or long trips, competitive races).

The Algodones Dunes are a natural treasure for which the neglect and abuse of the past is no longer acceptable. As in all ecosystems, there is a need to first actively protect and manage the natural values and resources. Then one can allow other uses (e.g., ORV operation) when and where such activities do not cause loss of species—especially sensitive or threatened forms—or lead to declines in the abundance of native flora and fauna. Such action would normally protect the majority (occasionally all) of the land in natural state or with minimal disruption, while permitting activities such as ORV recreation in defined areas. This is a distinct management system that could be more easily enforced than other proposals. The biological option is offered as a workable alternative to other confusing, piecemeal plans that cannot provide adequate protection of natural resources and wildlands in arid regions.

Management of Sand Dunes and the Theory of Island Biogeography

Germane to the management of sand dune areas are the theories of island biogeography (MacArthur and Wilson, 1967). Since sand dunes are distinctive habitat "islands" within deserts, these theories should apply to the colonization and extinction of biota of these regions. The MacArthur-Wilson theory suggests that small islands have low immigration rates and high extinction rates. If dunes are fragmented and effectively made into small habitat islands by vehicular recreation or management schemes, then immigration rates would be expected to become lower while extinction rates would increase. Thus, we should avoid any management plan which causes the fragmentation of a dune system.

Dunes often lack adjacent or nearby colonization sources and much of the biota may be endemic. Millennia may be required before species make adaptations necessary to colonize and thrive on dunes. For example, in the Algodones Dunes, there is no ecological equivalent of the *Uma* in the surrounding desert. Plant species of the Algodones are also psammophytic and it is doubtful that any other desert plant could readily colonize the harsh dune environment.

The sizes of protected areas are critical to the survival of many species. Although Simberloff and Abele (1976) suggested that under certain circumstances the sequestering of a series of small reserves could be the best approach to faunal preservation, it is now known that small reserves can fail to preserve faunas (e.g., Diamond, 1975; Terborgh, 1975; Whitcomb et al., 1976; Wilson and Willis, 1975). Studies of the effects of fragmentation of eastern deciduous forests (MacClintock et al., 1977; Whitcomb, 1977; Whitcomb et al., 1976) demonstrated that many of the neotropical migratory species that were once dominant in the forest interior tend to disappear from fragmented forests. Further, these dominant species are not replaced by other species. In dune systems, no evidence has been found to support the idea that small reserves are advantageous over large ones.

A paradigm for the management of desert dune systems should follow the recommendations of Whitcomb et al. (1976), who urge that ecological preserves be kept as large as possible because (1) large areas have low extinction rates and high immigration rates; (2) some taxa require very large areas for survival; (3) preservation of entire ecological communities, with all trophic levels represented, requires large areas; (4) large preserves are a better buffer against human disturbance; (5) large areas are necessary to minimize the predation, parasitism, and competition exerted by species abundant in the disturbed area surrounding reserves; (6) the failures of small reserves have been adequately documented; and (7) because fragmentation is irreversible, a conservative preservation strategy needs to be adopted.

Elsewhere in the world's desert regions, sand habitats do not usually occur in isolated dunes but are found instead in large sand bodies known as sand seas (the *ergs* of the Saharan region). Often the active eolian portions of these *ergs* may be as large as 125 km^2 (Cooke and Warren, 1973). While the proper management of sand seas might seem to be different from that necessary for isolated dunes, the two sand habitats actually require similar approaches. Management plans should recognize that the primary production base of dunes or *ergs* is small, and large tracts are needed to maintain trophic-dynamic stability within these ecosystems. The management of both areas should emphasize the integrity of local ecosystems through establishment of preserves of large size, minimization of isolation, and maintenance of corridors connecting fragmented sections in order to ensure the preservation of maximum biotic diversity.

Acknowledgments

We are grateful for the field assistance of D. M. Jorde, R. D. Fisher, W. Moffet, R. R. Ramey II, J. Schubert, A. Spolsky, and H. H. Welsh, Jr. during various phases of research on the Algodones biota. G. Flechsig assisted in the running of sand sweep surveys. We thank P. A. Medica, F. B. Turner, and V. H. Reid for their reviews of the paper and helpful advice.

One of us (Luckenbach) received financial aid through the Merten's Fund (Museum of Vertebrate Zoology, University of California at Berkeley) and the

Environmental Field Programs of the University of California at Santa Cruz. Field work for both of us in 1977 and 1979 was supported by the U.S. Fish and Wildlife Service.

References

Armstrong, W. P. 1980. Sand food: a strange plant of the Algodones dunes. Fremontia 7(4):3–9.

Benson, S. B. 1933. Concealing coloration among some desert rodents of the southwestern United States. Univ. Calif. Publ. Zool. 40:1–70.

Berry, K. H. 1980. A review of the effects of off-road vehicles on birds and other vertebrates. In: R. M. DeGraff (Tec. Coord.). Management of Western Forests and Grasslands for Nongame Birds. U.S. Dept. Agriculture Forestry Service, General Technical Report INT-86, pp. 451–467.

Brown, J. H. 1973. Species diversity of seed-eating desert rodents in sand dune habitats. Ecology 54(4):775–787.

Brown, J. H. 1975. Geographical ecology of desert rodents. In: M. L. Cody and J. M. Diamond (Eds.), Ecology and Evolution of Communities. Belknap Press, Cambridge, Massachusetts, pp. 315–341.

Bury, R. B. 1980. What we know and don't know about off-road vehicle impacts on wildlife. In: R. N. L. Andrews and P. F. Nowak (Eds.), Off Road Vehicle Use: A Management Challenge. U.S. Dept. Agriculture, The Office of Environmental Quality, pp. 110–120.

Bury, R. B., R. A. Luckenbach, and S. D. Busack. 1977. Effects of off-road vehicles on vertebrates in the California Desert. U.S. Fish and Wildlife Service, Wildlife Research Reports 8:1–23.

Clements, T., et al. 1957. A study of desert surface conditions. Headquarters Quatermaster Research and Development Command, Environmental Protection Research Division, Technical Report EP 53, 110 pp.

Cooke, R. U., and A. Warren. 1973. Geomorphology in Deserts. University of California Press, Berkeley, California, 374 pp.

DeDecker, M. 1979. Can BLM protect the dunes? Fremontia 7(2):6–8.

Diamond, J. M. 1975. The island dilemma: lessons of modern biogeographic studies for the design of natural preserves. Biol. Conserv. 7:129–146.

Dixon, J. R. 1967. Aspects of the biology of the lizards of the White Sands, New Mexico. Los Angeles Co. Mus. Contrib. Sci. 129:1–22.

Findley, J. S., A. H. Harris, D. E. Wilson, and C. Jones. 1975. Mammals and New Mexico. University of New Mexico Press, Albuquerque, New Mexico, 360 pp.

Franzreb, K. E. 1978. Breeding bird densities, species composition, and bird species diversity of the Algodones Dunes. Western Birds 9:9–20.

Hall, E. R., and K. R. Kelson. 1959. The Mammals of North America. The Ronald Press Co., New York, 1083 pp.

Hardy, A. R., and F. G. Andrews. 1976. A final report to the Office of Endangered Species on contract 14-16-0008-966. California Dept. Food and Agriculture, Insect Taxonomy Lab, unpublished report, 47 pp.

Henry, M. A. 1979. A rare grass on the Eureka Dunes. Fremontia 7(2):3–6.

Hill, S. J. 1965. Rodents of the Algodones Dunes, Imperial County, California. Unpublished M.Sc. thesis, University of Arizona, Tucson, Arizona, 59 pp.

Luckenbach, R. A., and R. B. Bury. In prep. Effects of off-road vehicles on the biota of Algodones Dunes, Imperial County, California. Submitted J. Appl. Ecology.

MacArthur, R. H., and E. O. Wilson. 1967. The theory of Island Biogeography. Princeton University Press, Princeton, New Jersey, 203 pp.

MacClintock, L., R. F. Whitcomb, and B. L. Whitcomb. 1977. II. Evidence for the value of corridors and minimization of isolation in preservation of biotic diversity. Am. Birds 31:6–12.

Norris, K. S. 1958. The evolution and systematics of the Iguanid genus *Uma* and its relation to the evolution of other North American desert reptiles. Bull. Am. Mus. Nat. His. 114:251–326.

Norris, R. M., and K. S. Norris. 1961. Algodones Dunes of southeastern California. Geol. Soc. Am. Bull. 72:605–620.

Sheridan, D. 1979. Off-road Vehicles on Public Lands. Council on Environmental Quality, Washington, D.C., 84 pp.

Simberloff, D. S., and L. G. Abele. 1976. Island biogeography theory and conservation practice. Science 191:285–286.

Stebbins, R. C. 1944. Some aspects of the ecology of the iguanid genus *Uma*. Ecology Mongr. 14:311–332.

Stebbins, R. C. 1974. Off-road vehicles and the fragile desert. Am. Biol. Teacher 36:203–208, 220, 294–304.

Terborgh, J. 1975. Faunal equilibria and the design of wildlife preserves. In: F. Golley and E. Medina (Eds.), Tropical Ecological Systems: Trends in Terrestrial and Aquatic Research. Springer-Verlag, New York.

U.S. Bureau of Land Management. 1977. Glamis-Imperial Sand Dunes—Area 66: Threatened and Endangered Plants in the Imperial Sand Dunes Complex. Information Pamphlet, 2 pp.

U.S. Bureau of Land Management. 1980. The California Desert Conservation Area: Plan Alternatives and Environmental Impact Statement. Draft. U.S. Dept. Interior, Bureau of Land Management, Riverside, California, 436 pp.

Vollmer, A. T., B. G. Maza, P. A. Medica, F. B. Turner, and S. A. Bamberg. 1976. The impact of off-road vehicles on a desert ecosystem. Environ. Management 1:115–129.

Webb, R. H., and H. G. Wilshire. 1978. A Bibliography of the Effects of Off-Road Vehicles on the Environment. U.S. Geological Survey Open File Report, 78–149, 38 pp.

Westec Services Inc. 1977. Survey of sensitive plants of the Algodones Dunes. Unpublished report, U.S. Dept. Interior, Bureau of Land Management, Riverside, California.

Whitcomb, R. F. 1977. Island biogeography and "habitat islands" of eastern forests. I. Introduction. Am. Birds 31:3–5.

Whitcomb, R. F., J. F. Lynch, P. A. Opler, and C. S. Robbins. 1976. Island biogeography and conservation: strategy and limitations. Science 193:1030–1032.

Wilson, E. O., and E. O. Willis. 1975. Applied biogeography. In: M. L. Cody and J. M. Diamond (Eds.), Ecology and Evolution of Communities. Harvard University Press, Cambridge, Massachusetts, 545 pp.

PART III

Rehabilitation Potential for Disturbed Arid Regions

11

Regeneration of Desert Pavement and Varnish[1]

Christopher D. Elvidge and Richard M. Iverson

Introduction

Desert pavements are stone-covered geomorphic surfaces characteristic of flat or gently sloping alluvial terrain in arid areas. Typically the stones are one layer thick and may be angular or rounded, closely or loosely packed, and are set in or on a matrix of fine-grained material. On many desert pavements the stones are covered with a dark patina known as desert varnish, whereas the stones beneath the surface generally lack desert varnish. Desert pavement surfaces are typically quite smooth and planar, with scattered incised drainage channels. Sparse perennial vegetation is generally present only along these drainages; the majority of the pavement is commonly devoid of significant vegetation. Known as gibbers, hammadas, regs, or sai in various arid regions around the world, desert pavements are especially prevalent on alluvial fans, bajadas, and terraces composed of sediments derived from metamorphic and volcanic rocks.

Although the surface cover of stones is the most readily observable characteristic of desert pavement (Fig. 11-1), the underlying soils are also distinctive. Relative to most desert soils, they are typically rather saline and contain considerable clay minerals, which are usually high in exchangeable sodium; pavement beneath paved surfaces are thus rather alkaline (Musick, 1975). The soil composing the substrate in the first few decimeters beneath the pavement surface may be stony, but commonly it is relatively stone free compared to the

---

[1]The views and conclusions contained in this chapter are based on the authors' studies or experiences and do not necessarily represent the official viewpoint of any U.S. government agency.

Figure 11-1. Close up view of desert pavement surface on a river terrace along the Gila River near Gila Bend, Arizona. The photograph shows how barren desert pavement surfaces can be.

Figure 11-2. Aerial photograph of the same desert pavement surface shown in Fig. 11-1. The vehicle tracks along the lower margin stand out due to the lower density of stones remaining after the ORV traverse. Photograph by Mike Martin.

underlying materials (Cooke, 1970; Denny, 1965; Mabutt, 1965). In the first few centimeters below the pavement surface the soil is typically fine-grained with an open, vesicular structure that is thought to result from thermal expansion of trapped soil air (Evenari et al., 1974; Springer, 1958).

Desert pavement soils typically have low infiltration capacities (Musick, 1975). Denny (1965), for example, describes the upper 30 to 50 mm of a Death Valley pavement soil after a day of rain as a jelly-like mud layer, with dry soil underneath. Several factors may contribute to the low infiltration capacities. Foremost, the clay constituents of desert pavement soils have intrinsically low permeabilities. Additionally, when they are wet, clays high in exchangeable sodium tend to defloculate to form a dispersed colloid that clogs soil pores and reduces infiltration (Jewitt, 1966; Musick, 1975). Desert pavement soils are also typically high in montmorillonite and other expanding lattice clays (Bales and Péwé, 1979; Howard et al., 1977) that swell upon wetting to close cracks that conduct water into the soil profile. Caliche (a $CaCO_3$-enriched zone) is present near the surface of some pavement soils and may be extensive enough to effectively plug soil pores (Péwé, 1978). Finally, the pavement stones themselves may retard infiltration because they constitute a considerable area of impervious surface.

The barreness of desert pavements has been noted by several authors (Denny, 1965; Hayden, 1976; Musick, 1975). Sparse desert scrub commonly occupies the washes and gullies that generally dissect desert pavement surfaces but the pavements themselves often support only a few annuals. Shrubs that do colonize pavements typically exist in islands of bare soil that interrupt the surface stone cover. Musick (1975) examined the barren pavements around Yuma, Arizona and concluded that the low infiltration capacities of the pavements made them exceedingly xeric. Once the pavement soil surface has saturated during a rain, overland flow begins to carry water off the pavement and the rate of downward movement of the infiltrating soil water is commonly slower than the rate at which the soil is dried by evaporation. The resulting dearth of soil moisture at many desert pavement sites inhibits seed germination and plant growth, leaving them virtually devoid of vegetation.

Recovery of Desert Pavement Disturbed by Off-Road Vehicle Traffic

Once established, desert pavement tends naturally to be a stable and long-lived feature of the landscape, a fact evidenced by the presence of slow-forming desert varnish on many pavement stones. However, because desert pavements comprise only a thin layer of stones underlain by unconsolidated, readily compressible soil material, they are very susceptible to artificial disruption. The shearing, compressing action of off-road vehicles (ORVs) traveling over desert pavements is especially effective in displacing surface stones and in disrupting and compacting the underlying soil (Chapter 4). Even slight changes in stone coverage density and microtopography caused by ORV disturbances leave highly visible trails across desert pavement surfaces (Fig. 11-2), and such marks may remain visible for at least tens of years (Wilshire and Nakata, 1976). To evaluate the prospects for regeneration of disturbed desert pavement it is necessary to understand the processes of desert pavement evolution and to review the past behavior of disturbed pavement surfaces.

Desert Pavement Evolution Processes

Three distinct processes have been postulated to be responsible for the evolution of stone pavements in deserts: (1) removal of fine soil material by wind, thus leaving a residual of coarse particles too large for eolian transport; (2) removal of fine soil materials by rainfall runoff, similarly leaving a residual lag deposit of stones; and (3) migration to the surface of stones originally buried in the soil. At any particular location it is possible that all of these processes may have contributed to the formation of desert pavement, although the efficacy of one process may have been predominant.

Most early researchers who addressed the origin of desert pavement usually evoked deflation by wind as the formative process (Blake, 1904; Gilbert, 1875). This process involves the removal of fine particles by wind, thus leaving behind the material the wind is incompetent to move. On rare occasions wind storms sufficient to cause saltation of gravel-sized particles may occur in arid areas, and formation of a residual cover of stones during a single event of this magnitude has been documented (Wilshire et al., 1980). Chepil (1950), however, has demonstrated that as a larger percentage of the ground surface becomes covered by coarse, immobile particles, eolian transport of interstitial finer particles becomes progressively more unlikely owing to the development of relatively quiescent wind conditions in the interstices. Hence, once the stone cover is fairly complete it tends to shield the remaining fine material from further erosion (Symmons and Hemming, 1968; Chapter 3). Development of dense, interlocking stone pavements exclusively through deflation is thus unlikely. Surficial crusts commonly present on desert soils also hinder the effectiveness of deflation (Cooke, 1970; Chapter 6), although crusts may be readily broken, especially by artificial disturbances.

Symmons and Hemming (1968) studied the effect of deflation on an experimentally disturbed desert pavement plot in the Sahara Desert. The plot surface was first cleared of stones and then the soil crust was broken apart. After only 1 month the surface of the plot had been lowered by an average of 7 mm and to a localized maximum of 20 mm. A neighboring plot from which only the stone cover had been removed showed an average surface lowering of 2.5 mm during the same month. These observations document some of the wind erodibility changes likely incurred by desert pavement as a result of disruption by vehicle use (Chapter 6). Once broken up, the protective crust may require months for reformation in an arid environment (Eckert et al., 1979). Thus disturbance of the stone cover and surface crust will likely lead to accelerated wind erosion that may possibly enhance pavement regeneration, depending on the stoniness of the substrate.

A second process that may aid formation of desert pavements is erosion by water. The low infiltration capacities of pavement soils suggests that large amounts of runoff may be generated on pavement surfaces. Although no rigorous documentation presently exists, it is likely that this runoff is regularly (perhaps once every few years in the Mojave Desert) capable of transporting considerable fine sediment; thus a residual surface covering of stones forms with time. Lowdermilk and Sundling (1950) demonstrated under controlled conditions that a coarse-grained surficial layer comprising stones included in the soil matrix of experimental plots was developed during periods of rainfall erosion. The efficacy of rainfall and runoff in generating the stone cover increased with increasing rainfall volume and slope steepness.

Several researchers have experimentally removed the stone covers from desert pavement plots to study the rate of ensuing water erosion and pavement regeneration. Sharon (1962) removed the surface stone covers from desert pavement plots in Israel and found that within 5 years the stone covers were 60 to 80% regenerated. Erosional surface lowering on the plots was found to be 15 to 20 mm, whereas nearby control plots were lowered by about 10 mm during the same period. Sharon (1962) concluded that the new stone covers developed largely through erosional exposure of buried stones and that water erosion was important in desert pavement regeneration. Cooke (1970) performed similar experiments in which stones were removed from a pair of 1.6-m^2 plots in the Mojave Desert of California. Sediment traps placed on the downslope sides of the plots yielded close to a kilogram of soil in a single year. Stones had emerged on the surface during this time, and Cooke and Warren (1973) reported that after 4 years the new desert pavements were rapidly becoming established.

The third major process contributing to the development of desert pavements is the upward migration of stones through the soil profile. This process, which may occur as the result of freezing and thawing or wetting and drying, is important because it accounts for the relatively stone-free layer of soil that commonly underlies desert pavement surfaces. Freeze-thaw cycles, which may be rather numerous in high altitudes or high-latitude deserts (Cooke and Warren, 1973), can cause stone migration through either frost-pull or frost-push mechanisms. Frost-pull of stones (Inglis, 1965) occurs when upward heaving of the soil profile results from expansion of soil water during downward passage of the freezing front. Stones are drawn upward with the heave of soil surrounding their upper projections, and the cavity left beneath the stones is filled by yet unfrozen soil that moves into the void. Upon thawing, which occurs from the top down, the entire soil profile settles but the stones have undergone a net upward migration because of the movement of soil into the spaces beneath them. Frost-push of stones (Bowley and Burghardt, 1971) results from preferential growth of ice lenses beneath stones. Because stones have a higher thermal conductivity than the surrounding soil, freezing at a given horizon in a soil may first occur beneath stones. Surrounding soil water is then drawn to the loci of freezing by chemical potential gradients, and growth of ice lenses ensues. The pressure of the growing ice lenses pushes the overlying stones toward the surface. Repeated

many times, these processes result in the accumulation of stones at the soil surface and the removal of stones from the underlying material. Where freezing and
thawing are presently common, or have in the past been common, these mechanisms may be important in explaining desert pavement formation.

Upward migration of stones may also be accomplished by expansion and contraction of desert pavement soils resulting from cyclic wetting and drying. When
wet, expanding lattice clays, common in pavement soils (Bales and Péwé, 1979;
Howard et al., 1977), absorb water into their lattice structure, causing a general
expansion of the soil mass and resulting upward heave. As the soil subsequently
dries and contracts, buried stones tend to retain their uplifted position. Additionally, contraction creates cracks into which soil particles may blow, wash, or
fall, resulting in a net downward soil movement. Repeated many times, these
processes lead to a net upward migration of stones and development of stone
covers on the soil surface. Springer (1958), using Nevada desert pavement soil,
and Jessup (1960), using Australian desert pavement soils, observed upward
stone migration of 10 to 22 mm after 22 wet-dry cycles in the laboratory.
Péwé (1978) and Bales and Péwé (1979) found evidence for upward stone migration in the regeneration of stone cover on a plot they had experimentally cleared
of surface stones. Based on the weight of stones collected in a pit dug nearby,
they estimated that 75 mm of soil would need to be removed to completely regenerate the pavement. The stone cover was 25% regenerated in 2 years' time,
while the amount of surface lowering was negligible. Apparently the stones had
moved upward to the surface.

Although no documentation presently exists, it is probable that upward stone
migration is hindered in areas subject to ORV use. Increases in soil density and
strength, and consequent decreases in infiltration capacity caused by ORV use,
are effects that likely impede all processes of upward stone migration, which also
cause loosening of compacted soil (Chapter 14). Where desert pavements have
formed through stone migration and are subsequently disrupted by ORV activity, their recovery will likely be relatively slow. Where well-developed stone-free
horizons underlie such pavements, or where relic climate conditions have been
responsible for stone migration, natural recovery may be impossible.

Behavior of Disturbed Desert Pavement Surfaces

There are numerous archaeological and historical cases wherein disturbed desert
pavement has been partially or wholly regenerated. Intaglios, features created
hundreds of years ago when native desert peoples scraped away varnish desert
pavement stones to expose bare soil in patterns or figures, are typically found to
have redeveloped some degree of stone cover. Rogers (1939) described a number
of intaglio sites in southeastern California where desert pavement has been
reestablished. Setzler (1952) reported in intaglio figures near Blythe, California
that largely have reformed desert pavement, but not desert varnish. Hayden
(1976) studied intaglios in the Sierra Pinacate of Sonora, Mexico and found that
all of them had reformed desert pavements and some had developed desert
varnish.

Desert pavement has been partially regenerated at the Ha-ak Va-ak intaglio site southeast of Chandler, Arizona, where pavement stones and perhaps some of the underlying soil were scraped away about 500 to 1000 years ago. A slight depression persists on which a new desert pavement, consisting of stones smaller than those of the original pavement, has formed (Fig. 11-3). Faint traces of new desert varnish are evident on some of the fresh pavement stones. Regenerated desert pavement also exists at the Topock Maze intaglio site near Needles, California (Fig. 11-4), although no traces of new desert varnish are present. Evidence from a variety of intaglio sites thus suggests that over a period of several hundred years disrupted desert pavement will be largely regenerated, at least where the pavement disruption is limited to removal of stone cover. The new pavement, however, is very slow to acquire a coating of desert varnish similar to that of the original pavement.

There are also many sites at which more recently disturbed desert pavements have been regenerated. In Death Valley National Monument such sites are common and stand out sharply owing to their lack of desert varnish (Fig. 11-5). Engel and Sharp (1958) investigated a roadbed scraped across desert pavement south of Barstow, California. Made in 1931, this road had by 1956 already developed a stone cover similar to that of the surrounding undisturbed pavement. The soil beneath the roadbed and adjacent pavement contains many buried stones, a fact which undoubtedly speeded the recovery. Such evidence suggests that disturbed desert pavement may, under the right conditions, recover rather quickly even when the underlying soil has been compacted and disrupted by vehicle traffic.

Figure 11-3. A segment of Ha-ak Va-ak, located at the edge of the Santan Mountains of Arizona. The linear depression is about a third of a meter wide and has reformed a stone mosaic consisting of smaller stones than the original.

Figure 11-4. Topock Maze near Needles, California is beside the Colorado River and is cut in the background by Interstate 40. Although what remains of the maze is fenced, several small roads cross it. The stones composing the regenerated pavement are about the same size as the originals and lack desert varnish.

Figure 11-5. Regenerated desert pavement on an abandoned road in Death Valley National Monument. The stones that emerged to form the new desert pavement are smaller than the originals. Lateral movement (human assisted) has brought the larger stones into the disturbed area.

Expectations for Recovery from ORV Disturbances

Available evidence suggests that disturbed desert pavements usually recover relatively rapidly—probably within a few decades and almost certainly within several hundred years. Pavement-forming processes appear to be presently quite active in many areas, and it is possible that removal of stone covers stimulates some pavement-forming processes (i.e., deflation and water erosion). The pavements regenerated in disturbed areas, however, commonly consist of stones smaller than those of the original pavement, and the stones are very slow to acquire desert varnish.

In some cases, where desert pavements owe their origin to relic climatic conditions, pavements disrupted by ORV or other activity will not be regenerated. Disturbed pavements underlain by well-developed stone-free soil will tend to regenerate new stone cover slower than pavements underlain by soil with abundant stone material. Another important consideration is that ORV effects on soil substrates (compaction, structural disruption, increased strength) may inhibit pavement regeneration processes. Because data bearing on this issue are insufficient to allow meaningful conclusions, estimates of recovery times for ORV-disturbed desert pavements must be conservative. Recovery periods on the order of tens of years should be considered minimum estimates for substantive regeneration of stone covers disrupted by ORVs.

Desert Varnish

Desert varnish is a dark brown to black ferromanganese coat, usually 10 to 200 μm thick that forms on exposed rock surfaces in arid regions around the world. Where it is well developed desert varnish forms a major aspect of sparsely vegetated desert landscapes. The operation of vehicles or construction of roads, buildings, or mines across varnished terrain results in rock scars that are visible for considerable distances, especially where the underlying rock is lighter in color than the varnish.

The unexposed surfaces of varnished rocks either are bare or have a red-orange coat. These orange coats on the cracks and undersides of varnished rocks are similar to the black desert varnish except they are lower in manganese (Potter and Rossman, 1979). Varnished rocks imbedded in soil commonly have thicker varnish at the air-soil interface, forming a dark ground-line band.

The mineralogy of desert varnish has been defined by Potter and Rossman (1977, 1979). Typical desert varnish is about 70% clay, predominantly illite and mixed-layer illite-montmorillonites. The dark color of desert varnish results from the presence of microcrystalline iron (Fe) and manganese (Mn) oxides. The Fe is largely in the form of hematite and the common Mn mineral is birnessite. The clays in desert varnish act as a substrate for the microcrystalline Fe and Mn oxides which cement the varnish.

Perry and Adams (1978) discovered that many desert varnishes consist of alternating red and black layers. The layers range from 0.25 to 20.0 μm thick, but most are about 1.0 μm thick. The black layers are high in Mn while the red layers are low in Mn. Desert varnish commonly forms botryoidal mounds containing the alternating red and black layers. The cavities between the mounds collect a variety of detrital material that becomes trapped as the varnish continues to form. The sequential layering and botryoidal mounds are interpreted as primarily depositional features. The alternating red and black layers are thought to result from changing climatic conditions. At present there are two quantitative techniques developing to date varnished surfaces (Bard et al., 1978; Knauss and Ku, 1980).

For many years desert varnish was considered to be the result of capillary action moving dissolved Fe and Mn from rock and soil up onto exposed rock surfaces for deposition (Blake, 1905; Engel and Sharp, 1958; Hooke et al., 1969; Merrill, 1898). Other researchers have emphasized the possible role of organisms in accumulating and precipitating Fe and Mn (Bauman, 1976; Krumbein, 1969; Laudermilk, 1931; Scheffer et al., 1963; White, 1924). All of the more recent researchers agree that desert varnish forms by the accretion of material from windblown dust to rock surfaces (Allen, 1978; Elvidge and Moore, 1979; Perry and Adams, 1978; Potter and Rossman, 1977).

There are a number of facts that indicate a windblown origin for desert varnish. Varnish forms on such rocks as quartzite that lack the necessary ingredients. It occurs on surfaces without an underlying Fe- and Mn-depleted zone (Allen, 1978). The bulk composition and mineralogy of desert varnish is not affected by that of the substrate rock. The clay minerals in desert varnish are the same clay minerals found in desert dust (Péwé et al., 1981). Desert varnish is found on the tops of ridges, peaks and outcrops above any possible runoff. Finally, varnish consists of a sequence of layers and botryoidal mounds that are primary depositional features and dust particles are trapped in cavities as the varnish forms.

Conditions for Desert Varnish Formation

Fe and Mn precipitates have a strong tendency to form as coatings on mineral surfaces (Hem, 1963). To form a desert varnish, these precipitates cement clay to rock surfaces. Thus the chemical behavior of Fe and Mn contains the key to understanding the chemistry of desert varnish formation. The Eh-pH relations of Fe and Mn are presented in Figure 11-6; the chemical behavior of the two is very similar. Fe and Mn are in the soluble 2+ state under acidic conditions but are oxidized and precipitated if conditions become alkaline. Interestingly, the stability field for Mn^{2+} is larger than that of Fe^{2+}. This results in Mn being more mobile than Fe (Krauskopf, 1957).

One of the distinctive characteristics of deserts is alkaline surface materials (Jewitt, 1966). It is the desert's alkalinity, resulting from salt accumulations, that makes the desert particularly favorable for the formation of ferromanganese deposits. Desert soils commonly have a pH in the range of 8.0 to 10.0 (Chapter 2). Alkaline soil and playa materials that make up desert dust contain all the

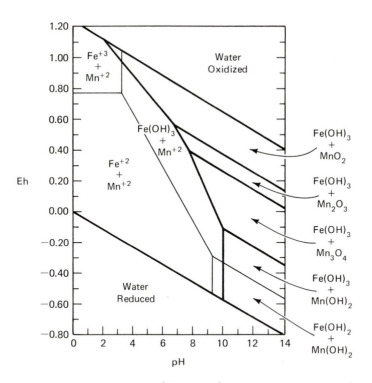

Figure 11-6. Eh-pH diagram for Fe^{2+} and Mn^{2+} concentrations of 10^{-5} molar at atmospheric pressure and $25°C$.

components necessary for desert varnish formation. Because of the low solubilities of Fe and Mn under alkaline conditions it is necessary to dissolve and reprecipitate Fe and/or Mn from the alkaline dust while it is on the rock surface to accrete some varnish. The chemical behavior of Fe and Mn suggests that desert varnish accretion occurs during an Eh and/or pH fluctuation in the dust.

It is during dust storms that the largest quantity of dust is brought into contact with rock surfaces. In Arizona and other parts of the southwestern United States, dust storms are often followed by brief rainshowers (Idso, 1974; Idso et al., 1972). Rainwater is slightly acidic, normally having a pH of 5.0 to 6.0 (Carroll, 1962). It may be that the pH fluctuates during the mixture of alkaline dust with rainwater to accrete some desert varnish. Dust that is washed off rock surfaces has the opportunity to accrete varnish along its way, forming varnish on vertical faces.

The Fe to Mn ratio of crustal rocks is about 50:1 (Krauskopf, 1957), which is also the ratio of Fe to Mn in desert dust (Péwé et al., 1981). The Fe to Mn ratio of desert varnish is typically about 2:1 (Elvidge, 1979). This indicates that a considerable amount of fractionation occurs in the formation of desert varnish. Engel and Sharp (1958) and Hooke et al. (1969) hypothesized that the excess Fe was deposited before the varnishing solutions reached a rock surface because of the lower solubility of Fe compounds relative to Mn compounds. This fit their model of migrating solutions supplying the varnish materials. To achieve the fractionation from dust on a rock surface implies that Mn is preferentially dissolved and reprecipitated. During Eh-pH fluctuations of systems containing ferromanganese deposits, Mn is preferentially mobilized and redeposited (Collins and Buol, 1970; Ryan et al., 1974). It is probable that some of the Fe and Mn of desert varnish enters as soil-formed ferromanganese coatings on the clay minerals (Anderson and Jenne, 1970) that are accreted.

The dependence of desert varnish on the chemical behaviors of Fe and Mn indicates that desert varnish is in chemical equilibrium with its environment. Well-developed desert varnish occurs where the chemical climate is favorable for desert varnish formation or preservation. Where these conditions are not met, desert varnish is eroding or absent. Elvidge (1979) examined the distribution of desert varnish in Arizona and found that conditions for the desert varnish formation are met in areas with alkaline soils, dust storm events, and less than about 250 mm of annual precipitation. Surrounding the areas of well-developed desert varnish in Arizona are areas of eroded desert varnish extending out to regions of about 400 mm annual precipitation.

Rainwater is acidic and in sufficient quantities is actually corrosive to desert varnish. In an experiment, desert varnish samples from desert pavement in Death Valley were allowed to weather outdoors in Illinois. The average annual precipitation at the Illinois site is 750 to 800 mm, whereas the precipitation at the Death Valley site is only about 50 mm per year. Removed from the alkaline environment in which they formed, it only took 8 months for the Illinois samples to become visibly eroded, with the rock surface visible through varnish in places.

Rate of Desert Varnish Formation

The recent activity of humans in desert areas has created innumnerable opportunities for desert varnish to be regenerated on disturbed rocky surfaces. The consistent absence of new desert varnish on these recent rock scars suggests that the rate of desert varnish formation is indeed slow. Fresh rock surfaces only a hundred to several hundred years old cannot be expected to have reformed a visible desert varnish, even if conditions are favorable for desert varnish formation.

The most rapid reported rate of desert varnish formation in the world is cited by Engel and Sharp (1958). They describe an abandoned roadbed across a patch of desert pavement south of Barstow, California where they believe desert varnish fomed in only 25 years. The road was constructed in 1931 with a bulldozer, and a low berm was scraped up along one side. When discovered by Engel and Sharp in 1956, the stones in the roadbed were found to have the same dark desert varnish as the stones in the adjacent desert pavement. Therefore Engel and Sharp concluded that the varnish on the roadbed stones has been completely regenerated since the road construction.

The senior author located the site described by Engel and Sharp in 1979 and found evidence that refutes the claim of 25-year-old desert varnish (Elvidge, 1982). Stones buried near the surface of the roadbed and the adjacent desert pavement already have the same dark desert varnish as the stones at the surface. Orange coats on stones overturned during the disturbance and imbedded in the berm and roadbed have not developed desert varnish. This is a case of desert pavement regeneration where the stones that emerged already had desert varnish on them. This situation deceptively appeared to indicate a rapid rate of desert varnish formation.

Because no recent rock disturbances have developed visible coats of desert varnish, archeological evidence must be used to examine the rate of desert varnish formation. Generally the archeological evidence gives only a vague notion of the rate of desert varnish formation because it is typically not known when a particular artifact was discarded or when a particular petroglyph or intaglio was constructed.

Studies of lithic artifacts and man-made rock disturbances in the southwest indicate some regional regularity in the rate of desert varnish formation. Rogers (1939) studied cultural remains in southeastern California and found that progressively older materials have darker varnishes. Setzler (1952) found the intaglios near Blythe, California to be unvarnished. Clements and Clements (1953) reported that crude artifacts estimated to be 10,000 years old from desert pavement in Death Valley have well-developed desert varnish. Malde and Schick (1964) found desert varnish on the brow of Thorne Cave in northeastern Utah that is presumed to have formed since the cave was exhumed 3000 years ago. Hunt and Mabey (1966) found no desert varnish on artifacts less than 2000 years old in Death Valley. Hayden (1976) describes a series of aboriginal occupations in the Sierra Pinacate southeast of Yuma, Arizona, where unvarnished materials are less than about 5000 years old. Two degrees of varnish are found on older materials, which include stone tools, intaglios, sleeping rings, and rock cairns. Materials with thin varnish coats are about 11,000 years old, whereas heavily varnished materials are about 21,000 years old. Bard et al. (1978) described petroglyphs at the Grimes Point site in western Nevada. Desert varnish at the site is presumed to have formed since being uncovered by the recession of Lake Lahontan some 10,000 years ago. Petroglyphs at the Grimes Point site show several distinct stages of varnish regeneration.

The senior author has visited numerous archeological sites looking for evidence of desert varnish regeneration. Topock Maze near Needles, California (Fig. 11-4) shows no signs of reformed varnish. Faint traces of new desert varnish can be found at Ha-ak Va-ak site near Chandler, Arizona (Fig. 11-3). Heavily revarnished petroglyphs have been observed at Petrified Forest National Park, Arizona. Partially revarnished petroglyphs have been observed in South Mountain Park in Phoenix, Arizona.

The archeological evidence indicates that desert varnish coats have formed in the southwestern United States within the past 10,000 years. Generally it takes 3000 to 5000 years to form a visible coat of varnish and 10,000 or more years to form heavy coats of desert varnish. Thick desert varnish found on outcrops may be more than 50,000 years old. Considering the long time required for desert varnish formation, the role of surface stability becomes apparent. Friable rocks, such as some sandstones and granites, can crumble before a desert varnish coat has time to form. Likewise, carbonate rocks are generally too soluble, even in the desert, to form a desert varnish.

Artificial Desert Varnish

Desert varnish formation is a slow process, taking thousands of years to form a visible coat. In contrast, revegetation and desert pavement reformation are typically initiated in a few years and completed within several centuries. Many disturbed desert pavements have reformed their stone covers rapidly but are still highly visible because of their continued lack of desert varnish. Vegetation can act to obscure desert disturbances only where it can be reestablished. Some disturbed surfaces such as those on barren desert pavement or rocky road cuts cannot be expected to support enough vegetation to camouflage the conspicuously unvarnished rock surfaces.

A technique has been developed for making artificial desert varnish by precipitating Fe and Mn compounds onto rock surfaces. The technique takes advantage of the tendency of ferromanganese oxides and hydroxides to form as coatings on mineral surfaces. Artificial desert varnish has been used successfully to repair defaced petroglyphs at several sites in Arizona (Elvidge and Moore, 1980).

Artificial desert varnish is made by applying two types of solutions in sequence to rock surfaces. One of the solutions provides alkalinity and is made with NaOH. The other solution contains Fe^{2+} and Mn^{2+}; the soluble Fe and Mn are supplied by metallic salts such as manganeous sulfate ($MnSO_4$), ferrous sulfate ($FeSO_4$), or ferrous ammonium sulfate [$Fe(NH_4)_2(SO_4)_2$]. All of these chemicals are inexpensive when purchased in bulk quantities.

The soluble Fe^{2+} and Mn^{2+} are oxidized and precipitated under the alkaline influence of the NaOH. The Fe precipitates contribute a yellow-brown color while the Mn precipitates produce a black color. As a byproduct the varnish reaction produces the soluble salt $NaSO_4$, which is generally not visible on the treatment and is removed by infiltration and runoff.

On large-scale treatments such as rock scars the solutions should be sprayed on. The NaOH solution is corrosive to human skin and should be used with care. Plastic spray tanks are preferable as they will not be corroded by the solutions. One person working with a hand-held 8-liter garden sprayer can cover a considerable area in a single day.

There are two possible sequences of application: NaOH first or Fe and Mn first. The NaOH first reaction is slow, taking up to 2 weeks for completion. The Fe and Mn first sequence results in a fast reaction (24 to 48 hr), but a less durable varnish on rocks that are not highly porous. Application of the NaOH solution first is recommended for most rock scar treatments for this reason. The scheduling of the treatment should be designed to avoid rain during the week or so after the treatment if the NaOH first sequence is used.

Variation in the color of artificial desert varnish is achieved by varying the following parameters: (1) Fe to Mn ratio, (2) concentration of Fe to Mn, and (3) volume of solution used per area. In general, the concentration of Mn should be in the range of 0.5 to 1.5 molar depending on whether a brown, dark brown, or black color is desired. The Fe concentration in broadcast spray applications should be kept low (0.01 to 0.1 molar). At higher Fe concentrations it is possible for the color to dominate the varnish. The NaOH concentration should be about 1.5 times the combined molarity of the Fe and Mn. The volume of each solution applied per area should be between 6.5 and 15.3 m^2 $liter^{-1}$. Because of differences in the rock types to be varnished and variation expected between individual applicators, no standard set of solutions can be described that will give the same colored varnish in all cases. The only way to determine the proper treatment for a particular set of scars is to spray test patches over small areas and see what colors develop. Because Fe is less soluble than Mn, the Fe color develops before the Mn color, especially when the NaOH first sequence is used.

Several test patches of artificial desert varnish have been sprayed along Skyline Road near the Furnace Creek Ranger Station in Death Valley National Monument, California. The site is an abandoned road across a desert pavement, and as such is representative of an abandoned ORV trail. The stone mosaic has been regenerated with stones that are generally smaller than the surrounding pavement. Lacking desert varnish the road was distinctly visible against the

Figure 11-7. Abandoned road across desert pavement in Death Valley National Monument stands out because of the lack of desert varnish on the stones composing the new stone cover.

darkly varnished background (Fig. 11-7). The test patches were sprayed between August 1978 and January 1979. At first the surface soil between the stones developed a brown stain, lighter than the color that developed on the rocks. However, after the first rain this soil stain disappeared and the soil regained its natural color. The resulting test patches make a considerable improvement in the landscape (Fig. 11-8).

The effect of artificial desert varnish on soil has not been studied in detail. The process introduces a strong base (NaOH) into the environment which may not be completely consumed during the reaction. It is known that the reaction produces $NaSO_4$, but this salt is already common in desert soils (Jewitt, 1966). The effect of artificial desert varnish on vegetation has also not been investigated. Most rock scars to be treated with artificial desert varnish are barren or sparsely vegetated, but considerable growth of annuals can occur in wet years (Chapter 7). The decision about whether to use artificial desert varnish on a rock scar must weigh the visual benefits against the possible damage to vegetation and soil. The benefit of artificial desert varnish is cosmetic, restoring the natural appearance to a disturbed area. Without the use of artificial desert varnish, it could easily take 20,000 years for freshly scarred rock surfaces to blend in with their varnished surroundings. Based on observations of the effects of artificial desert varnish made thus far it can be concluded that whatever damage to the desert environment caused by the treatment is of short duration when compared with the regeneration time for natural desert varnish.

Figure 11-8. Abandoned road across desert pavement in Death Valley with artificial desert varnish.

Conclusion

Because of the very long time required for the reestablishment of desert varnish on disturbed rocky surfaces, disruption of varnished surfaces by ORVs must be considered permanent on a human time scale. Only through artificial means can the visual esthetics of disrupted varnished surfaces be returned to their original condition. In contrast, many disrupted desert pavements typically heal relatively rapidly by natural means, although regenerated pavements may appear somewhat different from the originals. Planning for off-road vehicle use in stone-covered desert areas should therefore take into account the long-lasting physical and esthetic changes resulting from ORV disruption of these desert surfaces.

References

Allen, C. C. 1978. Desert varnish of the Sonoran Desert: Optical and electron probe microanalysis. J. Geol. 86:743–752.

Anderson, B. J., and E. A. Jenne. 1970. Free-iron and -manganese content of reference clays. Soil Sci. 109:163–169.

Bales, J. T., and T. L. Péwé. 1979. Origin and rate of desert pavement formation—a progress report. J. Arizona-Nevada Acad. Sci. 14:84.

Bard, J. C., F. Asaro, and R. F. Heizer. 1978. Perspectives on dating of prehistoric Great Basin petroglyphs by neutron activation analysis. Archeometry 20:85–88.

Bauman, A. J. 1976. Desert varnish and marine ferromanganese nodules: congeneric phenomena. Nature (London) 259:387–388.

Blake, W. P. 1904. Origin of pebble-covered plains in desert regions. Trans. Am. Inst. Min. Eng. 34:161–162.

Blake, W. P. 1905. Superficial blackening and discoloration of rocks, especially in desert regions. Trans. Am. Inst. Min. Eng. 35:371–375.

Bowley, W. W., and M. D. Burghardt. 1971. Thermodynamics and stones. Trans. Am. Geophys. Union 52:4–7.

Carroll, D. 1962. Rainwater as a Chemical Agent of Geologic Processes—A Review. U.S. Geological Survey Water Supply Paper 1535-G, 18 pp.

Chepil, W. S. 1950. Properties of soil which influence wind erosion: the governing principle of surface roughness. Soil Sci. 69:149–162.

Clements, T., and L. Clements. 1953. Evidence of Pleistocene man in Death Valley, California. Geol. Soc. Am. Bull. 64:1189–1204.

Collins, J. F., and S. W. Buol. 1970. Effects of fluctuation in the Eh-pH environment on iron and/or manganese equilibria. Soil Sci. 110:111–118.

Cooke, R. U. 1970. Stone pavements in deserts. Ann. Assoc. Am. Geogr. 60:560–577.

Cooke, R. U., and A. Warren. 1973. Geomorphology in Deserts. University of California Press, Berkeley, California, 374 pp.

Denny, C. S. 1965. Alluvial Fans in the Death Valley Region, California and Nevada. U.S. Geological Survey Professional Paper 466, 59 pp.

Eckert, R. E., M. K. Wood, W. H. Blackburn, and F. F. Peterson. 1979. Impacts of off-road vehicles on infiltration and sediment production of two desert soils. J. Range Management 32:394–397.

Elvidge, C. D. 1979. Distribution and formation of desert varnish in Arizona. Unpublished M.S. thesis, Arizona State University, Tempe, Arizona, 109 pp.

Elvidge, C. D. 1982. Reexamination of the rate of desert varnish formation reported south of Barstow, California. Earth Surface Processes and Landforms, 7:345–348.

Elvidge, C. D., and C. B. Moore. 1979. A model for desert varnish formation. Geol. Soc. Am. Abstr. 11:271.

Elvidge, C. D., and C. B. Moore. 1980. Restoration of petroglyphs with artificial desert varnish. Stud. Conserv. 25:108–117.

Engel, C. G., and R. P. Sharp. 1958. Chemical data on desert varnish. Geol. Soc. Am. Bull. 69:487–518.

Evenari, M., D. H. Yaalon, and Y. Gutterman. 1974. Note on soils with vesicular structure in deserts. Z. Geomorphol. 18:162–172.

Gilbert, G. K. 1875. Report on the Geology of Portions of Nevada, Utah, California and Arizona. Geographical and Geological Explorations and Surveys West of the 100th Meridian (Engineers Dept., U.S. Army) 3:21–187.

Hayden, J. D. 1976. Pre-altithermal archeology in the Sierra Pinacate, Sonora, Mexico. Am. Antiquity 41:274–289.

Hem, J. D. 1963. Chemistry of Manganese in Natural Waters: Deposition and Solution of Manganese Oxides. U.S. Geological Survey Water Supply Paper 1667-B, 42 pp.

Hooke, R. L., H. Yang, and P. W. Weiblen. 1969. Desert varnish: An electron probe study. J. Geol. 77:275–288.

Howard, R. B., B. Cowen, and D. Inouye. 1977. Reappraisal of desert pavement formation. Geol. Soc. Am. Abstr. 9:438–439.

Hunt, C. B., and D. R. Mabey. 1966. Stratigraphy and structure: Death Valley, California. U.S. Geological Survey Professional Paper 494-A, 162 pp.

Idso, S. B. 1974. Summer winds drive dust storms across the desert. Smithsonian 5:68–73.

Idso, S. B., R. S. Ingram, and J. M. Pritchard. 1972. An American haboob. Bull. Am. Meteorol. Soc. 53:930–935.

Inglis, D. R. 1965. Particle sorting and stone migration by freezing and thawing. Science 148:1616–1617.

Jessup, R. W. 1960. The stony tableland soils of the southeastern portion of the Australian arid zone and their evolutionary history. J. Soil Sci. 11:188–196.

Jewitt, T. N. 1966. Soils in arid lands. In: E. S. Hills (Ed.), Arid Lands. UNESCO, Paris, pp. 112–116.

Knauss, K. G., and T. L. Ku. 1980. Desert varnish: Potential for age dating via Uranium-series isotopes. J. Geol. 88:95–100.

Krauskopf, K. B. 1957. Separation of manganese from iron in sedimentary processes. Geochim. Cosmochim. Acta 12:61–84.

Krumbein, W. E. 1969. Uber den Einfluss der Mikroflora auf die exogene Dynamik. Geol. Rundsc. 58:333–363.

Laudermilk, J. D. 1931. On the origin of desert varnish. Am. J. Sci. 5:51–66.

Lowdermilk, W. C., and H. L. Sundling. 1950. Erosion pavement, its formation and significance. Trans. Am. Geophys. Union 31:96–100.

Malde, H. E., and A. P. Schick. 1964. Thorne Cave, northeastern Utah. Geology. Am. Antiquity 30:60–73.

Mabutt, J. A. 1965. Stone distribution in a stony tableland soil. Austral. J. Soil Res. 3:131–142.

Merrill, G. P. 1898. Desert varnish. U.S. Geol. Surv. Bull. 150:389–391.

Musick, H. B. 1975. Barreness of desert pavement in Yuma County, Arizona. J. Arizona-Nevada Acad. Sci. 10:24–28.

Perry, R. S., and J. B. Adams. 1978. Desert varnish: Evidence for cyclic deposition of manganese. Nature (London) 276:489–491.

Péwé, T. L. 1978. Geology field trip log along the Lower Salt River, Arizona. In: D. M. Burt and T. L. Péwé (Eds.), Guidebook to the Geology of Central Arizona. Arizona Bureau of Geology and Mineral Technology Special Paper 2, pp. 14–45.

Péwé, T. L., E. A. Péwé, R. H. Péwé, A. Journaux, and R. M. Slatt. 1981. Desert dust: Characteristics and Rates of Deposition in Central Arizona. In: T. L. Péwé (Ed.), Desert Dust: Origin, Characteristics and Effect on Man. Geol. Soc. Am. Spec. Paper 186, pp. 169–190.

Potter, R. M., and G. R. Rossman. 1977. Desert varnish: The importance of clay minerals. Science 196:1446–1448.

Potter, R. M., and G. R. Rossman. 1979. The manganese and iron oxide mineralogy of desert varnish. Chem. Geol. 25:79–94.

Rogers, M. J. 1939. Early lithic industries of the lower basin of the Colorado River and adjacent desert areas. San Diego Museum Papers 3, 75 pp.

Ryan, J., S. Miyamoto, and J. L. Stroehlein. 1974. Solubility of manganese, iron, and zinc as affected by application of sulfuric acid to calcarious soils. Plant and Soil 40:421–427.

Scheffer, R., B. Mayer, and E. Kalk. 1963. Biologische Ursachen der Wusternlackbildung. Z. Geomorphol. 7:112–119.

Setzler, F. M. 1952. Seeking the secret of the giants. Natl. Geog. 102:390–404.

Sharon, D. 1962. On the nature of hamadas in Israel. Z. Geomorphol. 6:129–147.

Springer, M. E. 1958. Desert pavement and vesicular layer of some soils of the desert of the Lahontan Basin, Nevada. Proc. Soil Sci. Am. 22:63–66.

Symmons, P. M., and C. F. Hemming. 1968. A note on wind stable stone mantles in the southern Sahara. Geog. J. 134:60–64.

White, C. H. 1924. Desert varnish. Am. J. Sci. 207:413–420.

Wilshire, H. G., and J. K. Nakata. 1976. Off-road vehicle effects on California's Mojave Desert. Calif. Geol. 29:123–132.

Wilshire, H. G., J. K. Nakata, and B. Hallet. 1980. Field observations of the December, 1977 windstorm, San Joaquin Valley, California. In: T. L. Péwé (Ed.), Desert Dust: Origin, Characteristics, and Effect on Man. Geol. Soc. Am. Spec. Paper 186, pp. 233–251.

12
Control of Rills and Gullies in Off-Road Vehicle Traffic Areas[1]

Burchard H. Heede

Introduction

Equilibrium conditions of deserts depend on a delicate balance between their ecosystem, soil structure, and landforms. In the context of this treatise, the balance is best described as dynamic equilibrium. It does not imply absolute equilibrium, but that adjustment to a new situation is attainable within a relatively short time, perhaps within a few years. Obviously, if considered in geologic time spans, dynamic equilibrium has not taken place, because land denudation is the long-term process.

Any abuse of one component of deserts will have grave consequences on the other components. Of particular interest here is the effect of changing a component on the erosional stability of deserts. For instance, destruction of the sparse but important plant cover will lead to surface soil movement that in turn destroys the soil structure and, in time, accelerates micro- and macrolandform changes. Because these processes are combined with degradation or aggradation, the overall results are local base level changes (lowering or raising of drainage elevations). These may trigger a chain reaction throughout the upstream watershed or hill slope—lowering of base level leading to degradation, raising of base level to aggradation throughout the system—until a new equilibrium topography is attained. In certain situations, hundreds or even thousands of years may elapse before a stable plant cover becomes reestablished (Wilshire, 1977; Chapter 14), which signifies that a new equilibrium has been achieved.

---

[1] The views and conclusions contained in this chapter are based on the author's studies or experiences and do not necessarily represent the official viewpoint or policy of any U.S. government agency.

If we consider the combined weight of a motorcycle and its rider, concentrated on two small wheel segments touching the ground, it becomes obvious how serious the impact on fragile arid soils is (Chapter 4). The stresses exerted by acceleration, turning, and braking of the wheels substantially add to this impact. The same is true for four-wheel vehicles whose imprints on the ground surface may be manifold. These vehicles can leave continuous imprints on the landscape which become available for the channelization of overland flows during rainstorms (Chapter 5). It is therefore not surprising that the recent literature is replete with examples of rill and gully development caused by off-road vehicle (ORV) traffic.

Instead of waiting for long time spans for the attainment of a new equilibrium condition, man can accelerate rehabilitation of ORV use areas by introducing artificial controls. If a system degrades because of a lowered local base level, the present base level may be maintained, thereby preventing future degradation in the system. Even more desirable, a new equilibrium can be reached by raising the base level. A raise, as outlined earlier, will introduce aggradation to the new elevation of the base level and thus lead to stabilization. This chapter will deal with proven control methods based on the concept of maintaining or raising the local base level.

Characteristics of Rills and Gullies Resulting
from Off-Road Vehicle Traffic

In contrast to the initiation of rill and gully processes by other land uses such as grazing, ORV-induced rilling and gullying proceed much more rapidly. When vehicles are not involved, rills and gullies are often discontinuous (Heede, 1970). Discontinuous water courses do not allow continuous concentrated flows, and therefore flow velocities and energies do not reach the large magnitudes attained by continuous flows. Usually, discontinuous rills and gullies are short and discharge their flows on undissected hill slopes or valley bottoms where water spreads and velocities decrease. The tracks of ORVs, especially on erosion-sensitive soil surfaces, form continuous rills and, in soft materials, continuous channels (Chapter 5). Both can quickly grow into continuous gullies (Wilshire, 1977). Rills must therefore be viewed as severe ground surface disturbances—as a beginning stage in gully development (Heede, 1974).

The formation of gullies may also be caused by indirect impact from ORV traffic, and at early gully development stages may be far removed from the use area. Because infiltration losses due to soil compaction by vehicles (Eckert et al., 1979; Chapter 4) lead to increased overland flow (Chapter 5), areas located below or downstream receive usually high flows, and gullying may occur. Thus, cause and effect may be spatially far apart from each other. In time, however, the gullies on the lowland will progressively extend into the remotest headwater and uphill areas, unless they are interrupted by natural controls such as hard bedrock outcrops. Thus the soil in the ORV use area, already compacted and disrupted by the vehicle traffic (Chapter 4), will finally be completely eroded by the gully processes advancing upstream if erosion is not controlled by artificial means.

Immediate Control Objectives and Strategies

Under severe conditions, such as disturbed desert environments which require extended periods of time to reach a new equilibrium, it is important to differentiate between quickly achievable and time-consuming objectives. From the preceding section it follows that the elevation of the mainstream gully mouth represents the local base level of the gullied area. If this elevation increases by sedimentation, aggradation throughout the gully system may follow where sufficient volumes of sediment are available. On the other hand, if the local base level lowers, degradation and extension of the gully system into the headwater areas will follow. Excellent examples of this process due to ORV use were documented by Knott (1978). Developments of bedscarps on the gully bottom are responsible for degradation, and gully headcuts of the mainstream and tributaries extend the gully upstream. Because bedscarps are similar to head-cuts, the local base level must be controlled before treatment of upstream gully sections and tributaries can be successful. This is also true for hill slope treatments, because otherwise gully bedscarps could advance into the hillsides.

From the base level concept, as expressed here, it also follows that treatments must begin at the gully mouth and advance upstream, never vice versa. Where natural controls (such as bedrock) exist in gully systems, treatment may begin at these controls. On the basis of expected future erosion and treatment effects, it should be decided whether gully sections downstream from natural controls require treatment. Since local base level control is the key to treatment success, the land manager must assure that the natural control is of substantial and lasting quality, or that the structure used in its place is the strongest in the treatment system.

Long-Term Control Objectives and Strategies

In desert regions, reestablishment of vegetation cover in eroding areas takes a long time; often thousands of years were required before the undisturbed vegetation became established (Chapter 7). Yet, plant cover establishment is a highly desirable treatment objective because only plants can offer permanent ground surface control. Structures are required first, however, to diminish or stop excessive surface soil movement. In serious erosion situations, some time may be required between structural installations and planting. Plantings should be done prior to the season having the highest probability for precipitation (Chapter 17), or when soil moisture is highest. A combination of physical structures and plants enhances gully control, since plants also add to stabilization of the engineering measures (Heede, 1977).

Control Measures on Hill Slopes

Stabilization of desert hill slopes is difficult, especially if ORV traffic has disrupted the soil surface and destroyed a sparse vegetation cover. Once the surface seal is broken, rills and gullies can develop quickly. Generally, there is no hope to reestablish a vegetative cover within a human lifespan, or to effectively construct check dams on steeper gullied slopes because of foundation problems and the need for very close dam spacing, requiring many structures. Thus hill slope stabilization becomes too costly for general use.

In semidesert regions, Heede (1975) successfully used a new method for surface-soil stabilization on a hill slope with continuous rills, which could have led to gullies if not controlled. In essence, the methods are designed for controlling local base levels. One experiment was conducted on a 50% denuded road-cut slope, and the other was conducted on waterways that replaced gullies on hills with slopes up to 22%.

The basic method consists of two parts:

1. Folded burlap strips 30 cm wide are placed vertically into the ground. The strips are placed on the contour 0.5 to 1 m from each other to form a reinforcing grid in the upper soil mantle (Fig. 12-1). A strip cannot prevent soil creep or slides along its full length; however, it can prevent or reduce soil movement when only part of the strip length is endangered. Also, the strips cannot stabilize slides that are seated deeper than strip depth. This method has another important benefit: the excavations for the strips relieve soil compaction caused by the ORV traffic, which will enhance plant establishment (Chapter 16) in addition to increasing infiltration rates.

2. The strips are placed to protrude between 5 and 8 cm above the ground surface to serve as a barrier to surface soil movement, thus increasing surface stability. Because surface soil movement can hinder the establishment of plants with undeveloped root systems, surface stability is especially important where seeds or young plants are to be planted. Since several layers of burlap are used for the strips, stiffness in the burlap prevents the protruding portion of the strip from flattening. With time, the protrusion attains a convex cross section that acts as a water spreader and miniature check dam for surface flows. Flow concentrations and flow velocities are thus reduced. This change of flow regimen is especially important immediately following treatment when erosion hazards are greatest.

On the road-cut slope, burlap strips reduced net erosion by a factor of 14 after $2\frac{1}{4}$ years in spite of severe testing by high-intensity storms. All strips were still intact $4\frac{1}{4}$ years after treatment. Water overfalls did not undermine the burlap, and the flexibility of the burlap allowed the strips to conform with the ground surface.

On the waterway area, where precipitation for the growing season averaged 142 mm, the burlap remained fully intact for 5 to 6 years; 12 years after treatment, segments of the strips were still in place. Although rills were up to 15 cm

Figure 12-1. Submerged burlap strip 1 year after installation. Note that the protruding part of the burlap behind the lightmeter acted as check against surface soil movement, although some sediment overtopped the strip. Flow is from right to left.

deep before treatment, the transformation of the continuous rills to discontinuous channels by the strips prevented gully development and, in combination with plant growth, stabilized the waterways.

It is expected that in desert climates the lifespan of burlap will at least double, but other materials such as erosion cloth may be more desirable and much longer lasting. This cloth must be of the type that resists sun radiation; otherwise the exposed parts will quickly disintegrate. The method and material must be tested in deserts before life expectancy of burlap or other material can be projected.

Other control measures for hill slope stabilization exist. Different types of mulches can be used, such as straw or a mixture of straw and chemicals that hold the mulch in place. Netting may be applied instead of chemicals. On steeper slopes, the netting should be stapled to the ground.

Measures that change the ground surface are contour ripping and water bars. Both are intended to spread flows. The literature of mulches, netting, and contour measures is too large to be quoted here.

A word of caution appears to be in place if ground surfaces will be modified because any surface modification disturbs the soils. In fragile desert environments, this disturbance should be held to a minimum. It is therefore advisable to keep earth structures (contour rippings, water bars, etc.), if required at all, as small as possible.

Control Measures on Valley Bottoms

The most serious impact of ORV traffic on valley bottoms is the lowering of the local base level by gullies. Gully control is an old human undertaking dating back thousands of years, but research in this field is rather recent and therefore our knowledge is limited (Heede, 1976). Basically, there are two approaches to gully control: diversion of the water from the gully, and control of flow within the channel. The first approach requires earth movement, a new channel, or diversion ditches, all depending for stability on rapid establishment of a plant cover. Obviously, shallow soils and slow plant growth do not allow this approach in deserts generally. The second approach, usually less risky, uses check dams, sometimes called gradient control structures. A check dam is an effective base level control.

A check dam may be built above ground, or submerged with its spillway flush with the gully cross section. In the first case, sediment will accumulate behind the dam, leading to reduced channel gradient and flow energies, and to a raised local base level. In the second, future deepening of the gully will be prevented by maintaining the present base level. Depending on the treatment objective, either method may be used.

Unless natural gradient controls such as hard bedrock outcrops exist, gully treatments with above-ground check dams require numerous structures, because sediment deposits induced by dams may lead to drastic breaks in channel gradients (nickpoints). As mentioned before, deposits have a much shallower gradient than the original gully gradient. Generally, gully gradients are steeper than the respective equilibrium gradient. A bedscarp may therefore develop at the nickpoint that in time, advances toward headwaters and thereby deepens the upstream gully section. Check dams will prevent bedscarp development if installed at the location of future nickpoints, i.e., at the upstream toe of the expected sediment wedge to be accumulated by a dam.

Sediment deposits in gullies are aquifers, as demonstrated by ancient agriculture (Heede, 1976), and may be one of the factors responsible for converting ephemeral to perennial flows. Heede (1977) induced such a conversion in a semiarid environment after 7 years of check dam treatment.

Types of Check Dams

Many different types of construction materials can be used in check dams, and selection of material will often also be based on cost. Only the more important materials and their physical aspects in dam construction will be discussed here.

Earth Dams. Experiences in semidesert environments in the western United States have shown that soil generally is the least desirable construction material for check dams. Earth dams allow for the possible formation of new critical locations where the flows are returned from the spillway to the gully, or pipe inlets may be plugged if standpipes are used to convey water beneath the dam. After the dam is filled with sediment, soil moisture remains longest at the inlet and enhances plant growth there that can also lead to clogging. The installation of rakes to prevent clogging did not prove successful under most wildland conditions. If the water is conveyed by a spillway in the approximate center of the earth dam, materials such as rock or concrete are required for lining as well as to dissipate energy where the flow is discharged onto the gully bottom. Hence, besides a clay core or other dam membrane, much additional work is required for the construction of a stable earth check dam.

Concrete Dams. Heede (1965) designed a prefabricated, prestressed concrete check dam consisting of nine individual members that can be put in place with a backhoe. This structure has the advantage of ease and quickness of installation, plus the potential for mass production which would substantially decrease unit cost. Heede (1965) presented stability calculations that can be followed also for design changes. The disadvantage of the concrete dam is its imperviousness, which creates high pressures against the keys in the gully banks that hold the concrete in place. Deep keys and soil compaction at the keys by special equipment are therefore required. Hauling costs could be substantial if there is no commercial concrete prestressing plant nearby. Usually, pouring conventional concrete dams in place is not much cheaper because water, concrete, aggregates, and steel still must be transported to the site.

Loose Rock Dams. Loose rock, a product of the land in many regions, is very effective as construction material for check dams (Heede, 1977). Loose rock dams not only release much of the hydrostatic pressure through the structure at a very vulnerable time—right after construction and before the dam is filled by sediment—but also have the advantage of some flexibility. Voids or scour holes will be quickly filled by rock due to gravitation, if a favorable mixture of rock sizes is used. Angular rock is preferable to round (stream-worked) rock because the former anchors itself more securely into a structure. The rock should be resistant to weathering and erosion and should initially be of good quality.

Different designs for rock check dams were developed (Heede, 1966). Some dams require reinforcing materials such as steel posts and/or mesh wire, but the field of check dam design is wide open to the imaginative land manager. The simplest way to reinforce a loose rock dam is to encase the structure in wire mesh. The dam slopes can then be steepened from the usual 1.5:1 to 1.25:1, with savings in the required amount of rock as well as greater structural stability. The use of wire mesh is not feasible where gully flows carry sediment loads of boulder size, however, because the wire would break under the impact of the bedload.

If steel posts and wire mesh are used, either single-fence or double-fence dams can be designed. The single-fence structure consists of a fence strung across the gully, reinforced by steel posts driven into the gully bottom and anchored with guy wires to other posts upstream from the dam. Loose rock is piled with a slope of 1.25:1 against the upstream side of the fence (Fig. 12-2). The guys must be strong enough to prevent the fence from being pushed over by the weight of the rock and the dynamic and hydrostatic pressures of future flows.

Double-fence dams consist of two parallel fences strung across the gully, with a rock fill in the interspace (Fig. 12-3). Heede (1966) used a spacing of 0.6 m between the fences; if greater stability is required, the structure should be designed with a base wider than the breadth of the dam crest. The fences should

Figure 12-2. View across a single-fence rock check dam. Note the loose rock apron below the structure to prevent bed scour. Ephemeral discharge will flow from right to left.

Figure 12-3. Upstream view of a double-fence rock check dam installed in a semiarid environment. Bank protection work is reinforced by wire mesh and steel posts. Length of rod in center of dam is 1.7 m.

be guyed to each other for stability. The rock size distribution must range from large to small to avoid formation of larger voids during filling operations, especially in double-fence dams. High porosity would prevent sediment catch and could also create water jets, which may hit the banks with great force, causing additional erosion. Spillway design and construction require special consideration because spillway size is easily reduced during fence installation.

In recent years, gabion dams have been used frequently. These dams consist of box-shaped wire baskets filled with loose rock. Depending on structural height, many baskets are required for one dam. It is estimated that the cost of this dam type is two to five times that of rock dams.

A special application of check dams is in the control of gully headcuts. Headcuts are located at the upstream end of discontinuous gullies and usually involve a steep or even vertical drop from the undissected valley floor into the gully. Headcut control may greatly reduce soil loss in large valleys, but it is also a difficult task requiring full attention of the designer and construction supervisor. Heede (1966, 1977) proposes the application of a rock wedge placed against the headcut and sloped into the gully at a slope of 3:1. The wedge should be swaled to such an extent on its centerline that the flows do not touch the banks. The location where the water flows from the soil into the wedge is critical. Inverted filter or erosion cloth applied to the interspace between soil and structure can be used to prevent the sudden increase of pore size from soil to rock wedge that can lead to scour and—in time—loss of the structure. The lip of the headcut must be protected to prevent flow from entering the gully from below the rock wedge. Instead of a wedge, other types of structures such as fence dams could also be used in certain situations.

Design of Check Dams

Spacing. To avoid over- or underdesign, check dams should be spaced to allow utilization of the full sediment catch capacity of the individual structures. The expected upstream extent of the sediment wedge must therefore be determined. Heede (1977) has shown that the sediment deposit gradient is strongly related to the original gully gradient. Although sediment processes change with flow regimen and therefore have one sediment profile for high flows and another for low flows, vegetation invasion in ephemeral streams leads to "freezing" of one depositional gradient. The relationship between the original and the sediment-deposit gradients can be obtained from inspection of sediment retention structures such as stock ponds that have been in place for at least a decade. Once this ratio is found, an equation for the determination of dam spacing S (in m) can be used[2]:

$$S = \frac{H_E}{KG \cos \alpha} \qquad (12\text{-}1)$$

where H_E is effective dam height as measured from gully bottom to spillway crest (meters), G represents the gully gradient as a ratio, and α is the angle corresponding to the gully gradient ($G = \tan \alpha$). The equation is based on the finding that the gradient of the sediment deposits is $(1 - K)G$. K is a constant, derived from the equation:

$$K = 1 - R \qquad (12\text{-}2)$$

where R is the ratio between the sediment deposit gradient and the original gully gradient.

Keys. If expected peak flows are larger than 0.3 m^3 sec^{-1}, check dams must be keyed into the gully bottom and banks. The key prevents undermining of the structure and bank cutting. The rocks used for the keys should be smaller than those for the dam proper to avoid formation of larger voids. A key breadth of 0.6 m had proved to be sufficient. The key in the gully bottom should be 0.6 m deep, while depth of the bank keys depends on the type of soil. In clay-rich soils, 0.6-m depth emplacement will be enough, while in sandy soils a depth of 1.2 to 1.8 m is recommended.

Height. The effective height of a check dam is one of the most important variables in the design. It influences dam spacing, and with this the number of structures required, and also the volume of sediment the dam can hold. A check dam

---

[2] A list of symbol meanings for all equations in this chapter is provided in Appendix 1.

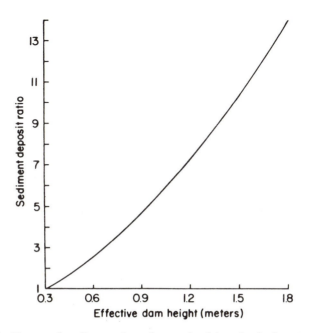

Figure 12-4. Expected sediment deposits retained by check dam treatment as a function of effective dam height (Heede, 1976). The sediment deposit ratio relates the volume of sediment deposits to the volume of sediment deposits at effective dam height of 0.3 m. Thus, deposits in a treatment with 1.2-m dams are more than seven times larger than those caught by 0.3-m dams. Note that this graph is general—the actual volumes depend on the geometry of the gully behind the dam.

system consisting of higher structures catches more sediment than one using low dams (Fig. 12-4), but check dam heights will be limited by stability considerations. Severely tested check dams (Heede, 1966) have maximum heights of 2.2 m for loose rock and wire-bound rock dams, and 1.8 m for fence-type rock dams (thickness 0.6 m). The effective height of dams may also be greatly restricted by the spillway requirements.

Spillway. Spillways should be sufficiently large to convey the design peak flow; otherwise overtopping may destroy the structure. Spillways of rock check dams can be considered as broad-crested weirs; therefore, the discharge equation for that type of weir is applicable:

$$Q = CLH^{3/2} \tag{12-3}$$

where Q is the discharge in $m^3 \ sec^{-1}$, C is the coefficient of the weir, L is the effective length of the weir in meters, and H is the head of flow above the weir crest in meters. A mean value of 1.65 should be used for C. If possible, spillway length should equal that of the gully bottom to prevent the water overfall from

hitting the banks. This is not always possible either due to large spillway requirements or V-shaped gully cross sections. In such cases, stability of the bank protection work must be emphasized in design and construction.

Apron and Bank Protection. Apron and bank protection below check dams are
required to dissipate flow energy and control erosion. Without an apron, water
overfall would form a scour hole that eventually would cause dam failure. Bank
protection guards against eddies developing on the apron against the banks. A
loose rock layer 0.3 m thick was shown to be effective for apron and bank protection (Heede, 1966).

Aprons must be sufficiently long to cushion the impact of the waterfall. As a
rule of thumb, on gully gradients ⩽15%, the length of the apron is 1.50 times
dam height, while on gradients >15% this length increases to 1.75 times dam
height. The gully banks must be protected for the total length of the apron.

Rock Volumes. Loose rock dams must be designed differently with angular and
round rock, because the angle of repose varies with rock shape and influences
the side slopes of the dam (Heede, 1976). The generalized equation is expressed
in metric units, as are all equations that follow:

$$V_{LR} = \left(\frac{H^2}{\tan A_R} + 0.6H\right) L_A - V_{SP} \qquad (12\text{-}4)$$

where V_{LR} is the volume of the dam proper, H is dam height, 0.6 is the breadth
of the core, L_A is the average length of the dam, $\tan A_R$ is the tangent of the
angle of repose of the rock type, and V_{SP} is the volume of the spillway. It is
assumed that the angle of repose for angular rock is represented by a slope of
1.25:1.00, corresponding to $\tan A_R = 0.80$, and the slope for round rock is
1.50:1.00 with $\tan A_R = 0.66$. L_A is given by the equation:

$$L_A = L_B + \frac{L_U - L_B}{2D} H \qquad (12\text{-}5)$$

where L_B is the bottom width of the gully, L_U is the upper width of the gully,
and D is the depth of the gully. V_{SP} is calculated by the equation:

$$V_{SP} = H_S L_{AS} B_A \qquad (12\text{-}6)$$

where H_S is the depth and L_{AS} the effective length of the spillway, and B_A
is the breadth of the dam, measured at half the depth of the spillway and derived
from the formula:

$$B_A = \frac{H_S}{\tan A_R} + 0.6 \qquad (12\text{-}7)$$

where 0.6 is the breadth of the dam at H.

From Equation (12-4) it follows that less rock is required if angular shapes
are used.

Volumes of rock for the structural key can be derived from the generalized equation (Heede, 1976):

$$V_K = (L_A + 2Y)(0.6H + 0.36) - 0.6HL_A \qquad (12\text{-}8)$$

where Y represents the depth of key and 0.6 and 0.36 are constants referring to depth and width of bottom key and width of bank key, respectively. Field experience indicates two groups of gully gradients should be considered for calculating rock volumes of apron and bank protection, each 0.3 m thick. The generalized equation is:

$$V_A = cHL_B + 2cH^2 \qquad (12\text{-}9)$$

where V_A is the rock volume and c is a constant whose value depends on the gully gradient. On gradients $\leqslant 15\%$, $c = 1.50$, and on gradients $> 15\%$, $c = 1.75$. Equation (12-9) is valid for all dam types discussed here.

For calculating rock volumes for single-fence dams, a zero gully gradient was assumed. This results in overestimates that compensate for simplification of the equation for volume calculation. While the construction plan calls for a dam with a 0.6-m breadth, for ease of calculation, the cross section of the dam parallel to the thalweg (the line joining the deepest points of a stream channel) is taken as a triangle with a dam side slope of 1.25:1.00. The equation is:

$$V_{SF} = \frac{H^2}{2 \tan A_R} L_A - V_{SSF} \qquad (12\text{-}10)$$

where V_{SF} is the rock volume of the dam proper, and $\tan A_R$ represents the tangent of a slope of 1.25:1.00. V_{SSF} is the volume of the spillway, calculated by the equation:

$$V_{SSF} = H_S L_{AS} B_{SF} \qquad (12\text{-}11)$$

where B_{SF} is the breadth of the dam, measured at half the depth of the spillway and given by the formula:

$$B_{SF} = \frac{H_S}{2 \tan A_R} \qquad (12\text{-}12)$$

The rock volume of a double-fence dam is expressed by the equation:

$$V_{DF} = 0.6HL_A - V_{SDF} \qquad (12\text{-}13)$$

where V_{DF} is the volume, 0.6 is the breadth of the dam, and V_{SDF} is the volume of the spillway, computed by the formula:

$$V_{SDF} = 0.6H_S L_{AS} \qquad (12\text{-}14)$$

The volume requirements for a headcut control structure are given by the equation:

$$V_{HC} = \left(\frac{3D^2}{2}\right)\left(\frac{L_U + 3L_B}{4}\right) \qquad (12\text{-}15)$$

where V_{HC} is the rock volume, D is the depth of the gully at the headcut, 3 is a coefficient that refers to a structure with a slope gradient of 3:1, and

$$\frac{L_U + 3L_B}{4}$$

is the weighted average length of the structure.

Wire Mesh and Fence Posts. Wire mesh and steel fence posts are used in most of the rock dam types. If dam height is equal to or larger than 1.2 m, the bank protection work should be reinforced with wire mesh and fence posts. The equation for square meter of wire mesh and number of posts includes a margin of safety to offset unforseen additional needs. To assist in construction, size of the mesh is given in length and width. The length measured along the thalweg is:

$$M_{LB} = 2(1.75H) \tag{12-16}$$

where M_{LB} is the length of the wire mesh for the bank protection on both banks and $1.75H$ is the length of bank protection for gradients $>15\%$. The width of the wire mesh equals the total dam height.

The number of fence posts is calculated by the equation:

$$N_B = 2\left(\frac{1.75H}{1.2} + 1\right) \tag{12-17}$$

where N_B is the number of fence posts for the bank protection rounded up to a whole even number, and the constant 1.2 refers to the spacing of the posts. All posts are 0.75 m taller than the dam. This equation is based on the rule of thumb that 8, 10, or 12 posts will be required, depending on dam height (H), if H is $\leqslant 2.3$ m. For most cases these amounts include a surplus that should be used to offset losses, and/or for horizontal structure members in single- and double-fence dams. Horizontal members were not included in the post-number equations for these dam types.

For wire-bound dams, the length of the wire mesh is taken as the length of the dam crest, which includes a safety margin and is calculated by the equation:

$$M_L = L_B + \frac{L_U - L_B}{D}H \tag{12-18}$$

where M_L is the length of the wire mesh. The width of the mesh, measured parallel to the thalweg, depends not only on dam height but also on rock shape. The equation for the width of the wire mesh is:

$$M_W = 2\left(\frac{H}{\tan A_R} + \frac{H}{\sin A_R} + 0.6\right) + 2 \tag{12-19}$$

where M_W is the width and A_R is the angle of repose of the rock. Equation

(12-19) provides for an overlapping of the mesh by 2 m. Only the dam proper will be encased in wire mesh.

For a single-fence dam, the length of the wire mesh is given by Equation (12-18), and the width of the wire mesh is equal to dam height. The number of fence posts is calculated by the equation:

$$N_{SF} = \frac{L_B}{1.2} + \frac{L_U - L_B}{1.2D}H + 1 \qquad (12\text{-}20)$$

where N_{SF} is the number of posts for the dam proper of a single-fence dam rounded up to a whole number, 1.2 signifies a distance of 1.2 m between the posts, and 1 is for an end post. Of the total number of posts, half should be 0.75 m taller than the dam, the other half are dam height.

For double-fence dams, the length of wire mesh is given by:

$$M_{LD} = 2L_B + \left(\frac{L_U - L_B}{D}H\right) \qquad (12\text{-}21)$$

where M_{LD} is the length of the mesh. The width of the wire mesh equals dam height. The number of fence posts is computed by the equation:

$$N_{DF} = \frac{L_B}{0.6} + \frac{L_U - L_B}{0.6D} + 2 \qquad (12\text{-}22)$$

where N_{DF} is the number of posts of the dam proper of a double-fence dam, rounded up to a whole even number. One-half of the number of posts are dam height, while the other half should be 0.75 m taller than the dam.

Relative Costs and Sediment Benefits

Check dams are effective structures, because they change the regimen of gully flows from turbulent to more tranquil flows. The result is a substantial reduction of channel erosion. Heede (1977) estimated that 90% of the sediment load in gullies he studied was derived from channel erosion. After 11 years of treatment, he reported a 92% decrease in suspended sediment load.

Sediment values can be realistically determined, since generally data can be obtained from sediment withholding structures such as stock ponds or dams. Thus, in contrast to other benefits from gully control (saving of topsoil, recreational use, etc.), sediment trapping is a tangible benefit. These other benefits cannot be omitted in the final decision making, however. Because the intangible values of benefits fluctuate immensely between different locations and conditions, they will not be examined further here.

Costs can be evaluated on a relative scale by comparing the different types of rock check dams. A project in semiarid Colorado provided the data for this comparison (Heede, 1966), which is expected to be valid also for other regions because physical characteristics such as bed gradient and structural type are

primarily responsible for cost differences. Thus expressed by indices, cost relationships between the different dam types were found to be as follows:

Double fence	1.00
Single fence	0.87
Wire bound	0.73
Loose rock only	0.68

The Colorado project, consisting of 132 rock check dams, demonstrated that
labor cost can be insignificant (7% of the total), while cost of rock is the main
expense. Relative costs and rock volumes can therefore be placed on the same
scale.

In Figure 12-5, the cost and rock-volume ratios relate the cost of treatment
to those of a treatment with loose rock dams 0.3 m high installed on a 2%
gradient. Thus, a treatment with single-fence dams, 0.3 m high and installed
in a gully with a 22% gradient, requires 15 times more rock and costs about 15
times more than one on a 2% gradient. If 1.8-m-high single-fence dams were used
for the 22% gradient, cost and rock volume requirement would increase to 18
times those of a treatment with loose rock dams 0.3 m high placed on a 2%
gradient.

The curves (Fig. 12-5), considered by themselves, convey even a more important design criterion: all curves have a low point at which the ratios are
smallest. Costs and rock volumes are minimum at this optimal dam height. For
example, this height is 0.7 m for single-fence and 1.1 m for double-fence dams
on a 22% gradient.

The relatively rapid increase in costs and rock volumes with decreasing dam
height below the optimum is explained by the large increase in the number of
dams required. At heights greater than optimum, the ratios increase again but at
a slower rate because dam height has a greater influence on costs and rock
volume than does number of dams.

If sediment deposit values are related to costs, it can be shown that treatments using dams higher than about 0.7 m, installed on relatively low gradients,
have a beneficial ratio. As mentioned previously, other benefits will always enter
the decision-making process. All curves (Fig. 12-6) indicate increasing sediment
benefits with effective dam height, because sediment catch is directly related to
structural height.

A computerized program for the design of gully control is available (Heede
and Weatherred, 1981). This program greatly eases the design and delivers several
options in type of structure and effective dam height related to sediment catch
and treatment costs. Consisting of two phases, it requires only few field survey
data. While phase 1 gives estimates based on selected representative gully cross
sections and segments, phase 2 delivers construction plans for each dam, material
requirements, sediment catch and benefit, and costs. For phase 2, gully bottom
and bank width, and depth for each structural site must be determined. Phase 1,
which is well suited for inventory purposes, shows the magnitude of projects
in terms of material and funding requirements and thus helps in decision making.

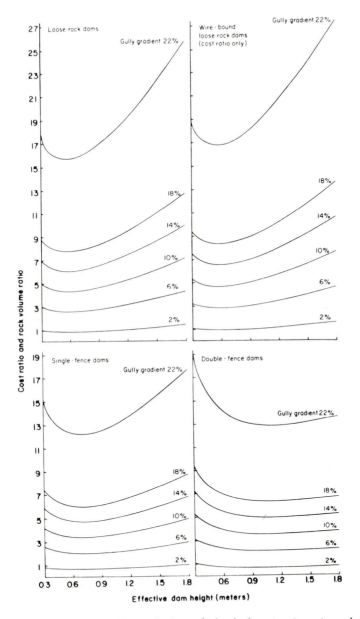

Figure 12-5. Relative cost of installation of check dam treatments and relative angular rock volume requirements in gullies with different gradients as a function of effective dam height (from Heede, 1976).

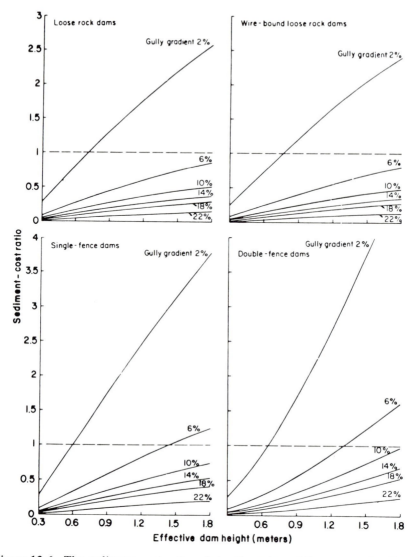

Figure 12-6. The sediment-cost ratio relates the value of the expected sediment deposits to the cost of treatment (Heede, 1976). The graphs show this ratio as a function of effective dam height on gully gradients ranging from 2 to 22%. The base cost was taken as \$20 m^{-3} of angular rock dam; the value of 1 m^3 of sediment deposits was assumed to be one-tenth of that cost.

Conclusion

In most desert environments, ORVs can cause plant and surface soil destruction that leads to local base level changes and loss of equilibrium condition—in other words, erosion. If nature is left alone, long time spans are required before dynamic equilibrium is reestablished. Although it is costly, man can hasten the adjustment processes by raising or stabilizing local base levels, thus reducing erosion and downstream sediment delivery and speeding plant establishment. A lasting plant cover, however sparse, and possibly representing an ecosystem quite different from the original, will signify attainment of a new equilibrium condition.

In semidesert environments, submerged burlap strips were used successfully for erosion control on road-cut slopes and on steep waterways. For gullies, however, larger structures are required to stabilize base levels and help plant growth. Check dams have proved to be very effective. Effective height is the most important criterion in the design of dams, because it controls number of dams, costs, sediment catch, and final depth of gully. Functional relationships and design criteria have been established to guide the land manager toward successful gully control projects.

References

Eckert, R. E., Jr., M. K. Wood, W. H. Blackburn, and F. F. Peterson. 1979. Impacts of Off-Road Vehicles on Infiltration and Sediment Production of Two Desert Soils. J. Range Management 32(5):394–397.

Heede, B. H. 1965. Multipurpose Prefabricated Concrete Check Dam. U.S. Dept. Agriculture Forest Service Research Paper RM-12. Rocky Mountain Forest and Range Experiment Station, Fort Collins, Colorado, 16 pp.

Heede, B. H. 1966. Design, Construction and Cost of Rock Check Dams. U.S. Dept. Agriculture U.S. Forest Service Research Paper RM-20, Rocky Mountain Forest and Range Experiment Station, Fort Collins, Colorado, 24 pp.

Heede, B. H. 1970. Morphology of Gullies in the Colorado Rocky Mountains. Bull. Intl. Assoc. Sci. Hydrol. 15:79–89.

Heede, B. H. 1974. Stages of Development of Gullies in Western United States of America. Z. Geomorphol. 18(3):260–271.

Heede, B. H. 1975. Submerged Burlap Strips Aided Rehabilitation of Disturbed Semi-Arid Sites in Colorado and New Mexico. U.S. Dept. Agriculture Forest Service Research Note RM-302, Rocky Mountain Forest and Range Experiment Station, Fort Collins, Colorado, 8 pp.

Heede, B. H. 1976. Gully Development and Control: The Status of Our Knowledge. U.S. Dept. Agriculture Forest Service Research Paper RM-169, Rocky Mountain Forest and Range Experiment Station, Fort Collins, Colorado, 42 pp.

Heede, B. H. 1977. Case Study of a Watershed Rehabilitation Project: Alkali Creek, Colorado. U.S. Dept. Agriculture Forest Service Research Paper RM-189, Rocky Mountain Forest and Range Experiment Station, Fort Collins, Colorado, 18 pp.

Heede, B. H. 1978. Designing Gully Control Systems for Eroding Watersheds. Environ. Management 2(6):509–522.

Heede, B. H., and J. Weatherred. 1981. CAGCOM, a Program for Designing Dams for Gully Control. WSDG Applications Document WSDG-AD-00003, Watershed Systems Development Group, Fort Collins, Colorado, 20 pp. and 2 appendices.

Knott, J. M. 1978. Reconnaissance Assessment of Erosion and Sedimentation in the Cañada de Los Alamos Basin, Los Angeles and Ventura Counties, California. U.S. Geological Survey Open-File Report 78-873, 31 pp.

Wilshire, H. G. 1977. Study Results of Nine States Used by Off-Road Vehicles that Illustrate Land Modifications. U.S. Geological Survey Open-File Report 77-601, 22 pp.

Appendix : Symbols

α	angle referring to the gully gradient
A_R	the angle of repose of rock
B_A	the breadth of loose rock or wire-bound loose rock dams, measured at one-half the depth of spillway
B_{SF}	the breadth of single-fence dams, measured at one-half the depth of spillway
C	the discharge coefficient, taken at 1.65
c	a constant referring to the gully gradient
D	the depth of the gully
G	gully gradient in percent
H	the total height of dam
H_E	the effective height of dam, the elevation of the crest of the spillway above the original gully bottom
H_S	the depth of spillway of a dam
K	constant, referring to the expected sediment gradient
L	effective length of the weir
L_A	the average length of dam
L_{AS}	the effective length of spillway
L_B	the bottom length of the gully
L_U	the width of the gully between the gully brinks
M_L	the length of the wire mesh of a wire-bound dam
M_{LB}	the length of the wire mesh of the bank protection, measured parallel to the thalweg
M_{LD}	the length of the wire mesh for a double-fence dam
M_W	the width of the wire mesh of a wire-bound dam, measured parallel to the thalweg
N_B	the number of fence posts of the bank protection work
N_{DF}	the number of fence posts of the dam proper of a double-fence dam
N_{SF}	the number of fence posts of the dam proper of a single-fence dam
Q	the rate of the peak flow in $m^3 sec^{-1}$ based on the design storm
R	ratio between sediment gradient and original gully gradient
S	spacing of check dams
V_A	the volume of the apron and bank protection
V_{HC}	the volume of a headcut control structure
V_{DF}	the volume of the dam proper of a double-fence dam
V_K	the volume of the key
V_{LR}	the volume of the dam proper of a loose rock dam
V_{SF}	the volume of the dam proper of a single-fence dam
V_{SP}	the volume of the spillway of loose rock and wire-bound loose rock dams
V_{SDF}	the volume of the spillway of a double-fence dam
V_{SSF}	the volume of the spillway of a single-fence dam
Y	the depth of the key

13

Recovery of Perennial Vegetation in Military Maneuver Areas[1]

Earl W. Lathrop

Introduction

The California deserts have been used for many years as training grounds for the armed forces of the United States. Figure 13-1 shows the distribution of military camp and vehicular exercise impacts related to the World War II General Patton training areas in the early 1940s, the "Desert Strike" operation in 1964, and "Bold Eagle" joint readiness exercise in 1976 in the California Desert as interpreted from aerial photographs (K. Berry, personal communication, 1978). In addition to these full-scale training exercises, ongoing military impacts arise from the active military bases at Fort Irwin, Twenty-nine Palms, China Lake, and the Chocolate Mountains in California, and in many other areas throughout the world's deserts.

Two sites of General Patton's World War II training areas were studied to survey the impacts of armored maneuvers on perennial vegetation of the eastern Mojave Desert, California. These data on heavily concentrated use between the years 1938 and 1942 can be useful for determining recovery rates of vegetation and predicting the longevity of disturbances created by off-road vehicle use.

Two time periods were studied to assess recovery. First, aerial photographs were analyzed to determine recovery between 1953 and 1974. The second phase of the study was an on-site ground analysis of differences between the disturbed and control (undisturbed) sites to detect the extent of recovery from the original disturbance over a period of approximately 36 years. Measurements of the

---

[1]The views and conclusions contained in this chapter are based on the author's studies or experiences and do not necessarily represent the official viewpoint or policy of any U.S. government agency.

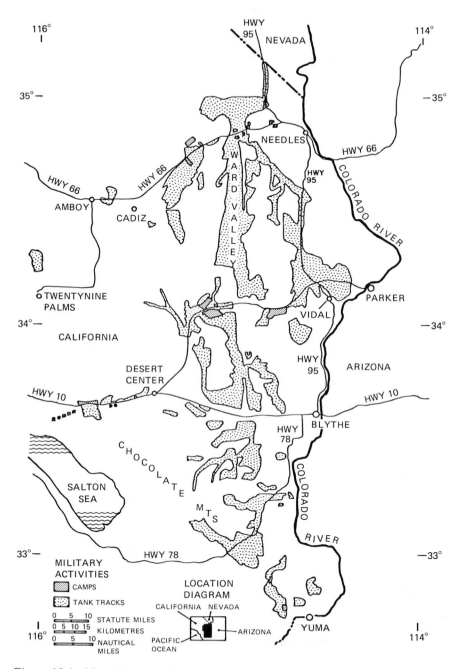

Figure 13-1. Map showing distribution of historic military maneuvers in the California Desert (map drawn by S. Stielstra; K. Berry, personal communication, 1978).

ground transects were made in approximately the same locations as the aerial photographic analyses (Lathrop, 1978). While absolute values of the aerial photographic analyses were not directly comparable to ground measurements due to lower resolution of the aerial photographs, relative values were useful to assess recovery over the 21-year period.

General Patton's Tank Maneuver Areas:
Camps Ibis and Essex

The two Patton training areas studied were Camp Ibis, 32 km northwest of Needles, and Camp Essex, 4.5 km north of Essex, San Bernardino County, California. The areas consist of gravelly alluvial substrate with gentle slopes at elevations of 510 m and 615 m for Camps Ibis and Essex, respectively. Soil surface conditions at both sites are approximately 80 to 90% gravel-pavement. Rainfall averages 152 mm or less annually, with a wide range of diurnal and seasonal temperatures (Iwasiuk, 1979).

The dominant plant community of the sites is creosote bush scrub (Thorne, 1976). Perennials associated with creosote bush *(Larrea tridentata)* are burrobush *(Ambrosia dumosa)*, krameria *(Krameria parvifolia)*, cheesebush *(Hymenoclea salsola)*, and others (Table 13-1).

The impacts of General Patton's armored maneuvers were assessed in three use categories: (1) tank areas (Fig. 13-2); (2) tent areas (Fig. 13-3); (3) roadways (Fig. 13-4).

Methods

The techniques used in aerial photographic analyses are outlined in Chapter 8. Ground transects utilized the point-quarter method (Brower and Zar, 1977) to assess differences/similarities between tank tracks, tent areas, and roadways (use categories) and their respective controls. Determinations of productivity, diversity, and stability from which impacts were assessed, followed procedures similar to those of Vasek et al. (1975a, b), Johnson et al. (1975), and Lathrop and Archbold (1980a, b). Productivity was determined from density, expressed as number of individual perennials per hectare (No. ha^{-1}) and cover, expressed as percentage of ground covered by the plant crowns.

Diversity is expressed as richness (R) or number of species in the transect; by evenness (V), a measure of how equally the species are represented in the sample; and by equibility (E_c), another measure of evenness (McIntosh, 1967). Stability was estimated from data provided by (a) percentage composition (relative cover); (b) percentage cover in relation to relative age span of perennial species, expressed as a community quality index (CQI) as proposed by Vasek et al. (1975a, b) and Johnson et al. (1975); and (c) mean percentage recovery for perennials in test (disturbed) and control transects.

Table 13-1. Ground Transect Comparison of Mean Relative Cover of Perennial Plants in Control and Test Areas of Camps Ibis and Essex

Creosote bush scrub community species	N	Control	N	Tent	N	Tracks	N	Road
Ambrosia dumosa	168	34.1	191	47.7	88	17.4	158	49.4
Brickellia incana			17	6.8			29	11.0
Krameria parvifolia		2			10	2.3		
Echinocactus polycephalus			1	0.1				
Eriogonum fasciculatum			2	1.0				
Hymenoclea salsola					1	0.1	1	1.0
Larrea tridentata	83	63.3	65	43.9	141	77.9	34	38.4
Lycium cooperi			1	0.2				
Opuntia ramosissima	2	0.4			6	2.2		
Stephanomeria pauciflora	1	2.0	3	0.2			2	0.1

Relative cover[a]

[a]Relative cover is percentage of total cover contributed by each species. N, number of plants sampled.

Figure 13-2. Tank tracks 36 years after use in Camp Ibis, T11N, R21E, Sec. 28 (January 28, 1978).

Figure 13-3. Tent area in Camp Essex, T8N, R16E, Sec. 11 (December 18, 1977).

Figure 13-4. Roadway in an armored maneuvers area of Camp Essex T11N, R21E, Sec. 28 (January 29, 1978).

Values for V range from 0 to 1; the greater the number the more even the number of individuals represented in each site. Values for E_c range from zero. The greater the value of E_c, the more equible or evenly represented is each individual in each site. Values for CQI range from zero. The larger the number, the more stable long-lived perennials there are in a community. Transect similarity was compared by Jaccard's coefficient of community similarity (CCj) (Brower and Zar, 1977). Values for CCj range from 0 to 1. Generally a similarity of about 0.7 or higher indicates virtual indentity between communities.

Results

Results of on-site ground transect comparisons of test and control areas, approximately 36 years after the end of the Patton maneuvers, are shown in Tables 13-1 and 13-2 and Figure 13-5. Table 13-1 shows differences in composition between control and test areas, indicating that diversity of the dominant perennials has been altered. It was not feasible to construct an accurate picture of diversity using the values of R, E_c, and V alone because of the low richness (R) in the two study sites and the relatively low N values of the subdominants (Table 13-1). However, the diversity index (DI) values of Table 13-3, reported for Camps Ibis and Essex by Iwasiuk (1979), indicate a decrease in diversity in all disturbed transects as compared to their respective controls.

Table 13-2. Ground Transect Comparison of Density and Cover Means of Perennial Plants in Control and Test Areas of Camps Ibis and Essex

Area	Number of transect points	N^a	Density (No. ha^{-1})	Cover (%)
Control	64	256	2338	8.2
Tent	70	280	1699	4.2
Track	62	248	1077	2.9
Road	56	224	782	1.4

[a]N, number of plants sampled.

Productivity, as represented by density and cover, also has been affected by the original disturbance. Table 13-2 shows significant reduction of density and cover in disturbed areas compared to the control. Tent areas show the least reduction in productivity, with a drop of 27 and 29%, respectively, for density and cover. Tank track areas show a reduction of 54 and 65% for density and cover, respectively.

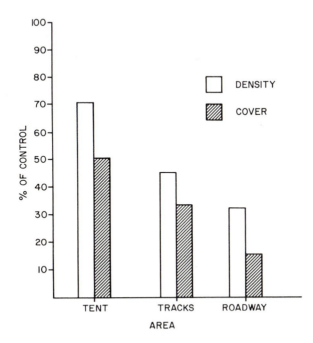

Figure 13-5. Ground transect comparison of mean percentage recovery between the years 1942 and 1978 for perennial plants of Camps Ibis and Essex.

Table 13-3. Diversity Measurements Computed from Densities (No. ha^{-1}) of Perennial Vegetation at Camps Ibis and Essex

Area[a]	Transects[b]			
	Tank tracks	Roadway	Tent area	Control
Ibis				
R	5	5	7	4
E_c	4.00	4.03	4.37	3.01
V	.600	.514	.363	.589
Essex				
R	5	2	3	3
E_c	4.10	1.38	2.05	2.10
V	.656	.321	.631	.494

[a]R, richness (number of species); E_c, equibility; V, evenness.
[b]Calculations based on ground measurements.

Recovery Rates

Recovery of perennial vegetation in the disturbed areas between the years 1942 and 1978, as determined from the ground transects, is graphically shown in Figure 13-5. Percentage recovery to control levels is greatest for tent areas, less so in tank track areas, and least for roadways.

Recovery between the years 1953 and 1974, as determined from aerial photographic analyses, is shown in Table 13-4 and Figure 13-6. Recovery over the 21-year period was highest in roadways, showing a positive change of 23 and 62% for density and cover, respectively. The increase in density and cover of vegetation in the control areas, over the same period of time, was 6 and 5%,

Table 13-4. Aerial Photographic Comparison of 1953 and 1974 Density and Cover Means of Perennial Plants of Camps Ibis and Essex

Area	Number of quadrats	N^a	Density (No. ha^{-1})		Cover (%)	
			1953	1974	1953	1974
Control	240	2986	310		19.1	
		3167		330		20.1
Tent	240	1839	192		9.4	
		2127		222		12.0
Tracks	240	2359	245		10.9	
		2958		270		13.7
Road	240	255	27		1.1	
		340		35		2.9

[a]N, number of plants sampled.

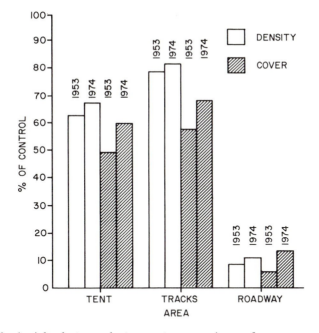

Figure 13-6. Aerial photograph transect comparison of mean percentage recovery between the years 1953 and 1974 for perennial plants of Camps Ibis and Essex.

respectively. Tent areas showed the next highest recovery, with tank tracks showing the least recovery between the years 1953 and 1974.

Estimated Time Span for Recovery

Study site values for density and cover were averaged and compared with the year of disturbance to determine estimates of time span for recovery. There are many variables and assumptions to be taken into consideration in assessing time for vegetation recovery following a disturbance (Lathrop and Archbold, 1980a, b; Chapter 14). Any time span arrived at is only a rough estimate at best. However, assuming a linear relationship, based on quantitiative data from field sites, estimates of recovery time for vegetation for Camps Ibis and Essex are shown in Table 13-5. These values, however, are based only on return to quantitative control levels of density and cover. Recovery time for the vegetation to a predisturbance percentage composition quality would be much greater if at all.

Recovery time is also a function of the amount of initial compaction (Webb and Wilshire, 1980; see Chapter 14). Thus, roadways will require the greatest time period for recovery, followed by tank tracks and tent areas.

In comparing recovery time of Patton's maneuver areas with those of utility corridor construction in the Mojave Desert, Vasek et al. (1975b) indicate 33

Table 13-5. Mean Recovery Estimates of Perennial Vegetation Density and Cover for Camps Ibis and Essex

	Time span for recovery (years)		
Unit	Tank track	Tent	Roadway
Density	65	45	112
Cover	76	58	212

years for significant recovery under pylons of powerlines following initial disturbance. Vasek et al. (1975a), in reference to recovery from pipeline construction, state that the creosote bush scrub community is fragile and easily destroyed but does have a long-term potential, probably measured in many centuries, for recovery from even drastic disturbance such as a pipeline. This is higher than the approximately 70 years recovery estimate for plant biomass of the Los Angeles aqueduct constructions in Kern County, California (Lathrop and Archbold, 1980a). Rice and Walgren (1972) and Kay (1979) also comment on recovery along the Los Angeles aqueducts. Mean recovery of biomass from construction of seven powerlines and five pipeline utility corridors in the Mojave Desert, studied by Lathrop and Archbold (1980b), is estimated to be approximately 100 years.

Conclusions

Productivity

In both ground (Table 13-2) and aerial (Table 13-3) measurements of density and cover, it can be readily observed that the use categories can be ranked according to disturbance category. Roadways display the greatest reductions in density and cover followed by tank tracks and tent areas. This may be due to the fact that building roadways and repeated passage of heavy equipment (tanks, trucks, etc.) eliminated individuals and altered the substrate by removal and/or compaction of topsoil. The sequence suggests that the tent areas did not undergo substrate alteration to the extent that the tank tracks and roadways did.

It is apparent that of the two values of productivity used here, cover appears to be more involved in recovery than does density. Observation of Figure 13-6 shows comparatively little increase in shrub density over the 21-year period compared to a greater increase in cover. While there was little change in numbers of individuals over the 21 years compared to control vegetation, the few individuals that survived would be expected to measureably increase the area they cover in these transect sites.

Table 13-6. Jaccard's Coefficient of Similarity (CCj) for Pairs of Transects at Camps Ibis and Essex

| Area | Transects compared[a] | | |
	A/B	A/C	A/D
Ibis	.55	.35	.20
Essex	.51	.35	.19

[a]Calculations based on total percentage cover of ground measurement data. A, control; B, tent area; C, tank tracks; D, roadway.

Stability

Table 13-6 shows a trend of decreasing community similarity, as compared to the control, with increased disturbance and use intensity. Comparisons between control and roadway transects (A/D) show the least similarity. The values of CCj decrease with increasing dissimilarity between the control and disturbed site transects.

Table 13-7 clearly shows a pattern in community quality index values between transects in both study areas. The values of CQI decrease with increasing disturbance intensity.

In summary, concentrated use at the Patton training camps has resulted in significant reductions in vegetation densities and covers, despite the long period of time (36 years) for recovery. There are also differences in percentage composition between disturbance and control areas, indicating alteration of both plant stability and diversity. The degree of negative impact on the plants tends to vary with intensity of use. The differences which can be seen in ground transect comparisons of test and control areas may be a function of the amount of original compaction of the soil or possibly postabandonment use of roads by off-road vehicles. Roadways display the greatest reduction in density and cover followed by tank tracks and tent areas.

Table 13-7. Community Quality Indices (CQI) for Perennial Vegetation at Camps Ibis and Essex

| Area | Transects | | | |
	Tank tracks	Roadway	Tent area	Control
Ibis	2.6	1.0	3.8	7.5
Essex	3.1	1.7	4.5	8.7

[a]Calculations based on percentage of perennial cover in relation to percentage of long-lived species.

Recovery estimates indicate that the time required for recovery of density and cover to predisturbance levels is somewhat greater than the time which has elapsed between the original disturbance and this study. In any case, recovery time of community vigor and composition will apparently be many times greater than that estimated for recovery of density and cover alone and could possibly not even occur at all in the foreseeable future.

All parameters analyzed show significant levels of negative results with the exception of richness, which shows perhaps a slight increase. This fact, however, may contribute to community instability, depending on species composition.

Management Recommendations

The fact that Patton's maneuver areas and camps are still clearly outlined in the desert vegetation and soil (Fig. 13-2, 13-3, and 13-4) after approximately 36 years attests to the longevity of the impact of military maneuvers. The visible scars left on the vegetation and landscape at the Ibis and Essex Camps might well be reflective of what is to be expected in the future in the California Desert as a result of the impact of off-road vehicle (ORV) use there (Chapter 8). Results observed at the Patton camps and ORV use sites in the California desert should be similar to what might be expected in other arid climates receiving similar intensity of use.

Acknowledgments

This study was supported by the U.S. Bureau of Land Management, Desert Plan Program, Riverside, California. Special appreciation goes to Hyrum B. Johnson and other members of the Desert Plan Program for the guidance and help they gave. Thanks goes to Robert F. Thorne for help in determination of plant specimens during the field work phase of these studies and for his critical review of pertinent portions of the manuscript.

References

Brower, J. E., and J. H. Zar. 1977. Field and Laboratory Methods for General Ecology. Wm. C. Brown Co., Dubuque, Iowa, 194 pp.

Iwasiuk, R. J. 1979. Plant response parameters to General Patton's armored maneuvers in the eastern Mojave Desert of California. Unpublished M.A. thesis, Loma Linda University, Loma Linda, California, 85 pp.

Johnson, H. B., F. C. Vasek, and T. Yonkers. 1975. Productivity, diversity and stability relationships in Mojave Desert roadside vegetation. Bull. Torrey Bot. Club 102:106–114.

Kay, B. L. 1979. Summary of Revegetation Attempts on the Second Los

Angeles Aqueduct. Mojave Revegetation Notes No. 22, Dept. of Agronomy and Range Science, University of California, Davis, California, 23 pp.

Lathrop, E. W. 1978. Plant Response Parameters to Recreational Vehicles in the California Desert Conservation Area. Final Report, Contract Ca-060-CT7-2824, Desert Plan Program, Bureau of Land Management, Riverside, California, 240 pp.

Lathrop, E. W., and E. F. Archbold. 1980a. Plant response to Los Angeles adueduct construction in the Mojave Desert. Environ. Management 4(2):137–148.

Lathrop, E. W., and E. F. Archbold. 1980b. Plant response to utility construction in the Mojave Desert. Environ. Management 4(3):215–226.

McIntosh, R. P. 1967. An index of diversity and the relation of certain concepts to diversity. Ecology 48:392–404.

Rice, C. M., and L. Walgren. 1972. Rehabilitation of Disturbed Arid Areas with Native Desert Species in the Mojave Desert. File Report, U.S. Bureau of Land Management, Bakersfield, California, 12 pp.

Thorne, R. F. 1976. The vascular plant communities of Southern California. In: J. Latting (Ed.), Plant Communities of Southern California. California Native Plant Society Special Publication No. 2, Riverside, California, pp. 1–31.

Thorne, R. F., B. A. Prigge, and J. Henrickson. 1981. A flora of the higher ranges and the Kelso dunes of the Eastern Mojave Desert in California. Aliso 10(1):71–186.

Vasek, F. C., H. B. Johnson, and D. H. Eslinger. 1975a. Effects of pipeline construction on creosote bush scrub vegetation of the Mojave Desert. Madrono 23:1–13.

Vasek, F. C., H. B. Johnson, and G. D. Brum. 1975b. Effects of power transmission lines on vegetation of the Mojave Desert. Madrono 23:114–130.

Webb, R. H., and H. G. Wilshire. 1980. Recovery of soils and vegetation in a Mojave Desert ghost town, Nevada, U.S.A. J. Arid Environ. 3:1–15.

14

Natural Recovery of Soils and Vegetation Following Human Disturbance[1]

Robert H. Webb, Howard G. Wilshire, and Mary Ann Henry

Introduction

Strange how long the soil keeps the impression of any continuous treading, even after grass has overgrown it. Twenty years since, a brief heyday of mining at Black Mountain made a stage road across the Ceriso, yet the parallel lines that are the wheel traces show from the height dark and well defined. Afoot in the Ceriso one looks in vain for any sign of it. (Austin, 1904)

Humans have disturbed desert soils and vegetation since man began to occupy arid lands. These disturbances were usually restricted to areas adjacent to towns or villages and resulted from tillage, mining, or access trails and roads. With increasing population, development of off-road vehicles (ORVs), and over-grazing, ever larger areas of the desert have been affected. These disturbed areas usually are partially or totally denuded and the soils compacted, causing an acceleration of the natural erosion rate. As the demand for use of these lands changes, disturbed areas are commonly abandoned to recover as best they can. An important management consideration for desert areas is the amount of time required for disturbed areas to recover naturally, because artificial reclamation techniques are very expensive and prone to failure when applied to large arid areas (Chapters 15 through 17).

The response of desert areas to disturbance can be observed at numerous sites in the southwestern United States which have been abandoned in prehistoric or

[1] The views and conclusions contained in this chapter are based on the authors' studies or experiences and do not necessarily represent the official viewpoint or policy of any U.S. government agency.

historic time. Examples of such sites include the prehistoric Anasazi pueblos and road systems around Chaco Canyon, New Mexico, abandoned approximately 800 years BP (Ware and Gumerman, 1977); prehistoric intaglios and associated trails in the Mojave and Sonoran Deserts (see Chapter 11); historic routes of travel such as Emigrant Trail, the Pony Express Trail, the Old Government Road (Casebier, 1975), and others; ghost towns and mining areas (e.g., Paher, 1971); agricultural fields, cleared and abandoned; livestock exclosures (Blydenstein et al., 1957; Gardner, 1950); abandoned military maneuver areas (see Chapter 13); aqueduct and powerline construction corridors (Lathrop and Archbold, 1980a, b; Vasek et al., 1975a, b); and abandoned subdivision streets. Because of the increasing accessibility of the desert to motorized recreation, most abandoned sites have undergone further disturbances which render them useless for measurement of soil and vegetation recovery. However, some sites have been undisturbed since abandonment because of their unique locations within military installations or national parks, fencing on private property, inaccessibility, or large areal coverage, and these are suitable for quantitative study of recovery rates.

"Recovery" of disturbed soils and vegetation is a concept that has different meanings in different contexts. The term is used here to mean that a "recovered" area has soil and vegetation with properties comparable to those of ambient undisturbed conditions, and the "recovery time" is the amount of time required for restoration of a disturbed area to this condition. Implicit in this definition of recovery is the assumption that soils and vegetation, given sufficient time after disturbance, will revert to a state comparable to the ambient undisturbed condition. In some cases, such as the partial or complete erosional loss of a relic soil or removal of relic vegetation, recovery may never take place. However, this usage of the recovery concept does take into account the long-term fluctuations in desert vegetation which may result from periodic drought and possible grazing influence because the vegetation on the abandoned disturbed site is always compared with the current assemblage of undisturbed vegetation.

Processes of Soil Recovery from Compaction

The recovery of soil properties to ambient conditions is a complicated process that involves numerous factors. The discussion here is limited to noneroded, compacted soils, because rates of soil formation in arid regions are so slow that recovery on a time scale relevant to humans is not possible. Moreover, Charley and Cowling (1968) estimated conservatively that removal of 0.1 m of an arid-region soil would reduce nitrogen, phosphorus, and organic material by 27%, 21%, and 38%, respectively, in the upper 0.45 m of soil; such depletion would obviously be an additional factor retarding revegetation.

The most important factor determining recovery from compaction is the magnitude of the density increase and the variation of the density increase with depth (see Chapter 4). The magnitude of compaction is very important because some lightly compacted soils may not undergo change [as suggested by Heinonen (1977)] or may recover at an imperceptible rate; the important management consideration for a lightly compacted soil is the magnitude of the influence the compaction exerts on plant growth and frequency of runoff generation. However, highly compacted soils should loosen upon abandonment, more quickly at shallow depth than deeper. Thorud and Frissel (1976) remarked that it is indeed fortunate that the greatest soil compaction occurs near or at the soil surface because it receives the most weathering and environmental extremes and hence recovers most rapidly.

Loosening of highly compacted soils is generally ascribed to the physical processes of clay-mineral expansion during wetting and freeze-thaw heaving in combination with biological activity. Clay-mineral expansion, or shrink-swell, is most prevalent in smectitic (montmorillonitic) clay soils and the rate at which a compacted soil loosens is dependent on the amount of expansive clay in the soil, the depth of water penetration, the frequency of wetting and drying cycles, and the depth of the compaction in the soil. In desert areas with a winter-dominated rainfall pattern and cool weather, the frequency of wetting and drying cycles is relatively low because the soil tends to remain moist throughout the winter and early spring when sufficient rainfall has occurred. However, soils in areas with a summer-dominated rainfall have more frequent wetting and drying cycles as a result of recurring thunderstorms and subsequent hot weather.

Freeze-thaw loosening reduces soil compaction in colder regions (Orr, 1975) although the loosening may only occur above 0.2 m (Blake et al., 1976; Larson and Allmaras, 1971; van Ouwerkerk, 1968). The effectiveness of freeze-thaw loosening is dependent upon the amount of soil water, soil texture, and depth and rate of frost penetration, and the depth of compaction in the soil. The effects of frost heaving are inseparable from wetting and drying because the freezing of water in the soil involves a dessication of clay minerals (Larson and Allmaras, 1971). Freeze-thaw loosening would probably be most effective in deserts with cold winters (e.g., Great Basin Desert) as opposed to deserts that experience only periodic frost (e.g., Mojave Desert).

One recent experiment showed the effectiveness of these processes. Akram and Kemper (1979) applied both wetting and drying and freeze-thaw cycles to compacted samples of silty clay, clay loam, sandy loam, and loamy sand. They found that most of the change in infiltration rate, which can be considered as an index of the amount of compaction a soil has undergone, occurred during the first three cycles although the resulting infiltration rates were still below the pre-compaction rates; these data indicate that some form of exponential-decay model would be appropriate in modeling the loosening of compacted soils empricially. Both freeze-thaw and wetting and drying were most effective in clay-rich soils while the loamy sand tested changed very little after four cycles.

Biological activity is probably more important than physical processes in loosening compacted, coarse-grained desert soils. Soil fauna and rodents are very important in loosening compacted soils, especially at depth, although the invasion of animals into areas with compacted soil is somewhat dependent upon the rate of secondary plant succession. Roots penetrating the soil cause very local compaction near the root surface (Larson and Allmaras, 1971) but can cause a volume expansion near the soil surface; and small channels are left in the soil after the root dies. This suggests that loosening would best be accomplished by plants with diffuse root systems as opposed to plants with central taproots because the small diffuse roots displace less of the high-strength, compacted soil per root while penetrating the soil with more roots per unit volume. The effectiveness of biological activity in loosening compacted soil is dependent on the availability of these types of plants, usually annuals, for invasion and the ability of these plants to overcome high stress conditions.

Many recent studies have discussed the rate of recovery from compaction as a product of a combination of these processes. Vorhees et al. (1978), studying the compaction of a silty clay loam, found that bulk densities remained high at 0.15 to 0.45 m depths while tillage and freeze-thaw loosening had rendered the 0 to 150 mm depth densities not statistically different from the uncompacted soil densities over one winter. Orr (1975) studied grazing exclosures in South Dakota and measured significant recovery of a sandy loam after 2 years (probably resulting from freeze-thaw loosening), but compacted subsurface soil had not shown signs of recovery by the end of the 4-year study. Thorud and Frissel (1976), studying the compaction of a sandy loam/loamy sand soil in Minnesota, measured a recovery time of between $4\frac{1}{2}$ and $8\frac{3}{4}$ years for soil in the 0 to 76 mm depth range, while compaction at a depth of 0.15 to 0.23 m was unchanged after 8 years. Ivanov (1976) reported that recovery from compaction in well-drained soils required 5 to 7 years, while poorly drained soils required 15 years in spruce forests in the USSR; no soil textures were given. Ivanov's study illustrates the importance of moisture content cycling to recovery from compaction.

Greacen and Sands (1980) reported that vehicle tracks on sandy soils in South Australia pine forests were still compacted compared to ambient undisturbed soil after 50 years. Blake et al. (1976) found that compacted clay loam at 0.3 to 0.4 m depth had not shown significant recovery after 9 years in Minnesota. Dickerson (1976) measured significant loosening of soils at 0 to 50 mm depth, ranging in texture from a loamy sand to a silty clay loam compacted by logging skidders in northern Mississippi; he predicted a complete recovery time of 12 years on the basis of a linear-regression model but did not specify the soil texture to which this recovery time applies. Van Ouwerkerk (1968) measured no change in the pore space of compacted soil at greater than 70 mm depth over a $3\frac{1}{2}$ year period; compacted subsoil cropping and manure treatments caused no amelioration of compaction over a $6\frac{1}{2}$ year span. These studies were all made in regions of greater than 500 mm year^{-1} of rainfall; only one study of soil recovery has been completed in an arid region (Webb and Wilshire, 1980; see Example IV).

Secondary Plant Succession in Compacted Soils

Recovery of vegetation may take place by secondary plant succession in compacted soils. We recognize the problems of application of the term "succession" to recovery of desert vegetation (see Chapter 7) but nonetheless use the concept here to describe the changes a plant assemblage undergoes during recovery. Secondary plant succession is a special case of plant succession in general but follows a somewhat different pattern. Vasek (1982) listed the trend of secondary succession in deserts as (1) an early state of invasion by pioneer annuals and shrubs with low stature and short life span; (2) an increase in biomass, height, and cover of perennial species as the pioneer species are replaced by inter-mediate- and long-lived species; (3) an increase in species diversity as changes in microclimate and soils occur; and (4) a shift from a producing to a maintaining state as the composition of long-lived species approaches the predisturbance level. Succession in disturbed areas is partly controlled by changes in soil prop-erties with time, which influence the types of productivity of species that can grow in the soil. One property of soil that greatly impedes plant growth is the increased density resulting from compaction (see Barnes et al., 1971); hence, the rate at which plant succession occurs is also somewhat dependent upon the rate of soil loosening.

This model of secondary succession involves the assumption that natural restoration of the composition of species present before the disturbance or present under ambient conditions is possible. Although this assumption has been used to predict full recovery times of "many centuries" (Vasek et al., 1975a), several "millenia" (Vasek, 1981), or "thousands of years" (Webb and Wilshire, 1980), and less than a century (Lathrop and Archbold, 1980a, b) in the Mojave Desert, it has yet to be demonstrated that succession into compacted soil ends with a vegetative assemblage the same as the predisturbance or ambient vegeta-tion with respect to cover, composition, and biomass of the long-lived, dominant species. Data from some areas suggest that opportunistic species not found in abundance before disturbance may become established in the disturbed soil to the possible exclusion of the dominant, predisturbance species. Studies of archaeological sites in the southwestern United States have found that certain species which are not found in significant quantities in the surrounding vegeta-tion are present on prehistoric Indian ruins abandoned 600 to 1000 years BP (Clark, 1968). This invasion may be a temporary state of the successional trend but could also be the end point of vegetation recovery because soil moisture may be controlled by the invading species to the exclusion of other species (Webb and Wilshire, 1980). Considering the longevity of some desert species (Chap-ter 17, Table 17-2), any succession will necessarily require large amounts of time if species are systematically displaced.

Introduction of nonnative species which may be at a competitive advantage under the harsh conditions of compacted soil poses an additional complication in the trend of secondary succession into disturbed soil. Livestock grazing can promote growth of nonnative brome grasses (*Bromus tectorum;* Robertson and Kennedy, 1954) in the southwestern United States and possibly enhance the spread of other nonnative species (*Erodium circutarium* and *Schismus barbatus;* Webb and Stielstra, 1979). Russian thistle *(Salsola iberica)* is a common invader in disturbed areas throughout the southwest. These species may become well established in both the undisturbed and disturbed areas following introduction into the disturbed area (Beatley, 1966).

Another influence on the rate of plant reestablishment is the presence or ab-sence of mycorrhizal fungi in the soil. Reeves et al. (1979) studied vegetation invading an abandoned road in a western Colorado sage assemblage. They found that plants comprising 99% of the total cover were infected by mycorrhizal fungi while only 1% of the total cover in the road was contributed by infected plants. Plants infected by microrrhizal fungi have an increased ability to absorb phosphorus and possibly other elements, greater water absorption capacities, and faster growth rates (see references in Moorman and Reeves, 1979) and thus are able better to compete in a natural ecosystem than noninfected plants. Moorman and Reeves (1979) found that 2% of corn *(Zea mays)* planted in the soil in the old roadway became infected by micorrhizal fungi while 77% of corn planted in the undisturbed soil became infected. They conclude that disturbance can cause reductions in the number of mycorrhizal spores available for infection of plants, hence retarding succession. Reeves et al. (1979) noted that while most species comprising an undisturbed sage assemblage are mycorrhizal, many of the common pioneer species are nonmycorrhizal; they suggest that the early invasion of nonmycorrhizal species may regard subsequent invasion of mycorrhizal species because the nonmycorrhizal species do not promote the required fungi source for the other mycorrhizal-dependent species.

Examples of Recovery in Disturbed Desert Areas

Sites of disturbed soil and vegetation from which quantitative information on recovery has been obtained include controlled motorcycle impacts, abandoned agricultural fields, two abandoned townsites, areas used for military maneuvers (Chapter 13), and utility corridors.

Example I:
Controlled Study of Motorcycle Impacts on Soil and Vegetation

A controlled study of motorcycle impacts was created in March 1979 in a loamy sand near Fremont Peak in the western Mojave Desert, California (see Chapter 4; Webb, 1982). The motorcycle trails, representing 1, 10, 100, and 200 passes with a 175-cc motorcycle, were allowed to recover for 1 year before remeasurement of soil density. The results, shown in Table 14-1, indicate that compacted soil has been loosened somewhat near the soil surface but is unchanged at depth. The greatest loosening occurred in soils which were highly compacted while the density in the one-pass trail was unchanged, and the most important loosening agent was probably the invasion of a nonnative annual *(Schismus barbatus)* in the trails. Two *Larrea tridentata* shrubs which had all but the root crown destroyed during the motorcycle compaction had shown vigorous growth after 1 year, but several damaged *Atriplex torreyi* showed no signs of revival following destruction of above-ground foliage.

Example II: Abandoned Agricultural Land

Numerous agricultural fields have been abandoned in the western Mojave Desert for a variety of reasons. One such field, located near Ridgecrest, California at NW $\frac{1}{4}$ NW $\frac{1}{4}$ Sec. 30, T26S R40E, was abandoned and fenced approximately 20

Table 14-1. Comparison of Soil Densities Measured Immediately After Motorcycle Use with Densities Measured After One Year, Fremont Park, Western Mojave Desert

| Number of motorcycle passes | Mean of bulk densities (t m^{-3}) | | | | | |
| | 0 to 3 mm depth | | 30 to 60 mm depth | | 0 to 60 mm depth | |
	1979	1980	1979	1980	1979	1980
Undisturbed	1.49		1.58		1.54	
1 pass	1.57	1.55	1.62	1.64	1.60	1.60
10 passes	1.68[a]	1.57	1.67	1.68	1.68[a]	1.62
100 passes	1.78[a]	1.67	1.76	1.78	1.77[b]	1.73
200 passes	1.77[c]	1.67	1.77	1.81	1.77	1.74

[a]Densities significantly different at 0.0005 alpha level, Student's t test.
[b]Densities significantly different at 0.005 alpha level, Student's t test.
[c]Densities significantly different at 0.01 alpha level, Student's t test.

years before our observation. An adjacent area of undisturbed vegetation was present immediately to the west of the abandoned field. Line intercepts measured in May 1979 confirmed the visually obvious fact that the perennial vegetation in the abandoned field was entirely *Atriplex polycarpa* while the adjacent control was the *Larrea-Ambrosia* assemblage typical of the Indian Wells Valley (Table 14-2). While the total areal coverage of vegetation (percentage cover) was the same in both areas, the density of *Atriplex* in the abandoned field was much higher than the total density of all species in the control area because of numerous seedlings and young plants. This illustrates that a disturbed, noncompacted soil can become "stabilized" in a relatively short time span, but a return time to predisturbance conditions is difficult to predict.

Table 14-2. Comparison of Vegetation in an Alfalfa Field Abandoned 20 Years with Adjacent Undisturbed Vegetation, Western Mojave Desert, California

| Species | Abandoned alfalfa field | | Undisturbed | |
	Density[a]	% cover[b]	Density[a]	% cover[b]
Ambrosia dumosa	Not present		2490	14.7
Larrea tridentata	Not present		510	2.6
Oryzopsis hymenoides	Not present		30	0.2
Acamptopappus	Not present		25	0
Ceratoides lanata	Not present		Present	
Opuntia echinocarpa	Not present		Present	
Atriplex polycarpa	7580	17.4	Not present	
Total	7580	17.4	3480	17.4

[a]Number per hectare measured using 200 m of 2-m-wide belt transects.
[b]Number per hectare, measured using 200 m of line intercepts.

The vegetation present in the alfalfa field is an example of how a disturbance can create an opportunity for a species which is not normally a part of the vegetative assemblage to become established and dominate the successional trend. Although salt concentrations from irrigation were not noticeable in the soils, *Atriplex* could be favored in this area because of such accumulations. More likely, this species behaves like *Chrysothamnus nauseosus* which has invaded other nearly disturbed areas where active revegetation efforts have failed (Chapter 16). Reeves et al. (1979) list *C. nauseosus* as a mycorrhizal species while members of the *Atriplex* genus are nonmycorrhizal. It should be noted that the invading *Atriplex* seedlings did not have to overcome the handicap of compacted soil although some residual compaction may have been present beneath the plow layer as a result of farm equipment passage.

Romney et al. (1979) examined a flood-irrigated alfalfa/barley field near Daggett, California that was abandoned in 1956. The field has been affected significantly by wind erosion as shown by mounds of eolian material around nearby shrubs, and some hard clay lenses were exposed in the field. Twenty-three years after abandonment, total cover of perennials varied between 3.5 and 8.1%, whereas the cover in a nearby undisturbed area varied between 10.2 and 18.5%. The principal shrub species present was *Atriplex polycarpa* with some *Larrea tridentata* and *Ambrosia dumosa;* the ratios of cover in the abandoned field to cover in a nearby undisturbed area were 1.39, 0.29, and 0.38 for *Atriplex*, *Larrea*, and *Ambrosia*, respectively. The abandoned field also has fewer species but with a higher density and biomass of annuals than the undisturbed area. Romney et al. (1979) suggest that the growth of annuals is promoted by the lower use of soil moisture by perennials in the abandoned field.

Example III: Utility Corridors

Numerous utility corridors in the Mojave Desert have provided information on recovery of vegetation following severe disturbances. Although utility corridors are the most often used sites for artificial revegetation attempts (Chapters 15 through 17), most disturbed land near utility corridors is simply abandoned to recover naturally once the pipeline or transmission line is in place. Vasek et al. (1975a) studied a pipeline in the southern Mojave Desert which had been constructed 12 years previously. They found that revegetation was highly variable; in general, the better sites, in terms of quality of soil and amount and frequency of rainfall, showed the most recovery in terms of reestablishment of long-lived perennials. Vasek et al. (1975a) used a linear extrapolation to estimate 30 to 40 years for restoration at the best sites but state that the linear model is unrealistic and that "centuries" are probably a more realistic estimate for recovery times.

Vasek et al. (1975b) studied 33-year-old transmission line corridors in the same general area with varying degrees of disturbance: undisturbed vegetation, slight disturbance under transmission wires, "drastic" disturbances under pylons, and road-edge effects. Vasek et al. found that the recovery under the pylons was variable after 33 years but that in all five study areas the cover contributed by *Larrea tridentata* to the total cover under the pylons was 12 to 73% lower than its contribution in the undisturbed area. The total ground cover, however, was higher under the pylons than in the undisturbed area in four of the study areas with a large contribution in cover coming from short-lived species, including *Hymenoclea salsola*. The predictability of vegetation recovery under the pylons was low compared with the less disturbed areas under wires; Vasek et al. (1975b) conclude that after 33 years revegetation has occurred to the extent that the quality of vegetation, as measured with an arbitrary index of cover contribution by long-lived perennials, approaches that of the undisturbed area. Vasek et al. also found that vegetation under the wires and along road edges were slightly enhanced because of water harvesting (Johnson et al., 1975).

Lathrop and Archbold (1980a) studied revegetation along the two Los Angeles aqueducts in the Mojave Desert constructed in 1913 and 1970. Using a linear estimate of above-ground biomass calculated from total percentage cover data, they estimated a recovery time of about 60 years for the aqueduct right-of-way and access-road edges. However, with respect to species composition they expected the recovery time to be "three or more times greater than that estimated for biomass recovery." The known-pioneer shrubs *Chrysothamnus nauseosus* and *C. paniculatus* contributed the greatest amount of biomass (34 to 38%) of any genus of perennial shrub in the 1913 right-of-way and road edges but was insignificant (1.5%) in the control area; similarly, the biomass contribution of *Chrysothamnus* was high along the 1970 aqueduct (19.5 to 21.7% compared to 0.9% in the control) but the pioneer *Hymenoclea salsola* has a greater biomass (25.1 to 30.6%). They conclude that the vegetation along the 1913 aqueduct, while virtually recovered with respect to total cover, biomass, and total cover contributed by long-lived species, is "subclimax vegetation" and in this respect does not equal the characteristics of the ambient vegetation. Note that use of the term "subclimax" implies that indeed the classical model for plant succession applies in deserts, which is a subject of debate (see Chapter 7).

Lathrop and Archbold (1980b) studied numerous powerline and pipeline corridors throughout the southern Mojave Desert. They reached the same general conclusion expressed by Vasek et al. (1975a, b) that the predictability of the recovery times for desert vegetation is very difficult and highly dependent on the degree of disturbance; site productivity characteristics including soil quality, climate, and kinds of plant species in the undisturbed vegetation; the proximity and relative age spans for invader species; and the inherent variability of vegetation, soil, and amount of disturbance within the area. Again using a linear estimator for biomass, Lathrop and Archbold (1980b) predict a recovery time of a century for pipeline berms and trenches, pipeline road edges, and powerline pylons and road edges. They state that an estimate of recovery based on vegetative composition could be "at least three times greater" than the estimate for biomass, again assuming that recovery follows a linear trend.

Example IV: Wahmonie Townsite, Nevada

Wahmonie townsite, located on the Nevada Test Site at latitude 36°49′N and longitude 116°10′W, was established and abandoned in 1928 in response to a mining boom (Paher, 1971). The site is in the northern Mojave Desert at an elevation of 1320 m and has an annual rainfall of about 180 mm year^{-1}. The town consisted of a main tent camp housing the 1000 to 1500 residents and a system of eight streets and five avenues that were apparently stripped of vegetation in anticipation of expansion of the townsite. In addition, the main street through the town was used as a major east-west route until about 1961 when it was replaced with a paved road on an alignment that bypasses the townsite. An actively used dirt road traverses the site.

The townsite and surrounding area has been protected from grazing or recreational activities since the early 1950s because of its location on the Nevada Test Site, although local construction activities have disrupted parts of the townsite. Thus, Wahmonie as a study area offers the attributes of three well-defined areas with known abandonment times (townsite, 51 years; old road, 18 years; active road, 0 years) in addition to control areas (Webb and Wilshire, 1980). Also, because of the presence of both cleared but not compacted streets and a compacted townsite that were abandoned at the same time, a comparison can be made of secondary plant succession in compacted as opposed to uncompacted soils.

A comparison was made between three indices of soil compaction measured in the townsite, old road, active road, and control area (Table 14-3). This comparison required the assumption that the soil in the three disturbed areas was compacted to a similar high level before abandonment, which is reasonable considering the mechanics of compaction and the spatial variability of the soil at Wahmonie (Webb and Wilshire, 1980; Chapter 4). The results indicate that soil in the townsite had not recovered to the ambient condition, as exemplified by the properties of adjacent undisturbed soil, after 51 years. Moreover, exponential-decay and linear models of the recovery, based on the three time-dependent soil property measurements, were used to predict a full-recovery time of approximately one century for the soil. Although the actual recovery-time estimates varied between 70 and 680 years, the resolution achieved with only four measurement times (∞, 51, 18, and 0 years) and the assumption of uniform high compaction in the three disturbed areas reduces the estimate of recovery time to an order of magnitude precision.

The vegetation present in the uncompacted streets and avenues was still markedly different from the undisturbed vegetation after 51 years of recovery (Table 14-4, Fig. 14-1). The streets and avenues have a high density and cover contribution from *Stipa speciosa*, a perennial grass common in the area, while the control area is dominated by the long-lived *Larrea tridentata* and *Grayia spinosa* assemblage. *Larrea* and *Grayia* are present in the streets and avenues although some could be predisturbance plants which sprouted from root crowns (Wells, 1961).

The vegetation present in the townsite and old main road differ substantially from the control area (Fig. 14-1, Table 14-5). The undisturbed assemblage is composed mainly of *Larrea*, *Grayia*, and *Coleogyne ramosissima* as dominants, while the recovering disturbed areas supported mainly *Stipa*, the perennial grass *Oryzopsis hymenoides*, and a known pioneer shrub *Hymenoclea salsola*. *Ephedra nevadensis*, a shrub reported as long-lived in the literature (see footnotes, Table

Table 14-3. Comparison of Soil Physical Properties in Disturbed Versus Undisturbed Areas of the Wahmonie Townsite, Northern Mojave Desert, Nevada

Area	Time since abandonment (years)	Bulk density (t m^{-3})		Penetration depth[a] (mm)		Infiltration rate[b] (mm hr^{-1})	
		Mean[c]	Standard deviation	Mean[c]	Standard deviation	Mean[c]	Standard deviation
Northeast control	–	1.50 (10)	0.08	107 (356)	18	227 (4)	48
Townsite	51	1.66 (10)	0.07	83 (326)	19	128 (3)	44
Old main road	18	1.71 (10)	0.08	47 (184)	7	34 (4)	20
Active road	0	1.96 (7)	0.06	19 (61)	5	26 (4)	12

[a]Penetration depth is an integrated measure of soil density, texture, and moisture centered. Measurements were made in dry soil.
[b]Infiltration rate under a 0.1-m head after 2 hr. A double-ring infiltrometer was used (for a description of methodologies used, see Webb and Wilshire, 1980).
[c]Numbers in parentheses are the numbers of samples taken.

Table 14-4. Comparison of Perennial Vegetation in Streets and Avenues with Adjacent Control, Wahmonie, Nevada

Perennial species	Streets and avenues			Southwest control		
	Cover (%)	Density (No. ha^{-1})	Composition (%)	Cover (%)	Density (No. ha^{-1})	Composition (%)
Larrea tridentata	1.4	25	0	9.1	350	4
Grayia spinosa	0.4	40	1	8.4	1350	15
Ephedra nevadensis	3.5	510	8	3.6	1140	13
Stipa speciosa	4.3	4160	68	2.0	3800	43
Lycium andersonii	1.4	210	3	1.7	1060	12
Thamnosoma montana	1.8	540	9	0.4	400	5
Acamptopappus shockleyi	0.2	40	1	0.4	60	1
Hymenoclea salsola	1.5	360	6	0.2	50	1
Coleogyne ramosissima	0.1	6	0	0.1	250	3
Salazaria mexicana	0.9	190	3	0	240	3
Total	15.9	6140	99	25.9	8700	100

Figure 14-1. Vegetation at Wahmonie townsite, Nevada. (a) Old main road, abandoned 18 years. Principal grass visible is *Oryzopsis hymenoides*. *Larrea tridentata* lines the road edges. (b) Vegetation in townsite, abandoned 51 years, consists mainly of *Stipa speciosa* (foreground), *Oryzopsis hymenoides* (middle ground), and the shrub *Hymenoclea salsola*.

(c)

Figure 14-1. (c) Undisturbed vegetation showing wide diversity of shrubs, principally *Larrea tridentata*.

14-6), occurs in surprising quantity in the old main road indicating an ability for this species to pioneer in compacted soil.

The vegetation measurements made at Wahmonie townsite are summarized in Table 14-6 with respect to total cover. The total cover (shown in Tables 14-4 and 14-5) was separated into the categories of short-lived, intermediate-lived, and long-lived species according to published accounts of the longevity of each species. The results show an interesting contrast between vegetative recovery in the uncompacted streets and avenues and the compacted townsite. According to the index of recovery, nearly half of the long-lived species have returned in the streets and avenues, whereas only 3% of the long-lived perennial cover has returned in the townsite. This dramatically illustrates the retardation of secondary succession by soil compaction; while the vegetation in the streets and avenues is in a midsuccessional stage of replacement of pioneers by dominants of the undisturbed assemblage, the vegetation in the townsite consists almost entirely of short-lived pioneers. The old main road has a high percentage of its cover contributed by *Ephedra*, which created the apparent discrepancy in Table 14-6. While these data are not sufficient for an estimation of a full-recovery time through a mathematical model, reasonable estimates of the full-recovery time might be a century for vegetation in the unused streets and avenues and probably greater than a thousand years for vegetation in the compacted soil (Webb and Wilshire, 1980), if this vegetation ever recovers to the ambient condition.

Table 14-5. Comparison of Perennial Vegetation in the Old Main Road, Townsite, and Adjacent Control, Wahmonie Townsite, Nevada

Perennial species	Old main road			Townsite			Northeast control		
	Cover (%)	Density (No. ha^{-1})	Comp. (%)	Cover (%)	Density (No. ha^{-1})	Comp. (%)	Cover (%)	Density (No. ha^{-1})	Comp. (%)
Larrea tridentata	0	0	0	0	0	0	9.5	450	6
Grayia spinosa	0	0	0	0	0	0	2.6	910	12
Coleogyne ramosissima	0	0	0	0	0	0	2.4	1,630	21
Ephedra nevadensis	2.3	1,450	22	0.6	310	2	1.8	1,010	13
Stipa speciosa	1.2	2,080	31	12.5	14,000	72	1.6	2,640	34
Oryzopsis hymenoides	2.3	2,400	36	0.7	740	4	0.4	490	6
Lycium andersonii	0	0	0	0	90	0	0.3	230	3
Thamnosoma montana	0	50	1	0.4	320	2	0.2	100	1
Acamptopappus shockleyi	0.1	50	1	0.2	140	1	0.1	50	1
Haplopappus cooperi	0.7	330	5	0	0	0	0.1	130	2
Hymenoclea salsola	0.1	240	4	6.7	3,630	19	0	130	2
Salazaria mexicana	0	0	0	0.1	160	1	0	0	0
Total	6.6	6,630	100	21.1	19,500	101	19.0	7,800	101

Table 14-6. Comparison of the Percentage of the Total Cover Contributed by Long-Lived, Intermediate-Lived, and Short-Lived Perennials in Study Areas at the Wahmonie Townsite[a]

	Percentage of total cover contributed by:				
	Long-lived[b]	Inter-mediate[c]	Short-lived[d]	Total	Total percent-age cover
Southwest control	88.4	3.1	8.5	100.0	25.9
Streets	40.0	20.0	40.0	100.0	15.9
Northeast control	87.4	1.6	11.0	100.0	19.0
Townsite	2.8	3.3	93.9	100.0	21.1
Old main road	34.3	1.5	64.2	100.0	6.6

[a]References: Wells (1961), Vasek et al. (1975b), and Johnson et al. (1975).
[b]Long-lived perennials are *Larrea tridentata, Grayia spinosa, Coleogyne ramosissima, Lycium andersonii,* and *Ephedra nevadensis.*
[c]Intermediate-lived perennials are *Acamptopappus shockleyi, Salazaria mexicana,* and *Thamnosoma montana.*
[d]Short-lived perennials are *Stipa speciosa, Oryzopsis hymenoides,* and *Hymenoclea salsola.*

Example V:
Skidoo Townsite, Death Valley National Monument, California

Skidoo townsite, located at latitude 36°26′N and longitude 117°9′W at an elevation of 1707 m, was established in 1906 in response to a gold rush and abandoned in 1917 (Paher, 1973). Although mining and ore processing continued until the late 1930s around the minesite area (Paher, 1973), the townsite, located in a nearby valley, was dismantled quickly after abandonment and left undisturbed because of its inclusion in Death Valley Monument in 1933. The area attracts recreationists to abandoned mine sites approximately 1 km to the northwest, and the townsite shows evidence of grazing by burrows and limited human trampling.

The Skidoo townsite appears to be nearly recovered from an esthetic point of view (Fig. 14-2). By 1980, only a few of the old streets were still noticeable from the ground, although the main portion of the townsite is littered with cans and broken bottles, masonry, and boards. However, aerial photography from 1948 and 1976 clearly shows the outlines of streets in the old townsite. In addition, the pads for all of the buildings shown in Figure 14-2 can still be found.

An investigation based on Figure 14-2, the aerial photography, and evidence at the site suggested streets where the soil was compacted during townsite occupation and the a street where the soil probably was not compacted yet the vegetation was cleared. The latter, called Montgomery Street on the townsite map, appears at left rear in the 1907 photograph (Fig. 14-2), while the compacted streets, identified as First and Second Streets, are in the middle ground.

(a)

(b)

Figure 14-2. Skidoo townsite, abandoned 63 years. (a) 1907 photograph showing numerous buildings at the townsite (courtesy Death Valley National Monument Museum). Evidence at the site suggests that the town was fully developed by 1907. (b) 1960 photograph showing same scene as (a) (courtesy Death Valley National Monument Museum).

(c)

Figure 14-2. (c) 1980 photograph. Measurements of the townsite were made between the wash and the main road (middle of photograph) while the undisturbed area was to the left of the main road where it disappears from view.

Penetrometer measurements in these areas reveals little if any residual compaction in Montgomery Street, while First and Second Streets have some remaining compaction. A simple linear recovery model based on the data in Table 14-7 suggests a complete recovery time of about 80 years. Again, due to the paucity of time points and variability in the data, a recovery time estimate of a century is appropriate.

Although little difference is discernible between vegetation in the streets and adjacent controls, important differences were measured (Table 14-8). The cover of the dominant *Grayia spinosa* has not returned to the undisturbed level in either First and Second Streets or Montgomery Street; however, recovery of this species has been much faster in the uncompacted Montgomery Street. *Artemisia spinescens,* a low-stature shrub, apparently is favored in noncompacted areas although it also has a greater density and cover in First and Second Streets than in the control. *Ephedra nevadensis* again shows an unpredictable behavior, increasing in Montgomery Street while remaining under the undisturbed levels in First and Second Streets. The main invader species in the area, *Chrysothamnus viscidiflorus,* is a dominant species in First and Second Streets and is slightly increased in Montgomery Street. This *Chrysothamnus* is abundant in the center of active roads, recently cleared areas, and active washes.

The vegetation in Montgomery Street has nearly recovered during the 63+ years since abandonment (it is unlikely that the street was cleared after 1906, giving a probable abandonment time of 75 years). The total cover is greater in

Table 14-7. Penetration Measurements in Streets and Control Areas at Skidoo Townsite

	Penetration depth (cm), mean ± 1 S.D.
Montgomery Street	9.1 ± 1.5
East control	9.9 ± 1.8
West control	9.4 ± 1.5
First and Second Streets	8.4 ± 1.5
Active road	4.3 ± 0.8

the street than in the control area, but the differences in *Grayia* and *Artemisia* between the street and control area will require additional time for amelioration. However, it is unlikely that more than a century to several centuries will be required for these differences to be eliminated. Recovery in the compacted First and Second Streets will require much longer. The live cover in these streets is only about 70% of the undisturbed cover. *Chrysothamnus viscidiflorus* must be reduced through the process of secondary succession, before other species, especially *Grayia,* can increase to the undisturbed levels. Total recovery in First and Second Streets will require additional centuries, and, like Wahmonie, the total recovery time cannot be estimated because of lack of data.

Conclusions and Management Recommendations

Recovery of desert soils and vegetation from land use such as ORV activity will require at least decades and probably centuries. The full recovery time required for any disturbed desert area is dependent upon the type of soil present, the magnitude of soil compaction, the propagation rates of the surrounding vegetation, the amount and temporal distribution of rainfall, the severity of the winter climate, and the degree to which the area is left undisturbed from additional human impacts. In addition, in most steep terrain where soil erosion is most severe, soil recovery is probably not possible without erosion control (Chapter 12). In areas where invading vegetation controls soil moisure, the predisturbance dominant species may be effectively excluded on the scale of a human lifetime.

The unpredictability of recovery times is a key problem in the management of ORV areas. Recovery is strongly dependent upon the amount of use an area receives; light ORV use may not cause the severity of impact that occurs in some ghost towns, but ORV pit areas usually have more soil and vegetation disruption as a result of the constant churning of vehicle tires than do the ghost town sites studied. Moreover, Example I illustrated the fact that although the appearance of disturbed soil may resemble the nearly undisturbed soil, subsoil compaction

Table 14-8. Comparison of Density and Cover of Perennial Vegetation in Compacted Streets, a Cleared Street, and Control Areas, Skidoo Townsite, Death Valley National Monument, California[a]

Species	Compacted First and Second Streets		Western control		Eastern control		Uncompacted Montgomery Street	
	Density (No. ha⁻¹)	Cover (%)	Density (No. ha⁻¹)	Cover (%)	Density (No. ha⁻¹)	Cover (%)	Density (No. ha⁻¹)	Cover (%)
Shrubs								
Grayia spinosa	5,450	5.5	5,000	14.0	7,400	14.6	5,900	9.8
Artemisia spinescens	7,650	2.1	6,400	1.7	12,400	4.8	28,350	10.1
Ephedra nevadensis	650	3.3	2,100	7.2	750	3.2	1,500	4.1
Lycium andersonni	350	0.3	1,100	1.2	950	0.8	1,150	1.1
Chrysothamnus viscidiflorus	2,900	4.2	300	0.6	150	0.2	700	0.5
Atriplex canescens	50	0.6	0	0.0	0	0.0	0	0.0
Hymenoclea salsola	900	0.6	300	0.0	Tr	0.1	Tr	0.1
Artemisia tridentata	0	0.0	100	0.2	0	0.0	0	0.0
Ceratoides lanata	50	0.2	0	0.0	0	0.0	50	0.0
Chrysothamnus nauseosus	50	0.1	0	0.0	0	0.0	0	0.0
Tetradymia spinosa	0	0.0	0	0.0	50	0.0	0	0.0
Acamptopappus shockleyi	0	0.0	50	0.0	0	0.0	0	0.0
Subtotal for shrubs	18,050	16.9	15,350	24.9	21,700	23.7	37,650	25.7

Herbaceous perennials								
Sphaeralcea rusbyi	3,400	0.1	1,200	0.0	350	0.0	1,000	0.1
Mirabilis bigelovii	0	0.0	100	0.0	0	0.0	0	0.0
Stanleya elata	0	0.0	350	0.0	500	0.1	100	0.1
Subtotal	3,400	0.1	1,650	0.0	850	0.1	1,100	0.1
Grasses[b]	9,050	0.3	18,700	0.4	2,400	0.6	2,700	0.5
Dead[c]	1,350	4.4	1,050	4.0	1,650	—	1,800	—
Total live	30,500	17.3	35,700	25.3	24,950	24.4	41,450	26.3
Total	31,850	21.7	36,750	29.3	26,600	—	43,250	—

[a] Data based on four 50 × 2 m² belt transects and eight 50-m line intercepts in each area.
[b] Includes *Hilaria jamesii*, *Sitanian hystrix*, *Stipa speciosa*, and *Oryzopsis hymenoides*.
[c] % cover calculations include dead parts of live plants.

may persist long after the impact and influence plant regrowth. Often the vegetation which is damaged or destroyed during use either is relic or propagates slowly. It is clear that the full-recovery time required to ameliorate severe ORV impacts probably should be estimated in terms of human lifespans.

Natural recovery is generally an infeasible means of reclamation in heavy ORV-use areas because of the long recovery times, although it is by far the least expensive reclamation method. Artificial reclamation techniques (Chapters 15 through 17) combined with exclusion of vehicles offer the most reasonable means for rehabilitation in arid regions. For any artificial recovery method to be effective, a careful monitoring program must be instituted and standards adopted that will allow reclamation to begin in a timely manner and provide full protection from future impacts.

References

Akram, M., and W. D. Kemper. 1979. Infiltration of soils as affected by the pressure and water content at the time of compaction. Soil Sci. Soc. Am. J. 43: 1080–1086.

Austin, M. 1904. The Land of Little Rain. University of New Mexico Press, Albuquerque, New Mexico, 171 pp.

Barnes, K. K., W. M. Carleton, H. M. Taylor, R. I. Throckmorton, and G. E. Vanden Berg. 1971. Compaction of Agricultural Soils. American Society of Agricultural Engineers Monograph, St. Joseph, Michigan, 450 pp.

Beatley, J. C. 1966. Ecological status of introduced brome grasses (*Bromus* sp.) in desert vegetation of southern Nevada. Ecology 47(4):548–554.

Blake, G. R., W. W. Nelson, and R. R. Allmaras. 1976. Persistence of subsoil compaction in a mollisol. Soil Sci. Soc. Am. J. 40:943–948.

Blydenstein, J., C. R. Hungerford, G. I. Day, and R. R. Humphrey. 1957. Effect of domestic livestock exclusion on vegetation in the Sonoran Desert. Ecology 38(3):522–526.

Casebier, D. 1975. The Mojave Road. Tales of the Mojave Road Publishing Company, P.O. Box 307, Norco, California, 91760, 192 pp.

Charley, J. L., and S. W. Cowling. 1968. Changes in soil nutrient status resulting from overgrazing and their consequences in plant communities of semi-arid areas. Proc. Ecol. Soc. Austral. 3:28–38.

Clark, A. B. 1968. Vegetation on archaeological sites compared with non-site locations at Walnut Canyon, Flagstaff, Arizona. Plateau 40(3):77–90.

Dickerson, B. P. 1976. Soil compaction after tree-length skidding in northern Mississippi. Soil Sci. Soc. Am. J. 40:965–966.

Gardner, J. L. 1950. Effects of thirty years of protection from grazing in desert grassland. Ecology 31(1):41–50.

Greacen, E. L., and R. Sands. 1980. Compaction of forest soils. A review. Austral. J. Soil Res. 18(2):163–189.

Heinonen, R. 1977. Towards "normal" soil bulk density. Soil Sci. Soc. Am. J. 41:1214–1215.

Ivanov, B. N. 1976. Dynamics of density of soil in clearings of spruce forests. Lesovedenie 4:26–30.

Johnson, H. B., F. C. Vasek, and Y. Yonkers. 1975. Productivity, diversity, and stability relationships in Mojave Desert roadside vegetation. Bull. Torrey Bot. Club 102(3):106–115.

Larson, W. E., and R. R. Allmaras. 1971. Management factors and natural forces as related to compaction. In: K. K. Barnes, W. M. Carleton, H. M. Taylor, R. I. Throckmorten, and G. E. Vanden Berg (Eds.), Compaction of Agricultural Soils. American Society of Agricultural Engineers Monograph, pp. 368–427.

Lathrop, E. W., and E. F. Archbold. 1980a. Plant response to Los Angeles Aqueduct construction in the Mojave Desert. Environ. Management 4(2):137–148.

Lathrop, E. W., and E. F. Archbold. 1980b. Plant response to utility right of way construction in the Mojave Desert. Environ. Management 4(3):215–226.

Moorman, T., and F. B. Reeves. 1979. The role of endomycorrhizae in revegetation practices in the semi-arid west. II. A bioassay to determine the effect of land disturbance on endomycorrhizal populations. Am. J. Bot. 66(1):14–18.

Orr, H. K. 1975. Recovery from soil compaction on bluegrass range in the Black Hills. Trans. Am. Soc. Agric. Eng. 18(6):1076–1081.

Paher, S. W. 1971. Nevada Ghost Towns and Mining Camps. Howell-North Books, Berkeley, California, 492 pp.

Paher, S. W. 1973. Death Valley Ghost Towns. Nevada Publications, Las Vegas, Nevada, 48 pp.

Reeves, F. B., O. Wagner, T. Moorman, and J. Kiel. 1979. The role of endomycorrhizae in revegetation practices in the semi-arid west. I. A comparison of incidence of mycorrhizae in severely disturbed versus natural environments. Am. J. Bot. 66(1):6–13.

Robertson, J. H., and P. B. Kennedy. 1954. Half-century changes on northern Nevada ranges. J. Range Management 7(3):117–121.

Romney, E. M., A. Wallace, and R. B. Hunter. 1979. Revegetation Studies Pertinent to the Barstow 10 MEw Solar Thermal Power System and to Potential Power Plants Elsewhere in the Mojave Desert. UCLA 12/1224 UC 11, Laboratory of Nuclear Medicine and Radiation Biology, University of California, Los Angeles, California, 44 pp. (Available through National Technical Information Service).

Thorud, D. B., and S. S. Frissell, Jr. 1976. Time changes in soil density following compaction under an oak forest. Minnesota Forestry Research Notes No. 257, 4 pp.

Van Ouwerkerk, C. 1968. Two model experiments on the durability of subsoil compaction. Netherlands J. Agric. Sci. 16:204–210.

Vasek, F. C. 1982. Plant succession in the Mojave Desert. In: W. Wright (Ed.), California Deserts—Fragile Ecosystems. Symposium Proceedings, Southern California Botanists, Ranch Santa Ana Botanical Gardens, Claremont, California (in press).

Vasek, F. C., H. B. Johnson, and D. H. Eslinger. 1975a. Effects of pipeline construction on creosote bush scrub vegetation of the Mojave Desert. Madrono 23(1):1–13.

Vasek, F. C., H. B. Johnson, and G. D. Brum. 1975b. Effects of power transmission lines on vegetation of the Mojave Desert. Madrono 23(3):114–130.

Vorhees, W. B., C. G. Senst, and W. W. Nelson. 1978. Compaction and soil structure modification by wheel traffic in the northern corn belt. Soil Sci. Soc. Am. J. 42:344–349.

Ware, J. A., and G. J. Gumerman. 1977. Remote sensing methodology and the Chaco Canyon prehistoric road system. In: T. R. Lyons and R. K. Hitchcock (Eds.), Aerial Remote Sensing Techniques in Archaeology. Reports of the Chaco Center No. 2, University of New Mexico, Albuquerque, New Mexico, pp. 135–167.

Webb, R. H. 1982. Off-road motorcycle effects on a desert soil. Environ. Conserv. (in press).

Webb, R. H., and S. S. Stielstra. 1979. Sheep grazing effects on Mojave Desert vegetation and soils. Environ. Management 3(6):517–529.

Webb, R. H., and H. G. Wilshire. 1980. Recovery of soils and vegetation in a Mojave Desert ghost town, Nevada, U.S.A. J. Arid Environ. 3:291–303.

Wells, P. V. 1961. Succession in desert vegetation on streets of a Nevada ghost town. Science 134:670–671.

15

Recovery Rates and Rehabilitation of Powerline Corridors[1]

Gilbert D. Brum, Robert S. Boyd, and Susan M. Carter

Introduction

Off-road vehicles (ORVs) and power transmission line construction and maintenance can result in similar environmental disturbances. Both activities directly damage vegetation, disrupt animal life, and considerably alter soil characteristics. These disturbances are usually more obvious and persistent in arid areas, where recovery is very slow (Vasek et al., 1975). Together, power transmission lines and ORVs can lead to greater environmental damage than either one can alone. For example, power transmission line rights-of-way can provide ORV access to previously inaccessible areas and ORV use of transmission line rights-of-way will disrupt or prevent vegetation recovery.

Power transmission lines are present in nearly all civilized nations, in all types of natural and developed areas (Robinette, 1973). A power transmission line is part of an electrical power system which functions in transferring electrical energy from either a generating plant or a transforming facility to a distribution station (Weinbach, 1948). Presently in the United States there are more than 3600 electric utility companies, generating more than 300,000 megawatts (MW) of electricity a year (Robinette, 1973). Distribution of this electrical output requires more than 92,000 km of overhead transmission lines and, based on an average width of 34.3 m, impacts more than 1,012,000 ha of land (Robinette, 1973). The national demand for electricity has at least doubled every 10 years

---

[1] The views and conclusions contained in this chapter are based on the authors' studies or experiences and do not necessarily represent the official viewpoint or policy of any U.S. government agency.

since 1930 and projected demand of more than 1,000,000 MW has been estimated for 1990 (Federal Power Commission, 1971; Robinette, 1973). This projected demand will require an almost quadruple generating and transferring capacity by 1990. As in the past, some of the demand for increased transferring capacity will be met by upgrading power transmission lines to carry increasingly larger voltages (Woodruff, 1938). Even with the increased transferring capacity, Robinette (1973) has estimated that more than 600,000 ha of additional land will be required to accommodate the transmission lines necessary to satisfy the projected demand.

Currently more than 8000 km of overhead power transmission lines are present in the California Desert area (this estimate is based on mapped transmission lines from the U.S. Department of the Interior, Bureau of Land Management, 1980), impacting more than 28,000 ha of arid land. These transmission lines provide between 25 and 27% of the electrical energy demand for southern California (U.S. Department of the Interior, Bureau of Land Management, 1980). An estimate of a threefold increase in electrical power transmission across the California Desert (from 5000 to 20,000 MW) is expected by the year 2000 to meet the increasing southern California energy demands (U.S. Department of the Interior, Bureau of Land Management, 1980). Assuming that very high voltage transmission lines (50 kV), are used to transfer this energy, about 15 new transmission lines will have to be constructed to meet the 15,000 MW growth projection. The total land area impacted from the construction of these new transmission lines will depend upon where the new power generating plants are located and the extent to which existing transmission corridors are utilized. A conservative estimate of an additional 50,000 ha of land would be required to accommodate the projected increased electricity transmission across the California deserts.

Environmental Impact of Transmission Lines

Power transmission lines affect the environment in a number of different ways. The U.S. Department of the Interior and the U.S. Department of Agriculture (1970) published guidelines to "safeguard aesthetic and environmental values" during all phases of power transmission line construction, including the selection of the transmission line route, the design and materials for construction for transmission line towers, clearing methods, construction activities, cleanup and restoration practices, and maintenance procedures. The degree of environmental disturbance will depend upon how closely these guidelines are followed. Many direct environmental disturbances occur during the clearing and construction phases. Major disturbances to the soil and plant and animal communities occur as a result of (1) grading access and service roads, construction roads, campsites, storage areas and tower sites; (2) excavating, blasting, and grading for terracing purposes; (3) assembling transmission towers using heavy ground equipment; and (4) stringing cables and transmission wires using heavy ground equipment.

Robinette (1973) estimates that between 25 and 40 ha of land are impacted for each kilometer of transmission line due to these activities. The care taken and the extent of cleanup procedures will affect the extent and duration of the disturbances.

Although the greatest source of direct environmental disturbance ceases following the construction phase, transmission line maintenance through continued use of access and service roads by maintenance patrols and repair teams, chemical and/or mechanical vegetative control to maintain access and transmission line functioning, and multiple use of access roads (including recreational ORVs) result in continued, long-term disturbances.

The presence of transmission line access and service roads affect both plant and animal life. Changes in bird and mammal species diversity (Anderson et al., 1977; Johnson et al., 1979), mammal foraging territory and movement patterns (Oxley et al., 1974; Schreiber and Graves, 1977), and introduction of unique mammal species to an area (Schreiber et al., 1976) have been reported. Access and service roads allow for the invasion of exotic plant species (Frenkel, 1970) and changes in species vigor, productivity, phenology, and diversity (Johnson et al., 1974; Vasek et al., 1975).

During the operation of a high-voltage transmission line, electric fields, electromagnetic fields, and acoustical vibrations are produced (King, 1955; Weinbach, 1948; Woodruff, 1938). Although there is some debate on whether ground level fields or vibrations are high enough to influence organisms, many studies have been conducted showing that these side effects have varying affects on plant and animal life (Alt, 1963; Anthrop, 1970; Bankoske et al., 1976; Barnothy, 1964; Barthold, 1971; Blackman and Jorgensen, 1917; Boe and Salunkhe, 1963; Bonneville Power Administration, 1975; Brown and Chow, 1973; Goodman et al., 1976; Libber, 1970; Murr, 1963; Presman, 1970; Shrader, 1978; Strong, 1966). The effects of electric fields from very high voltage power transmission line (500 kV) on humans have been reported by Korobkova et al. (1972). This study reported changes in the nervous and vascular system, and reduced sexual potency in workers associated with the operation of these lines. All effects disappeared within a month when workers were assigned to posts away from transmission lines or high-voltage substations.

The intensity of the electric field, electromagnetic field, and acoustical vibration increases, in part, proportionally to the line voltage (Weinbach, 1948). Today, extreme high-voltage (500- and 765-kV) transmission lines are in operation and ultra-high-voltage (1100-kV) lines are being planned to meet future transmission needs (Robinette, 1973). With the use of more ultra-high-voltage lines, the effects electrical fields, electromagnetic fields, and acoustical vibrations have on plants and animals may become more pronounced in the future.

Other side effects from energy transmission are (1) the ionization of the atmosphere surrounding the transmission wire (Krueger et al., 1962), (2) the production of ozone and oxides of nitrogen by transmission line coronas (Weinback, 1948; Shrader, 1978), and (3) radiation leakage to the magnetosphere (Hartline, 1979). Controversy still exists concerning what significance, if any, these side effects have on the biota of an area (Anthrop, 1970; Hartline, 1979; Homan, 1937; Krueger et al., 1963, 1964).

Natural Recovery Following Transmission Line Construction

Natural vegetation recovery rates following the construction of a power transmission line will vary depending upon the extent of disturbance during construction and maintenance of a transmission line, the type of natural vegetation, climatic conditions, and soil characteristics. Access and service roads may also allow entrance into disturbed areas for recreational activities (including ORV activity) and thereby delay, impede, or prevent vegetation recovery.

Natural recovery along two power transmission lines was assessed by Vasek et al. (1975) in the Mojave Desert (San Bernardino County, California). They report that the effects of disturbances were still present 33 years after construction of a transmission line. Considering the estimated longevity of the dominant *Larrea tridentata* (creosote bush) in this region (Vasek, 1980), vegetation recovery may take thousands of years (see Chapters 7 and 14).

Power Transmission Lines and ORVs

Power transmission line rights-of-way are used for a number of different purposes including parks, golf courses, access to recreation areas, equestrian paths, bicycle paths, orchards, storage facilities, wildlife areas, and recreation vehicle routes (Robinette, 1973; U.S. Department of the Interior, Bureau of Land Management, 1980). ORVs utilize transmission line access and service roads directly for recreational purposes; however, these roads may also serve as a means of gaining access to undisturbed areas for ORV recreational activities. The addition of a number of new transmission line rights-of-way in the California Desert in the near future will open portions of the desert that were previously inaccessible to ORV and recreational activities (U.S. Department of the Interior, Bureau of Land Management, 1980). ORV activity along transmission line rights-of-way will restrict or prevent the recovery of the native vegetation and reduce the effect of restoration or inhibit attempts to revegetate, rehabilitate, or restore areas disturbed during transmission line construction (Brum, 1980; Chapter 17).

Coolwater-Kramer 220-kV Transmission Line
Revegetation Study

A 2-year study designed to test various revegetation procedures was conducted for the Southern California Edison Company to determine whether it would be possible to rehabilitate areas disturbed during the construction of the Coolwater-Kramer 220-kV Transmission Line (Mojave Desert, California). The Coolwater-Kramer Transmission Line originates at the Coolwater generating station, 1 km

east of Daggett, California, traverses 70 km of mainly creosote bush scrub vegetation, and terminates at Kramer Junction, California. Rehabilitation of the
disturbed areas was to include the restoration of native plant species diversity
and abundance along the transmission line, particularly in areas of greatest
disturbance (i.e., under and near transmission line towers, and in equipment,
storage, and line stringing sites). At present, no standardized revegetation me th-
odology exists for arid areas (McKell, 1978). Very few revegetation studies have
been completed in the California Desert area (see Chapters 16 and 17), and previous attempts to rehabilitate habitats in the Mojave Desert area using native
plant species have not been highly successful (Graves, 1976; Smith et al., 1978).

The Coolwater-Kramer Revegetation Study included tests designed to: (1)
determine germination and establishment rates for four dominant native plant
species under different seeding and postseeding irrigation regimes; (2) monitor
the survival of transplanted native species seedlings; (3) attempt to define the
role mycorrhizae play in seed germination and seedling survival of the dominant
species in disturbed areas along the transmission line. All field tests were conducted in three study areas along the transmission corridor.

Larrea tridentata Germination Studies

Based on importance value calculations, the most dominant species found along
the Coolwater-Kramer 220 kV Transmission Line corridor is *Larrea tridentata.*
Thirty-six pretreatment tests were conducted on 2150 seeds under greenhouse
and field conditions. Germination rates varied from 1 to 54% for greenhouse
tests, while field germination rates averaged 1.5%. None of the field germinated
seedlings survived longer than 6 months, even those that were protected from
herbivore foraging pressure by wire exclosures. The results of this study also
showed that germination rates varied considerably between seeds that had been
collected from different *Larrea* individuals. In another study using 7806 hand-
collected seeds from different individuals from different populations along the
transmission line corridor, the results showed a significant difference (0.05
probability level) in germination rates of seeds produced in different *Larrea*
populations and of seeds collected from different *Larrea* individuals. The average
overall germination rate for *Larrea* seeds was only 1.5%. These results are similar
to those found in other studies (Barbour, 1968; Graves et al., 1975; Kay, 1975).

Seeding and Postseeding Irrigation Studies

Twelve, 5-m radius field test plots were established in each study area and
seeding and postseeding irrigation studies were conducted during the fall of
1977, spring of 1978, summer of 1978, and fall of 1978. Test plots were either
seeded with seeds of *Larrea, Ambrosia dumosa, Ceratoides lanata,* and *Atriplex
spinifera*; seeded and irrigated with a sprinkler; seeded and irrigated with flood
irrigation (bulk spray); irrigated with a sprinkler; irrigated with flood irrigation;
or not treated (control test plots). The fall, 1977 and spring, 1978 irrigated test

plots were reirrigated on August 21 and 22, 1978. A total of 13,818 hand-collected seeds was broadcasted into raked and unraked portions of test plots. Initial germination (Table 15-1) in all test plots (seeded, seeded and irrigated, and irrigated), discounting the number of seedlings found in the control test plots, was 252 (germination rate, 1.8%). All of these seedlings were found in the seeded or seeded and irrigated test plots; however only one was found in the seeded-only test plot. These data show that field germination rates for these species during this study were very low. Postseeding irrigation did improve germination rates. The number of seedlings surviving to the end of the project (September 19, 1979) dropped to 47. It is important to point out that 41 of these seedlings (or 87%) are seedlings that resulted from seed germination taking place between the date of initial test plot censusing and September 19, 1979. Therefore, only a few of the surviving seedlings were seedlings that had germinated soon after test plot treatments (seedling survival rate for initial seedlings was 2.4%). The majority of the surviving seedlings (28, or 60%) were seedlings of *Ambrosia,* followed by *Atriplex* (11, or 23%), *Ceratoides* (5, or 11%) and *Larrea* (3, or 6%). There was no significant difference (0.05 probability level) between seed germination rates or seedling survival rates for the two irrigation techniques. Soil moisture profile analyses showed, however, that more irrigated water was deposited and percolated to greater depths in the test plots that received sprinkler irrigation than in those that received flood irrigation. These data suggest that postseeding sprinkler irrigation would be more conducive for seedling survival than flood irrigation.

The importance of herbivore exclosures to seed germination and seedling survival was assessed during the fall of 1978 seeding and postseeding irrigation study. Initial germination was 249 out of 6400 seeds. Over 94% (245) of the germinants were protected by wire herbivore exclosures. Most of these seedlings did not survive to the end of the project (mortality rate was 98%); however, the four surviving seedlings were inside herbivore exclosures. Climatic conditions and/or edaphic conditions may be responsible for this high seedling mortality rate for exclosed seedlings.

Table 15-1. Number of Seeds Broadcast, Initial Germination, and Number of Seedlings Surviving to September 19, 1979 for All Seeding and Postseeding Irrigation Studies, Coolwater-Kramer 220-kV Transmission Line

Species	No. seeds broadcast	Initial germination	No. seedings surviving to September 19, 1979
Larrea tridentata	5,252	5	3
Ambrosia dumosa	6,046	117	28
Ceratoides lanata	1,532	48	5
Atriplex spinifera	988	82	11
Total	13,818	252	47

Seeding Transplant Study

Seeds of *Larrea, Ambrosia,* and *Ceratoides* were hand collected, sorted, and germinated in the greenhouse. Resultant seedlings were transplanted on different dates to field test plots established in each study area. Results of the transplant studies are presented in Table 15-2.

On May 15, 1978, 211 *Larrea, Ambrosia,* and *Ceratoides* seedlings were transplanted to the field test plots. One-half of the seedlings were protected from herbivores by wire exclosures and all seedings were irrigated at regular intervals. Seedling mortality rates were very high for all seedlings (Table 15-2). None of the *Ceratoides* seedlings survived longer than 25 days and only one *Larrea* and three *Ambrosia* seedlings remained alive on September 19, 1979.

Fifteen seedlings each of *Ceratoides* and *Ambrosia* were transplanted on July 7, 1978; August 13, 1978; and August 21, 1978. None of the seedlings was placed in a herbivore exclosure but all seedlings received periodic irrigation. None of the *Ceratoides* seedlings survived longer than 24 days, while 14 *Ambrosia* seedlings survived to September 19, 1979. Additional seedlings of

Table 15-2. Survival of Transplanted Seedlings of Three Dominant Species Found Along the Coolwater-Kramer 220-kV Transmission Line

Species	Date of transplan- tation	Number of transplants	Initial survival	No. surviving to 9/19/79
Larrea tridentata	5/15/78	53	8	1
Ambrosia dumosa	5/15/78	65	20	3
	7/07/78	30	4	0
	8/13/78	30	27	7
	8/21/78	30	1`5	7
	1/02/79	75	21	16
	1/27/79	50	1	0
	2/17/79	75	73	49
	3/11/79	75	75	46
Ceratoides lanata	5/15/78	93	11	0
	7/07/78	30	0	0
	8/13/78	30	0	0
	8/21/78	30	0	0
	1/02/79	75	20	14
	1/27/79	50	0	0
	2/17/79	75	59	50
	3/11/79	75	70	51
Total		941	404	241

Ceratoides and *Ambrosia* were transplanted to field test plots on January 2, January 27, February 17, and March 11, 1979. The results show that herbivore foraging pressure on *Ceratoides* seedlings was very high, but not for *Ambrosia* seedlings transplanted on these dates.

Mycorrhizae Study

A bioassay test for potential mycorrhizal development (Moorman and Reeves, 1979) was conducted. Results showed that the potential for mycorrhizal development is significantly lower in disturbed desert areas (0.05 probability level) than in undisturbed areas. Since mycorrhizal associations have been reported to be beneficial to seedling survival in disturbed arid areas (Moorman and Reeves, 1979; Reeves et al., 1979), the high seedling mortality rates found during this study and the slow reported recovery rates (Vasek et al., 1975), may be due to the lack of mycorrhizal association development.

Conclusions

Revegetation efforts employed during the Coolwater-Kramer 220-kV Revegetation Study resulted in low, long-term seedling establishment for the tested species. Overall germination-establishment rate for the seedling and postseeding irrigation procedures was only 0.3%, and the overall seedling establishment rate for transplanted seedlings was 26%. The most dominant species found along the Coolwater-Kramer Transmission Line corridor, *Larrea tridentata,* responded very poorly to all revegetation attempts, suggesting that before a restoration effort is attempted in any area containing this species more information on its germination and establishment requirements will have to be known. Since overall germination and establishment rates were very low for all tested species, even those placed in herbivore exclosures, the chances of successfully rehabilitating disturbed areas in this desert region are minimal. Total restoration of the plant composition and structure would be impossible using the techniques tested during this study if environmental conditions are similar to those which occurred during this project. The cost projected for a restoration attempt involving seeding and periodic postseeding irrigation based upon the results of this project is $9,225.00 per hectare or approximately $5,400,000 for the 70-km transmission line. It is important to point out that the germination and seedling survival rates may change from one year to the next for any species as environmental conditions change. Results from revegetation tests, such as those presented here, usually apply only to the period of time covered during the project.

Conclusions and Management Implications

Revegetation efforts in disturbed arid areas frequently result in limited success partly because the precise germination and seedling establishment requirements of the desert plant species cannot be completely duplicated using available revegetation techniques. Even when some success is obtained, long-term establishment may be very low because of both the harsh climatic conditions present and the high herbivore foraging pressure. Considerable revegetation success may occur, however, when revegetation efforts fortuitously coincide with favorable climatic conditions and low herbivore population levels.

The success of the revegetation efforts used in the Coolwater-Kramer 220-kV Transmission Line Revegetation Study was less than that reported in other studies in the Mojave Desert (Graves, 1976; Chapter 16). A partial explanation for this very limited success is the extent of disturbance during construction activities. However, continued long-term disturbance during construction along the transmission corridor by maintenance crews and ORV recreationalists also contributed to the poor success of the revegetation effort. Habitat restoration is impossible in areas that experience any form of continued disturbance. Therefore, efforts at restoring power transmission line habitats will fail unless maintenance crews and ORV use are restricted. Partial restoration might be possible if only maintenance crews were allowed access, and these crews were aware of the specifics of the revegetation procedures.

The potential for habitat restoration following power transmission line construction using currently available revegetation techniques is very low, while the cost for such an effort is very high. Since power transmission line construction and ORV environmental impacts are similar, it is expected that the same would be true for areas damaged by ORVs alone. When combined, both can lead to severe and long-term environmental damage, leaving little or no chance for habitat restoration.

Acknowledgments

Funding for the Coolwater-Kramer 220-kV Transmission Line Revegetation Study was provided by the Southern California Edison Company.

References

Alt, F. (Ed.). 1963. Proceedings of the First National Biomedical Sciences Instrumentation Symposium. Vol. I. Plenum Press, New York, 475 pp.

Anderson, S. S., K. Mann, and H. H. Shugart, Jr. 1977. The effect of transmission line corridors on bird populations. Am. Midl. Naturalist 97:216–221.

Anthrop, D. F. 1970. Environmental side effects of energy production. Bull. Atomic Sci. 26:39–41.

Bankoske, J. W., D. F. Poznaniak, and H. G. Mathews. 1976. Simulation of transmission line ground-level gradient for biological studies on small plants and animals. Westinghouse Electric Corporation, East Pittsburgh, Pennsylvania, pp. 2–8.

Barbour, M. G. 1968. Germination requirements of a desert shrub, *Larrea divaricata*. Ecology 49:915–923.

Barnothy, M. F. 1964. Biological Effects of Magnetic Fields. Plenum Press, New York, 324 pp.

Barthold, L. O. 1971. Electrostatic effects of overhead transmission lines: Hazards and effects. In: International Symposium on High Power Testing, pp. 422–426.

Blackman, V. H., and I. Jorgensen. 1917. The overhead electric discharge and crop production. J. Board of Agric. 24:45–59.

Boe, A. A., and D. K. Salunkhe. 1963. Effects of magnetic fields on tomato ripening. Nature (London) 199:91–92.

Bonneville Power Administration. 1975. Electrical Effects of Transmission Lines. Bonneville Power Administration, U.S. Dept. Interior, Portland, Oregon, 22 pp.

Brown, F. A., and C. S. Chow. 1973. Interorganistic and environmental influences through extremely weak electro-magnetic fields. Biol. Bull. 144:437–461.

Brum, G. D. 1980. Coolwater-Kramer 220 kV Transmission Line Revegetation Study. Final Report. Southern California Edison Company, Rosemead, California, 124 pp.

Federal Power Commission. 1971. The 1970 National Power Survey: Guidelines for Growth of the Electric Power Industry. U.S. Government Printing Office, Washington, D.C., 951 pp.

Frenkel, R. E. 1970. Ruderal Vegetation Along Some California Roadsides. University of California Publications in Geography, Vol. 20, VII, 163 pp.

Goodman, E. M., B. Greenebaum, and M. T. Marron. 1976. Effects of extremely low frequency electromagnetic fields on Physarum polycephalum. Radiat. Res. 66:531–540.

Graves, W. L. 1976. Revegetation of disturbed sites with native shrub species in the Western Mojave Desert. In: B. L. Kay (Ed.), Tests of Seeds of Mojave Desert Shrubs. Progress Report, Contract Number 53500 CT 4-2(N), U.S. Bureau of Land Management, Davis, California, pp. 11–31.

Graves, W. L., B. L. Kay, and W. A. Williams. 1975. Seed treatment of desert shrubs. Agron. J. 67:773–777.

Hartline, B. K. 1979. Powerline radiation in the magnetosphere. Science 205: 1365 pp.

Homan, C. 1937. Effects of ionized air and ozone on plants. J. Plant Physiol. 12:957–978.

Johnson, H. B., F. Vasek, and T. Yonkers. 1974. Some effects of roads on Mojave Desert vegetation: In: Biological Impact Evaluation for the Southern California Edison Company, University of California, Riverside, California, Chapter 9, pp. 9-1 to 9-25.

Johnson, W. C., R. K. Schreiber, and R. L. Burgess. 1979. Diversity of small mammals in a powerline right-of-way and adjacent forest in East Tennessee. Am. Midl. Naturalist 101:231–235.

Kay, B. L. 1975. Test of Seeds of Mojave Desert Shrubs. Progress Report, Contract 53500-CT4-2(N), U.S. Bureau of Land Management, Davis, California, 24 pp.

King, R. W. 1955. Transmission Line Theory. McGraw-Hill Book Co., Inc., New York, 509 pp.

Korobkova, V. P., Y. A. Morozov, M. D. Stolyarov, and Y. A. Yakub. 1972. Influence of the Electric Field in 500 and 750 KV Switch Yards on Maintenance Staff and Means for Its Protection. International Conference on Large High Tension Electric Systems, Paper 23-06, 23 pp.

Krueger, A. P., S. Kotaka, and P. C. Andriese. 1962. Studies on the effects of gaseous ions on plant growth: I. The influence of positive and negative air ions on the growth of *Avena sativa*. J. Gen. Physiol. 45:897–904.

Krueger, A. P., S. Kotaka, and P. C. Andriese. 1963. A study of the mechanism of air-ion-induced growth stimulation in *Hordeum vulgaris*. Intl. J. Biometeorol. 7:17–25.

Krueger, A. P., S. Kotaka, and P. C. Andriese. 1964. The effect of air containing O_2-, O_2+, CO_2-, and CO_2+ on the growth of seedlings of *Hordeum vulgaris*. Intl. J. Biometeorol. 8:17–25.

Libber, L. M. 1970. Extremely low frequency electromagnetic radiation biological research. Biol. Sci. 20:1169–1170.

McKell, C. M. 1978. Establishment of native plants for the rehabilitation of Paraho processed oil shale in an arid environment. In: R. A. Wright (Ed.), The Reclamation of Disturbed Arid Lands. University of New Mexico Press, Albuquerque, New Mexico, pp. 13–32.

Moorman, T., and F. B. Reeves. 1979. The role of endomycorrhizae in revegetation practices in the semiarid West II. A bioassay to determine the effect of land disturbance on endomychorrhizal populations. Am. J. Bot. 66:14–18.

Murr, L. E. 1963. Plant growth response in a simulated electric environment. Nature (London) 201:1305–1306.

Oxley, I. J., M. B. Fenton, and G. R. Carmody. 1974. The effects of roads on populations of small mammals. J. App. Ecol. 11:51–59.

Presman, A. S. 1970. Electromagnetic Fields and Life. Plenum Press, New York, 366 pp.

Reeves, F. B., D. Wagner, T. Moorman, and J. Kiel. 1979. The role of endomycorrhizae in revegetation practices in the semiarid West. I. A comparison of incidence of mycorrhizae in severely disturbed vs. natural environments. Am. J. Bot. 66:6–13.

Robinette, G. O. 1973. Energy and Environment. Kendall/Hunt Publishing Company, Dubuque, Iowa, 302 pp.

Schreiber, R. K., and J. H. Graves. 1977. Powerline corridors as possible barriers to the movements of small mammals. Am. Midl. Naturalist 97:504–508.

Schreiber, R. K., W. C. Johnson, J. D. Story, C. Wenzel, and J. T. Kithcings. 1976. Effects of powerline rights-of-way on small, nongame mammal community structure. In: R. Tillman (Ed.), International Symposium on Environmental Concerns in Rights-of-Way Management. Mississippi State University Press, Starkville, Mississippi, pp. 263–273.

Shrader, V. L. 1978. The effects of high voltage transmission lines on some aspects of plant growth and development. Unpublished Masters thesis, California State Polytechnic University, Pomona, California, 125 pp.

Smith, P. D., J. Edell, F. Juak, and J. Young. 1978. Rehabilitation of eastern Sierra Nevada roadsides. Calif. Agric. 32(4):4–5.

Strong, C. L. 1966. Stimulating plant growth with ultrasonic vibrations. Sci. Am. 215:100–102.

U.S. Department of the Interior, Bureau of Land Management. 1980. The California Desert Conservation Area. Plan Alternatives and Environmental Impact Statement. U.S. Government Printing Office, Washington, D.C., 436 pp.

U.S. Department of the Interior and U.S. Department of Agriculture. 1970. Environmental Criteria for Electric Transmission Systems. U.S. Government Printing Office, Washington, D.C., 52 pp.

Vasek, F. C. 1980. Creosote bush: Long-lived clones in the Mojave Desert. Am. J. Bot. 67:246–255.

Vasek, F. C., H. B. Johnson, and G. D. Brum. 1975. Effects of power transmission lines on the vegetation of the Mojave desert. Madrono 23:114–130.

Weinbach, M. P. 1948. Electrical Power Transmission. The MacMillan Co., New York, 362 pp.

Woodruff, L. F. 1938. Principles of Electric Power Transmission (2nd ed.). John Wiley and Sons, Inc., New York, 257 pp.

16
History of Revegetation Studies in the California Deserts[1]

Burgess L. Kay and Walter L. Graves

Introduction

Revegetation studies in the California deserts are relatively few and all were completed in recent years. They are apparently the result of recently increased public awareness of the environment and increased destructive activity in the desert ecosystem. This chapter outlines all known studies (except that discussed in Chapter 15) and discusses the problems involved in reestablishing vegetation. While none of these studies has involved ORV areas specifically, the problems appear to be the same.

The disturbances caused by ORV activities are similar to those caused by construction activities. They occur on a varied topography consisting of flat areas (pit areas) and trails on shallow to very steep slopes. The soil is always compacted to some degree, except perhaps on sand dunes, and will require ripping to relieve compaction before vegetation can be most successfully established. Unless a revegetation program is started immediately after the disturbance, the soil is usually eroded to some degree by wind and water action (Chapters 5 and 6). Water erosion is the most severe, with gullying occurring on slopes as low as 20%. All of these studies emphasize the need to stop ORV activities and to control animal use if revegetation is to be successful.

---

[1] The views and conclusions contained in this chapter are based on the authors' studies or experiences, and do not necessarily represent the official viewpoint or policy of any U.S. government agency.

Los Angeles Aqueduct

The second Los Angeles Aqueduct was constructed in the western Mojave Desert, Califoria, during 1968 through 1970 and involved clearing an area 60 m wide by 200 km long. This clearing also provided ready access for ORV activity which had its impact on adjacent areas (Fig. 16-1). Recognizing the need to re-establish native shrubs, the U.S. Bureau of Land Management and the City of Los Angeles Department of Water and Power cooperated in plantings in February 1972. Seed of seven native shrubs was collected by a professional seed collector in 1970 and 1971. Compaction along most of the aqueduct was relieved by ripping the soil 25 cm deep on 60-cm centers. Experimental planting was at six sites, each of 2 to 15 ha, from Mojave to Little Lake, totaling 40 ha. A rangeland drill was used to distribute the seed and evenly plant it about 1 cm deep in the ripped soil. Essentially no effective rain fell until December 1972 (9 months after seeding).

Seeding results eight growing seasons later were measured on each site (Kay, 1979). The number and height of plants were determined in belt transects 1.8 m wide on both seeded and unseeded areas, totaling 4.7 ha. Planting *Ambrosia*

Figure 16-1. Los Angeles Aqueduct. Construction corridor is about 100 m wide. Constructed in 1970; photograph August, 1980. Note considerable erosion on slope in foreground and intensive motorcycle use in left background.

dumosa improved establishment over that of volunteer plants on three of six areas, but on only one site did numbers approach those on adjacent undisturbed sites. Two areas have fair stands while the remaining three have less than 10% of the original number. Similarly, stands of *Larrea tridentata* were improved by planting on four sites. Only on a portion of one seeding, however, does the aspect (originally dominated by *Larrea*) appear at all restored. All plants, but especially *Larrea,* are much smaller than adjacent undisturbed plants. Seeding of *Atriplex polycarpa, Ephedra nevadensis, Hymenoclea salsola* var. *salsola,* and *Lepidospartum squamatum* was totally unsuccessful.

Atriplex canescens, where established, was very heavily grazed (all of the aqueduct is grazed by cattle and/or sheep). Because of the long, narrow nature of the disturbance it was not practical to fence the seedings. Satisfactory establishment under small cages and fenced areas indicates that this species could be grown successfully if protected (Fig. 16-2A and B). A few head of domestic livestock have quickly eliminated reclamation efforts in other southwestern deserts (Packer and Aldon, 1978).

Chrysothamnus nauseosus, the most abundant shrub species along the aqueduct, was not seeded and is not present in great numbers in the adjacent undisturbed desert. This species seems well adapted to disturbances although it contrasts with the undisturbed areas, dominated by the darker green creosote bush.

Rehabilitation of the total construction project has been very slow. Virtually all of the aqueduct is still a highly visible scar and increased ORV activity on adjacent areas has added to the problem. While a few areas have a high density of shrubs, much of the area, including the steeper slopes, is bare and eroding. The better natural revegetation has been with short-lived species that contrast visually with the natural vegetation, a result which has been observed in the natural recovery of ghost towns (Chapter 14).

Conclusions of this study are that more attention should be paid to establishing the visually dominant species, *Larrea*. Establishment of all species would probably have been better if seeding had been done as soon as possible after construction, since highly competitive resident annuals such as *Erodium cicutarium* and *Amsinckia* sp. had become established on the site before the shrubs were seeded. Protection from grazing and vehicles would have increased establishment, and *Chrysothamnus nauseosus* seed would be desirable in the seeding mix. To avoid poorly adapted ecotypes, seed of all species should be collected as close as possible to the site where they are to be planted. *Atriplex polycarpa* established well at one one site along the aquaduct, apparently from adjacent stands rather than the planted seed. The planted seed of *Atriplex polycarpa* was of good quality but may have been poorly adapted since it was collected in San Louis Obispo County, California, away from the Mojave Desert seeding site. Finally, when clearing *Larrea* sites for construction, the shrub crown should be left intact. If only the top is removed *Larrea* will resprout and grow rapidly.

(a)

(b)

Figure 16-2. (a) *Atriplex canescens* protected from grazing by fence. Note close grazing by cattle. (b) Same scene as 2a. Note recovery of plant with one season of non-use by cattle. Rabbits have still used lower part of plant.

Other Aqueduct Seedings

The transplanting of container-grown shrubs, a much more expensive revegetation method, is generally more successful than planting from seed. Therefore, tests were conducted both at a site near Mojave, California and at one near Highway 178 (South Freeman site) on the Los Angeles aqueduct to compare transplanting with direct seeding (Graves et al., 1978). Estimated mean annual precipitation at the two sites is 200 and 180 mm, respectively. The same seed collections as used in the direct seeding project were used to start plants in the greenhouse in the fall of 1972. Transplants were hardened outdoors for 2 weeks before planting, in early January. A second lot of *Ambrosia dumosa* was started and transplanted in February 1973. At each site an area of about 0.4 ha was fenced to exclude rabbits and other grazing animals. Revegetation treatments were designed to test the effects of a single irrigation on stand establishment and the value of transplanting as opposed to direct seeding. The rate of direct seeding per plot was 18 fruits of *Ambrosia dumosa,* 10 fruits of *Atriplex canescens,* 22 fruits of *Atriplex polycarpa,* 10 hulled thiourea-treated seeded of *Larrea tridentata,* and 10 fruits of *Lepidospartum squamatum.* Treatments were replicated four to eight times and completely randomized at each site. Water was applied at 2 liters per transplant or spot seeding for the one-time-irrigated treatment.

The results of spot seeding and transplanting varied widely among the five shrub species on both sites. Rainfall approximated average conditions during the initial growing season of December 1972 through June 1973, but rainfall in the second and third seasons was below normal. At both sites, *Atriplex canescens* was superior in its ability to establish from spot seeding and was comparable to the best transplant establishment species, *Ambrosia dumosa* (Table 16-1). The pooled seed spot establishment of *Atriplex canescens* (44%) at the Mojave site matched the *Ambrosia dumosa* pooled transplant establishment (44%) and was similar at the south Freeman site (53% vs. 48%). Spot seeding gave very poor results with the other four species.

Transplants of *Atriplex polycarpa, Lepidospartum squamatum,* and *Larrea tridentata* did not survive well at the South Freeman site, and the survival of *Lepidospartum* and *Larrea* transplants was poor at the Mojave site. The lack of *Larrea* establishment was particularly disappointing because it is the dominant vegetation at both sites. This lack of establishment tends to confirm our previous findings that late fall and winter seedings are inappropriate for *Larrea* because it requires warm temperature for germination (Kay et al., 1977, Monograph 9).

The one-time irrigation did not significantly improve spot seeding or transplant establishment of any species at either site. Seed production occurred on about 20% of the transplants of *Ambrosia dumosa, Atriplex canescens,* and *Atriplex polycarpa* at the Mojave site during the first year, but almost no seed was produced at the other site. The use of an "antistress" agent, sarsaponin, was not an effective treatment.

Table 16-1. Percentage Seed Spot Emergence and Survival and Transplant Survival for Different Seeding Treatments of Five Shrub Species Planted at two Mojave Desert Sites[a]

| | Mojave site | | | | South Freeman site | | | |
| | Seed spot | | Transplant | | Seed spot | | Transplant | |
Observation date	Irrig.	Control	Irrig.	Control	Irrig.	Control	Irrig.	Control
Ambrosia dumosa								
4/17/73	0	4	75	69	0	4	58	58
3/25/75	0	4	44	44	0	0	42	54
Atriplex canescens								
4/17/73	50	75	31	19	81	62	19	12
3/25/75	31	56	28	19	62	44	19	12
Atriplex polycarpa								
4/17/73	12	12	31	25	0	12	12	0
3/25/75	12	6	31	25	0	6	0	0
Lepidospartum squamatum								
4/17/73	50	38	0	17	8	12	—	—
3/25/75	0	8	0	8	0	0	—	—
Larra tridentata								
4/17/73	0	0	17	21	4	0	0	6
3/25/75	0	0	12	12	0	0	0	0

[a]The irrigated plots received 2 liters of water after planting, while no water was provided for the control plots.

This study, though limited in scope, shows that artificial revegetation is feasible on these low-rainfall sites. If seeding or transplanting is done in late fall or early winter, a one-time irrigation at planting is not helpful in a year with normal rainfall.

Solar Thermal Power Systems

Romney et al. (1979) measured natural establishment of vegetation on an abandoned agricultural clearing near Yermo, California. Measurements 23 years later show the disturbed area supports fewer species of annuals, but a higher density and biomass of annuals, and a lower biomass and cover by perennials compared to undisturbed areas. However, significant numbers of shrubs have returned. The densities of the shrubs were 383 and 1880 per hectare of *Ambrosia dumosa,* 2447 and 1400 per hectare of *Atriplex polycarpa,* and 340 and 630 per hectare of *Larrea tridentata* on disturbed and undisturbed plots, respectively.

Transplants of *Larrea tridentata* and *Ambrosia dumosa* were made in May 1979. Reporting in November 1979, they conclude that:

> Initial results indicate that shrubs can be transplanted successfully on site, if supplemental irrigation and protection from grazing rabbits is provided.

Romney et al. (1979) found initial inhibitive effect from fertilization with manure. This study is being expanded to look at direct seeding as well as transplanting of propagated materials.

Highway Seedings

Transplanting of container-grown shrubs was tested in cooperative studies on desert highways (Smith et al., 1978). Tests were made at the foot of Sherwin Grade (Highway 395 near Bishop, California) and an off ramp in Mojave, California, as well as at higher elevation sites. Average survival of the 100 transplants made at Sherwin Grade in November 1975 was 89% 12 months after planting and 32% at 50 months (Smith, personal communication). Seven other plants were killed by a wildfire. The species with the greatest survival were *Atriplex polycarpa, Atriplex canescens, Chrysothamnus nauseosus,* and *Ephedra nevadensis.* The 57 seedlings planted in Mojave in October 1973 and February 1974 had 90% survival in May 1974. Heavy rains eroded the soil by December 1974, exposing the roots, and all plants were dead by October 1975.

The authors concluded that container-grown desert shrubs were feasible for transplant seeding but are too costly. They suggest that techniques of direct seeding should be developed.

Other Roadside Studies

The Soil Conservation Service, U.S. Department of Agriculture, under contract with the California Department of Transportation, is investigating both direct seeding and transplanting of shrubs and direct seeding of grass. Studies center in the Lancaster, Ridgecrest, and Barstow areas of the Mojave Desert of California. Early results indicate that the best success has been with direct seeding or transplants of *Atriplex polycarpa*. The success of this species appears to be a result of its relative unpalatability to rabbits. Most shrub species became established better if planted (or transplanted) in February or March than in November. The greatest obstacle to the success of either direct seeding or transplanting of all species has been overgrazing by jackrabbits and competition from *Salsola iberica* (Rai Clary, personal communication).

Laboratory Studies

An extended series of studies was made of 21 Mojave Desert shrub species by the University of California at Davis and partially funded by the U.S. Bureau of Land Management (BLM). Initial interest by the BLM was in the possibility of harvesting seed of desert shrubs in "good seed years" and determining the conditions under which the seed could be safely stored until needed for planting. Seed is being stored under various conditions and sampled periodically over a 20-year period. These studies were expanded to include methods of harvest, breaking seed dormancy, optimum germination temperature, depth of planting, and a literature review of uses the plant may have as well as other studies on revegetation. A series of monographs summarizing this work has been prepared for *Acamptopappus sphaerocephalus, Ambrosia dumosa, Atriplex canescens, Atriplex polycarpa, Cassia armata, Ceratoides lanata, Chrysothamnus nauseosus, Encelia virginesis* ssp. *actoni, Ephedra nevadensis* and *E. viridis, Eriogonum fasciculatum* ssp. *polifolium, Grayia spinosa, Isomeris arborea, Larrea tridentata, Lepidium fremontii, Lepidospartum squamatum, Lycium andersonii, Lycium cooperi, Salazaria mexicana, Prunus andersonii* and *Hymenoclea salsola,* and *Yucca brevifolia* var. *herbertii* (Kay et al., 1977; Chapter 17). Studies of an additional 60 desert shrub species are continuing under a U.S. Bureau of Land Management grant.

Among the conclusions of these studies is that most of the seeds were ready to germinate as soon as ripe; hence seed dormancy was not a serious factor with any species. Seed treatments did, however, increase the germination of some species (Graves et al., 1975). Activated carbon was the most effective treatment in improving germination of *Larrea tridentata, Atriplex polycarpa, Hymenoclea salsola, Ephedra nevadensis,* and *Ambrosia dumosa.* Seeds were mixed with moistened 12 X 50-caliber activated carbon in loosely sealed plastic bags and stored for 30 days at 2 C. Stratification in moist sand at 2°C for 30 days was effective on *Atriplex polycarpa, Atriplex canescens,* and *Ambrosia dumosa.* Thiourea (3%) was effective in improving the germination of both the carpels and seeds of *Larrea*. Ineffective treatments were 6% hydrogen peroxide, 1000-ppm ethylene, 4-hr 80°C dry heat, 6% sodium hypochlorite, and hot water bath (5 min).

The germination of some species was increased by various storage treatments. Storage of *Ceratoides lanata* in a sack in a warehouse reduced an initial germination of 22% to none by 13 months. Storage in sealed containers at room temperature, refrigerated (4°C), or frozen (−15°C) resulted in 26, 22, and 24% germination, respectively, at 69 months. Similarly, *Lepidospartum squamatum* stored in sacks in a warehouse declined from 58% to 3% (germination) by 18 months but was still 25% at 69 months for sealed and frozen seed. Optimum seeding depth of all species is related to seed size with a depth two to three times the diameter of the seed being best.

Discussion

Because of the harsh environment of the desert (low and erratic rainfall and high temperatures), revegetation efforts resulted in many failures. Even the relatively more expensive and reliable techniques of transplanting container-grown shrubs or irrigation have had very limited success.

If growing conditions are favorable, seed is abundant, and rodent, bird, and herbivore populations are low, natural establishment may be quite good and reseeding or transplant efforts can be expected to be very good. Unfortunately, all of those factors are almost never favorable at the same time. Good seed years serve mostly to feed the wildlife of the desert, and are seldom followed by good growing conditions. Even if shrub seedlings become established, they must face the probability of being eaten as well as the usual struggle to survive in the harsh environment.

Results from revegetation efforts in arid regions can be expected to be poor and erratic even if the best techniques are used. Site disturbances should be avoided if possible, and they should be kept to a minimum if unavoidable. For the best revegetation success, seeding should be as early as possible after the disturbance, using local seed, covered with soil to a depth two to three times the diameter of the seed, and protected from subsequent grazing by animals and disturbance by vehicles. Even the best revegetation successes will probably not replace the original ecosystem as measured by number of plants or species diversity.

References

Graves, W. L., B. L. Kay, and W. A. Williams. 1975. Seed treatment of Mojave Desert shrubs. Agron. J. 67:773–777.

Graves, W. L., B. L. Kay, and W. A. Williams. 1978. Revegetation of disturbed sites in the Mojave Desert with native shrubs. Calif. Agric. 32(3):4–5.

Kay, B. L. 1979. Summary of revegetation studies on the second Los Angeles

Aqueduct. Mojave Revegetation Notes No. 22. Dept. Agronomy and Range Science, University of California, Davis, California, 23 pp.

Kay, B. L., C. M. Ross, W. L. Graves, C. R. Brown, and J. A. Young. 1977. Mojave Revegetation Notes. (Twenty-one separate monographs of 2–10 pages each.) University of California, Dept. of Agronomy and Range Science, Davis, California.

Packer, P. E., and E. F. Aldon. 1978. Revegetation techniques for dry regions. In: M. Stelly (Ed.), Reclamation of Drastically Disturbed Lands. American Society of Agronomy, pp. 425–450.

Romney, E. M., A. Wallace, and R. B. Hunter. 1979. Revegetation Studies Pertinent to the Barstow 10 MWe Pilot Solar Thermal Power System and to Potential Power Plant Sites Elsewhere in the Mojave Desert. UCLA 12/1224, UC 11, Laboratory of Nuclear Medicine and Radiation Biology, University of California at Los Angeles, 44 pp. (Available through U.S. Dept. of Commerce, National Technical Information Service.)

Smith, P. D., J. Edell, F. Jurak, and J. Young. 1978. Rehabilitation of eastern Sierra Nevada roadsides. Calif. Agric. 32(4):4–5.

Stelly, M. (Ed.). 1978. Reclamation of Drastically Disturbed Lands. American Society of Agronomy Monograph, 742 pp.

Thames, J. L. (Ed.). 1977. Reclamation and use of disturbed land in the southwest. University of Arizona Press, Tucson, Arizona, 362 pp.

Vasek, F. C., H. B. Johnson, and D. H. Eslinger. 1975a. Effects of pipeline construction on creosote bush scrub vegetation of the Mojave Desert. Madrono 23:1–13.

Vasek, F. C., H. B. Johnson, and G. D. Brum. 1975b. Effects of power transmission lines on vegetation of the Mojave Desert. Madrono 23:114–130.

17

Revegetation and Stabilization Techniques for Disturbed Desert Vegetation[1]

Burgess L. Kay and Walter L. Graves

Introduction

Vegetation is very important in protecting the soil and providing cover and food for native and domestic animals. Once this vegetation is destroyed by off-road vehicles (ORVs), grazing, farming, mining, or construction it is important that it be replaced with a similar protective cover as soon as possible as the best means to mitigate the disturbance (McKell et al., 1979; Stelly, 1978; Thames, 1977).

Revegetation studies in semiarid and arid regions of the world are numerous. Most relate to improving forage for livestock or wildlife (range improvement) or rehabilitation following mining. However, very few studies have been attempted in true desert conditions because it is recognized that the problems are excessive and the resulting forage or cover will be minimal and very slow to develop. The techniques described here are borrowed from both range management and reclamation studies as well as experience gained from the studies described in Chapters 15 and 16.

Temporary Erosion Control

The establishment of a protective plant cover in disturbed arid areas will probably take a very long time. Most of the native desert cover is provided by shrubs which are difficult to establish and have a slow growth rate. The soil may be eroded by water (Chapters 5 and 12) or wind (Chapter 6) before the plants can be reestablished, which makes revegetation more difficult. Thus, the revegetation

---

[1] The views and conclusions contained in this chapter are based on the authors' studies or experiences and do not necessarily represent the official viewpoint or policy of any U.S. government agency.

efforts should begin as soon as possible after the disturbance to minimize problems resulting from erosion.

The first step is to correct the source of the disturbance, such as halting ORV activity or limiting and completing construction activities. Vehicles and grazing animals must be kept off the site being revegetated. Water diversion and protection of the soil surface from the impact of raindrops or effects of wind are important temporary measures which should be attended to immediately after the disturbance. While rainfall is generally confined to predictable seasons, desert winds are less seasonal and can always be a problem.

Water should not be allowed to run for great distances over disturbed soils without being diverted to undisturbed surfaces or into drainage structures. The water should be diverted before it has sufficient volume to cause gullies on either the disturbed areas or the area to which it is diverted. The Soil Conservation Service (U.S. Department of Agriculture, 1977) suggests the following rule-of-thumb formula for spacing cross drains.

> Divide the slope in percent into 300 and the resulting answer will provide a guide for the spacing of cross drains. Example—slope equals 10%, $300/10 = 30$, thus, cross drains would be spaced about 30 m apart.

Vehicles must be kept off as they readily destroy the cross drains. (Also see Chapter 12 for more erosion-control methods.)

Soil ripping, a form of deep, wide plowing, effectively reduces runoff and erosion from semiarid watersheds (Aldon, 1976) in addition to alleviating compaction resulting from vehicle use. Rips 0.1 m wide and 0.7 m deep located 2.2 m apart along the contour were effective in reducing surface runoff 85% and erosion 31% 3 years after treatment. Treatment effectiveness declines after 3 to 5 years depending on the amount and intensity of summer thunderstorms. Properly located along contours, ripping may eliminate the need for water-control structures. Ripping on the Los Angeles Aqueduct effectively discouraged ORV traffic except for occasional crossings.

Surface treatments which might be used to reduce erosion are straw, chemicals, or fabrics. These treatments will also influence the establishment of plants because of their mulch effect and are discussed in detail later in this chapter under seeding techniques. Straw is very effective, but it must be rolled or crimped into the soil; the vertically oriented straws will then trap blowing or washed soil. Chemicals can be sprayed on to form a crust. However, the crust allows only limited water penetration (Chapter 3) and may peel off if the wind has access to a break such as is caused by animals or vehicles. Fabrics are the most expensive and would require considerable maintenance to repair wind damage.

Choice of Plants for Vegetation

Growing conditions of the desert generally limit the choice of plants to natives, particularly shrubs. In addition, state and federal land rehabilitation laws place a high priority on native plant species for revegetation of disturbed lands (Imhoff et al., 1976).

The immediate environment to be revegetated must be considered in choosing the best plant. Variations of soil properties (texture, structure, pH, salinity, and moisture retention), exposure, rainfall, etc., determine which species will perform the best. The species composition of the plants on the site should be measured before the disturbance (or in areas immediately adjacent to the disturbance). Other measurements which may prove useful are plant density, size (height/diameter), and percentage of ground covered by each species.

Experience in growing native desert shrubs is limited. The following is a discussion of the species which we or others have tried to grow in the Mojave Desert of California. A more complete discussion of experiments with each of these species may be found in a series of monographs (Kay et al., 1977); additional seed characteristics are listed in Table 17-1.

The species of the *Acamptopappus* genera studied were *shockleyi* and *sphaerocephalus*. Both are low (0.2 to 0.9 m) yellow-flowered shrubs common to the Mojave and Colorado Deserts of California, with *A. sphaerocephalus* also found in Utah and Nevada, generally below 1200 m. Seeds of *A. sphaerocephalus* var. *hirtellus* collected near Mojave, California, had only 13% achene fill and

Table 17-1. Collection Date, Germination (Percent) Shortly After Collection, and Numbers of Seeds per Kilogram of Seed Collected in the Mojave Desert

	Collection date	Germi-nation	Number seeds per kg (thousands)	Processing needed
Acamptopappus sphaerocephalus	June–July	2	1038	None
Ambrosia dumosa	May–July	8–10	280	None
Atriplex canescens 4,000'	Nov–Jan	3–23	37+	H&F
Atriplex polycarpa	Nov–Dec	23	1210	F
Cassia armata	June–Aug	55	39	B&F
Ceratoides lanata	June–Aug	44	143	None
Chrysothamnus nauseosus	Nov–Dec	22	5000	None
Encelia virginensis	June–July	78	477	None
Ephedra nevadensis	July–Aug	21	41	F
Ephedra viridis	July–Aug	38	55	F
Eriogonum fasciculatum	July–Aug	2–4	1180–1480	B&F
Grayia spinosa	May–June	36	506	F
Hymenoclea salsola	May–June	67	83	F
Isomeris arborea	June–July	40	16	B&F
Larrea tridentata	June–Aug	6–17	180	None
Lepidium fremontii	May–June	6–18	1411	F
Lepidospartum squamatum	Nov–Dec	58	682	None
Lycium andersonii	July–Aug	3	428	––
Lycium cooperii	July–Aug	16	468	––
Prunus andersonii	June–July	2	3.5	None
Salazaria mexicana	June–July	84	211	None
Yucca brevifolia var. *herbertii*	Fall	85	12	B&F

Note: H = hammermilling; F = fanning mill; B = belt sheller.

11% germination. This declined rapidly in the first year to 2% at 13 months. Sealing and storing at $-15°C$ resulted in 5% germination at 13 months but only 1% at 30 months. Germination of *A. shockleyi* was also low (9%). Optimum germination temperature of *A. sphaerocephalus* and *A. shockleyi* was 5°C and 20°C, indicating that they may germinate in the winter and spring, respectively.

Ambrosia dumosa is a low, gray, rounded shrub 0.2 to 0.6 m high. It is abundant on well-drained soils through much of the southwest in creosote bush scrub and joshua tree woodland communities (Munz, 1974) and is an important forage plant for sheep. The flowering season is February to June (the flowers are inconspicuous) with the seed ripening in early June in the Mojave area. The fruits are 5 to 6 mm long and resemble cockleburs. Germination of field-collected seed has been low (8 to 20%) with optimum germination between 15 and 25°C. The seed stores well with the germination being unchanged after 69 months of storage. *Ambrosia* is easier to establish by transplanting than by spot seeding (Graves et al., 1978; Kay et al., 1980). Transplanting nursery-grown seedlings in February at two Mojave test sites resulted in 42 and 54% establishment. Success from spot seeding was 0 and 4%. A one-time-irrigation treatment did not improve results of either transplanting or spot seeding. Drill planting improved *Ambrosia* stands in three of six trials on the Los Angeles Aqueduct (Kay, 1979).

Atriplex canescens, important in all deserts of North America, is found from eastern Oregon to North Dakota and southward to Mexico. It is common on dry slopes, flats, and washes below 2100 m in alkali sink, creosote bush scrub, and pinyon-juniper woodland. It is drought and salt tolerant and can live for 20 years (Table 17-2), and because it is a preferred browse plant of domestic stock and wildlife it has been the subject of many studies. The literature was reviewed and local studies reported by Kay et al. (1977). *Atriplex canescens* is a much branched erect shrub 0.4 to 2.0 m tall; the flowers are generally inconspicuous, with male and female flowers usually on separate plants. The distinctive four-winged fruits remain on the plants for extended periods. Seed may be collected November through January by hand stripping into hoppers. Seed fill will be quite variable with location and year, but a fill percentage of less than 40% is substandard. Germination of seed collected near Mojave occurred equally well at temperatures from 2 to 40°C. The seed stores well under warehouse conditions with no loss in germination after 69 months. Removal of the wings from the fruit is a common practice to achieve faster germination and easier handling of the seed. Our studies show direct seeding in early winter, without irrigation, to be more reliable (68% of seed spots had a plant) than transplanting (16% survival). A one-time irrigation at planting was not helpful in a year with normal rainfall (Graves et al., 1978).

Atriplex polycarpa is a gray shrub, 1 to 2 m tall, found on alkaline plains and occasionally gravelly slopes in desert or grassland at elevations of 120 to 900 m. It is less extensive and cold tolerant than *A. canescens,* but is more drought resistant. It is an important browse species for deer, cattle, sheep, and goats and a fair browse species for horses. Male and female flowers are borne on separate plants from May to August, with seed ripening from October through December.

Table 17-2. Maximum Ages Reported for Selected Arid and Semiarid Vegetation (P. G. Rowlands, personal communication)

Species	Common name	Maximum reported age (years)	References
Shrubs			
Artemisia tridentata	Great Basin sagebrush	40–100	Wallace and Romney (1972), West et al. (1979)
Atriplex canescens	Four-wing saltbush	20±	Wallace and Romney (1972)
Coleogyne ramosissima	Blackbrush	400+	Nord (1965)
Grayia spinosa	Spiny hopsage	20±	Wallace and Romney (1972)
Gutierrezia sarothrae	Snakeweed	8	West et al. (1979)
Larrea tridentata	Creosote bush	100++	Hollick (1932)
Larrea tridentata clones		9400–12000	
Lepidium fremontii	Desert alyssum	8±	
Purshia glandulosa	Bitterbrush	115±	
Yucca brevifolia	Joshua tree	200–1000	Wallace and Romney (1972)
Yucca schidigera	Spanish bayonet	200–1000	Wallace and Romney (1972)
Grasses			
Oryzopsis hymenoides	Indian rice grass	19	West et al. (1979)

Seed germinates well from 2 to 20°C, and large seeds give better germination than small ones. The seed stored well in the warehouse for up to 30 months but declined significantly after that. Drying the seed and storing in sealed containers shows complete retention of viability at 69 months at all temperatures (room temperature, 4°C, and −15°C). Graves et al. (1978) found transplants to be more successful than spot seeding under western Mojave Desert conditions.

Atriplex confertifolia is a compact, rounded spinescent shrub, 3 to 10 cm tall, which is very common on alkali soils from Canada to Mexico at 300 to 2135 m elevation and is very important in the Great Basin. It is common on both fine and gravelly textured soils. It is palatable, but use is limited by its spiny growth habit. Studies are limited by its very poor germination under artificial conditions. Seed may be collected in the fall and should be planted immediately. The combination of winter temperatures (stratification) and rainfall (leaching) will overcome germination problems. It has been observed to spread readily on disturbed sites. Stem cuttings root well from late winter through summer when treated with 0.3% IBA powder (McKell et al., 1979).

Cassia armata is a low bush to over 1 m high, leafless much of the year, having golden yellow blossoms covering the plant. It occurs mainly in sandy soils or gravelly washes of both the Mojave and Colorado deserts. Seed matures in July or August and can be removed from the pods before planting. Seedlings emerged from planting as deep as 40 mm but was best from 10 mm. Germination is favored by warm temperatures (15 to 20°C). Seed stored in warehouse conditions has 5% hard seed at 43 months, while seed dried, sealed, and stored at −15°C has 56% hard seed. Total germination was 88% and 96%, respectively. The hard seed coat apparently has a protective function, allowing the seed to remain unaffected through the winter in moist, cold soil. After establishing a long tap root, the seedling emerges in the spring.

Ceratoides lanata is another important browse plant which has been studied extensively (Kay et al., 1977). This whitish, erect shrub 0.3 to 0.8 m high, usually occurs in subalkaline areas on mesas and flats above 660 m from Canada to Mexico in the western United States, including the Great Basin. It is highly drought resistant, with deep spreading roots, but is only moderately tolerant of high-salt-ion content in the soil. Seed matures as early as June in the Mojave area. Removing the seed from the fruit may be excessively damaging to the seed, so it is recommended that the entire fruit (utricle) be planted. The seed germinates well at temperatures from 2 to 30°C. Seed does not store well under normal conditions, with complete loss of viability if stored in a bag in the warehouse for 13 months. By contrast, the viability was not reduced at 69 months when sealed in containers and stored at either room temperature, 4°C, or −15°C.

Chrysothamnus sp. are shrubs 0.5 to 2.0 m tall which are important in all North American deserts and are noted for their showy yellow flowers in late summer. This genus is represented by several species in the desert with subspecies of *C. nauseosus* being the most common. Also frequently seen in the Mojave are *C. paniculatus* and *C. teretifolius.* They are generally rated low in palatability to livestock but may be heavily utilized locally by rabbits. Seed may be harvested between November and December in the Mojave area. Seeds of *C. nauseosus* germinated well at temperatures of 2 to 15°C. Low germination of this species is not uncommon, with 20% not unusual. Seed viability declines rapidly when sack stored in the warehouse, with 50% loss of viability by 18 months and no live seed at 30 months. By contrast seed sealed in containers and stored at 4°C or −15°C retained full viability for 58 months and was reduced to 50% at 69 months. Seeding of this species is uncommon because of its low palatability. However, in evaluating the natural revegetation of the Los Angeles Aqueduct it was shown to be the most important shrub revegetating species, even where it does not occur naturally (Kay, 1979) (Fig. 17-1). *Chrysothamnus* may produce viable seed in its second growing season which further accelerates its spread.

Encelia sp., common in the Great Basin as well as southern deserts, is a rounded shrub up to 1 m tall, found commonly in washes or disturbed sites such as roadsides and noted for its sunflower-type blooms from February to July. Seed of *E. virginensis* ssp. *actoni* was collected in late June near Mojave. Preferred germination temperature is 10 to 20°C. The seed stores well for 13 months but declines about 75% by 18 months irrespective of storage treatment. The remaining viability (20% germination) did not decline further through 69 months.

Figure 17-1. Natural establishment of *Chrysothamnus nauseosus* on Los Angeles Aqueduct. Larger plants on left are over pipe trench.

Ephedra sp. are evergreen, leafless shrubs 0.5 to 1.5 m in height, and are represented on the desert by *E. nevadensis* at lower elevations (below 1400 m) and *E. viridis* at higher elevations (900 to 2100 m). The former is the most palatable. Seed of both may be collected May through July. Germination of both species is good at 10 to 20°C, and seed stores well under warehouse conditions.

Eriogonum fasciculatum is a low, rounded shrub 0.3 to 0.6 m tall which has white or pinkish flowers in bundles at the end of naked stalks and is most famous as a bee (honey) plant. The subspecies *polifolium* is found on dry slopes below 2100 m in both the Mojave and Colorado Deserts. The seed persists on the plants during the summer, allowing for flexibility in harvest time (August through October). Germination temperatures of 5 to 20°C are satisfactory. The seed stores well for at least 30 months under warehouse conditions and at least 69 months if dried and stored in sealed containers at either room temperatures, 4°C, or −15°C.

Grayia spinosa is an erect or spreading shrub up to 1 m high with flowers in dense terminal spikes. The seeds are in reddish-tinged, dense, many bracted clusters. It is found from the upper limits of the *Larrea* distribution to as low as 800 m as well as in the Great Basin, and ages of 20 years for individuals have been reported (Table 17-2). Though usually excluded from saline soils, *Grayia* is common on alkaline soils of mesas and flats from 76 to 2290 m. It is a preferred browse plant for livestock and wildlife. It has been grown from seed or rooted cuttings. Germination is best at 10 to 15°C; in warehouse storage the germination declined rapidly after 18 months but showed no decline at 69 months in sealed containers at room temperature, at 4°C, or −15°C.

Hymenoclea salsola is an erect or twiggy bush 0.6 to 1.0 m high with white flowers in March through July. It is found only on sandy soils or most commonly in desert washes from the lower to upper limits of *Larrea* in California, Nevada, Utah, and Arizona. It is short lived but has the ability to colonize disturbed sites (Chapter 16). Seed collection near Mojave, California is in early June. Optimum germination temperature was 15 to 25°C, and seedling emergence was good from 10-mm planting depth but poor at 20-mm depth. Treating seed with activated carbon both hastened and increased germination. The seed stores well, with seed of original germination of 68% still being 50% at 43 months but decreasing to 6% at 69 months. By contrast seed stored in sealed containers at −15°C was 61% at 69 months.

Isomeris arborea is a rounded shrub, 1 to 1.5 m tall, with large yellow flowers and elliptical inflated bladder-like pods which contain the smooth spherical seeds. It is found in dry washes of the creosote bush scrub and joshua tree woodland in western Mojave and Colorado Deserts. Seed may be collected in late June and July. Germination is best at 5 to 15°C, and the seed stores well under warehouse conditions. *Isomeris* is relatively easy to grow from seed and is planted as an ornamental and as food and cover for wildlife.

Larrea tridentata is a long-lived dark green shrub, 1 to 3 m tall, strongly scented and resinous. Flowers are yellow, and the fruit is a hairy capsule which separates into five single-seeded densely white mericarps. It is the most prevalent scent of the North American deserts and is dominant over great areas below 1500 m but not in the Great Basin. Individual *Larrea* can be over 100 years old, and *Larrea* clones in the southern Mojave are reported to have been in the same location for 9000 to 12,000 years (Table 17-2). It is not usually found on markedly saline soils (pH above 8.4 or 173 ppm sodium or above). *Larrea* is a largely unpalatable to browsers, but the seeds are a preferred food of the kangaroo rat. Optimum germination temperature is 23°C (15 to 25°C) (Barbour, 1968) suggesting that it should be planted in the early spring if moisture is available. Seed quality is very low, but it does store well. Seeding tests have been largely unsuccessful. Better, though not outstanding, results have been obtained with transplanting of seedlings started in the greenhouse (Graves et al., 1978; Romney et al., 1979).

Lepidium fremontii is a low, rounded, bushy shrub about 50 cm tall, and its white flowers in the spring contrast with the more common yellow flowers of the other shrubs. *Lepidium fremontii* is common in rocky and sandy places below 1500 m in the deserts of California, Nevada, Utah, and Arizona and can live for 8 years (Table 17-2). Seed is easily stripped from the plant when ripe but is generally of poor quality, with 20% germination being exceptional. Emergence tests were unsuccessful at any depth. Seed does not store well at any condition tested.

Lycium species, including *L. andersonii* and *L. cooperi*, are spiny shrubs 1 to 2 m high. *Lycium andersonii* has a fleshy fruit which is difficult to harvest and process. *Lycium cooperi* is a hardened pear-shaped fruit which is easily knocked from the bush when ripe. *Lycium cooperi* occurs in both the Mojave and Colorado Deserts as well as the San Joaquin Valley in California and in Nevada, Utah, and Arizona. Shallow planting is important as only a few plants emerged from 10 mm and none from 20 to 40 mm. The seed stores well at room temperature in sealed containers with no loss in germination at 69 months.

Prunus andersonii occurs between 1100 and 2300 m in the Sierra Nevada of California and in Nevada. The plants are easily established from the mummified fruits. The seeds will have very low germination unless treated, and the best results have been obtained with cool-moist stratification (4 weeks at 2°C). The seed stores well but dormancy problems may increase.

Salazaria mexicana is a dense shrub up to 1 m high which is best known for its bladder or paperbag-like fruits. It is common in dry washes and canyons below 1500 m in the deserts of California, Utah, and Texas to northern Mexico. The dry bladders were collected in June near Mojave, California. The fill was poor, with only 64 seeds in 100 bladders. Germination was best (24%) at 15°C. Emergence was best at 10 mm but fair at 20 mm and a few emergences at 40 mm. The seed stores well, decreasing from the original 84% germination to 32% in sacked storage at 69 months but still 84 to 87% if kept in sealed storage at a variety of temperatures.

Yucca brevifolia grows in the Mojave and Colorado Deserts of California as well as Nevada and Arizona at elevations between 600 and 1800 m. The largest recorded "tree" was 24 m tall and estimated to be 1000 years old (Table 17-2). Native Americans ate the seeds and fruits and used the fibers for sandals, rope, baskets, and soap. More recently the fibers have been used to produce paper and livestock feed, and the fruits are a preferred cattle feed. Seed may be difficult to find because of the demand by many animals. However, when found the seed is generally of good quality (88% germination at 15°C) and stores well in sealed containers (84 to 87% at 69 months at different temperatures) compared to 32% when sacked in a warehouse.

Perennial grasses are sometimes the first to naturally invade disturbed desert soils (if the source of the disturbance is removed). Two of the most common are *Oryzopsis hymenoides* and *Stipa speciosa*. *Oryzopsis* is prominent on very sandy soils but is not restricted to them and is found throughout western North America below 3350 m. Individuals have been reported to be up to 19 years old (Table 17-2). *Stipa speciosa* is confined to dry rocky places below 2000 m on both California Deserts. Both *Oryzopsis* and *Stipa* invade disturbances readily if ungrazed (Chapter 16).

Annual plants commonly provide an effective ground cover. The most effective are the forb *Erodium cicutarium* and the grasses *Bromus rubens* and *Schismus arabicus* or *S. barbatus*. All are introduced from the Old World and are so well adapted that they grow to the exclusion of the more colorful native annuals in both California deserts. At higher elevations, and in the Great Basin, *Bromus tectorum* occupies a similar position. All of these species are well regarded by the livestock industry but are disliked by desert ecologists because of their threat to native species. Not only do they reduce the colorful display of wildflowers, but they may preclude the natural establishment of nonsprouting shrubs following fire or other disturbance. The replacement of *Artemisia tridentata* by *Bromus tectorum* following fire in Great Basin ranges is an excellent example (Young and Evans, 1978).

Seed Availability

Seed of desert species is not commonly available and must be collected from wild stands. There are people in the business of collecting wild seed for special orders, but seed must be requested well in advance of the anticipated planting date because seed is only produced at certain times of the year and not at all in some years.

Seed collection sites should be chosen as close as possible to the area where the seeds are to be planted. There is great ecotypic variation within desert species and seed collected at some sites may not be sufficiently cold or drought tolerant at the new site. Also some ecotypes are more palatable than others and their use would increase the risk of overgrazing.

Seed collection, cleaning, and storage are not complicated and can be done by amateurs if the simple steps are followed (Young et al., 1978). Timing of collection is critical, because too early collection of immature seeds results in low viability or dormancy and too late a collection will find the seeds fallen and lost. Collection can often be mechanized with strippers or vacuum harvesters. Excessive cleaning of the seed should be avoided as seed damage may result.

Storage of most seeds for several years is practical as is noted in the preceding discussion of suitable plants. The storage life can often be improved by storing the dry seed in air-tight containers. Storage life may be further extended by storing the containers at cold or freezing temperatures.

Direct Seeding Techniques

Once quality seed of the desired species is obtained it must be placed in a favorable position to germinate and grow. This generally means covering the seed with soil, but not so deep that it cannot emerge. Depth of seeding studies have been conducted for the species mentioned earlier; covering deeper than 10 mm reduced emergence. A good rule-of-thumb is to cover the seed to a depth two to three times the diameter of the seed. Plant at the time of year which will take advantage of expected moisture, usually in the fall or early winter. Seeding rate will vary between species depending on seed size and expected germination. Increased seeding rates offer some insurance against degradation by rodents and other hazards. Larger seeds with high germination such as *Yucca brevifolia* might require about 4 seeds m^{-2} or 4 kg ha^{-1} while *Chrysothamnus* might require at least 1000 seeds m^{-2} or 2 kg ha^{-1} (Table 17-1).

Seed may be planted in spots by hand, placing several seeds in each hole and covering with soil. A more mechanized method requires use of a planter called a drill (Fig. 17-2). A rugged modification of drills used by farmers is the rangeland drill designed by the U.S. Forest Service, which will evenly distribute seeds and cover them with soil at the desired depth any place a crawler tractor can pull it. Hydroseeding (spraying a slurry of water and seed) is not generally successful on arid or semiarid lands (Packer and Aldon, 1978).

Seed coverage is more important in the desert than other wildland seedings. Covering seed not only puts it in a more favorable position to grow, it helps hide it from birds and small animals. Desert animals survive by finding these seeds in nature and are very effective at digging up planted seeds. A poisoning program may be necessary to temporarily reduce rodent populations if seeding is to be successful.

Some site or seedbed preparation may be necessary before planting. Water diversion was discussed earlier. Compaction of the soil where vehicles have been repeatedly driven may need to be relieved by ripping the soil using heavy equipment. Cultivation, such as by disking or plowing, may be desirable to prepare a seedbed and control weeds. Water diversion structures may need to be replaced after all other operations are completed.

Mulching nearly always shortens the time needed to establish a suitable plant cover. The conventional mulches of agricultural or industrial residues have recently encountered competition from many chemical stabilizers or mulches

Figure 17-2. Rangeland drill seeding the Los Angeles Aqueduct.

which are introduced largely as supplements to the increasingly popular hydro-seeding method. Showing the most promise in excessively dry areas are mulches applied after the seed has been covered to the proper depth with soil, as with a grain drill (Kay, 1978; Springfield, 1971). Besides the advantages of a mulch effect (modifying the extremes of moisture and temperature) most mulches protect the soil surface from the impact of raindrops and may trap soil which would otherwise wash or blow away. They generally increase water infiltration which is important because desert soils often repel water, increasing runoff and decreasing the amount available for plant growth. Mulches further enhance plant establishment by holding seed in place, retaining moisture, and preventing crusting of the soil.

Straw and hay are the mulches most commonly used in the western United States. Clean grain straw, free of the seed of noxious weeds, is preferred. The straw can be expected to contain cereal seed which may result in considerable plant cover the first year. This provides additional erosion protection but may also be prohibitively competitive with the planted species. Straw may be applied with specially designed straw blowers or spread by hand. The amount of straw to be used will depend on the erodibility of soil at the site and the amount of protection required. Increasing rates of straw give increasing protection; rates from 2 to 9 metric tons ha^{-1} are commonly used. Straw needs to be held in place until plant growth starts, and erosion by wind is more of a problem than water erosion. Water puddles the soil around the straw and helps hold it in place. Common methods of holding straw in place are crimping, disking, or rolling into the soil; covering with a net or wire; or spraying with a chemical tackifier. The latter method would probably not be adequate with the persistent high-velocity winds encountered in deserts.

Hydromulching, the application of a slurry of water and mulch over properly planted seeds, provides a weed-free mulch which is quite wind resistant. It will not trap as much soil as straw and the availability of water for the slurry may be a problem in the desert. Satisfactory mulches are made from wood fibers or recycled paper products. Gums and glues are sometimes added to the slurry, but their value under arid conditions has yet to be proved (Kay, 1978).

Wood residues (woodchips and bark) can be used effectively if locally available as waste from the forest products industry (Meyer et al., 1972). Smaller wood-residue particles such as shavings or sawdust would be subject to wind loss. The rate must be twice that of straw to obtain the same soil protection.

Fabrics or mat, including jute, excelsior, and woven paper or plastic fibers, are provided in rolls to be fastened to the soil with wire staples. Fiberglass roving (which is applied with compressed air and tacked with asphalt emulsion) is also available as a nonbiodegradable substitute. Use of these products is limited by their cost and effectiveness. They require high labor inputs for installation, cost at least four times as much as tacked straw, are not adapted to fitting to rough surfaces or rocky areas, and are subject to wind damage.

Soil and rock are often overlooked as the most practical solution to plant establishment and soil protection problems. The microsites created by rough seedbeds of rock provide seed coverage and a mulch effect. Mulches of crushed stone or gravel 25 mm deep provided more effective erosion control than 4480 kg ha^{-1} of straw, and heavier rates of stone were even more effective (Meyer et al., 1972). Field observations in Nevada and California also show a groundcover of gravel to be effective for reducing wind and water erosion and encouraging invasion by indigenous plant species, particularly annuals.

Fertilization of shrubs in low-rainfall areas is of questionable value. Until it can be demonstrated to be beneficial it should not be generally used. The plant species recommended are adapted to conditions of low fertility. The addition of nutrients may only encourage weed growth which would provide excessive moisture competition for the seeded shrubs.

Transplanting Shrubs

Generally more effective than direct seeding is transplanting of container-grown plants, although the practice is also much more expensive. Plants are started from seed or cuttings under greenhouse conditions, hardened off in a lath-covered area, and then transplanted to the field. Another option is to transplant wild seedlings (wildings). The plants would be irrigated, at least at the time of planting and perhaps several times during the first growing season. Planting should take place in late winter when moisture conditions are the most favorable and temperatures are the lowest.

When collecting wildings, care should be taken to avoid root damage. After digging, wildings should immediately be put into predampened plastic bags and the bags placed in an insulated chest and shaded from the sun. They may be either planted in containers for later transplanting or planted as soon as possible on the desired site (McKell et al., 1979).

Management of Seeded Areas

Grazing, particularly by rabbits, is the single greatest cause for failure of seeded shrubs to survive (Kay, 1979; Kay et al., 1980; McKell et al., 1979; Packer et al., 1978; Romney et al., 1979). Shrubs must be protected by fencing or cages, or revegetation efforts will be largely wasted. Grazing by livestock is of course also to be avoided for several years after planting. Use of the least palatable species is worth considering but may not be adequate to avoid loss. The possibility of less palatable ecotypes is being investigated. Control of small rodents during seeding and for one season after planting may be required to protect the seed and small plants. This can be effectively done with poison bait if regulations permit.

Control of weeds is essential if shrub seedlings are to survive. Moisture is extremely limited and if the supply must be shared with vigorous weeds such as *Salsola iberica* the shrubs will not survive. Early establishment of perennial grasses has been observed possibly to have the same effect (Chapter 16).

Irrigation may be essential to establishment of direct seedings or transplants in some years and on some sites for all years. Irrigation should not be necessary after the first year on any site if the correct species are planted.

Another way to create a favorable soil moisture content is by water harvesting. Directing runoff from short slopes to planting basins may increase the available moisture (McKell et al., 1979). Water spreading has been used successfully in areas of less than 100-mm rainfall and has been practiced for centuries in the middle east. This may also be one of the beneficial effects of ripping.

Vehicles must be kept off the new seeding. This seems obvious, but vehicle operators often are not aware of the amount of money and effort that has been spent on revegetation projects and must be informed.

Conclusions and Recommendations

Revegetation efforts under desert conditions will meet with many disappointing results. Plans should include funds for repeated seedings until weather conditions are favorable for successful plant establishment. These plants rarely become established under natural conditions and many failures can be expected from artificial revegetation efforts.

There are no shortcuts to successful plant establishment. Good seed or plants must be carefully planted and the new plants protected or the effort will be just one more failure.

The cost of the revegetation practices has not been discussed here but is high. Care has been taken to point out the most cost-effective practices and some of the more expensive were deleted from the discussion. In light of the difficulties, uncertainties, and expenses of attempting to revegetate disturbances in the desert it is important that such disturbances be kept as small and infrequent as possible.

References

Aldon, E. F. 1976. Soil ripping treatments for runoff and erosion control. In: Proceedings of the Federal Inter-Agency Sediment Conference, Denver, Colorado, March 1976, 3:2-24 to 2-29.

Barbour, M. G. 1968. Germination requirements of the desert shrub *Larrea divaricata*. Ecology 51:676-700.

Christensen, E. M., and R. C. Brown. 1963. A blackbrush over 400 years old. J. Range Management 16:118.

Graves, W. L., B. L. Kay, and W. A. Williams. 1978. Revegetation of disturbed sites in the Mojave Desert with native shrubs. Calif. Agric. (3):4-5.

Hollick, A. 1932. Deserts of the southwest. N.Y. Botanical Garden J. 33:247-250.

Imhoff, E. A., T. O. Friz, and R. LaFevers, Jr. 1976. A Guide to State Programs for the Reclamation of Surface Mined Areas. U.S. Geological Survey Circular 731, U.S. Government Printing Office, Washington, D.C.

Kay, B. L. 1978. Mulch and chemical stabilizers for land reclamation in dry regions. In: M. Stelly (Ed.), Reclamation of Drastically Disturbed Lands. American Society of Agronomy, pp. 467-483.

Kay, B. L. 1979. Summary of Revegetation Studies on the Second Los Angeles Aqueduct. Mojave Revegetation Notes No. 22, Dept. Agronomy and Range Science, University of California, Davis, California, 23 pp.

Kay, B. L., C. M. Ross, W. L. Graves, C. R. Brown, and J. A. Young. 1977. Mojave Revegetation Notes. (Twenty-one separate monographs of 2-10 pages each.) University of California Dept. of Agronomy and Range Science, Davis, California.

Kay, B. L., G. D. Brum, and W. L. Graves. 1980. Problems of revegetation after disturbance. In: J. Latting (Ed.), The California Desert: An Introduction to Natural Resources and Man's Impact. California Native Plant Society Special Publication, in press.

McKell, C. M., G. A. Van Epps, S. G. Richardson, J. R. Baker, C. Call, E. Alvarez, and K. A. Crofts. 1979. Selection, propagation, and field establishment of native plant species on disturbed arid lands. Bulletin 500, Utah Agricultural Experiment Station, 49 pp.

Meyer, L. D., C. B. Johnson, and G. R. Foster. 1972. Stone and woodchip mulches for erosion control on construction sites. J. Soil Water Conserv. 27:264-269.

Munz, P. A. 1974. A Flora of Southern California. University of California Press, Berkeley, Califoria, 1086 pp.

Nord, E. C. 1965. Autecology of bitterbrush in California. Ecol. Monogr. 35:307-334.

Packer, P. E., and E. F. Aldon. 1978. Revegetation techniques for dry regions. In: M. Stelly (Ed.), Reclamation of Drastically Disturbed Lands. American Society of Agronomy, pp. 425–450.

Romney, E. M., A. Wallace, and R. B. Hunter. 1979. Revegetation Studies Pertinent to the Barstow 10 MWe Pilot Solar Thermal Power System and to Potential Power Plant Sites Elsewhere in the Mojave Desert. UCLA 12/1224, UC 11, Laboratory of Nuclear Medicine and Radiation Biology, University of California, Los Angeles, California, 44 pp. (Available through U.S. Dept. of Commerce, National Technical Information Service.)

Shreve, F. 1931. Foquieriaceae, *Larrea tridentata, Carnegiea gigantea.* Die Pflanzenareale Ser 3:4–6.

Springfield, H. W. 1971. Selection and limitations of mulching materials for stabilizing critical areas. In: W. F. Currier and D. L. Merkel (Eds.), Proceedings of the Critical Area Workshop, 27–29 April 1971, Albuquerque, New Mexico. U.S. Dept. Agriculture-ARS, Box 698, Las Cruces, New Mexico, pp. 128–161.

Stelly, M. (Ed.). 1978. Reclamation of Drastically Disturbed Lands. American Society of Agronomy, 742 pp.

Thames, J. L. (Ed.). 1977. Reclamation and Use of Disturbed Land in the Southwest. University of Arizona Press, Tucson, Arizona, 362 pp.

U.S. Department of Agriculture. 1977. Guides for Erosional Sediment Control. Soil Conservation Service, U.S. Government Printing Office, Washington, D.C., 32 pp.

Vasek, F. C. 1980. Creosote bush: long-lived clones in the Mojave Desert. Am. J. Bot. 67:246–255.

Wallace, A., and E. M. Romney. 1972. Radioecology and Ecophysiology of Desert Plants at the Nevada Test Site. National Technical Information Service, U.S. Dept. Commerce, Springfield, Virginia, 439 pp.

Webber, J. M. 1953. Yuccas of the Southwest. U.S. Dept. Agriculture Monograph 17, 195 pp.

West, N. E., Rhea, K. H., and Harniss, R. O. 1979. Plant demographic studies in sagebrush-grass communities of southeastern Idaho. Ecology 60:376–388.

Young, J. A., and R. A. Evans. 1978. Population dynamics after wildfires in sagebrush grasslands. J. Range Management 31:28–289.

Young, J. A., R. A. Evans, B. L. Kay, R. E. Owen, and J. Budy. 1978. Collecting, Processing, and Germinating Seeds of Western Wildland Plants. U.S. Dept. Agriculture-SEA, Agricultural Reviews and Manuals -W-3, 44 pp. (Available from Science and Education Administration, 920 Valley Rd., Reno, Nevada.)

PART IV

Case Histories of Off-Road Vehicle Impacts

18

Off-Road Vehicular Destabilization of Hill Slopes: The Major Contributing Factor to Destructive Debris Flows in Ogden, Utah, 1979[1]

John K. Nakata

Introduction

The Wasatch Mountains in northern Utah are a north-south trending range with steep slopes caused by faulting less than 10,000 years ago. Through the natural processes of rain, frost-wedging, gravity, and earthquakes these slopes are slowly being eroded. A geologic history of instability is recorded at the base of the range in the form of landslide deposits, debris flows, and rock-fall deposits.

Within the last few decades, the pressure of urban growth has caused development to move closer and closer to the range. Here a conflict arises between natural processes and man-made structures. In this precariously balanced system, this conflict is exacerbated when human activities that tip the balance farther toward instability combine with the effects of severe storms.

One activity of modern man that changes the balances on steep slopes quickly is recreational off-road driving. Near Ogden, Utah, slopes of the Wasatch Mountains above residential developments had been denuded of vegetation and rutted by such activity. On August 17 and 18, 1978, this effect on the land combined in a unique way with a severe rainstorm. The storm dropped at least 3.85 cm of rain in 7 hr. Debris washed from the surfaces damaged by ORVs flowed into a canal above a residential area. The debris clogged the canal, diverting it onto slopes above homes. This sudden discharge of large volumes of water produced debris flows seriously damaging a number of residences.

[1] The views and conclusions contained in this chapter are based on the author's studies or experiences and do not necessarily represent the official viewpoint or policy of any U.S. government agency.

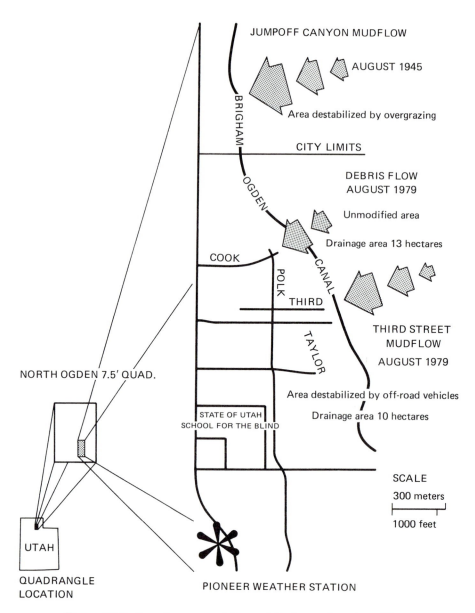

Figure 18-1. Location map of the east Ogden rock and mudflows.

The purpose of this investigation is to ascertain the sequence of events that followed the storm, and to quantify the processes insofar as possible. An inspection of the area near Third, Taylor, and Polk Streets (Fig. 18-1) on September 21 through 25, 1979 and the subsequent study indicated that the principal cause of damage was a combination of two factors: (1) channelization of runoff and erosion of off-road vehicle (ORV) trails clogged the Brigham-Ogden Canal, and

(2) the diverted canal water eroded a notch in the alluvial fan and terrace deposits below, which then combined with the debris eroding from the ORV trails to bury downslope structures.

Physical Setting

Surficial materials along the mountain front in east Ogden are derived primarily from the Precambrian Farmington Canyon Complex, which consists of medium- to coarse-grained gneissic quartz monzonite (Sorensen and Crittenden, 1972). Older alluvial fan and terrace deposits from Pleistocene Lake Bonneville at the base of the range front are locally covered by unconsolidated material consisting of boulders, cobbles, gravel, sand, and silt. These areas are partly stabilized by grasses, small shrubs, smooth sumac, and Gambel oak.

Many of the houses damaged by the flood were built on surfaces of terraces and alluvial fans that are actively aggrading during heavy rains and are fed by west-facing catchment areas that capture the maximum amount of precipitation from eastward moving storms. Even without destabilization of adjacent hill slopes by ORVs, the continuing processes of erosion and deposition were dramatically illustrated in the drainage just east of Cook Street (Fig. 18-2). There boulders of Tintic Quartzite (Cambrian) and crystalline rock, as large as 1.5 m in diameter, were deposited along braided distributary channels. Designers of the

Figure 18-2. Rocks as large as 1.5 m in diameter were deposited on the covered segment of the canal east of Cook Street. The upstream drainage system is unmodified by man.

Brigham-Ogden Canal were aware of the hazard of high erosion rates, and as a result the canal is covered where it intersects natural distributary channels. This precautionary measure prevented clogging of the canal at those points, including that just east of Cook Street.

The bedrock underlying the upper catchment area is primarily Cambrian quartzite, limestone, and dolomite overlain by shallow soils that do not support a mature vegetative cover. The shallow soils, sparse vegetation, and steep slopes of the Wasatch Range front lead to high discharge after intense rains. The discharge from most storms is accommodated without major damage to cultural features. However, this natural system is precariously balanced, and any disturbance within it tends to increase the potential for erosion and downslope damage to man-made structures.

Historical Perspective

Cloudburst floods along the Wasatch Range front are historically very common. Butler and Marsell report (Marsell, 1971) that 373 floods occurred during the 124-year span between 1845 and 1969. The geologic record suggests that there were debris flows in the past, but the frequency and intensity of floods have increased (Marsell, 1971). Whether increased flooding is related to overgrazing, logging, road building, and other factors that destroy the vegetative cover or to recent changes in climatic conditions is still unresolved.

A man-induced debris flow occurred in August 1945 when a rock and mud-flow covered farmland at the mouth of Jumpoff Canyon, 1.5 km north of the August 1979 mudflow (Fig. 18-3) (Robert Eldard, written communication, October 29, 1979). Overgrazing during the spring and summer months had denuded the hillsides and left the land extremely vulnerable to erosion. Under similar circumstances, the southern San Joaquin Valley of California was devastated by wind and subsequent rains in December 1977 (Wilshire et al., 1981). The loss of vegetative cover in both the Ogden and Bakersfield areas contributed to increased runoff sufficient to overload the drainage systems. Records from the Pioneer Weather Station in Ogden indicated that 3.58 cm of rain was sufficient to trigger the 1945 mudslide.

Methods of Study

Erosion of the ORV trails was examined by profiling methods described by Wilshire and Nakata (1978). The profiles allow calculation of minimum total volumes of surficial material eroded from the ORV trails up to the time the measurements were made. Soil samples were taken for bulk density measurements (Table 18-1). Mass losses by erosion of the ORV trails were then computed from volume losses and bulk density values.

Figure 18-3. A 1945 photograph shows overgrazed hillsides in Jumpoff Canyon (a), and the debris flow after August 1945 rains (b) (photographs courtesy of the Ogden City Planning Commission).

Table 18-1. Bulk Density of Soil Samples

Location	Bulk density range $(t\ m^{-3})$
Above canal	1.74 to 1.92
Below canal	1.66 to 1.98

Results

The major destabilized areas above the canal are hillclimbs that have been stripped of their vegetative and soil cover by ORVs and, as a result, have been altered both physically and chemically. Studies by Wilshire and Nakata (1976), Webb et al. (1978), and Wilshire et al. (1978a) have demonstrated that soil in denuded areas responds with a systematic increase in surface strength, bulk density, and diurnal temperature range, accompanied by a marked decrease in nutrients, infiltration, moisture, and organic material (see Chapter 4). All these factors combine to decrease productivity in the soil and inhibit regrowth of vegetation. These denuded areas are then extremely susceptible to erosion (Fig. 18-4). In the study area, the material eroded from these gullies combined to form a debris flow sufficient to block the Brigham-Ogden Canal.

Figure 18-4. Anastomosing gullies formed after August 1979 rains in all denuded areas. The string marks profile 7 (Fig. 18-5) along trail 1 and is approximately 11 m long.

Erosion of ORV Trails

To ensure that most of the volumetric loss from the ORV trails was the result of water erosion from the August storm and not prestorm mechanical erosion by ORVs, calculations were biased to that end. Where applicable, transect-area calculations were made from the ORV trail surface and not from the original ground surface. In addition, deep gullies that appear on the 1975 aerial photograph supplied by the Ogden Planning Commission were not included in the calculations of mass loss. Living grasses still attached at their root tips in the bottom of many gullies provide additional evidence that most of the gullies were the result of the August rainstorm. The length of the exposed roots indicated the amount of soil that had been eroded.

Profiles were made of two trails located above the canal to establish the order of magnitude of material eroded from the impacted hillside (Fig. 18-5). A 330-m section of a trail located on an interfluve with a slope range of $10°$ to $35°$ was profiled to determine soil loss. The volume lost was 187 m^3 with a mass loss of 325 or 359 metric tons, which corresponds to dry bulk density measurements of 1.74 t m^{-3} and 1.92 t m^{-3}. A second trail 120 m long with a slope range of $10°$ to $23°$ lost 72 m^3 of soil, yielding values of 125 or 138 metric tons depending on which bulk density measurement is used.

The total minimum loss from the two trails is estimated as 450 metric tons of material. This figure does not apply to the entire destabilized area, nor does it account for natural erosion. Consequently, the volume loss reported represents only a partial estimate of the material eroded from the hills above the canal. However, the material displaced and channeled by ORV trails was sufficient to block the Brigham-Ogden Canal which measures only 2.8 m^2 in cross-sectional area (Fig. 18-5).

Vegetative and Soil Factors

Vegetation cover and soil type significantly affect erosion potential. The importance of vegetation in retarding erosion on ORV sites is discussed by Wilshire et al. (1978b) (see also Chapters 3, 5, 6, 12, 16, 17). In addition, recent studies by Wilshire and Nakata (unpublished data) have shown that sandy soils derived from crystalline rock are the most vulnerable to erosion.

Vegetation in the form of grasses, shrubs, and trees decreases erosion potential by: (1) forming a canopy to decrease rain impact, (2) adding humus to the soil to increase absorption, (3) decreasing the velocity of sheetwash, and (4) binding soil particles together with root systems. However, road construction, overgrazing, logging, and ORV use that denude areas have the reverse effect.

The immature soils underlying most of the ORV trails are derived from a medium- to coarse-grained gneissic quartz monzonite. This rock weathers into sand-size particles with little clay and combines with cobbles and boulders brought in by the distributary system and mass wasting to form a moderate to poorly sorted soil horizon of low erosional stability.

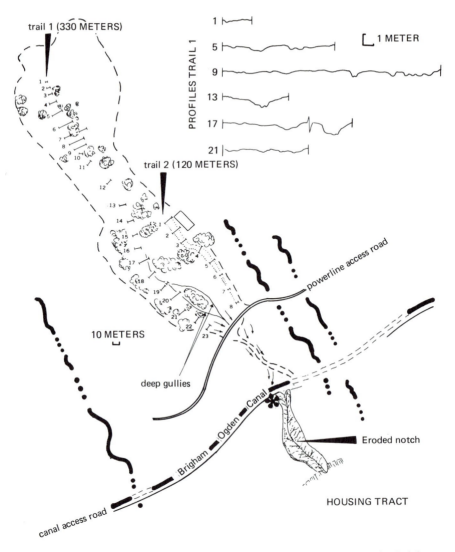

Figure 18-5. Sketch map of the off-road vehicle area in relation to the Brigham-Ogden Canal. Inset are typical profiles along the trail 1 and a cross section of the canal at Third Street.

In the area above the canal (Fig. 18-5), two 75-m^2 plots, each with the same slope, slope aspect, and soil and both receiving excess runoff from denuded upslope terrain, were profiled to determine volume loss. The plot that was partially denuded by moderate ORV use lost 10 m^3 of soil, whereas the adjacent area subjected to light ORV use lost 4 m^3. In areas not used by ORVs, the grass was matted by sheetflow, but the soil horizon was virtually intact.

Erosion Below the Canal

According to the Ogden Water Users Association, the Brigham-Ogden Canal was shut down on the morning of August 18 at 2:45 a.m. and was dry by 3:20 a.m., a running time of 35 min (Bill Burbidge and Ralph Bird, oral communication, September 24, 1979). They also reported a flow rate of 55–60 sec foot^{-1}, which translates to approximately 3.0 to 3.4 $\times$ 10^6 liters of water diverted over the canal embankment. According to the August 18, 1979 issue of the *Ogden Standard-Examiner,* boulders were being swept along Third Street just after 2:00 a.m.; therefore the canal may have topped before 2:00 a.m., and the running time may have been 80 min. If so, approximately 7.6 $\times$ 10^6 liters of water was diverted. Using the cross-sectional area of the water in the canal, 2.07 m^2, and the distance from the surge tank to Third Street, 2.56 km, but not the flow rates, a value of approximately 5.3 million liters is computed. These values are approximate orders of magnitude of water diverted over the canal embankment.

Grading done after the mudflow to protect houses from subsequent rains changed the configuration of the notch below the canal. Consequently, only crude measurements were made on this notch. A conservative estimate of the volume displaced is 12,000 m^3 or approximately 21,000 metric tons, on the basis of an average bulk density of 1.82 t m^{-3}. The erosion that occurred below the canal is dramatically illustrated in Figure 18-6, which shows the hillside before and after the debris flow.

Summary

Damage from the 1979 storm can be traced directly to several geologic processes which constitute hazards in the Ogden area. The steep slopes of the Wasatch Range front are the result of Holocene faulting. Along the range front, mechanical weathering of the Tintic Quartzite cliffs by frost wedging forms unstable talus slopes. Below these talus slopes, immature alluvial fans still grow after intense rains.

The historical record of debris flows along the Wasatch front, in particular at Jumpoff Canyon in 1945, constitutes evidence of land instability. The designers of the Brigham-Ogden Canal were aware of these constraints and took precautions to cover the canal at all active distributaries.

The areas upslope from Cook and Third Streets (Fig. 18-1) have similar drainage sizes, slopes, slope aspects, rock types, and vegetative communities. The only significant difference is ORV modification to the Third Street area. Within this precariously balanced natural system, the added burden of material eroded from and channeled by the ORV trails blocked the canal and diverted canal water, contributing significantly to the damage of structures downslope. Kaliser (1979) also concluded that terrain modification by ORVs was the major contributing factor to the chain of events leading to flood damage.

Figure 18-6. Before (a) and after (b) photographs of the notch eroded by diverted canal water at the end of Third Street [photograph (a) courtesy of Mr. and Mrs. L. Haun].

Acknowledgments

I thank the Ogden City and Weber County Planning Commissions, particularly Mr. Robert Eldard for supplying photographs and data concerning the 1945 rock and mudflow in Jumpoff Canyon. I am grateful to Mr. Ralph Bird of the Ogden River Water Users Association, and Mr. and Mrs. L. Haun, flood victims, who contributed valuable information concerning the 1979 flood.

References

Kaliser, B. N. 1979. Off-Road Vehicle Tracks Trigger Ogden Flood. Utah Geological and Mineral Survey, Survey Notes, Vol. 13, No. 4, p. 3.

Marsell, R. E. 1971. Cloudburst and snowmelt floods. In: Environmental Geology of the Wasatch Front, 1971. Utah Geological Association, Salt Lake City, Utah, Publication 1, pp. N1–N18.

Sorensen, M. L., and M. D. Crittenden, Jr. 1972. Preliminary Geologic Map of Part of the Wasatch Range near North Ogden, Utah. U.S. Geological Survey Miscellaneous Field Studies Map, MF-428, U.S. Government Printing Office, Washington, D.C.

Webb, R. H., H. C. Ragland, W. H. Godwin, and D. Jenkins. 1978. Environmental effects of soil property changes with off-road vehicle use. Environ. Management (3):219–230.

Wilshire, H. G., and J. K. Nakata. 1976. Off-road vehicle effects on California's Mojave Desert. Calif. Geol. 29:123–132.

Wilshire, H.G., and J. K. Nakata. 1978. Erosion off the road. Geotimes 22(7/8): 27.

Wilshire, H. G., J. K. Nakata, S. Shipley, and K. Prestegaard. 1978a. Impacts of vehicles on natural terrain at seven sites in the San Francisco Bay Area. Environ. Geol. 2(5):295–313.

Wilshire, H. G., S. Shipley, and J. K. Nakata. 1978b. Impacts of off-road vehicles on vegetation. Transactions of the 43rd North American Wildlife and Natural Resources Conference, 1978, Wildlife Management Institute, Washington, D.C., pp. 131–139.

Wilshire, H. G., J. K. Nakata, and B. Hallet. 1981. Field observations of the December 1977 windstorm, San Joaquin Valley, California. In: T. L. Péwé (Ed.), Desert Dust: Origin, Characteristics, and Effects on Man. Geological Society of America Special Paper 186, pp. 233–251.

19

The Impacts of Off-Road Vehicles in the Coorong Dune and Lake Complex of South Australia[1]

David Gilbertson

Introduction

The management of off-road vehicles (ORVs) being driven in areas of natural or seminatural vegetation has become a subject of great concern in the coastal areas of North America, Australia, and New Zealand (Australian House of Representatives Standing Committee on Off-Road Vehicles, 1977; Crozier et al., 1977; Gilbertson and Foale, 1977; Godfrey et al., 1978; Hall, 1975; Hozier and Eaton, 1980; Robertson and Wood, 1977; Steiner and Leatherman, 1979; Welsh, 1975; Wood, 1978). The widespread ownership of four-wheel-drive vehicles and trail bikes for normal work or travel purposes in a large cross section of the rural and urban communities of Australia has led inevitably to extensive use of ORVs for recreational purposes. Increasingly, such activity is enjoyed on sites such as abandoned quarries or forestry plantations often close to urban areas, where the magnitude and frequency of use can be managed by state officials or private owners to ensure maximum enjoyment and minimum damage.

However, in the more distant areas, such as the Coorong Dune and Lake system in South Australia, severe management problems have arisen for several reasons. First, comparatively little is known of the ecology and geomorphic processes operating in these areas. Second, it commonly is not clear whether a particular effect is the result of ORV impact, natural environmental changes, or the legacy of early European agricultural and pastoral activity or earlier aborigi-

---

[1]The views and conclusions contained in this chapter are based on the author's studies or experiences and do not necessarily represent the official viewpoint or policy of any U.S. government agency.

nal firing of the land. Third, the social composition and expectations of the ORV users are not well established, although the recreational vehicle sales trade and ORV clubs and organizations frequently put forward their views (RVCC, 1975). Fourth, difficulties exist concerning the related issues of (1) the interpretation and enforceability of Acts of Parliament or local bylaws concerning technically illegal ORV use, and (2) the extent to which responsible potential ORV users are misinformed by parties with commercial interests about their right to use public land.

There are also important differences in the various interested parties' perceptions of what constitutes damage and of the time scales at which damage or change become important. It is essential not to polarize the situation unneces-

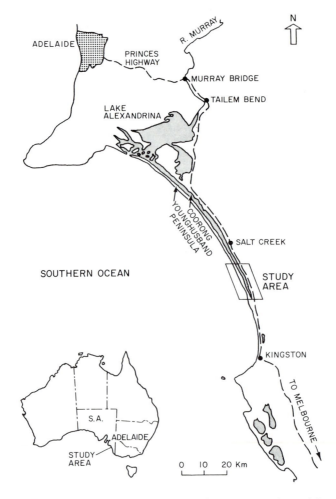

Figure 19-1. The location of the study area of dunes, marsh, and lagoon at the southern end of the Coorong National Park, South Australia.

Figure 19-2. Oblique aerial photograph showing the Southern Ocean, the Younghusband Peninsula, and the main Coorong lagoon.

sarily; many professional scientists own and use ORVs for work and pleasure, while many ORV users are ecologically responsible and do not wish to destroy the source of their relaxation and recreation.

This account addresses the first two questions. It integrates, summarizes, and brings up to date recent geomorphic and ecological studies of the impact of ORVs on a fairly representative area of a major dune and lake complex on the South Australian coast—the Southern Coorong and lower Younghusband Peninsula (Figs. 19-1 and 19-2). In this example the major cause of environmental concern was the problem of accelerated coastal dune drift and the impact of ORVs on plant and animal life in the region.

Geomorphic and Ecological Setting

An understanding of the main study area's geomorphology and major habitats (Figs. 19-3 and 19-4) is essential to a satisfactory appreciation of the overall significance of ORV activity. The climate of the area is semiarid with marked summer drought. A coastal barrier of carbonate dune sands interbedded with paleosols and aboriginal shell middens overlies an older calcrete-cemented beach-dune system. Up to 40% of the surface area of this dune barrier is occupied by mobile sand sheets (Fig. 19-2) with an occasional thin cover of scrub and the sand-binding grasses *(Spinifex hirsutus* and the introduced *Ammophilia arenaria).* The remaining dune area comprises dense scrub dominated by *Acacia sophorae* and *Leucopogon parviflorus,* with occasional pockets of gum trees, *Eucalyptus diversifolia.* Aerial photography clearly indicates that the mobile sand sheets represent the mobilization of "fixed" older parabolic dunes. Precipitation percolating into these dunes reemerges as a line of freshwater "soaks"

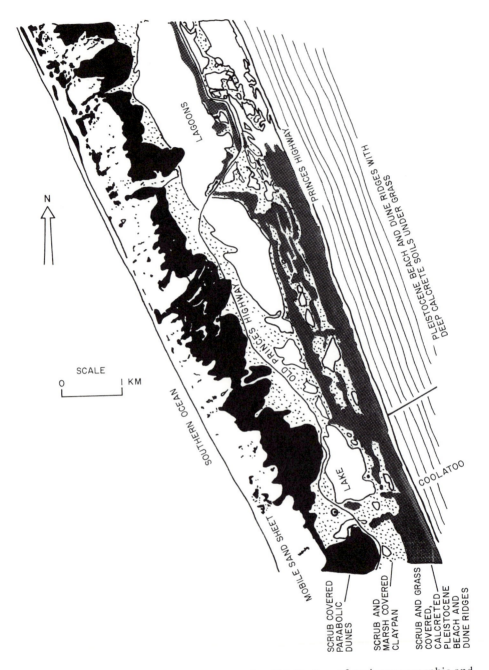

Figure 19-3. Simplified map showing the distribution of major geomorphic and habitat types near Coolatoo in the lower Coorong.

or springs along both margins of the dunes (Fig. 19-3). The landward margin of the dunes is 10 to 20 m high with a slope of 25 to 30°.

These dunes enclose a complex of hypersaline lakes, prone to complete dessication in summer. These lakes are separated by the calcrete-cemented remnants of Mid-Holocene or earlier beach or lake-shoreline deposits. The lakes have a rich vegetation of *Ruppia* grasses and an unusual invertebrate fauna, with the larger crustaceans including an apparently new species of brine shrimp of the genus *Paratemia* found by Geddes and Brock (1977). These feed a spectacular and well-known bird fauna with 88 aquatic species in a total of 153 indigenous species for the area (Glover, 1975; Hawkes, 1975). The lake shores are fringed in saltmarsh and scrub, with Ti tree *(Melaleuca helmaturorum)* evident. The calcrete-cemented ridges either are scrub covered (principally *Acacia sophorae*) or when cleared they are covered in swards of short grass grazed by rabbits. The strongly calcrete-cemented Late Pleistocene parallel beach ridges further inland from the Princes Highway are covered in structurally complex mallee form eucalypt scrub characterized by *Eucalyptus diversifolia* and a fairly diverse understory of tall shrubs.

There are major areas of cleared ground reverting from pasture around the early colonial farms, as exemplified by Coolatoo homestead abandoned at the turn of the century. A major consequence of this early pastoralism is that of the 258 species of vascular plants collected by Alcock and Symon (1977) in the area, no less than 92 (35%) were aliens—principally from South Africa or western Europe. These species are either garden escapes, species deliberately introduced as fodder or grain crops, species introduced in dune stabilization programs, or accidental introductions.

Patterns of ORV Use and Their Geomorphic Impacts

Access

The region currently forms the southern limit of the Coorong National Park, designated and managed for nature conservation and extending north as far as the mouth of the Murray Mouth (Fig. 19-1), where the River Murray, having entered Lake Alexandrina, breaches the coastal barrier of the Younghusband Peninsula. Access to the northern area is difficult because of the lake and main Coorong lagoon; however, ORV users enter these areas in several ways. First, users may drive the 50 to 90 km along the beach from Kingston to the south, or from the present study area. Second, users may ferry trailbikes on small boats from trailers parked off-road east of the lagoon. Third, ready access is provided from the Sir Richard Peninsula to the north when sediment, moving onshore and along shore, completely blocks the Murray Mouth. This occurred most recently in 1981.

The study area itself has been one of the most intensively used areas for

ORV use (Figs. 19-4, 19-5, and 19-6), especially until 1977 when this section of the coast was incorporated into the national park. This latter factor coupled with increased fuel costs and possible adverse publicity has caused ORV use to decline; for example, official ORV clubs of 20 to 50 vehicles no longer spend long weekends in the area (Fig. 19-4). In the recent past an immense variety of vehicles have travelled off-road, that is, away from established tracks and the sur-faced roads of the old and new Princes Highways: family vans of four-wheel-drive vehicles, often towing a trailer, or caravans carrying trail bikes, trikes, or dune buggies (Fig. 19-5); and four-wheel-drive vehicles of both newer lightweight and older heavier designs, and dune buggies. At popular holiday weekends at least 250 ORVs might have been in use in the actual study area. These vehicles principally entered the region along the "old" Princes Highway (Fig. 19-3) and from there penetrated further afield using the disused tracks linking derelict farmsteads to the main highways; and the old "Bullock Track," a telegraph maintenance track which travels between the landward margin of the dunes and the edge of the ephemeral lakes.

Most users travel 250 km south from Adelaide (population ca. 950,000); however, important, fairly continuous, but lower intensity use is enjoyed by ORV users from the local towns of Murray Bridge, Tailem Bend, and Kingston. Several of these local people use their ORV to gain access to the beach for sea angling.

Figure 19-4. Clearance of produne scrub for camping, runways, and "pioneer" tracks into vegetated dunes.

Figure 19-5. Movement of sand downslope and forward by ORVs on the main mobile dune face; note the runways leading to the face.

Figure 19-6. Intensity of trailbike and dune buggy activity on the middune area prevents the growth of sand-binding grasses.

ORV User Landscape Preferences

Gilbertson (1981) established a hierarchy of ORV users with different requirements in the area, shown in Figure 19-7. Many trails are initiated or reopened
from homestead-pastoral days by individuals on trail bikes seeking to explore the
wilderness in isolation. Once opened, the track is used by more individuals or
groups on fairly long-distance explorations. Inevitably, track widening occurs
until a recognizable route is obvious to gregarious trail bike and four-wheel-drive
users who wish to traverse steep slopes at speed in large groups. Substantial areas
of cleared ground are needed in front of the dunes to allow for communal camping, and "runways" are cleared long enough for vehicles to gain speed and climb
the steep landward dune face. While its steepness is attractive to trailbike and
dune buggy users, steep slopes are a problem for four-wheel-drive users. These
users seek lower gradients by traversing diagonally up the mobile face and more
commonly gain access to the dunes via the beach and old cross-dune routes.
However, in the saltmarsh, lake, and produne areas the compaction and rutting
of the clay soils by ORVs usually results in large, poorly drained depressions in

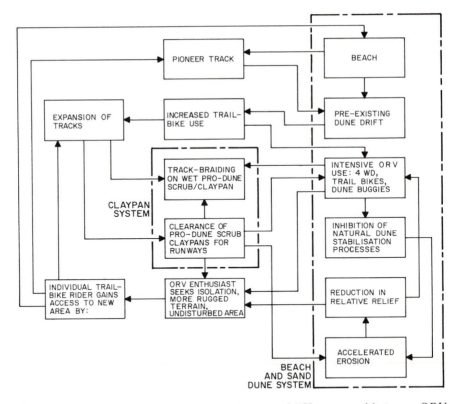

Figure 19-7. A model of the interaction between ORV users, and between ORV
users and geomorphic change in the lower Coorong (redrawn from Gilbertson,
1981).

routes during the winter and spring rains. Individuals using passenger cars, trail bikes, dune buggies, and to a lesser extent, four-wheel-drive vehicles avoid these areas, cause tracks to spread into an anastomosing network of 4 to 10 tracks, 20 to 80 m across, in these areas prone to waterlogging. The original "lone" user is usually horrified by both the trailer and vehicle camps and the intensity of use and travels further into "unexplored" country, whereupon the process starts again.

Causes of Accelerated Dune Drift

Studies by Gilbertson (1981) indicated that it was important to distinguish the effects or legacies of past environmental changes or land-use practices to assess the impact of ORVs on the landscape. The conclusions were as follows:

1. The entire study region has in the past experienced major oceanographic or climatological changes which have caused the dunes to become mobile and then stabilize. This occurred at some point in the Mid-Holocene. However, there is no reliable evidence to suggest that any such changes are associated with the present dune-drift problem.
2. Aboriginal firing was probably only responsible for small-scale drifting.
3. Much of the apparent topographic stability and apparent resistance to erosion was the result of the exposure of archaeologically rich paleosols of relatively high resistance to vehicles. However, ORV use was indicated to be destroying the exposed and important cultural remains. It was unclear how long the paleosols would retard erosion.
4. The legacy of European pastoralism is evident in the flora and fauna of the region, with many alien plants, rabbits, feral dogs, cats, and foxes. However, with one exception, it was not possible to discern noticeable modern accelerated dune drift attributable directly or indirectly to European pastoralism in the period up to approximately 1937.
5. Modern accelerated dune drift is associated with and is probably attributable to ORV use. Figure 19-8 employs the most recent aerial photography, taken in January 1981, and indicates a continuance to the present of substantial rates of dune advance, sufficient to warrant concern for the soaks, salt-marshes, and lakes in 1977 (Gilbertson, 1981). The period from 1954 to the present coincides with the start and great expansion of ORV use in the area.

Mechanisms involving ORV impact as a major cause of this accelerated dune drift may be hypothesized but are difficult to substantiate because of interplay with past European activity and the impact of vehicles and vandals on monitoring equipment. It is clear that vehicles entering the dunes from the beach rip, push down, or bury the back beach and produne sand-binding vegetation, which would otherwise help to trap the wind-blown carbonate sand near its source on the beach (Figs. 19-4 and 19-5). Constant vehicle use has a similarly deleterious effect on middune sand-binding vegetation (Fig. 19-6). At the landward dune

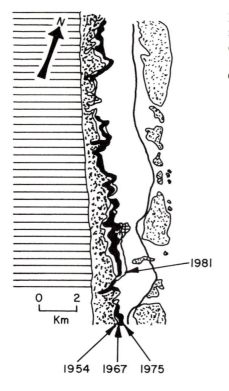

Figure 19-8. Relative position of the main mobile sand space near Coolatoo drawn from aerial photographs 1954 to 1981 (1954 to 1975 data redrawn from Gilbertson, 1981).

face, the passage of vehicles up and down the face directly displaces sand down-face and forward, while the necessity for runways and cleared camp areas removes or suppresses tree and shrub species which otherwise may offer a barrier to sand drift (Fig. 19-4). These mechanisms interact with the sequence of ORV users and their various expectations and may be expressed in the multiple feedback geomorphic-ORV use model (Fig. 19-7, from Gilbertson, 1981).

The relationship between ORV use and dune drift has been explored in more detail by using the changing frequency of tracks (observed on aerial photographs) per unit area in the period 1954 to 1975 as a surrogate measure for spatial variations in the intensity of past ORV use. The results for the Coolatoo area are shown in Figures 19-9 and 19-10. The general trend is clear: the most accelerated dune drift is associated with higher track frequencies in this particular area. However, because of the exploitation or reopening of tracks which naturally cluster around old homesteads, higher track density and more accelerated dune advance may also be shown to be negatively correlated with increasing distance from the old homesteads. This relationship may be interpreted in the following way: areas of currently high rates of dune advance are a legacy of the greater impacts of clearance and grazing closer to the homesteads. The ORVs, it could be argued, are only taking advantage of those areas of

Figure 19-9. The relationship between the rate of advance of the
main mobile dune face near Coolatoo in the lower Coorong and the
total length of tracks per km^2 observed in 1975 aerial photographs.

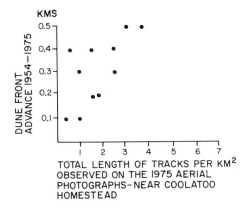

already accelerated dune advance. In these most disturbed areas the rates of
recovery and stabilization deleteriously affected by the many now wild grazing
animals—sheep, rabbits—adapted to the cleared area.

More rigorous photogrametrically based studies of aerial photograph sequences for the entire length of the peninsula, especially of those areas where
pastoralism was less intense, are needed to resolve these problems. However, if
the current rate of dune drift eventually causes sufficient concern for the survival of springs, marshes, and lakes, then the problem of establishing the relative
impacts of vehicles and European pastoralism becomes unimportant, because
any stabilization strategy involving planting and/or surface treatments will
inevitably be incompatible with continued ORV use.

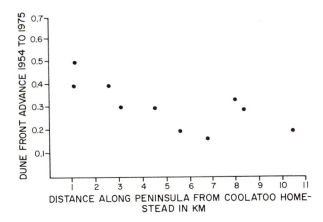

Figure 19-10. The relationship between the rate of advance of the main mobile dune face and the distance along the Peninsula from Coolatoo in the lower
Coorong.

The Impact of ORVs on Plant and Animal Life

The following data derive mainly from the 1975 biological surveys of the Nature Conservation Society of South Australia (Gilbertson and Foale, 1977). Experimental or controlled studies of ORV impact are impracticable for several reasons. Continuous monitoring programs are often frustrated by loss or damage to field equipment, while it is impossible or impolitic for conservation bodies to replicate in controlled studies the types of ORV impacts they deprecate. Similarly, it is not possible to monitor spatial and temporal variations in the types and intensities of ORV use. Consequently, most studies have compared biological data from areas of intensive and relatively infrequent ORV use. As discussed previously, the association of ORV activity with preexisting disturbed ground introduces complications.

The principal effects of ORVs on the plant and animal life in the area are (a) soil surface compaction; (b) accelerated soil erosion; (c) accelerated rates of burial in sand; (d) destruction of vegetation, especially shrub and tree cover; (e) prevention of natural regeneration of a grass or scrub cover; (f) decreased diversity of habitats, and the number of species and often individuals; (g) noise; (h) direct physical impact on plants and animals and associated illegal shooting, hunting, etc.; (i) impairment of resting places on longer distance coastal migration routes; (j) and accelerated spread of alien plants and animals.

Vascular Plants

Vegetation is usually completely absent in the areas of most intensive ORV such as the preferred camping grounds and runways adjacent to the main inland dune face (Figs. 19-5 and 19-6) (Alcock and Symon, 1977; Symon and Gilbertson, 1977). In areas where vehicle pressure is reduced on claypans or dune soils, the primary colonists are alien weeds, often species classified as noxious or "Proclaimed Weeds" under the Weeds Act (South Australia) of 1956 to 1969. These species include *Arctotheca calendula* (L.) Levyns, *Asphodelus fistulosus* L., *Oxalis pes-carprae* L., *Reseda lintea* L., *Marrubium vulgare* L., *Cirsium vulgare* (Savi) Ten., *Carthamus lanatus* L., *Carduus tenuiflorus* Curtis, and other plantains, clovers, and grasses.

Transects across tracks and routes intensively used by ORVs are shown in Figures 19-11, 19-12, and 19-13. The sites include rush (*Juncus* spp.)-covered claypans of dried-up lake margins, scrub-covered stable dune, and grazed, pasture-covered calcrete soils. Alien species are identified on the figures. The claypan site is very rutted by wheels, with marked subsurface compaction (Gilbertson, 1981). There is a gradual decrease in vegetation height from essentially undisturbed vegetation until the track margin is reached, whereupon it declines suddenly. Not surprisingly, the taller *Juncus* are easily killed when hit by vehicles. The distribution of *Juncus* spp. parallels plant litter on the soil surface. The native grass *Zoysia metrella* is most noticeably successful, occurring with alien taxa well known for their tolerance of trampling and compacted

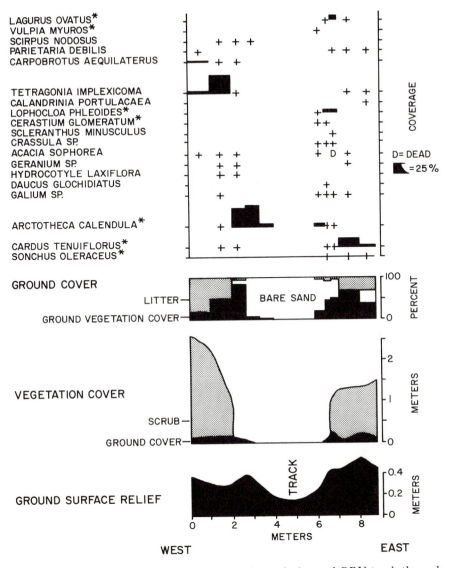

Figure 19-11. Vegetation transect across an intensively used ORV track through the rush-covered claypans of former lake margins. Alien species are shown with an asterisk (redrawn from Symon and Gilbertson, 1977).

soils—*Agrostis* spp., *Poa poaeformus* (Labill) Druce, and *Acaena anserinifolia* (Forst) Druce.

The soils beneath the track crossing the carbonate sands of the scrub-covered vegetated dune are not compacted; rather they are eroding. Vegetation cover and height both decline dramatically at the track margins. The South African cape-weed *(Arctotheca calendula)* is noticeably more resistant to erosion and vehicle

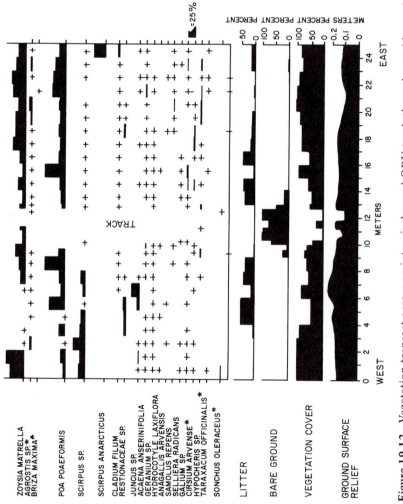

Figure 19-12. Vegetation transect across an intensively used ORV track through a stable scrub covered dune. Alien species are shown with an asterisk (redrawn from Symon and Gilbertson, 1977).

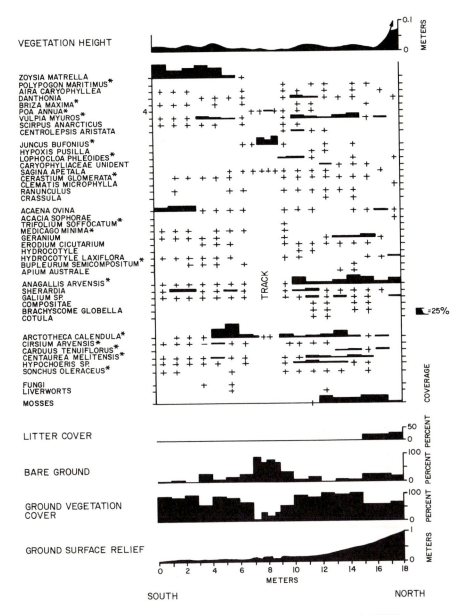

Figure 19-13. Vegetation transect across an intensively used ORV route on grazed pasture over calcrete. Alien species are shown with an asterisk (redrawn from Symon and Gilbertson, 1977).

pressure as a result of its low rosette growth form. Surface plant litter, important for soil fauna, does not survive in the vicinity of the track.

The calcreted soils are resistant to compaction and erosion. As with grazed limestone pastures in many parts of the world, the flora of these areas is relatively rich. The vegetation as a whole is comparatively more resistant to vehicle wear than the two previous examples. *Poa annua* and *Arctotheca* survive in the most intensely pressured areas. Not surprisingly, mosses, fungi, and liverworts are intolerant of vehicle pressure.

In all cases, increasing vehicle pressure causes a decline in vegetation height, structural complexity, species numbers, and diversity. Most native species are seen to be poorly tolerant or intolerant of either, or both, direct or indirect vehicle impacts. A major effect of vehicle pressure is the introduction and spread of more resistant alien species from the land disturbed by earlier pastoralism. One example, *Arctotheca,* like many other alien species, currently has a useful sand-binding role. It does not otherwise appear able to penetrate into scrub-covered areas.

The impact of vehicles on the unusual flora of the lake beds exposed during the summer drought is largely unknown. One effect is for the usually precise vegetation zonation to be displaced in wheel ruts. Its significance for the *Ruppia* grasses, blue-green algae, and burrowing lake fauna is unknown.

Invertebrates

Arthropods living on or near the air-soil interface, on the soil surface, in litter, or on low-growing vegetation have been shown to be sensitive to trampling, and the fauna of grassland litter has been suggested as being affected by trampling levels lower than those required to produce change in the vegetation (Duffey, 1975). Ants and Collembola were studied on transects across disturbed and undisturbed habitats by Greenslade and Greenslade (1977). These authors found that species diversity and population numbers were lower on the tracks and disturbed ground, with edge effects slightly increasing species numbers across transitional zones.

Vertebrates

Few differences were observed in the mammal faunas of disturbed as opposed to relatively undisturbed sites (James, 1977), the survey emphasizing the richness of the introduced European fauna and the decline of the native fauna. Studies of the frog, lizard, and snake faunas (Chesson, 1977; Roberts, 1977) were restricted in scope and failed to detect any species changes attributable to ORV impact. The bird fauna is very well known (Glover, 1975; Hawkes, 1975; Swaby and Jenkins, 1977) and includes several very rare species, such as the Cape Barren goose *(Ereopsis novae hollandiae)* which feeds on grasses around the freshwater springs along the dune margins. This coastal strip is also the last refuge of the orange-bellied parrot *(Neophana chrysogaster),* the beautiful firetail *(Emblema bella),* and the southern emu-wren *(Stipiturus malachuras).* Several rare species are especially secretive and readily lost through habitat disturbance and noise. Currently, the most endangered species is the rufous bristle bird *(Asyornia broadbenti).* Once the habitat of this unique bird is damaged, it is unclear how vegetation may be restored in an appropriate manner for the bird (Swaby and Jenkins, 1977).

Management Possibilities

The data currently available indicate that sand dune drift is a real threat to the freshwater springs, many claypans, and lakes, while loss of habitat continues as a result of dune-scrub habitat damage. This is a threat first to the local plant and animal life (especially to species sensitive to noise or having unusual habitats). It is possible that the loss of such linear coastal lines of habitats between the ocean and the "Little Desert" immediately inland may represent disruption of long-distance bird migration routes. Only in the case of the vascular flora and soil invertebrates have the general nature of the ORV impact been identified. If such problems are viewed by national park and planning authorities as reinitiating a more active management strategy for the region, then several further issues must be resolved.

Attempts to control dune drift by planting, barriers, and/or soil treatments must commence in the sand source areas (i.e., back beach and foredunes) as well as the active dune front and middune areas. There are already so many European and South African species in the problem areas that attention might be given to their extensive use as stabilizing agents. The annual coastal spurges (*Euphorbia* spp.) merit special attention. These prolific self-seeding species trap sand to form a complex pattern of closely spaced 0.5 to 1 m high mounds, resembling an "inverted egg-box" topography. The morphology is similar to World War II tank traps. This microtopography is extremely difficult for most ORVs to cross. Any stabilization policy must exclude ORVs from these areas. This in turn raises questions on how to achieve the management objectives with minimal resources: the extent to which alternative sites will be offered as "honey pots" for ORV owners; how any such policy may be enforced and/or supported.

A major key to any management program lies in the monitoring of access, the sequence of ORV users, and the spreading geomorphic impact discussed previously. Control of the initial exploring trailbike user is imperative. This is achievable by closing the main access route of the Old Melbourne Road (Princes Highway) to all except family vehicles; second, by instigating prosecution against the trailbike-transporting trailers and vans which are parked off-road in the area; third, by excavating ditches with backhoes, and/or sowing with native trees or the well-established locally present thorn-bearing shrubs.

The provision of resistant 20 to 50 m long routes using calcrete rubble, linking the many small areas of pasture-covered calcretes, would facilitate camping and recreation for families and aid educational or scientific parties without the present necessity of driving across the lake and claypan surfaces with their more sensitive flora, fauna, and soils.

The posting of signs and warning information at the southern perimeter of the reserve, especially near the beach area, indicating the importance of the Coorong reserve and the impacts upon it of ORV use, would probably have a gratifying response from the many responsible ORV users who gain access to the area from Kingston beach.

Finally, public and private concerns might be further advised of the recreational potential of routes measuring 100 to 200 km in length which could be sited on the 2 to 3 m deep calcrete soils overlying the inland paleodunes systems. These extend in lines parallel to the coast inland from the Coorong until the area of Naracoorte, 80 km inland. Many long-distance routes are practical on these paleodunes. Removal of the calcrete in the usual manner using explosives over 50 to 400 m areas would provide the type of attraction sought by those who wish to make very intensive use of an area. Nevertheless, the solution to the ORV problem in such areas may lie ultimately in the price of fuel rather than local and regional management policies.

References

Alcock, C. R., and D. E. Symon. 1977. The flora. In: D. D. Gilbertson and M. R. Foale (Eds.), The Southern Coorong and Lower Younghusband Peninsula of South Australia. Nature Conservation Society of South Australia Inc., Adelaide, pp. 25–44.

Australian House of Representatives Standing Committee on Environment and Conservation. 1977. Off-Road Vehicles: Impact on the Australian Environment. Australian Government Publishing Service, Canberra.

Chesson, P. L. 1977. Reptiles. In: D. D. Gilbertson and M. R. Foale (Eds.), The Southern Coorong and Lower Younghusband Peninsula of South Australia. Nature Conservation Society of South Australia Inc., Adelaide, pp. 55–56.

Crozier, M. J., S. L. Marz, and I. J. Grant. 1977. Off-road-vehicle recreation: the impact of off-road-motorcycles on soil and vegetation conditions. In: T. J. Hearn and R. P. Hargreaves (Eds.), Proceedings of the 9th New Zealand Geographical Conference, Dunedin, pp. 76–79.

Duffey, E. 1975. The effects of human trampling on the fauna of grassland buttes. Biol. Conserv. 7:255–274.

Geddes, M., and M. Brock. 1977. Limnology of some lagoons in the southern Coorong. In: D. D. Gilbertson and M. R. Foale (Eds.), The Southern Coorong and Lower Younghusband Peninsula of South Australia. Nature Conservation Society of South Australia Inc., Adelaide, pp. 47–49.

Gilbertson, D. D. 1981. The impact of past and present land use on a major coastal barrier system. Appl. Geogr. 1(2):97–119.

Gilbertson, D. D., and M. R. Foale (Eds.). 1977. The Southern Coorong and Lower Younghusband Peninsula of South Australia. Nature Conservation Society of South Australia Inc., Adelaide, p. 121.

Glover, B. 1975. A list of aquatic birds of the Coorong. In: J. Noye (Ed.), The Coorong. Publication 39, Department of Adult Education, University of Adelaide, South Australia, Appendix 7a.

Godfrey, P. J., S. P. Leatherman, and P. A. Buckley. 1978. Impact of off-road vehicles on coastal ecosystems. In: Proceedings of a Symposium on Technical, Environmental, Socioeconomic, and Regulatory Aspects of Coastal Zone Planning and Management. San Francisco, pp. 581–600.

Greenslade, P., and P. M. Greenslade. 1977. Effects of vehicles on arthropods inhabiting the soil surface. In: D. D. Gilbertson and M. R. Foale (Eds.), The Southern Coorong and Lower Younghusband Peninsula of South Australia. Nature Conservation Society of South Australia Inc., Adelaide, pp. 93–98.

Hall, R. D. 1975. Can public land be protected from motorized vehicles. Victorian Resources 17(2):21–24.

Hawkes, W. R. 1974. Wildlife of the Coorong Area. In: J. Noye (Ed.), The Coorong (rev. ed.). Publication 39, Department of Adult Education, University of Adelaide, South Australia, Appendix 8.

Hozier, P. E., and T. E. Eaton. 1980. The impact of vehicles on dune and grassland vegetation on a south-eastern North Carolina barrier beach. J. Appl. Ecol. 17:173–182.

James, C. T. 1977. Mammals. In: D. D. Gilbertson and M. R. Foale (Eds.), The Southern Coorong and Lower Younghusband Peninsula of South Australia. Nature Conservation Society of South Australia Inc., Adelaide, pp. 67-68.

Noye, J. (Ed.). 1975. The Coorong (rev. ed.). Publication 39, Department of Adult Education, University of Adelaide, South Australia.

Paton, J. B. 1977. Historical notes on the Coorong. In: D. D. Gilbertson and M. R. Foale (Eds.), The Southern Coorong and Lower Younghusband Peninsula of South Australia. Nature Conservation Society of South Australia Inc., Adelaide, pp. 99–105.

Roberts, J. D. 1977. Frogs. In: D. D. Gilbertson and M. R. Foale (Eds.), The Southern Coorong and Lower Younghusband Peninsula of South Australia. Nature Conservation Society of South Australia Inc., Adelaide, pp. 51–54.

Robertson, J. P., and R. Wood. 1977. Off-road Vehicles in Australia. Australian Institute of Parks and School of Applied Science, Canberra College of Advanced Education, Australian Capital Territory, Australia.

Recreational Vehicles Co-ordinating Council of South Australia (Inc.). 1975. Recommendations on the Control and Management of Recreational Vehicles in South Australia. Report submitted to the Department of Environment and Conservation, State Government of South Australia. (Available for inspection in the library of the Department of Environment and Conservation, Adelaide.)

Steiner, A. J., and S. P. Leatherman. 1979. An Annotated Bibliography of the Effects of Off-Road Vehicles and Pedestrian Traffic on Coastal Ecosystems. The Environmental Institute, University of Massachusetts, 87 pp.

Swaby, R. J., and C. R. Jenkin. 1977. Birds. In: D. D. Gilbertson and M. R. Foale (Eds.), The Southern Coorong and Lower Younghusband Peninsula of South Australia. Nature Conservation Society of South Australia Inc., Adelaide, pp. 39–43.

Welsh, A. 1975. Report of Off-Road-Recreational-Vehicles. South Australian Department of Environment and Conservation, Environment Division, SADEC 3, Adelaide.

Wood, J. P. 1978. ORV planning and management workshop—Canberra. School of Applied Science, Canberra College of Advanced Education, Australian Capital Territory, Australia.

20

Chrysotile Asbestos in a Vehicular Recreation Area: A Case Study[1]

William Popendorf and Hans-Rudolph Wenk

Introduction

The popularity of off-road vehicle (ORV) recreation provides fresh evidence that not only can man have an adverse impact on particular ecosystems, but these systems in turn can have a negative effect on man. Severe injuries incurred while using recreational vehicles are obvious hazards, but they may be blamed on the participants themselves. A less readily recognized danger lies in the development of chronic or latent diseases related to the geological setting itself. This chapter describes investigations of a California ORV area to evaluate the potential for respiratory diseases attributable to repeated and prolonged exposures to very high concentrations of chrysotile asbestos in ambient-soil and user-generated airborne dust.

Geology

The Clear Creek Recreational Area is located in the Southern Diablo Range, San Benito County, California, about 185 km southeast of San Francisco, and is part of more than 250 km^2 of federally owned land in this region that is supervised by the Bureau of Land Management (BLM). Among its major attractions are sparsely vegetated and erosion-resistant slopes which attract adventurous cyclists. The Clear Creek area is centered in a large serpentinite body 6 km wide and 22 km long, which is exposed over 130 km^2 (Fig. 20-1).

---

[1] The views and conclusions contained in this chapter are based on the authors' studies or experiences and do not necessarily represent the official viewpoint or policy of any U.S. government agency.

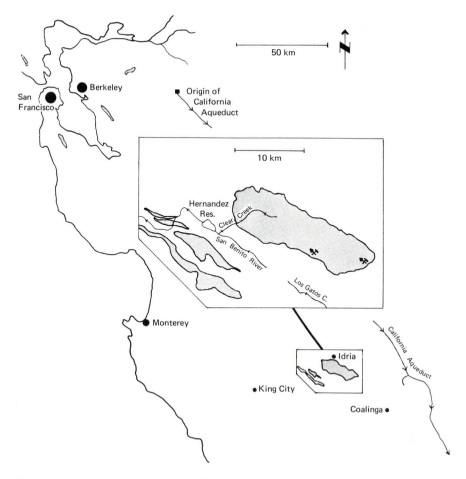

Figure 20-1. Regional setting of the Clear Creek Recreation Area. Largely serpentine ultramafic rocks are indicated by shaded zones. Inset shows details of New Idria complex.

The petrography and minerology of the area have been described by Eckel and Myers (1946), Bailey et al. (1964), and Mumpton and Thompson (1975). Coleman (1961) concluded that the ultramafic body originally consisted of 30% perdotite and 10% dunite which was almost completely serpentinized at depth to chrysotile, lizardite, and antigorite, leaving only occasional relics of the original olivine-pyroxene assemblage. In addition to serpentine minerals, 10 to 15% brucite is present along with magnetite, chromite, and calcite; the latter minerals occur mainly in veinlets (Mumpton and Thompson, 1975). The presence of brucite suggests that serpentinization proceeded below 400°C via the reaction olivine + water → serpentine + brucite, isochemically and was accompanied by a volume increase of 40%. The decrease in bulk density may have been the main driving force for the upward tectonic intrusion of this ultramafic mass as a more or less continuous body into the sedimentary rocks of the Coast Ranges. Serpentine rocks composed of antigorite and relics of peridotite are massive, forming cliffs and ridges, but parts have been brecciated and highly sheared during uplift. The bulk of the friable and fractured serpentine surface exposures and soils consists of 75% chrysotile (Cooper et al., 1979), making the San Benito complex an unusual ultramafic body.

Vegetation

Despite the fact that annual rainfall in the Clear Creek Basin is typically 500 mm, falling mainly between November and April, vegetation is sparse and confined to clusters of chaparral, principally leather oak *(Quercus durata)* and manzanita *(Arctostaphylos glauca* and *A. pungens),* with scattered stands of Coulter *(Pinus coulteri),* Digger *(P. sabiniana),* and Jeffrey *(P. jeffreyi)* pine trees. Many of the slopes and ridges are totally devoid of vegetation. This pattern is the result of typical nutrient imbalances in serpentine soils and is enhanced by numerous landslides. Griffin (1974) reported an available magnesium:calcium ratio of 9:1, with only 0.006% total nitrogen and nearly undetectable amounts of phosphorus. Few native plants and practically no commercial agricultural crops can tolerate such low nutrient levels, and as a consequence no homesteaders settled the land.

History

The development of major cinnabar mines and mercury smelters during the late 1800s resulted in the decimation of much of the pine and cedar forests on the eastern edge of the area by the turn of the century. Later needs for domestic sources of chromite spurred rampant trail development during the early part of the twentieth century. In 1958 Rice and Matthews of the California Division of Mines reported a white, "mountain-leather-like" material which covered many hillsides and suggested that it might be asbestos (anonymous, 1957; Matthews, 1961). More surface scarring resulted from asbestos exploration, which led to the discovery of one of the world's largest asbestos deposits on the southern slopes of the complex, and California soon became the largest asbestos-producing state in the United States with three mines supplying over 100,000 t in 1973. Commercial chrysotile fibers from these open pit mines are relatively short, attaining a maximum length of only a few millimeters.

Except for a brief period from 1907 to 1916, when the area was part of the Monterey National Forest, most of the San Benito complex has been administered by the BLM. Until recently the area received little recreational usage except by rock collectors, botanists, and occasional game hunters. However, during the past 10 years the dramatic growth in high-performance ORVs and increasing restrictions on other hill-climbing ORV recreational areas has led the BLM to develop the San Benito area for heavier recreational use. The naturally barren slopes, the network of bulldozed mining trails, the unique property of serpentine soils even when wet to support vehicles, and the isolated location further contributed to its rapidly increased uses, particularly during the rainy season.

Because of its isolation the area is not patrolled/managed by a BLM ranger every day, and use statistics are therefore incomplete; however, recent estimates seem to lie between 20,000 and 40,000 visitor-days per year, consisting principally of trail motorcyclists and a much smaller number of four-wheel-drive enthusiasts, including many families with children who plan weekend (and sometimes longer) camping excursions into the area. Access by pickup-campers and similar vehicles which many of the visitors use is restricted primarily to the main unpaved road running along Clear Creek. A majority of ORV users operate from campsites along this road, which parallels Clear Creek. From there the riders fan out across many large, bald ridges, hillsides, and dirt trails. The undulating terrain and frequent clusters of chaparral provide the riders with a feeling of isolation while they restrict any attempts by the BLM to manage use patterns by visual surveillance.

Against this background and with the increasing recognition of asbestos as a long-term health hazard, the BLM initiated a series of studies to verify and quantify the dust exposures of users and rangers within the Clear Creek Basin. A preliminary survey reported by Cooper et al. (1979) demonstrated that, as expected, the aerosols generated by vehicles in this area contained high levels of chrysotile fibers. However, more information was needed concerning the spatial and temporal patterns of airborne dust as they might relate to potential health risks and to various management options. Further measurements were therefore collected of dustfall, soil moisture, rainfall, and aerosols from March through June 1979, during the transition from wet spring to dry summer conditions.

Experimental Procedures and Results

Dustfall

Dustfall samples (American Public Health Association, 1977) were collected at five points along the main canyon road to evaluate the dispersion and drift of settled road dust, to monitor its mineral composition over this 3-month transition season, and to provide an index of area use patterns and intensities. Metal dustfall cans 13.6 cm in diameter were irregularly painted on the outside (olive drab and flat black) to blend with nearby chaparral in a largely successful effort to avoid tampering. Five sample containers were placed on 2-m stakes within 2 m of the road and replaced at variable intervals depending upon area use intensities and soil dryness, as shown in Table 20-1. These five roadside stations were located at distances of approximately 3, 3.5, 4.2, 4.9, and 5.8 km from the nominal entrance to the recreational area, extending from the second of three popular campsites to the head of the canyon (where the road abruptly begins

Table 20-1. Dustfall Along Main Clear Creek Road (values in g m^{-2} month^{-1})[a]

Station	Inclusive period					
	23 Mar 6 Apr	6 Apr 9 Apr	9 Apr 22 Apr	22 Apr 6 May	6 May 19 May	19 May 17 Jun
1	5.0	55.	15.5	9.3	5.0	11.4
2	b	39.	13.1	8.9	4.9	b
3	1.8	29.	10.6	6.8	5.3	5.2
4	b	22.	6.1	3.6	2.8	4.8
5	5.0	9.7	8.8	5.5	4.7	6.4
Average vehicles per day	35.	132.	30.	16.	6.	9.
Soil moisture (%)	∿9.	3.5	3.	2.	1.5	0.5

[a]Vehicles estimated from BLM reports and average soil moisture from model estimates.
[b]Samples vandalized in the field.

to climb the northern ridge). In addition, three other containers were set along each of two transects extending laterally up to 50 m in a prevailingly downwind (southeasterly) direction from the road at stations 2 and 4.

The dust collected at each station was measured for mass and analyzed later by x-ray powder diffraction (XRD) techniques. XRD patterns indicated that in most locations, dust consisted almost entirely of serpentine minerals with minor amounts of olivine and pyroxene (Fig. 20-2a is typical of the majority of samples). Only near the metamorphic inclusion near the center of the canyon (Coleman, 1961) did we observe a greater variety of components (Fig. 20-3b). As the season progressed, only slight changes were observed in the relative mineralogical composition of the collected dust at each station. This consistency indicated to us that there were negligible changes in the composition of particles resuspended from local soils as a function of soil moisture.

The rate of dustfall at each roadside station is shown in Table 20-1. Dustfall along the transects is represented graphically in Figure 20-3 as a percentage of the roadside dustfall at their respective location. It can be seen that the bulk of the suspended roaddust settles within the first 10 to 15 m of the road, beyond which levels rapidly stabilize at values near the limit of sensitivity for this technique (0.2 g m^{-2} month^{-1}; American Public Health Association, 1977).

Vehicle-use and soil-moisture data recorded by the BLM rangers were then examined in an attempt to explain temporal patterns in dustfall along the road. BLM rangers patrol the area in a four-wheel-drive pickup truck 3 to 5 days a week. Their records of the number of vehicles observed in the area were used to estimate average vehicle-days during each period as listed in Table 20-1. Multiple linear-regression analyses indicated that vehicular activity had the most pro-

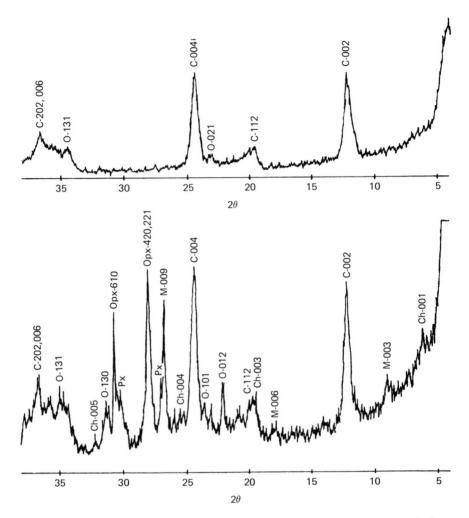

Figure 20-2. X-ray powder diffraction patterns of dust samples collected along Clear Creek road. Cu K_α-radiation, graphite monochromatized; ordinate gives diffraction angle 2θ. C, serpentine (chrysotile); Ch, chlorite; M, muscovite; O, olivine; Opx, orthopyroxene; Px, clinopyroxene.

found effect on dustfall (see regression coefficients, Table 20-2). This is not surprising given the fact that soil moisture only establishes the potential for aerosolization but the vehicles actually provide the mechanism. The number of visitors per day varied considerably both because of the seasonal weather and when an organized ORV event was scheduled (e.g., the weekend of 7 and 8 April). The regression constant values remaining after accounting for the effect of vehicles (a in Table 20-2) range from 2.1 to 5.4 g m^{-2} month^{-1}, values very similar to the background levels of 1.5 to 3.0 g m^{-2} month^{-1} collected at transsect stations 10 m from the road.

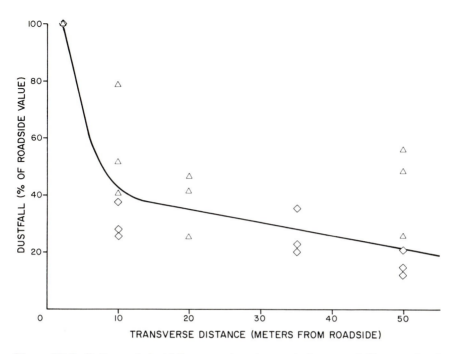

Figure 20-3. Pattern of dustfall among two transects from road ($\Diamond$ = station 2; $\triangle$ = station 4). Note the apparent increase in dustfall 50 m from station 4 during two periods from April 22 to June 17.

By calculating dustfall per vehicle, the independent effect of soil moisture can be isolated as shown in Figure 20-4. Two patterns can be noted here. One is the tendency for dustfall per vehicle to decrease for stations further from the main canyon entry portal. This tendency is even more clearly seen in the slopes of the regression lines (b as listed in Table 20-2) and is thought to be caused by more frequent vehicular traffic near the entrance and central portions of the canyon

Table 20-2. Regression of Dustfall as a Linear Function of Average Number of Vehicles per Day Reported or Estimated in the Area (dustfall) = $a + b$ (vehicles/day), the Regression r^2, and the Probability (p) that this Correlation Was a Random Occurrence

Station	a	b	r^2	p
1	2.23	0.38	.915	.01
2	4.3	0.26	.997	.001
3	2.5	0.19	.86	.01
4	2.1	0.15	.988	.001
5	5.4	0.30	.55	.1

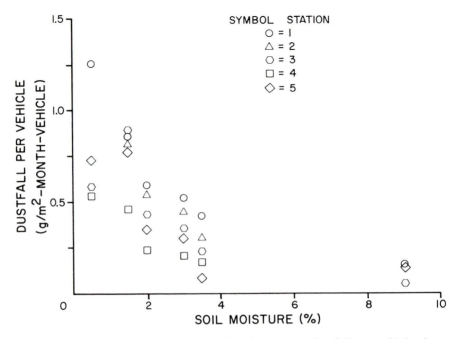

Figure 20-4. Relationship between soil moisture and dustfall per vehicle along the main canyon road.

than at the head of the canyon. Second is the apparent nonlinear relationship between soil moisture and dustfall, a relationship perhaps better described by an exponential $(Y = Y_o e^{-ax})$ or "threshold" model, as discussed in the next section.

The use of dustfall measurements in ORV management programs thus shows some promise but also has limitations. For instance, local sources of pollen can increase apparent sample mass and variability. This may well have occurred at station 5 and could have been verified and corrected by determining only the inorganic fraction. Dispersion measurements can also be affected by local secondary sources such as a small undeveloped bike path which was discovered late in this study near the distal station of the second transect as shown in Figure 20-3. Furthermore, the apparent contribution of each vehicle to roadside dustfall is probably specific to each soil/road composition. However, it is also apparent that dustfall can be used as an inexpensive, passive technique within a generally homogeneous environment to evaluate both temporal and spatial ORV use patterns.

Aerosol Sampling

The evaluation of personal exposures to respiratory hazards is one traditional role of industrial hygienists within the occupational setting. The standard industrial personal air sampling (PAS) method employs a 37-mm open-face filter cassette (e.g., Gelman Instrument Co., Ann Arbor, Michigan, or Millipore Corp., Bedford, Massachusetts) aspirating at a rate near 2 liters min^{-1} [National Institute for Occupational Safety and Health (NIOSH), 1977]. The application of this PAS technology to ORV users is not wholly satisfactory. Significant inaccuracies result because air entering the cassette is not isokinetic with average motorcycle speeds (0.04 m sec^{-1} versus 4 to 10 m sec^{-1}), increasing the measured concentration above ambient levels (Fuchs, 1975; Sehmel, 1970). The significance of this error is mitigated by the fact that the rider's nose and mouth are similarly anisokinetic (Wood and Birkett, 1979). Stationary area sampling is an unacceptable alternative to sampling near the ORV rider's breathing zone because of the rapid dispersion of aerosols from the source. The evaluation of nonfibrous aerosols would permit the use of a cyclone preselector, greatly decreasing the cross-sectional area of the orifice, reducing the velocity difference, and thereby improving the sampling accuracy (Lippmann, 1970; Seltzer et al., 1971). However, for asbestos aerosol sampling the standard open-face cassette remains the best highly mobile method available and allows a more direct comparison of results to an established data base.

Nine sets of personal aerosol samples were collected on groups of 5 or 6 motorcyclists who rode along one of two fixed circuits. On one circuit (run A) cyclists stayed single file on a well-traveled dirt road leading from the creek to the top of a prominent ridge, completing the 8 km round trip in 15 to 18 min. Within broad guidelines the riders on the second circuit (run B) had more latitude to vary their group sequence and path; a loop of 19 to 22 km was generally traversed in 50 to 70 min. Eight other aerosol samples were collected on the ranger or in campsites.

Analyses of these aerosol samples were made for asbestos fibers principally using phase contrast light microscopy at 450X to determine airborne fiber concentration, fibers cm^{-3} (NIOSH, 1977). By convention when using this method, only particles with a greater than 3:1 aspect ratio and 5 μm length are counted. Sample mass was measured but it soon became clear that on wet terrain, droplets or large clumps of mud or dried dirt fragments frequently struck the filter, making direct measurement of aerosol mass concentration an unreliable estimate of respiratory exposure.

Six of the filters were also prepared for transmission electron microscope (TEM) analysis as described by Ortiz and Isom (1974). Fibers were counted and sized in the TEM at magnifications of 10^3X and 10^4X, and their mineralogical and chemical composition was frequently verified by selected area diffraction (SAD) and energy dispersive x-ray analysis (see Cooper et al., 1979). Both TEM and light microscopy (LM) indicated that more than 90% of the particles were fibrous. TEM displayed the tubular morphology and SAD of chrysotile (Fig. 20-5). Flakes of antigorite and fibers of tremolite were rarely observed (Cooper et al., 1979). Chrysotile was clearly the dominant component in these samples.

The results of LM analyses are shown in Table 20-3. An evaluation of the experimental methods can be made by an examination of Table 20-3 and the duplicate LM and TEM counts shown in Table 20-4. The agreement between

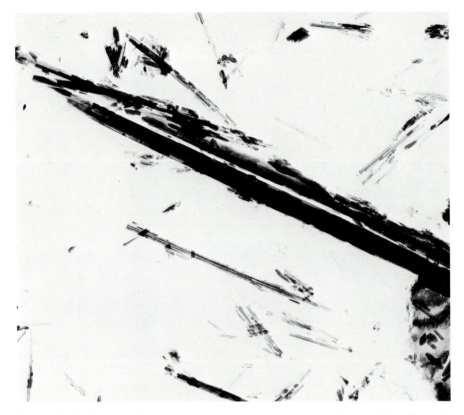

Figure 20-5. Typical electron microscope image of dust particles collected on air filters of motorcyclists. Notice the tubular morphology of chrysotile.

microscopes is quite good. The consistency both between and within these data is characteristic of these experimental methods [Joint (American Conference of Governmental Industrial Hygienists [ACGIH] and American Industrial Hygiene Association [AIHA]) Committee on Aerosol Hazards, 1975]. There seem to be proportionally fewer fibers 5 μm long than were reported in the preliminary study of Murchio et al. (1978). The toxicological importance of fiber size, especially its length, is a point of some controversy, but most of the evidence indicates that the longer fibers (5 μm) are more fibrogenic than the shorter fibers (Harrington, 1976; NIOSH, 1976). The effect of fiber size on the carcinogenicity of asbestos is less certain.

On the first set of runs (March 24, 1979), the soil was still relatively wet (Figs. 20-6 and 20-7), and aerosol concentrations did not exceed 0.5 fibers cm^{-3}. Values thereafter ranged from 1 to 10 fibers cm^{-3}. This range can be compared with campsite measurements of 0.05 when quiescent and 0.5 when vehicles were active. When comparing the two runs, it can be seen that, in general, exposures were greater on run A than B. The major factor contributing to

Table 20-3 Aerosol Concentration, fibers cm^{-3}, for Samples Collected on Clear Creek Motorcycle Riders

	Rider position						
	1	2	3	4	5	6	Mean[a]
Run A							
24 Mar 79	0.1	0.1	0.13	0.13	0.13	0.26	.13 ± .09
15 Apr 79	0.30	3.0	7.1	4.5	7.0		5.4 ± 2.0
22 Apr 79	0.13	2.0	2.4	7.7	3.9		5.4 ± 3.8
19 May 79	0.1	2.9	3.9	1.6	1.5	7.0	3.4 ± 2.3
17 Jun 79	0.16	2.4	5.2	1.0	2.7		2.8 ± 1.7
18 Jun 78[c]	0.9	5.6	2.3	4.3	2.8	5.3	4.1 ± 1.5
Mean[b] ratio to mean	.1 ± .1	.8 ± .5	1.3 ± .7	1.0 ± .5	2.2 ± .5		
Run B							
24 Mar 79	0.05	0.26	0.10	0.25	0.45	0.05	.26 ± .14
22 Apr 79	0.9	2.0	2.0	1.2	2.9	3.2	2.3 ± 0.8
19 Apr 79	0.31	0.9	0.74	0.19	0.39	1.4	0.7 ± 0.5
17 Jun 79	0.31	1.1	1.7	0.44	0.48		0.9 ± 0.6
18 Jun 78[c]	0.3	1.9	3.2	2.9	1.7	2.9	2.5 ± 0.7
Mean[b] ratio to mean	.3 ± .2	1.2 ± .2	1.2 ± .6	0.8 ± .5	1.1 ± .7	1.3 ± .8	

[a]Mean and standard deviation of aerosols at the second through last positions, inclusive.

[b]Mean and standard deviation of the ratios of each measurement at that position (column) to the mean for that row as calculated in note a above.

[c]From Cooper et al. (1979).

Table 20-4. Comparison Between Concentration of Fibers Above and Below 5 m Using Light Microscope (LM) and TEM Techniques

	Position	Fibers <5 μm long		Fibers >5 μm long		
		TEM	LM	TEM	LM[a]	LM[b]
Run						
24 Mar	3	19–62		0.4	0.13	0.13
22 Apr	4	1.0–2.4	1.3	0.2–1.1	0.7	1.2
19 Jun	3	8.9–12.	12.	0.5–11.	1.9	5.2
18 Jun	4		1.3	3.7–4.9	1.6	1.0
Camp samples						
24 Mar		1.8	0.2	.17	.47	0.08
19 May		0.9	0.1	0.1	.03	0.04

[a] Separate analyses which may not agree with Table 20-3.
[b] Corresponding samples from Table 20-3.

this difference was probably the greater degree of latitude available to the riders on run B to vary their intragroup spacing and position, and thereby avoid some visible dust clouds.

The first rider in a group was always in significantly cleaner air than those in the remaining positions. The mean fiber concentration for these remaining positions was calculated for each run (mean in Table 20-3). It can be seen that exposures are relatively uniform from the second rider on back. This is important not only from the point of view of the direct health implications but also because it indicates that future evaluations of a similar sort could be made with as few as two or three motorcycles. In fact, given the variability noted above, more consistent results could be expected from two or three well-disciplined riders than from the larger group of locally available volunteers participating in this study.

The effect of soil moisture upon aerosol exposures is depicted in Figure 20-7. There is only a slight linear correlation between moisture and aerosols on run B ($r^2 = 0.33$) and a negligible correlation on run A ($r^2 = 0.17$). The variability among the riders and their actions is thought to be one factor in the low correlations, but again as for dustfall, a linear correlation may be totally inappropriate. For instance, aerosols may only become a problem for soil moisture below a certain threshold similar to that described by Chepil (1956) who characterized wind erosion forces as having to overcome a particle adhesion threshold, the magnitude of which is dependent upon soil moisture and soil type. Based on data contained in Figures 20-5 and 20-7, the threshold for vehicles to generate significant aerosols from these serpentine soils seems to lie between 3 and 5% moisture by weight.

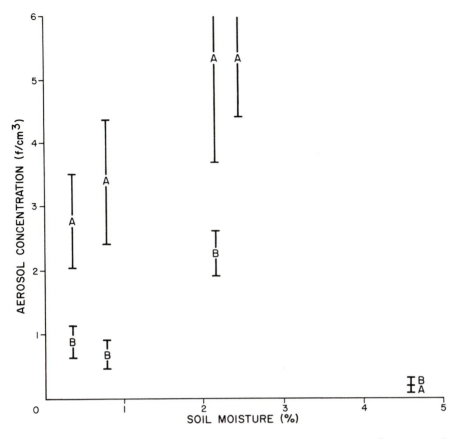

Figure 20-6. Pattern between measured soil moisture and mean fiber aerosol concentration excluding the first motorcycle rider for run A and run B, as indicated. Vertical bars indicate standard error of the mean. Scale: 4 cm = 1 μm.

Soil Moisture

Because of the importance of moisture as a predictor of ORV-generated aerosols, an empirical model relating soil moisture to rainfall was developed as a prospective management tool. The first-order kinetic form of this model is similar to the "antecedent-precipitation index" (API) proposed by Kohler and Linsley (1951) and Linsley et al. (1975). Rather than use an index per se, for our purpose "predicted moisture" (M, percentage of soil by weight) was preferred, although converting from rainfall to soil moisture required an additional empirical coefficient. Whereas the API was applied to seasonal water basin accounting schemes, M in surface soils can vary much more rapidly than the bulk soil moisture. Two compartments were therefore included in this model to characterize the superimposed patterns of slow, seasonal moisture accumulation (M_1) with

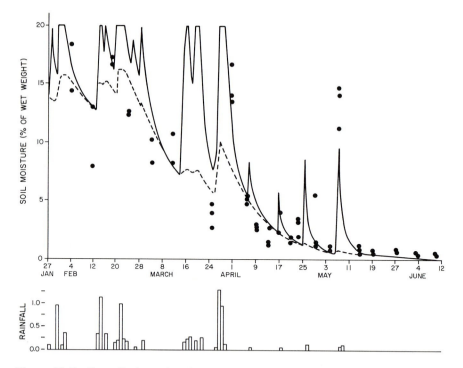

Figure 20-7. Compilation of soil moisture measured at three points and daily rainfall reported at two nearby recording stations (16 to 18 km north and south of test area). The results of moisture model (Equation 20-1 shown by dashed line; Equation 20-3 by solid line) are superimposed.

transient spikes (M_2) following a rain (R, inches of water). The physical analogy of M_1 is "capillary water" which relates to the retention and evaporation of moisture within the internal and interstitial pore spaces of the soil particles: and for M_2, "gravity water," the more rapid accumulation, percolation, and evaporation characteristics of particle-free surface water (Chepil, 1956; Linsley et al., 1975). The physical measurement of soil moisture is the sum of these two components.

The mathematical form of the moisture equations is indicated by Equations (20-1) to (20-3) which calculate M stepwise (day by day) based on the previous day's moisture (M') and recorded or expected rainfall.

$$M_1 = k_1 M_1' + k_3 R \qquad (20\text{-}1)$$

$$M_2 = k_2 M_2' + k_4 R \qquad (20\text{-}2)$$

$$M = M_1 + M_2 \qquad (20\text{-}3)$$

As with the "recession factor" $(1 - k)$ used in the API, the factors k_1 and k_2 should be adjusted for seasonal variations in potential evaporation. Linsley et al. (1975) described "evaporation pan" measurements which we found to be a convenient index on which to base such seasonal adjustments. United States Weather Bureau reports from the nearest evaporation station (National Oceanographic and Atmospheric Administration, 1979; San Luis Dam, approximately 85 km north in a setting similar to Clear Creek) indicate that monthly evaporation ranged in a pseudosinusoidal manner between roughly 1.5 inches (3.8 cm) in January and 17.5 inches (44 cm) in July, or expressed mathematically with advancing calendar date

$$\text{Pan evaporation (mm)} = 440 \left[0.543 - 0.457 \cos \left(2\pi \text{ date}/365 \right) \right] \quad (20\text{-}4)$$

Thus Equation 20-5 was patterned after Equation 20-4 and used to seasonally adjust the k_1 coefficient as follows:

$$k_1 = 1 - \alpha \left[0.54 - 0.46 \cos \left(2\pi \text{ date}/365 \right) \right] \quad (20\text{-}5)$$

where α is the maximum fraction of capillary water which will evaporate per day. Together Equations (20-1) and (20-5) are equivalent to Kohler's and Linsley's API translated into percentage moisture. These equations account for evaporative losses. In water basin applications it could be assumed that other "losses" from the surface, such as percolation, would remain within the basin. However, it was felt that any loss from the surface would affect the aerosolizability of the soil, and a second compartment was therefore included in this model.

Percolation affects particle-free surface water much more readily than capillary water, and this effect is not expected to be seasonally variable. Some evaporation may still affect M_2. A reasonable adjustment to the coefficient k_2 was found to be

$$k_2 = 1 - \beta \left[0.90 - 0.10 \cos \left(2\pi \text{ date}/365 \right] \right) \quad (20\text{-}6)$$

where β is the maximum fraction of gravity water which will be lost per day. In future studies it may well prove that k_2 can be assumed to be a constant as are k_3 and k_4.

Other considerations which should be accounted for in surface moisture are saturation and runoff. These factors were not measured in this study but a convenient maximum moisture content of 20% was somewhat arbitrarily selected. It is within the range of other soils (Linsley et al., 1975) and was never exceeded during this study even for measurements collected during a storm (see Fig. 20-8). During the stepwise calculations of M, whenever $M_1 + M_2$ exceeded 20%, the excess M_2 was assumed to run off and was therefore deleted from M_2. This may be an unrealistic simplification, but it is one which is consistent with the empirical nature of the model, the limited resolution of daily rainfall, and the spotty nature of the field moisture data.

To supply data for this model (as well as for the prior correlations with dustfall and aerosols), soil moisture measurements were performed by BLM rangers at three locations using a Soiltest Speedy Moisture Tester (Soiltest, Inc., Evanston, Illinois). This device is a convenient field kit in which water from a 6-g sample reacts with calcium carbide in a sealed container and the resulting pressure is read directly as moisture percentage of wet weight in approximately 5 to 10 min. Although these readings were used throughout this report, Equation (20-7) may be used to convert their readings to the more common percentage of dry weight.

$$\% \text{ dry} = \frac{M}{1 - M} \tag{20-7}$$

The combined results of these measurements along with publicly reported daily rainfall (National Oceanographic and Atmospheric Administration, 1979) are shown in Figure 20-8. In general, the selection of soil sampling locations should consider the effects of solar heating, wind, water drainage, proximity to vegetation, and soil compaction. The three locations monitored during this study were simply representative of terrain subject to ORV use, but as can be seen in Figure 20-8, the variation in soil moisture between locations at any given point in time was relatively insignificant in comparison to the variation of M over the course of the season. Empirical values for the above coefficients (and for the seasonal factors in Equation 20-6) were estimated from this data using an IMSL (International Mathematical and Statistical Libraries) (IMSL Library, 1979) optimization algorithm with the result that

$$\alpha = 0.13 \text{ day}^{-1} \text{ or } 0.87 \leqslant k_1 \leqslant 0.98$$

$$\beta = 0.40 \text{ day}^{-1} \text{ or } 0.60 \leqslant k_2 \leqslant 0.68$$

$$k_3 = 2.5\% \text{ inch}^{-1} \text{ or } 0.098\% \text{ cm}^{-1}$$

$$k_4 = 60\% \text{ inch}^{-1} \text{ or } 2.4\% \text{ cm}^{-1}$$

The value of k_1 is exactly in accord with the range quoted by Linsley et al. (1975). M was thereafter calculated stepwise (day by day), beginning with the first rainfall in September, resulting in the superimposed soil moisture line (solid line) shown in Figure 20-8. The dashed line indicates the values for M_1.

Rather than hoping to characterize all factors and mechanisms affecting soil moisture and accounting for daily fluctuations in evaporation, this model should be looked upon as a convenient management tool to predict soil moisture and potential dust exposures and to plan appropriate recreational use management schedules. In one application, the model could be regularly "updated" by calculating M for each day since the rainfall season began. At any point in time, the moisture n days forward without rain could be predicted by Equation (20-8).

$$M = (\bar{k}_1)^n M_1 + (\bar{k}_2)^n M_2 \tag{20-8}$$

where the bar notation indicates an average coefficient for the season in question.

As an alternative approach, necessary where rainfall data are not available or useful as a check on the seasonal rainfall calculation, such predictions could be made from soil moisture purposefully measured in the ORV area late in the spring. In this case the relative contributions of M_1 and M_2 to the measured M

are unknown unless a sufficient interval (i) is allowed to elapse between the most recent rainfall, R, and the measurement M, such that M_2 is negligible. A ratio of $M_1 \geqslant 10M_2$ provides reasonable accuracy to future estimates. Combining this ratio with Equations (20-3) and (20-8) yields:

$$M_1 = M - M_2 \geqslant 10M_2 = 10(\bar{k}_2)^i M_2 = 10(\bar{k}_2)^i k_4 R \qquad (20\text{-}9)$$

and solving for i:

$$i = \frac{1n(M/11\bar{k}_4 R)}{1n(\bar{k}_2)}$$

While this equation can be useful given any M and R, from an inspection of Figure 20-8 one can see that this interval need be no more than 20 days.

An even more general management application of such a model would be to examine historic weather patterns, to develop a statistical profile of expected soil moisture during the spring season, and to plan a seasonal control strategy based upon this profile and aerosol exposures which might be expected. Figure 20-8 presents data for 1979. Soil moisture can be seen to decrease into the 3 to 5% range around April 5 to 14. For other years, the statistical profile could be used to establish the earliest probable date at which such levels of moisture would occur. An efficient control strategy could then rely on moist soils before that date and implement one of the above monitoring approaches after that time.

It can be seen in Figure 20-8 that late spring rains provide only a very transient respite from dry, easily aerosolized soil. In this regard it should be expected—and can be seen again by the dashed line in Figure 20-8—that the interstitial moisture (the analog of the API) is the more reliable index for long-range moisture predictions. It is helpful in this regard that M_1 can be analyzed independently of M_2 in Equations (20-1) to (20-3), thereby greatly simplifying model calculations.

Discussion and Conclusions

The previous sections of this chapter describe several approaches used to quantify human exposures to a respiratory disease hazard in an ORV recreational area. It was shown by dustfall measurements that ORV traffic along the roads and trails of the area is the major source of airborne dust. Both airborne dust and dustfall are predominantly chrysotile asbestos. The influence of rainfall and soil moisture upon these dusts has also been demonstrated. The Clear Creek case represents to our knowledge the first instance in which naturally occurring airborne asbestos, not the result of mining, milling, or other industrial activity, occurs at levels comparable to those in the workplace. The airborne fibers in the Clear Creek recreational area are in diameters, lengths, and concentrations which could be hazardous to health if inhaled over long periods of time.

The methodologies, findings, and implications of this case study are qualitatively applicable to other serpentine areas and to other soil components such as quartz (a source of silicosis). This study does not, however, define either the magnitude of the health risk or the conditions at which controls should be instituted. As stated in the preliminary report of these aerosols (Cooper et al., 1979), quantitative knowledge concerning the health implications of asbestos exposures such as these does not exist. Even if the moisture-aerosol relationship were more clearly defined, the existence of a safe threshold below which no measurable disease will result is unknown.

Nonetheless, an equivalent time-weighted average (TWA) exposure can be calculated for comparison to occupational health standards. If one were to assume that a rider spends a weekend at Clear Creek (36 hr), of which 4 hr were spent riding each day, and concentrations of 5 and 0.1 f cm^{-3} were assumed for trail (8 hr) and camp exposures (28 hr), respectively, then the equivalent TWA for the weekend equals

$$\text{TWA}_{\text{(weekend)}} = \frac{(5 \times 8)}{36} + \frac{(0.1 \times 28)}{36} = 1.2 \text{ f cm}^{-3} \qquad (20\text{-}11)$$

If the area were visited only one weekend per month, then

$$\text{TWA}_{\text{(month)}} = \frac{(1.2 \times 1.5) + (0 \times 28.5)}{30} = 0.06 \text{ f cm}^{-3} \qquad (20\text{-}12)$$

and if only half the year were dry, the annual TWA would be 0.03 f cm^{-3}; these TWAs can be compared to current permissible 40-hr weekly occupational exposure limits of 2 f cm^{-3} [29 CFR (Code of Federal Regulations), 1910] and proposed standards of 0.5 f cm^{-3} (NIOSH, 1976). Thus, asbestos exposures to ORV users while in the Clear Creek Recreational Area can be expected to exceed proposal occupational health standards, but intermittent usage would reduce these time-weighted average exposures to more acceptable although not necessarily "safe" levels.

This case study was limited to on-site hazards. A further issue concerns the spread of asbestos beyond the ORV area. One general question is how does it affect others who do not participate in ORV use? Dustfall profiles (Fig. 20-4) have demonstrated that airborne dispersion of large fibers beyond 10 m from the road is barely above background. This is in agreement with findings of John et al. (1976) that airborne fiber concentrations downwind of asbestos mills decrease very rapidly with distance. Therefore it seems that exposures to hikers and rock collectors not associated with vehicles is minimal.

An additional problem which we have not addressed concerns the continued exposures of area users to fibers carried home on their clothes and vehicles. This is reported to be a significant risk from occupational exposures to asbestos (Anderson et al., 1976). Wetting or washing these dusts from their vehicles and clothing will reduce their immediate respiratory exposure potential, but asbestos will not dissolve or be degraded by water. Dried and resuspended, it is equally hazardous.

Another serious consideration is effects on water pollution. While we have not studied the direct impact of ORV riders on water quality, exploratory water

Table 20-5. Chrysotile Asbestos Concentration (f liter^{-1}) and Turbidity (Hach Units) of Some Streams Draining the San Benito Complex[a]

Location	Date	f liter^{-1}	Hach units
Clear Creek at lowest public	4 Jul 77	10^8–10^9	2.1
stream crossing	27 Feb 78	10^8	2.3
San Benito River below Clear Creek	27 Feb 78	10^8–10^9	0.4
Hernandez Reservoir near shoreline	11 Jun 78	10^9	21.
San Benito River 20 km downstream of Hernandez Reservoir	8 Jul 78	10^6	7.0
Los Gatos Creek just above Mexican Reservoir	27 Feb 78	10^8–10^9	0.5

[a]From Murchio et al. (1978).

analyses listed in Table 20-5 (from Murchio et al., 1978) show extremely high fiber concentrations in all streams with direct runoff from the San Benito ultramafic complex. These values are similar to concentrations recently measured in the California Aqueduct which is believed to be contaminated by local surface runoff just east of Coalinga (McGuire and Cohen, 1980). Most of the asbestos fibers apparently settle in local reservoirs (Hernandez Reservoir on the San Benito River and presumably in the Mexican Reservoir on Los Gatos Creek). The contribution to the aqueduct contamination from San Benito runoff via Los Gatos Creek below Mexican Reservoir has not yet been demonstrated. Neither has the additional contribution of ORV use to natural erosion been established.

Given this background and our present knowledge concerning the public health risks of asbestos, the need for use restrictions or other protective measures for the general public must be considered. A general discussion of the complications of identification and liability for environmentally induced diseases, especially from asbestos, was presented by Ehrenreich and Selikoff (1977), but the justification for restricting children and freely consenting adults exposing themselves in the pursuit of recreation is at best debatable. The criteria for occupational health standards are based on perhaps the best epidemiologic evidence (British Occupational Hygiene Society, 1968; Harrington, 1976; NIOSH, 1976; Peto, 1978), but of course, they are not legally applicable and may also not be appropriate. Nonetheless, both Occupational Health and Safety Administration (U.S.) and Environmental Protection Agency regulations are precedents for legal action.

Management options to reduce the hazards include use restrictions, containment of the dust, personal protection, and public awareness programs. Restrictions up to and including prohibition of area usage are costly and difficult to enforce because of the remote setting, the terrain, the nature of the activity, and the many possible points of entry. Paving the main canyon road (currently maintained annually by the county government) would alleviate one highly visible source of aerosol but would not affect trail riders, and might eventually attract more users to the area. The general availability to the public of inexpensive, disposable respirators which can reduce inhaled air concentrations by about five-fold, offers yet another potential strategy for controlling exposures during the dry season, but again, enforcement of any requirement and proper use of respirators are obstacles to effective control.

As an interim measure the best short-term solution may be voluntary compliance through education. A large "Caution" sign has been posted to notify the public, but its effect in deterring use has not been tested. The seasonal aspect of rainfall, soil moisture, aerosols, and the general climatic attractiveness of the area could be coupled to a hazard-status warning sign (analogous to forest fire hazard signs) triggered by soil-moisture measurements or model predictions. Moisture below 3% should certainly be of concern to users and use managers. In the long run, a creative combination of approaches may be necessary to effectively deal with this problem. While the Clear Creek case is unusual, it clearly demonstrates that interference with the environment is not only the cause for serious ecological imbalances but that such action can have a direct impact on those who are involved.

Acknowledgments

We wish to acknowledge the support and cooperation of the Bureau of Land Management and the field support of their rangers (Mr. Artega and Mr. Reiger). We also appreciate the laboratory support of Ms. Janet Teshima and the participation of the many motorcyclists who volunteered their time and interest.

References

American Public Health Association. 1977. Tentative method of analysis for dustfall from the atmosphere. In: M. Katz (Ed.), Methods of Air Sampling and Analysis. American Public Health Association, Washington, D.C., pp. 585-587.

Anderson, H. A., R. Lilis, S. M. Daum, A. F. Fischbein, and I. J. Selikoff. 1976. Household-contact asbestos neoplastic risk. Ann. N.Y. Acad. Sci. 271:311–323.

Anonymous (1957). Proposed wildlife withdrawal. Calif. Div. Mines, Mineral Information Service 10, p. 6.

Bailey, E. H., W. P. Irwin, and D. L. Jones. 1964. Franciscan and related rocks, and their significance in the geology of western California. Calif. Div. Mines Geol. Bull. 183:1–177.

British Occupational Hygiene Society. 1968. Hygiene standards for chrysotile asbestos dust. Ann. Occup. Hyg. 11:47–69.

Chepil, W. S. 1956. Influence of moisture on erodibility of soil by wind. Soil Sci. Soc. Am. Proc. 20:288–292.

Code of Federal Regulations, Title 29, part 1910.0001. OSHA Safety and Health
    Standards for Asbestos. (See also Federal Register 41:11505, Mar. 19, 1976.)
Coleman, R. G. 1961. Jadeite deposits of the Clear Creek area, New Idria dis-
    trict, San Benito County, California. J. Petrol. 2:209–247.
Cooper, W. C., J. Murchio, W. Popendorf, and H. R. Wenk. 1979. Chrysotile
    asbestos in a California recreational area. Science 206:685–688.
Eckel, E. B., and W. B. Myers. 1946. Quicksilver deposits of the New Idria dis-
    trict, San Benito and Fresno Counties, California. Calif. J. Mines Geol. 42:
    81–124.
Ehrenreich, T., and I. J. Selikoff. 1977. Medicolegal aspects of occupational and
    environmental disease. In: C. G. Tedeschi, W. G. Eckert, and G. L. Tedeschi
    (Eds.), Forensic Medicine, Vol. III. W. B. Saunders Co., Philadelphia, Pennsyl-
    vania, pp. 1271–1292.
Fuchs, N. A. 1975. Review papers: sampling of aerosols. Atmos. Environ. 9:
    697–707.
Griffin, J. R. 1974. A strange forest in San Benito County. Fremontia 2:11–15.
Harrington, J. S. 1976. The biological effects of mineral fibers, especially asbes-
    tos, as seen from *in vitro* and *in vivo* studies. Ann. Anat. Pathol. 21:155–198.
International Mathematical and Statistical Libraries. 1979. Reference Manual.
    International Mathematical and Statistical Libraries, Inc., Houston, Texas.
    Vol. 3, p. ZXSSQ-1 to ZXSSQ-7.
John, W., A. Berner, G. Smith, and J. J. Wesolowski. 1976. Experimental Deter-
    mination of the Number and Size of Asbestos Fibers in Ambient Air. Final
    Report, Interagency Agreement ARB-3-688, California Department of
    Health, Berkeley, California, 36 pp.
Joint ACGIH-AIHA Aerosol Hazards Evaluation Committee. 1975. Background
    documentation on evaluation of occupational exposure to airborne asbestos.
    Am. Indus. Hyg. Assoc. J. 36:91–103.
Kohler, M. A., and R. K. Linsley. 1951. Predicting the Runoff from Storm Rain-
    fall. U.S. Weather Bureau Research Paper 34.
Linsley, R. K., M. A. Kohler, and J. L. H. Paulhus. 1975. Hydrology for Engi-
    neers. McGraw-Hill Book Co., Inc., New York, 482 pp.
Lippmann, M. 1970. Respirable dust sampling. Am. Indus. Hyg. Assoc. J. 31:
    138–159.
Matthews, R. A. (1961). Geology of the Butler Estate chromite mine, South-
    west Fresno County, California. Calif. Div. Mines, Special Report 71, p. 11-18.
McGuire, M. J., and R. S. Cohen. 1980. The Occurrence of Asbestos Fibers in
    Source Water Supplies Available to Metropolitan. A report by the Metropoli-
    tan Water District of Southern California, Los Angeles, California, 48 pp.
Mumpton, F. A., and C. S. Thompson. 1975. Mineralogy and origin of the
    Coalinga asbestos deposit. Clays and Clay Min. 23:131–143.
Murchio, J., H. R. Wenk, W. Popendorf, and W. C. Cooper. 1978. Asbestos in
    Clear Creek Recreation Area. Report to Bureau of Land Management, Fol-
    som, California, 33 pp.
National Institute for Occupational Safety and Health. 1976. Revised Recom-
    mended Asbestos Standard. National Institute for Occupational Safety and
    Health, Dept. Health, Education and Welfare (NIOSH) Publ. No. 77-169,
    Washington, D.C., 96 pp.
National Institute for Occupational Safety and Health. 1977. Manual of Analy-
    tical Methods, Vol. 1, 2nd ed. National Institute for Occupational Safety and

Health, Dept. Health, Education, and Welfare (NIOSH) Publ. No. 77-157A, Washington, D.C., pp. 239-1 to 239-21.

National Oceanographic and Atmospheric Administration. 1979. Climatological Data, California. National Oceanic and Atmospheric Administration, Environmental Data Service (for Hernandez 2 NW and Priest Valley, September 1978 through June 1979).

Ortiz, L. W., and B. L. Isom. 1974. Transfer technique for electron microscopy of membrane filter samples. Am. Indus. Hyg. Assoc. J. 35:423–425.

Peto, J. 1978. The hygiene standard for chrysotile asbestos. Lancet 1(8062): 484–489.

Rice, S. J. 1963. California Asbestos Industry. California Division of Mines and Geology, Mineral Information Service 16(9):1–7.

Sehmel, G. A. 1970. Particle sampling bias introduced by anisokinetic sampling and deposition within the sampling line. Am. Indus. Hyg. Assoc. J. 31:758–771.

Seltzer, D. F., W. J. Bernaski, and J. R. Lynch. 1971. Evaluation of size-selective presamplers II. Efficiency of the 10-mm nylon cyclone. Am. Indus. Hyg. Assoc. J. 32:441–446.

Wood, J. D., and J. L. Birkett. 1979. External airflow effects on personal sampling. Ann. Occup. Hyg. 22:229–310.

PART V

Management of Off-Road Vehicles

21
Management Concepts[1]

William J. Kockelman

Introduction

Off-road vehicle (ORV) use of public and private lands is an extremely controversial issue (Chapter 1). Other land uses—such as for missile sites, grazing,
surface mining, water diversions, timber cutting, waste disposal, nuclear-device
testing, and wilderness—are also controversial, but according to Sheridan (1979,
p. v) none is as controversial as ORV use.

An examination of the three primary aspects of ORV use—pleasure for ORV
users, conflict with other users, and destruction of resources—is necessary before
discussing management practices (Chapter 22) and regulations and education
(Chapter 23). This chapter includes a discussion of the three primary aspects, as
well as answers to four recurring questions. Although Chapters 2 through 20
cover the effect of ORV use on resources in detail, some of the effects are restated here in abbreviated form for the convenience of the nonscientist who
might skip the more technical chapters.

Users and Their Needs

Most ORVs are promoted and rated by the manufacturers according to their
ability to break new ground across wild land, to scale steep slopes, and to ford
natural streams. ORV users have many different behavioral characteristics and
desires. To many, an ORV is the means to an end—it's a way to get out, to explore, and to challenge oneself. Some users like trails in a variety of unrestricted

[1]The views and conclusions contained in this chapter are based on the author's studies or
experiences and do not necessarily represent the official viewpoint or policy of any U.S.
government agency.

areas. Others feel that riding the ORV is an end in itself. These users ride, jump, spin, slide, and play to their hearts' content, usually in a relatively small area. They may be satisfied with a so-called "sacrifice area" where most of the natural resources are already destroyed and no attempt is being made to conserve or reclaim it. Most ORV users interviewed agreed that ORVs gave them a feeling of adventure and freedom and that driving an ORV was their most important form of outdoor recreation (California Department of Parks and Recreation, 1974). ORV users' aims, preferences, and needs are identified by Nash (1979, pp. 29–89) in an off-road recreation survey for the State of Washington.

The machine itself is important to ORV users. Many ORV owners have invested a substantial share of their disposable incomes in their machines; according to Nash (1976, pp. 57–60), as much as 10%. According to the Motorcycle Industry Council, Inc. (1980a, p. 3), motorcycles are used off the road in every state, and riders may travel several hours to reach an open-use area. In Texas, where public land is relatively scarce, tens of thousands of Texans travel 2 or 3 hours to New Mexico in order to drive their ORVs. In Ballinger-Deer Park Canyon in California, Nash (1976) found that nearly 70% of those interviewed drove from $1\frac{1}{2}$ to $2\frac{1}{2}$ hours to reach the open-use areas.

Types of Users

ORV users can be divided into three types. The first type includes those who need to use an ORV for their work, including land managers, repairmen, emergency and utility personnel, and patrollers. The second group of ORV users is those who use them solely for recreational purposes and for having a good time; they are usually law-abiding citizens with respect for other users and the environment. The third group might be called the "bad-apple" group—users who simply do not care about others or the damage they cause.

The second group of users can be further divided into casual and endurance riders. The casual rider uses the machine as a means to reach a destination or get into the back country, usually on a trail. This user group includes hunters, fishermen, environmentalists, conservationists, and scientists. Usually esthetics are important, whereas challenge and competition are unimportant. The casual rider might traverse a developed trail for the pure enjoyment of reaching a vista, a geologic formation, or a campsite. The casual rider desires access to the back country, and if he is provided with a trail, he will probably remain on the trail. The conflicts with other users and with the environment are minor. For example, a bridge would be used to avoid fording a stream. Obstacles, such as logs and rocks, would be removed and the trails would be designed with shallow grades and wide turns.

The endurance rider is much different; he desires a challenge. He wants to participate in enduros, hillclimbs, motocross, and scrambles. These events have been defined by the American Motorcyclist Association (1982). The Motorcycle Industry Council, Inc. (1980a, p. 5) has developed a chart which lists three types of motorcycles—on-highway, dual purpose, and off-highway—and their use areas. The off-highway types are further divided into four specialized event-type motorcycles—each having distinctive features described by the Motorcycle Industry Council, Inc. (1980b, pp. 4, 5).

The endurance riders like hilly and rolling terrain. They desire open areas— areas the include natural or undeveloped terrain in which vehicles are permitted to go anywhere. More than anything else, they like land that will challenge them and their machines. They also like the freedom to travel in any direction they desire, because the real pleasure comes from having no rules or regulations. ORV use of the Ballinger-Deer Park Canyon was perceived by most of those interviewed as an important aggression-relieving, physically demanding, socially interactive activity which cannot be obtained in controlled areas, such as ORV parks. The results of one survey (Nash, 1976) indicate that an overwhelming number of ORV users believe that other sports are "unsubstitutable" (Table 21-1).

However, endurance riders need some safety rules. Despite normal precautionary measures, dangers exist. The possibility of death must be considered. This danger is generally understood and is regarded as an inherent element of competition by the U.S. Bureau of Land Management (BLM). In their evaluation of the 1973 Barstow-Las Vegas race, BLM (1975) reported 47 medical incidents, ranging from a severe stomach ache to death. Serious lacerations, contusions, and bone fractures were common. Even in well-designed and managed ORV facilities, injuries occur, for example, McEwen (1978, p. 20) reports:

> During the 48 sampling days, six minor scrapes or bruises and 4 injuries requiring medical attention were reported. The most serious injury was a broken back suffered by one motorcyclist who was thrown from his bike into a tree after hitting a deep rut. The three other serious injuries were a broken arm, a broken ankle, and some deep lacerations. The rate of reported injuries in proportion to the total number of cyclists riding, would be one for every 186 outings. If a Turkey Bay cyclist were to ride 30 to 40 times a year, this would mean he could expect injury every 4 to 5 years.

Behavior and Awareness

The behavioral problems of the "bad-apple" ORV users have been recognized by the California Department of Parks and Recreation (1975, pp. 12, 15). Careless use of ORVs results in deliberate or unintended damage to public and private property, such as damage to trails, fences, and other property. ORV users have destroyed geologic, paleontological, and archeological resources. Sometimes the ORVs are used to aid and abet antisocial or criminal activities. Because of their speed and versatility, ORVs can be used easily for undesirable activities in arid areas, such as trespass, vandalism, property damage, theft, littering, poaching, and malicious harassment of wildlife and passive recreationists according to the California Department of Parks and Recreation (1978, p. 29).

Some ORV users are aware that the desert is being damaged. For example, Briggs and Tellier (1977, p. 77) wrote an article for *Cycle Guide* to help

Table 21-1. Activity "Substitutability": Riding Versus Other Sports and Respondents Attitudes[a]

Other sport	Number ranking other sport equally	Number ranking other sport ahead	Number saying "unsubstitutable"
Any other form of racing (excl. foot)	4	2	171
Racing on foot	1	0	178
Mountain or rock climbing	1	0	178
Skydiving	0	0	179
Hunting	8	4	167
Backpacking	5	2	172
Picnicking	9	0	170
Fishing	3	0	176
Surfing	7	2	170
Scuba diving	3	1	175
Horseback riding	4	0	175
Sailing	0	0	179
Dunebuggying	1	2	176
Canoeing/whitewater kayaking	0	0	179
Crew	1	0	178
Football	12	0	167
Basketball	3	4	167
Ice hockey	1	0	178
Lacrosse	1	0	178
Baseball	2	1	176
Snow skiing	10	6	163
Water skiing	11	4	164
Boxing	0	0	179
Wrestling	0	0	179
Karate or other martial arts	0	0	179
Tennis	4	0	175
Golf	0	0	179
Other contact sports	7	0	172
Other noncontact sports	14	2	159

[a] From Nash (1976).

motorcyclists understand the kind of impact that is being made on the desert environment. They conclude that the desert racer does abuse the desert, that the damage does not go away, and that the racer will probably not be allowed to continue to operate at will. But a survey by McKenzie and Studlick (1980, p. 7) of over 1000 ORV users in Ohio found that almost three-quarters of the user-responders perceived the overall environmental impact of ORVs operating in state forests as being minor or nonexistent, with only 5.5% recognizing the effect as being major or potentially dangerous. However, in response to a specific question on the types of impact caused by ORVs, erosion was cited by 27.7% of the respondents, litter by 26.1%, wildlife destruction by 19.6%, and vegetation destruction by 10.9%. Almost half (46.9%) indicate noise as a major problem if the public image of dirt biking is to be improved. McKenzie and Studlick (1980, pp. 7, 8) report that about 60% of the respondents indicated that they had a "quiet bike" but agreed that noise was a problem that ORV users must address among themselves if the sport is to win friends and expand.

Besides the benefits to ORV users, secondary benefits flow to others—manufacturers, dealers, salespersons, financial institutions, sponsors and promoters of events, and small businesses, such as repair shops, gas stations, restaurants, and motels. But Sheridan (1979, p. 4) points out:

> The overall economic benefits of this recreation have never been determined. . . . large numbers of ORVs are imported and therefore represent a negative factor in the nation's balance of payments.

Conflicts with Other Users

Arid areas are used in many ways: some for urban, suburban, and rural developments; Indian reservations; military uses, such as weapon testing and war games; economic uses, such as grazing and mineral and fuel extraction; resource conservation, such as reforestation, timber harvesting, reservoirs, and watershed protection; agricultural uses, such as dry-land and irrigated farming; and various recreational uses, other than for ORV use. Because of location, fencing, danger, unsuitability, management, or policing, many of these uses do not come into conflict with ORV use. It is educational, scientific, and other recreational uses with which ORV users usually come in conflict. Kemsley (1980, p. 235) identifies two aspects of ORV conflicts with other users:

> First, there is the terrible intrusion of a machine. When you walk several miles along a deserted beach, it is disturbing to have to look out for vehicles. You cannot lie down to sunbathe without fear of being run over by a vehicle. This is not only a competition for space problem. I believe there is a definite safety problem involved.
>
> The second aspect of the problem is an environmental one. When you walk these beaches now, you do not see windswept expanses any more. You see tire tracks criss-crossing the sands. . . . there is a violent psychological damage to other users, like myself when I am on foot. In no way can you confront a wide expanse of beach, no matter how many miles it runs on, and think of it as wild, if there are tire marks on it.

Public Reaction

Until the last 10 years, there was little interest in how the arid areas were used for recreation. However, the results of a recent poll by the Gallup Organization, Inc. (1978), prepared for the BLM, showed that only 23% of the people who responded wanted more areas for ORVs, while 46% wanted fewer. The Field

Table 21-2. Attitudes Concerning Types of Land Uses: A Comparison of 1978 Results, 1977 Statewide, and Nationwide Results[a]

	Net support score[b]			
	Desert residents (%)	Statewide[c] visitors (%)	Statewide[d] non-visitors (%)	Nationwide[e] opinion givers (%)
Protection of desert wildlife and ecology	+64	+78	+71	+82
Developed campgrounds	+55	+47	+40	+21
Control over recreational and other public use of the desert	+40	+40	+43	+54
Primitive areas	+38	+50	+37	+53
Roads for four-wheel-drive use	+11	−2	−8	−17
Open areas for use of off-road vehicles such as dune buggies and motorcycles[g]	−8	−15	−20	−41
Number of cases	1210			629

[a] From Stanford Research Institute International (1978).
[b] Net support score is proportion who said they would like to see more of a type of land use minus the proportion who said they would like to see less of or eliminate that type of land use. [Denominator for these proportions include respondents who had no opinion ("can't say").]
[c] Statewide residents who have visited the desert in the past year or so.
[d] Statewide residents who have not visited the desert in the past year or so.
[e] Nationwide residents who agreed to give their opinions about how the desert should be used.
[f] 0.5% or less.
[g] Nationwide wording was: "Unrestricted open areas . . . ."

Research Corporation (1975) conducted a statewide survey of California residents for the BLM to obtain preliminary data regarding use, recreational demands, and attitudes toward the California Desert. The results of the survey showed a substantial use of the desert by the public, a demand for a variety of recreational activities, and a general concern for protecting the desert. Adding areas for ORV use was not considered very important. Adding hotels, eating places, and ORV areas was ranked as the least important. The results of the interviews with visitors and nonvisitors, and people from both southern and northern California, indicated that sightseeing, camping, picnicking, fishing, photography, and hiking were the most popular recreational activities, ranging from one-third to two-thirds of the responses. Riding or racing motorcycles, jeeps, and dune buggies was ranked 13 and below. Racing was included by fewer

	Percentage wanting to eliminate activity			
	Desert residents (%)	Statewide[c] visitors (%)	Statewide[d] non-visitors (%)	Nationwide[e] opinion givers (%)
Protection of desert wildlife and ecology	1	f	1	0
Developed campgrounds	1	1	3	3
Control over recreational and other public use of the desert	2	3	1	1
Primitive areas	1	f	1	1
Roads for four-wheel-drive use	8	9	11	9
Open areas for use of off-road vehicles such as dune buggies and motorcycles[g]	14	12	14	20
Number of cases	1210			629

than 10% of the respondents. Another survey of land use attitudes and activity preferences by desert residents and visitors for the BLM by Standard Research Institute International (1978) showed similar attitudes and preferences (Tables 21-2 and 21-3).

The desert is becoming more popular for extensive nonconsumptive uses; ORV use conflicts with these nonconsumptive uses. The dust, noise, odor, wide-ranging presence, and complete mobility of the ORV are usually the source of complaints. For example, under the best of conditions, as in a forest, the noise from the average motorcycle can be heard more than 4000 feet (1 km) away, and a loud one, over 2 miles (3 km) away (Michigan State University Department of Park and Recreation Resources, 1971, p. 138). The effect of ORVs on the nation's resources, as discussed in the next section, also serves as a major

Table 21-3. Respondents' Activity Preferences: A Comparison of 1978 Desert Residents, and 1977 and 1975 Statewide Residents[a]

Activity	Have done or would like to do[b]		
	Desert residents (1978) (%)	Statewide residents[c] (1977) (%)	Statewide residents[c] (1975) (%)
Horseback riding	29	20	28
Water-based activities on Colorado R.	33	19	NCI[d]
Camping—developed campground	44	30	NCI
Camping—undeveloped sites	35	22	NCI
Photography	40	27	37
Backpacking	22	19	24
Dune buggying	23	12	13
Hang gliding	9	5	7
Hiking	40	25	36
Picnicking	59	38	44
Sightseeing and exploring	46	35	NCI
Water-based activities, Salton Sea	20	8	NCI
Motorcycle riding (noncompetitive)	26	14	17[e]
Prospecting as a hobby	11	7	NCI
Rock and mineral collecting	19	14	NCI
Sand sailing	8	4	8
Educational activities	28	12	NCI
Four-wheel driving	27	11	14
Painting	13	5	12
Hunting	23	11	17
Sightseeing, driving on paved roads	60	36	59[f]
Rock climbing	23	12	23
Scientific research	6	4	NCI
Target shooting	26	10	20
Bird watching	14	7	NCI
Motorcycle riding (competitive)	3	1	8[g]
None of these	N/A	N/A	N/A
Number of cases	1210	1031	1124

[a] Adapted from Stanford Research Institute International (1978).

[b] 1977 and 1978 values are the sum of the proportions of residents reporting having done an activity and the proportion saying they would like to try that activity (Questions 11 and 13 on 1978 questionnaire). 1975 values are based on the following item: "This card contains a list of some different types of recreation activities that take place in the California desert. Please tell me which of the things on this list, if any, you do or would you like to do in the California desert (19 items)."

[c] Statewide adults (18 years and older) residing in residential dwelling units.

[d] NCI, no comparable item on 1975 survey.

[e] "Motorcycle riding or play."

[f] "Sightseeing."

[g] "Motorcycle racing."

source of conflict with most other recreational users. Sheridan (1979, p. 17) reports on an interview with a biologist:

> Before the ORV's, Dove Springs Canyon was a popular spot for hikers, campers, birdwatchers, and fossil hunters. Today. ORVs dominate the canyon. On a Memorial Day weekend, there may be as many as 500 machines at play in the once tranquil canyon.

Some ORV users can cause distress to private land owners. Their trespass onto private property impairs the land owner's peace and tranquility. Conflicts between ORV use and economic uses of the land also occur. For example, ranchers complain about trespass, cut fences, broken gates, polluted water for livestock, new roads, noise, gully erosion, and interference with livestock operations. Some ranchers on public lands have not reapplied for grazing permits, citing conflicts with ORV users as their reason (Scott et al., 1978, p. 45). Such problems also occur in nonarid areas. In the words of a dairy farmer from Michigan's Upper Peninsula (Suchovsky, 1980, p. 174):

> Deliberate acts of vandalism have led to serious confrontations. Vandalistic activity such as packs of ORVs ploughing through muddy roads until they get stuck, ransacking and destroying remote cabins, knocking over corner posts so fence lines fall down, seeing how many fence posts one can knock over before the vehicle becomes entangled in wire, going into forested areas and trying to see how big a tree they can push over, cutting fences, and driving through row crops during various stages of growth occur all too regularly throughout the country.

In some cases, the public seems to be overwhelmingly opposed to ORV uses. For example, part of the Los Padres National Forest has been subjected to uncontrolled use by a variety of ORVs. The U.S. Forest Service participated in working sessions with a number of interested groups, agencies, and individuals to ensure that all possible routes and resource considerations were analyzed. News media coverage provided overall public awareness of the management situation. According to one survey for BLM, competitive and noncompetitive motorcycle riding were found particularly objectionable by both residents and visitors to the desert (Table 21-4). Another example of conflicts between neighbors and ORV areas was raised by the plans of San Mateo County, California to reestablish a legal off-road motorcycle park—a 1200-acre (480-ha) site, for 30,000 to 50,000 ORV users (*Peninsula Times Tribune,* August 20, 1980).

The U.S. Bureau of Outdoor Recreation (1976) reports that there is a widespread and severe conflict between ORV users and other users. Most nonmotorized forms of outdoor recreation are disrupted or hurt by the operation of ORVs nearby, especially for those whose recreational goals include solitude, tranquility, relaxation, observation of wildlife, and the appreciation of wild environments. An attitude survey by the Motorcycle Industry Council, Inc. (1980c, p. 7) reveals that ORV users blame neither the land manager nor the environmentalist for his "where to ride" problems but rather blames himself or the "bad apples." In the *Cry California* magazine, Badaracco (1979, p. 73) reports on new

Table 21-4. Objectionable Activities: A Comparison of 1978 Desert Results and 1977 Statewide Results[a]

	Percentage who find activity "particularly objectionable"		
Activity	Desert residents (1978) (%)	Statewide visitors[b] (1977) (%)	Statewide non-visitors[c] (1977) (%)
None of the listed activities	38	37	50
Motorcycle riding (noncompetitive)	34	38	30
Motorcycle riding (competitive)	29	36	29
Dune buggying	23	31	22
Hunting	14	21	15
Target shooting	14	20	22
Four-wheel driving	13	20	14
Camping at undeveloped sites	2	6	3
Hang gliding	2	4	5
Scientific research	1	<1	<1
Sand sailing	1	5	6
Rock climbing	1	3	2
Bird watching	1	<1	<1
Hiking	1	<1	<1
Sightseeing and driving for pleasure on paved roads	<1	3	3
Rock and mineral collecting	<1	2	1
Water-based activities on Colorado R.	<1	2	1
Camping in developed campground	<1	1	3
Water-based activities on Salton Sea	<1	2	1
(Other listed activities named by fewer than 1% of respondents in each of the three categories shown here)			
Number of cases	1210	433	598

[a] From Stanford Research Institute International (1978).
[b] Statewide residents who have visited the desert within the past year or so.
[c] Statewide residents who have not visited the desert in the past year or so.

kinds of recreation and identifies the ORV as causing the most change to the outdoor environment:

> They have markedly altered recreational environments—physically, socially, and esthetically. The ORV owners love their machines; other recreationalists are outraged by the noise, dust, commotion, rowdy behavior, and environmental damage ORVs bring with them.

Multiple-Use Concept

Multiple use of public lands is a management concept that assumes that many uses can be made of the same land and that such uses would not be in conflict with each other, such as grazing and horseback riding, sustained-yield forestry and backpacking. Section 601 of the Federal Land Policy and Management Act governing most public arid areas in the United States (U.S. Congress, 1976) defines "multiple use" as:

> the management of the public lands and their various resources values so that they are utilized in the combination that will best meet the present and future needs of the American people; making the most judicious use of the land . . . ; a combination of balanced and diverse resource uses that takes into account the long-term needs of future generations for renewable and nonrenewable resources, including, but not limited to, recreation, range, timber, minerals, watershed, wildlife and fish, and natural scenic, scientific and historical values; and harmonious and coordinated management of the various resources without permanent impairment of the productivity of the land and the quality of the environment with consideration being given to the relative values of the resources and not necessarily to the combination of uses that will give the greatest economic return or the greatest unit output.

Stebbins (1974) describes multiple use as a concept that a given use must not jeopardize or destroy other legitimate uses of public lands and notes (p. 208) that "ORV use tends to be consumptive. . . . Unless greatly confined, it will gradually damage—in some places permanently—opportunities for many of the other uses." Krutch (1969) writes that Coral Dunes in southern Utah is an area that is not suitable for multiple use, because the undeveloped state park cannot be used for sand buggy racing and also the quiet enjoyment of esthetic, ecological, and geologic resources. According to Badaracco (1978), generally the noisier, more consumptive, and less contemplative recreation activities, such as ORV riding, preempt and drive out the activities that are quieter, less consumptive, and more contemplative.

Clearly multiple use cannot include ORV use. ORV use is exclusive and conflicts with most other uses whether they be residential, military, mining, grazing, or recreational. In the words of Rosenberg (1976, p. 176):

> In terms of total recreational use, ORVs are inefficient in that they cause serious user-conflicts. That is, one ORV operator can effectively restrict a larger public area to his own use through the emission of loud engine noise, obnoxious smoke, gas and oil odors, and dangerously high speeds. Whereas previously many persons of all ages and wealth could observe the beauty of unspoiled land, now a single ORV can reign supreme.

In effect, ORVs shrink the amount of land available to other recreational users. If the ORVs stay on specific trails, then the amount of shrinkage is confined to the trails and the land immediately adjacent to them—they become the corridors of ORV noise. If they roam anywhere in an area, then the amount of

land available to the quiet-seeking, non-ORV recreationists in that area shrinks
to zero (Sheridan, 1979, p. 33). ORV use, if unregulated, becomes an infringe-
ment on other people's right to recreation. ORV user needs cannot be met if
one is to consider the needs and rights of others in a multiple-use context. It is
an irreconcilable difference. Whereas a backpacker might intrude upon a bird
watcher's sanctuary, such intrusions are rare and repairable. However, the mobility and numbers of ORV users disturb all other recreational users.

Hikers and campers do not trek far into the wilds to hear a chorus of gasoline engines, however polite the driver is, however well-tuned their engines,
although a good muffler and a courteous driver certainly would make the experience less unpleasant than it might otherwise be. Direct encounters with ORV
machines simply are not compatible with the quality of outdoor experience
being sought by a majority of Americans. Sheridan (1979, p. 30) points out that
it is a mistake to believe that skilled, courteous, well-intentioned ORV users can
operate ORVs with minimal effect on the environment and with no conflict with
other users. He adds that St. Francis of Assisi (an environmentalist among other
things) while driving an ORV on wildlands could not avoid diminishing the
recreational experience of the non-ORV users of the same area.

One of the consequences of ORV use is the creation of conflicts with almost
every other use. The issue becomes one of an intensive consumptive exclusionary
use versus extensive nonconsumptive multiple uses. If conflicts with other uses
are to be avoided, ORV use must be separated from them. Areas specifically selected and managed for ORVs cause the fewest user conflicts.

Effects on the Nation's Resources

A primary consequence of ORV use is its effect on the nation's resources—both
physical and biological. The natural resources that are affected include soil,
water, plants, wildlife, solitude, and air. Other resources affected include archeological and paleontological sites, historic features, relic landforms, and other
cultural, esthetic, and scientific legacies. While the rights and conflicts of users
are well expressed by organized groups, only a few scientists, managers, and
poets have praised the life of the arid areas. However, the effects of ORV use
have been well documented (Webb and Wilshire, 1978), and additional evidence
is presented in this volume (Chapters 2 through 20). Damage to every type
of ecosystem in the nation from the eastern coastal beaches to the mountain
ranges, deserts, and beaches of the west has been documented. In some cases,
the effects have actually been anticipated, for example, in the BLM (U.S. Bureau
of Land Management, 1974) environmental impact statement on a proposed
Barstow-Las Vegas motorcycle race.

Recently, the BLM (U.S. Bureau of Land Management, 1980) identified 18
resources and uses in their final environmental impact statement and proposed
plan for the 12 million-acre (4.8 million-ha) California Desert Conservation
Area. Vehicle access and ORV use are identified as having a significantly negative effect on 10 of these resources and uses. The resources identified as being

negatively affected are air quality, soil, vegetation, wildlife, visual quality, cultural resources, Native American values, wilderness, recreation, and livestock grazing. In addition, the BLM (1980, pp. E87, E88) noted four resources that will receive unavoidable and irreversible impacts from ORV use. "Open areas" for vehicles will cause dust and soil compaction and disturbance, animals will be lost wherever they are directly impacted by vehicles, and inadvertent losses to cultural and historical resources will occur.

Off-road vehicles have adverse effects not only in the arid areas with their particularly fragile ecosystems, but in forest, prairie, tundra, and mountain areas throughout the United States. In the California Desert alone, areas scarred by ORVs include Jawbone Canyon, Johnson Valley, Stoddard Valley, Horse Canyon, Sage Canyon, Rainbow Basin, Spangler Hills, Rand Mountains, Ricardo Fossil Beds, and the Salton Sea marshes. Sheridan (1979) discusses some of these effects and the federal response in his *Off-Road Vehicles on the Public Lands* report. The Geological Society of America's (GSA) Committee on Environment and Public Policy report (Geological Society of America, 1977) addressed the effects of ORVs on resources. Many of the following subjects were introduced in its report.

Soil

Natural soils evolve in response to the entire environment. Their physical, chemical, and biological qualities depend on the associated plants and animals, as well as on the natural stability of the soil. Impacts that kill the living organisms or that change the natural stability could destroy the soil. Soils are naturally stabilized by the combined effects of soil structure, plant cover, and the development of crusts (Chapter 3). Soil sensitivity to vehicles is highly variable, but all data indicate that the natural stability of soils is damaged by vehicle use (Chapters 4, 5, and 6).

Soils which are very wet, loose, or on steep slopes tend to be particularly susceptible to damage by ORVs (Chapter 4). The U.S. Bureau of Outdoor Recreation (1976) reports that certain ORV users find these types of terrain especially attractive and, accordingly, subject them to heavy use. Such use has a particularly adverse effect because soil damage causes the air and water quality to be reduced; the biotic productivity and esthetic quality also suffer. When moving rapidly, particularly uphill, ORV tires and treads tear up and dislodge the soil (Chapter 4). If the soil is dry, some of it then blows away as dust (Chapter 6); if rained on, soil is washed away in the runoff (Chapter 5). Soil that reaches lakes and streams lowers water quality for human use, kills beneficial aquatic organisms, and hurts valuable fisheries. On thin soils in arid areas, vehicles can destroy the protective "desert pavement" (Chapter 11) and can cause excessive soil movement that may require thousands of years for natural repair (Chapter 2; California Department of Parks and Recreation, 1978). ORV effects on the soil include:

Compaction and disruption of surface soil (Chapter 2)
Destruction and dispersal of surface stabilizers (Chapter 3)

Reduction of infiltration capacity (Chapter 4)
Increased frequency and intensity of runoff (Chapter 5)
Concentration and channeling of runoff (Chapter 5)
Increased erosion and sediment yield (Chapter 5)
Increased wind erosion and fugitive dust (Chapter 6)

For example, the soil compaction effect of ORVs is described by Luckenbach (1975, pp. 3, 4):

> When an ORV crosses desert soil, several things happen. Most desert soils have a mantle formed by the cementing action of various carbonates or by the filaments of lichens or soil fungi or both in combination. There may also be a cobble of large gravel or pebbles that gives the appearance of a pavement. When this "desert pavement" or mantle is broken, the soft friable soil beneath is no longer protected and is susceptible to desiccation and erosion by water and by wind (deflation). The amount of dust put into the air by ORV events is staggering.

A two-wheel ORV compacts soil, on the average, across a track about 5 in. (13 cm) wide. Thus, a single track ORV compacts 1 acre (0.4 ha) of soil in traveling 20 mi. (32 km). Tracks made by four-wheel ORVs are typically 18 in. (0.5 m) wide and, accordingly, disturb about 1 acre (0.5 ha) in 6 mi. (10 km) of travel. The degree of compaction varies with the nature and wetness of the soil, the character of the terrain, and the frequency of ORV impact, but some compaction is an inevitable consequence of vehicular travel. The effects of compaction increase logarithmically, the greatest changes occurring during the first passes according to Webb (Chapter 4).

Even the static weight of a standing ORV compacts the soil and alters its structure. In motion, an ORV not only compacts the soil but imparts a shearing stress by which soil particles slide over one another, closing some voids between particles and enlarging others. Thus, the soil structure is disrupted, the plant cover is stripped, and the crust, if present, is destroyed. The effects are a loss of stability and a reduced capacity of the soil to maintain its natural barriers to erosion. Compaction also reduces the capacity of the soil to absorb water, and the water that remains is held more firmly. Hence, even the reduced amount of water is less available to plants and animals (Geological Society of America, 1977).

Increased runoff, increased sediment yield, changes in patterns of surface runoff, increased wind erosion, and increased sedimentation are some of the indirect effects of physical changes in the soil. Increased runoff acts to accelerate erosion and promote soil loss. Increased depositions of fine sediments have several adverse effects: reduced intake of groundwater (Snyder et al., 1976); burial of stable, biologically productive surfaces (Wilshire, 1977); and production of dust (Péwé, 1981).

Disturbance of soil structure by ORVs, stripping of plant cover, and the loss of a soil crust facilitate the processes of erosion. Soil erosion is of three kinds:

1. Direct mechanical abrasion of the ORVs themselves (Chapter 3)

2. Accelerated removal by runoff (Chapter 5)
3. Accelerated movement by wind (Chapter 6)

In Redrock Canyon, geologists have watched a hillside used by ORVs for about 5 years and have calculated that the hillside, which is about a mile long and a couple of hundred yards (meters) wide, with a slope of about 18 to 28°, has lost 12,000 tons (11,000 tonnes) of soil (Wilshire and Nakata, 1977). In other places, ORVs have cut notches in the ridge line 3 (1 m) to 6 (2 m) feet deep. At breaks in slope, particularly on hills and sharp divides, the mechanical erosion notches the surface, making grooves as much as 6 feet (2 m) deep in terrain of soft rocks and even 2 feet (0.7 m) deep in hard rock.

Spinning wheels with knobby tires quickly tear out the protective plants and churn the soil downhill. This direct mechanical erosion strips slopes. The result of mechanical erosion by ORVs is a rapid loss of soil and a corresponding exposure of infertile bedrock. The effects are especially noticeable on steep slopes where the soil is usually shallow (Geological Society of America, 1977). In many ORV areas that have been used for 5 to 10 years, the entire soil mantle has been worn away by abrasion and by running water. In other places, ORVs have made grooves that runoff deepened to the point that the sites have become impassable for the ORVs that made them.

In 1979, the U.S. Soil Conservation Service (SCS) issued new guidelines for rating soil limitations for ORV trails (Chapter 3, Table 3-2). Although slope does not limit the machines until it exceeds 40%, the erosion becomes severe if the slope exceeds 10 to 20%. Under the SCS rating system, most desert soils would be rated severe-fragile. This range of slopes is incompatible with the hillclimbs and trails desired by many ORV users.

Although rainfall is scarce in arid areas, it tends to come in heavy downpours that last only a few minutes, and most of the water quickly runs off. The erosive power of this runoff is very great. Water erosion of land in arid areas stripped of its vegetative cover by ORVs is widespread and severe, especially where the infrequent rains are especially heavy. In Chapter 5, Hinckley et al. conclude that ORV activity nearly always results in greatly increased erosion.

Increased runoff, resulting from a reduced capacity of the soil to absorb rainfall, and from the associated loss of soil by erosion, is usually evident in ORV areas. In a study by Snyder et al. (1976), runoff from an ORV area in central California was eight times greater than in a neighboring unused area, and the eroded sediment amounted to 3,200 tons per square mile (1120 tonnes km^{-2}) in a 2-year period. Adjoining unused areas had no measurable yield of sediment. Hinckley et al. (Chapter 5) report 10 to 20 times greater sediment yields from used hill slopes at Dove Spring Canyon, as compared with the unused slopes. Floods resulting from the runoff and sediment washed from ORV sites may degrade the animal habitat along streams and can damage valuable areas of agricultural soil (Geological Society of America, 1977). ORV use has increased the erosion rate eight times in the Hungry Valley subbasin of Ventura and Los Angeles counties, California. The most serious impact of ORVs on the environment of Hungry Valley has been the establishment of major networks of gullies, which may in time reduce both recreational and alternative land uses (Knott, 1980, p. 18).

In Ballinger Canyon, a heavily used ORV site in Los Padres National Forest, California, erosion rates are now more than five times greater than the natural erosion rates for the area. The total loss of soil from hill slopes adjacent to the ORV campground averages 54,000 tons per square mile (19,000 tonnes km^{-2}) per year, which exceeds by a factor of 86 the soil-loss tolerance standards used by SCS for upland soils in this area (Stull et al., 1979, p. 19). Chabot, a regional park east of San Francisco Bay, is losing soil at the rate of about 32,000 tons per square mile (11,000 tonnes km^{-2}) a year after 20 years of ORV use, thereby exceeding the tolerance level suggested by SCS by 46 times. Former one-time ORV paths at Chabot are now 6-ft (2 m) deep gullies (Wilshire et al., 1978b).

In arid areas, the destruction of natural barriers to erosion by ORVs also results in exposure of soils to wind erosion. A documented dust storm originating from a site used by ORVs on the El Mirage Dry Lake covered an area greater than 170 square miles (450 km^2) and dissipated only after the plume had been carried 23 miles (38 km) from its source. According to a Geological Society of America (1977) report, the weight of airborne particles generated by direct mechanical erosion in the 1974 Barstow-Las Vegas race amounted to more than 600 tons (550 tonnes). Dust from such activity was considered to result in permanent losses of fertility and hazards to life, health, and property while in transit and to cause immeasurable degradation of the environment where the dust was deposited. Similarly studies by Gillette and Adams (Chapter 6) indicate that most desert soils are very sensitive to disturbances that accelerate wind erosion. The indirect impacts of wind erosion on air quality, safety, and health are well documented by Reinking et al. (1976).

Sand dunes are terrain that truly challenges the capability of ORVs, and is therefore especially attractive to many ORV users, even though it is notably susceptible to erosion. This conflict between machine capability and land sensitivity is one of the most crucial issues. The physical changes and losses of plant cover caused by ORV traffic on dunes can lead to various degrees of instability. Because ORVs open the area to wind erosion, stabilized dunes become unstable and begin to migrate. According to Gilbertson (Chapter 19) modern accelerated dune drift is associated with and is probably attributable to ORV use. The dunes continue to migrate as long as heavy ORV traffic is permitted (Godfrey et al., 1978). Where ORV use has broken the vegetal cover that anchors inactive sand dunes, the sand is put in motion and spreads as a sheet downwind, where it buries and kills vegetation not directly damaged by the ORVs. In time and without additional vehicle use, the zone of unanchored sand is enlarged, and the area subject to wind erosion is thereby correspondingly enlarged.

Water

ORVs have adverse effects on the quantity and quality of surface and ground waters. For example, the amount of water available at an ORV site is reduced by the increased runoff that results from removal of plant cover and soil compaction. As much as 90% of the surface soil moisture is lost along some ORV trails, and the loss even as deep as 3 feet (1 m) has been found to be 14% at several sites. This loss of water intensifies erosion by causing mechanical breakdown of the soil, by retarding plant growth, and by inhibiting the activities of moisture-dependent soil organisms (Geological Society of America, 1977).

Increased runoff—which is tantamount to a reduced ability to absorb rainfall—and loss of soil by erosion are always evident in ORV areas. Accelerated runoff can begin with the passage of a single vehicle, which makes a track that becomes partly sealed to infiltration and that acts as a channel for overland flow. The sealing results from compaction, as well as from the closing of pore spaces, animal burrows, and the like. The equilibrium between the soil, rainfall, and surface processes, besides the plants and animals, is thereby disturbed; without disturbance, the equilibrium might otherwise persist indefinitely (Geological Society of America, 1977).

The hydrologic or water-related hazards to people from ORV use include the increased frequency and magnitude of floods. For example, Nakata (Chapter 18) reports that an estimated million dollars worth of damage was done to a housing subdivision at Ogden, Utah in August 1979 by a sequence of events linked to erosion of ORV trails. According to the *Salt Lake Tribune* (1980), several Ogden homeowners are seeking damages and the city is accused of failing to keep ORVs out of the area.

Two widely separated sites in California were studied by Snyder et al. (1976) to evaluate the impact of ORVs on water resources. At Panoche Hills in central California, an area formerly used by ORVs together with an adjacent unused area, were monitored from 1971 to 1975 together with an adjacent unused area. The observations included measurements of precipitation, runoff, soil moisture, soil bulk density, plant cover, and erosion. Further, at Dove Spring Canyon in southern California, erosion was measured on a site that is currently being used for ORVs. At the Panoche Hills site, the area used by ORVs produced about eight times as much runoff as the unused area. At the Dove Spring Canyon site, which is still being used for hill climbing, surveys show that degradation in trails has been as much as 12 in. (0.3 m) in the period 1973 to 1975. The transported sediment clogs downstream drainages and has buried some roadways and agricultural lands.

The unique hydrologic conditions in sand dunes are particularly vulnerable to ORV use. Rain is held in the sand for long periods, often until the moist sand is exposed by changes in the dune surface. The moisture sustains animals that live on and beneath the surface, and its eventual drainage from the dune provides water for peripheral plants and animals. Loss of this water when the dune surface is disturbed by vehicles causes a corresponding loss in wildlife—a loss that persists even when the dune is reshaped by subsequent wind (Geological Society of America, 1977).

Off-road vehicle use has two kinds of adverse effects on surface water quality—increased chemical and biological contamination and added sediment. Small quantities of gasoline and lubricating oils spilled or leaked from ORVs enter surface waters or groundwaters via adjacent soils. Body wastes of ORV users also enter surface waters where they contribute to organic and microbial contamination (U.S. Bureau of Outdoor Recreation, 1976). In addition, increased runoff can reduce the groundwater quantity and quality. Much of the soil that is eroded from the land by ORV use ultimately enters surface waters, where it contributes to sediment load and accelerates siltation of streams and lakes. The sediment may become a serious local problem where the discharge is into valuable high-quality waters (U.S. Bureau of Outdoor Recreation, 1976). Destabilization of soils rich in asbestos increases its abundance in surface waters according to Popendorf and Wenk (Chapter 20).

Plants

Small plants are quickly eliminated by ORVs, and shrubs soon deteriorate under repeated impact. Even trees can be toppled when undermined by erosion. ORVs often cause injury to roots by breakage and soil compaction, so that larger perennials eventually die, although perhaps appearing at first to be unharmed. Seeds upon and within the surface layers of soil are crushed, abraded, and displaced (Geological Society of America, 1977). Luckenbach (1975, p. 4) notes that:

> Desert perennials have been there for some time; they have become established against great odds and have the potential to remain for some time. There is little turnover in individual plants; some creosote bushes and burro-weeds must be very old. How long it will take to replace them, or even if it is possible to replace them once the soil environment has been so badly damaged, is not known.

Plants associated with dunes, meadows, or arid areas are most vulnerable to ORV activity. Bury et al. (1977) examined 16 sites in the desert and discovered that "moderate" ORV use reduced the shrub biomass by about 50% and heavy use reduced the biomass by 70%. It was found that in those areas where ORV users congregate—parking their trucks, cars, and campers in the so-called "pit areas"—shrub biomass was reduced by about 95% as compared to undisturbed areas. Lathrop (Chapter 8) examined six heavily used ORV areas in the Mojave Desert and measured an average of 59% reduction in total plant cover in areas of high vehicle concentration.

A single pass across vegetated soft sandy soil can completely destroy the small plants, but larger and tougher plants are only destroyed by multiple vehicle passes. Because the largest plants are at first avoided, they are usually broken down bit by bit. However, direct destruction of trees that are more than 9 ft (3 m) tall by four-wheel vehicles has been observed, and four-wheel vehicles have cut swaths through dense chaparral that is 13 ft (4 m) high. Motorcycles have cut trails through dense chaparral that was nearly 3 ft (1 m) high (Wilshire et al., 1978a). On slopes steeper than 15°, junipers are especially vulnerable because soil erosion exposes their root systems and eventually the whole tree topples over.

Running over and through vegetation in a heavily used ORV recreation area causes an almost total loss of plant cover. In an area of sand dunes, Bury and Luckenbach (Chapter 10) note a dramatic difference in the vegetation remaining in a closed area as compared with adjacent land used by ORVs, and they conclude that ORVs have a major detrimental impact on the plant communities.

Denuded areas, if not artificially reclaimed, may require many centuries for complete recovery, if in fact such recovery is even possible (Chapters 13 and 14). For cases in which plant species are relics of former climatic conditions, recovery may never occur. Even a few vehicle passages affect plant regrowth; some data from the southern Mojave Desert (Chapter 7) suggest that one pass of a truck can substantially impede plant growth.

Wildlife

The impact of ORVs on wildlife is pervasive and long lasting. After damage to the soil by compaction, even wildlife that escapes direct harm is adversely affected. In compacted soil, as the plants decline in numbers, so do the animals that depend on them for food and shelter. The rise of soil temperature caused by decreases in plant cover and by purely physical factors, may discourage animals from living in denuded areas. The ecology of an area is more than just a food web; it entails a whole series of dynamic interactions (Fig. 21-1).

The U.S. Bureau of Outdoor Recreation (1976) reports that ORV users frequently frighten both wild and domesticated animals. The frightened animals either are often driven from shelter and are thereby exposed to predators, or their feeding, resting, reproducing, and rearing of young is disrupted. When the disruption is severe, the wildlife population may be reduced below the natural carrying capacity of the land. Where ORV use on the land is heavy, the impact on wildlife lasts longer and is harder to correct than the impacts from harassment. Bury and Luckenbach (Chapter 10) find that arid areas closed to ORV use have more species of animals, more individuals, and more biomass.

The killing and maiming of animals, long observed on roadways, is extended by ORVs to open areas, in three ways:

1. Animals are accidentally killed by ORVs.
2. Animals are deliberately molested and maimed by some ORV users.
3. Animals are carried off by some ORV users.

Frogs, salamanders, insects, and other animals that assemble in small areas to breed are particularly threatened by ORVs, to the degree large numbers of prime adults can be killed along a single track. Later, the young that linger at their birthplace are equally defenseless. In virtually all habitats, large numbers of animals take shelter within and under logs, in leaf litter, beneath rocks, and in burrows in the soil—the particular kinds of shelters that are easily destroyed by ORVs (Geological Society of America, 1977). Stebbins (oral communication, March 5, 1982) estimates that about 80% of terrestrial vertebrates in arid areas (exclusive of birds and larger mammals) are sequestered underground during the

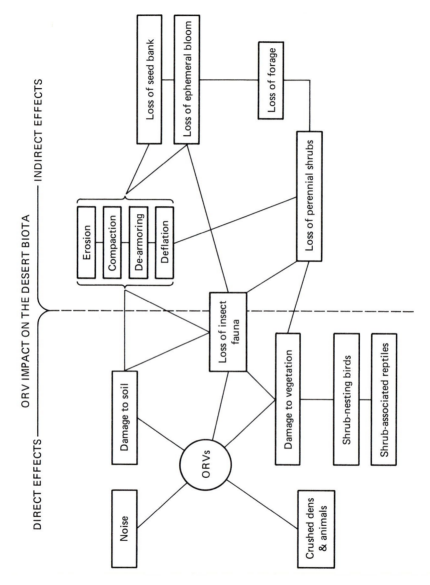

Figure 21-1. ORV impact on desert biota (from Luckenbach, 1975, p. 5). Published with permission.

winter months—November through February—and that a large percentage are probably within the first 12 inches (30 cm). He suspects that many animals are being crushed by ORVs and die unseen; that since the early 1970s the number of animals (vertebrate and invertebrate) destroyed by ORVs in arid areas number in the millions; and that deaths are the result of direct vehicle impacts or habitat deterioration.

Few animals can successfully avoid ORVs by moving elsewhere, because neighboring sites are usually filled to capacity, and a wild animal has limited chances for survival on unfamiliar ground. Although most animals are capable of adjusting to gradual change, the sudden impact of man often brings changes that are overwhelming. The slow process of natural adaptation cannot then take place. Such is the effect of ORVs on wildlife, because these vehicles bring noise, frightening movements, shaking ground, and polluted air, in addition to their power to cripple or cause sudden death. The noise of ORVs, for example, drowns out the calls of animals that are essential for mating, warnings, territorial behavior, and other social interactions. Further, because ORVs have caused hearing losses in humans, it can be expected that other animals will be similarly affected according to Brattstrom and Bondello (Chapter 9).

Besides generally degrading wildlife, ORVs threaten isolated species, remnant populations, colonies of naturally occurring hybrids, and populations of other uncommon or highly restricted species. Several species and isolated populations threatened by ORVs are now officially classed as rare or endangered and are protected by law, but some of their restricted habitats have already been intruded illegally, and significantly damaged, by ORVs, for example, the habitat of the endangered long-toed salamander (Geological Society of America, 1977, p. 5).

Bury et al. (1977, pp. 13–15) discovered that extensive reduction in wildlife accompanies the destruction of plant life by ORVs. It was found that "moderate" ORV use reduced the biomass of an area's terrestrial vertebrates by almost 60%. Heavy-use areas suffered a 75% decline in vertebrate biomass, a 45% decline in the number of such animals, and about a 10% drop in the species present. Desert tortoises, for example, depend almost entirely on spring ephemeral vegetation; a female tortoise must be able to store enough energy at this time to breed and lay eggs and then survive the summer and winter. If the spring vegetation is diminished by ORV use, the tortoise cannot store enough energy prior to egg laying or during the following summer. Hence it is unlikely she will survive the winter (Luckenbach, 1975, p. 5).

Initial studies of the effects of ORVs on animal diversity and density demonstrate destructive impacts. Animals are displaced from their accustomed places of refuge, and the disoriented animals may temporarily attract predators from surrounding areas. Stebbins and Cohen (1976) find that desert washes are fragile natural environments, which contain many plants and animals, some of which are restricted to this habitat. In their survey of ORV use of washes along state or federal highways in the desert, Stebbins and Cohen found the "growing incidence of ORV damage truly alarming." The long-term ecological consequences of widespread destruction of small mammals are especially noteworthy. These creatures form an important part of an area's food chain. According to the Geological Society of America (1977, p. 5), where ORV use is heavy, virtually all existing life is ultimately destroyed.

Solitude

One of the most commonly voiced criticisms of ORV users concerns the noise created by the machines. Even when the noise is muffled to the legal level, many people feel that it is intrinsically offensive in natural settings and an invasion of privacy and solitude. Many people enjoy the out-of-doors for its solitude and are angry when the sounds of ORVs disrupt this quiet. At the extreme, excessive ORV noise may be detrimental to the ORV user and can cause temporary or permanent hearing damage. The "sounds" of silence dominate arid areas. A U.S. Bureau of Land Management (1974, pp. 11-13) environmental impact statement noted that:

> Silence is a resource. These sounds which man typically associates with the pristine natural environments are perceived by the senses as solitude. The solitude of the desert is one of its . . . valuable resources.

The noise of an ORV shatters that solitude. Sounds generally associated with arid areas are very subtle and muted, such as light winds through shrubs, and they give the feeling of solitude. They are normal sounds associated with natural conditions. Man-made noises, however, have become commonplace throughout some of the arid areas. Most ORVs emit noise loud enough to disturb or annoy persons in their general vicinity. The contrast between this noise and the quiet surroundings serves to magnify the hearer's perception of the disturbance. The U.S. Bureau of Land Management (1974, p. V-5) notes that:

> The noise level generated by a single motorcycle is approximately 10,000,000 times greater than that experienced by a person in a quiet suburban residential area . . . .

Noise is highly obnoxious to all but the maker. According to Brattstrom and Bondello (Chapter 9), people are annoyed by intermittent or unpredictable sounds. Heart rates increase, and symptoms of stress such as vasoconstriction, stomach spasms, headaches, fetal convulsions, and ulcers can be expected. The noise levels created by competitive ORV events are extremely high. At any given time, the noise can increase from almost total silence to high levels that last up to 5 hours, depending on the type of event and the number of participants. Obviously noise from casual ORV use persists as long as the users are in the area. The fact is that most ORV noise is unnecessary; even motorcycles can be muffled to a relatively unobjectionable noise level.

ORV noise is also disruptive and often destructive to native wildlife according to Brattstrom and Bondello (Chapter 9). They indicate that merely the noise of vehicles can seriously disrupt wildlife populations, even leading to death. The Indiana Department of Natural Resources (1972, p. 52) notes that:

Some of life's functions are dependent on quietness. Many animals and birds depend upon it to find their mates, and to protect themselves from attack. Some embryos still in the egg communicate with siblings in adjacent eggs and synchronize their hatching. Some birds lean down to the ground to listen for a worm. The radar of bats, the trilling of toads, and the prolonged symphonies of thrushes can be affected if their home range is invaded by man-made noise. It is known that the pileated woodpecker, the broad-winged hawk, Cooper's hawk, sharp-shinned hawk, great horned owl, and barred owl are very sensitive to sound disturbances.

Air

The operation of ORVs creates two principal types of adverse effects on air quality—fugitive dust and gaseous exhaust emissions. Dust is created when ORVs dislodge small particles from the soil surface, which are suspended for a time in the air. Also, the disturbed surface may product fugitive dust through wind erosion long after the ORVs have passed. Even visibility and driving safety become problems. The U.S. Bureau of Outdoor Recreation (1976) in its draft environmental impact statement on implementing Executive Order 11644 which concerns the use of ORVs on public lands (Chapter 1, Fig. 1-3) finds that fugitive dust is the principal cause and concern when evaluating the effect of ORVs on air quality. Dust is particularly bad in arid areas or near areas with little or no vegetation. The arid-area soils most susceptible to wind erosion are in the drier parts of the western states. Wind erosion in these areas can cause poor air quality and limit visibility during certain seasons of the year. At other times, even without wind, ORV activity produces dust in arid areas. Indeed, the impact of an ORV race in raising dust is so enormous that it is hard for the uninitiated to imagine. Consider an excerpt from Villalobo's (1975, p. 12) dustfall study of a Barstow to Las Vegas motorcycle race:

> The amount of dustfall contributed by 3000 motorcycles and probably 2000 vehicles such as dune buggies, campers, trucks, automobiles and numerous campfires was very high. Within three to four hours, the concentration of dust was six to ninety times higher than the norm for the area. The peak concentration of dust could be one thousand times higher during the first fifteen minutes of the race when a crescendo of dust was reached.

Furthermore, competitive events can be expected to temporarily increase oxidant levels as well as dust levels. Rosenberg (1976, pp. 182, 183) observes that:

> although ORVs are recognized as polluting, a lack of regulation of air pollution emission exists, notwithstanding the agencies' apparent authority to control air emission by virtue of the Executive Orders' language directing agency operating regulations to "preserve public health." This failure to impose exhaust emission controls is compounded by the exemption of ORVs from EPA requirements estab-

lished pursuant to the Clean Air Act, which defines a motor vehicle as
". . . any self-propelled vehicle designed for transporting persons or
property on a street or highway."

Off-road vehicle engines, particularly the oil-burning, two-cycle type, create
exhaust fans that are heavy with unburned fuel, which cause chemical and visual
contamination of the air. Both the two-cycle and the four-cycle engines emit
unburned hydrocarbons and oxides of nitrogen that are the primary ingredients
of photochemical smog. According to the California Department of Parks and
Recreation (1978), chemical air contamination caused by vehicle exhaust emissions may be directly toxic to plant and animal life, as has been demonstrated
by the slow death of ponderosa pines from smog on the east side of the Los
Angeles Basin.

Other Resources

Off-road vehicles with improper exhaust systems may emit sparks and start fires
in dry plant materials. This problem is particularly serious in arid areas during
hot summers when most of the plants are tinder dry. The problems of fire
control are also increased because ORVs bring large numbers of people into
remote areas, where accidental fires (or those deliberately set by some ORV
users) are difficult to reach and extinguish (California Department of Parks and
Recreation, 1975).

The U.S. Bureau of Outdoor Recreation (1976) finds that most of the damage caused by ORVs also diminishes the attractiveness of the land. The esthetic
damage is especially noticeable where heavy ORV use has seriously damaged the
soil or vegetation. Many ORV users, moreover, tend to litter the landscape just
as many thoughtless picnickers litter. However, an ORV user covers 20 times
more land per day than less mobile users, and he or she can carry more disposable items for a longer time. Consequently, the litter problem is intensified.

Historic ruins and paleontological and archeological sites are commonly
abundant in arid areas. Until recently, they have been preserved by their remote-
ness. According to Gilbertson (Chapter 19) even the archeologically rich paleosols of relatively high resistance are being destroyed by ORVs. The intaglios
near Blythe, California have suffered significant degradation by ORV use. All of
the figures at the Blythe site, together with another figure in the nearby Yuha
Desert, were completely destroyed after a protective fence was cut (Wilshire,
1977, p. 4). The President's U.S. Council on Environmental Quality (1979, p.
422) reports that:

> Concern is growing over the damage ORVs are doing to intaglios in
> Arizona and southern California. Intaglios are large human and animal
> figures carved into the earth by ancient peoples and held sacred by
> them. These rare archeological figures exist in only two places in this
> hemisphere—Peru and the U.S. Sonoran Desert. Associated with the
> intaglios are rock carvings called petroglyphs. There are at least 29
> known site concentrations—containing approximately 150 individual

intaglios and less than 100 major petroglyph loci—all of which are on BLM-administered land.

Only four of these intaglio sites have been fenced in, and at one of the four, the famous Blythe intaglio, a portion of the fence was broken through 8 years ago and has not yet been repaired. The rest of the unprotected sites are constantly endangered by ORV use and particularly so by the Parker 400, an annual BLM-authorized ORV race.

Sustained-Yield Concept

In any discussion of management concepts, it is necessary to have an understanding of the "sustained-yield" concept alongside the magnitude of impact of ORV use on the nation's resources. Section 601 of the Federal Land Policy and Management Act (U.S. Congress, 1976) requires the federal public lands in the California desert to be administered within the framework of a program of "sustained yield" which is defined in Section 103 as:

> the achievement and maintenance in perpetuity of a high-level annual or regular periodic output of the various renewable resources of the public lands consistent with multiple use.

The Geological Society of America (1977, pp. 5, 6) set forth the magnitude of ORV use on the nation's resources:

> living systems are inherently stable, reflecting an evolutionary background that extends far into the past. Each species in the system, plant or animal, is adapted to its particular habitat, which has been built by physical and biological processes that change only slowly with the passage of time.
>
> The harsh impacts of vehicles on these closely adjusted systems—the living forms and the physical environment in which life literally takes root—have destroyed evolutionary gains of such antiquity that recovery will be exceedingly slow. Indeed, it seems certain that many delicate interdependencies between organisms and their habitats, having been obliterated by ORVs, can never be restored.

In this volume, it can be seen that ORV use is an exclusive use and is not compatible with the "multiple-use" concept as defined by the U.S. Congress (1976). It can also be seen that ORV use is consumptive of vulnerable resources and therefore cannot be compatible with the "sustained-yield" concept. According to Dregne (Chapter 2), there is no possibility of setting a realistic level of use; any use will be destructive. Lathrop and Rowlands (Chapter 7) conclude that ORV use cannot be attempted under the "sustained-yield" or "carrying capacity" concept as can be done with livestock grazing.

One advantage of the environmental impact statements required by the National Environmental Policy Act (U.S. Congress, 1970) is that some federal land managers have become aware that ORV use is not compatible with the concepts of "multiple use" and "sustained yield." This awareness is shown by the analysis and statements presented in Figure 21-2.

B. Living Components:

1. Vegetation: There have been several recent studies on the effects of motorcycle races on the vegetation in the Mojave Desert. The studies not only discuss general effects, but quantify impacts and give specific impacts for pits, camping area, start areas (bomb runs), and along racecourses. In general, these studies show that off-road vehicle use will:

    a. Reduce the number of shrubs.
    b. Reduce diversity of shrub species by selectively impacting the smaller, more fragile species.
    c. Reduce the numbers of annual wildflowers that will germinate and flower the following years.
    d. Reduce the diversity of annual wildflowers.
    e. Enhance the growth and extend the range of exotic weeds.
    f. Increase impacts as numbers of motorcycles increase.
    g. Intensify the damage with repeated use.
    h. Cause a lengthened period of recovery with repeated use.
    i. Compact the soil which plays an important role in determining plant growth. Compaction of soil decreases moisture available to plants, increases surface runoff, and decreases germination of plant seeds.

2. Wildlife: As a result of the direct impacts on vegetation mentioned above, competitive off-road vehicle use will cause a loss of wildlife habitat. Reduction of vegetation sets off a series of events which are complex but predictable, because plants form the base for all food chains. Generally, damage to plants, especially shrubs, can affect animal populations by:

    a. Reducing cover used for protection from extremes of weather, and from predators.
    b. Reducing sites for placement of burrows and nests.
    c. Reducing insectivore and herbivore populations which reduces the carnivore population

Not only will there be a loss of habitat, but also a direct loss of habitat, but also a direct loss of animals. Direct mortality of some animals occurs at the time of a competitive event even though many of the desert reptiles and mammals are nocturnal or may be hibernating during the winter months. Some, especially the reptiles, have shallow burrows beneath the soil surface and are crushed as vehicles pass over. Others that are active during an event may be unable to avoid being run over. One species of particular concern, the desert tortoise, is threatened by man's encroachment upon its habitat.

C. Human Interest Values:

1. Aesthetics: The overall aesthetic quality of the UJVCA is not expected to change to any significant extent. The UJVCA has already been heavily aesthetically impacted by the high degree of ORV use. Short-term degradation of the visual aesthetics is normally caused by the dust created by a competitive event. This impact is largely dependent on the weather conditions and on the type of soils traversed.

2. Recreation: The impact of the proposed action on recreation in the UJVCA varies greatly depending on the type of recreationist involved. The vehicle oriented recreationist would receive a great deal of benefit from the proposed action. Being able to compete in an organized ORV event is a tremendously rewarding experience to many desert recreationists. Others enjoy watching a competitive event or enjoy participating in an event by serving as a pit crewman or a flagman.
On the other hand, competitive events tend to exclude many other recreationists from the area. A competitive event can be a great distraction to anyone seeking to enjoy the desert in a non-vehicle oriented way. Hikers, campers, photo enthusiasts, artists, hunters, and "nature lovers" in general are denied the chance to enjoy the desert in its natural state.

3. History: No additional impacts to historical resources are anticipated. A large amount of vandalism, whether related to competitive events in the vicinity or not, has already occurred at all of the old mining camps.

4. Archaelogy: Impacts of the proposed action on the archaelogical resources will be very minimal since no important or major sites are known. Archaeological sites in general are extremely fragile and should an event cross over a valuable yet unknown site, the information they could yield would be lost forever.

Figure 21-2. ORV effects, excerpted from the Environmental Analysis Record for Competitive ORV Events in Designated Vehicular Use Area 30—Upper Johnson Valley (from U.S. Bureau of Land Management, 1976).

ORV use may be typical of our time; it is a consumptive use. While hunting or fishing consumes animals, ORVs consume entire landscapes. In destroying resources, ORVs make demands on petroleum energy and on the manpower and funds of public agencies—all in pursuit of a pastime that could be discontinued. Aldo Leopold (1966, p. 240) in *A Sand Country Almanac* gently but clearly perceives right and wrong:

> A thing is right when it tends to preserve the integrity, stability, and beauty of the biotic community. It is wrong when it tends otherwise.

Four Questions

We have seen that benefits to ORV users can be provided, but that the costs are substantial both to virtually all other users (who are excluded) and to the nation's resources (which are damaged or destroyed). However, some questions persist and should be answered before management practices are addressed. The most pertinent questions are:

1. Does unrestricted ORV use always have a negative effect on arid areas?
2. Will the arid areas naturally recover after unrestricted ORV use?
3. Can ORV use be effectively regulated?
4. Does anyone really care about the arid areas?

Always a Negative Effect?

In arid areas where soils are shallow, the cover of ephemeral vegetation provides no significant protection against ORVs. A single ORV pass can strip this cover and expose the soil surface, although several passages are required for substantial damage to the soil. Hinckley et al. (Chapter 5) report that ORV activity in arid areas nearly always results in greatly increased erosion and that, while some areas may be affected more than others, evidence indicates that significant damage occurs virtually everywhere. Observations by the U.S. Bureau of Land Management (1975), as well as other studies (Webb and Wilshire, 1978), indicate that even single ORV traverses can eradicate 100% of annual flora in the track and can have substantial impact on sensitive perennial shrubs.

In arid-area sand dunes, certain animals bury themselves just beneath the surface of the sand; others make their dens in depressions. These animals are easily crushed by vehicles passing above. Bury and Luckenbach (Chapter 10) conclude that even a limited amount of ORV activity could have dire consequences for certain sensitive species. They further conclude that ORV use and biological wellbeing are mutually exclusive and that closure of the majority of arid-area dunes is the only choice if plant and animal communities are to exist.

Trail breaking by ORV users is the antithesis of commonly understood soil conservation practices. Wilshire (Chapter 3) reports that the algal and lichen mats, short grasses, small shrubs, lag gravels, and thin chemical crusts that help stabilize large areas in deserts are all easily broken by a single ORV incursion. A single pass of an ORV across a mature desert pavement of the type in which the intaglios were made can be sufficient to destroy it (Chapter 11). Luckenbach (1975, p. 11) queries: "When the passage of one dirt bike can make a 'trail,' where is the protection of the roadless areas?" And he concludes that "any area conceded to ORV use sacrifices all other recreational uses of that area."

Godfrey et al. (1978, p. 587) in their study on the impact of ORVs on coastal ecosystems report that the first 175 vehicle passes over beach grass inflict maximal damage; after that, incremental damage is less because most of the harm is already done. Thus, a "minimum" number or a "carrying capacity" cannot be stated in ecological terms because such a number would not allow even light use. The "carrying capacity" of dune vegetation for vehicles is quite low, since any track can require several years to return to preimpact conditions, and an established ORV track through dunes can be considered to be an almost permanent feature. The California Department of Parks and Recreation (1978) observes that:

> while each individual machine may itself do only a little damage, the cumulative effect of millions of ORVs is large, even if it is not easily calculated, and there may be significant damage to the soil mantle, even when the machines move very slowly and do not actually tear away the soil.

In heavily used ORV areas, habitat loss is virtually complete, as can be readily observed in ORV staging sites. These "pit" areas appear as greatly compacted and denuded parking lots; no studies are needed to document the profound ecological damage. A parallel between ORV use and graded roads can be drawn. Graded roads which are commonly associated with rural land developments have seriously affected the environment of the arid areas. Campbell (1972, p. 147) reports that these roads cause major destruction of the natural environment. Roads (like ORV trails) make no compromise with the natural vegetation, wildlife habitat, or even the local topography. Local ecosystems are totally disregarded. Graded roads (like ORV trails) destroy the arid areas' meager plant cover and expose the dry soil to the wind. This exposed surface provides a potential source of dust. While the impact of one or a few ORVs causes adverse impacts on the natural environment, a large ORV event such as the Barstow-Las Vegas motorcycle race of 1974 causes catastrophic and irreversible impacts that should make even the most "macho" person feel uncomfortable (U.S. Bureau of Land Management, 1975).

Off-road vehicle damage can last hundreds of years—in some arid areas just the tracks of the vehicles may last thousands of years. Vehicle tracks are analogous to the furrows of Indian intaglios near Blythe, California, which are believed to have been made several hundred years ago, if not earlier (U.S. Bureau of Land Management, 1974). Unused trails more than 60 years old can be seen in Death Valley (Hunt and Mabey, 1966). Wagon trails over a century old can be seen between Needles and the San Bernardino Mountains (Davis and Winslow, 1966). Tracks made by General Patton's tanks and jeeps on practice maneuvers in the Mojave Desert, California in the early 1940s remain clearly visible today (Chapter 13).

Do all drivers have some negative effect? Of course not. ORV users who remain on, or are restricted to paved roads or paved facilities do not cause any additional damage. For example, Sheridan (1979, p. 59) reports that the Jeep Corporation, in cooperation with members of the Outdoor Writers Association of America, developed a code of environmental ethics for ORV drivers:

> I will appreciate the solitude and beauty of our natural environment, and respect the feelings of others. . . . I will not drive where I cannot leave the land essentially the same as before I drove across it.

Sheridan concludes that if these ethics guided the ORV manufacturers, the advertisers, the ORV users, and the regulatory agencies managing public lands, then ORV use would not be an issue.

It should be noted that the interactions of vehicles on soil, water, plants, wildlife, solitude, and air however, are physical phenomena independent of the attitudes of the ORV user. The distinction between "responsible" and "irresponsible" ORV operators is not relevant to arid areas. Some operators are sensitive to the needs of others and to the conservation of resources, but it is not in the nature of their machine with its aggressive tread patterns and noisy engine to leave the medium of travel unaffected like fish through the water, or birds through the air.

Is Natural Recovery Possible?

There are usually three levels of ORV effects on natural resources—disturbance, impairment, and destruction. The question heading this section can be rephrased into three subquestions relating to these levels:

1. Can disturbed arid areas recover naturally?
2. Can impaired resources be rehabilitated or restored?
3. Can destroyed lands be reclaimed?

Can Disturbed Arid Areas Recover Naturally? Lathrop (Chapter 13) reports that concentrated ORV use has resulted in significant reductions in vegetation density and cover, despite the long periods of elapsed time for recovery (36 years). Once the soil surface in arid areas is disturbed, recovery is extremely slow according to Dregne (Chapter 2). Natural recovery is generally an unsatisfactory means of reclamation in heavy ORV-use areas because of the long recovery times—at least decades and probably centuries (Chapter 14). According to the Geological Society of America (1977, p. 2), the capability of the land and its biota to sustain ORV impact is as varied as the invaded habitats and that:

> damage by ORVs in even the least vulnerable areas will require periods for recovery measured in centuries or millennia. Losses of soil and changes in the land surface will be long lasting, and certain natural life

systems will never recover from the intensive ORV impacts already sustained.

To generate soil over hard rock in arid areas requires thousands of years; softer rock provides inorganic soil material faster, but the productivity will depend on the nutrient content of the rock and the remaining plants. The buildup of topsoil is the result of a very slow process. Dregne (Chapter 2) reports that it requires anywhere from as little as 1000 years to several tens of thousands of years to form a soil, depending on climate, slope, and type of parent material. Even under optimum conditions, it may take nature several hundred years or longer to generate an inch of topsoil in arid areas. Some soils are so old that their character was formed under climatic conditions that no longer exist and hence cannot be replaced.

Wilshire and Nakata (1976, p. 128) describe two types of damage from ORVs on alluvial fans:

> 1) in light use zones, stripping of pavement and vegetation exposes the soft underlayer to erosion by wind and water; 2) in heavy use zones, compaction reduces wind-erosion but will substantially increase run-off of rain and hence has increased the potential for water erosion. The desert pavement protection, however, is for practical purposes destroyed because its rate of formation is extremely slow. Compaction further inhibits seed germination and regeneration of the plant cover. It is possible, if granted relief, that plant growth could recover in the light use zones sufficiently to afford some protection to the surface before the infrequent heavy rains hit them. Compaction is so severe in heavy use zones that it is very unlikely that plants will recover in time to afford any protection from water erosion.

Increased sediment loads in surface runoff, as a result of soil destabilization, is another serious problem. In areas of sensitive soils and steep terrain, the increased runoff is commonly accommodated by diversion to vegetated areas which are themselves then degraded. The result over a period of years is that these downstream areas become erosion centers even though never directly touched by ORVs.

The Geological Society of America (1977, p. 6) concluded that the interactions of vehicles with closely adjusted systems have destroyed evolutionary gains of such antiquity that recovery will be exceedingly slow. Indeed, it seems certain that many delicate interdependencies between organisms and their habitats, having been obliterated by ORVs, can never be restored. Disruption by ORVs of surfaces otherwise preserved by desert varnish must be considered permanent on a human time scale according to Elvidge and Iverson (Chapter 11). Briggs and Tellier (1977)—both ORV users and earth scientists—advise ORV users to "accept the certainty of unrecoverable damage from motorcycle races . . . ."

Litter is common along motorcycle race courses. Some types of litter will decompose relatively quickly; others decompose by oxidation; but many others—such as rubber and plastic objects—undergo only mechanical breakdown and become a permanent part of the landscape. But won't one good rain heal the disturbed arid areas? In effect, what happens is the removal of plant cover and an increase in erosion. Instead of the desert healing with rainfall, a scar is formed. Webb et al. (Chapter 14) report that compaction resulting from motorcycle use persisted after 1 year, although the tracks were not visible. The effect of one good rain is mainly cosmetic and merely hides instead of heals the damage. The U.S. Bureau of Land Management's (1974) final environmental impact statement on a proposed Barstow-Las Vegas race anticipated that motorcycle tracks and ruts across 692 acres (280 ha) of wet playas could be expected to be visible for 30 or more years; the recovery of vegetation was estimated at 1 to 10 years or more for annuals; as much as decades for perennials; and centuries for the return of climax communities.

Some people feel that when an area is disturbed the animals, being mobile, simply go somewhere else. This is only partly true, as the new arrivals inevitably displace, or crowd, the established animals. Vast numbers of animals may exist in a small area, but the natural biotic community is extremely complex. Many of the organisms have low mobility. Others have good powers of locomotion but may simply refuse to move or, if they do, are soon eliminated by predation, accidents, lack of food, or competition on unfamiliar ground. Probably in many instances a wild animal displaced by an ORV is as good as dead because surrounding areas will usually be fully occupied.

Since the contemporary ORV user is not the first user of the arid areas, how could the Indians and Spaniards who occupied the arid areas even before the first English settlement on the Atlantic Coast leave such little trace? The answer lies in the Indian's natural-ethic lifestyle and the Spaniard's lack of motorized equipment. An excerpt from *Death Comes for the Archbishop* by Willa Cather (1928, pp. 235–236) illustrates this answer:

> When they left the rock or tree or sand dune that had sheltered them for the night, the Navajo was careful to obliterate every trace of their temporary occupation. He buried the embers of the fire, and the remnants of food, unpiled any stones he had piled together, filled up the holes he had scooped in the sand. . . . Father Latour judged that, just as it was the white man's way to assert himself in any landscape, to change it, make it over a little (at least to leave some mark or memorial of his sojourn), it was the Indian's way to pass through a country without disturbing anything; to pass and leave no trace, like fish through the water, or birds through the air.

Can Impaired Soils, Vegetation, and Wildlife Be Rehabilitated or Restored by Rest, Rotation, or Ceasing ORV Use? Webb et al. (Chapter 14) conclude that rest-rotation practices are impractical for management of ORVs in arid areas because the rest periods would have to be considerably longer than the use periods. Scott et al. (1978), in their resource assessment and management analysis of the Ballinger-Deer Park Canyon ORV open-use area, evaluated a provision for rest-rotation on hillclimb areas and found that the system would not be practical. They felt that to be done properly, resting areas should receive some rehabilitation to aid in a "healing" process, although erosion problems could never be corrected (p. 56). Such a project would require considerable capital investment. The findings confirmed a 1972 Ballinger Canyon soil management survey recommendation that a rest-rotation plan would be pointless in this area because of soil types and conditions.

A rest-rotation system, where a particular open area is closed to permit revegetation, is not feasible according to Lathrop (Chapter 8). Where plants, water quality, and habitat have been impaired, only limited success for revegetation in arid areas has been achieved. The reasons are the harsh climatic conditions— low and erratic rainfall and high temperatures—and the high pressure from grazing animals. Snyder et al. (1976, p. 29) showed that the runoff from one ORV use area was eight times that from an adjacent unused basin such that even after closing the use area, natural revegetation did not take place. Kay and Graves (Chapters 16 and 17) also found that efforts to revegetate arid areas were disappointing. Plants rarely reestablish under natural conditions, and artificial plantings result in many failures. Even the most dominant species respond very slowly to revegetation according to Brum et al. (Chapter 15). The chances of successfully rehabilitating disturbed areas in arid areas seem to be minimal. Total restoration of the plant composition and structure using techniques tested by Brum et al. under the environmental conditions along a 220-kV transmission line was found to be impossible.

On the other hand, where plants, water quality, and habitat have been impaired, Kay and Graves (Chapter 16) suggest that restoration is possible provided that growing conditions are favorable, seed is abundant, and rodent, bird, and herbivore populations are low. Then, reseeding or transplanting probably would be effective, but Kay and Graves go on to say that all these factors are seldom favorable at the same time. Good seed years serve mostly to feed the wildlife and are seldom followed by good growing conditions. Even expensive techniques such as transplanting container-grown shrubs or irrigating have had very limited success on arid sites. They conclude that revegetation in arid areas can be expected to be slow and erratic even if the best techniques are used. For the best success, seeds should be sown as soon as possible after the disturbance using local seed, covered with soil, and protected from animals and vehicles. However, even under these optimum conditions, the original ecosystems cannot be replaced, as measured by numbers of plants or diversity of species (Chapter 16). According to Lathrop and Rowlands (Chapter 7) attempts at artificial rehabilitation and revegetation in arid lands have never been an unqualified success, or even a qualified success.

Wind erosion in ORV areas persists even when such areas have been abandoned. Such erosion is especially common in arid lands where vehicles readily destroy the delicate crusts that protect the soil from wind. Sand and soil blown from these denuded sites may be deposited far from the area of vehicle use. Nakata et al. (1976) have identified ORV use as one of the causes of Mojave Desert dust plumes photographed from a satellite in space. By destroying vegetation on sand dunes and disrupting their stability, ORVs may cause the dunes to advance on neighboring areas (Geological Society of America, 1977, p. 3).

It is interesting to note that four of the five state approaches for managing an ORV facility, as reported by Rasor (1977), are somewhat successful only in areas of high average rainfall: the Buttgenbach Mine Recreation Area, Florida, 52 to 64 in. (1300 to 1600 mm) a year; the Cheniere Lake Bicentennial Park, Louisiana, 52 to 56 in. (1300 to 1400 mm) a year; the Finger Lakes State Park, Missouri, 30 to 40 in. (760 to 1000 mm) a year; and the Washington statewide system of ORV facilities, 48 to 96 in. (1220 to 2440 mm) a year. Plants obviously grow better in humid areas than in arid areas, and hence, rehabilitation efforts can be effective. In addition, existing vegetation or other natural barriers tend to prevent ORVs from leaving the trails and thereby limit their overall damage.

Closing disturbed ORV areas is often suggested as a means to permit natural recovery. In arid areas, ceasing ORV use is not enough. Scientists have found that for years after closing, the land used by ORVs continues to lose soil and plants grow slowly, if at all. Ostby (1979) observes that rotation of trail segments to provide for rehabilitation seems impossible. Old trails remain visible for a long time and their continued use ordinarily can be prevented only by screening and by explicit marking of crossings by new trails. Continued ORV use would require dedication of a trail specifically for ORVs.

With respect to wildlife, certain desert animals are so scarce and mature so slowly that their removal would result in a long-term loss, not only of the individuals, but also of their reproductive potential (Bury et al., 1977). Brattstrom and Bondello (Chapter 9) conclude that there is little or no recovery of hearing losses in wildlife. In short, recovery of animal populations in deserts would be slow, even where there are no further ORV activities.

Can Destroyed Lands Be Reclaimed? Rocks can be replaced, soil can be hauled in and graded to the original contours, and plants and animals can be carried in, but the cost is astronomical. Wilshire (1980) finds that the cost of reclamation can be especially high in arid areas. In Richmond, California, Shay (1979, p. 316) reports that the park district is trying to reclaim an ORV area and that the cost so far is $2,000 per acre. Brum, et al. (Chapter 15) project reclamation costs greater than $3,600 per acre ($9,000 per ha) for lands disturbed by transmission line construction, disturbances they consider comparable to those caused by ORVs. A demonstration that reclamation is possible for any of a number of specific habitats relating to ORV use of public lands cannot be found in any documents published by the U.S. Department of Agriculture. The usual practice in specific areas where trails are no longer used or desired by ORV operators has been simply to abandon them. According to Kay and Graves (Chapter 17) transplanting shrubs or wild seedlings is not only expensive but requires great care and vigilant protection from grazing livestock, rabbits, and rodents, and all foot and vehicular traffic.

The difficulties and potential cost of reclaiming disturbed areas are well known from studies of reclamation of mined land. Despite efforts to restore native vegetation in the California Aqueduct construction corridor in the area of Dolan Springs Canyon, the corridor remains a bare zone with accelerated ero-

sion. In Panoche Hills, a semiarid area south of San Francisco, efforts were made
to rehabilitate an area used for 2 years by ORVs. Restabilization of the surface
was successful at a cost of $80 per acre in a terrain with low relief but failed on
steep slopes where erosion rates are still, 8 years after closure, nearly 50 times
the natural rate (Wilshire, 1977, p. iii). Attempts to revegetate disturbed arid
areas are described by Brum et al. (Chapter 15), and by Kay and Graves in both
Chapters 16 and 17.

The impossibility of reclamation in arid areas for other uses has been recognized. For example, Box (1974, p. 2) notes that:

> The dryer areas, those receiving less than ten inches (250 mm) of an-
> nual rainfall . . . pose a more difficult problem. Revegetation of these
> areas can probably be accomplished only with major, sustained inputs
> of water, fertilizer, and management. Range seeding experiments have
> had only limited success in the dryer areas. Rehabilitation of the dryer
> sites may occur naturally on a time scale that is unacceptable to society,
> because it may take decades, or even centuries, for natural succession
> to reach stable conditions.

Certain features of the landscape cannot be restored at any price, for example,
irreplaceable historic, scenic, or archeological sites and endangered species. In
1969, Los Angeles County placed three benchmarks imbedded in concrete and
inserted to depths of 1 to 2 feet (0.3 to 0.6 m) in a hill in Hungry Valley. By
1977, they were gone. The ground around them was eroded away by ORVs so
that there was nothing left to hold them in place, and the markers, concrete
and all, rolled to the bottom of the hill.

Stebbins and Cohen (1976) in assessing overall ORV damage to the arid areas,
point out that natural areas severely damaged by ORVs cannot be reclaimed in
the sense of restoring the original natural ecosystem. It is not humanly possible
to reconstruct complex and delicate interrelationships that have evolved over a
vast stretch of time. They concluded that a reclaimed area will always be something less desirable than that created by natural processes.

Can ORVs Be Effectively Regulated?   Regulation is often suggested as the
answer to ORV conflicts with other users and to their destruction of resources.
However, regulation of open areas is a monumental and probably impossible
task. For example, the Indiana Department of Natural Resources (1972) concluded that it simply did not have the personnel to supervise or maintain ORV
trails or areas on its lands:

> Maintenance of quality and recreational environment is related closely
> to constant and efficient management of all facilities. Poor mainte-
> nance, whether in high-use areas or natural settings, encourages further
> vandalism, litter, and the destruction of many native plants . . . .

In 1978, the BLM State Director for New Mexico (Zimmerman, 1978), was
administering 13 million acres (4.8 million ha) of land which received approximately 120,000 visitor-days of motorcycle use each year, and an additional
115,000 visitor-days by other forms of ORVs, such as jeeps and pickups. He

states that "this unregulated use has caused conflicts with other land uses which we have not been able to control with our existing limited staff." The U.S Bureau of Outdoor Recreation (1976) in its draft environmental impact statement on implementation of Executive Order 11644, notes that:

> in practice, particularly in the case of the Bureau of Land Management, which lacks the staff to effectively patrol its vast holdings, unauthorized off-road vehicle use will occur in these areas in the interim. Some of these lands will later be found to contain unique and fragile bio-physical, archeological, or historic resources, and will be designated as closed to ORVs. Certain of these resources will have been damaged or destroyed irreversibly as a result of ORV use during the undesignated period.

Examples of manpower and budgetary constraints abound. For example, severe ORV problems at the Tejon Administrative Site has forced attention away from Ballinger Canyon during the implementation phase of the ORV plan. ORV patrolmen have been working almost exclusively at the Administrative Site, thus diluting the enforcement and public contact necessary to reduce trespass outside the ORV boundary (Scott et al., 1978, p. 48). ORV users normally cross areas closed for habitat protection to reach sites used for Enduro events according to Scott et al. (p. 49). In Chapter 7, Lathrop and Rowlands conclude that attempts to regulate the number of ORVs would be difficult if not impossible.

The process of designating areas or trails as open or closed to ORV use is a laborious undertaking for public land managers. For example, the BLM administers 474 million acres (191 million ha) of public land, and the task is compounded by the fact that they have not been able to exercise much control over ORV use in the past. Hence, a behavior pattern for millions of ORV users has already become established. In the past, BLM's lack of presence in the California desert was caused by their having had only slightly more than a dozen rangers to patrol 12 million acres (4.8 million ha) of land. In fact, BLM has fewer men and women per acre (ha) than the other public land management agencies.

Public-land managers' past efforts to control ORV use have run into severe problems. An evaluation report by the U.S. Bureau of Land Management (1975) after the Barstow-Las Vegas motorcycle race showed that the environmental impact analysis had underestimated the damage because of ineffective controls. The exhaustive environmental impact analysis that preceded the 1974 Barstow-Las Vegas motorcycle race listed the procedures to be followed. They included: checking for compliance, monitoring the course, requiring a performance bond, requiring the permittee to provide 100 course marshals, and clearly marking and flagging the entire course route. The race entrants were limited to 3,000—the maximum number of riders that the sponsors stated their organization could handle (U.S. Bureau of Land Management, 1974). The postrace evaluation (U.S. Bureau of Land Management, 1975) reported great devastation: a 90% reduction in the small mammal population; damage to archeological sites; extensive damage to rare plant habitats, the protection of which had been assured; and immeasurable damage to the soil, plant life, and wildlife.

The BLM monitored the 1974 Barstow to Las Vegas motorcycle race closely. The race affected 25% more land than the 1973 race and damaged more soil and vegetation than expected. Attempts to protect Indian archeological sites along the way proved less than successful because the racers did not stay on course; also the race covered previously undiscovered sites, which became known only after the damage was done.

In its final environmental impact statement to the proposed Barstow-Las Vegas motorcycle race, the U.S. Bureau of Land Management (1974, p. V-1) predicted that unavoidable adverse impacts would occur despite the proposed mitigation efforts and noted that the scope of mitigation was constrained by: (1) their limited manpower resources; (2) the funds available to implement certain mitigation measures; (3) the nature of the race itself, namely a "thrill" event pitting man against his environment with concomitant threats to human safety and the environment; and (4) the time required to effect certain mitigation measures.

In addition, the U.S. Bureau of Land Management (1974, p. V-13) noted that traffic and human congestion will occur despite efforts to minimize these problems:

> Ten to twelve thousand spectators in addition to 3,000 racers are expected at the starting area. Many of these spectators will themselves be riding motorcycles around the general vicinity of the start. An anticipated 6,000 casual ORV riders are expected to be "joy riding" within a radius of three miles of the start area. While this general area is already severely impacted by past use, additional destruction to vegetation and soils is expected. Similar "joy riding" is expected by lesser numbers of spectators at other concentration areas mentioned, *viz.* 500 riders at each of the three pit stops, and 2,000 at the finish area.

Wilshire and Nakata (1976, p. 132) note that significant damage was caused by the 1974 Barstow-Las Vegas race even though many steps were taken by both BLM and the sponsoring motorcycle club to reduce environmental impact. Except for control of litter and damage to cultural sites, the other adverse effects caused by racing cannot be adequately mitigated.

Effective regulation requires many marshals and careful monitoring. In some cases the magnitude of the event or problem is so great that it discourages proper management. For example, in the case of the Ballinger Canyon, no devices, such as catchment dams or diversions, are used to prevent damage outside of the use area. No water bars or diversions to retard erosion on site are in evidence. In the case of the Blythe intaglios, figures were damaged before protective fencing was erected, or access was gained through a gate in the fence or by breaking down the fence. In Red Rock State Recreation Area, Jawbone Canyon, and Hungry Valley, no erosion control devices are used to mitigate off-site effects of accelerated erosion. In the case of the Barstow of Las Vegas course, efforts to reduce damage during the 1974 race by channeling the course failed. Damaged surfaces have not been restored, nor has any attempt been made to mitigate erosion. In Wilshire's (1977) study of nine sites used by ORVs, no effort was made by the various private or public land managers to mitigate the damage; or if attempted, the efforts were thwarted.

In arid and semiarid areas, high erosion rates are common even in regulated ORV use areas. For example, the Hollister Hills ORV facility south of San Francisco has been used by ORVs for about 20 years, and it is currently losing soil at the rate of 18,200 tons per square mile (6400 tonnes km^{-2}) a year—26 times the "tolerance level" suggested by the U.S. Soil Conservation Service. Previous efforts to reduce erosion by using water bars and diversions were unsuccessful in coping with the massive runoff, or the effort created other problems by burying plants and diverting erosion to unused slopes.

Even when carefully regulated and when the land managers are assured of a promoter's cooperation, problems arise. A U.S. Forest Service resource officer (Ostby, 1979) commenting on an Enduro ORV event in the Greenhorn Ranger District of Sequoia National Forest states: "The permittee did not honor his agreement with the Forest Service regarding racing on private land where the camp was. This is greatly discouraging to me as a breach of trust." Keith Axelson (1979) made a field inspection of the Kelso Creek Camp area after the regulated ORV Enduro and commented:

> Even after 16 days of virtual non-use, the camping area bore the marks of heavily compacted soil and the previous ground cover of grasses was non-existent. Motorcycle tracks were clearly visible throughout the creek bottom. . . . I noted new hillside trails adjacent (east side) to the camp site. All of this was in contradiction to the guarantee by the event promoter that no riding was to be done other than on existing roads within the camp area.
>
> I believe we are deluding ourselves if we think, for a moment, that an event of this magnitude has a place in this highly vulnerable ecosystem. . . . It will not sustain such tremendous local pressure. The removal of downed wood from the creekbottom for campfires eliminates undergrowth which is essential to the riparian system. Each time a large group descends here this occurs.
>
> Lastly, the event promoter did not keep his agreement concerning the start/finish line. The start was to have originated on Kelso Valley Road. Instead he opted to begin the event from the southeast edge of the camping area. It was not surprising to me. The exhilaration of a start in a cloud of dust is undeniable.

Some ORV uses have proved nearly impossible to regulate; no public lands are free from ORV abuse. Ed Carlson, a park ranger in Joshua Tree National Monument, says his efforts to close off ORV routes into protected areas of the monument have been continually frustrated. In one case rangers built a virtual tank trap from concrete, steel cables, and blades from road graders. Shortly after it was built, Aleshire (1979, p. 145) reports that someone with a welder's torch cut through the steel blades and pulled them aside with a winch.

In some cases the destruction is accidental, but in others, it is intentional. Near El Centro, the BLM erected a fence to protect a 5000-year-old design. Someone tore down the fence and then some ORV users drove in circles over the prehistoric artwork, until they had wiped out more than 75% of it. An excerpt from an article by Aleshire (1979, p. 144), a reporter for *The Desert Sun* in Palm Springs, illustrates this problem:

> In recent years, the Barstow-to-Las Vegas race has received the most publicity. In 1974 environmental groups forced the BLM to do an environmental impact report on the 130-mile event which drew 3,000 motorcycles. The report found that the motorcycles kicked up 600 tons of dust, damaged plants and animals, and increased erosion rates. Since then, the BLM has refused to issue a permit for the event, as required by the bureau's management plan. But last November, Louis H. McKey, a Fontana motorcyclist nicknamed the "Phantom Duck," led off-road vehicle clubs in defying the BLM ban. The run was widely publicized in motorcycle magazines, and 600 riders turned up for the Thanksgiving Day race.
>
> Helpless BLM rangers stood by, taking pictures, while the event went off as scheduled. After mulling over this defiance for several months, BLM finally filed a motion in Los Angeles District Court to show cause why McKey, Rick Sieman, William Brinson, and Albert Fols, all of Phantom Duck of the Desert Incorporated, should not be brought to trial for contempt of court.
>
> "The special interests have a very major role," says one BLM source. "The economics of off-road vehicles is quite a big thing. Frankly, I'm at a loss to explain it. But a BLM manager who takes a stand against the special interests is apt to get himself removed."

A hydrologist for the Arizona Water Resources Agency (Briggs, 1979, p. 35) observes that, "Closing a popular area will just move the use to an adjacent area—creating enforcement problems and perhaps chewing up more terrain." The Chief of the Branch of Land for the Bonneville Power Administration (BPA) (Kornelis, 1979, pp. 27, 28) in writing about ORVs quotes from an Oregon newspaper article and observes that the accompanying pictures "do not, and could not, show adequately the deplorable condition of ruts, scarred hillsides, mudholes, debris, hard-packed soil, and total disregard for property owned by others that are also evident." He goes on to report that the:

> Signs on BPA towers are nearly indiscernable because of accurate—or inaccurate—target practice. The area looks as though war games had just been held. . . . Locked gates are crashed down or pulled up by the practical use of the winch attached to the bumper of the vehicle . . . "No trespassing" signs are quickly removed and not to be found on the premises.
>
> Although ORV users are not to be blamed exclusively, transmission line insulators are also used for target practice, challenging the reliability of the electric transmission grid upon which the whole Northwest depends.
>
> The cost of maintaining access roads, repairing and replacing gates, etc., is greatly increased. Last year we spent $260,000 replacing insulators, most of which had been shattered by rifle fire.

Foreman (1979, pp. 15, 16) quotes from a trip leader's letter to the supervisor of the Gila National Forest—a regulated public recreation facility which was being managed under the multiple-use concept:

> As Memorial Day weekend approached, I noticed that the cattle down in the canyon were herded out. Then I began to see why: four-wheel drives, ORVs of all kinds started coming down the canyon. It turned a beautiful river canyon into a noisy motorized playground . . . . Some of the people had guns and were shooting at anything that moved . . . some people had big rifles . . . . We camped along the river at night and people would come by in their vehicles, shining their spotlights on the canyon walls. There were a group of bighorn sheep in the immediate area. They began to fire shots . . . . We saw a camp of ORVers drinking beer and throwing the cans into the river, then shooting them as they floated by.

There are also shortcomings in regulations adopted by public land managers. Rosenberg (1976, p. 190) concludes after examining the largest federal regulators that "Clearly the regulations established by the four agencies fall far short of the level of environmental protection contemplated in Executive Order 11644 . . . ." Rosenberg notes that while the majority of states now have some form of ORV legislation, the statutes vary in comprehensiveness and in the types of vehicles regulated. As is true with the federal agencies' programs, a complete detailed state program for controlling ORV use does not yet exist (p. 191). For example, most states have established specific maximum noise-emission levels. Although all states strive for a reasonably low noise level, the levels vary widely from state to state. This variation makes it difficult for the individual or manufacturer to comply with the regulations unless the individual is willing to limit his travels to within one state, the manufacturer is willing to limit his sales to within one state, or the manufacturer is willing to construct all his vehicles so as to comply with the standard of the most stringent state (p. 193).

But even ORV use under the most stringent regulations, carefully and meticulously enforced, causes irreversible impacts on the nation's resources. For example, the U.S. Bureau of Land Management (1977) prepared an environmental assessment for an interim program in a critical area—No. 37, Cadiz Valley/ Danby Lake. The mitigation and regulatory measures included numerous prohibitions, constant patrols, avoidance of sensitive land, signs, education, limitation of participants, the possibility of immediate cancellation or postponement of an event, and the sponsor policing his own ranks. The U.S. Bureau of Land Management (1977, pp. 81, 82) nonetheless recognized, and clearly stated, that the proposed ORV use under these regulations would result in permanent loss of soil; destruction of unique vegetation of great age; consumption of 39,000 gallons (150,000 liters) of fuel above what would have been needed if an alternate site had been used; severe disturbance of the habitat requiring decades or centuries for rejuvenation; great reductions in the numbers of mammals, reptiles, and birds; and destabilization of the ecosystem causing further irreversible impacts to wildlife not yet fully understood.

Some public land managers have suggested self-policing, but under this system illegal use takes place according to Bury and Luckenbach (Chapter 10). The California Department of Parks and Recreation (1975, p. 15) reports that many ORV users will probably resist regulatory effort even though they may be aware of the problems; their desire for noise and speed will remain just as strong as ever; and strict geographic limitations on ORV use will also be strongly opposed by most users because the ORVs give them freedom and allow them to explore large remote areas unhampered.

Even in success stories, problems occur. For example, in the Turkey Bay ORV area, McEwen (1978, p. 13) points out that although cyclists are asked to follow the practices recommended by the American Motorcyclist Association, no detailed safety rules are stated. It was felt that such rules would be resented by the cyclists because they would unduly restrict them from riding as they please. He adds that these cyclists would probably ignore the rules; and, without frequent patrols, it would be impossible to enforce them.

Who Cares?

It is not just the environmentalists who care. The silent majority care too. A Field Research Corporation (1975) survey prepared for the BLM showed that the great majority of visitors and nonvisitors, and of northern and southern Californians, are united in wanting more protection of desert wildlife, ecology, and historic resources, and less development of all kinds. Of those who responded, 45.5% identified more places for use of ORVs as the least important use of the California Desert. The most popular recreational activities were sightseeing and camping, followed by picnicking, fishing, photography, and hiking. Motorcycle riding ranked thirteenth in preference. Jeeping, dune buggying, and motorcycle racing ranked close to the bottom of the list.

The results of a poll showed that 81% of the people who responded wanted more protection of wildlife and the ecology; 73% wanted more protection of scenery and the natural character; 67% wanted more protection of historic areas. In its analysis of the results of the poll, the Gallup Organization, Inc. (1978, p. 5) noted:

> The prevalent attitude among those interviewed is support for the type of land use that would preserve the natural environment. This sentiment is held by the majority of people regardless of their sex and socioeconomic background and regardless of the region of the country in which they live.

Another survey, by the Stanford Research Institute International (1978) for the BLM, showed strong support for the protection of desert wildlife and ecology, for control over use of the desert, and for eliminating open areas for ORVs (Table 21-2). Among preferred activities were sightseeing, picnicking, exploring, camping, hiking, and photography, while ORV use ranked much lower; competitive ORV use received 3% of the vote by desert residents, and only 1% by statewide residents (Table 21-3).

One hundred and forty-five professional biologists from throughout California petitioned the BLM in 1975 to protect the desert from further ORV damage. They warned that if present rates of destruction continued, "opportunities for the study of native flora and fauna and natural interrelationships will be reduced," and "the future of arid lands teaching and research will be compromised" (Stebbins, 1975).

The Bottom Line!

The three primary aspects of ORV use examined in this chapter are:

1. Pleasure for ORV users
2. Conflict with other users
3. Destruction of resources

In an economic sense, the first aspect can be considered as a benefit to the ORV user, the second as a cost to other users, and the third as a cost to the public at large. Previous sections of this chapter have explained that the benefits that accrue to ORV users have corresponding costs borne by others.

ORVs obviously have done much damage to every kind of ecosystem found in arid areas, not because the drivers are irresponsible (although some are), but because their machines are inherently destructive. We have seen that there are almost always adverse effects on the ecology whenever ORVs leave an existing trail, that the ecosystems do not recover naturally, that rehabilitation is practically impossible, and that reclamation requires large capital outlays. We have also seen that policing and attempts to reduce the damage are not very successful in preventing conflicts, and that there is a great deal of interest by other users and the public to protect the arid areas. Thus, this chapter emphasizes that ORV activities are an exclusive type of land use and conflict with virtually all other legitimate uses. Sheridan (1979, p. 56) concludes that:

> there are, in reality, very few natural areas suitable for cross-country motorized recreation—that is, areas where the machines will either not cause "considerable adverse effects on the soil, vegetation, wildlife," or will not impair the recreational experience of others.

We have seen that ORV activities even when regulated have negative impacts on various other users and on the nation's resources. State and federal public lands are held in trust for citizens in general and are supposed to be managed under "multiple-use" and "sustained-yield" concepts. Public-land managers are supposed to manage the lands for all Americans—not just those who happen to live nearby, but for everyone, even those who have never seen nor will ever set foot on the land. Rosenberg (1976, pp. 201, 202) notes that:

> the costs of operating ORVs fall upon other recreationers and the public in general, not upon those who are causing them. Since the costs of ORV operation are not "internalized," *i.e.*, borne by ORV users, the public is in effect providing a subsidy to those creating the social costs

. . . . Reduction of noise, air pollution emissions, and conflicts with other users of the same land are only reductions of ORV costs—any costs remaining are still borne by the innocents.

In a simple economic sense, every human activity has some benefits and some costs. When the costs of such activities are voluntarily borne by those receiving the benefits, whether they be individuals, families, communities, states, or nations, there is usually little conflict; but when the costs are shifted to others who are receiving none of the benefits, the result is injustice and conflicts, causing discontent, lawsuits, disobedience, riots, and sometimes war. Almost all the ORV costs are borne by people other than the ORV users. The ORV user currently pays none of the costs resulting from conflicts with other recreational users, and none of the costs resulting from destruction of resources. All these costs are borne by innocent citizens. This situation suggests three questions:

1. Should other recreation users bear the cost of the benefits derived by ORV users?
2. Should other citizens bear the cost of the destruction of the nation's resources?
3. Is it just—politically, ethically, or morally—for others to bear the costs of a use whose benefit accrues solely to the ORV user?

The answer in a plutocracy or oligarchy could be "yes"; in a mobocracy, sometimes "yes"; but in a healthy and mature democracy, the answer is obviously "no." Surely no one, neither other users of the land nor distant citizens, should be asked to bear any costs that benefit only one kind of user. Of course, examples abound in the United States where benefits, such as subsidies, grants, entitlements, tax exemptions, education, defence, and quasipublic and private corporate loan guarantees accrue to one person or one segment of society, while the costs are borne by others. Public policy is often given as the reason for these inequities, and the costs to the public are justified on the grounds of benefit to the general economy, national security, domestic tranquility, and similar socioeconomic goals. However, most honest and mature Americans would be hard pressed to justify ORV use of public lands when the costs and bearers of the costs are so readily apparent and where no public benefit is apparent.

Some public-land managers or their consultants raise the question of who should be responsible for repairing the damaged resources and bearing the costs of administering the regulations. A U.S. Forest Service recreation planner (Dymkoski, 1979) after field checking an Enduro event site raised some questions:

Will we assume the responsibility for destruction of critical habitat (if it is critical) by allowing the enduro to become an annual and traditional event?

Should we be in the business of providing trails with a "challenge" and "thrills," and if we don't provide them, are we prepared to cope with bikers that find their own places for challenge?

Are we prepared to react to the application for the annual event with 75–90 man-days of our time, and do we recover our costs?

A resource officer for the Greenhorn Ranger District, Sequoia National Forest (Ostby, 1979), in his memorandum to the district ranger, estimated the administrative costs of an Enduro event at $3450 and concluded: "I strongly believe proponents of special privileged uses should be required to reimburse the government for administration of the event activities." Keith Axelson (1979) concludes his report on the ORV effects on the Sequoia National Forest managed by the U.S. Forest Service (USFS) as follows:

> Should the USFS and the public be responsible for reparation of National Forest land for damage produced by the off-road vehicle? Why isn't the promoter of the enduro considered responsible for the cost of reconditioning the entire course? When will the costs of the event be made public? . . . Consequently, the field inspection of July 10 brings me to the conclusion that a compromise of forest values to accommodate off-road vehicle activity is not in the best interests of the public or the USFS.

To paraphrase a Republican congressman from Illinois' 16th District John B. Anderson's (1980) description of conservatives:

> Real conservatives believe that, in order to work correctly, the free-market system must allow all of the costs of pleasure to be included in the price to the user. Such costs must therefore incorporate the price of exclusive use and resource destruction established either through sound regulation or, perhaps better yet, through user taxes. The marketplace can then reward the least abusive user. Pseudo-conservatives believe in eliminating sound regulation and allowing the costs of exclusive use and resource destruction to be passed on to the public in the form of "hidden taxes," and damage to people's health, private property, and public resources.

The answer for both the conservationist and the "real conservative" is that ORV users should bear their own costs much as do exclusive users of public lands or rights-of-way, such as ticket-buying alpine skiers on leased national forest lands or gas tax-paying drivers on the interstate highway system. The costs of right-of-way acquisition, leasing, construction, repair, maintenance, and safety are paid through users' fees. Most of the costs of separating the skiers or drivers from all other users and of soil and water conservation practices are also paid through users' fees.

The premise that local, state, or federal governments are obligated to provide public lands and the services of public employees for a use that is consumptive of resources and that conflicts with virtually every other use cannot be defended and sets a poor precedent. Based on such a premise, any time in the future that a group of people develop an interest in a particular indoor or outdoor recreational pastime, the government would be obliged to provide public land on which to do it. Sheridan (1979, p. 38) reveals the absurdity of such an idea as a basis for public policy:

> If, for example, the power chain saw becomes a recreational tool, must the . . . government provide RCSers (recreational chain sawers) with public trees and shrubs to cut down?

References

Aleshire, P. 1979. High-stakes conflict over the California desert: Dune buggies versus flowering cactus. Calif. J. 10(4):143–145.

American Motorcyclist Association. 1982. Amateur and Semi-Professional Competition Rule Book. Westerville, Ohio, 60 pp.

Anderson, J. B. 1980. Unmasking fake conservatives. This World, December 21, p. 31.

Axelson, K. A. 1979. Comments on the July 10 Field Review of the United Enduro Association's Event held June 24, 1979. Keith Axelson & Associates, Los Angeles, California, July 25, 1979, letter to Don Ostby, 4 pp.

Badaracco, R. J. 1978. Recreational Planner, California Desert Plan Staff, U.S. Bureau of Land Management, interview with David Sheridan, U.S. Council on Environmental Quality, January 11, 1978.

Badaracco, R. J. 1979. Recreation. Cry California, Annual Review Issue, Summer 1979, 14(3):70–76.

Box, T. W. 1974. Rehabilitation Potential of Western Coal Lands. Study committee on the potential for rehabilitating lands surface mined for coal in the Western United States, Ballinger Publishing Company, Cambridge, Massachusetts, 198 pp.

Briggs, P. C. 1979. The dirtbike as a form of outdoor recreation. In: Planning for Trailbike Recreation, U.S. Heritage Conservation and Recreation Service, Washington, D.C., pp. 32–36.

Briggs, P. C., and A. H. Tellier. 1977. The desert alternative. Cycle Guide, January 1977, pp. 70–77.

Bury, R. L., R. A. Luckenbach, and S. D. Busack. 1977. Effects of off-road vehicles on vertebrates in the California desert. U.S. Fish and Wildlife Service, Wildlife Research and Rept., Washington, D.C., pp. 2–19.

California Department of Parks and Recreation. 1974. California Outdoor Recreation Resources Plan. Sacramento, California, 188 pp.

California Department of Parks and Recreation. 1975. The Off-Road Vehicle; A Study Report. Sacramento, California, 62 pp.

California Department of Parks and Recreation. 1978. Summary, California Recreational Trails Plan. Sacramento, California, 44 pp.

Campbell, C. E. 1972. Some environmental effects of rural subdividing in an arid area. A case study in Arizona. J. Geogr, Vol. 71, No. 3, March 1972, pp. 147–154.

Cather, W. 1928. Death Comes for the Archbishop. Knopf, New York, 303 pp.

Davis, E. L., and S. Winslow. 1966. Giant ground figures of the prehistoric deserts. Proc. Am. Phil. Soc. 109:8–21.

Dymkoski, M. S. 1979. Enduro Event. U.S. Forest Service, Sequoia National

Forest, Porterville, California, July 17, 1979, memorandum to Greenhorn District Ranger, 2 pp.

Field Research Corporation. 1975. Summary of the Preliminary Desert Market Analysis of the California Desert. Prepared for the U.S. Bureau of Land Management, San Francisco, California, 12 pp.

Foreman, D. 1979. ORVs Threaten a Wild Canyon. Report from the Southwest. Living Wilderness, September 9, 1979, pp. 14–18.

Gallup Organization, Inc. 1978. National Opinions Concerning the California Desert Conservation Area. Prepared for the U.S. Bureau of Land Management, Princeton, New Jersey, January 1978, 30 pp.

Geological Society of America. 1977. Impacts and Management of Off-road Vehicles. Report of the Committee on Environment and Public Policy, Boulder, Colorado, 8 pp.

Godfrey, P. J., S. P. Leatherman, and P. A. Buckley. 1978. Impact of off-road vehicles on coastal ecosystems. In: Coastal Zone '78, Vol. II, American Society of Engineers, New York, pp. 581–600.

Hunt, C. B., and D. R. Mabey. 1966. Stratigraphy and structure. Death Valley, California. U.S. Geological Survey Professional Paper 494-A, pp. A1–A162.

Indiana Department of Natural Resources. 1972. Off the Road Vehicle Study. Indianapolis, Indiana, 138 pp.

Kemsley, W. 1980. ORV user conflicts. In: R. N. L. Andrews and P. F. Nowak (Eds.), Off-Road Vehicle Use: A Management Challenge. Cosponsored by the U.S. Department of Agriculture and University of Michigan, Washington, D.C., pp. 234–238.

Knott, J. M. 1980. Reconnaissance Assessment of Erosion and Sedimentation in the Canada de los Alamos Basin, Los Angeles and Ventura Counties, California. U.S. Geological Survey Water-Supply Paper 2061, prepared in cooperation with California Department of Water Resources, 26 pp.

Kornelis, T. 1979. BPA and ORV. In: Planning for Trailbike Recreation. U.S. Heritage Conservation and Recreation Service, Washington, D.C., pp. 26–29.

Krutch, J. W. 1969. The Best Nature Writing of Joseph Wood Krutch. William Morrow and Company, New York, 196 pp.

Leopold, A. 1966. A Sand County Almanac. Oxford University Press, New York, 269 pp.

Luckenbach, R. A. 1975. What the ORVs are doing to the desert. Fremontia 2(4):3–11.

McEwen, D. N. 1978. Turkey Bay Off-Road Vehicle Area at Land Between the Lakes. An Example of New Opportunities for Managers and Riders. Research Report No. 1, Department of Recreation, Southern Illinois University, Carbondale, Illinois, 28 pp.

McKenzie, G. D., and J. R. J. Studlick. 1980. A Survey of Off-Highway Motorcyclists and Their Perceived Environmental Impact in Ohio—A Summary. In: The Recreational Trailbike Planner. Motorcycle Industry Council, Inc., Newport Beach, California, Vol. 1, No. 10.

Michigan State University Department of Park and Recreation Resources. 1971. Proceedings of the 1971 Snowmobile and Off the Road Vehicle Research Symposium. Technical Report 8, East Lansing, Michigan, 110 pp.

Motorcycle Industry Council, Inc. 1980a. The Recreational Trailbike Planner, Newport Beach, California, Vol. 1, No. 10.

Motorcycle Industry Council, Inc., 1980b. Motorcycle types: Which is which? In: The Recreational Trailbike Planner, Newport Beach, California, Vol. 1, No. 11.

Motorcycle Industry Council, Inc., 1980c. The Recreational Trailbike Planner, Newport Beach, California, Vol. 1, No. 7.

Nakata, J. K., H. G. Wilshire, and G. G. Barnes. 1976. Origin of Mojave Desert Dust Plumes Photographed from Space. Geology 4(11):644–648.

Nash, A. E. K. 1976. Off-Road Riding on Forest Lands as a Public Policy Problem. Report prepared for the U.S. Forest Service, Washington, D.C., 162 pp.

Nash, A. E. K. 1979. Understanding and Planning for ORV Recreation: The 1978–1979 Washington Offroad Recreation Survey. Prepared for the State of Washington Interagency Committee for Outdoor Recreation, Tumwater, Washington, 159 pp.

Ostby, D. 1979. Enduro Motorcycle Event. U.S. Forest Service, Greenhorn Ranger Sequoia National Forest, California, September 10, 1979, memorandum to Greenhorn District Ranger, 3 pp.

Peninsula Times Tribune. 1980. Dirt Cyclists Get a Racing Track—Neighbors Angry. August 20, 1980.

Péwé, T. L. (Ed.). 1981. Desert Dust: Origin, Characteristics, and Effects on Man. Geological Society of America Special Paper 186, Boulder, Colorado, 303 pp.

Rasor, R. 1977. Five State Approaches to Trailbike Recreation Facilities and Their Management. American Motorcyclist Association, Westerville, Ohio, 64 pp.

Reinking, R. F., L. A. Mathews, and P. St.-Amand. 1976. Dust storms due to the dessication of Owens Lake. In: Intl. Conf. Environmental Sensing and Assessment, September 14–19, 1975. Institute of Electrical and Electronics Engineers, Publishers Las Vegas, Nevada, Vol. 2, Paper No. 37-4, 9 pp.

Rosenberg, G. A. 1976. Regulation of off-road vehicles. Environ. Affairs. 5(1): 175–206.

Salt Lake Tribune. 1980. Ogden Homeowners File Flood Charges. March 23, 1980.

Scott, R., N. Ream, and D. Trammell. 1978. A Resource Assessment and Management Analysis of the Ballinger-Deer Park Canyon ORV Open-Use Area. U.S. Forest Service, Mt. Pinos Ranger District, Los Padres National Forest, California, 62 pp.

Shay, R. 1979. Management problems in off-road-vehicle recreation. In: Recreational Impact on Wildlands Conference Proceedings. U.S. Forest Service, pp. 314–317.

Sheridan, D. 1979. Off-Road Vehicles on Public Land. Council on Environmental Quality. U.S. Government Printing Office, Washington, D.C., 84 pp.

Snyder, C. T., D. G. Frickel, R. F. Hadley, and R. F. Miller. 1976. Effects of Off-Road Vehicle Use on the Hydrology and Landscape of Arid Environments in Central and Southern California. U.S. Geological Survey Water-Resources Investigations 76-99, prepared in cooperation with U.S. Bureau of Land Management, 45 pp.

Stanford Research Institute International. 1978. Survey of residents of the California Desert. Final report prepared for U.S. Bureau of Land Management, Menlo Park, California, 114 pp.

Stebbins, R. C. 1974, Off-road vehicles and the fragile desert. Am. Biol. Teacher 36(4 & 5):203–208; 294–304.

Stebbins, R. C. 1975. Scientists' Petition Requesting Reduction in Off-Road Vehicle Recreation on National Resource Lands in the California Desert. Submitted to the U.S. Bureau of Land Management and other agencies and persons concerned with the control and regulation of off-road vehicle recreation, October 31, 1975.

Stebbins, R. C. 1977. Interview with David Sheridan, U.S. Council on Environmental Quality, Washington, D.C., November 17–18.

Stebbins, R. C., and N. W. Cohen. 1976. Off-road menace. Sierra Club Bulletin, July-August 1976, 38 pp.

Stull, R., S. Shipley, E. Hovanitz, S. Thompson, and K. Hovanitz. 1979. Effects of off-road vehicles in Ballinger Canyon, California. Geology 7(1):19–21.

Suchovsky, W. 1980. A private landowner's viewpoint. In: R. N. L. Andrews and P. F. Nowak (Eds.), Off-Road Vehicle Use: A Management Challenge. U.S. Department of Agriculture and University of Michigan, Washington, D.C., 348 pp.

U.S. Bureau of Land Management. 1974. Final Environmental Impact Statement, proposed Barstow-Las Vegas Motorcycle Race. California State Office, Sacramento, California, October 22, 1974, 390 pp.

U.S. Bureau of Land Management. 1975. Evaluation Report, 1974 Barstow-Las Vegas Motorcycle Race. Sacramento, California, 108 pp.

U.S. Bureau of Land Management. 1976. Environmental Analysis Record for Competitive Off-Road Vehicle Events Designated Vehicle Use Area 30—Upper Johnston Valley. District Office, High Desert Resource Area, Riverside, California, 50 pp.

U.S. Bureau of Land Management. 1977. Environmental Assessment Record for Interim Critical Management Program Area No. 37, Cadiz Valley/Danby Lake. Riverside District Office, Riverside, California, 236 pp.

U.S. Bureau of Land Management. 1980. The California Desert Conservation Area. Final Environmental Impact Statement and Proposed Plan. California State Office, Sacramento, California, September 1980, 273 pp., 22 maps.

U.S. Bureau of Outdoor Recreation. 1976. Draft Environmental Impact Statement on the Departmental Implementation of Executive Order 11644 Pertaining to Use of Off-Road Vehicles on the Public Lands. U.S. Department of the Interior, Washington, D.C., 119 pp.

U.S. Congress. 1970. National Environmental Policy Act of 1969, as Amended. Public Law 91-190, 83 Stat. 852, 42 USC 4321 et seq.

U.S. Congress. 1976. Federal Land Policy and Management Act of 1976, as Amended. 94 Public Law 579, 90 Stat. 2747, 43 U.S. Code 1701 et seq.

U.S. Council on Environmental Quality. 1971. Third Annual Report, pp. 139; 1974, Fifth Annual Report, pp. 207–210; 1975, Sixth Annual Report, pp. 243–245; 1976, Seventh Annual Report, pp. 93–94; 1977, Eighth Annual Report, pp. 81-83; 1978, Ninth Annual Report, pp. 303–305; 1979, Tenth Annual Report, pp. 421–422; 1980, Eleventh Annual Report, pp. 48, 357. U.S. Government Printing Office, Washington, D.C.

U.S. Soil Conservation Service. 1979. National Soils Handbook Notice 42, NSH PART II, Guide for Rating Soil Limitations for Motorcycle Vehicle Trails, Section 403.6(b). April 19, 1979, Washington, D.C.

Villalobos, M. L. 1975. Dustfall study of the 1974 motorcycle race, Barstow to Las Vegas. San Bernardino County, California Air Pollution Control District, 13 pp.

Webb, R. H., and H. G. Wilshire. 1978. A Bibliography on the Effects of Off-Road Vehicles on the Environment. U.S. Geological Survey Open-File Report 78-149, 15 pp.

Wilshire, H. G. 1977. Study Results of 9 Sites Used by Off-Road Vehicles That Illustrate Land Modifications. U.S. Geological Survey Open-File Report 77-601, 22 pp.

Wilshire, H. G. 1980. Overview of ORV Impacts on the Environment. Speech presented at a conference on recreational use of ORVs cosponsored by the U.S. Department of Agriculture and University of Michigan, Menlo Park, California.

Wilshire, H. G., and J. K. Nakata. 1976. Off-road vehicle effects on California's Mojave desert. Calif. Geol. 29(6):123–132.

Wilshire, H. G., and J. K. Nakata. 1977. Erosion off the road. Geotimes 22(7/8): 27.

Wilshire, H. G., S. Shipley, and J. K. Nakata. 1978a. Impacts of off-road vehicles on vegetation. In: Transactions of the 43rd North American Wildlife and Natural Resources Conference. Wildlife Management Institute, Washington, D.C., pp. 131–139.

Wilshire, H. G., J. K. Nakata, S. Shipley, and K. Prestegaard. 1978b. Impacts of vehicles on natural terrain at seven sites in the San Francisco Bay area. Environ. Geol. 2:295–319.

Zimmerman, A. W. 1978. New Mexico State Director, U.S. Bureau of Land Management. Letter to David Sheridan, February 24, 1978.

22
Management Practices[1]

William J. Kockelman

Introduction

The management practices discussed here are designed to meet the needs of ORV users, to protect the nation's resources, and to minimize the conflicts with various other recreational users. The practices are based upon discussions and conclusions in Chapter 21, Management Concepts.

An understanding of the goals of management practices requires a familiarity with the concepts "multiple use" and "sustained yield," and with the scientific findings in Chapter 21. A consideration of the goals of management practices for ORVs must begin by recognizing that the concepts "multiple use" and "sustained yield" are inappropriate for ORV activity. That is, any plan to accommodate ORV use must be recognized as one that permits an exclusive and consumptive use, which is disruptive to other recreation, and which destroys resources in or near its path.

Although the management practices discussed here are designed for arid areas, some examples are taken from humid areas. The reader should realize that the practices for humid areas are usually more successful because natural recovery rates are comparatively rapid; higher and denser vegetation provides screening; and a relatively large number of patrol persons is available.

Many of the practices described here were briefly discussed in a Geological Society of America (GSA) (1977) committee report. The practices are based on

---

[1]The views and conclusions contained in this chapter are based on the author's studies or experiences and do not necessarily represent the official viewpoint or policy of any U.S. government agency.

accepted management principles and are believed to be applicable to the recreational programs of federal, state, and local agencies of government in the United States, as well as to similar government levels elsewhere. The practices described include: meeting user needs; making land-use and resource inventories; selecting sites; designating or zoning ORV areas; designing and constructing facilities; managing facilities and events; and monitoring, closing, and reclaiming sacrifice areas. The management practices selected are based upon the following five interdependent conditions:

1. Citizens and their government representatives are fully cognizant of the problems with unrestricted ORV use (Chapter 21).
2. Environmentalists will accept some ORV use as legitimate if conflicts with all other users are avoided, or greatly minimized, and if resources are destroyed only within carefully selected and carefully managed sacrifice areas (Chapter 22).
3. Congress and state legislatures are willing to provide the necessary revenue and regulatory authority (Chapter 23).
4. Public land managers have the staff and funding to inventory, select, design, construct, and patrol ORV facilities (Chapter 22).
5. Most ORV users are law-abiding citizens willing to assume the true costs of their recreation (Chapter 21).

The U.S. Presidential Executive Orders concerning federal management of ORVs (Chapter 1, Fig. 1-3) serve as a start toward realizing many of the above conditions—awareness of the problem, implicit recognition of legitimate ORV use, designating ORV areas, promoting safety, protecting resources, minimizing conflicts, and requiring immediate closing of an ORV facility if the manager determines that continued use will adversely affect resources.

Meeting User Needs

Types of Riders

Three types of ORV users—vocational, recreational, and "bad apples"—were described in Chapter 21. The needs of those using ORVs for their work can usually be accommodated by existing roads, trails, and rights-of-way, and careful off-road use. The needs of the recreational ORV user—casual and endurance uses—are addressed here. In the context of the management concepts defined in Chapter 21, the desire of certain ORV users to leave paved cycleways or sacrifice areas and wander without restriction across the country—breaking new ground—cannot be met rationally. In the words of Sheridan (1979, p. 56):

> There are, in reality, very few natural areas suitable for cross-country motorized recreation—that is, areas where the machines will either not cause "considerable adverse effects on the soil, vegetation, wildlife" or will not impair the recreational experience of others.

No attempt is made here to accommodate the unrestricted user, for the reason that such use must be considered illegitimate, and the user (albeit sadly) must be considered a "bad apple." Meeting the desires of "bad apples" is outside the scope of this book.

The casual rider usually uses the machine as a means to an end and does not ordinarily stress himself or the machine. He or she is aware of his surroundings—vista, stream, landscape—and can remain on a paved cycleway. He or she likes long routes, although younger or inexperienced users are satisfied with lesser distances.

The endurance rider usually uses the machine as an end in itself. He or she desires a challenge that stresses himself and his or her machine, either alone or by participating in an organized event—enduros, hillclimbs, motorcrosses, and scrambles—as defined by the American Motorcyclist Association (1982) in their *Amateur and Semi-Professional Competition Rule Book.* Participants in events are usually oblivious of their natural surroundings during the event, and according to the Motorcycle Industry Council, Inc. (1973, p. 4) generally "best enjoy dirt surfaces, deep sand, deep gravel or pebbles (such as dry streambeds), leaf cover, and shallow mud."

Terrains Best Suited to ORV Use

Most ORV users like hilly and rolling terrain—subdued and rolling for beginners, steep and rough for endurance riders—which provides a diverse spectrum of features to challenge their skill. Emetaz (1980, p. 8) reports that:

> Forest trail bikers seek scenery but also have a keen interest of the terrain under wheel. A difficult and demanding trail that requires skill and a machine specifically designed for the terrain are an integral part of the experience—at least for most participants. As in other trail activities, scenery often has greater appeal when it can only be reached by overcoming some degree of difficulty.

Moreover, terrain needs vary with the type of rider, whether casual or endurance. For example, the Motorcycle Industry Council, Inc. (1973, p. 4) observes that the ORV operation:

> requires a variety of topography—flat areas, gentle hills, slopes, meandering trails, gullies, etc.—ranging from the easy to the difficult. . . . the motorcross area, if possible, should be situated in a depressed section of the site—cutting down noise transmission and also providing ready-made observation points around its periphery for spectators.

Size, Accessibility, and Type of Facility

ORV users desire large areas for maximum variety, but the type of ORV use, supporting facilities, neighboring land uses, and the availability of land determines the size. The Motorcycle Industry Council, Inc. (1973, p. 4) reports that:

a small community cycle park, restricted to small bikes (100 cc and less), could be developed on 35 acres; whereas, a large-scale park should contain from 300 to 1,500 or 2,000 acres if a large-scale operation is planned for the future.

The California Department of Parks and Recreation (1975, p. 57) advises that relatively small ORV areas are appropriate and desirable in urban and suburban areas, and that they could be from 10 to 100 acres (4 to 40 ha). On the other hand, regional ORV areas should be large enough to accommodate various-sized motorcycles and suitable acreage would be between 100 and 3,000 acres (40 to 1200 ha) (California Department of Parks and Recreation, 1975, p. 58).

The majority of ORV users are from urban areas (Motorcycle Industry Council, Inc., 1980a, pp. 2, 3) and therefore desire facilities in or near metropolitan areas. Proximity is particularly important for those who desire to ride after work or after school. In all cases, a minimum two-lane paved public highway is required for access to a facility. The need for on-site support facilities—first-aid stations, fueling stations, overnight accommodations, concessions, and lavatories—depends upon the size, neighboring land uses, and type of user.

Two types of facilities can meet the needs of the casual ORV users. These can be labeled cycle parks and cycleway systems. However, different types of facilities are required to meet the needs of the endurance ORV users. These can be labeled sacrifice areas and mechanical compounds. The following discussions generally pertain to facilities for two-wheel ORVs. Similar but separate facilities can be designed for four-wheel ORVs.

Cycle Parks. Cycle parks can be attractive, pleasant, and safe places for ORV users and their friends and relatives, and they can be located in or close to urban areas. The parks should consist of *paved* cycleways interspersed with vegetation offering some shade, and picnic areas similar to those in modern public parks. Such facilities would generally be smaller than those located on state and federal lands, serving only the needs of a locality and or the immediate region. Most would be operated by an appropriate city or county agency or by private enterprise if a potential for profit exists.

The smaller cycle parks from 10 to 100 acres (4 to 40 ha) would be designed to accommodate minibikes, small motorcycles, go-carts, and vehicles that are owned by persons too young to have access to more distant facilities. Ideally, such areas should be within a few minutes' drive of the users' homes. Support facilities would include only parking, water, lavatories, and concessions.

The larger cycle parks from 100 to 500 acres (40 to 200 ha) would be designed for a variety of ORV users with a wide range of age and experience, but would *not* include areas for endurance riders. These parks would be appropriate for individual and family day-use activities. They would ordinarily be located within a 1-hr drive of the user's home, and such parks could be operated by an appropriate county or regional governmental agency or by private enterprise. Support facilities would include parking spaces for autos, trucks, and trailers; sanitation, potable water; and picnic sites, concessions, and family play areas all free of ORVs. Large grassy areas and many trees would improve the environmental quality, particularly in the areas set aside for picnicking and other non-ORV activities.

The cycle parks would be carefully managed for the protection of the user, the facility, and its neighbors. The parks should have limited and fully controlled access and be staffed by qualified people. The staff should be trained in safety and first aid and should have good rapport with the ORV users. The California Parks and Recreation Department (1975, p. 58) suggests that such areas:

> should be maintained in a condition free of hazards and unpleasant or unsightly conditions and should be patrolled regularly. Admission would be granted only to identified individuals with demonstrated minimum ability (or under parental supervision), who had signed an appropriate liability release form. Upon each admission, the machines would be inspected for mufflers, spark arrestors, and apparent safety problems. Admission would be granted only to licensed machines, registered either as ORVs or for regular street use.

Cycleway Systems. A cycleway system is an extensive network from 100 to 300 miles (160 to 480 km) of *paved* trails or *paved* lanes for the exclusive use of ORV users; narrow corridors would provide variety and privacy. The system would usually be located on state or federal lands and would take advantage of existing rights-of-way, but access could be provided to private or public utility rights-of-way where needed for continuity and where consent has been obtained.

The cycleways would not interfere or intermingle with the large cycle parks; they would complement one another. Basically, this system of cycling will be reasonably smooth and safe, having the beauty and ease that meet the needs of the casual ORV user. The design and terrain of cycleways *would not* meet the needs of the endurance rider.

Sacrifice Areas. A sacrifice area would be for the exclusive use of endurance riders; it would be unpaved and not designed to satisfy anyone's esthetic needs. Dirt surfaces, deep sand, deep gravel or pebbles, leaf cover, and shallow mud would be the nature of the ground. Major sacrifice areas would include flat tracks, hillclimbs, warmup trails, jumps, tight corners, stream fords, steep grades, mud holes, sandy areas, scramble tracks, obstacle and motorcross courses, poker runs, enduros, and trail loops.

Sacrifice areas would accommodate all types of events and all types of motorcycles; they should also provide less demanding trails for family members or user warmups. The location of the sacrifice areas would depend upon the availability of the land and its geographic relationship to other land uses. Areas already seriously degraded would be prime candidates. Because sacrifice areas would usually be remote and because a large number of spectators could be involved, a full range of support facilities will be required—large parking areas, first-aid stations, heavy maintenance equipment, fencing, sanitation, concessions, and camping and picnic areas.

A very heavy and concentrated use is expected, and vegetative cover is not practical. Soil erosion and serious environmental degradation is anticipated. Mechanical grooming would be used in an attempt to reduce the movement of soil and rock downhill. Sacrifice areas would be dusty, damaged, and eroding. Public-land managers and adjoining property owners would attempt to keep the adverse effects under control and completely within the facility. Careful site selection, design, construction, and maintenance are required. Large performance bonds, scrupulous monitoring, and legal techniques for immediate closing would be necessary. User fees as well as performance bonds would be used to pay for the maintenance, monitoring, and reclaiming. The inconvenience to the users because of frequent closings and the continuing cost to the operator or manager for maintaining the facilities, will eventually lead to conversion to a mechanical compound, discussed below.

Mechanical Compounds. A mechanical compound is an entirely *paved* or artificially *surfaced* area selected, designed, and constructed to meet all the needs of the endurance rider with no adverse effects on the environment or neighboring lands. It would be similar to a skating-board park, or race-car track—the impact of the vehicle being separated from the ground. The compound would be encircled with a natural or artificial sound barrier. All desires of the endurance rider for dirt, sand, gravel, water crossing, steep climbs, jumps, sharp turns, leaf cover, shallow mud, pot holes, terrain that requires gear changing, rock obstacles, and so forth would be provided and maintained artificially. Costs would be fully met by user fees.

The capital outlay required for construction will be much higher than for the sacrifice area, but the maintenance and reclamation costs will be lower; performance bonds and closing would not be necessary. It could be an attractive and regularly operated facility. Peripheral areas of the compound could be planted with grass, trees, and shrubs, and some of the needs of the users' friends and relatives, and of inexperienced users, could be provided.

Inventorying Land Uses and Resources

In the previous section, four ORV facilities that will meet the needs of recreational ORV users were described. Good land-use management requires a knowledge of existing land uses and existing resources before planning and developing these facilities. Therefore, before potential areas for ORV facilities—cycle parks, cycleway systems, sacrifice areas, and mechanical compounds—are identified, inventories and evaluations of land uses and resources must be made by both the public land manager and the regional or community planner. The inventory will also identify those terrains that are attractive to ORV users, and to recreation land managers and private entrepreneurs. The next step is to select those areas for ORV facilities that will minimize destruction of the resources and conflicts with other users and that will meet user needs.

Executive Order 11644 (Chapter 1, Fig. 1-3) sets forth the conditions to which these areas and trails must conform if they are to be designated for ORV use on federal lands. For example, damage to "soil, watershed, vegetation or other resources of the public lands" and "harassment of wildlife or disruption of wildlife habitats" must be minimized. It is obvious that before areas and trails can be located so as to minimize such damage, an inventory must be made of what and where the resources are. The California State Attorney General (undated written communication, p. 12) in an appeal before the Chief Forester, U.S. Forest Service argued:

> It is simply impossible to minimize damage to soil, watershed, vegetation, wildlife, and other resources unless the resource base is adequately assessed.

Recommendations for Making Inventories

Federal, state, and local units of government should complete, as soon as possible, an inventory of all lands within their jurisdiction and identify all uses and resources requiring protection, preservation, or conservation. The inventory would be made within geographic areas that are related by climate, terrain, soils, geology, and biology. Most local communities have made such inventories of land uses, and some public land managers have inventoried and evaluated resources within their areas of jurisdiction. For example, a U.S. Bureau of Land Management (BLM) study (1980, pp. P 16-94) has divided the resources or land uses into the following elements: critical resources, Native American resources, wildlife, vegetation, wilderness, wild horse and burro, livestock grazing, recreation, motorized vehicle areas, geology, energy, minerals, energy production, and utility corridors. In addition, the U.S. Bureau of Land Management (1980, pp. P 95-102) has identified areas of critical environmental concern and "special" areas.

Resources To Be Identified

In arid areas, the resources to be identified and delineated on maps should include woodlands, brushlands, grasslands, riparian communities, dunes (Brattstrom and Bondello, Chapter 9), ecologically fragile areas, major wildlife habitats, unusual plant and animal species, and populations of isolated species classified as rare or endangered; critical animal breeding and shelter sites; historical, geologic, archaeological, and cultural sites; educational and scientific areas; scenic and esthetic features; existing natural and man-made recreational areas; undisturbed native soils; groundwater recharge areas, their catchment basins and surface-water supplies; woodlands; designated wilderness areas; and grazing lands.

According to the Geological Society of America (1977, p. 6) these resources should be evaluated and ranked by those with recognized professional knowledge of each resource. For example, bird habitats would be evaluated and ranked by bird watchers and ornithologists, grazing lands by ranchers and range conservationists.

Land Uses To Be Inventoried

In arid areas, the land uses to be identified and shown on maps should typically include: ORV uses and all non-ORV uses, such as grazing, utility lines, dry farming, irrigated farming, recreation facilities, military reservations, mining, urban, and suburban areas, transportation facilities, unused rights-of-way, disposal sites, and abandoned lands.

Land uses and areas that would be dangerous and unhealthy for ORV users should be identified. Such areas would include sites for testing, disposal, or storage of radioactive wastes, sewage, toxic materials, weapons, and ammunition; areas having naturally occurring health and safety hazards such as valley fever, quicksand, air- and waterborne asbestos (Chapter 20); and terrain used for military maneuvers.

The time, cost, and staff capabilities required for making resource inventories and evaluations is very high, especially when the great extent of the arid areas is considered. For example, the U.S. Bureau of Land Management (1980, p. 16) indicates that "only about five percent of the California Desert has been inventoried for cultural resources," and concludes "contingent on budget allocation, 2,000 acres or more per resource area will be inventoried each year. Volunteers will be used where feasible."

There is another way. Instead of inventorying all the resources, the land uses could be inventoried and the areas having potential for ORV facilities selected. Problems of resource destruction and use conflict arise primarily because of unrestricted use. The cycle parks, cycleway systems, sacrifice areas, and mechanical compounds labeled and described in this chapter are restricted-use areas. If the inventories required to identify and locate vulnerable resources and conflicting land uses are limited to potential ORV facilities, the inventory and evaluation becomes much more manageable.

Effects Related to Type of Facility

In 1969, the BLM in California convened the Off-Road Vehicle Advisory Council (ORVAC), a group of comprised of ORV organization representatives, environmentalists, ranchers, and businessmen. Despite the members' many differences, this group reached a consensus on a number of issues. Sheridan (1979, pp. 36, 37) reports that:

> ORVAC wrote 24 specific criteria for defining areas where ORV use should *not* be allowed. These include, for example, "areas where soils are classified as highly susceptible to erosion," or "sites with scientific values such as historical, biotic, archaelogical and paleontological where damage would occur," or "known, potential and existing camp and picnic grounds or other appropriate recreation development."

Whatever resources are present and whatever impacts ORV use has on such resources, soil is rarely absent and the ORV impact on it is always degrading. In arid areas, the machine's power drive and direction of tire-tread movement combined with gravity, wind, and rainfall generally result in a rapid displacement of the soil and severe erosion. Use of restricted facilities, such as sacrifice areas or where the tire and earth are separated, as on paved cycleways or in paved mechanical compounds, is the only way to protect soil, water, and the other resources.

All direct resource impacts can then be confined to the restricted facilities—cycle parks, mechanical compounds, and sacrifice areas. By confining ORVs to paved cycleways the impacts are also confined. The impacts of ORVs on the cycleway system, although extensive, are in relatively narrow corridors. The mechanical compound completely supplants all living resources, but unlike the sacrifice area, problems of soil erosion and water pollution can be technically solved. In all cases, wildlife is displaced by paved cycleways, and of course, they are also completely displaced or destroyed in the sacrifice areas. Although contained, the paved cycle parks and mechanical compounds must be considered biological sacrifice areas just as most physical improvements—buildings, highways, or parking lots—replace the natural system of soils, plants, and wildlife.

The conflicts with other non-ORV uses can be effectively avoided by complete segregation of the cycle parks, sacrifice areas, and compounds. Conflict near the cycleway systems can be minimized by carefully selecting the route and by warning other users.

Selecting the Sites

The criteria on which to base site selection must include meeting user needs, protecting resources, and minimizing conflicts with other users. In addition, the specific criteria discussed here also meet the mandates of Executive Order 11644 (Fig. 1-3, Chapter 1):

1. Minimize damage to soil, watershed, vegetation, or other resources of the public lands
2. Minimize harassment of wildlife or significant disruption of wildlife habitats
3. Minimize conflicts between off-road vehicle use and other existing or proposed recreational uses of the same or neighboring public lands and ensure the compatibility of such uses with existing conditions in populated areas, taking into account noise and other factors

Because of the great differences that exist among the various local, state, and federal agencies, it is not possible to draw up specific criteria for the selection of ORV facilities that would be applicable in all cases. Therefore, the following guidelines are general in their discussion of potential sites, user needs, protection of resources, and avoidance of conflict. Guidelines concerning the size, configuration, characteristics, and location of potential sites are helpful, but each specific site will have to be developed to fit the particular environmental and user needs unique to that location and user market.

Full consideration should be given to existing and planned ORV facilities in evaluating and selecting the most appropriate potential sites. Other recreational and general land-use planning agencies of government should be consulted so that coordination between agencies is established.

Sites To Be Considered

The Geological Society of America (1977) suggests that lands already damaged by surface mining or by ORV use probably are the most likely candidates from an environmental point of view for ORV areas. Sheridan (1979, p. 56) notes that old surface-mine sites which have been abandoned and never reclaimed account for over two million acres (800,000 ha) of land in the United States and might make acceptable ORV areas. Florida, for example, opened the 2,600-acre (1040-ha) Buttgenbach motorcycle area in a state forest. The area had been extensively mined for phosphate in the last century, and today the pits are favorite ORV areas. The State of Missouri has acquired old strip coal mines and ORV facilities are being designed for them. The Iowa Department of Transportation con-structed an ORV park around several lakes that had previously been a strip mine area (Motorcycle Industry Council, Inc., 1980a, p. 4).

Nicholes (1980) suggests several other possibilities that have not been tried or fully exploited in many parts of the country. These possible sites include dis-continued airport facilities; active airports with abandoned runways or with property held for future development and not in current use; utility rights-of-way; underused secondary roads; completed landfills; and future highway cor-ridors during the right-of-way acquisition period. The Missouri motorcycle trail guidelines (Rasor, 1977, p. 57) include abandoned roads, abandoned railroad beds and rights-of-way, canal banks, dry canals, and river levees. The Geological Society of America (1977, p. 7) suggests that:

> those areas now designated as natural preserves (Wilderness Areas; Primitive Areas; National Parks, Monuments, and Historic Sites; Natural Areas; Natural Wildlife Refuges; National Recreational Areas and Game Ranges; and the like) and those areas under study for such designation would not be considered for ORV use.

This suggestion would accommodate the Federal Land Management Agency regulations required by Section 3(a)(4) of Executive Order 11644 (Fig. 1-3, Chapter 1).

Meeting User Needs

A combination of flat and gently rolling terrain would best satisfy the casual riders who use the cycle parks and cycleway systems. Steep and rough terrain is needed for endurance riders. Grassy areas and trees are desirable near cycle parks and cycleway systems. In size, the facility should be large enough to accommodate the ORVs and their support facilities—lavatories, first-aid stations, fueling stations, and concessions. Good access by paved highways is necessary, and Wells (1980) points out that use drops off considerably if the facility is more than 125 miles from the users' home base. Medical and ambulance services should be a part of the facility. The Motorcycle Industry Council, Inc. (1973, p. 5) lists the following desirable criteria:

> Reasonable distance from a suitable user/draw area; overnight parks could be 2 or 3 hours away
> Relatively close to sufficient services—gas stations, restaurants, motorcycle dealers
> Availability of telephone, electricity, and sanitary facilities
> Suitable availability of community services—fire department, medical, police
> Ample level space for parking cars and support vehicles.

Dangerous and unhealthy areas should be avoided. Such areas might include sites for testing, disposal, or storage of radioactive wastes, sewage, toxic materials, weapons, and ammunition; areas having naturally occurring health hazards, such as valley fever; and terrain used for military maneuvers (Geological Society of America, 1977, p. 7). Open vertical mine shafts are extremely dangerous and should be filled or permanently sealed. The probability of wild fires occurring on or near the facility should be considered. Fire prevention and protection measures should be coordinated with governmental fire departments.

Protecting Resources

After concluding that ORV use and the protection of biological resources are mutually exclusive, Bury and Luckenbach (Chapter 10) suggest that the two uses be separated from one another through distinct management units. Such separation is possible in cycle parks and mechanical compounds. In the cycleway systems, it can be accomplished by careful route selection, paving of all trails and lanes, strict compliance by ORV users, and stringent enforcement by the facilities' managers.

Since all natural resources in the sacrifice areas will be destroyed or seriously depleted, these irreversible impacts should be contained insofar as possible. Sites with easily eroded soils should be avoided, and the trail and open-use areas should be designed to minimize the need for cuts and fills and subsequent soil movement. Wilshire (Chapter 3) advises that ORV sites should be selected by identifying the areas that have the most stable and resilient soils. Where ORV use is permitted, it should be confined to small drainage basins where the off-site effects of increased runoff, erosion, and sedimentation can be properly monitored and controlled (Chapter 5). The U.S. Bureau of Outdoor Recreation (1976, p. 33) notes that the soil which erodes as a result of ORV use ultimately enters surface waters, where it contributes to sediment load and to the siltation of stream and lake bottoms. ORV use should never be permitted in or near reservoir watershed areas or in groundwater recharge areas. Sites should be avoided where material damage will be caused to the hydrologic balance outside the ORV area. This balance can be simply defined as the equilibrium established between the groundwater and the surface-water system of a drainage basin and between the recharge and discharge to and from that system.

Wilshire and Nakata (1976, p. 132) list some criteria for ORV sites which may minimize damage. They advise that areas be selected having closed-basin drainage with minimal soil-plant variation between catchment and discharge area, and having prevailing wind conditions that minimize airborne removal of material from the site. They point out that:

> perfectly ideal conditions of containment of damage cannot be realistically expected. Expansion of damage, by erosion and deposition, beyond the areas of direct use will occur.

Bury and Luckenbach (Chapter 10) suggest that ORV use be confined to specific, clearly defined areas, and that such "biological sacrifice areas be limited in size." Brattstrom and Bondello (Chapter 9) recommend specific measures to protect the unique habitats and wildlife of arid areas.

Avoiding Conflicts

Three conflicts occur: conflicts between ORV users and non-ORV users, conflicts with neighbors, and conflicts with the traveling public. These conflicts involve safety, noise, trespass, and esthetics. The major conflicts with other recreational users can be resolved by completely separating the casual and endurance riders from all other users. The four facilities described in this chapter—cycle parks, cycleway systems, sacrifice areas, and mechanical compounds—can be and should be designed to accomplish such a separation. The noise of the machines, trespass of the users, and the appearance of the facilities create the remaining conflicts.

Off-road vehicle facilities should never be located near existing residential, park, resource conservation, or recreational areas, or where the land is zoned for these uses. The California Department of Parks and Recreation (1978, p. 84) suggests that industrial, commercial, open-space, and agricultural land-use zones are more compatible with ORV use. In all cases, noise should be so buffered by distance, protective hills, berms, embankments, ridges, or solid noiseproof fences as to completely protect existing and potential neighboring land uses. Existing and potential ORV facilities should be incorporated into community comprehensive plans or state and federal recreation plans so that future land-use proposals will not conflict. The California Department of Parks and Recreation (1975, p. 57) suggests that:

> Small urban ORV areas will generally be best located where there is already substantial commotion and noise, such as near airports, freeways, and in industrial areas. Residential and quiet park areas should be avoided.

All noise should be kept within a facility's boundaries. In some sites, the noise is captured by enbankments or natural ridges. Sites with flat terrain will require larger buffer zones or carefully designed structures to limit the sound.

The site should also have boundaries, walls, or fences that would discourage or restrict trespassing onto adjoining closed areas—private or public. The California Department of Parks and Recreation (1978, p. 84) suggests that to avoid offending the general public, ORV facilities be situated so that they are not readily visible to non-ORV users. However, complete isolation of ORV facilities is difficult to achieve. Sacrifice areas, no matter how badly ravaged the land may be, are still part of a natural system and the effects of misuse continue. Generally, ORV facilities should be located only where their use:

Causes comparatively little damage to resources
Creates no safety or health hazards to non-ORV users
Causes no environmental impacts outside the boundaries of the facility
Creates no conflicts with other existing or proposed uses of neighboring
    lands

After those sites that meet these general criteria are selected and before the design and construction of the ORV facilities are addressed, the designation or zoning of the land by the government agencies having jurisdiction is required.

Designation or Zoning

As early as 1971, a U.S. Department of Interior Task Force Study (1971, p. 68) reporting on off-road recreational vehicle (ORRV) use stated that it believes:

essentially what is necessary to plan adequately for outdoor recreation and ORRV use is a land classification system specifically designed to protect the resources, provide for safe and sane recreation, and allow for as rational and balanced, yet diversified, an outdoor recreation program as possible. Providing a place for the motorized vehicle user on public lands within this framework should be possible without lowering other outdoor recreation standards.

Either open, restricted, or closed designations can be used for ORV facilities on state and federal public lands. Special local land-use zoning districts such as public or commercial recreational districts, together with conditional use regulations, can be applied to cycle parks or mechanical compounds on city, county, or private lands. The unit of government having jurisdiction, usually in cooperation with other governments, would select areas that could be designated or zoned for ORV facilities after considering at least the following:

Value and ranking assigned to each resource
Existing lands used by ORVs
Desires of ORV users
Mission and plans of the governmental unit having jurisdiction
Character and recreational needs of adjoining communities

State and Federal Public Lands

The unit of government having jurisdiction may designate certain public lands as open, restricted, or closed to ORV use. The "open" designation would be appropriate for sacrifice areas or mechanical compounds. The "restricted" designation would be appropriate for cycle systems and cycle parks. All other areas would be designated "closed." For example, the U.S. Bureau of Land Management (1974b, Sec. 6292.3) bases its "restricted" and "closed" designations on criteria such as:

> Ability of the land and its resources to withstand and sustain ORV use impacts
>
> Consideration of the scenic qualities of the land, and its ecological and environmental values
>
> Need for public areas for recreation use and consideration of ORV impacts on other lands, uses, and resources
>
> Potential hazards to public health and safety, other than the normal risks involved in ORV use
>
> Existing or potential quality and quantity of recreational experiences available
>
> Consideration of the need to minimize harassment of wildlife or significant disruption of wildlife habitats

Use of "Open" or "Closed" Designations

There are two ways of designating whether public lands are open or closed: (1) by designating "closed" only those areas whose resources are to be protected, and leaving "open" all other lands; or (2) designating "open" those lands where ORVs are permitted, and designating "closed" for all other lands. The latter is preferred, and authorization for it is included in Section 9(b) of Executive Order 11989 (Chapter 1, Fig. 1-3):

> Each respective agency head is authorized to adopt the policy that portions of the public lands within his jurisdiction shall be closed to use by off-road vehicles except those areas or trails which are suitable and specifically designated as open to such use . . . .

Reames (1980, p. 6) argues that the Executive Order is very clear in directing that areas and trails be designated as either "open" or "closed" to ORV use in order to minimize resource damage and user conflicts, and that the amending Executive Order provides further clarification—ORV use must be restricted to protect the natural resources of the public lands.

Because inventorying and evaluating resources is a time-consuming task, great environmental damage can occur while such studies are being made, unless the land is closed while the inventory is in progress. The practice of closing all lands not designated "open" substantially reduces the time and averts such damage. To emphasize this approach, the Society of American Foresters (1975) adopted the position that:

In order that control be effective, off-road vehicles should be allowed only on forest roads, trails and areas . . . which are explicitly designated for off-road vehicle use. Experience shows this approach to be less costly, and easier to enforce than a restriction in which off-road vehicles are allowed on all forest roads, trails, and areas except where designated to the contrary.

A former acting chairman of the President's Council on Environmental Quality (Busterud, 1976) commenting on a federal agency's position that "blanket closure" was not authorized by Executive Order 11644, was adamant:

We do not agree; the Executive Order permits no such cramped reading of its goals and policies . . . If data available . . . suggests that blanket closure or regulation is necessary . . . then such alternatives are unquestionably available to and should be adopted . . . under the Executive Order.

In the preceding chapters, several scientists make management recommendations that bear on this issue. For example, Hinckley et al. (Chapter 5) suggest that every effort be made to prevent extension of existing ORV use to any as yet unimpacted arid areas. Because of the difficulties, uncertainties, and expenses of attempting to revegetate disturbed arid areas, such disturbances should be as infrequent as possible according to Kay and Graves (Chapter 17). The American Association for the Advancement of Science Committee on Arid Lands (1974, p. 501) observed that there is no time for a prolonged study of the problem and recommended:

Designating a number of large easily accessible areas for unrestricted ORV use

Designating portions of the desert as wilderness or other kinds of areas in which access is permitted to nonmotorized travel only

Prohibiting ORV travel on the remaining desert lands

Establishing buffer strips approximately one mile (1.6 km) wide in the open country along the major highways and permitting no ORV traffic in the buffer strips except in areas designated for recreational use

After designating those areas that are open or restricted, all other lands and waters would be deemed closed. This legal procedure is similar to the enactment of a modern zoning ordinance by which all uses not specified as "principal permitted uses" are prohibited. Restated—the lands and waters requiring study before designation or zoning should be considered closed until inventoried, evaluated, ranked, and discussed at public hearings.

Examples of "Closed" and "Restricted" Areas

Several examples of state and federal "closed" and "restricted" areas exist. The U.S. Fish and Wildlife Service regulations restrict ORV access to most of the national wildlife refuges. The regulations provide that public recreation will be allowed in wildlife refuges only when such recreational use is practicable and consistent with the areas' primary objectives and is not disturbing to wildlife. The National Park Service strictly prohibits motor vehicles outside established public roads or parking areas. In national park recreational areas, ORV use is prohibited except where designated by area superintendents. Rosenberg (1976, p. 187) notes that national park lands are presumed closed unless the agency head determines that ORV use would not adversely affect "the natural, esthetic, and scenic values" of the land. All water resource development projects administered by the U.S. Army Corps' Chief of Engineers are closed to ORV use except those areas and trails specifically designated for use. The U.S. Bureau of Reclamation has closed most of its lands to ORV use according to the U.S. Bureau of Outdoor Recreation (1975, p. 6). The Tennessee Valley Authority (TVA) designated one part of its 170,000-acre (68,000-ha) "Land Between the Lakes" area in western Tennessee and Kentucky for ORV use and put the remainder of the area out of bounds. The U.S. Council on Environmental Quality (1975, p. 245) reports that TVA finds this arrangement easier to enforce than trying to confine ORV use to roads and trails.

The U.S. Department of Defense (1973) decided that all its 26 million acres (10.5 million ha) of land and water would be closed to ORV use except those areas and trails specifically designated for such use. The department's decision was partially based on an assessment that "Practically no area on Department of Defense land would be free from potential danger by ORV use." In accord with the U.S. Secretary of Agriculture's regulations, U.S. Forest Service supervisors have the power to restrict the use of ORVs on national forest lands. For example, an order prohibiting the use of ORVs on all national forest system lands except for designated trails in the Allegheny National Forest in Pennsylvania was issued by Butt (1977a).

Several states have also restricted ORV use. Washington has virtually prohibited all cross-country ORV use on state land; ORVs must stay on designated roads and trails. Sheridan (1979, p. 49) reports that Washington does provide sacrifice areas, such as abandoned gravel pits, for ORV users seeking to "bust loose and drive wide open." Connecticut forbids ORV use on government-owned land without the written permission of the agency under whose control such land falls, either state or municipality. Rosenberg (1976, p. 196) notes that:

> This method of presuming land closed except where able to withstand ORV activity is the best means of ensuring protection of environmental interests (short of prohibiting all ORV use on all lands).

Massachusetts has restricted ORV use to designted trails. In Indiana, ORVs have been banned from all state lands since late 1972. The decision was based on an Indiana Department of Natural Resources (1972) study which gives an economic reason:

> it is very difficult for the private entrepreneur to compete with a public agency which builds its facilities (for ORVs) with tax money and charges only minimal user fees.

Zoning Ordinance

To accommodate ORVs in urban and rural areas under the jurisdiction of municipalities may require amending the zoning ordinance to create a special zoning district, such as a public or commercial recreational district. Usually, the primary function of a zoning ordinance is to implement a community's land-use plan; the secondary function is to protect desirable existing development. Zoning is used to encourage the most appropriate use of the land by confining certain land uses to those areas of the community which are peculiarly suited to and set aside for these uses.

Modern zoning ordinances permit only principal, accessory, and conditional uses in any zoning district; all other uses are prohibited. ORV use should be considered a conditional use in the recreational districts. Conditional uses are defined as uses having such a special nature that it is impractical to include them as the principal permitted use in a district without individual review. Additional requirements are imposed on conditional uses to protect neighbors from any noise, vibration, glare, traffic hazards, unsightliness, or odors which might be involved. The text of a zoning ordinance should specify the procedures for applying for a conditional use permit and for review and public hearing. The review procedure should provide for imposing special requirements upon the conditional use. For ORVs, such requirements might include landscaping, planting screens, type of fencing, control of operations, sound barriers, improved traffic circulation, increased yards, and larger parking areas. The City of Pomona, California, issued a cycle-park permit that was conditioned upon improving an access road, treating its surface for dust, fencing with barbed wire, providing 200 dustproof parking spaces, and obtaining the fire department's approval (Motorcycle Industry Council, Inc., 1973, p. 22).

Permits for conditional uses are not directly issued by the local zoning or building inspector. The local planning agency is usually empowered to grant or deny the application after a review and hearing. In many cases, the planning agency is the most qualified local government body for such review, because it usually has some professional assistance available. The conditional use permit can also require that the procedures approved for management and maintenance of the facility be fully guaranteed by a performance bond in an appropriate amount. The Motorcycle Industry Council, Inc. (1973, p. 12) recommends that:

> Legislative bodies and administrative departments and officers should establish the principle that it is an appropriate role of local and regional governments to set aside areas in certain public lands where practicable in which use of motorized recreation vehicles may be permitted under suitable conditions and enforceable regulations.

and that:

> Private enterprise should be encouraged in efforts to establish motorcycle riding reserves by reasonable zoning requirements and tax incentives.

Requiring Public Hearings

Public participation in scheduled public hearings is necessary if federal public lands are to be designated as available for ORV use; Section 3(b) of Executive Order 11644 (Chapter 1, Fig. 1-3) provides that:

> The respective agency head shall ensure adequate opportunity for public participation in the promulgation of such regulations and in the designation of areas and trails . . . .

Public hearings are usually required by state legislatures when local governments amend the text or map of the zoning ordinance to accommodate ORV use. Local governments usually require public hearings when applications are made for ORV conditional use permits.

The U.S. National Park Service provides for a period of 30 days during which the public may comment on proposed designations of land for ORV use. The U.S. Bureau of Land Management (1974b, Sec. 6292.4) provides that the land manager:

> will consult with interested user groups, Federal, State, county, and local agencies, local landowners, and other parties in a manner that provides an opportunity for the public to express itself and have those views taken into account.

Acquiring Land for ORV Facilities

In addition to designating state and federal public lands for ORV use or rezoning private lands, acquisition of lands by state, local agencies, or private developers may be feasible. It was the opinion of a U.S. Department of the Interior Task Force Study (1971) that the contribution of private lands is vital to the continued expansion of ORV use. The California State Legislature (1971, Sec. 38270) provides that the Off-Highway Vehicles Fund may be used for acquisition of ORV facilities. Several counties have made such acquisitions.

Proper Ways to Post Signs

Although posting of signs is a function of managing an ORV facility or event (discussed later in this chapter), it is necessary to discuss it in the context of designating public lands. There are three ways to sign ORV areas:

1. Just the areas that are closed
2. Just the areas that are open
3. Both the closed and open areas

Providing signs for both closed and open areas is expensive and unnecessary. For example, the U.S. Department of Defense would have to design, purchase, erect, and maintain "closed" signs for all their lands since all their lands are closed. The more economical and rational practice is to sign just those areas designated for

ORV use on state and federal public lands; all other lands being deemed closed to ORV use. Appropriate signs for those areas designated "open" is very important both for the users' information and the land managers' enforcement. For example, if only the closed areas were signed and the "bad apples" destroyed the "closed" signs, both the law-abiding ORV users and the patrol persons would be in the impossible position of not knowing whether violations are taking place. The signs should be posted along the cycleways, or on the periphery of the sacrifice areas or mechanical compounds. Section 5 of the Executive Order (Chapter 1, Fig. 1-3) gives clear instructions for marking "open" areas:

> The respective agency head shall ensure that areas and trails where off-road vehicle use is permitted are well marked and shall provide for the publication and distribution of information, including maps, describing such areas and trails and explaining the conditions on vehicle use.

Rosenberg (1976, p. 189) summarizes the arguments for "open-use" area marking:

> First, if signing was limited solely to open-use areas, less signing would be done, since less area would be open to ORV's than would be closed. Also, the impact of unsightly signing would be lessened if limited to those open areas where less emphasis is placed on aesthetics. Finally, enforcement would be simplified if signing was limited to designating open lands, because vandalism to signs in a "closed-area" signing system would effectively negate the closure, since enforcement without the signs would be questionable. The closed-area without signs would thus be converted into "open" land, resulting in a potential for harm to fragile, "closed" areas.

To conclude, all ORV use should be prohibited on state and federal lands unless signed "open." All ORV use should be prohibited on private and local public lands unless zoned for such use and a conditional use permit has been issued.

Design and Construction

This section contains some general design and construction considerations but makes no attempt to address the complete range of criteria that would result in detailed plans or specifications. The design criteria and standards vary with the type of facility—whether it is a small or large cycle park, cycleway system, sacrifice area, or mechanical compound—site characteristics, site resources, and adjoining land uses and users. Spolar (1979, p. 284) observes:

> Most trails are not designed with proper grades, tread width, drainage and switchbacks. All of these affect user experience. Excessive grades magnify drainage problems. Poorly designed and constructed switchbacks can lead to cutting and in some cases, hillclimbing. Narrow tread

width can pose safety problems, particularly on steep side slopes. Good
redesign, particularly of switchbacks, can ward off many of the problems associated with our inherited trail systems.

The discussion will pertain primarily to cycleway systems, since these may
satisfy the needs of the majority of ORV users. Cycle parks and mechanical compounds require more intensive site analysis and design by specialists such as
urban motorcycle-park designers. The design of sacrifice areas is oftentimes not
practical as the users' needs are satisfied by no design or no prearranged routes.

General Design Criteria

Generally, a system of cycleways should provide for diversity of experience for
the casual rider. Desirable elements include distance, variety, and elevation
changes such as are provided by large loop systems and a meandering course.
The cycleways should avoid all non-ORV use areas and as many plant and wildlife habitats as possible. Where ORV use cannot avoid damage to soil and water
resources, bridges, culverts, or pavement will be required. The reader should be
reminded that the challenges required by endurance riders cannot be met by
cycle parks or cycleway systems. Perhaps a mechanical compound meeting their
needs could interconnect to a cycleway system. Obviously, motorcycle events
would not be permitted on a cycleway system because it is designed for casual
riders.

The Motorcycle Industry Council, Inc. (1981, p. 2) stresses that riders want
their trails to be challenging but still have an "unimproved" or "primitive"
appearance, even though they were carefully planned and laid out. However,
challenging trails for endurance riders cannot retain a truly rustic appearance.
Such an appearance can be maintained for cycleway systems, but any attempt to
maintain a natural environment for sacrifice areas is impossible. For example,
the U.S. Forest Service (1977, p. 90) notes that:

> Motorized vehicle competition events, such as speed races and hill
> climbs, are not generally consistent with resource management objec-
> tives and the type of recreation experiences appropriate to the National
> Forest . . . .

Several reports are available which suggest design and construction criteria
and standards. However, most of these reports make no distinctions as to
whether the standards apply to cycle parks, cycleway systems, or sacrifice areas.
For example, Bury and Fillmore (1977, p. 63) make many specific preliminary
design recommendations, several of which are appropriate only for sacrifice
areas. The following excerpt illustrates the point:

> Trails should traverse available hills. Novices considered hills of 30 to
>   40 percent too steep, while experienced riders thought the 5 to 10
>   percent slopes of the other two sites were not steep enough.
> Trails should be located to maximize the number of natural jumps avail-
>   able from existing topography. Ten small jumps in a one-quarter-mile
>   course were not considered excessive by the riders.

> Trails should be designed to place demands on the rider's ability to handle his machine. Not only is a tortuous trail more challenging, but it uses less area per linear foot of trail.
>
> Areas for experienced riders should be constructed in taller vegetation; parts of the trail should be separated by vegetation, distance, and/or variations in terrain to create a feeling of isolation from most other cyclists.
>
> Rockiness was approved by experienced riders, but not by novices. Rocky areas need not be cleared for trail cycle use if rocks are cherty plates less than 5 inches in length.

Some reports give helpful suggestions concerning cycleway routes, cycleway construction, drainage, stream crossings, underpasses, support facilities, resources to be avoided, daily travel distances, system configuration, appearance, grades, types of pavement, and cycleway lengths, widths, clearances, junctions, alignments, switchbacks, and turning radii. Some of the sources for these design and construction standards include: U.S. Soil Conservation Service (1979) (Chapter 3, Table 3-2), Emetaz (1980), Motorcycle Industry Council, Inc. (1980c, p. 2), the State of Missouri Motorcycle Trail Recommendations (Rasor, 1977, pp. 57-59), Bury and Fillmore (1977), the U.S. Forest Service (1977), and the technical guides found in the U.S. Soil Conservation Service field offices. Wells (1980), an ORV planner for the Idaho State's Park and Recreation Department, discusses and provides diagrams of several basic layouts, such as the simple loop, stacked loops, primary loop with satellites, point to point, dendritic, spoked wheel, and maze.

Examples of the various types of ORV facilities used in Florida, Louisiana, Missouri, and Washington have been described by the American Motorcycle Association (Rasor, 1977) and include some successful design and construction standards. The reader should be reminded, however, that four of the examples are for nonarid areas. One area described by Rasor (1977, p. 13) has an average rainfall of 8 to 16 inches (200 to 400 mm) per year and is an arid area. This example—Hollister Hills, originally a sacrifice area—is California's first attempt at developing an ORV facility and will probably be successful only if all cycleways are *paved* or if the facility is converted to a mechanical compound. If the area continues to be used by the unrestricted endurance rider, the area will remain a sacrifice area. Attempts to restrict the endurance riders and retain what soil and plants are left will cause the area to evolve into a mechanical compound.

Meeting User Needs

Trails should be designated for one-way traffic and signs posted, as many ORV users have complained of being unsure of the intended direction of travel. Except in sacrifice areas, obstacles near the sides of the trail should be cleared; outcropping tree roots, rocks, logs, deep treads, and overhanging branches can be hazardous. Turns on slick surfaces in sacrifice areas should be avoided, and water bars should be placed perpendicular to the ORV crossing. To keep ORVs on bridges and puncheons, edge or low rail barriers should be used.

The Motorcycle Industry Council, Inc. (1973, p. 7) recommends that spectator areas be separated by a fence from the track where ORV events are held. Other measures to minimize hazards would include the construction and maintenance of fire breaks. The use of cattle-guard type crossings are preferred to automatic gates and barbed wire gates. The Motorcycle Industry Council, Inc. (1980b, p. 2) has been compiling information for a guide on planning, development, and maintenance of ORV facilities.

Numerous ORV support facilities are necessary or desirable to meet user needs. Such facilities include parking areas, potable water, sanitation, concessions, medical bulletin boards, trash receptacles, loading ramps, fire rings, picnic tables, showers, small parts and accessories shops, repair stations, ORV rentals, safety equipment rentals, shelters, overnight camping facilities, tent camping areas, staging areas, pit areas, and vehicle washing facilities. The type and number of support facilities needed vary with the type of ORV facility and its distance from urban areas where such facilities may be found. Discussions of supporting facilities can be found in Wells (1980), Motorcycle Industry Council, Inc. (1973, p. 8), and in the examples reported by the American Motorcyclist Association (Rasor, 1977).

Protecting Resources

Kay and Graves (Chapter 16) advise that disturbances of resources should be avoided, but if unavoidable, kept to a minimum. Selecting sites carefully, designating or zoning them for restricted ORV use, and closing all other public and private lands will help protect the resources. Paved cycleways or trails with bridges over streams, paved staging, parking, and pit areas, and mechanical compounds, all help to avoid direct impacts on the soil and water. Of course, the vegetation and the animals and their habitats in the way or adjacent to the cycleways and supporting facilities will be displaced, supplanted, or destroyed.

Cycle parks, cycleway systems, and mechanical compounds should be designed by engineers in accordance with the soil and water conservation practices developed and approved for arid areas. Cycleways and other supporting facilities should be located and designed to follow the contours insofar as possible. Natural drainage patterns should be retained so as to minimize cuts and fills and resulting soil movement. Boggy and wet areas should be avoided. Culverts, bridges, and ditches should be designed so that they can pass flood waters and withstand ORV traffic.

Sacrifice areas require the most attention, not only to confine the destruction from wind erosion and sedimentation within the facility, but to so maintain the facility that it will continue to meet the endurance riders' needs—intensive use and consumptive of resources. Some of the erosion can be reduced by placing water bars in the stream crossings. Some of the water pollution and sedimentation can be reduced through the use of debris dams and settling ponds so that eroded debris will not leave the facility. Air pollution can sometimes be reduced by watering to control dust or by regulating the use if wind conditions are unfavorable.

   To protect the resources, management should include the design, installation, and maintenance of those soil-erosion and sediment-control practices appropriate to the local area. Such practices are enumerated in the technical guides found in the U.S. Soil Conservation Service field offices. They include providing access roads, seeding ranges, planting critical areas, building debris basins and windbreaks, protecting streambanks, stabilizing grades, planting trees, and managing wildlife habitats. Heede (Chapter 12) notes that burlap strips on slopes and check dams on gullies have been effective in reducing erosion. Catchment dams and diversions can be used to lessen soil damage, flooding, and sedimentation outside the sacrifice area. Catchment basins will ensure that soil and other debris do not leave the area. Local conservation district offices, assisted by the U.S. Soil Conservation Service, can provide specific information on soil conditions and assist in planning ORV use areas and trails. They can also provide technical assistance in reclaiming damaged areas.

   If an attempt is made to convert a sacrifice area to a cycle park or mechanical compound, the disturbed and impaired areas that are no longer needed should be rehabilitated. For example, the California Department of Parks and Recreation (1978, pp. 42, 43) requires that:

> When it becomes apparent that any type of use is resulting in uncontrollable soil erosion, that use will be restricted or stopped until the problem can be mitigated.
>
> Roads, scars, trails, firebreaks, and other man-made intrusions that are no longer used for off-road vehicles, maintenance purposes, or other visitor uses will be restored, revegetated, or stabilized to help alleviate erosion generating from these open areas.

Wilshire (1980) notes that:

> minimization of soil resource damage, as required by Presidential directive, can be achieved by site selection that emphasizes soils with low erodibility, and engineering techniques that reduce effective slope and slope length.
>
> These factors have been taken into account in the Soil Conservation Service Guidelines for ORV Trails . . . which list a number of soil-terrain factors that should alert managers to potential problems. Especially important for western public lands is . . . the soil erosion hazard. Since typical soil erodibility factors . . . for western soils are in the range 0.2 to 0.4, slopes of only 10% to 20% will generally be in the SEVERE category. This range of slopes is incompatible with most hillclimbs . . . .

   Although protecting the soil resource is incompatible with the concept of an unrestricted sacrifice area, several design and construction measures can be taken to reduce the more serious impacts. Some of Knott's (1980, pp. 22-24) recommendations for Hungry Valley illustrate the point:

> Hillclimbs are located away from established stream channels, and slope lengths are reduced on steep hillsides.
> Hillclimbs are located on south- and west-facing slopes, where vegetation

is sparse and soil-moisture retention is low, thus reducing the impact on wildlife habitat and esthetics.

Cross-country trails follow natural contours and avoid landslide- or slump-prone areas.

Debris basins, windbreaks, and gully-control structures are used to reduce or delay sediment transport from ORV sites.

Debris basins, revegetation, and diversion of flow to spreading areas are used to reduce storm runoff.

Once a suitable location has been selected by a qualified planner, special protection measures are designed to safeguard sensitive sites along the route. Before the final location is chosen, many alternatives will be examined and rejected. The number of sites requiring special protection should be minimized. Special protection measures are physical features built into the facility to prevent adverse impact or excessive maintenance costs. Protective features should be planned for and built into the trail during initial construction; however, in most cases, they can be built into existing trails.

Drainage Dips. Drainage dips are developed during initial construction by reversing the prevailing grade for a distance of 4.7 m (15') or more. They are used to divert run-off from the trail tread. Drain dips are effective, inexpensive, and do not detract from the natural setting.

Water Bars. Water bars are small—12.7 cm (5") in diameter or less—log barriers placed perpendicular to the direction of travel and staked into position. They serve the same purpose as drainage dips. Water bars are inexpensive, and unlike drain dips can be placed on an existing trail. They are "less" natural and may constitute a hazard to novice riders if not properly constructed.

Culverts. Culverts are used to keep traffic out of the water source. They are difficult to transport and should not be less than 30 cm (12") in diameter. Bare metal ends may be unsightly, and adequate diameter is essential to prevent plugging up. Routine maintenance is necessary.

Bridges. Bridges are used on larger streams and serve the same purpose as culverts. Rustic construction utilizing native materials is the key to eye pleasing facilities.

Ditches. Ditches are used to intercept water and prevent saturation of the trail. They can be hazardous to the rider and should be placed as far from the trail as practical.

Tread Armor. Tread armor is a protective covering of borrow material (crushed rock, for example) placed on top of the native soil. It is expensive and difficult to transport extended distances. Armor is an effective tread protection, but it is unsightly when first applied.

Concrete Blocks. Concrete blocks imbedded in the trail provide a solid, unyielding surface. They are quite effective, but expensive and difficult to transport, and can be hazardous if improperly used. There are still technical problems to be worked out, and this treatment should be used sparingly and only for short distances.

Puncheon. Puncheon is essentially a "land bridge" constructed with hand split planks and round logs. Puncheon is used to cross water saturated soil. As in all features of this type, rustic construction and native materials should prevail. Costs are highly variable and the effective life span of this treatment is uncertain.

Turnpike. Turnpike is a method used to elevate the trail tread above wet soil. It is constructed by placing parallel log "sideboards" 91.4 to 152.4 cm (3 to 5') apart and backfilling with soil containing a high proportion of fractured rock. Turnpike must be "crowned" to provide drainage. Properly applied, turnpike is an effective treatment.

Wire Mesh. Wire mesh covering the trail tread and fastened to parallel log stringers is presently under evaluation. It appears to greatly reduce "rutting" in soft clay soils.

Figure 22-1. Special soil protection features (from Wernex, 1979, pp. 250, 251).

In addition, Knott (1980, p. 24) recommends stabilization devices to reduce erosion and runoff. Various stabilization or "soil-hardening" devices described by Wernex (1979, pp. 250–251) are listed in Figure 22-1. In addition to preventing vehicle wheels from churning up the surface and causing further erosion, these protective features also serve to improve traction on steep slopes and reduce maintenance costs chargeable to ORV users. As these special protection features are installed, the sacrifice area is evolving into a mechanical compound.

Reducing Conflicts

All cycle parks, sacrifice areas, and mechanical compounds should be fenced. Fencing provides the following benefits:

> Decreases the manager's or owner's liability
>
> Prevents "bad apples" from avoiding payment of user fees
>
> Prevents users of ORV facilities from deliberately or inadvertently leaving the restricted area and causing damage to resources outside the area and conflicts with non-ORV users

Construction of paved cycleways will avoid conflicts with other users. Sheridan (1979, p. 56) advises that *"Trails* specifically designed and maintained for ORVs . . . will cause the fewest user-conflict and environmental problems." Although vegetation and distance are helpful in reducing the visual conflicts with other users, they do not serve as noise barriers in arid areas. Real isolation and natural terrain barriers, or constructed earth works, are required for sound-proofing. For example, Bury and Fillmore (1977, p. 63) recommend that:

> Trails should usually be at least 600 feet from the nearest camping site. This distance may be shortened if substantial hills and/or vegetation lie between the two areas. The distance may need to be longer if prevailing winds blow from the riding area toward the camping sites.

The U.S. Forest Service (1977, p. 88) suggests:

> A minimum distance of 1500 feet shall separate ORV routes which may have to parallel non-motorized trails for short distances.

Managing ORV Facilities

Facility management includes managing ORV operation (discussed here), site resources, and ORV events (discussed in the next section). The objectives of facility management should be to: meet user needs, protect resources, and minimize conflicts with various other users. Even if the site is selected carefully and the facility designed and constructed properly, the objectives cannot be realized if the facility is poorly managed. Also important are installation of signs (discussed below); monitoring and closure (discussed in a following section); and regulation, enforcement, funding, and education (discussed in the following chapter).

Post Signs

The careful location and wording of signs to indicate areas open to ORV use and to identify permissable behavior are prerequisites for effective monitoring, regulation, enforcement, and education. Section 5 of Executive Order 11644 (Chapter 1, Fig. 1-3) specifically provides that federal public land managers:

> shall ensure that areas and trails where off-road vehicle use is permitted are well marked and shall provide for the publication and distribution of information, including maps, describing such areas and trails and explaining the conditions on vehicle use.

Reames (1980, p. 11) stresses that the public land managers are legally required "to adopt a *positive* signing policy (*i.e.,* signing of areas and trails *open* to ORV use). . . ." Some states specifically authorize signs, for example the California State Legislature (1971, Sec. 38280) provides:

> Federal, State, or local authorities having jurisdiction over public lands may place or cause to be placed and maintained, such appropriate signs, signals and other traffic control devices as may be necessary to properly indicate and carry out any provision of law or any duly adopted regulation of such governmental authority or to warn or guide traffic.

Properly located and worded cycleway markers, warning and caution signs, and posted regulations contribute to meeting the objectives. Standardized signs, symbols, and flags indicating entrances, exits, major junctions, major turns, special conditions, mileage, identification of travel mode, operating conditions, hazard warnings, nearest emergency assistance, cycleway difficulty ratings, distances to destination points, camping areas, directional signs, caution signs for steep sections, crossings, turns, or slick areas, resource conflicts, event courses, and park regulations all contribute to meeting user safety needs, avoiding resource damage, and warning non-ORV users. In addition, ORV users should have easy access to publications which explain the rules and regulations, location of riding areas, and designation of trails.

Meet User Needs

Once developed, ORV facilities should be carefully managed for the protection and safety of the user. The size of the staff managing the facility can range from one man to a large full-time staff depending on the size and type of facility. The California Department of Parks and Recreation (1975, pp. 58, 59) recommends:

> Any ORV area should have limited and fully controlled access and be staffed by qualified people whenever open for public use. The staff should be trained in safety and first aid . . . . The ORV area itself should be maintained in a condition free of hazards and unpleasant or unsightly conditions and should be patrolled regularly. Admission would be granted only to identified individuals with demonstrated minimum ability (or under parental supervision), who had signed an appropriate liability release form. Upon each admission, the machines would be in-

spected for mufflers, spark arrestors, and apparent safety problems. Admission would be granted only to licensed machines, registered either as ORV's or for regular street use.

Adult supervision should be provided for juveniles. A useful practice noted by the Motorcycle Industry Council, Inc. (1973, p. 11) is that:

> All riders under 18 should present a consent form signed by their parents before the park management allows them to use the site. The waivers generally contain a consent to available medical care which could prove quite important, if properly drawn. The minimum age of riders varies from nine to twelve years old in most cycle parks.

Families should be expected to supervise their younger members. The smaller cycle parks are sometimes used for babysitting purposes; parents deposit their children in the morning and return for them in the afternoon. If this practice is followed, the small park must be staffed with qualified adult personnel to supervise the children according to the Motorcycle Industry Council, Inc. (1973, p. 9). Unnecessary ORV riding near supporting facilities should be avoided. Bury and Fillmore (1977, p. 63) state that "Ideally, the dirt bikes should either be pushed or transported from the campsite to the riding area."

The U.S. Bureau of Outdoor Recreation (1976, p. 43) notes that user safety and public safety is enhanced when operating regulations are enforced, and where ORV use is restricted to properly located and managed trails. When artificial materials—wire mesh, concrete blocks, or puncheons—are used to stabilize sacrifice areas, they must be checked for safety. Facility managers should make users aware of any unsafe or unhealthy conditions, whether manmade or natural, such as airborne asbestos or valley fever. For example, Popendorf and Wenk (Chapter 20) suggest use restrictions, dust containment, personal respirators, and education as techniques to reduce some of the public health risks of asbestos. The guidelines provided by the U.S. Bureau of Outdoor Recreation (1975, pp. 15, 16) should be followed to reduce injuries:

> Know your machine. Know its capabilities and limitations, and handle it properly at all times. See that your machine regularly receives proper maintenance to keep it in good working condition.
> Use extreme caution in crossing all highways and side roads. Beware of barriers such as cables strung across old roadways, fences, bridge abutments, logs across the trail, etc.
> Never travel alone. An adult should accompany children and assume responsibility for their actions and safety.
> Always check your vehicle before leaving on an ORV trip. Carry water, tools, an emergency repair kit, and a first-aid kit.
> Always dress in appropriate and safe attire. Wear proper clothing and safety equipment suited to your particular type of riding, terrain, and weather conditions involved.

Park patrolers are necessary for user safety; some parks provide volunteer patrolers with a bright yellow jacket and free admission. At TVA's Turkey Bar cycle system, safety considerations are emphasized; ORV users are required to wear safety helmets and protective eye gear; and ORV use is allowed only during daylight hours (McEwen, 1978, p. 13). The Motorcycle Industry Council, Inc. (1973, p. 9) reports that serious injuries are surprisingly infrequent at motorcycle parks; however, the park operator must be ready to react quickly if one occurs, and recommends:

> At least one member of the park staff must be knowledgeable in first aid; and a telephone and a four-wheel drive emergency/maintenance/ patrol vehicle are absolute essentials. It is, of course, far better if all park officials have an understanding of first aid techniques and emergency procedures.

Protect Resources

After providing paved cycleways in the cycle parks and cycleway systems, and specifying and fencing the sacrifice areas, ORVs must remain on such paved cycleways or in such sacrifice areas. Any cross-country or unrestricted ORV use should be prohibited and the prohibition stringently enforced. For example, the U.S. Forest Service (1977, p. 88) prohibits all cross-country ORV use in their Allegheny National Forest, and U.S. Bureau of Outdoor Recreation (1976, p. 50) closes ORV areas to mitigate damage, as follows:

> During winter months when wildlife is extremely hungry or weakened
> On occasions when snow is so low that vegetation and soils would be
>   damaged by the weight of ORVs
> When trails are unusually muddy or unstable, such as after extensive
>   rains or rapid spring thaws
> During periods of extreme fire hazard
> During breeding, nesting, and calving seasons

In order to reduce impacts in a sacrifice area, the course widths should be limited and to avoid course cutting and additional impacts on the resources, the course should be well marked and flagged. In some cases, the course can be routed along existing roads or existing unpaved trails. Even sacrifice areas must be groomed and maintained. Soil erosion can be reduced by grading and proper drainage control. Garbage cans should be placed in the staging, pit, spectator, and other support areas.

The most crucial management problem lies in restricting ORV use to the capability of the land to sustain it (Wilshire, 1980). For example, weather conditions affect the number of ORV users a sacrifice area can accommodate. If adverse weather conditions accelerate erosion, use in those areas should be restricted. Temporary and seasonal closings are helpful in reducing the impacts on animals as well as limiting the adverse effects of climate. For example, the U.S. Bureau of Outdoor Recreation (1976, p. 50) suggests that "decisions to close certain areas seasonably or temporarily to avoid significant adverse environmental effects, will be exercised by designated land managers" and suggests that such closings take place.

Fires caused by ORV users or their machines can create a safety hazard for the users and the spectators. Great damage can be caused to adjacent watersheds and other natural resources when a fire spreads from a sacrifice area onto adjacent wildlands. The California Department of Parks and Recreation (1978, p. 43) provides that "prescribed burning techniques may be employed to achieve ecological stability on chapparal, forested, and grassland areas." A fire-hazard severity scale (U.S. Forest Service, 1976) taking into consideration fuel loading, fire-weather frequency, and slope has been developed to enable planners to classify and delineate areas with varying degrees of hazard in California's wildlands. The facility manager or public land manager should counsel with the local fire protection agency to develop a total fire protection system. They should consider the special fire problems, hazard reduction, and risk related to vegetation, topography, weather, transportation systems, water supply systems, and building density. Fire protection affects all three of our management objectives—meeting user safety needs, protecting resources, and reducing conflicts with other users. Facility managers should provide fire-fighting equipment and make every effort to prevent, report, control, and suppress any fire in their areas.

Although most coastal ecosystems do *not* lend themselves to paved ORV facilities, many of the preliminary management recommendations made by Godfrey et al. (1978, p. 597-599) for coastal areas are also applicable to arid areas:

Restrict traffic to marked routes with borders of cable or dense, impenetrable shrubs. Such tracks should only be established after careful study to minimize environmental impact.

Wooden ramps should be built and maintained over dune lines where beach access must be through the dune zone.

Dune routes should be oriented in such a way that prevailing winds cannot create blow-outs. Adequate borders of vegetation can prevent such wind erosion.

Close off all sensitive habitats such as heathlands and shrublands. Areas that are stable, but experience some natural stress, such as aridity, are likely to be most in need of protection.

Increase enforcement of trail regulations and develop public awareness that "dune busting" and "wheeling" are environmentally unacceptable. Seek the aid of conservation-oriented off-road vehicle organizations to help foster this attitude.

Although some managers avoid erecting signs that indicate resource areas so as not to attract illegitimate ORV use, the U.S. Bureau of Land Management (1977, pp. 5-2 and 3) has suggested posting signs indicating that a site has historic value, research is underway, and all cultural remains are protected by the Antiquities Act of 1906. Gilbertson (Chapter 19) points out that the posting of signs and warning information indicating the importance of a resource and ORV impacts on it would probably have a gratifying response from responsible ORV users.

Reduce Conflicts

The complete separation of ORV users by distance or visual and sound barriers from other recreational users is the key to avoiding or reducing conflicts. When ORV use is restricted to properly located and carefully designed cycle parks, cycleway systems, sacrifice areas, and mechanical compounds, little conflict with other users should occur. In addition, the erection of fences or the installation of barriers or gates so as to prevent egress from the facility onto lands that are closed or private is vital. Other management practices that may be helpful include limiting the hours of operation, creating buffer zones, limiting egress and ingress, treating sacrifice areas to reduce dust, and preventing or controlling fugitive dust.

Off-road vehicle support facilities, such as picnicking and camping areas, should be located where non-ORV users would be safe from ORV activities. ORV use that draws spectators should be located away from roads that are near the perimeter of the facility. Such location prevents passing motorists from slowing or stopping and thereby creating a traffic hazard on a public thoroughfare.

Some cyclists tamper with their exhaust equipment to raise the noise levels. All loud and unusual exhaust noise should be prohibited, and the prohibition should be strictly enforced. All ORVs must be equipped with mufflers in good working condition. An ORV equipped with a muffler cutout bypass or similar device producing excessive noise should not be permitted access to the facility.

An important consideration in managing the facilities is the protection of the spectators and other non-ORV users. Public liability insurance is usually required by private facility managers and should be required by all facility managers—whether of cycle parks, cycleway systems, sacrifice areas, or mechanical compounds. The Motorcycle Industry Council, Inc. (1973, p. 10) reports that:

> Insurance for a small, community operated riding reserve can generally become part of the recreational package at no increase in rates. For the largest privately owned riding reserves the premium can range as high as 7 to 10% of the annual gross receipts, but experience has shown that rates can be expected to decrease. Between these two extremes insurance costs can be adjusted depending upon the type of riding being done at the facility and several other factors.

Insurance underwriters often base their rate on the degree of safety of the spectator. The cycle park developed by the Iowa Department of Transportation is insured for one million dollars under a single combined limited liability policy (Motorcycle Industry Council, Inc., 1980a).

The ORV users' attitude and knowledge are key factors in reducing conflicts. The following guidelines provided by the U.S. Bureau of Outdoor Recreation (1975, pp. 15, 16) illustrate the point:

> Never trespass on any lands while riding your machine. Strictly observe any land posted . . . and obtain consent from the landowners before riding on such lands.

Know the laws regarding ORV use at the Federal, State, and local levels.

Obtain any license required to operate your vehicle, and register it if the law requires. Also, become informed of the liability, property damage, and insurance laws relating to your machine.

Managing ORV Events

Because of the large number of ORV users and spectators who gather for events and the limited number of patrol persons, special management is required. Permits, marshals, fees, and performance bonds are needed.

Require Permits

Prerequisite to proper management of events is the application for a use permit, which is issued subject to conditions of use. According to the U.S. Forest Service (1977, p. 90) such a permit would include:

> provisions for protection of the environment, site clean-up and restoration, law enforcement, crowd control, public safety and sanitation. In addition, performance bond and liability insurance will be required by the permittee . . . .

Generally, the permit applicant, in addition to the special conditions attached to the permit, is required to take full responsibility for public safety and health during the event, and to place the necessary number of course marshals at strategic locations in order to ensure participant and spectator safety, protect resources, control traffic and crowds, and prevent straying from the marked course. The BLM for the Lakeview District in Oregon (Motorcycle Industry Council, Inc., 1980b, p. 7) requires applicants to:

Provide the District Manager with a plan showing proposed traffic control measures (including traffic flow patterns), camping areas, sanitary facility locations, concession locations, staging, refueling, and other related event use areas, prior to the issuance of a permit

Ensure that all State and local laws, including motor vehicle laws, are obeyed at all times during the event

Contact State and local law enforcement agencies regarding the event

Publish rules and regulations governing the conduct of the event which incorporates the terms of the permit which are applicable to the participants and spectators

Brief participants and spectators of the rules and regulations and enforce compliance within the permitted area

The U.S. Forest Service management of the Allegheny National Forest, Pennsylvania, requires that all ORVs operated in the forest be registered and/or licensed according to state law (Butt, 1977b, p. 124). In addition, the U.S. Bureau of Land Management (1974a), has included the requirement that a permit holder:

provide a minimum of 100 course marshals who will be placed at strategic locations identified by the BLM . . . in order to insure participant and spectator safety, resource protection, traffic and crowd control, and adherence to the marked course . . . .

The permit holder should be required to mark and flag the entire course, including the start and finish areas, and provide warning signs at all crossings such as public roads, railroads, and supporting facilities prior to the event. For example, the U.S. Bureau of Land Management (1974a), has required an average of at least 10 flags per mile; special course markings in locations that are susceptible to adverse impacts; and flags at spectator, pit, refueling, and camping areas.

Meet User Needs

In managing events, an adequate number of marshals are necessary along the course. The course marshals protect ORV users by acting as flagmen to provide warnings to the users, keeping the spectators off the course, lining up racers, stopping participants when railroad or other public road crossings are unsafe, ensuring participant and spectator safety, and generally controlling traffic and crowds.

In order to meet users' needs and minimize hazardous conditions, the permit holder can be required to do the following:

Ensure adequate sanitation facilities for participants and spectators
Obtain the services of a fully equipped and trained desert first-aid and rescue organization
Coordinate the removal of disabled vehicles and riders from the course
Distribute written instructions and hold a pre-event briefing to inform participants of routes, regulations, and safety procedures
Require all ORVs to be equipped with proper brakes
Provide an ambulance on standby and radio communication to all checkpoints
Water spectator areas so as to keep the area free of dust

Sometimes additional conditions are necessary. For example, the U.S. Bureau of Land Management (1974c) has required:

The permittee shall provide for a minimum of ten chemical toilets at the first pit stop, six chemical toilets at the second pit stop, six chemical toilets at the third pit stop, 22 chemical toilets at the start, and 16 chemical toilets at the finish area.

The U.S. Bureau of Land Management (1974a) has also required that a permit holder provide first aid, communications, and search and rescue personnel and equipment, including a radio base station, 11 mobile radio sites, portable radios, fully equipped ambulance, mobile field hospital, and personnel trained in field first aid. Some states have special requirements, for example, the Missouri Department of Natural Resources in its service contract for competitive events requires the permit holder to obtain an insurance policy in the amount of $300,000 (Rasor, 1977, p. 55).

Protect Resources

Although a sacrifice area would be located so as to avoid areas containing valuable resources, event courses should also be routed so as to minimize the impacts on all resources. For example, Webb (Chapter 4) suggests limiting ORV use to areas such as playas where soils are not susceptible to compaction during dry times of the year; and to reduce wind erosion, Gillette and Adams (Chapter 6) recommended discouraging ORV use on alluvial fans and desert flats. Pit stops and areas for staging and camping should be well marked and flagged, and course marshals should prevent illegitimate use outside these areas. Wide courses can be narrowed across more sensitive soil areas or where animal and plant resources exist. Access to ridges along the course should also be blocked. Before, during, and after ORV events, the permit holder can be required to:

Prevent misuse of ORVs by spectators

Manage user and spectator parking so as to minimize disturbance of vegetation and soil

Make every effort to prevent, report, control, and suppress any fire

Confine participants to the marked course and limit spectator and support vehicles to designated areas

Pick up all trash and litter, discarded motorcycle parts, and disabled ORVs

Block, post, and provide marshals to prevent any participant or spectator from leaving approved course or support areas if sensitive resources might be damaged

Restrict the ingress and egress of cleanup crews and support vehicles to existing roads.

These and other similar requirements are necessary for ORV events. For example, the U.S. Bureau of Land Management (1974c) has required that courses be narrowed, channeled, and in one instance, limited to a width of only 15 feet (5 m). To minimize adverse effects on vegetation, the U.S. Bureau of Land Management (1977, p. 5-1, 2) has suggested using the following measures:

Prohibiting racing when the soil is wet and during peak annual and perennial growth periods

Maintaining the width of the race course so as not to exceed 200 feet (60 m)

Retaining the same camping and pit areas for succeeding events

Fencing and stationing personnel near creosote rings

and to minimize adverse effects on wildlife, the U.S. Bureau of Land Management (1977, p. 5-2) has suggested:

Requiring surface restoration to preclude the need for moving the courses to new locations when they become unusable for ORVs

Prohibiting competitive events from mid-February to mid-May to protect breeding and migrating wildlife

Prohibiting any night use, both competitive and noncompetitive, to minimize the destruction and harassment of resident wildlife

Prohibiting use of significant catchments in selected drainage areas to prevent indirect effects of increased runoff

To mitigate adverse effects on cultural resources, the U.S. Bureau of Land Management (1977, p. 5-4) has suggested advising participants and spectators during the events of their responsibility to protect the resources, patrolling specific sites to prevent any inadvertent loss or disturbance of cultural remains, and patrolling in an unobtrusive manner in order to prevent loss or disturbance, and yet not attract attention to the location. To protect scenic and visual resources, the U.S. Bureau of Land Management (1977, p. 5-4 and 5) has suggested:

Restricting access to and egress from the event course to specific locations so as to reduce the alteration of form, line, color, and texture adjacent to highways

Routing courses no closer than 1 mile (1.6 km) from area boundaries in order to reduce the visibility of the land disturbances

Confining courses to previously disturbed areas wherever possible and having curbs follow existing landforms to retain harmony with the natural landscape

Prohibiting course routes within 200 feet (60 m) of well-developed washes

The BLM Lakeview District, Oregon (Motorcycle Industry Council, Inc., 1980b, p. 8) requires that:

Stakes, flagging materials, litter equipment, temporary facilities, and all other event-related material shall be removed from the route immediately following the event or within three days after the event. Painting of rocks or trees and establishment of other permanent markers or improvements is prohibited.

Reduce Conflicts

To reduce conflicts with other users, permit holders can be required to:

Protect telephone, telegraph, and electrical transmission lines, fences, ditches, roads, trails, and other existing improvements

Advise state and local patrols and law enforcement agencies of the event well ahead of time

Submit a signed affidavit assuring that all private land owners whose property is affected by the event have been contacted and have given their consent

Inform all participants in the event of all pertinent state and federal requirements

Obtain an insurance policy for general liability coverage indemnifying the permit holder and the public land manager for any damage or injury to persons and property which may occur during the event or as a result of the event

These and other conditions have been required of event permit holders by public-land management agencies. For example, the BLM Lakeview District, Oregon (Motorcycle Industry Council, Inc., 1980b, p. 8) requires:

The event course may cross fences at cattleguards or gates only. A guard will be posted at each gate used during the event to ensure that no livestock pass through any gate during the event. The guard shall ensure that the gate is closed before leaving.

and the U.S. Bureau of Land Management (1974c) has required a permit holder to:

indemnify, defend, and hold harmless the United States and/or its agencies and representatives against and from any and all demands, claims, or liabilities of every nature whatsoever including but not limited to damages to property, injuries to or death of persons, arising directly or indirectly from or in any way connected with, the permittee's use and occupancy of the lands described in this permit or with the event authorized under this permit.

The U.S. Bureau of Land Management has also required a permit holder to maintain comprehensive liability insurance, insuring the United States in the following minimum amounts: $100,000 for bodily injury to any one person and $300,000 for any one occurrence, and $10,000 for property damage for any one occurrence. The permit holder was also required to give 10 days' notice prior to cancellation or modification of the insurance, and to provide a copy of the actual insurance policy to the district manager, who would forward it to the Regional Solicitor's Office for approval.

Private land owners authorizing ORV use on their lands can require users to assume all risk and release the owners through an indemnification agreement. For example, the Motorcycle Industry Council, Inc. (1973, p. 23) in their *Motorcycle Park Planning and Management* guide include an agreement between an ORV association and its members wherein the users assume all risk incident to their use of specific private lands and waive any claims or rights that arise out of the ORV activity.

Hold Permittees Responsible

The public-land manager or private owner should require the permit holder to be financially responsible for:

Faithful conformance to all terms and conditions of the permit including public safety and health during any phase of the event

Any damage by ORV users or spectators to soil and water conservation practices or structures

Supervision of all participants, spectators, and other persons associated
with the event using the lands in the permit area

Damage to any government-owned or private structures, property,
roads, or resource harmed or damaged by the permit holder, participants, or spectators

Suppression of fire and cost of any damage resulting from fire on public
or private lands caused by the participants or spectators, deliberately
or through negligence

These and other responsibilities have been assigned to permit holders by
public-land managers and private owners. For example, the U.S. Bureau of Land
Management (1974c) requires such harm or damage to be:

> reconstructed, repaired, rehabilitated, and restored as may be required
> by BLM within 30 days after the event so that the condition thereof, in
> the judgement of BLM, is at least equal to the condition thereof im-
> mediately prior to such damage or destruction. Permittee further shall
> abate, as soon as possible, any condition existing which may cause harm
> or damage to any person, structure, property, land, wildlife, vegetation,
> and/or other resources.

The U.S. Forest Service (1977, p. 93) suggests that:

> Any Government-owned structures, property, land, or resource harmed
> or damaged by an event permit holder, participants, or spectators
> associated with the permit shall be reconstructed, repaired, rehabili-
> tated, and restored so that the condition thereof is at least equal to the
> condition thereof immediately prior to such damage or destruction.

Require Fees and Bonds

Public-land managers and private owners should require fees of all permit holders. These fees are intended to cover all costs related to an event, including:
review of the application; consultations with adjoining land owners, engineers,
soil and water conservationists, and attorneys; preparation of the use permits
and performance bonds; and the cost of hiring, equipping, and provisioning all
patrolmen, monitors, and marshals to ensure that all conditions of the permit are
fully complied with.

A record of the full cost should be prepared and made public. It should include cost of the staff time to prepare the environmental assessment reports,
staff time for course approval and monitoring during the event, staff time to
oversee and monitor mitigation work, and the costs of equipment and materials.
These costs should be included in the fees required of the permit holder.

In addition, permit holders should provide a bond guaranteeing the faithful
performance of all terms and conditions of the permit including the payment of
the fees and the cost of monitoring, closing, and reclaiming (discussed in the
next section). The Geological Society of America (1977, p. 8) suggests that
"Reclamation costs should be paid entirely from revenues generated by ORV

use . . . ." that is, by fees or bonds required of permit holders. The bond shall remain in force as long as necessary to ensure compliance with all terms and conditions of the permit and until the permit holder is notified in writing that all obligations incurred under the permit are satisfied and that all rights are terminated.

The amount of the bond should be determined by the manager or owner before the permit is issued and after considering such factors as the type of the events, number of entrants and spectators, estimate of damage, requirement for removal of course markings and other debris, and cost of rehabilitating or reclaiming the course and other support areas. The U.S. Bureau of Land Management (1974a, p. IV–4) has provided that:

> If BLM personnel making the post-race compliance check do not find all areas mentioned . . . at least as free of trash and litter as they were prior to the event, the permittee will be required to return and complete the cleanup before the bond will be released.

The U.S. Bureau of Land Management [1974b, Sec. 2924.3-1(c)] has also provided in its special land-use permits for ORV events:

> As a condition of permit issuance, the authorized officer shall require the permittee to furnish bond, surety or other guarantee in such amounts as may be required to cover cost of restoration and rehabilitation of the trails and areas used, and such other special costs attributable to the events.

The manager or owner should check for compliance with the conditions of the permit before, during, and after the event. For example, pre-event compliance would entail the time necessary to confirm that the permit holder has alerted the appropriate law-enforcement agencies, that the search and rescue field organization has been retained, and that adjoining private landowners have been contacted. Compliance during the event requires that an adequate number of marshals be posted throughout the spectator areas, support areas, and along the course. Compliance after the event requires checking all areas for resource damage (particularly unanticipated damage), property damage, litter, and debris. If there has been noncompliance with any condition, all the administrative costs, attorney fees, and court costs as well as the cost of performing should be fully assigned against the performance bond.

Monitoring, Closing, and Reclaiming

In cycle parks, cycleway systems, and mechanical compounds, ORVs do not come in contact with soil or water; they are restricted to *paved* cycleways. If the regulations of these facilities are stringently enforced by the managers and if action for trespass is taken by private owners, the problems with "bad apples" will be reduced, and ORVs will destroy only the resources in the sacrifice areas.

Monitoring, closing, and reclaiming are management techniques intended to reduce the effects of ORV use on resources in sacrifice areas. Monitoring of the physical and biological systems in ORV facilities and closing are prerequisites to reclaiming damaged areas; however monitoring is impossible unless ORV use is restricted (Chapter 21). Monitoring becomes possible only when ORV use is permitted in designated or zoned sacrifice areas. Reclamation or the slow change of a sacrifice area into a mechanical compound might reduce some of the destruction. The full cost of monitoring, closing, and reclaiming should be covered by user fees or performance bond assessments.

Monitor Impacts

If resources are to be protected, monitoring is a prerequisite to closing and reclaiming. Public land managers should initiate a program by which trained and experienced personnel will be available to monitor ORV impacts. Wilshire (1980) notes that:

> The need for such monitoring systems, tied to effective mitigation programs, is evident from obvious risks to the public . . . from the clear indications of topical monitoring studies that deterioration of the physical and biological systems in ORV areas is extremely rapid, and from the need for information that will allow timely rehabilitation of sites before deterioration has exceeded limits of feasible reclamation.

Executive Order 11644 (Chapter 1, Fig. 1-3) requires public-land managers to monitor the effects of the use of ORVs on lands under their jurisdictions. An effective monitoring system requires the establishment of baseline information and threshold levels. In the plan for the California Desert, the U.S. Bureau of Land Management (1980, p. P-112) proposes a monitoring system that includes:

> Measurement of impacts and measurement of mitigations covering broad areas such as common vegetative types or ecosystems, focusing on the resources impacted from cumulative sources, with analyses for trends
>
> Measurement of impacts and mitigation effectiveness of one particular use on all the resources, *e.g.,* ORV use in an area inhabited by a sensitive wildlife species

Knott (1980, p. 24) suggests that an adequate ORV impact monitoring program could be established to determine areas of unacceptably severe erosion, effectiveness of erosion-control structures, and impacts on downstream reaches. He suggests further that monitoring techniques might include:

> Periodic interpretation of aerial photographs.
>
> Debris-basin surveys to determine area erosion rates.
>
> Soil surveys to determine thickness and composition of remaining soil; standards for permissible deterioration could be adopted in terms of a preplanned rehabilitation program.

Vegetation surveys to determine viability of native vegetation and intrusions of exotic species.

Stream-channel surveys to determine channel migration and changes in hydraulic geometry.

Monitoring is a complex and rigorous scientific operation, and a thorough discussion is beyond the scope of this section. For example, the use of sacrifice areas by ORVs is contingent on producing no effects on resources, including the hydrologic balance, outside the sacrifice areas. The U.S. Congress (1977) describes hydrologic balance as:

the equilibrium established between the groundwater and surface water of an area, between the recharge and discharge to and from that system. Some of the measurable indicators of hydrologic balance include: flow patterns of groundwater within aquifers; the quantity of surface water as measured by the volume, rate, and duration of flow in streams; the erosion, transport, and deposition of sediment by surface runoff and stream flow; the quality of groundwater and surface waters, including both suspended and dissolved materials.

In their final environmental impact statement for an ORV race from Barstow to Las Vegas, the U.S. Bureau of Land Management (1974a) has described the environmental sampling plots and aerial photograph points that are required to provide for proper monitoring of the race and related activities (Fig. 22-2). Besides being work of a complex and highly skilled nature, some kinds of monitoring require persistent, dedicated attention. For example, Bucher (1979, p. 26) recommended that within a week after the "Red Garter Enduro" event proposed by the Dirt Diggers Motorcycle Club, Inc., the entire route be ridden by U.S. Forest Service personnel including a soil scientist and a hydrologist to identify areas which required repair.

Off-road vehicle events draw many participants and spectators. This intensified use requires additional costly monitoring by facility managers to ensure that overuse does not occur. New trails and facilities have to be carefully monitored during the first 2 years. According to Emetaz (1980, p. 4) problems that develop should be quickly resolved through use of special protective measures and, in extreme cases, relocation. Existing erosion problems resulting from past use also have to be closely monitored.

In the U.S. Forest Service management of Ballinger Canyon, Scott et al. (1978, p. 34) recommend that a system for monitoring soil compaction and erosion from ORV traffic be established on each soil unit involved and suggest the following method:

The photo-plot location be pin-pointed on aerial photos, and a picture be taken from an easily identifiable spot. If the picture is taken in a way that distinctive limbs, stumps, or structures frame one or more sides of the print, then the print can be used to duplicate positioning of future takes. Photogenic measuring devices or gimmicks should be used and positioned in each photo taken.

---

3. Establishing Environmental Sampling Plots and aerial photo points to provide proper monitoring of the race and related activities.

Baseline photographic plots will be established before the race to document the present state of key resources along the proposed course. Photography will be used to record precise sizes, shapes, and density of vegetation, soils, archaeological features, and other resources that are not accurately remembered by observers.

Ground and aerial photos will be included at each established Environmental Sampling Plot (E.S.P.). On the ground, a series of 11 oblique photos will be taken from a leveled tripod at 4½ feet above ground to include a 360-degree view. With a 360-degree view, the plot can be relocated even if reference stakes were inadvertently destroyed. The photos will be taken with 35 mm color film.

The aerial photos will be vertical, low-level (large-scale), 70 mm transparencies. These photos will allow a quantification of changes in vegetation density and composition and soil alterations. Flight height, ground datum, camera, and lens type will be recorded so that the horizontal scale of the photos can be calculated. Approximately six aerial photos will be taken to cover each ground photo plot.

Twenty-five E.S.P.'s will be established to assess the critical vegetative, soils, visual, archaeological, and historical resources. These will be photographed before and after the race. The exact E.S.P. locations and subjects are not included here to avoid encouraging alterations of each plot. (For location of E.S.P. plots, see Sheet Index Map E-1).

In addition to photos, one or more representative soil samples will be collected and analyzed for each E.S.P.

E.S.P.'s will be rephotographed on the ground after the race. Plots where environmental changes are evident will also be rephotographed from the air. Plots will be checked monthly during February through June at the lower elevations, 1500 to 4000 feet; April through September at the higher elevations. These plots will be rechecked on an annual basis.

Figure 22-2. Monitoring the Barstow to Las Vegas race course (from U.S. Bureau of Land Management, 1974a, pp. IV-1 and 2).

Photo points should be established at the base, midpoint and upper portion of runs, climbs and trails. The photo points should be retaken at both the season's beginning and end, and during or after unusual storms and moisture conditions they may relate directly to use.

In arid areas, the monitoring of erosion is difficult. For example, transects for measuring erosion were placed at two locations in Ballinger Canyon in February 1978. One transect was located on a hillclimb north of the campground; the other was placed on a hillclimb known as Suicide Hill. Remeasurement of the transects was made in July 1978, but according to Scott et al. (1978, p. 35), some of the data could not be used because they were not representative, not comparable, or not valid.

In response to Executive Order 11644, the TVA established an environmental monitoring plan for the 2350-acre (950-ha) Turkey Bay ORV area, in the 170,000-acre (68,000-ha) National Recreation Area "Land Between the Lakes." The Chief of the TVA Recreation and Interpretive Services (McKnelly, 1980, p.

92) reports that prior to opening the ORV area, TVA was required to establish a monitoring plan designed to measure the environmental impact caused by the vehicles. The task was extremely difficult because of the previous use of the area by ORVs. He adds that "It was not a highly scientific study, but rather a modest attempt to identify the impact of vehicles on soils, woody vegetation, and wildlife within funding and manpower limitations."

The design results and evaluation of the monitoring plan are described by McEwen (1978, pp. 14–17). The reader should be reminded that the Turkey Bay ORV area lies in a humid region with a stable soil and an oak-hickory woodland ecosystem. Therefore, while some techniques of the monitoring system may apply to arid areas, the ORV effects on the resources are not comparable.

On private lands, the Council of State Governments Committee on Suggested State Legislation (1973, p. 17) recommends periodic inspections to ensure compliance with the erosion and sediment control plan and to determine whether the measures required in the plan are effective.

Close Damaged Areas

The results of the monitoring should be periodically published and the facility managers should close damaged ORV areas until they are reclaimed or until the sacrifice area evolves into a mechanical compound. Temporary closings should also be considered when the area is abnormally vulnerable, such as when there are heavy snowfalls, muddy trails, or fire hazards; after fires; or during breeding, nesting, and calving seasons. Sacrifice areas in which the resources have become so degraded as to affect resources outside the facility should be closed and reclamation efforts begun. For example, Bury and Luckenbach (Chapter 10) suggest that closing the majority of arid-area dunes is the only choice if plant and animal communities are to survive. Executive Order 11989 (Chapter 1, Fig. 1-3) provides that the federal public land manager shall:

> whenever he determines that the use of off-road vehicles will cause or is causing considerable adverse effects on the soil, vegetation, wildlife, wildlife habitat or cultural or historic resources of particular areas or trails of the public lands, immediately close such areas or trails to the type of off-road vehicle causing such effects, until such time as he determines that such adverse effects have been eliminated and that measures have been implemented to prevent future recurrence.

The U.S. Council on Environmental Quality (CEQ), which is responsible for overseeing the implementation of the executive orders (Chapter 1, Fig. 1-3), issued a memorandum interpreting this provision. According to Reames (1980, pp. 20, 21), the CEQ memo should be interpreted as meaning that "the requirements . . . are mandatory and involve not merely the authority but the obligation to make protective closures in prescribed circumstances." In determining when "considerable adverse effects" exist, the CEQ directs that the term "considerable" should be liberally construed to provide the broadest possible protection. And, finally, when "considerable adverse effects" are observed by land managers, the CEQ emphasizes that those managers "must act immediately, if possible that very day."

The U.S. Forest Service (1977, p. 91) may temporarily close ORV areas not only to prevent soil damage but to ensure adequate public safety and resolve user conflicts. For example, if significant conflicts develop between hunters and ORV users, closure should be considered. The U.S. Bureau of Land Management (1974b, Sec. 6292.4) provides that the land manager may:

> act independently of the planning system if he/she deems emergency action to close or restrict areas and trails is essential to attain the objectives of the regulations . . . .

Webb et al. (1978, pp. 229, 232) recommend that:

> Trails should be closed before the soil mantle is removed . . . . One important means of ORV management is the prevention of accelerated erosion . . . .

Reclaim Damaged Areas

According to Wilshire (1977, p. 6), reclaiming arid areas damaged by ORVs is likely to be very expensive, probably more than $2000 to $6000 per acre in sacrifice areas. After one illegally staged motorcycle race with 250 participants that broke 4.5 miles (7.2 km) of new trails with an average width of 7.9 feet (2.4 m), the reclamation costs were estimated to be more than $23,000, or $21.90 per participant per mile (1.6 km). According to Wilshire (1977, p. 8), this figure, based on a 50% shrub loss, was considered low by the official making the estimate and did not include those replantings which failed or those animals destroyed. If unrestricted ORV use is permitted in arid areas, irreversible destruction of resources will occur. The only effect of reclamation efforts is to mitigate the longterm adverse effects and reduce the soil and water erosion. Sheridan (1979, p. 58) stresses that:

> If reclamation is not technically or economically feasible, then the public land management agency should not allow ORV use in the first place.

Eroded soil cannot be replaced, and even the steps required to reduce the erosion potential may significantly modify the surface. The meaning of the term "reclamation" should be clearly and fully stated in terms of the physical and biological damages that will need to be corrected. The extent to which the permit holder or other users are responsible for reclamation and repairs of damage caused by the participants or spectators should be specified and included in the performance bond. The Geological Society of America (1977, p. 8) suggests that:

> A reclamation program should specify final contours, topsoil replacement, revegetation, drainage patterns, additional practices for control

of soil erosion and the discharge of sediment, and a schedule for completion of successive stages of work.

Reclamation costs can be assessed for specific events, but reclamation costs
for widespread random use are more difficult to calculate. Wilshire (1980) notes
that coherent plans for reclamation or a demonstration that reclamation is even
possible are not found in any documents published by the U.S. Department of
Agriculture relating to ORV use of public lands. Very few examples can be provided; see Brum et al. (Chapter 15) and Kay and Graves (Chapters 16 and 17).
However, Webb et al. (1978, p. 232) note that:

> If trails are eroded to bedrock, soil should be imported and stabilized
> to replace the displaced soil mantle. Mulches such as hay can be ap-
> plied to minimize erosion and provide a seedbed, or the modified soil
> can be loosened by plowing or discing and seeded for revegetation;
> fertilizer applications may be necessary.

A U.S. Forest Service resource assistant (Spolar, 1979, p. 284) reported on
some of his experiences in the Wenatchee National Forest, Ellensburg, Washington, as follows:

> My experience shows that grade and tread rehabilitation is best accom-
> plished by filling the old tread with plenty of brush. This slows down
> runoff and provides microsites suitable for the establishment of native
> vegetation or seeding.
>
> Four-wheel-drive routes can be water-barred and seeded. On some
> sites, if accessible, a road grader may be used to scarify the tracks. They
> may then be water-barred by hand and left for adjoining native vegeta-
> tion to invade. I plan for three to five years for satisfactory site
> recovery.
>
> Dry meadows and grasslands require scarification, soil replacement
> and protection from use for long periods of time. These sites can be
> protected with brush, fallen trees and logs.

The Geological Society of America (1977, p. 8) suggests that:

> Some ORV areas, depending on their nature and size, could be divided
> into parcels for sequential use and reclamation, thus providing the least
> inconvenience to ORV users. The use and reclamation of successive
> land units could allow reclamation plans to be modified as experience
> is gained. This practice also could ensure that the success of reclamation
> efforts is evaluated before use of another land parcel is permitted.

The reader should be reminded that the reclamation of successive land units is
not a system of rest-rotation. In the Ballinger-Deer Park Canyon area, Scott et
al. (1978, p. 56) pointed out that a rest-rotation system is not practical and
would be pointless because of the type and condition of the soil.

For private lands, the Council of State Governments Committee on Suggested State Legislation (1973, p. 12) developed a model state act for soil erosion and sediment control. The principal elements of the model act which are
applicable to the effects of ORV use include:

Establishment of a comprehensive state soil-erosion and sediment-control program applicable to different types of land use and soil conditions, with identification of areas having critical soil-erosion and sediment problems

Adoption of statewide guidelines including conservation standards for the control of erosion and sediment resulting from land-disturbing activities

Establishment of district soil erosion and sediment control programs and conservation standards consistent with the state program and guidelines

Prohibition of certain land-disturbing activities unless conducted in accordance with approved soil-erosion and sediment-control plans

Use of existing regulatory mechanisms, such as building, grading, and other permits applicable to land-disturbing activities, to implement erosion and sediment-control plan requirements

Inspection, monitoring, and reporting requirements

Penalties, injunctions, and other enforcement provisions

TRAIL USERS CODE OF ETHICS

*I will appreciate the solitude and beauty of the trail and the surrounding environment. I will respect the feelings of others toward it.

*I will do my best to preserve the natural and historic features which attracted me to the trail.

*I will not disturb plant and animal wildlife along the trail.

*I will use only established campsites and rest areas when available.

*I will reduce the litter problem by carrying out all that I take in, and more.

*I will take care to conserve the improvements that have been placed along the trail.

*I will use a trail only for its designated purpose.

*I will not promote activities or create situations that disturb others.

*I will promote the use of maps, educational materials and equipment that will help trail users achieve maximum enjoyment.

*I will exercise utmost care with open fires.

*I will not exceed my physical or technical capabilities and will travel equipped to meet emergency situations.

*I will treat property of others with the same care I would give my own property by:
   *not entering posted land
   *observing laws and regulations, and discouraging violations of them
   *getting permission before entering private property
   *not disturbing livestock, nor passing over cultivated fields.

Figure 22-3. Trail Users' code of ethics (adopted by Michigan State Department of Natural Resources Trails Advisory Council).

Closing Comment

The best management program for ORV use depends on accurate and adequate scientific information that can be used to make resource inventories, select sites, designate or zone areas, design and construct facilities, manage facilities and events, and monitor, close, and reclaim sacrifice areas. Godfrey et al. (1978, p. 599) conclude that when such information is lacking, "the ORV plan should err, if it must, on the conservative side."

Finally, the adoption of, and committment to, a users code of ethics—similar to that established by the Michigan State Department of Natural Resources Trails Advisory Council—would be best for all concerned with good management practices (Fig. 22-3).

References

American Association for the Advancement of Science Committee on Arid Lands. 1974. Off-road vehicle use. Science 184(4135):500, 501.

American Motorcyclist Association. 1982. Amateur and Semi-Professional Competition Rule Book. Westerville, Ohio, 60 pp.

Bucher, D. R. 1979. Short-Form Environmental Assessment Reports on Red Barter Enduro. U.S. Forest Service Los Padres National Forest (September 14 and December 7, 1979), California.

Bury, R. L., and E. R. Fillmore. 1977. Motorcycle area design and location. Impacts on the recreational experience of riders and non-riders. In: R. Rasor, Five State Approaches to Trailbike Recreation Facilities and Their Management. American Motorcyclist Association, Westerville, Ohio, Appendix V, pp. 61–64.

Busterud, J. 1976. Letter to Secretary of Interior on the draft environmental impact statement on the Department of Interior's implementation of Executive Order 11644 (October 8, 1976). U.S. Council on Environmental Quality, Washington, D.C., 4 pp.

Butt, J. P. 1977a. Order of the Forest Supervisor Restricting the Use of Off-Road Vehicles on the Allegheny National Forest, Pennsylvania. U.S. Forest Service, Warren, Pennsylvania, 2 pp.

Butt, J. P. 1977b. Notice of Limited Closure to Off-Road Vehicle Use, Allegheny National Forest, Pennsylvania. U.S. Forest Service, Warren, Pennsylvania, 4 pp.

California Department of Parks and Recreation. 1975. The Off-Road Vehicle, A Study Report. Sacramento, California, 62 pp.

California Department of Parks and Recreation. 1978. Summary, California Recreational Trails Plan. Sacramento, California, 44 pp.

California State Legislature. 1971. Chappie-Z'berg Off-Highway Motor Vehicle Law of 1971, as Amended. Vehicle Code, Sec. 38000 et seq., West's annotated codes.

California State Attorney General. (Undated). Brief before the Chief Forester, U.S. Forest Service in re appeal of the Sequoia National Forest off-road vehicle plan. Los Angeles, California, 14 pp.

Council of State Governments Committee on Suggested State Legislation. 1973. Model State Act for Soil Erosion and Sediment Control, Volume XXXII. Lexington, Kentucky, 19 pp.

Emetaz, R. V. 1980. Management—the Solution to the Problem. Dispersed Recreation Group. U.S. Forest Service, Pacific Northwest Region, 16 pp.

Geological Society of America. 1977. Impacts and Management of Off-Road Vehicles. Report of the Committee on Environment and Public Policy, Boulder, Colorado, 8 pp.

Godfrey, P. J., S. P. Leatherman, and P. A. Buckley. 1978. Impact of off-road vehicles on coastal ecosystems. In: Coastal Zone '78, Vol. II. American Society of Engineers, New York, pp. 581–600.

Indiana Department of Natural Resources. 1972. Off the Road Vehicle Study. Indianapolis, Indiana, 138 pp.

Knott, J. M. 1980. Reconnaissance Assessment of Erosion and Sedimentation in the Canada de los Alamos basin, Los Angeles and Ventura Counties, California. U.S. Geological Survey Water-Supply Paper 2061 prepared in cooperation with California Department of Water Resources, 26 pp.

McEwen, D. N. 1978. Turkey Bay Off-Road Vehicle Area at Land Between the Lakes. An Example of New Opportunities for Managers and Riders. Research Report No. 1, Department of Recreation, Southern Illinois University, Carbondale, January 1978, 28 pp.

McKnelly, P. K. 1980. Turkey Bay off-road vehicle area: Its use and monitoring system. In: R. N. L. Andrews and P. F. Nowak (Eds.), Off-Road Vehicle Use: A Management Challenge. U.S. Department of Agriculture and University of Michigan, Washington, D.C., pp. 91–99.

Motorcycle Industry Council, Inc. 1973. Motorcycle Park Planning and Management. Washington, D.C., 24 pp.

Motorcycle Industry Council, Inc. 1980a. The Recreational Trailbike Planner. Newport Beach, California, Vol. I, No. 10.

Motorcycle Industry Council, Inc. 1980b. Lakeview BLM provides for its own. In: The Recreational Trailbike Planner. Newport Beach,* California, Vol. I, No. 11, pp. 7, 8.

Motorcycle Industry Council, Inc. 1980c. Washington trail building workshop "Works." Wealth of information unveiled. In: The Recreational Trailbike Planner. Newport Beach,* California, Vol. I, No. 12, pp. 1, 2.

Motorcycle Industry Council, Inc. 1981. The Recreational Trailbike Planner. Newport Beach,* California, Vol. II, No. 1.

Nicholes, G. E. 1980. Creative planning. In: The Recreational Trailbike Planner. Motorcycle Industry Council, Inc., Newport Beach,* California, Vol. I, No. 10, pp. 1, 2.

Rasor, R. 1977. Five State Approaches to Trailbike Recreation Facilities and Their Management. American Motorcyclist Association, Westerville, Ohio, 64 pp.

Reames, D. S. 1980. Statement of Reasons in Support of Appeal. In the matter of Forest Service Manual Title 2300—Recreation Management Amendment 86 (Chapter 2355: Off-road vehicle use management) before the Secretary of Agriculture. Sierra Club Legal Defense Fund Inc., San Francisco, 25 pp.

Rosenberg, G. A. 1976. Regulation of off-road vehicles. Environ. Affairs 5(1): 175–206.

Scott, R., N. Ream, and D. Trammell. 1978. A resource assessment and management analysis of their Ballinger-Deer Park Canyon ORV open-use area. U.S. Forest Service, Mt. Pinos Ranger District, Los Padres National Forest, California, 62 pp.

Sheridan, D. 1979. Off-Road Vehicles on Public Land. Council on Environmental Quality. U.S. Government Printing Office, Washington, D.C., 84 pp.

Society of American Foresters. 1975. The Use of Off-Road Vehicles on Public Forest Lands: A Position of the Society of American Foresters. Washington, D.C., November 12, 1975.

Spolar, T. J. 1979. ORV site restorations: In: R. Ittner, D. R. Potter, J. K. Agee, and S. Anschell (Eds.), Recreational Impact on Wildlands Conference Proceedings, Seattle, Washington, October 27–29, 1978, U.S. Forest Service No. R-6-001-1979. Washington, D.C., pp. 284–285.

U.S. Bureau of Land Management. 1974a. Final Environmental Impact Statement, Proposed Barstow-Las Vegas Motorcycle Race. California State Office, Sacramento, California, October 22, 1974, 390 pp.

U.S. Bureau of Land Management. 1974b. Public lands. Use of off-road vehicles. Fed. Reg. 39(73):13612 et seq.

U.S. Bureau of Land Management. 1974c. Special Land Use Application and Permit Application. East Desert Area manager, Serial No. 04 060-SLY-133, 16 pp., 11 maps.

U.S. Bureau of Land Management. 1977. Environmental Assessment Record for Interim Critical Management Program Area No. 37, Cadiz Valley/Danby Lake. Riverside District Office, Riverside, California, 236 pp.

U.S. Bureau of Land Management. 1980. The California Desert Conservation Area. Final Environmental Impact Statement and Proposed Plan. California State Office, Sacramento, September 1980, 273 pp., 22 maps.

U.S. Bureau of Outdoor Recreation. 1975. Off-Road Vehicle Use on Federal Lands. Washington, D.C., 16 pp.

U.S. Bureau of Outdoor Recreation. 1976. Draft Environmental Impact Statement on the Departmental Implementation of Executive Order 11644 Pertaining to Use of Off-Road Vehicles on the Public Lands. U.S. Department of the Interior, Washington, D.C., 119 pp.

U.S. Congress. 1977. Mineral Lands and Mining. Public Law 95-87, 91 Stat. 486, 30 USC 1265 et seq.

U.S. Council on Environmental Quality. 1971, Third Annual Report, pp. 139; 1974, Fifth Annual Report, pp. 207–210; Sixth Annual Report, pp. 243–245; 1976, Seventh Annual Report, pp. 93–94; 1977, Eighth Annual Report, pp. 81–83; 1978, Ninth Annual Report, pp. 303–305; 1979, Tenth Annual Report, pp. 421–422; 1980, Eleventh Annual Report, pp. 48, 357. U.S. Government Printing Office, Washington, D.C.

U.S. Department of Defense. 1973. Use of Off-Road Vehicles. Draft environmental impact statement, Office of the Assistant Secretary (Health and Environment), Washington, D.C.

U.S. Department of the Interior Task Force Study. 1971. Off-Road Recreation Vehicles, Pacific Southwest Region. San Francisco, California, 123 pp.

U.S. Forest Service. 1976. Environmental Analysis Report; Off-Road Vehicle Use on National Forest Land. Off-Road Vehicle Management Plan for Trabuco Planning Unit, Cleveland National Forest, Trabuco Ranger District, California, 128 pages.

U.S. Forest Service. 1977. Final Environmental Statement. Off-Road Vehicles. Allegheny National Forest, Eastern Region, Warren, Pennsylvania, 216 pp.

U.S. Soil Conservation Service. 1979. National Soils Handbook Notice 42, NSH PART II, Guide for Rating Soil Limitations for Motorcycle Vehicle Trails, Section 403.6(b). Washington, D.C., April 19, 1979.

Webb, R. H., H. C. Ragland, W. H. Godwin, and D. Jenkins. 1978. Environmental effects of soil property changes with off-road vehicle use. Environ. Management 2(3):219-233.

Wells, C. 1980. Recreational Trailbike Program. An Outline of the Basic Criteria Needed to Develop a Trailbike Program. Idaho State Parks and Recreation Department, Boise, Idaho, 18 pp.

Wernex, J. J. 1979. Successful methods of design and construction for managing impact on trailbike trails. In: R. Ittner, D. R. Potter, J. K. Agee, and S. Anschell (Eds.), Recreational Impact on Wildlands. Conference Proceedings, Seattle, Washington, October 27-29, 1978. U.S. Forest Service No. R-6-001-1979, Washington, D.C., pp. 250-252.

Wilshire, H. G. 1977. Orphaning Desert Land—Dirt Bikes Move Faster Than Planners. Cry California 13(1):5-7.

Wilshire, H. G. 1980. Overview of ORV Impacts on the Environment. Speech presented at the Conference on Off-Road Vehicle Use: A Management Challenge at Ann Arbor, Michigan. Cosponsored by the U.S. Department of Agriculture and University of Michigan, March 1980, Menlo Park, California.

Wilshire, H. G., and J. K. Nakata. 1976. Off-road vehicle effects on California's Mojave Desert. Calif. Geol. 29(6):123-132, 139.

23
Regulations and Education[1]

William J. Kockelman

Introduction

Regulations and education are required to make the management practices discussed in Chapter 22 effective. In addition, techniques for enforcing the regulations, penalties for their violation, and methods of raising revenue are required. The discussions in this chapter are also directed to meeting the needs of ORV users, protecting resources, and minimizing conflicts with other users. Some of the topics discussed were introduced in a 1977 Geological Society of America (GSA) committee report. The laws and techniques discussed are based on experience and accepted jurisprudence; they are believed to be applicable to the recreation programs of federal, state, and local units of government in the United States.

Regulating ORVs

Off-road vehicle registration, operator licensing, proper equipment, safety inspection, prudent operation, and equipment testing are necessary to meet user needs, protect resources, and minimize conflicts. According to Baldwin and Stoddard (1973, p. 42), one of the most obvious needs is for states to establish comprehensive legislation and regulation of all ORVs. The Geological Society of

---

[1]The views and conclusions contained in this chapter are based on the author's studies or experiences and do not necessarily represent the official viewpoint or policy of any U.S. government agency.

America (1977, p. 7) recommended that state legislatures provide for the registration and inspection of ORVs and the licensing of their operators. In their ORV study, the U.S. Department of the Interior Task Force Study (1971, p. 67) concludes:

> that it is at the State level where responsibility for basic legislative authority regarding the use of these vehicles as a recreation activity must be assumed. Such legislation should include vehicle registration, operator licensing, fees, liability coverage requirements, and safety requirements. State laws should also provide proper regulation for State land use and, where appropriate and constitutional, for local public land and private land use to assure that the environmental impact caused by the use of these vehicles will be minimal.

Each unit of government having jurisdiction—federal, state, or local—should adopt relatively uniform equipment and operating regulations for ORVs. For example, the regulations would deal with control of noise, sparks, and other emissions; prohibition of ORVs on unmarked trails or in undesignated areas and unzoned lands; inspection of brakes, lights, and other equipment; possession of an operator's license and a safety inspection certificate; visible registration numbers; rules of the road and speed limits; financial liability and responsibility; operation while intoxicated; negligent or careless operation; and the use or carrying of firearms while operating ORVs.

Registration and Licensing

All ORVs should be registered by a state except for those operated on the owner's property. Applicants should pay a fee and receive a registered certificate number. Dealers should register the vehicle, affix the required identification number, transfer the fee to, and record the registration with, the state. According to the Motorcycle Industry Council, Inc. (1981b), 16 states have provided for registration of ORVs.

Baldwin and Stoddard (1973, p. 55) suggest that every ORV should display its registration number as a permanent label. The most comprehensive state legislation is the Chappie-Z'Berg OHV Act (California State Legislature, 1971). This act provides for issuance and display of identification plates; application for identification; change of address; identification kept with vehicle; stolen, lost, or damage identification; renewal and transfer of title; and fees. All ORV users should be licensed by a state to operate a particular class of vehicle, but according to the Motorcycle Industry Council, Inc. (1981b) only two states have provided for ORV licensing—Maryland and Ohio. The U.S. Bureau of Land Management (1974, Sec. 6295.2) provides that:

> No person may operate an off-road vehicle on public lands without a valid operator's license or learner's permit unless accompanied by an adult who has a valid operator's license and who is responsible for the acts of that individual.

Equipment

All ORVs should be required to have proper mufflers to prevent any unusual or excessive noise, brakes in good working condition, spark arresters, and lights. Some states require lights, brakes, mufflers, spark arresters, and pollution-control devices (California State Legislature, 1971, Sec. 38325 et seq.). According to the Motorcycle Industry Council, Inc. (1981b) a few states require helmets; only one state requires reflector material. Safety equipment is required by many states for on-road motorcycles (Motorcycle Industry Council, Inc., 1980b), but not for ORVs.

The U.S. Bureau of Land Management (1974, Sec. 6295.3) provides that no ORV may be operated on public lands unless equipped with proper brakes and a muffler in good working condition. On some public lands, no ORV may be operated unless equipped with a properly installed spark arrester capable of trapping at least 80% of the carbon particles at all flow rates for at least 1000 hours of normal use. Baldwin and Stoddard (1973, p. 57) recommended that no ORV be operated if it emits obnoxious exhaust fumes, or if it makes unusual or excessive noise and:

> An off-road vehicle that produces a sound level of 73 decibels or more on the "A" scale at 50 feet shall be deemed to make an unusual or excessive noise. Sound pressure levels in decibels shall be measured on the "A" scale of a sound level meter having characteristics defined by American Standards Association S1.4-1961 "General Purpose Sound Meter."

Operation

The following operating regulations are applicable to all lands—federal, state, local, and private. ORVs shall not be operated at any time:

In a reckless, careless, or negligent manner
In excess of established speed limits
While the operator is under the influence of alcohol or drugs
In a manner likely to cause damage to or disturbance of the land, water, animal, plant, or other natural resources
In the evening or night without lighted headlights and taillights
Without brakes, muffler, and spark arrester in good working order
Without a valid operator's license or vehicle registration in the possession of the operator
Off paved cycleways or outside sacrifice areas
On any private property without permission of the owner or his agent
If the operator is carrying firearms or bows unless unstrung, unloaded, and securely encased

These operating regulations have been required by several states and by federal agencies in accordance with Executive Order 11644 (Chapter 1, Fig. 1-3) which provides that each federal public land agency shall:

develop and publish, within one year of the date of this order, regulations prescribing operating conditions for off-road vehicles on the public lands. These regulations shall be directed at protecting resource values, preserving public health, safety, and welfare, and minimizing use conflicts.

For example, the U.S. Forest Service (Butt, 1977, pp. 124, 126), U.S. Bureau of Land Management (1974, Sec. 6295.2), the California State Legislature (1971, Sec. 38305 et seq.), and the Washington State Legislature (1971, Secs. 46.09.120 and 46.09.130) have all adopted operating regulations. In addition the Washington State Legislature (1971, Sec. 46.09.180) has empowered any city, county, or other political subdivision or any state agency to regulate ORV operation on public lands and other properties under its jurisdiction by regulations or ordinances provided they are not less stringent than those of the state. The Pennsylvania State Legislature (1981) specifies the following noise limitations:

	DBA measured perpendicularly 50 ft. from source	
	35 mph or less	More than 35 mph
Motorcycles and trailbikes	90	92
4-wheel vehicles		
Over 7000 lbs.	90	92
Any other motor vehicle	82	86

The prohibition against operations off paved cycleways or cross country is one of the most important. The TVA specifically prohibits driving in woods, fields, foot trails, or utility rights-of-way (McEwen, 1978, p. 26). In addition, ORV users should be prohibited from littering or causing any other environmental damage. For example, the California State Legislature [1971, Secs. 38320.(a) and 38321.(a)] provides that:

No person shall throw or deposit, nor shall the registered owner or the driver, if such owner is not then present in the vehicle, aid or abet in the throwing or depositing, upon any area, public or private, any bottle, can, garbage, glass, nail, offal, paper, wire, any substance likely to injure or kill wild or domestic animal or plant life or damage traffic using such area, or any noisome, nauseous or offensive matter of any kind.

Any person who drops, dumps, deposits, places, or throws, or causes or permits to be dropped, dumped, deposited, placed, or thrown, upon any area any material described . . . shall immediately remove the material or cause it to be removed.

In addition, Baldwin and Stoddard (1973, p. 58) suggest that the provisions of the state motor-vehicle financial-responsibility laws apply to ORVs; that the application of such laws not be restricted to public roads but of general application; and that the ORV operator and owner be responsible and held account-able to the owner of any lands where trees, shrubs, crops, or other property have been damaged as a result of travel over their premises. Of course, events should be carefully regulated and permits required for each one (Chapter 22). For example, the U.S. Bureau of Land Management (1974, Sec. 6293.1) specifies that:

> No person or association of persons may conduct any race, rally, meet, contest, or other type of organized event involving the use of off-road vehicles, on public lands without first obtaining a permit to do so from the authorized officer . . . .

Trespass

Church (1979, pp. 29-33) proposes new model legislation to protect private owners from recreational trespass. The model act lists prohibited activities and provides for: limiting landowners' liability, enforcement procedures, restitution to landowner for damage and attorneys' fees, punitive damages, revocation of license, seizure of property, and arrest without a warrant. After finding that ORV activity has adversely impacted many areas of the county, the Santa Clara County Board of Supervisors (1980) adopted an ordinance prohibiting ORV use on any lands owned or occupied by another except where a use permit has been obtained (Fig. 23-1).

Enforcing Regulations

Consistent enforcement of ORV regulations and penalties is necessary to accomplish the goals of meeting user needs, protecting resources, and avoiding conflicts. Enforcement of ORV use is difficult; LeValley's (1979, p. 72) observa-tions illustrate the point:

> Most of us who patrol forest roads and trails have attempted to stop a trailbike rider; and we are well aware a special skill is needed to appre-hend one who will not stop willingly. Pursuing trailbikes with a patrol car is not at all practical and even trailbike versus trailbike is extremely hazardous. In fact, chasing fleeing trailbikes at all, for the most part, is an exercise in futility.

Without enforcement and penalties, all the other work—resource inventory, designation or zoning, site selection, facility design, management, and regula-tions—would be for nought. State legislatures, local governments, and federal public-land managers should provide for enforcement of the regulations, such as providing adequate enforcement personnel, techniques, and methods for en-forcement; immediate prevention of any further damage; and appropriate penalties.

Particular attention should be given to the enforcement of the requirement that ORVs stay on paved cycleways or within sacrifice areas. ORV users should

ORDINANCE NO. NS-1019.1

An Ordinance Amending Article 7 of Chapter II of Division B-12 of the Santa Clara County Ordinance Code to Include all Types of Off-Road Motor Vehicles and to Prohibit Operation of Off-Road Motor Vehicles on Private Property Without a Permit

The Board of Supervisors of the County of Santa Clara, State of California, do ordain as follows:

SECTION 1. Findings and Intent.

The Board finds that off-road motor vehicle activity has a strong potential for adversely impacting upon both the site of the activity, the surrounding neighborhood and surrounding land, and has adversely impacted upon many areas of the county.

The Board finds that off-road motor vehicle use has resulted in the destruction of natural soil stabilizer, soil displacement, stripping of vegetation and mechanical erosion. The Board finds that these impacts have greatly reduced soil moisture, increased temperature increase in the soil, and increased runoff of rain water. The Board finds that these effects combine to increase the erosion potential and decrease the land's ability to restore its barriers to erosion.

The Board finds that regulation is necessary to avoid or mitigate soil erosion, destruction of natural vegetation and wildlife habitat, fire hazard, and similar adverse environmental consequences of off-road motor vehicle activites. Regulation is also necessary to assure the participants and spectators at motor vehicle events of adequate crowd control measure, parking areas, and sanitation facilities. Regulation is necessary to minimize disruption of the surrounding neighborhood as the result of noise, dust, litter, and traffic congestion generated by the motor vehicle activities. Regulation is necessary to reduce unauthorized off-road vehicle operation on private and public land since such use can result in the adverse environmental impacts, including soil erosion.

This article is intended to prohibit off-road motor vehicle operation on property in private ownership as well as public land unless such activities are being conducted under the authority of a valid permit or by permission of the public authority.

SECTION 2.

Article 7 of Chapter II of Division B-12 of the Santa Clara County Ordinance Code is amended to read:

ARTICLE 7. OFF-ROAD MOTOR VEHICLE ACTIVITIES

Sec. B12-90. Off-Road Motor Vehicles Defined.

As used in this article, "off-road motor vehicle" includes, but is not limited to, the following:

(a) Any motorcycle or motor driven cycle;

(b) Any motor vehicle commonly referred to as a sand buggy, dune buggy, or all terrain vehicle;

(c) Any motor vehicle commonly referred to as a jeep, pickup truck, or four-wheel drive vehicle.

(d) Any motor vehicle when such motor vehicle is operated on land to which this article applies.

Sec. B12-91. Regulation of Operation of Off-Road Motor Vehicles; Prohibition.

No person shall operate an of-road motor vehicle on any lands owned or occupied by another, except on property for which a use permit has been issued pursuant to this article.

No owner, tenant, lessee of real property or other person shall authorize or allow off-road motor vehicle operation, riding, racing, parking, or hill climbing on such property without first obtaining the permit provided for under this article. No person shall operate off-road motor vehicles or otherwise engage in off-road motor vehicle operation, riding, hill climbing, or other activities for which a permit is required hereunder unless the necessary permit has been obtained. The burden shall be on the off-road motor vehicle operator to ascertain that a permit has been issued by viewing the original permit prior to engaging in off-road motor vehicle operation, riding, racing, hill climbing, or other activities for which a permit is required. No person shall knowingly violate any terms or conditions of a permit issued hereunder.

Sec. B12-92. Application; Fees; Powers of Secretary.

Any owner, tenant, or lessee of real property desiring to allow off-road motor vehicle riding, racing, or hill climbing on such property shall file an application therefor with the central permit office.

For the purpose of recovering the administrative expense in processing an application for a permit, a filing fee in an amount prescribed by resolution of the board of supervisors shall accompany the application.

The secretary of the planning commission shall hear and decide all applications for permits authorized by this article.

Sec. B12-93. Time and Place of Hearing; Notice; Grant of Permit.

Upon the filing of sufficient and proper application and the payment of a filing fee, the secretary of the planning commission shall fix a time and place for a public hearing.

At least five (5) days before the date of said hearing, the secretary of the planning commission shall cause notice of such hearing to be mailed to owners of all property within three hundred (300) feet from the exterior boundaries of the property upon which an application for a proposed use has been made. Said notice shall be mailed to said property owners at their last known address using the addresses from the last adopted tax roll of the County of Santa Clara.

Upon the grant of an application for a permit, the secretary of the planning commission shall prepare and deliver to the applicant a formal statement thereof stating the fact of the grant and any conditions attached thereto. No decision of the secretary of the planning commission shall become final upon an application for a permit authorized by this ordinance until the time in which an appeal may be filed with the planning commission has elapsed without an appeal having been filed.

Sec, B12-94. Permit required; Issuance; Conditions.

A permit issued pursuant to this article shall be required when any person operates an off-road motor vehicle on private property. Following the public hearing, the Secretary shall issue the off-road motor vehicle event permit if all of the following findings are made:

(1) The off-road motor vehicle event or activity, if conducted at the proposed location, would not be in violation of the Zoning Ordinance (NS-1200, as amended) or of any other County Ordinance;

(2) The property in question is suitable in terms of terrain, size and location for off-road motor vehicle activities of the nature and scope requested by applicant; and

(3) The off-road motor vehicle event or activities can be conducted without adverse environmental consequences and without adverse effect upon the health, safety, tranquillity and general welfare of persons residing within the surrounding area and the surrounding land. The potential adverse effect upon such persons is to be measured in terms of noise, dust, flood hazard, litter, soil erosion, and traffic congestion generated by the proposed off-road motor vehicle activities.

In issuing a permit under this article, the secretary may impose conditions intended to avoid or mitigate potential adverse environmental consequences and to preverve the public health, safety, tranquillity and general welfare. The secretary may refer the application to any county department, agency, committee, official or employee and to other public entities or agencies for review, comment and assistance in formulating conditions of approval. In filing an application for a permit hereunder, the applicant shall agree and assure that police, health, fire and other county offices to whom the application is referred shall be given reasonable access to the property for the purpose of inspection and to insure compliance with the permit when issued. Conditions imposed by the secretary may include but are not limited to: date(s) and hours of off-road motor vehicle activities, maximum number of participants, fire protection, traffic control, parking requirements, crowd control, noise attenuation, litter control and cleanup, water supply and sanitation facilities. Conditions imposed by the secretary may also include limitation with regard to use when soils are wet.

Sec. B12-95. Permit Appeal Procedure.

Section 12-95.1: Appeal from decision of secretary of the planning commission. Within fifteen (15) calendar days after the decision of the secretary of the planning commission on an application for a permit, any person dissatisfied with the action of the secretary of the planning commission may file an appeal to the planning commission by filing such appeal with the central permit office. At the time of the filing of the appeal, the appellant shall pay a nonrefundable filing fee in an amount prescribed by resolution of the board of supervisors,

Sec. B12-96. Exemptions.

The provisions of this article shall not apply to any of the following:

1. Off-road motor vehicle operation on real property by the owner, tenant, lessee or employee thereof of such property and members of owner's, tenant's or lessee's immediate family. For purposes of this exemption, "owner" is deemed to be the owner of record and a "tenant" or "lessee" is any person or persons entitled to exclusive possession of the property with a minimum month-to-month tenancy. For the purposes of this exemption, "immediate family" is deemed to include spouse, children, grandchildren, parents, grandparents, brothers and sisters. Operaion of an off-road vehicle by an employee shall be exempt when such operation is within the course and scope of employment.

2. Off-road motor vehicle operation on real property having a valid use permit or other entitlement under the County Zoning Ordinance to conduct such activities.

3. Off-road motor vehicle operation on any paved (asphalt or concrete) surface.

SECTION 3. Violation.

A violation of any provision of this article shall be punishable as a misdemeanor.

PASSED AND ADOPTED by the Board of Supervisors of the County of Santa Clara, State of California, on May 13, 1980, by the following vote:

AYES: Supervisors — Cortese, Steinberg, Diridon.

NOES: Supervisors — None.

ABSENT: Supervisors — McCorquodale,, Wilson.

GERALDINE F. STEINBERG,
Chairperson, pro tempore
Board of Supervisors

DONALD M. RAINS,
Attest: Clerk
Board of Supervisors

(May 27, 1980 - L50)

Figure 23-1. County ORV Ordinance (from Santa Clara County Board of Supervisors, 1980).

be expected to know all public and private land ownerships and the regulations for operating ORVs within the state and on public or private lands. It is important to emphasize that only those facilities open to ORV use need be marked. If a facility or area is not marked "open," the user must presume it is "closed."

ORV Recognition

Both managers and enforcement personnel should be able to recognize the different types of motorcycles so that they can determine if the vehicles are being used properly. For example, highway and dual-purpose motorcycles are easy to identify because they are equipped with license plates, head- and taillights, mirrors, horns, and other equipment required by both federal and state laws. The Motorcycle Industry Council, Inc. (1980b) has provided an aid for identifying off-highway vehicles. Recognition is important for enforcing certain regulations—noise, for example. Motorcross motorcycles are inherently louder than other ORVs because they are intended by the manufacturers for closed course competition events only, in other words just in sacrifice areas or mechanical compounds which would be located in non-noise-sensitive areas or would be fully soundproofed. The Motorcycle Industry Council, Inc. (1980a, p. 3) discusses some of the different types in their periodical *The Recreational Trailbike Planner*.

Enforcement Techniques

Patrol persons and patrol vehicles are needed for enforcement. Fixed-wing or helicopter aircraft, ORVs, or car patrols may be used as appropriate, the objective being to concentrate manpower in order to contact as many ORV users as possible. Parking areas for ORVs and commonly used access points to ORV facilities are the main targets. A patrol person should be fully authorized to issue citations, hold a valid Red Cross first-aid card, and be in an identifiable official uniform. Night patrols, if deemed necessary, should consist of two patrol persons. When the potential for a serious problem exists, contact should be made with a state or local police officer; vehicular pursuits should also be handled by state or local police officers.

A complete communication system is essential for effective enforcement. For example, the U.S. Forest Service (1977a, p. 119) law enforcement plan for ORVs provides that:

> Centralized communications services (dispatching) will be provided by Allegheny National Forest personnel, during regular working hours of the Allegheny National Forest personnel, or during any other periods designated. This is normally 7:30 a.m. through 4:00 p.m., Monday through Friday, except National holidays. On weekdays and holidays during primary summer recreation season, Forest Service Radio System communications and monitoring is available through Kinzua Point Information Center at Allegheny Reservoir (10:30 a.m.–6:00 p.m.). This monitoring service will be provided on 24 hour, 7 day per week basis by the Warren County Sheriff Department. To facilitate communications during use of aircraft, consideration will be given to use of a loud speaker system to establish air to ground contact.

In addition to the patrol persons assigned by federal, state, and local public-land managers, all other federal, state, and local law-enforcement personnel should cooperate in enforcing regulations on any public and private lands where they possess such powers. For example, under the wildlife protection agreements, signed by the Tennessee Valley Authority and the states of Kentucky and Tennessee, the TVA patrol persons have the power of arrest to enforce their ORV use regulations (McEwen, 1978, p. 13). In the case of the Allegheny National Forest, the U.S. Forest Service (1977a, p. 111) relies upon local law-enforcement agencies.

Each patrol person and other law-enforcement officer should be empowered to issue citations. A typical citation would include the name, address, and license number of the alleged violator; name of the issuing patrol person; violation alleged to have been committed; amount of penalty, forfeiture, and other costs; date, time, and place to appear in court; and a deposit and stipulation by the defendant in lieu of a court appearance.

Executive Order 11644 provides that public land managers shall establish procedures for the enforcement of their regulations and may enter into an agreement with state or local government agencies for cooperative enforcement of laws and regulations relating to ORV use. Baldwin and Stoddard (1973, p. 60) suggest that state police, regional statepark police, conservation officers, regional and assistant regional conservation officers, forest rangers, and all peace officers enforce ORV regulations.

Issuance of warning notices instead of citations should be the exception. ORV user behavior such as complete disregard for state laws, local ordinances, or facility regulations; excessive or abusive language; threats to the patrol persons or repeated violations should always result in a formal citation. For example, the U.S. Forest Service (1977a, p. 113) provides for firm and aggressive law enforcement in areas closed to ORVs.

A University of Wisconsin Law School professor (Church, 1979, p. 30) in a report cosponsored by the National Rifle Association (among others) recommends in proposed model legislation that the following be prohibited:

> Recreational trespass
> Destruction or removal of any property of the landowner or operator, or vandalism of any sort while engaged in recreational use of the land of another
> Littering while engaged in recreational use of the land of another
> Failure to leave any gates, doors, fences, roadblocks and obstacles, or signs in the condition in which they were found, while engaged in recreational use of the land of another

It should be *prima facie* evidence that an ORV user has trespassed if he is on land of another without the owner's permission. The absence of posting, by itself, should not be sufficient to imply consent. It should be *prima facie* evidence that an ORV user is in violation of the facility regulations if such user is off a paved cycleway in a cyclepark or cycleway system or has crossed the marked or fenced boundaries of a mechanical compound or sacrifice area.

Enforcement Remedies

In addition to issuing a citation, there are several other remedies that a patrol person or law-enforcement officer can take. These remedies range from one suggested by the Motorcycle Industry Council, Inc. (1973, p. 11):

> Any rider not obeying reserve rules should be warned, and if need be, evicted. Motorcycle patrols are often used to escort a rider from a distant part of the reserve to the office or main gate.

to that suggested by the Geological Society of America (1977, p. 7):

> State legislatures, local governments, and the Congress should give enforcement officers power to (1) cite ORV operators for violations, (2) impound unregistered vehicles and those operated by unlicensed persons, and (3) immediately immobilize an ORV when its operator trespasses on private land or is found in closed areas or unzoned lands.

Obviously the remedy "Misuse a bike, lose a bike" is the most effective. In addition, private and public nuisance actions are available. A nuisance is defined as anything which is injurious to health, or is indecent or offensive to the senses, or is an obstruction to the free use of property—public or private. Some courts have construed this definition to apply to threatening as well as to existing nuisances. In the case of a public nuisance affecting an entire community or neighborhood, state legislatures provide that city or district attorneys are authorized to remedy the nuisance. A private nuisance occurs when the property rights of a private party have been injured; remedies include civil action or abatement. State legislatures usually provide that the nuisance may be stopped and damages recovered. In the case of ORV noise, the California State Legislature (1971, Sec. 38370) provides special limits.

In the case of aggravated violations, Church (1979, pp. 32, 33) suggests seizure of the ORV if the culprit refuses or is "unable to pay promptly a deposit in the amount of the forfeiture, costs and taxes applicable . . . ." Church suggests arrest without a warrant if the user refuses to accept a citation, to make a deposit, or to identify himself satisfactorily. Aggravated violations are defined as:

> Driving of any motorized vehicle in such a way as to endanger others
> Intentional or accidental lighting of a fire, or conduct that is otherwise inherently dangerous to persons or property
> Shooting of any firearm or bow and arrow or the setting of traps for animals

Costs of Enforcement

Additional personnel at the local, state, and federal levels are required to enforce the regulations. Sheridan (1979, p. 50) notes that some state and federal public-land managers have "faced squarely the problem of enforcing ORV regulations" while others have stated that enforcement would depend on levels of funding and manpower.

Few public-land managers have adequate personnel and equipment. For example, the Indiana Department of Natural Resources asked its land managers whether they had the personnel necessary for additional ORV supervision and maintenance. Forty-six said they did not; four said they did; and one did not respond. Asked the same question, 76 enforcement officers said they did not; 17 said they did; and 20 did not respond. In addition, many state land managers indicated that they would also need more equipment if ORV activities were expanded in their areas (Sheridan, 1979, p. 50). The Indiana Department of Natural Resources (1972, p. 72) concluded that it simply did not have the personnel to supervise or maintain ORV trails or areas on its lands:

> Maintenace of quality in recreational environment is related closely to constant and efficient management of all facilities. Poor maintenance, whether in high-use areas or in natural settings, encourages further vandalism, litter, and the destruction of many native plants . . . .

The costs of enforcement personnel and their equipment should be paid for by the ORV user of the facility. All enforcement costs should be borne by the ORV user through a system of user fees or special-event fees.

Penalties

Enforcement without strict penalties is ineffective. Some of the penalties that should be considered are fines, imprisonment, restitution, punitive damages, and license revocation. All of these penalties have been suggested or enacted as law. For example, Executive Order 11644 provides that federal public-land agency heads shall, where authorized by law, prescribe appropriate penalties for violation of regulations. The U.S. Forest Service (1977a, p. 93) provides "Violators shall be subject to a fine of not more than $500 or imprisonment by not more than six months, or both (16 U.S. Code 551)."

Church (1979, p. 32) in his proposed model legislation provides for reasonable punitive damages and for restitution as follows:

> A court to which any forfeiture or deposit is paid hereunder may apply all or part of that amount paid over to the owner of the land in question, if it concludes that justice would thereby be served, as recompense to such owner for damages or attorney's fees or inconvenience suffered due to the violations of this Act that gave rise to the forfeiture or deposit. Such restitutionary payment shall not prejudice or affect any other civil action which such owner may have for such damages or inconvenience.

The California State Legislature (1971, Sec. 38317) provides that whenever reckless driving of an ORV causes bodily injury to any person, the person driving the vehicle shall, upon conviction thereof, be punished by:

imprisonment in the county jail for not less than 30 days not more than six months, or by fine of not less than one hundred dollars ($100) nor more than five hundred dollars ($500) or by both such fine and imprisonment.

In addition to a fine of not less than $25.00, the Washington State Legislature [1971, Sec. 46.09.130(2)] provides that the ORV owner or operator:

shall be liable for any damage to property including damage to trees, shrubs, growing crops injured as a result of travel . . . . The owner of such property may recover from the person responsible three times the amount of damage.

Enforcement—An Educational Technique

Emetaz (1980, p. 15) emphasizes that law enforcement can be an educational tool, that a good, positive program of law enforcement that develops rapport between users and enforcement personnel will lead to self-policing by the users themselves, and that:

The law enforcement officer often becomes somewhat of a mediator. It is important that the law enforcement officer is able to relate to both groups on a logical and reasonable level. An important goal of a positive program is not to arrest violators but to educate the user. One cannot go from zero enforcement to 100% enforcement without alienating the very people that we want compliance from. An enforcement program that allows for personal contacts and exchange of information will build rapport and create a great deal of self-policing by the users themselves.

Raising Revenues

Money is needed to plan, acquire, design, develop, and maintain ORV facilities. In addition, the monitoring of ORV use, the preparing and adopting of regulations, and the enforcing of those regulations requires money. The cost of paving cycleways, stabilizing sacrifice areas, and constructing mechanical compounds is high. For example, Rasor (1977, p. 29) reports that trail costs for the Washington State Department of Natural Resources vary "from $3,000 . . . to $12,000 per mile."

Sources of funds include facility user fees, registration and license fees, excise or sales taxes, manufacturer's taxes, state or local bond issues, oil and gasoline taxes, donations, state and federal recreational grants, event fees (including participant, spectator, and concessionaire fees), and fines and forfeitures collected from violators of ORV regulations. Baldwin and Stoddard (1973, p. 55) suggest that revenues from registration fees should be used to cover not only registration costs but enforcement costs and to compensate private property owners for damage when the identity of the vehicle or operator cannot be determined.

State legislatures and the U.S. Congress can enact laws to raise the necessary revenues. The primary source of such revenues should be the ORV user. Examples of how some states have raised revenues include:

> Florida Department of Agriculture and Consumer Services (1979) in the case of the Buttgenbach Mine ORV facility established a permit system to provide funds for day-to-day operation and maintenance. The fee is $12.00 per year; $1.00 per month if issued for less than 1 year, with a minimum fee of $3.00.

> Idaho earmarks 1% of gasoline taxes up to $300,000 per year for ORV facilities (Wells, 1980).

> New Hampshire requires snowmobile users to pay $9.00 per year registration fee ($15.00 per year for out-of-staters). Of the funds collected from registration fees, 45% are earmarked for use by the Bureau of Off-Highway Recreational Vehicles, 40% for the Fish and Game Department, and 15% for the Department of Safety. The state makes grants-in-aid to local governments and to ORV clubs for the construction and maintenance of snowmobile trails (Sheridan, 1979, p. 49).

> Wisconsin created a Motorcycle Recreation Program to assist local government to meet ORV needs. Cost sharing is available for acquisition (100%), development (75%), operation (50%), and maintenance (50%) of land and ORV facilities. The money comes from an addition of $2.00 to the annual registration fee of all motorcycles (Motorcycle Industry Council, Inc., 1980c, p. 7).

The Missouri Department of Natural Resources for the Finger Lakes ORV facility obtained funding for initial park development through a grant from the Federal Land and Water Conservation Fund. In addition, the state raised revenues by entering into an agreement or service contract with club promoters for the use of the facilities for competitive events (Fig. 23-2).

Washington State obtains its revenues from a $5.00 registration fee and a percentage of a tax on gasoline used by ORVs. The money is distributed to state and local units of government on the basis of the amount of present or proposed ORV facilities, thereby providing funding only for those facilities actually being constructed or planned (Rasor, 1977, p. 29). The Washington State Legislature [1971, Sec. 46.09.170(3)] provides:

> ORV moneys shall be expended only for the acquisition, planning, development, maintenance, and management of off-road vehicle trails and areas; for education and law enforcement programs related to non-highway vehicles; to construct campgrounds and trailheads which are necessary for the convenient use of designated ORV trails and areas; and to maintain those campgrounds and trailheads specifically constructed with ORV moneys.

The California State Legislature (1971, Sec. 38225) created an ORV fund as the principal source of money for purchasing and developing ORV facilities. According to the California Department of Parks and Recreation (1978b, pp. 48–50) the fund's monies come from ORV registration fees, ORV gasoline taxes, user charges at state facilities, in-lieu-of property taxes, and from fines and forfeitures collected for violations of the ORV code. Of the $15.00 biennial registration fee, $6.00 goes into the fund. Of the $15.00 in-lieu-of property tax, $4.00 goes into the fund.

The California State Legislature (1971, Sec. 38270) provides that the State Department of Parks and Recreation utilize the fund to plan, acquire, develop, construct, maintain, administer, and conserve ORV trails and areas. The California State Legislature [1971, Sec. 38240.(b)(2)] further provides that the in-lieu-of property tax be used for controlling the operation of motor vehicles in areas off the highways where the operation of motor vehicles is restricted or prohibited. The California State Legislature [1971, Sec. 38270(a)] also provides that some of the funds be made available for matching grants to local government for ORV facilities. Pertinent excerpts from the state law are set forth in Figure 23-3. In addition, the states of Colorado, Delaware, Indiana, Iowa, Maryland, Michigan, Ohio, and Utah provide for some ORV funding. According to the Motorcycle Industry Council, Inc. (1981b), the revenue sources include registration fees, gasoline tax refunds, state appropriations, and other fees.

STATE OF MISSOURI
SERVICE CONTRACT

The agreement made and entered this ___ day of _____ 19 , between the Department of Natural Resources, State of Missouri, hereinafter referred to as OWNER, and Columbia Motor Sports, a not-for-profit corporation, duly incorporated and registered under the laws of Missouri, hereinafter referred to as CONTRACTOR, witnesseth:

1. **Services.** The Contractor agrees to perform for the Owner, in a proper and competent manner, the following specific services at Finger Lake State Park, Boone County, Missouri, on a maximum of (number) dates during the period from _____, 19__, to _____, 19 , such dates subject to approval by Owner at least thirty (30) days in advance:

a. Complete administration of a motorcycle race program; such administration shall include printing of entry forms, handling registration at the site, collecting a motorcycle entry fee and a spectator admission fee, providing judges and timers for all events, and other items deemed necessary by the contracting parties for such administration.

b. Contractor agrees to provide suitable trophies to award to participants in each event.

c. Contractor agrees to provide a suitable concession operation, including food and drink, and sufficient personnel to properly operate said concession service.

d. Contractor agrees to provide an adequate first aide station with transportation or ambulance service to be immediately available for the duration of all events.

2. **Compensation.** In full compensation for the heretofore described services provided, Owner agrees to permit Contractor to retain all motorcycle entry fees collected, ninety-five percent (95%) of all spectator admission fees, and ninety-five percent (95%) of the gross receipts, if any, received from the concession service. Contractor will pay five percent (5%) of all spectator admission fees collected and five percent (5%) of the gross receipts, if any, received from the concession service to Owner. Contractor agrees to maintain proper records and to provide a financial statement, including an accurate and full accounting of all receipts and disbursements, within thirty (30) days of each event. Contractor agrees to provide any relevant information or make any pertinent record available, upon request, to Owner, the State Auditor, or the State Department of Revenue.

3. **Insurance.** Contractor agrees to obtain an insurance policy for general liability coverage indemnifying itself and Owner for the duration of all events conducted pursuant to this contract. The amount of liability coverage shall be three hundred thousand dollars ($300,000). Contractor shall provide a copy of such policy or policies to Owner prior to the applicable event.

4. Contractor agrees to obtain all licenses, permits, and other items of regulation as required by law, for the proper performance of its obligations, including a Missouri Retail Sales Tax License with posting of required bond.

5. **Publicity.** Contractor is responsible for all event publicity. Owner reserves the right to approve all public information, advertising, and other communications related to this event, before distribution, dissemination, and use. All publicity must state that the event is coordinated with or sanctioned by the Missouri Department of Natural Resources, Division of Parks and Recreation.

6. Owner reserves the right to suspend or cancel this contract with reasonable notice to the Contractor, at any time.

In Witness Whereof, the parties hereto have caused this agreement to be executed by their duly authorized officers the date first above written. Execution of this contract is contingent upon the approval of the Commissioner of Administration, or his designated representative.

OWNER

ATTEST _____
Director, Department of Natural
Resources, State of Missouri

APPROVED: _____
Commissioner of
Administration
CONTRACTOR

ATTEST: _____
President,
Columbia Motor Sports

Figure 23-2. State service contract for competitive ORV events.

Service Fee and Special Fee: Off-Highway Vehicle Fund

38225. (a) A service fee of five dollars ($5) shall be paid to the department for the issuance or renewal of identification of off-highway motor vehicles subject to identification, except as expressly exempted under this division.

(b) In addition to the service fee specified in subdivision (a), special fee of six dollars ($6) shall be paid at the time of payment of the service fee for the issuance or renewal of an identification plate or device. All fees received by the department pursuant to this subdivision, and all day use, overnight use, or annual or biennial use fees for designated off-highway state recreation areas received by the Department of Parks and Recreation, shall be deposited in the Off-Highway Vehicle Fund, which is hereby created. There shall be a separate reporting of special fee revenues by vehicle type, including four-wheeled vehicles, motorcycles, and snowmobiles. All money in the Off-Highway Vehicle Fund is continuously appropriated for expenditure by the Department of Parks and Recreation for the purposes specified in Section (   ) *38270.*

Additional Fee: In Lieu Tax

38230. In addition to the fees imposed by Section 38225, there shall be paid a four-dollar ($4) fee for the issuance or renewal of identification for every off-highway motor vehicle subject to identification. The fee imposed by this section is in lieu of all taxes according to value levied for state or local purposes.

Added Ch. 1816, Stats. 1971. Operative July 1, 1972.

Fees for Special Permits

38231. The fees for a special permit issued under Section 38087 shall be the prevailing identification fees as set forth in Sections 38225 and 38230 and shall be deposited and distributed as are identification fees under this chapter.

Added Ch. 973, Stats. 1972. Effective Aug. 16, 1972 by terms of an urgency clause.

Fee: Special Transportation Identification

38232. A special fee of three dollars ($3) shall be paid to the department for the issuance of a special transportation identification device issued pursuant to Section 38088 and shall be deposited in the Motor Vehicle Account in the Transportation Tax Fund. Such fee is in lieu of the fees provided in Section 38225.

Allocation and Use of Fees

38240. (a) The State Controller shall allocate the fees collected under Section 38230 in July and January of each fiscal year in the same manner fees are allocated under Section 11005 of the Revenue and Taxation Code.

(b) It is the intent of the Legislature that funds collected under Section 38230 be used for any one or more of the following purposes:

(1) Planning, acquiring, developing, constructing, maintaining, or administering, for the use of off-highway *motor* vehicles, trails, areas, or other facilities.

(2) Controlling the operation of motor vehicles in areas off the highways where the operation of motor vehicles is restricted or prohibited.

(3) Otherwise carrying out the provisions of this division.

Delinquency of Transfer Fees

38250. Whenever any person has received as transferee a properly endorsed certificate of ownership and identification certificate of the vehicle described on the certificates and the transfer fee has not been paid by this division within 10 days, the fee is delinquent.

Figure 23-3. State ORV fund. Excerpts from Chappie-Z'berg Off-Highway Motor Vehicle Law (from California State Legislature, 1971, Sec. 38000 et seq.).

Transfer Application and Fees

38255. Upon application for transfer of ownership or any interest of an owner, or legal owner in or to any off-highway motor vehicle identified under this division, there shall be paid the following fees:

(a) For a transfer by the owner $3

(b) For a transfer by the legal owner $3

(c) When application is presented showing a transfer by both the owner and legal owner $3

Fees for Duplicate Certificates, Plates, Stickers

38260. Upon application for duplicate ownership certificate, identification certificate, duplicate or substitute identification plate or device, tabs, stickers or device, there shall be paid a three-dollar ($3) fee.

Penalty Fee for Delinquency

38265. (a) The penalty for delinquency in respect to any transfer shall be three dollars ($3), and shall apply only to the last transfer.

(b) The penalty for delinquency in respect to the fees imposed by Sections 38225 and 38230, shall be equal to one-half the fee after the same has been computed.

Allocation of Fund

38270. The Department of Parks and Recreation shall, utilizing special fee funds in the Off-Highway Vehicle Fund created by subdivision (b) of Section 38225, revenue transferred from the Motor Vehicle Fuel Account to the Off-Highway Vehicle Fund created by subdivision (b) of section 38225, revenue transferred from the Motor Vehicle Fuel Account to the Off-Highway Vehicle Fund, and unexpended service fees, carry out programs of planning, acquisition, development, construction, maintenance, administration, and conservation of trails and areas for the use of off-highway motor vehicles. Such funds, revenues and fees shall be allocated as follows:

(a) An amount, not to exceed 50 percent of the special fee and Motor Vehicle Fuel Account transfer revenues of the Off-Highway Vehicle Fund, shall be made available for grants to cities, counties, and appropriate special-purpose districts for recreation projects for off-highway motor vehicles in accordance with local government planning and the statewide plans for trails for recreational motor vehicles developed by the Department of Parks and Recreation. Local governments, to be eligible for these funds, shall provide matching funds, or the value of services, material, or property used, in an amount equal to, but not less than 25 percent of, the total expense of the off-highway motor vehicle facility.

Portions of this amount not committed to cities, counties, and appropriate special purpose districts shall be available for the Department of Parks and Recreation to enter into cooperative agreement with federal agencies for acquisition projects, or development projects, or both, for recreational use of off-highway vehicles.

(b) The remainder of the special fee funds, Motor Vehicle Fuel Account transfer revenues, and all unexpended service fees, and all use fee funds, contained in the Off-Highway Vehicle Fund, shall be used by the Department of Parks and Recreation for purposes of funding recreational areas for the use of such vehicles and trails for the use of such vehicles.

Educating and Training

Educating and training ORV users is very important if we are to meet user needs, protect the resources, and minimize conflicts with other users. For example, Executive Order 11644 (Chapter 1, Fig. 1-3) requires that public-land management agencies provide for the publication and distribution of information, including maps, describing such areas and trails and explaining the conditions of vehicle use. The U.S. Forest Service (1977a, p. 111) believes that it is the intent of the order that the public be adequately informed as to where and under what conditions they may use ORVs on National Forest land. For example, the U.S. Forest Service (1977a, p. 112) indicated in an environmental impact statement that:

> During fiscal year 1977, the Allegheny National Forest will place major emphasis on providing the public with adequate information about the policy to give a clear understanding of rules and regulations which apply to ORV use on areas and trails. However, this will not preclude the issuance of formal law enforcement citations if circumstances dictate such use.

In order to reduce the severity of injuries, damage, and trespass caused by ORVs, the California Department of Parks and Recreation (1978a, pp. 41, 42) suggests an education and training program that would incorporate the following subjects:

Physical skill in operating and handling

Mechanical skill in maintaining and repairing

Basic first aid, survival, and search and rescue skills

Rules, regulations, laws, and other guidelines or restrictions on the various aspects of ORV use

Knowledge and appreciation of the natural environment that will increase the enjoyment of ORV users and develop awareness of damage that might occur through careless use

Code of conduct for ORV use that will encourage positive attitudes and respect for the rights and needs of others

Educational Techniques

Educational and training programs can include numerous techniques such as state recreation department newsletters; industry periodicals; seminars, workshops, and other discussions with ORV users; regulations and tips printed on facility maps or posted at staging areas; news media articles; exhibits and displays; tours to areas of historic, cultural, or natural interests; facility visitor information services; posting of instructional signs at facilities; safety training programs; industry advertising that stresses resource protection and the needs of other users; and preparation, publishing, and posting of ORV user codes of ethics. Stebbins (1974, p. 303) suggests that biology teachers undertake studies of ORV damage near their schools. Godfrey et al. (1978, p. 599) suggests establishing a series of interpretive displays which show how vehicles damage the marine resources. They feel that:

> Such information can help visitors understand why certain areas should be closed or controlled. The public is much more likely to support such actions when they understand that it is in their best interest.

Federal public-land managers and some states have inaugurated education and training programs and used many of these techniques, for example:

New Hampshire's trailrider education program uses a comprehensive trail-bike student safety manual covering protective clothing, ORV regulations, and user responsibilities (Motorcycle Industry Council, Inc., 1981a, p. 3). A code of ethics is taught to the students of the program.

U.S. Forest Service (1977b) maps of "Welcome to the Angeles National Forest" include tips to users on ORV operation and regulations on littering, speeding, clothing, and spark arresters; a list of prohibited activities; request for respect of private areas and property; and appropriate cartoons.

According to Emetaz (1980, p. 14) state operator safety training programs include both classroom and field instruction covering such topics as maintenance and machine operation, proper riding positions, proper clothing, terrain, and weather and stress environmental awareness, skill, courtesy, judgment, and common sense.

Motorcycle Industry Council, Inc., 35-mm color slides and an 11-min pre-recorded sound casette presentation explain how a simple, stationary noise test can be used to recognize excessively noisy ORVs.

The U.S. Department of Agriculture and the University of Michigan co-sponsored a conference and published its proceedings in *Off-Road Vehicles: A Management Challenge* (Andrews and Nowak, 1980).

The U.S. Geological Survey prepares exhibits of ORV impacts (Black and Tsoi, 1976).

The U.S. Heritage Conservation and Recreation Service (1979) cosponsored with several state recreational agencies eight workshops conducted by the Motorcycle Industry Council, Inc., on *Planning for Trailbike Recreation*.

Michigan appropriated funds and mandated the development and implementation of an ORV user's education program as an enforcement technique (LeValley, 1979, p. 72).

Education—An Enforcement Technique

An ORV user's education and training can be an important enforcement technique. A specialist in enforcement and safety education with the Michigan Department of Natural Resources Law Enforcement Division visualizes the educational process as serving as an enforcement technique for the ORV user.

LeValley (1979, p. 74) sums the importance of user education as an enforcement technique as follows:

> In closing, I want to leave you with a few thoughts to emphasize the role user education plays in the law enforcement officer's "tools of the trade." Laws govern everything we do. They tell us what our actions and attitudes should be. Effective law enforcement is a necessity of life. For the minority, agency law enforcement is the immediate and only solution. Apprehension and arrest (sometimes more than once) is the manner by which they must learn. For most of us, however, the educational approach is more effective. We are content to learn in the classroom and willingly comply.

Closing Comment

All education and training programs should be comprehensive, be required of all ORV users, and conclude with the award of a certificate for satisfactory completion. The certificate should be required for licensing and entry onto public ORV facilities. Such a program could introduce both the experienced rider and the inexperienced rider (and perhaps the parents) to the need for protective clothing, vehicle maintenance, riding skills, regulations, enforcement, and the user's duties and responsibilities toward the environment and non-ORV users.

In addition, before entering an ORV facility—public or private—information regarding the area's facilities, cycleways, regulations, prohibited activities, prohibited areas, and system of traffic signs should be provided to the user along with a release of the manager's liability.

A management approach combining education, regulation, and facilities specially designed for the exclusive use of ORVs will give the ORV user a safer and more satisfying experience, minimize resource destruction, and reduce non-ORV user conflicts.

References

Andrews, R. N. L., and P. F. Nowak (Eds.). 1980. Off-Road Vehicle Use: A Management Challenge. U.S. Department of Agriculture and University of Michigan, Washington, D.C., 348 pp.

Baldwin, M. F., and D. H. Stoddard, Jr. 1973. The Off-Road Vehicle and Environmental Quality. An Updated Report on the Social and Environmental Effects of Off-Road Vehicles, Particularly Snowmobiles, with Suggested Policies for Their Control. The Conservation Foundation, Washington, D.C., 61 pp.

Black, W., and D. Tsoi. 1976. Off-Road Vehicle Use of the Desert. U.S. Geological Survey (circulating exhibit), Menlo Park, California.

Butt, J. P. 1977. Notice of Limited Closure to Off-Road Vehicle Use, Allegheny National Forest, Pennsylvania. U.S. Forest Service, Warren, Pennsylvania, 4 pp.

California Department of Parks and Recreation. 1978a. Hollister Hills State Vehicular Recreation Area. Resource Management Plan, General Development Plan, and Environmental Impact Report. Sacramento, California, 128 pp.

California Department of Parks and Recreation. 1978b. Off Highway Vehicle Recreation in California. An Element of the California Recreational Trails Plan. Sacramento, California, 96 pp.

California State Legislature. 1971. Chappie-Z'berg Off-Highway Motor Vehicle Law of 1971, as Amended. Vehicle Code, Sec. 38000 et seq., West's annotated codes.

Church, W. L. 1979. Private Lands and Public Recreation. A Report and Proposed New Model Act on Access, Liability and Trespass. National Association of Conservation Districts, Washington, D.C., 33 pp.

Emetaz, R. V. 1980. Management—The Solution to the Problem. Dispersed Recreation Group, Pacific Northwest Region, U.S. Forest Service, 16 pp.

Florida Department of Agriculture and Consumer Services. 1979. Buttgenbach Motorcycle Area, Withlacoochee State Forest. Tallahassee, Florida, 2 pp.

Geological Society of America. 1977. Impacts and Management of Off-Road Vehicles. Report of the Committee on Environment and Public Policy, Boulder, Colorado, 8 pp.

Godfrey, P. J., S. P. Leatherman, and P. A. Buckley. 1978. Impact of off-road vehicles on coastal ecosystems. In: Coastal Zone '78, Vol. II. American Society of Engineers, New York, pp. 581–600.

Indiana Department of Natural Resources. 1972. Off the Road Vehicle Study. Indianapolis, Indiana, 138 pp.

LeValley, C. L. 1979. User Education as an Enforcement Tool. In: Planning for Trailbike Recreation. U.S. Heritage Conservation and Recreation Service, Washington, D.C., pp. 72–74.

McEwen, D. N. 1978. Turkey Bay Off-Road Vehicle Area at Land Between the Lakes. An Example of New Opportunities for Managers and Riders. Research Report No. 1, Department of Recreation, Southern Illinois University, Carbondale, Illinois, January 1978, 28 pp.

Motorcycle Industry Council, Inc. 1973. Motorcycle Park Planning and Management. Washington, D.C., 24 pp.

Motorcycle Industry Council, Inc. 1980a. Motorcycle types: Which is which? In: The Recreational Trailbike Planner, Newport Beach, California, Vol. I, No. 11.

Motorcycle Industry Council, Inc. 1980b. State motorcycle equipment requirements, November 1980 (Table). Newport Beach, California.

Motorcycle Industry Council, Inc. 1980c. The Recreational Trailbike Planner. Newport Beach, California, Vol. I, No. 7.

Motorcycle Industry Council, Inc. 1981a. The Recreational Trailbike Planner. Newport Beach, California, Vol. II. No. 1.

Motorcycle Industry Council, Inc. 1981b. State off-highway motorcycle requirements. April 1981 (Table). Newport Beach, California.

Pennsylvania State Legislature. 1981. Motor Vehicle Code, Secs. 828.2, 828.3.

Rasor, R. 1977. Five State Approaches to Trailbike Recreation Facilities and Their Management. American Motorcyclist Association, Westerville, Ohio, 64 pp.

Santa Clara County Board of Supervisors. 1980. Ordinance No. NS-1019.1 to

prohibit operation of off-road motor vehicles on private property without
a permit. San Jose, California (adopted May 13, 1980), 2 pp.

Sheridan, D. 1979. Off-Road Vehicles on Public Land. Council on Environmental Quality, U.S. Government Printing Office, Washington, D.C., 84 pp.

Stebbins, R. C. 1974. Off-road vehicles and the fragile desert. Am. Biol. Teacher 36(4, 5):203–208; 294–304.

U.S. Bureau of Land Management. 1974. Public lands. Use of off-road vehicles. Fed. Reg. 39(73):13612 et seq.

U.S. Department of the Interior, Task Force Study. 1971. Off Road Recreation Vehicles, Pacific Southwest Region. San Francisco, California, 123 pp.

U.S. Forest Service. 1977a. Final Environmental Statement, Off-Road Vehicles. Allegheny National Forest, Eastern Region, Warren, Pennsylvania, 216 pp.

U.S. Forest Service. 1977b. Welcome to the Angeles National Forest. (Map.) Pasadena, California.

U.S. Heritage Conservation and Recreation Service. 1979. Planning for Trailbike Recreation. U.S. Government Printing Office, Washington, D.C., 93 pp.

Washington State Legislature. 1971. Off-Road Vehicle Act, as Amended. Sec. 46.09.020 et seq., Washington Revised Code.

Wells, C. 1980. Recreational Trailbike Program. An Outline of the Basic Criteria Needed to Develop a Trailbike Program. Idaho State Parks and Recreation Department, Boise, Idaho, 18 pp.

Index

Springer Series on Environmental Management
Robert S. DeSanto, Series Editor

Natural Hazard Risk Assessment and Public Policy
Anticipating the Unexpected
by **William J. Petak** and **Arthur A. Atkisson**

This volume details the practical actions that public policy makers can take to lessen the adverse effects natural hazards have on people and property. Its step by step framework guides the reader through all phases of risk identification, assessment, analysis, decision making, implementation and review.
This strategy, applicable to most situations, illustrates the means with which one can attenuate the costs of natural disasters *before* they ocur.

1982/xvi, 489 pp./89 illus./cloth
ISBN 0-387-**90645**-2

Gradient Modeling
Resource and Fire Management
by **Stephen R. Kessell**

Gradient modeling is a promising new approach to resource management simulation and land management planning—a method that applies the tools of remote sensing, computer technology, and gradient analysis to resource management problems.

"[The] approach is both muscular enough to satisfy the applied scientist and yet elegant and deep enough to satisfy the aesthetics of the basic scientist. . . . Kessell's approach . . . seems to overcome many of the frustrations inherent in land-systems classifications."

—Ecology

". . . deserves to be read and understood by all those concerned with the wise management of land and resources."

—BioScience

1979/xv, 432 pp./175 illus./27 tables/cloth
ISBN 0-387-**90379**-8

Springer Series on Environmental Management
Robert S. DeSanto, Series Editor

Disaster Planning
The Preservation of Life and Property
by **Harold D. Foster**

"This book draws on an impressively wide range of examples both of man-made and of natural disasters, organized around a framework designed to stimulate the awareness of planners to sources of potential catastrophe in their areas, and indicate what can be done in the preparation of detailed and reliable measures that will hopefully never need to be used."

—Environment and Planning A

"This is an excellent book, the first academic survey in the whole disaster field. . . . There can be no doubt . . . that this book will become essential reading for all concerned with disaster planning. . . . The author must be congratulated."

—Interdisciplinary Science Reviews

1980/x, 275 pp./48 illus./cloth
ISBN 0-387-**90498**-0

Air Pollution and Forests
Interactions between Air Contaminants and Forest Ecosystems
by **William H. Smith**

"A definitive book on the complex relationship between forest ecosystems and atmospheric deposition . . . long needed . . . a thorough and objective review and analysis."

—Journal of Forestry

"It presents a tremendously useful framework for thinking about the problems it treats."

—Atmospheric Environment

"Recommend[ed] to anyone who would like a thorough overview of the interaction between air pollution and forests."
—Bulletin American Meteorological Society

1981/xv, 379 pp./60 illus./cloth
ISBN 0-387-**90501**-4